# From Lambs to Lions

# From Lambs to Lions

## Future Security Relationships in a World of Biological and Nuclear Weapons

Thomas Preston

ROWMAN & LITTLEFIELD PUBLISHERS, INC.
*Lanham • Boulder • New York • Toronto • Plymouth, UK*

ROWMAN & LITTLEFIELD PUBLISHERS, INC.

Published in the United States of America
by Rowman & Littlefield Publishers, Inc.
A wholly owned subsidiary of The Rowman & Littlefield Publishing Group, Inc.
4501 Forbes Boulevard, Suite 200, Lanham, Maryland 20706
www.rowmanlittlefield.com

Estover Road, Plymouth PL6 7PY, United Kingdom

British Library Cataloguing in Publication Information Available

**Library of Congress Cataloging-in-Publication Data**
Preston, Thomas, 1963-
   From lambs to lions : future security relationships in a world of biological and nuclear weapons / Thomas Preston.
       p. cm.
   Includes bibliographical references and index.
   ISBN-13: 978-0-7425-5502-0 (cloth : alk. paper)
   ISBN-10: 0-7425-5502-X (cloth : alk. paper)
   1. Weapons of mass destruction. 2. Security, International—Forecasting. 3. Biological warfare—Prevention. 4. Nuclear warfare—Prevention. 5. Nuclear nonproliferation—21st century. 6. Asymmetric warfare—Forecasting. I. Title. II. Title: Future security relationships in a world of biological and nuclear weapons.
   U793.P74 2007
   355'.031--dc22

                                                                    2006039722

Printed in the United States of America

This book is dedicated to the memory of Dr. Joseph J. Kruzel, deputy assistant secretary of defense for European and NATO policy (1993–1995), who died while serving the cause of peace as a diplomat on a rain-soaked mountain road above Sarajevo. His tireless efforts to negotiate peace in the Balkans and unflinching service to his country will always be remembered. But he was also a mentor and role model to a generation of young scholars who had the immense good fortune of working with him at The Ohio State University. He was an inspiration to us all, generous with his time, frank with his criticisms, and always a shining example of the kind of "scholar-practitioner" we hoped we could one day emulate. Thank you, Joe.

# Contents

Please see the book's website for additional materials:
www.rowmanlittlefield.com/isbn/0742555038

# Figures and Tables

## FIGURES

## TABLES

# Acknowledgments

As with all research endeavors of this size, I am deeply indebted to a great many people whose advice, support, reactions to earlier drafts, and patient tolerance made this project possible. Foremost among these are two individuals. Joseph Kruzel, to whom this book is dedicated, inspired my interest in nuclear proliferation issues and encouraged my original research that would eventually become this book with his many frank and insightful critiques. The other is Jeffrey Lantis, who has long provided me not only with his friendship, but also with immensely valuable feedback, sage advice, and unwavering support for this project. He has been a critical sounding board whose input on this book has been invaluable and greatly appreciated.

I would also like to express my deep thanks to Kenneth Waltz, whose own work on nuclear proliferation has greatly inspired me and who unexpectedly took the time to provide detailed and thoughtful handwritten comments on an earlier draft. I would also like to thank Richard Harknett, Bengt Sundelius, Eric Stern, Chet Herbst, Yaacov Vertzberger, Charles Hermann, Alexander George, T. V. Paul, Michael Young, Paul 't Hart, Margaret Hermann, and the countless graduate students in my security seminars over the years who provided advice, support, and thoughtful reactions to earlier drafts of this research.

In addition, I would like to express my great appreciation to a number of individuals who generously gave of their time to discuss their insights with me—James Woolsey, Ken Alibek, Sergei Popov, Eric Croddy, Anne Harrington, Charles Hickey, Esther Lietz, Scott Minnich, Robert McNamara, and a number of others who shall remain nameless. In particular, I would like to express my deep thanks to Ken Alibek, Sergei Popov, and James Woolsey for their willingness to be interviewed, their patience, and the invaluable assistance they provided to this endeavor. I would also like to thank my wonderful editors at Rowman & Littlefield, Jessica Gribble and Renée Legatt, for all of their encouragement and support. Finally, I would like to thank my sons, Tobias and Samuel, for letting their father work in peace on his book, my mother Velma, and my darling wife Frances for all of her love and continuing support (and tolerance) of my big projects.

# Abbreviations

| | |
|---|---|
| ALCM | air launched cruise missile |
| ASCM | antiship cruise missile |
| ASF | African swine fever |
| ATV | advanced technology vessel |
| AVLIS | atomic vapor laser isotope separation |
| BMD | ballistic missile defense |
| BSE | bovine spongiform encephalopathy |
| BW | bioweapons |
| CDC | Centers for Disease Control and Prevention |
| CW | chemical weapon |
| CWC | Chemical Weapons Convention |
| DIA | Defense Intelligence Agency |
| DMZ | demilitarized zone |
| DoD | Department of Defense |
| DRTF | Decade Radiation Test Facility |
| DTRA | Defense Threat Reduction Agency |
| EMP | electromagnetic pulse |
| END | exotic Newcastle disease |
| EPA | U.S. Environmental Protection Agency |
| FAD | foreign animal disease |
| FDA | U.S. Food and Drug Administration |
| FMD | foot-and-mouth disease |
| GAO | General Accounting Office |
| GPS | Global Positioning System |
| HEU | highly enriched uranium |
| HFV | hemorrhagic fever virus |

| | |
|---|---|
| IAEA | International Atomic Energy Agency |
| ICBM | intercontinental ballistic missile |
| IDF | Israeli Defense Forces |
| IRBM | intermediate-range ballistic missile |
| LACM | land-attack cruise missile |
| MPV | monkeypox virus |
| MTCR | Missile Technology Control Regime |
| NIE | National Intelligence Estimate |
| NMD | national missile defense |
| NPT | Nuclear Non-Proliferation Treaty |
| OTA | Office of Technology Assessment |
| PAC | physiologically active compound |
| PAL | permissive action lock |
| PCR | polymerase chain reaction |
| PONAST | postnuclear attack recovery process |
| RV | reentry vehicle |
| SEB | staphylococcal enterotoxin B |
| TEL | transporter-erector launchers |
| TMD | theater missile defense |
| UAV | unmanned aerial vehicle |
| USAMRIID | U.S. Army Medical Research Institute of Infectious Diseases |
| VEE | Venezuelan equine encephalitis |
| vCJD | variant Creutzfeldt-Jakob disease |
| VHF | viral hemorrhagic fever |
| WMD | weapons of mass destruction |

# 1

## The Challenge for Small States Seeking to Be Lions Rather Than Lambs

[Y]ou know as well as we do that, when these matters are discussed by practical people, the standard of justice depends on the equality of power to compel and that in fact the strong do what they have the power to do and the weak accept what they have to accept. . . . So far as right and wrong are concerned . . . there is no difference between the two . . . those who still preserve their independence do so because they are strong.

—Thucydides (1985, 402–4)

Through time immemorial, the relations between states have been captured by these words, expressed without remorse, by powerful Athenian invaders who had surrounded the beleaguered and vastly outnumbered Melian defenders of a small city-state during the Peloponnesian War. Calling out from atop their walls to the Athenians, who demanded their unconditional surrender, the Melians, who had remained neutral in the conflict between Athens and Sparta, cried out that these demands were unjust and unfair, and that they wished only to be left alone and had no intention of involving themselves with the Spartans. And the Athenian response was the same as those given by other great powers to smaller, weaker opponents over the following millennium—"the strong do what they will and the weak suffer what they must." It is an expression of *realpolitik*, of pure power politics—that "might makes right" and unless you have the strength to resist, nothing else matters. And the fate of the Melians, slaughtered to a man and their women sold into slavery, befell others over the ages in similar situations—the weak facing the strong, when lions descended upon lambs.

But this book is *not* about ancient history, nor is it purely a theoretical piece. Though looking to the past for its patterns, and mindful of existing theories of state behavior and international security, the argument advanced is a practical one—exploring how changes occurring in the world may alter the nature of this "Melian dilemma" between states. It explores the extraordinary depth and accelerating speed of the proliferation of nuclear and biological weapons technologies and capabilities to traditionally smaller, weaker opponents (whether they be small states or terror groups), and how this may challenge great power invulnerability (if not supremacy) in future security relationships. How might, for example, a "nuclear" North Korea or Iran *constrain* U.S. freedom of action in its foreign or military policies? How, on a practical level, could smaller opponents possessing WMD *deter* superpower threats to their freedom or sovereignty? What might be the impact of the biotechnical revolution and spread of bioweapons know-how to opponents? How might terror groups, like Al Qaeda, make use of such weapons in future attacks? These are the most *fundamental* questions facing American security policy over the coming decades, and we ignore the threats posed by such weapons and their impact upon security relationships at our peril. To do so is to only *invite* new September 11th–style surprises, but this time resulting in losses of life and property dwarfing those of the 2001 attacks. Instead of thousands, the toll could be in the hundreds of thousands or millions. Such are the nature of the security threats posed by WMD in the twenty-first century.

But how can future 9/11s be avoided? In truth, there are no "magic bullets" or solutions to perfectly protect a nation from future attacks, nor any way to defend every possible "soft" target available to determined terrorists. There is no such thing as perfect or absolute security. At the same time, an awareness of the nature of these threats can help us limit the damage inflicted and allow policy makers to more realistically appraise how opponents might limit or constrain their policy options. Of critical importance is avoiding being caught by surprise by opponents using weapons or tactics that analysts should already have anticipated given current trends in technology, military capability, and extremist ideology. For example, the Japanese attack on Pearl Harbor in 1941 was a "strategic surprise," but one that should have been anticipated had analysts paid attention to previous Japanese tactics—including their surprise, preemptive attack on the Russian Pacific Fleet at the start of the Russo-Japanese War of 1905. Similarly, though administration officials expressed surprise at the suicide hijackings of passenger airliners on September 11th, two years before the attacks, a federal report warned Al Qaeda might attempt hijacking an airliner and flying it into a government building like the White House, Pentagon, or CIA headquarters at Langley (Associated Press 2002). Today, while increased attention has been paid to bionuclear threats, the reality is that their *true potential* to alter future state security relationships has *still* not received the attention it deserves.

Why is this the case? To a great extent, it is caused by a lack of understanding about the utility of such weapons and how they could be used. This is especially true regarding bioweapons, where the biotechnical revolution requires us to fundamentally rethink what might be possible. More fundamentally, however, it is the lack of *future thinking* on our part when considering potential threats over the coming decades. All too often, we fall into the historical trap of "preparing to fight the last war" instead of considering where current trends are taking us. Indeed, until September 11th and the anthrax postal attacks, the terrorism literature confidently predicted (based on historical data sets) that terrorists were *not* interested in causing mass-casualty attacks on civilians and had little interest in pursuing bioweapons (cf. Mullen 1978; Jenkins 1985; Tucker and Sands 1999; Pate and Cameron 2001). As we discovered to our cost, past is not always a prologue.

In the nuclear proliferation literature, in contrast, the tendency has been to adopt a strongly normative tone in debates over WMD issues. The argument pits pessimists, who see only destabilization and deterrence breakdowns as a consequence of nuclear spread, against optimists, who take the position that deterrence relationships reduce the chances of war between nuclear-armed rivals. Though applying numerous theoretical approaches to buttress their competing arguments, the overall debate itself exhibits a strongly normative underlying tone, with the assumed "immorality" of relying on WMDs targeting civilians coupled almost seamlessly by pessimists to warnings about organizational malfunctions and the danger of accidental war. Indeed, the tone is similar to that adopted by governmental policy makers (usually when talking about *other* country's nuclear programs rather than their own) or by officials from international agencies, like the International Atomic Energy Agency (IAEA), whose primary organizational mission is to control and prevent nuclear proliferation. For both, the risks (no matter how slight) of nuclear war, and the immorality of the use (or threatened use) of such weapons is so great, it renders any arguments by nuclear optimists about deterrence and increased stability irrelevant and unduly risky.

Unfortunately, while both sides make legitimate and valuable points, debates too often center around what scholars believe *ideally* (in a perfect world) to be the most stable, risk-free security environment. Leaving aside for the moment the observation that what security situation is most desirable is an immensely subjective notion, depending greatly upon whether one takes the perspective of "nuclear-armed" Athenians or Melians, these arguments ignore the world as it *actually is*, and the motivations of state and nonstate actors alike to disagree with the negative view of academics regarding their possession of WMDs. Indeed, given existing nuclear states (like the U.S.) have clearly proven unwilling to surrender their arsenals in the foreseeable future due to their perceived security benefits, it is naive to imagine North Korea, Iran, Pakistan, or Israel (facing their own dire security needs) being swayed by such counterproliferation arguments. Especially in the absence of other means for ensuring their own survival and security.

This book makes no normative value judgments regarding the morality of nuclear or biological weapons, nor whether we would be better off in an alternate reality where the "genie" was conveniently shoved back inside its bottle and forgotten about. Analysts should look at the world as it *currently* is (and *will be* in the future), not how we *wish* it to be from theoretical or normative perspectives. Instead, I will look objectively at what is *actually* happening regarding WMD proliferation and how these trends will give rise to vastly different security relationships in the coming decades.

## THE NEW ASYMMETRICAL THREAT ENVIRONMENT

To understand the new security threat environment, it is necessary to view it not only from the perspective of great powers, like the U.S., but also from the perspective of smaller actors seeking to deter or constrain American power. Faced with an opponent possessing historically unprecedented levels of technical and conventional military superiority, these small state or nonstate terror groups have quickly learned—especially after the resounding nature of the military victories in the first two gulf wars and Kosovo—that it is impossible to successfully engage the U.S. in conflict on even terms and win (Cohen 1994; Hass 1999; Schmitt and Dao 2001; Easterbrook 2004). As former Indian army chief of staff Sundarji observed, the principal lesson of the Gulf War was that a state intending to fight the U.S. "should avoid doing so until and unless it possesses nuclear weapons" (Joseph and Reichart 1999, 2).

As a result, weaker actors have begun adopting an *asymmetrical* approach to deal with American hyperpower. One based upon a logic of warfare as old as Sun Tzu and predicated on never seeking direct conflict in areas of U.S. superiority, but instead striking at areas of weakness. It is a strategy Scales (1999) describes as being an "adaptive enemy"—who relies on unconventional weapons and tactics to confront U.S. areas of vulnerability rather than strength. The successful guerrilla campaigns by the Vietcong in Vietnam during the 1960s, the mujahideen in Afghanistan during the 1980s, and the current efforts of Iraqi insurgent groups illustrate how far weaker opponents may still actively contest the battlefield with great power opponents by becoming adaptive enemies. Similarly, 9/11 and the anthrax attacks illustrated the potential of opponents to take advantage of great power vulnerabilities using nonconventional strategies. And of all the asymmetric strategies available, few rival the potential effectiveness or impact of nuclear and biological weapons. They represent the "Holy Grail" of asymmetry, weapons allowing actors, regardless of size, to exact tremendous, disproportionate damage upon larger opponents regardless of their relative military capabilities. For terror groups, the potential of WMDs for blackmail is immense, especially if target governments know the capability is real and immune to preemption. For small states, WMD hold out the hope of deterring direct threats to key central interests (e.g., territorial integrity, sovereignty, regime survival) through the ability to deliver devastating attacks upon an opponent's military forces or homeland.

This growing threat has been recognized by some within government circles (e.g., Joseph and Reichart 1999; Falkenrath et al. 1999). Testifying before the Senate Select Committee on Intelligence in February 2000, Vice Admiral Thomas Wilson, director of the Defense Intelligence Agency (DIA), noted that asymmetric threats pose one of the most critical challenges to U.S. security interests and over the next fifteen years, "the prospects for limiting proliferation are slim, and the global WMD threat to U.S.-allied territory, interests, forces, and facilities will increase significantly" (*Military Threats* 2000). Indeed, so great are the potential constraints such capabilities place upon American freedom of action that writers like Hass (1999, 129) warn that the U.S. "must prevent a situation from evolving in which it is deterred from intervening militarily because of the unconventional capabilities of regional adversaries," even if this means pursuing preemptive military doctrines.

At present, conventional military relationships between the U.S. and the rest of the world resembles one in which "the strong do as they will and the weak suffer what they must." This unprecedented conventional dominance allows the U.S. to pursue with near impunity compellent or deterrent strategies through its unsurpassed ability to launch devastating attacks on opponents. As a result, potential opponents are revising their strategic thinking to seek ways to counteract this unilateral U.S. advantage. But, as Joseph and Reichart (1999, 20) note, "there is little or no information available regarding the employment doctrines of states with nuclear weapons and offensive BW programs." Further, as Gray (1999, 164–65) warns, just because "the first major work of theory worthy of the name has yet to be written . . . on "strategy for biological warfare" . . . the absence of a strategic theoretical literature . . . does not mean that polities and sub-state groups will not figure out strategically effective ways to use [biological] agents for coercion in peacetime and success in war." Indeed, Bracken (1999, 43) notes that in Clausewitzian terms, bioweapons "move the center of gravity of the battle from the front, where the United States has advantage, to the rear, where it does not." Moreover, introducing the potential costs inflicted by WMDs into calculations may render many potential interventions abroad too costly to consider.

Yet, while new nuclear states have historically been reticent about acknowledging any deployed capabilities (e.g., Israel, India, Pakistan, North Korea), there are times when they do choose to reveal them, describe their notions of use, and accept the consequences of international sanctions as a result (much as India and Pakistan did in 1998). Especially if such actions are perceived by policy makers to enhance their deterrent threats against powerful opponents (a likely explanation for North Korea's nuclear admission). However, for bioweapons, the rules of the game differ substantially. No state publicly admits to possessing an offensive BW program or arsenal, since such acknowledgment carries with it a heavy stigma and nearly automatic sanctions from the international community. As a consequence, though intelligence sources suggest at least nine to twelve (possibly more) states have ongoing, active BW programs, these remain more opaque than even the most secretive nuclear programs. But, acknowledged or not, nuclear and biological weapons have the potential to alter security relationships between states.

Further, the hypocrisy of the position taken by existing nuclear powers regarding additional members to the club undercuts any arguments regarding "safety" or "stability" that they make to nuclear aspirants. From the perspective of would-be nuclear states, American arguments about nuclear weapons being unnecessary for security are clearly contradicted by its own belief in the indispensability of its arsenal. As Under Secretary of Defense for Policy Walter Slocombe noted before the Senate Armed Services Committee in May 2000, "our overall nuclear employment policy [states that] the United States forces must be capable of and be seen to be capable of holding at risk those critical assets and capabilities that a potential adversary most values" (McKinzie et al. 2001, 12). In other words, the nation with the most powerful conventional military forces in the world, a hyperpower of unparalleled military superiority around the globe, argues it *still needs* nuclear weapons to guarantee its security. Given that states like Israel, North Korea, and Pakistan face far more powerful or numerous opponents *without* the overwhelming conventional superiority of the U.S., it is easy to see why Western protestations about the evils of nuclear weapons fall upon deaf ears. In fact, the same statement of U.S. security requirements given by Slocombe applies equally to smaller nuclear states as well—especially if they are to successfully create stable deterrent relationships with either regional or great power opponents. As Sundarji notes:

> Even for the sake of nebulous future threats, if the USA feels compelled now to hold on to a large nuclear arsenal, the message to regional powers with more live and immediate threats, some of them nuclear . . . [is] loud and clear. *There is no alternative to nuclear weapons and ballistic missiles if you are to live in security and with honor.* Those who cannot for whatever reasons go the nuclear and

ballistic missile route . . . have every incentive to go clandestinely down the chemical and biological route." (Sundarji 1996, 193)

And, despite concerns regarding the peaceful intentions of those who may obtain nuclear arsenals, Goldstein (2000, 279) notes that while there are strong reasons to believe counterproliferation efforts "will not be fully successful, it is important to keep in mind that there is room for tempered optimism in thinking about the consequences of nuclear spread . . . both logic and the experience of the Cold War (especially as illustrated in the Chinese, British, and French cases) suggest that nuclear weapons may be a stabilizing influence on international politics because they are most easily married to strategies designed to preserve the status quo, and not easily employed for other purposes." Indeed, Aron once described deterrence as "diplomacy which uses thermonuclear 'terrorism' to dissuade a possible aggressor from certain undertakings" (Gallois 1961, ix). Noting the hackneyed old bromide that "one man's terrorist is another man's freedom fighter," the hypocrisy of the U.S. position on nuclear weapons suggests an equally true formulation of "one country's illegitimate weapon of terror is another's legitimate nuclear deterrent." In reality, the appropriateness of these normative labels or rationalizations regarding legitimacy of possession remain immensely subjective notions, depending greatly upon whether one is an Athenian or Melian.

## WHAT ARE WEAPONS OF MASS DESTRUCTION?

What are true weapons of mass destruction? The term is often used as a "grab bag" by politicians, journalists, and scholars for any type of weapon capable of killing a lot of people they disapprove of (either morally or because of the negative, visceral responses they induce). Unfortunately, this has generally meant chemical weapons have been included on the list, along with the more appropriate nuclear and biological weapons, by writers on security topics. However, for analytical purposes, this makes absolutely no sense given that the characteristics of chemical weapons relative to those of nuclear or biological weapons are as similar as chalk to cheese.

Chemical weapons require massive quantities of agent to cause militarily significant effects on the battlefield or substantial casualties. In fact, during the First World War, chemical weapons were routinely employed before battles, with preparatory artillery bombardments consisting of *millions* of shells and *hundreds* of tons of chemicals being used by each side. Although the full tactical utility and effectiveness of chemical weapons during WWI is routinely misunderstood by modern-day analysts, who often have no more than a passing knowledge of the period, during the war itself, such weapons were immensely feared by troops. They caused substantial numbers of casualties (with many of the wounded suffering blindness or other serious physical ailments for the remainder of their lives), and substantially affected military operations (cf. Waitt 1943; Gilbert 1994; Keegan 1998; Cook 1999; Haber 2002; Arthur 2003). And the sophistication of chemical warfare increased as the war progressed, with only its conclusion in November 1918 preventing more extensive employment of chemical munitions on the battlefield that doubtlessly would have resulted in far higher casualties among the combatants. Simply put, the militaries of the day saw the value and effectiveness of chemical weapons as "force-multipliers" on the conventional battlefield and also the potential utility of such weapons against civilian targets.

Yet, this does not make chemical weapons any more of a weapon of mass destruction than it does gunpowder or conventional artillery, which killed far more soldiers than all the chemical weapons put together during World War I. Chemical weapons are cumbersome, require large quantities to be effective, and demand immense logistical and delivery system capabilities to be effectively employed on a massive scale against civilian or military targets, especially over substantial distances. Obviously, such limitations do not apply to either nuclear or biological weapons.

A more useful definition of weapons of mass destruction are "discrete weapons which have the potential, in small quantities, to kill tens or hundreds of thousands (perhaps millions) of people and/or cause immense physical or economic damage to an opponent's infrastructure." Using this definition, nuclear weapons provide the purest example of WMDs, with massive killing power housed in individual weapons capable of leveling cities. Though lacking the physical destructiveness of nuclear weapons, bioagents, if properly weaponized and deployed, can cause equivalent numbers of civilian casualties in city attacks and (depending upon the agent used) severe damage to an opponent's infrastructure and economy due to the need for decontamination and other clean-up costs. In fact, a 1993 study by the U.S. Office of Technology Assessment goes even further to warn that bioagents are "true weapons of mass destruction with a potential for lethal mayhem that can *exceed* that of nuclear weapons" (U.S. Congress, Office of Technology Assessment 1993, 73; emphasis added). As a 1996 report by the Pentagon's Office of Counterproliferation and Chemical and Biological Defense noted:

> Biological weapons are the most problematic of the weapons of mass destruction (WMD). They have the greatest potential for damage of any weapon. They are assessable to all countries, with few barriers to developing them with a modest level of effort. The current level of sophistication of BW is comparatively low, but there is enormous potential—based on advances in modern molecular biology, fermentation and drug delivery technology—for making sophisticated

weapons. . . . Genetic engineering give the BW developer a powerful tool with which to pursue agents that defeat the protective and treatment protocols of the prospective adversary. (Office of Counterproliferation 1996)

Obviously, based upon these criteria, chemical weapons are *not* weapons of mass destruction by any reasonable definition and will not be included in subsequent discussions.

## THE CURRENT SECURITY CONTEXT

Regardless of whether we like it or not, a new security environment is beginning to unfold for states as a result of the accelerating spread of nuclear and biological weapons know-how and technology, and the unstoppable pace of scientific and industrial advancement. In the realms of biomedical research and biotechnology, medical advancements and cures for disease have burst upon us at an unprecedented pace. Things that only a decade ago would have been in the realm of science fiction have become science fact, from mapping the entire human genome to using maps of genomes to artificially create life forms from their chemical components—as scientists recently did by manufacturing polio viruses from scratch. Unfortunately, all such technologies and breakthroughs are "Pandora's boxes," providing in equal measure the promise of alleviating human suffering and the ability to inflict immense harm.

Though the Soviet BW program of the 1970s and 1980s, the largest the world has ever known, involved massive industrial infrastructures and employed the services of over 60,000 personnel at its height, the world of the twenty-first century—with its technological advancement and widespread availability of equipment and know-how—holds out the possibility for states (or even nonstate actors) to obtain impressive and extensive biowarfare capabilities with only small production facilities. What in the past would have required a massive, state-run BW program with substantial infrastructure and technical support can today be accomplished by state and nonstate actors alike in buildings the size of a standard garage using easily acquired, off-the-shelf equipment and technically proficient personnel. The genie has been so far removed from the biowarfare bottle, and grown so huge, that thoughts of returning it to captivity are as great a fantasy as uninventing gunpowder!

According to a variety of estimates, the number of countries currently possessing ongoing BW programs, or conducting offensive bioresearch, numbers anywhere from nine to nearly twenty (Department of Defense, Office of the Secretary of Defense 2001; Cirincione 2002; Central Intelligence Agency, *Unclassified Report to Congress* 2002). And even amongst those states acknowledging the kind of "defensive" bioresearch programs allowed by the

Biological Weapons Treaty of 1972, the reality is all such work rests within a gray area, since any knowledge gained from defensive research can easily have offensive applications. Indeed, the difference between "offensive" and "defensive" biowarfare research is much like the difference between "offensive" and "defensive" weapons—they depend for their definition only upon which direction they are pointed and the motivations of their wielder.

As for nuclear weapons, in addition to the "official" nuclear powers (Britain, France, China, Russia, and the United States) acknowledged by the Nuclear Non-Proliferation Treaty (NPT), two declared nuclear powers (India and Pakistan) have conducted tests and several (Israel and North Korea) are widely assumed to possess nuclear arsenals of as few as eight to as many as 200 weapons. Moreover, given the widespread possession of nuclear technology and infrastructure arising from the civilian power industry elsewhere, it is estimated that nearly sixty states have the "capability" if not the motivation to become nuclear states were they to decide to do so (Cirincione 2002; Central Intelligence Agency 1993). Nuclear-capable nations like Japan or Germany, for example, could achieve nuclear status in months were they motivated—and the number of nuclear-capable states continues to rise. And, as the examples of Iran, North Korea, and Iraq illustrate, membership in the NPT or IAEA does not prevent states from expanding their nuclear capabilities by constructing clandestine facilities not open to inspection. We have now reached the point where counterproliferation policies based purely upon restricting access to technology and know-how have limited effectiveness in stopping most states from pursuing nuclear arsenals. Again, the genie has long since changed addresses and letters have ceased to be forwarded from the bottle.

The tendency to underestimate the nature of the current bionuclear threat is greatly facilitated by the fact that most ongoing weapons programs are shrouded in secrecy and seldom acknowledged by states. Further, blatantly pursuing nuclear or biological weapons instantly brings down the full wrath of fearful opponents (thereby increasing tensions and possibly resulting in attack), greater international scrutiny and sanctions (which hurts the acquisition process as well as the economy), and serves to increase a state's vulnerability in the short-term. For example, India and Pakistan both adopted clandestine, or opaque, nuclear programs during the 1980s and 1990s to avoid not only exacerbating tensions between themselves, but to evade the international sanctions and restrictions on imports that would have resulted from a more blatant program. Also, many states (though not all) who have pursued nuclear or biological weapons capabilities have been signatories to international treaties (such as the 1970 Nuclear Non-Proliferation Treaty or the 1972 Biological Weapons Treaty) forbidding such actions. In fact, for states like Iraq, Iran, and

North Korea, being signatories to the NPT has been a disadvantage, since it is used as a pretext by the international community (and especially the U.S.) to adopt harsh economic, or preemptive military policies against them for alleged treaty violations. It is hardly surprising that of the three most recent nuclear states (Israel, India, and Pakistan), all adopted clandestine approaches and denied the existence of active weapons programs until they reached advanced stages of development—with Israel still (as of this writing) denying (at least publicly) the existence of its arsenal. And as for bioweapons, they are universally condemned internationally and, hence, utterly denied by all states who pursue them.

However, this veil of secrecy has resulted in a tendency by many analysts to underestimate the nature of the current bionuclear threat. In the absence of declared policy or capability, analysts are forced to rely upon intelligence assessments of capability—which can often be wildly inaccurate or politically motivated, as the Bush administration's case for the war against Iraq illustrated quite vividly. At the same time, it is a serious mistake to dismiss analysis suggesting growing or potential WMD capabilities in countries just because of the political bias in one case. We tend to not like to hear bad news as a rule, and hope for the best. We also tend to selectively attend to information that we believe (or hope) to be true, while ignoring evidence to the contrary. Indeed, until only recently, much of the scholarly literature on bioweapons downplayed their value, effectiveness, or utility to either states or terrorist organizations—a position influenced in equal measure by nearly complete ignorance of biowarfare on the part of the writers and the strong personal repugnance they held toward such weapons. This should not be mistaken as an argument in favor of biowarfare, nor is it an expression of support for its morality. Rather, it is intended to warn against the tendency to ignore the threat potential which exists from the current spread of nuclear or biological weapons know-how due to our own personal or normative biases.

## AN OVERVIEW OF THE COMING CHAPTERS

While it might seem to some readers that this book takes a worst-case approach to bionuclear issues, in reality, a very conscious effort has been made to adopt a conservative approach to the issues and consider only reasonably plausible scenarios. That the conclusions are fairly dire results more from the objective nature of the bionuclear threat than from director's license. Unfortunately, even in the wake of September 11th, we continue—in both the academic and policy communities—to underestimate the degree to which the increasing spread of nuclear and biological weapons capabilities will alter security relationships among states and nonstate actors over the coming decades. Hopefully, this book will help to rectify this by providing an additional voice in support of policies designed to enhance U.S. biopreparedness and homeland security to limit our vulnerability to attack. Further, it is hoped the arguments advanced by this book will help begin the process of acquainting policy makers with the new realities of our current security environment, so that newly imposed limitations and constraints upon policy are recognized and realistically assessed, rather than ignored or dismissed. Without resorting to pure worst-case thinking, *future thinking* allows us to avoid the shock of strategic surprises that, with careful analyses, can be avoided.

In the next chapter, the growing nuclear weapons threat is examined and an elaborate analytical framework proposed for analyzing how changing nuclear capabilities among small states will affect and influence interstate security relationships—whether involving regional rivals or great powers like the U.S. The debate between nuclear optimists and pessimists is reviewed and placed into context, and the challenges of obtaining nuclear deterrence for modern-day Melians explored. How difficult is it for small states to develop viable nuclear capabilities to deter threats to their interests and what would be required? What of the potential impact of nuclear proliferation to nonstate actors (like Al Qaeda) upon state security relationships? How do the perceptions of policy makers matter? A broad range of new nuclear security relationships are proposed. In chapter 3, a practical application of this analytical framework is made by discussing the future trajectory of several *new nuclear states*—Israel, North Korea, India, and Pakistan—as well as that of *near-nuclear states*—like Iran—over the next ten to fifteen years. What types of capabilities do these states currently possess (in terms of nuclear infrastructure, production capabilities, and delivery technologies) and what changes would it be reasonable to expect these nations to exhibit in their nuclear capabilities or use doctrines in the coming decades? How will these changing capabilities affect their existing and future security relationships with potential opponents? A number of scenarios will be presented to illustrate some of the potential options available to these new nuclear states.

The growing threat of bioweapons proliferation (to both state and nonstate actors) is the subject of chapter 4. The potential of such weapons to cause extensive harm—as true WMDs—is explored through reference to past state-run bioweapons programs, field tests, and studies assessing the likely effectiveness of such weapons against a variety of targets. An analytical framework is developed to illustrate how varying degrees of bioweapons capabilities are likely to influence subsequent security relationships and the range of possible employment strategies available to state or nonstate possessors. The practical implications of advancements in biotechnology and genetic engineering for the enhancement and further proliferation of bioweapons capabilities is examined in great depth in chapter 5. A variety of potential bioagents likely to be considered for weaponization by new biostates (such as plague, anthrax, smallpox, etc.) are discussed in detail, as is the potential of these agents to be further enhanced by bioengineering. What would be the threat posed by such agents? How might novel pathogens be employed? What of the threat posed to agriculture by bioweapons? And, how difficult would it be to obtain, engineer, or modify pathogens for use by either state or nonstate actors? As will quickly become apparent, the potential of bioweapons is now virtually unlimited and poses a far greater threat to state security than will nuclear weapons in the coming years. Further, bioweapons will prove next to impossible to contain using traditional counterproliferation strategies (such as restriction of technologies and materials) that were at least of limited value in the nuclear realm.

Chapter 6 concludes with a review of the implications derived from the preceding chapters on nuclear and biological proliferation, and what these suggest for state security relationships in the twenty-first century. How will American foreign and defense policy have to be altered to adapt to this changing environment? How might American power be constrained? How might we avoid new "strategic surprises"—new bionuclear 9/11s—in the future? What limitations will exist in the power of these new nuclear or biological Melians in asserting their challenge to the invulnerability of the great powers? Finally, a number of policy recommendations will be made that are geared toward reducing U.S. vulnerability, and enhancing domestic preparedness against, the kinds of bionuclear threats we are likely to face. At a minimum, a greater awareness of these threats, and how likely they are to manifest themselves, should allow policy makers to develop more realistic foreign policy expectations, better recognize potential constraints or dangers surrounding certain policies, and reduce the damage inflicted should a bionuclear attack be carried out.

Unfortunately, no silver bullets are introduced. Though it is imminently practical to take steps to reduce our vulnerability to bionuclear attack, and reduce the damage that might result, it is clearly impossible to completely eliminate our susceptibility to attack. We will forever be dealing with "adaptive enemies," whether they be state or nonstate actors, who seek to challenge our areas of weakness rather than contest our areas of strength. These are the foreign and military policy implications of the increasing expansion of small state bionuclear capabilities over the coming decades, changes which will introduce new rules to the traditional game of power politics played since the time of the Athenians and Melians. No longer will "the strong do what they will and the weak suffer what they must." Instead, the new political reality will be one in which the weak can force the strong to suffer as well—disproportionately so—creating a situation which, for the first time in history, makes deterrence of the strong by the weak (at least regarding central interests like survival) obtainable at last.

# 2

# Nuclear Proliferation, Deterrence, and Evolving Security Relationships

The arrival of the U.S. atomic bomb upon the world stage in 1945, and subsequent spread of nuclear capability to other great powers, brought significant changes to interstate security relationships. A consensus formed among politicians and scholars alike that nuclear weapons had fundamentally altered the nature of the international system (cf. Brodie 1973; McNamara 1983). Direct threats to the continued existence, survival, or sovereignty of great power nuclear states were avoided, as were actions endangering their main allies or central economic interests. The immense dangers of conflict, and subsequent escalation, were seen to far outweigh any possible advantage to be gained by continuing to pursue unrestrained competition between nuclear states. At the same time, however, competition in peripheral areas of interest (such as the third world)—where potential losses were not great enough to merit the far greater losses inherent in a great power nuclear exchange—continued unabated during the Cold War. Relationships between nuclear states and their nonnuclear cousins remained characterized by the pure *power politics* dynamics of the realist tradition (Morgenthau 1948), where "the strong do as they will and the weak suffer what they must."

Of course, given this situation, the "eternal" question of what steps could be taken to increase the security and stability of states (nuclear proliferation or its absence) remained largely a matter of perspective, centering around *whose security or stability* one was considering. For the great powers, possession of immense conventional military strength, or absent that, nuclear weapons capabilities (for either deterrence or defensive purposes) have long been viewed as critical for ensuring their national security against threats from abroad (Freedman 1981; Bundy 1988; Goldstein 2000). As illustrated by the 2002 *Nuclear Posture Review* (NPR), even the most powerful

15

conventional military power of the twenty-first century, the U.S., continues to see the need for a large nuclear arsenal as a deterrent force against potential threats from other great power opponents (or in lesser forms, as a means of tactically preempting the WMD capabilities of lesser powers through earth-penetrating warheads).[1]

Yet, for great powers to maintain their own "freedom of action" to make the weak "suffer what they must," they cannot allow less powerful states to succeed in their quest for *offsetting military capabilities*. Quite clearly, the existing great power nuclear states already accept as fact that nuclear weapons provide deterrence—it is why they developed their arsenals in the first place and why they have no plans to ever relinquish them. The nuclear have-nots, the small states tempted to acquire them, also recognize that *if* they were able to develop such weapons, and the delivery systems rendered them invulnerable to preemption and able to retaliate against distant attackers, they could (just like the great powers) enhance their security against foreign threats. Given the self-serving nature of great power objections, it is hardly surprising Indian prime minister Vajpayee forcefully argued that Western criticism of India's decision to become a nuclear weapon state smacked of both hypocrisy and double standards (Swamy 1998).

For small states to escape the fate of the Melians, they must *offset* the immense conventional strength of great power opponents. Until the nuclear age, this asymmetrical struggle was confined to defensively waged resistance or guerilla wars against foreign invaders or occupying powers. And though sometimes successful (Vietnam, Afghanistan), far more representative historically were the many failed efforts to prevent great power control over small state territories or governments (e.g., the colonial period, numerous state-sponsored coups, and successful foreign military invasions). In recent years, however, increasing proliferation has marked the beginnings of a fundamental transfer of power away from great powers to smaller states—at least in the security arena. Small states acquiring offsetting WMD capabilities establish new "rules of the game" for larger states, who become progressively less able to utilize traditional power resources (military, economic, technical superiority) to achieve their foreign policy goals. Although small states still lack the material resources of larger states, nuclear weapons provide an ability to deter their threats for the first time in history. Irrespective of the relative power balance, small nuclear states will obtain the ability to deter encroachment on their vital interests with the advent of credible, survivable retaliatory capabilities. This does not require massive force structures or an ability to destroy great power attackers in a cold-war-mutual-assured-destruction sense. Instead, small states need only be *capable* of launching highly destructive attacks with certainty to gain some measure of deterrence.

That being said, it should be noted that while nuclear weapons alter the security relationships between great powers and small states in areas of central interest, *realist assumptions will continue to remain applicable to competition between states in more peripheral areas.* Indeed, active competition and conflict in peripheral areas of interest will continue between small and large nuclear states (or between small nuclear ones), just as they continued between the superpowers during the Cold War. The explanation for this rests in the "credibility of nuclear threats." Just as the credibility of U.S. "extended deterrence" was doubted by Europeans, who questioned America's willingness to respond to an attack on Western Europe by risking New York for Paris, nuclear threats by small states over peripheral areas of interest would similarly lack credibility (Gallois 1961). Only when small state *central* interests are *critically threatened* would nuclear threats against great powers appear nominally credible. For small states, growing nuclear capability will not be a carte blanche to deter great powers across the board, but instead represents a *limited* (but important) exception to the normal "power politics" game played between these actors.

## THE INEVITABILITY OF THE SPREAD OF NUCLEAR CAPABILITY

Scholars have long argued that structural changes in the distribution of power in the international system after the Cold War would lead to *increased* nuclear proliferation. For example, neorealist scholars say bipolarity within the system (a characteristic of the Cold War) inhibited proliferation among states, whereas multipolarity (after the Cold War) would accelerate it (Mearsheimer 1990; Frankel 1993). Moreover, multipolar systems are generally considered to be more war prone than bipolar systems. Indeed, Frankel (1993) contends only the combination of structural constraints imposed by the bipolar system and nuclear weapons led to stability during the Cold War. In a multipolar, post–Cold War world, Frankel (1993, 60–61) warns of greater incentives for states to proliferate, along with a general weakening of the stability provided by nuclear weapons. Though agreeing "security" motivations account for much of the rationale for new nuclear states, Sagan (1996/1997, 54–86) makes a compelling case for "domestic politics" (where nuclear weapons are political tools to advance parochial domestic or bureaucratic interests) and "normative symbolism" (where weapons acquisition or restraint provides important symbols of the state's modernity or identity) also playing important roles in accelerating proliferation. But, *whatever the motivation* driving states toward seeking nuclear capabilities, the pattern emerging over the past decade has been one of *increasing* numbers moving in that direction—which makes the issue of "how difficult" it would be for states to obtain various WMD capabilities of critical importance.

Unfortunately, scholars have also noted that significant spread of basic nuclear *know-how* and capabilities within the international system is almost inevitable, regardless of counterproliferation regime efforts, due to both the increasing industrialization and economic development of states and advances in available technology (Weltman 1981/1982; Zimmerman 1993; Preston 1997; Roberts 1999). Indeed, current counterproliferation regime efforts have been aptly demonstrated—in countries ranging from Iraq, Iran, and North Korea to India, Pakistan, and Israel—to have very limited ability to prevent determined states from pursuing nuclear arms if they decide to do so. As Betts (1993, 115) observes, "there has still been no case in which legal safeguards or inspections either revealed or derailed an attempt to build nuclear weapons" by a state motivated to obtain these capabilities.

In an excellent overview of the technical barriers to state nuclear weapons programs, Zimmerman (1993, 345) notes that over the past sixty years, the technological knowledge required for successful weapons design and development has become widespread and no longer poses a significant hurdle for determined states. Moreover, the physics behind simple, uranium-based nuclear weapons employing gun designs (which fire a projectile of uranium into a larger mass of uranium using a modified cannon to initiate the chain reaction) are so certain that they do not require actual weapons tests to ensure they will function. Indeed, this was the precise design used by the Hiroshima bomb in 1945, a weapon dropped by the U.S. without having conducted any prior test explosions. As Zimmerman (1993, 354) notes:

> Given the fact that the basics of nuclear weapon design and construction are now widely known, as is the technology for producing plutonium and enriched uranium, no nation with the technical capabilities of the United States in 1941 can ever be said to be more than five years from possessing a nuclear weapon, regardless of the state of its program at any given moment. There are no technical barriers to nuclear proliferation, only hurdles of greater or lesser size which can be leaped over at greater or lesser cost on time scales commensurate with the budget for the project and the skill of the workers . . . so far as is known, no nation which has attempted to detonate a nuclear explosive has failed on its first attempt.

Describing the "Nth Country" experiments carried out by the U.S. during the mid-1960s, Stober (2003) notes they conclusively demonstrated three new post-doc physicists, with no access to classified information and using only open literature, were capable of designing effective, Nagasaki-size nuclear weapons using plutonium. In explaining their choice to construct a plutonium-based weapon in the exercise, the young physicists, who wanted to impress their employers, felt a uranium gun-assembly weapon would be "too simple" a task to accomplish (Stober 2003, 59). In the end, the physicists not only completed a working plutonium bomb design (producing a 20-kiloton plus yield), but also a full set of blueprints to guide imaginary machinists in the fabrication of bomb parts (Stober 2003, 60–61). Amazingly, the team proceeded to develop thermonuclear-yield weapons designs with only another six weeks of work! (Stober 2003, 61)

Along the same lines, Zimmerman warns "should a nation determined to build a nuclear weapon quickly be able to *purchase* the fissile material (say from black market sources in the former Soviet Union), the costs for its project would probably plummet, and the time needed to construct its first weapon might decrease from years to months or weeks" (1993, 365). Although Russian police have regularly seized low-grade nuclear materials from individuals seeking to sell them on the black market, these materials had not been "weapons grade" in purity. This changed in late 2001 when Russian police arrested seven men seeking to sell more than two pounds of highly enriched weapons-grade uranium-235 in a town just south of Moscow ("Russia Says" 2001). The appearance of weapons-grade materials on the black market, as well as small amounts of plutonium, illustrate the continuing problem for counterproliferation efforts in the former Soviet Union—especially given the strong likelihood that only a fraction of the shipments are actually being intercepted.

Since the end of the Cold War, there have been over 175 incidents of smuggling or attempted theft of nuclear materials within the former Soviet Union, and at least 104 attempts to smuggle nuclear material into Turkey during the past eight years (Mansoor and Woolsey 2001; Frantz 2001). At least eighteen of these cases involved significant amounts of weapons-grade, highly enriched uranium or plutonium (Tagliabue 2001; Erlanger 2001). These included seizures of nearly three kilograms (6.6 pounds) of 90 percent enriched uranium-235 in St. Petersburg in March 1993, 360 grams of Russian-made plutonium in Munich in August 1994, and 2.7 kilograms (just over five pounds) of 80 percent enriched uranium-235 (part of what might have been an even larger shipment) that had apparently been stolen from the Russian nuclear research center in Obninsk (Erlanger 2001). In 1998, Russia barely succeeded in preventing the theft of more than forty pounds (18.5 kilograms) of highly enriched uranium from a military weapons facility near Chelyabinsk in the Urals, and twice in 2001, Russian forces discovered stakeouts by terrorists of a secret nuclear arms storage facility (Erlanger 2001).

At least 100 facilities around the former Soviet Union store weapons-grade material or warheads (only 40 percent of which meet U.S. security standards);

many of the nuclear power plants lack significant security; and up to eighty abandoned nuclear submarines lay rusting along Russia's eastern coast—all of which provide tempting targets for those seeking to obtain access to nuclear materials (Kluger 2001, 41–42). According to a 2002 Harvard University report, "there are hundreds of thousands of kilograms of military plutonium and highly enriched uranium spread across the former Soviet Union, much of it dangerously insecure, and smaller but still immense amounts in the other seven nuclear weapon states" (Nicoll 2002). Similarly, the National Intelligence Council (NIC) warned "Russian facilities housing weapons-usable nuclear material . . . typically receive low funding, lack trained security personnel, and do not have sufficient equipment for securely storing such material" (CIA 2002). Though it didn't know "the extent or magnitude" of nuclear thefts from Russian institutes (over 300 buildings in more than forty facilities), the NIC expressed concern about "the total amount that could have been diverted over the past 10 years" (CIA 2002).

But it is not only "weapons-grade" material that is of concern, since it is widely accepted that weapons can be easily fashioned from "reactor-grade" plutonium (Mark et al. 1986; Mark 1990; Garwin and Simonenko 1996). In fact, Mark (1990, 3) warns that while the use of "reactor-grade" plutonium *does* increase the probability yields obtained by warheads will fall short of the optimal yields achieved using "weapons-grade" material (so-called fizzle yields), these would nevertheless still produce explosions of hundreds to perhaps one thousand tons of TNT. Indeed, the nominal yields of an atomic bomb employing the very conservative 1945 Trinity design using reactor-grade plutonium would still reach a yield of ten kilotons or more (Mark 1990, 3). With modern materials and technical knowledge, Mark suggests "straightforward ways could be found to realize a faster-moving implosion, that would have the effect of increasing fizzle yields to higher levels" (1990, 3). Put another way, with increasing technical sophistication, terrorist groups or new nuclear states could achieve one-to-five-kiloton blasts from weapons which "fizzled" and did not achieve their nominal yields—something that would dramatically increase the potential "minimum" damage inflicted using even crude atomic weapons. As Garwin and Simonenko (1996, 4) observe regarding constructing nuclear weapons from reactor-grade plutonium:

[I]t is not much more difficult than making an implosion weapon from "weapon-grade" Pu-239, and the difficulties involved are not of a different type. The fact that there are no national nuclear weapon stockpiles built of reactor-grade plutonium does not in any way reduce the possibility that separated reactor-grade plutonium could be used to make one, a few, or even hundreds of nuclear weapons.

Of course, states seeking more powerful, "boosted" fission weapons (accomplished by placing deuterium and tritium gas inside the hollow pit of warheads) will be faced with the need to develop additional facilities capable of producing tritium gas, since it only has a half-life of 12.3 years and needs to be replaced to maintain the viability of weapons. Garwin and Simonenko (1996, 7) note "it has long been a rule of thumb that many thermonuclear weapons typically produce about half of their total energy from the thermonuclear fuel and half from the fission of uranium in the proximity of that thermonuclear fuel." Since the plutonium fission yields of weapons can be greatly increased by adding fusion fuel (such as deuterium) to the core, it is likely that new nuclear states, like Israel, will seek to develop higher yield weapons using this technique.

Equally dangerous from a proliferation standpoint are concerns about the "brain drain" of weapons expertise out of the former Soviet Union. The Soviet nuclear weapons community was estimated to consist of between 50,000 and 60,000 scientists, many of whom are now out of work, impoverished, and at high risk of selling their knowledge on the open market to the highest bidder (Smithson 1999). Over 2,000 of these scientists are considered by the U.S. government to be of "critical proliferation concern" due to their comprehensive knowledge of all aspects of designing and fabricating nuclear weapons—*knowledge that would vastly simplify and accelerate any state's nuclear development program* (Smithson 1999, 49). As Zimmerman (1993, 353) warns, "most experienced weapon designers are convinced that once a reliable implosion system has been designed and tested using inert material similar to plutonium or enriched uranium (e.g., natural uranium), a nuclear test is probably unnecessary in order for the proliferant to have confidence in the functioning of the weapon." Moreover, while "most advanced pure fission devices, boosted fission weapons, and true thermonuclear weapons probably cannot be constructed without a certain amount of experience with what 'works' and what does not," Zimmerman (1993, 354) notes the required expertise could be obtained "either by testing or by finding mercenary weapons experts who can replicate successful designs for well-to-do customers."

## HOW MUCH MATERIAL IS REQUIRED?

Although costly, analysts versed in nuclear weapons production argue these capabilities are clearly within reach of states with only modest technical or industrial bases. Estimates of the amount of material required for weapons varies with the degree of design sophistication and quality of materials involved, but has been shown by the UN to be between 15 and 25 kilograms

(33–55 pounds) of uranium-235 and between 4 and 8 kilograms (8.8–17.6 pounds) of plutonium-239 (Spiers 2000, 3). But Cochran and Paine (1995, 1–3) warn these standards—used by both the UN and the IAEA (the International Atomic Energy Agency) in calculating "significant quantity" (SQ), or the minimum amount of fissile materials required (if no further enrichment or enhancements needed to be done) to manufacture a weapon—are seriously overinflated. While the original Fat Man bomb dropped by the U.S. on Nagasaki in 1945 used 6.1 kilograms of weapons-grade plutonium (WGPu), modern boosted-fission primaries in current U.S. thermonuclear weapons are made with less than 4 kilograms of plutonium and lightweight, boosted-fission weapons of up to 15 kilotons require as little as 3.5 kilograms of plutonium! As Cochran and Paine (1995, 5–6) observe:

> For single-stage pure fission weapons, a spherically symmetric implosion design requires the least amount of fissile material to achieve a given explosive yield, relative to other possible designs. For this type of device the amount of fissile material required depends primarily upon the type of fissile material used, e.g., plutonium, U-233, or HEU, the desired explosive yield of the device, and the degree to which the fissile material is compressed at the time disassembly of the fissile material begins due to the release of energy from the rapid nuclear chain reaction. The degree of compression achieved depends on the sophistication of the design and the degree of symmetry achieved by the imploding shock wave . . . the Nagasaki bomb, *Fat Man*, which produced a 20 kilotons (kt) explosion with 6.1 kilograms (kg) of WGPU, falls on the "low technology" curve. However, only three kilograms of WGPU compressed the same amount would still have produced a 1 kt explosion. A non-nuclear weapons state today can take advantage of the wealth of nuclear weapons design information that has been made public over the past 50 years, and do even better . . . . We estimate, for example, that as little as 2 kilograms of plutonium or about 4 kilograms of HEU are required to produce a yield of 10 kilotons.

Further, Cochran and Paine (1995, 8) observe that so-called high sophisticated techniques were known to U.S. weapons designers in the late 1940s and early 1950s. Thus, countries with highly developed nuclear infrastructures (like Israel, India, and Pakistan) would have to be considered technologically sophisticated. They also note that "even for countries that are generally not sophisticated technologically, the key technical information needed to establish a program for achieving a high degree of compression by implosion techniques is now available in the unclassified literature."

## TRENDS IN THE PROLIFERATION
## OF DELIVERY SYSTEM CAPABILITIES

States also have a growing variety of means to deliver nuclear weapons onto opponents, ranging from clandestine delivery aboard commercial ships or aircraft to delivery using advanced cruise missiles, short- to long-range ballistic missiles, or advanced combat aircraft. Further, most states will have the option of using *a combination of these delivery modes*, creating essentially a *poor-man's quadrat*—mirroring the U.S. nuclear *triad* of missile, bomber, and submarine delivery systems. Obviously, the new nuclear state's quadrat will have qualitative limitations regarding range, reliability, and survivability, and will likely lack the assured nature of advanced U.S. delivery methods. However, for these states, the key to making a credible threat is having the clear capability to deliver *at least some* of their nuclear weapons over an opponent's targets. This does not require that all of the delivery systems perfectly penetrate the defender's defenses and survive—only that some do. The earliest *assured delivery capabilities* for new nuclear states are likely to be in local or nearby regional theaters of operation, where the short ranges of systems and limited geographic distances work to increase the chances of effective delivery. The last (and most difficult) capability is longer-range delivery against distant regional or intercontinental strikes against great power opponents. These require the most advanced and costly delivery systems, and are likely to be available only to new nuclear states who are close to making the transition to great power nuclear status themselves (like China during the 1970s). But, even for new nuclear states lacking such advanced delivery capabilities, attacks against distant opponents are still possible almost from the beginning using clandestine delivery of weapons concealed within cargo containers aboard ships or aircraft.

Perhaps the most widely proliferated, potential nuclear delivery system available to states are foreign-supplied advanced combat aircraft (Spector 1986; Harvey 1992). Indeed, noting Sweden developed (during its secret nuclear program of the 1960s) a prototype, 20-kiloton weapon weighing only 1,300 pounds (591 kilograms) designed for delivery from the exterior of an aircraft, Spector (1986, 143–44) observes that by the late 1980s, Israel, India, and Pakistan had similar capabilities. All three possess large inventories of advanced fighter-bomber aircraft, obtained from U.S., French, or Soviet/Russian sources, all of which can easily carry such payloads (or even heavier ones) and have effective combat radiuses of many hundreds of miles.

As Harvey (1992, 74) notes, "for nuclear missions, ballistic missiles are superior to strike aircraft in overall cost effectiveness (measured in total cost for one sortie)," yet "in evaluating the likelihood of a successful nuclear strike mission, no single military factor provides a compelling rationale for favoring ballistic missiles over aircraft." Moreover, there is no obvious reason why new nuclear states will view this as an "either/or" choice regarding missile or aircraft delivery of their weapons. States such as North Korea, India, Pakistan, and Israel will likely employ both to create redundancy of delivery systems and increase the chances of effectively penetrating an opponent's defenses. As Harvey observes:

> Because of the nature of regional *strategic* targets (few in number, soft, distributed and not time-critical), the attacker has a great deal of flexibility in the timing, routing to the target, and ground-zero location of nuclear strikes. Thus, while the probability of defense penetration for ballistic missiles is high, so too is the likelihood that a significant fraction of modern strike aircraft carrying appropriate ECM, and flying at low altitude along routes that permit terrain masking and defense avoidance, will penetrate unmolested to their targets. In any case, even an extremely high rate of aircraft loss (e.g., 50 percent per sortie) is not likely to preclude extraordinary destruction of the attacked state; even a few nuclear strike aircraft penetrating defenses would be disastrous (1992, 68).

As for ballistic missiles, despite the export restrictions imposed by the MTCR (Missile Technology Control Regime), the ability of states to indigenously develop ballistic missiles have not been eliminated. Scholars have long noted the potential utility of currently proliferated ballistic missiles as delivery vehicles for WMD (McNaugher 1990; Cohen and Miller 1991; Karp 2000). North Korea, India, Pakistan, Iran, and Israel all currently have indigenous ballistic missile development programs that have developed and deployed systems with ranges in excess of 1,000 kilometers (620 miles), and continue efforts to produce missiles with substantially longer ranges (Cirincione 2002, 74). Observing how even the *threat* to use long-range missiles against the U.S. would complicate American decision making during crises, the September 1999 the National Intelligence Estimate (NIE) warned:

> Acquiring long-range ballistic missiles armed with WMD will enable weaker countries to do three things that they otherwise might not be able to do: deter, constrain, and harm the United States. To achieve these objectives, these WMD-armed weapons need not be deployed in large numbers; with even a few such weapons, these countries would judge that they had the capability to threaten at least politically significant damage to the United States or its allies. They need not be highly accurate; the ability to target a large urban area is sufficient. They need not be highly reliable, because their strategic value is derived primarily from the threat (implicit or explicit) of their use, not the near certain outcome of such use . . . such weapons are not envisioned at the outset as operational

weapons of war, but primarily as strategic weapons of deterrence and coercive diplomacy. (CIA 1999, 4–5)

Mistry (2003, 120–23) notes the MTCR can only delay, not stop, regional powers from building missile arsenals, having already failed to prevent Israel, India, North Korea, Pakistan, and Iran from testing intermediate-range ballistic missiles (IRBMs) with ranges between 1,000 and 2,000 kilometers. Though development of intercontinental ballistic missiles have been delayed by the MTCR, many states (e.g., India, Israel, Brazil) are developing space-launch systems (ostensibly for satellites) that could be adapted into true ICBMs (Mistry 2003, 124). Most new nuclear states (and several potential future ones) possess sizable inventories of short-range to medium- and intermediate-range ballistic missiles.

As for cruise missiles, only a dozen states possess land-attack cruise missiles (LACMs) comparable to the U.S. Tomahawk. But, while the MTCR makes it more costly and difficult to obtain ballistic missiles, the same is not true for cruise missiles. Antiship cruise missiles and UAVs (unmanned aerial vehicles) have already been exported to more than forty countries, and by 2010, as many as ten more nations might possess LACMs (Gormley 1998, 98; Center for Counterproliferation Research 2001, 35). Further, the potential of states to indigenously develop or modify these weapons into strategic delivery systems increases with time, especially given the dual-use character of much of the hardware. For example, most structures, propulsion/navigation systems, and autopilots from manned aircraft are interchangeable with those in cruise missiles (Gormley 1998, 96). Unlike the past, where controls over the spread of advanced guidance systems effectively prevented states from obtaining the technology to make accurate cruise missiles, commercial guidance and navigation systems now available using the Global Positioning System (GPS) allow states to circumvent these controls (Gormley 1998, 95). Now, any state with the ability to produce aircraft, or the technical expertise to maintain existing foreign-produced aircraft, has the basic technical capability to begin cruise missile development. As Gormley (1998, 98) notes, "the technology required to produce a 1,000 km-range cruise missile is not fundamentally different from that needed for short-range systems."

Moreover, states can also convert *existing* antiship cruise missiles or UAVs into land-attack cruise missiles. Ironically, the best systems for such conversion are not newer ones (like the French *Exocet*, which is smaller and more densely packed with miniaturized components), but rather much older ones (like the Chinese Silkworm and Russian Styx missiles, which are larger and provide space for needed upgrades) (Gormley 1998, 97). Both Iran and North Korea have already modified existing Silkworm systems to increase their range, and at only $250,000 per missile, they are affordable and among the most widely proliferated systems (along with the Scud) in the world (Gormley 1998, 97). Advanced cruise missiles are also becoming available from exporters who creatively package them to circumvent MTCR export restrictions. For example, Russia offers a short-range version of its 3,000-kilometer AS-15 cruise missile (complete with GPS-equivalent navigation systems) and avoids MTCR restrictions by advertising payloads and ranges just beneath critical cutoff points (Gormley 1998, 99). Technical assistance provided by states, such as Russia and China, have also helped countries develop their own cruise missile programs.[2]

Cruise missiles provide a flexible and survivable delivery capability for states. They can be stored in canisters allowing for easy operation and maintenance in harsh environments, are relatively compact, require a smaller logistics burden, and allow for more mobility and flexible launch options (by ground launchers, commercial ships, or aircraft) than large ballistic missiles (Gormley 1998, 95). The aerodynamic stability of cruise missiles make them incredibly effective platforms for dispersing bioagents, producing lethal areas for given quantities of agent at least ten times greater than that provided by standard ballistic missiles (Gormley 1998, 96). Unlike long-range ballistic missiles that require highly visible flight and performance tests of rocket motors and stages, cruise missile development is very difficult to monitor since it doesn't require such tests. As Gormley (1998, 101) notes, "whereas ballistic-missile improvements tend to unfold sequentially over time, several levels of cruise-missile capability—including both early missile designs and advanced missiles with stealth features—could emerge simultaneously."

Further, covert conversion of commercial container ships into launching platforms for cruise missiles is a growing threat:

> There are thousands of commercial container ships in the international fleet, and U.S. ports alone handle over 13 million containers annually. Even a large, bulky cruise missile like the Silkworm—converted for land attack—could readily fit inside a standard 12-meter shipping container equipped with a small internal erector for launching. Such a ship-launched cruise missile could be positioned just outside territorial waters to strike virtually any important capital or large industrial area anywhere on the globe. And, because a cruise missile is an ideal means for efficiently delivering small but highly lethal quantities of biological agent, a state or terrorist group could forgo acquiring or building a nuclear weapon without sacrificing the ability to cause catastrophic damage.

Similarly, the December 2001 NIE observes that these systems have the advantage of being "less expensive, more reliable and accurate, more effective for disseminating biological warfare agents, [could] be used without attribution, and would avoid missile defenses" (Gormley 2002, 25 and 28).

## THE IMPACT OF PROLIFERATION ON
## DETERRENCE AS A CONTINGENT VARIABLE

Within the security studies field, an ongoing debate exists between scholars who take radically different views on the stabilizing/destabilizing effects of nuclear proliferation on interstate relations. As Schneider (1994, 210–16) observes, scholars disagree on whether proliferation is inevitable or not, as well as over whether the probable outcome of such spread will be positive, mixed, or negative upon the international system. Among scholars who take an optimistic view of proliferation, there is the belief that nuclear weapons provide deterrence, enhance crisis stability, and create more peaceful security relationships between states (e.g., Sandoval 1976; Rosen 1977; Waltz 1981; de Mesquita and Riker 1982; Feldman 1982; Goldstein 1992, 2000; Mearsheimer 1993; Hagerty 1995/1996, 1998). On the other hand, scholars taking a more pessimistic view of proliferation question whether nuclear weapons create more peaceful security relationships, arguing that crisis instability, the risk of war, and the danger of accidental/unauthorized use increase as more states cross the nuclear threshold (Dunn 1982, 1993; Quester 1983; Kaiser 1989; Miller 1993; Kincade 1993; Bracken 1993; Feaver 1993; Sagan 1994).

Other scholars have suggested proliferation might have *both* stabilizing effects (when advanced enough for mutual deterrent postures to develop), as well as destabilizing effects in the short-term (Weltman 1980, 1981/1982; Feldman 1997; Preston 1997). As Feldman (1997, 2) observes, "whether the overall effects of nuclear spread would be largely stabilizing or destabilizing is likely to depend primarily on the general political circumstances prevailing in the region when such proliferation takes place." Or, as Weltman (1980, 189) notes:

> The introduction of nuclear weapons into a regional conflict may produce an impetus either to stability or instability, depending on the specifics of the technology introduced, the pace of its introduction, and the extent to which that introduction is made on a symmetrical or asymmetrical basis between the parties to a regional conflict. There is no reason to assume, as a general proposition, that one or another outcome must eventuate.

In fact, Wirtz (1998, 137) foresees the possibility of "a series of bilateral deterrence relationships" between "an increasing number of relatively small nuclear arsenals" becoming much more prevalent in the post–Cold War system. At the same time, however, he argues that "it is impossible to avoid the conclusion that arms-race stability is unlikely until a robust situation of mutual assured destruction emerges between any possible combination of potential adversaries" (Wirtz 1998, 151).

Essentially, deterrence is the quintessential "contingent" relationship that varies in shape and form across differing situational contexts, military capability levels, political leaders, and psychological dynamics operating at the time. As George and Smoke (1974, 509) observe, despite the common presentation of abstract, deductivistic theories of deterrence in a normative-prescriptive mode, this "does not eliminate the necessity for situational analysis or act as a substitute for it." Though analysts typically try to apply the logics of "strategic deterrence as the paradigm case for thinking about deterrence in general," George and Smoke note that "deterrence of lower-level conflict, unlike Assured Destruction, cannot be implemented by threatening a specific level of damage; and it does not involve a single kind of military power" (1974, 45 and 51). Instead, differences in both the *objectives* of policy makers at differing strategic vs. nonstrategic levels of interaction and their *perceptions* become incredibly important. In fact, Joseph and Reichart (1999, 8) warn of the need to include "new factors" into thinking about deterrence (such as cultural/religious differences influencing risk hierarchies, risk tolerances, communications) which "are likely to vary substantially region by region and even country by country." As is discussed in later chapters, such a distinction becomes important when differentiating between how deterrence is likely to operate between nuclear state actors on the one hand, and nuclear nonstate actors (like Al Qaeda) on the other. Deterrence relationships are both contingent upon the situational context and upon the psychological characteristics of the policy makers on both sides. It is not a "one-size-fits-all" theoretical approach, and it is simplistic to treat it as such.

## THE PESSIMIST/OPTIMIST NUCLEAR PROLIFERATION DEBATE

Nuclear proliferation has been the subject of one of the longest and most bitterly contested debates within the academic security community, largely between two camps of scholars, the so-called optimists and pessimists. They differ radically from one another regarding their views of the likely impact of proliferation upon crisis stability and deterrence relationships between states. They differ widely regarding what solutions or policy approaches should be adopted. And it is a debate in which neither side has been very willing to consider the many valid points made by their opponents, who seldom are actually as extreme in their arguments as they are caricaturized. In fact, there is a wide spectrum of beliefs expressed across proliferation scholars which in reality spans the gap between the two poles of total optimism and pessimism. In the following discussion, I will seek to lay out these views and suggest where (and under what contexts) each might be correct. What should quickly become apparent is that it is often *not* the nature of some of the assertions made as much as the assumption that they are *always true* across any context that is the problem.

## The Essence of the Argument

Scholars who fall into the more "pessimistic" category regarding proliferation are by far the more numerous within the academic community (cf. Dunn 1982, 1993; Fetter 1991; Feaver 1993; Miller 1993; Cimbala 1998; Bracken 1999; Carranza 1999; Sagan 1994, 2004). Yet, those falling into the more "optimistic" category regarding proliferation, which began largely with Waltz's seminal (if controversial) arguments (see Waltz 1981, 1990), have evolved an equally strong body of work (cf. Rosen 1977; Bundy 1982; de Mesquita and Riker 1982; Hagerty 1995/1996, 1998; Karl 1996/1997; Feldman 1997; Preston 1997; Harvey 1997a; Goldstein 1992, 2000) which challenges pessimist assumptions. While a full review and critique of this immense literature is clearly beyond the scope or purpose of this book, it is useful to review some of the central arguments raised within this debate to assist in developing a new analytic framework which might bridge some of the gaps between the two perspectives by placing predictions about the consequences of proliferation into their proper situational contexts.

Essentially, the arguments raised by the pessimist school of thought on proliferation typically center around the following major themes:

*The Cost of Deterrence Failure Is Too Great*—Since deterrence can never be perfect, the more states that have nuclear weapons, the more likely they are to be used in some future conflict. This makes the potential losses of human life too great to trust to deterrence (Lebow and Stein 1989, 1990; Feaver 1993).

*Deterrence Theory Is Flawed*—This involves a long-standing debate between scholars who argue deterrence theory is flawed, seldom (or never) works, is too difficult to achieve, and is too dangerous to rely upon (Lebow 1987; Lebow and Stein 1989, 1990) versus those who see it as both empirically well-grounded and historically supported (Huth and Russett 1984, 1990; Harvey 1997a; Goldstein 2000).

*Deterrence Is Ineffective and Cannot Be Proved to Have Worked Even during the Cold War*—This involves the argument that the long peace between the U.S. and Soviet Union (held out as an example by optimists and deterrence supporters of the positive role of nuclear weapons) could have occurred *despite* (not because of) the presence of such weapons (Gjelstad and Njolstad 1996). The Cuban Missile Crisis is suggested (along with various nuclear alerts) as an example of risky superpower behavior that only good fortune prevented from becoming nuclear wars (Sagan and Suri 2003).

*Organizational Problems and Difficulties of Effective Command and Control Make Nuclear Weapons Too Risky for Less Politically Stable States to Possess during Crises*—Based upon organization theory arguments and the notion of normal "accidents" in complex, tightly coupled systems, it is argued that new nuclear states are unlikely to be politically stable enough (or be able to develop sufficiently effective organizational and C3I structures) to maintain positive control over their nuclear arsenals during crises or prevent accidents that could lead to war (Feaver 1992/1993; Sagan 1993, 1994). Examples of U.S.–Soviet organizational/C3I problems during the Cold War are used to buttress this argument. Since new nuclear states are likely to be politically unstable, there is concern this increases the chances of accidental or intentional use during civil wars or after the rise to power of extreme factions. Since many new nuclear states are in the developing world and have histories of civil unrest or military juntas, such arguments have little difficulty envisioning dire scenarios (Dunn 1982; Bracken 1999).

*New Nuclear States Will Not Act in the Same Rational, Mature Manner the Great Powers Did in the Stewardship of Their Nuclear Weapons*—An immensely ethnocentric line of argument, but one which basically argues developing states' leaders will not act like "rational" Western leaderships, but be driven by messianic, aggressive, even suicidal motivations drawn from extreme ideologies or religious beliefs (Dunn 1982; Martel 1998). Such states are viewed as "rogues" and governed by "crazy" leaders whose behavior will be neither rational nor predictable.

*New Nuclear States Are Less Likely to Be Democratic and More Likely to Be Authoritarian, Making Nuclear Use More Likely*—This argument is driven by the currently fashionable "democratic peace" theory, which argues democracies are more peaceful than authoritarian regimes and democracies don't fight other democracies (Ray 1993, 1995; Weart 1994, 1998; Russett and Oneal 2001). Authoritarian regimes are viewed as more aggressive, less responsive to domestic political constraints, and therefore, more likely to use nuclear weapons (either offensively or defensively).

*New Nuclear Arsenals Are Inherently More Vulnerable to Preemption Than Those of Established Nuclear Powers, Creating Greater Crisis Instability and Likelihood of Launch-on-Warning Postures*—Since new arsenals are likely to be small in number, housed in vulnerable basing modes, and use less advanced delivery system technologies, they face a far greater danger of being preempted and disarmed by an opponent's first strike. This means new states must "use them or lose them" when in doubt, and lacking an assured second strike retaliatory capability, this means effective, stable deterrence relationships are unlikely to be achieved—increasing the dangers of nuclear war (Dunn 1982; Feaver 1992/1993).

*The Stability-Instability Paradox*—The notion that possession of nuclear weapons increases the "comfort zone" states might feel as they enter into conventional confrontations with opponents, reducing their fear of escalation, and thereby increasing their willingness to escalate the intensity of such conventional conflicts in the belief that the threat of nuclear retaliation will prevent the conflict from getting out of hand. This creates a potential for miscalculation by policy makers who might inadvertently find themselves in a dramatically escalated conventional conflict that has become severe enough to force considering the use of nuclear weapons (Snyder 1961).

## 1.) The Cost of Deterrence Failure Is Too Great

Advocates of deterrence seldom take the position that it will *always* work or that it *cannot* fail. Rather, they take the position that if one can achieve the requisite elements required to achieve a stable deterrent relationship between parties, it vastly decreases the chances of miscalculation and resorting to war—even in contexts where it might otherwise be expected to occur (George and Smoke 1974; Harvey 1997a; Powell 1990, 2003; Goldstein 2000). Unfortunately, critics of deterrence take the understandable, if unrealistic, position that if deterrence cannot be 100 percent effective under all circumstances, then it is an unsound strategic approach for states to rely upon, especially considering the immense destructiveness of nuclear weapons. Feaver (1993, 162), for example, criticizes reliance on nuclear deterrence because it *can* fail and that rational deterrence theory can only predict that peace should occur *most* of the time (e.g., Lebow and Stein 1989).

Yet, were we to apply this standard of perfection to most other policy approaches concerning security matters—whether it be arms control or proliferation regime efforts, military procurement policies, alliance formation strategies, diplomacy, or sanctions—none could be argued with any more certainty to completely remove the threat of equally devastating wars either. Indeed, one could easily make the argument that these alternative means have shown themselves historically to be far less effective than nuclear arms in preventing wars. Certainly, the twentieth century was replete with examples of devastating conventional conflicts which were *not* deterred through nonnuclear measures. Although the potential costs of a nuclear exchange between small states would indeed cause a frightful loss of life, it would be no more costly (and likely far less so) than large-scale conventional conflicts have been for combatants.

Moreover, if nuclear deterrence *raises* the potential costs of war high enough for policy makers to want to *avoid* (rather than risk) conflict, it is just as legitimate (if not more so) for optimists to argue in favor of nuclear deterrence in terms of the lives saved through the avoidance of far more likely recourses to conventional wars, as it is for pessimists to warn of the potential costs of deterrence failure. And, while some accounts describing the "immense weaknesses" of deterrence theory (Lebow and Stein 1989, 1990) would lead one to believe deterrence was almost impossible to either obtain or maintain, since 1945 there has not been one single historical instance of nuclear deterrence failure (*especially* when this notion is limited to threats to key central state interests like survival, and not to minor probing of peripheral interests). Moreover, the *actual costs* of twentieth-century conventional conflicts have been staggeringly immense, especially when compared to the *actual costs* of nuclear conflicts (for example, 210,000 fatalities in the combined 1945 Hiroshima and Nagasaki atomic bombings compared to 62 million killed overall during World War II, over three million dead in both the Korean and Vietnam conflicts, etc.) (McKinzie et al. 2001, 28).[3]

Further, as Gray (1999, 158–59) observes, "it is improbable that policymakers anywhere need to be educated as to the extraordinary qualities and quantities of nuclear armaments." Indeed, the high costs and uncontestable, immense levels of destruction that would be caused by nuclear weapons have been shown historically to be facts that have not only been readily apparent and salient to a wide range of policy makers, but ones that have clearly been demonstrated to moderate extreme policy or risk-taking behavior (Blight 1992; Preston 2001) Could it go wrong? Of course. There is always that potential with human beings in the loop. Nevertheless, it has also been shown to be effective at moderating policy maker behavior and introducing an element of constraint into situations that otherwise would likely have resulted in war (Hagerty 1998).

## 2.) Deterrence Theory Is Flawed

The dispute between scholars critical of rational deterrence theory (Jervis 1976; Lebow 1981, 1987; Stein 1987; Lebow and Stein 1989, 1990) and those supporting it (Huth and Russett 1984, 1990; Achen and Snidal 1989; Huth 1988) has raged for decades without resolution. Again, while a full review of the details of this debate is far beyond the scope of this book, it is useful to briefly note the chief points made by both camps.

Deterrence critics Lebow and Stein (1989, 223) argue that "deterrence theories presuppose that leaders are (1) instrumentally rational, (2) risk-prone gain maximizers, (3) free of domestic constraints, and (4) able correctly to identify themselves as defenders or challengers"—assumptions which they suggest "are unrealistic and contradicted by empirical evidence." They suggest rational deterrence theory is not only conceptually unsound, but lacks both the ability to make good predictions of strategic behavior or provide guidance for successful strategies of conflict management. Moreover, as Feaver (1993, 161) observes, among all of the critiques of deterrence theory, "one criticism emerges as particularly relevant to the nuclear proliferation question: whether rational deterrence theory pays inadequate attention to the role of key factors, psychological and otherwise, which complicate deterrence calculations." As Lebow and Stein argue:

> The problem with rational models is not that they contain idealizations but that these idealizations are their fundamental assumptions. Such assumptions as the rational decision maker, perfect information, and a politically neutral environment are realizations that lack any empirical referent. Rational deterrence theories are accordingly "theories" about nonexistent decision makers operating in nonexistent environments. (1989, 224)

But, as Harvey (1997a, 10) points out, this description by Lebow and Stein represents a serious mischaracterization of how the concept of "rational" is used by the rational deterrence literature:

> Rationality does not require complete information or an exhaustive search for alternatives, objectives, and consequences; in fact, it is often irrational to undertake such a search if the marginal cost of continuing the investigation exceeds the marginal gain from doing so. Similarly, rational choice theory does not stipulate that decision makers actually calculate the costs and benefits associated with each option, or measure the probabilities and utilities of every alternative outcome. This too would be irrational in most cases.

Indeed, Harvey (1997a, 6) correctly observes that the end result of this long debate over deterrence theory has been to saturate the field primarily "with efforts to falsify theories by pointing out the flaws inherent in the methods used" by scholars to study them—not careful analysis of the concept of deterrence itself (separate from the methodology used to study it)! In fact, as Tetlock et al. (1991, 252) observe, Lebow and Stein's work could be criticized as being based upon an "unrepresentative sample of deterrence failures drawn from a much larger unspecified universe of cases" and that the failures they cite do not necessarily falsify the predictions of deterrence theory, since it actually predicts numerous failures. In other words, failures of deterrence policies are not necessarily failures of deterrence theory (Achen and Snidal 1989; Quester 1989). Further, as Harvey (1997a, 95) notes, though most studies of deterrence failure use the outbreak of war or conflict as the main indicator, a better (and more nuanced) approach to assessing outcomes would be to focus upon "the achievement or denial of the defender's and attacker's policy interests." In their study of Cold War conventional deterrence cases,

George and Smoke (1974, 520–21) found that since states seeking to challenge the status quo normally have more than one option for doing so, this leaves open the possibility of *mixed deterrence outcomes*, part success and part failure—since some options may have been successfully deterred, but others not foreseen. Moreover, from the standpoint of the initiator, his *perceptions* of the potential effectiveness of each option (i.e., their expected benefits, costs, risks, and probabilities of success) differ across the options (George and Smoke 1974, 521–22). Excellent overviews and critiques of this debate are provided elsewhere by several scholars (see Herring 1995; Harvey 1997a).

In reality, much of the debate centers less around whether deterrence really works, and more upon the difficulties of empirically measuring and testing hypotheses against historical cases whose interpretations are often open to dispute, plagued by incomplete records of the events (particularly those centering around individual policy makers), and the fact that most historical cases are seldom examples of only one case of deterrence, but a series of deterrence/compellence efforts across a long period of time throughout a crisis. Since the deterrence testing literature uses the success-failure strategy, Harvey (1997b, 12) notes scholars identify "the cases of immediate deterrence, coding these cases as instances of success or failure, isolating conditions that were present or absent during successes, and absent or present during failures, and, based on these differences, draw conclusions about why and how deterrence works." As a result, each of the single crisis cases examined by Huth/Russett and Lebow/Stein frequently consist of "several different types of interactions and outcomes"—and the reason each side can have radically different interpretations of the historical record in their data sets is that *both sides* are right since each "focused on different periods (and exchanges) throughout the crises" (Harvey 1997b, 12).

### 3.) Deterrence Is Ineffective and Cannot Be Proved to Have Worked Even during the Cold War

Disagreement also centers around the validity of one of the key examples cited by optimists of the stability enhancing effects of nuclear weapons, the so-called nuclear peace between the superpowers during the Cold War. Proponents of this argument note, among other things, the extreme arms race dynamic between the sides, the close proximity of their conventional forces to one another in Western Europe, the intense hostility and bitterness of their rivalry and competition, and the many political "flashpoints" (such as Germany and Cuba) that in the absence of credible nuclear deterrence would have made war almost inevitable (e.g., Schlesinger 1996; Gaddis 1996; Van Benthem van den Bergh 1996). The certainty of nuclear annihilation, the invulnerability of each side's arsenals to preemption, and the belief that escalation was largely uncontrollable made resorting to force and fundamentally threatening the other side's central interests untenable.

In contrast, critics of the nuclear peace argument have variously suggested: We were just lucky; neither superpower truly wanted war during this period; perhaps the USSR was not really the expansionist, aggressive power it was depicted as being; Soviet conventional forces in Europe or the inability of policy makers to control escalation (not deterrence itself) were responsible; or that numerous dynamics were at play in the international system (such as growing interdependence, international organizations, etc.) resulting in a peace that would have existed regardless of nuclear weapons (e.g., Mueller 1996, 1998; Russett 1996; Smith 1996; Cimbala 1998; Krepon 2001). The absence of war during the period is explained as due, not to deterrent threats that kept each side's aggressive intentions in check, but instead to a lack of such intentions. Though both sides make strong, logical arguments in support of their positions, it is essentially a dead-end debate requiring each to conclusively prove why a "nonevent" (World War III) didn't happen or would have happened based upon counterfactual argumentation.

Some of the strongest empirical support for the effectiveness of nuclear deterrence during the Cold War is a study by Blechman and Kaplan (1976) tracking U.S. uses of military force (1946–1975) to support political objectives. Among the nineteen cases where nuclear threats were implicitly or explicitly made, three-quarters of the incidents happened during the first fifteen years of American nuclear dominance, with only two such incidents occurring after the Cuban Missile Crisis (Blechman and Kaplan 1976, 48; Cimbala 1998, 27–28). This strongly suggests that once the Soviet Union obtained a credible counterdeterrent, American nuclear threats rapidly lost their credibility in all but extreme situations. Moreover, in an exceedingly detailed analysis of behavior patterns between the U.S. and USSR during crises from 1948 to 1988, Harvey (1997a, 112) also found strong support for nuclear deterrence theory. As Harvey (1997a, 113) noted, "crises involving nuclear states are more likely to exhibit characteristics of restraint, as Brodie predicted (1959a, b), because each side understands the dangers of any action that could raise tensions to the level of war." Further, despite changes in the distribution of nuclear capabilities between the U.S. and Soviets (from American superiority during the 1940s and 1950s to Soviet parity from the late 1960s onward), these basic interactional patterns remained the same (Harvey 1997a, 114).

In suggesting nuclear weapons likely prevented military skirmishes during the 1999 Kargil crisis between India and Pakistan from escalating to full-scale war, Waltz (2004, 386) notes "the evidence, accumulated over five decades, shows that nuclear states fight with nuclear states only at low levels, that accidents seldom occur, and that when they do they never have bad effects. If nuclear pessimists were right, nuclear deterrence would have failed again and again." Indeed, as Hagerty (1998, 185) points out, the fundamental dynamic between nuclear powers in conflict is that the very existence of nuclear weapons deters war:

> In superpower crises over Berlin, Cuba, and the Middle East, the Sino-Soviet crisis of 1969, and the Kashmir crisis of 1990, the main impact of nuclear weapons on the disputants was to slow escalation to war. Rather than operationalizing the nuclear doctrines devised by their military planners, leaders have chosen instead to focus on how not to use the nuclear weapons they command.

*4.) Organizational Problems and Difficulties of Effective Command and Control Make Nuclear Weapons Too Risky for Politically Less Stable States to Possess during Crises*

The dangers posed by immature nuclear organizations and C3I capabilities, as well as those associated with organizational malfunctions and accidents in any complex, tightly coupled system, have also been a concern (e.g., Sagan 1993, 1994; Feaver 1992/1993; Feaver and Niou 1996).[4] For many politically unstable regimes, there is always the risk of military coups (if civilians are in charge), more radical military factions seizing power (if they aren't), or in worst-case scenarios, civil war. Such scenarios obviously raise serious questions regarding the fate of a state's nuclear arsenal, ranging from concerns about a new regime's revanchist ambitions against neighboring states, the chances of weapons being used against domestic opponents, or the danger of arms falling into terrorist hands for use elsewhere. Organizational problems, accidents, and near accidents experienced by the Cold War superpowers are cited as examples of the risks such weapons would hold for less sophisticated and financed nuclear organizations within new nuclear states. Indeed, the shorter geographic distances separating many of the new nuclear states from their opponents, the highly vulnerable first-generation nuclear forces possessed, the short time frames available for warning of and responding to attacks, and the intense ethnic/religious/ideological disputes involving many of the potential new nuclear states are justifiably cited as sources of concern for crisis stability.

Unfortunately, pessimists often extend this argument beyond these quite legitimate concerns about early stability of arsenals and adopt the untenable position that such instability is an eternally constant, never-changing truth for such states. Indeed, the view that the early stages of nuclear development are potentially unstable is one upon which there is wide agreement, even among optimist scholars (Preston 1997; Karl 1996/1997; Goldstein 2000). The primary distinction, however, lies in the difference of viewpoint regarding whether such vulnerabilities and weaknesses remain an eternal verity, or can be meaningfully addressed by these states over time so their nuclear organizations more resemble the stable, mature forms possessed by established nuclear powers. As Waltz (2004, 390) observes:

> Students of organizations rightly worry about complex and tightly-coupled systems because they are susceptible to damaging accidents. They wrongly believe that conflicting nuclear states should be thought of as a tightly-coupled system. Fortunately, nuclear weapons loosen the coupling of states by lessening the effects of proximity and by cutting through the complexities of conventional confrontations. Organizational theorists fail to distinguish between the technical complexities of nuclear-weapons systems and the simplicity of the situations they create.

The normative undercurrents to these arguments are well illustrated by the negative reaction of pessimists to the suggestion that, in order to remove the potential danger of unauthorized use or diversion of weapons from a new nuclear state's arsenal, existing nuclear states should provide them with PALs (permissive action locks) or other security devices to improve control over their arsenals. Indeed, cooperation between existing nuclear states and new nuclear states (to improve their C3I capabilities or enhance arsenal security) are opposed for potentially encouraging further proliferation—all the while the dangers posed by these insecure arsenals are lamented by the same critics (e.g., Dunn 1982). And while it is fair to be concerned about encouraging proliferation by too readily assisting the nuclear ambitions of additional states, it is naive (and counterproductive) to take this attitude once it is clear states (like Pakistan and India) will develop their arsenals regardless of any outsider's counterproliferation views.

*5.) New Nuclear States Will Not Act in the Same Rational, Mature Manner the Great Powers Did in the Stewardship of Their Nuclear Weapons*

This represents an immensely ethnocentric line of argument, and one which is completely devoid of any historic empirical support. In fact, if anything, the history of new nuclear state behavior over the past decades has shown nothing but rational, mature stewardship of their arsenals—and no recourse to war. Early new nuclear states (Britain, France, China) went on to develop fairly similar minimal deterrent doctrines and could certainly not be argued to have been irresponsible or irrational regarding their weapons (cf.

*Chapter 2*

Lewis and Xue 1988; Hopkins and Hu 1995; Johnston 1995/1996; Goldstein 1992, 2000). Similarly, the second wave of nuclear states (Israel, Pakistan, and India) have behaved responsibly as well, with all three adopting notions of minimal deterrence to prevent external attacks threatening their survival, while moving to make their arsenals more stable and secure (cf. Hersh 1991; Sundarji 1996; Cohen 1998; Hagerty 1998; Kampani 1998; Ahmed 1999; Tellis 2001). Even would-be nuclear states like North Korea and Iran, the long-standing favorites of worst-case scenario pessimists seeking "rogue states" governed by "crazy" leaders whose behavior would be irrational and aggressive (e.g., Dunn 1982; Martel 1998), have not been shown to be any less rational (if one understands their cultures and societies) than other states.

*6.) New Nuclear States Are Less Likely to Be Democratic and More Likely to Be Authoritarian, Making Nuclear Use More Likely*

This argument is driven by the "democratic peace" theory, which argues democracies are more peaceful than authoritarian regimes and that democracies don't fight other democracies (Ray 1993, 1995; Weart 1994, 1998; Hermann and Kegley 1995; Russett and O'Neal 2001). Indeed, some have argued the spread of democracy and complex interdependence in the post–Cold War system should reduce the need for states to pursue nuclear weapons, resulting in enhanced stability (Chafetz 1993). Authoritarian regimes are viewed as more aggressive, less responsive to domestic political constraints, and therefore, more likely to use nuclear weapons (either offensively or defensively). Indeed, nondemocratic, perhaps fanatical regimes, are suggested by pessimists to be *extremely likely* to use their weapons with little or no regard to their own country's interests or welfare. As Martel (1998, 219 and 221) suggests, unlike the prospect of facing liberal democratic states (presumed by his argument to be responsible and rational wards of nuclear weapons), we could face what he describes as "millenarian" or "revolutionary" societies that would not respond to Western notions of deterrence:

> A distinctive feature of millenarian societies is that they hold a different image of costs and benefits that may extend beyond the traditional conception of rational behavior. This means that millenarians may be willing to sacrifice their society, if such action advances their revolutionary ideology or theology. Such sacrifice of the society may be instrumentally rational. . . . A revolutionary society . . . could be driven by fatalistic urges to destroy its adversary, and thus itself, rather than allow the enemy to prevail. Furthermore, revolutionary societies could justify the decision to use nuclear weapons as an act of martyrdom in service of their deity or because their adherence to a revolutionary ideology mandates radical actions against status quo powers.

Unfortunately, while Martel's suggestion that nonstate actors (like Aum Shinrikyo, or in the current context, Al Qaeda) are groups who could appropriately be viewed as holding millenarian images of nuclear weapons, his description of Iran, Iraq, and Libya as revolutionary societies that "could be drawn toward a millenarian image of nuclear possession based on radical political ideologies and beliefs that are animated by the desire to destroy status quo societies" is vastly overdrawn and inaccurate regarding these regimes (1998, 221). Further, his historical examples of revolutionary societies willing to consciously commit suicidal actions "for the sake of revolutionary or millenarian goals," most notably Stalin, Hitler, and North Vietnam, ignores the fact that none of these nations actually behaved in this fashion historically (1998, 226).

Others have suggested "hysterical nationalism" (where religious hatreds and rage drive decisions), unlike the wonderfully unhysterical type of nationalism possessed by the superpowers during the Cold War, will make it hard for Asian states to approach "nuclear warfare with detachment and rationality." As Bracken (1999, 113) warns, "the idea of budding defense intellectuals sitting around with computer models and debating strategy in Iran or Pakistan defies credulity." That this opens pessimists to the charge of engaging in ethnocentric thinking and simplistic analysis is a criticism often leveled upon them by optimists (Karl 1996/1997; Sagan and Waltz 2003). Moreover, the history of U.S. behavior during the Cold War, as Sagan and Suri (2003, 180–81) observe, suggests that even "enlightened" Western policy makers are not immune to "roguish" behavior:

> The history of the October 1969 alert provides . . . [a] discomforting insight into the nature of command and control of nuclear weapons. Americans tend to assume that democratic institutions will make better decisions about war and peace than less democratic alternatives. Check and balances, it is assumed, assure that a single irrational and ignorant figure cannot create disaster. In October 1969, however, Richard Nixon deliberately exceeded the strategic actions that he believed Soviet leaders would perceive as those of a "rational actor" with nuclear weapons . . . senior officials in the U.S. government, including the secretary of defense, firmly believed that the commander in chief and his national security adviser were taking unnecessary and risky actions with U.S. strategic nuclear forces. They could not, however, check the direct orders of the president.

For Sagan and Suri (2003, 182), whether a state has a democratic or authoritarian political system has *no impact* upon their nuclear decision making during crises because: "Leaders in democratic, undemocratic, and mixed regimes can behave irresponsibly with nuclear weapons. Leaders in both democracies and non-democracies are susceptible to poor decision-making and pressures that induce dangerous activities. Both can give commands that produce complex military operations that they cannot control." Further, seeking to obtain bargaining leverage by making nuclear threats is certainly not a phenomenon limited to Nixon (e.g., Eisenhower in Korea and the Taiwan Strait) and is hardly empirical evidence of anything other than *signaling* one's resolve to opponents. It certainly does not provide any proof Nixon was going to launch a nuclear war on the USSR—*pretending* to act irrationally and actually *being* irrational are too very different things. Moreover, wasn't the threat to retaliate in response to a first strike during the era of mutual assured destruction an equally irrational, suicidal threat? Indeed, it required nuclear strategists to adopt the "threat that leaves something to chance" (Schelling 1960), or the notion of states under crisis becoming "contingently unsafe actors" (Rhodes 1989) who might loose control, in order to provide the required credibility for a seemingly irrational deterrent threat. Instead, the historical record shows a kind of "cold shower, hot coffee" effect provided by nuclear weapons for states considering aggression or recourse to war. As Hagerty (1998, 184) observes:

> There is no more ironclad law in international relations theory than this: nuclear weapon states do not fight wars with one another. Although the number of such states constitutes a small sample from which to derive such a sweeping generalization, the law's power is enhanced by the fact that it has encompassed a wide variety of countries. Several of the most embittered international relationships in the postwar era—between the United States and the Soviet Union, the United States and China, the Soviet Union and China, China and India, and India and Pakistan—have now fallen under its rubric. . . . Also, the political nature of these states spans a continuum from totalitarian (the Soviet Union and China) to authoritarian (Pakistan) to liberal (the United States and India). . . . We now have evidence from a strikingly dissimilar political, cultural, and geographical milieu that adds to our confidence in the logic of nuclear deterrence.

Democratic peace scholars point to the period of American absolute nuclear superiority during the Cold War, when the U.S. did not attempt to conquer the Soviets, as evidence of democracies more peaceful stewardship of nuclear weapons. However, as Quester (1998, 176–77) notes, an equally likely explanation for the U.S. not taking advantage of its nuclear monopoly during the 1940s to preempt the Soviet program or military had less to do with the liberal benevolence of the democratic American system, and more to do with the "scarcity" of atomic weapons. Indeed, the U.S. nuclear arsenal between 1946 and 1947 consisted of fewer than a dozen bombs, all of which were disassembled and stored at a single New Mexico facility, 100 miles from the base housing of the only bombers converted to carry the heavy war-heads—a true minimal deterrent force (Quester 1998, 176–78). This was not a force that could be quickly assembled and used.

Although it is far too early to judge the validity of the "democratic peace" theory, in the realm of nuclear weapons, there is less than overwhelming historical evidence to support its assertion that there is a noticeable difference in behavior across different types of states.

*7.) New Nuclear Arsenals Are Inherently More Vulnerable to Preemption Than Those of Established Nuclear Powers, Creating Greater Crisis Instability and Likelihood of Launch-on-Warning Postures*

Since new arsenals are, at least initially, likely to be small in number, housed in vulnerable basing modes, and use less-advanced delivery system technologies, they face a far greater danger of being preempted and disarmed by an opponent's first strike. This obviously poses serious challenges to both the security of these states and to crisis stability. The extreme vulnerability of nuclear forces require states to "use them or lose them" when in doubt, adopt "launch-on-warning" postures, and with the likely lack of assured, second-strike retaliatory capabilities, stable deterrence relationships between parties would be difficult to establish—thereby increasing the chances of nuclear war.

Yet, while these are entirely legitimate concerns, and part of an inevitable "high-risk initial phase" all nuclear states (except the U.S.) have gone through, it does not represent a permanent phase for new nuclear states. Indeed, Hagerty (1998, 180) argues both the 1987 Brasstacks and 1990 Indo-Pakistani crises "strongly rebuts the notion that there is any inevitability to preemptive nuclear escalation during crises between states with small, crude nuclear capabilities." Further, Betts (2003, 36) notes nuclear states have fought each other only twice in history (China and the Soviet Union over the Ussuri River dispute in 1969, and India and Pakistan over Kargil in 2000), and both were instances involving states with small nuclear capabilities in which the clashes remained only skirmishes and the survival of neither regime was threatened. As Waltz (2004, 390–91) observes:

> Once countries have nuclear weapons any confrontation that merits the term "crisis" is a nuclear one. With conventional weapons, crises tend towards instability. Because of the perceived, or misperceived, advantage of striking first, war may be the outcome. Nuclear weapons make crises stable, which is an important reason for believing that India and Pakistan are better off with than without them. Yet because nuclear weapons limit escalation, they may tempt countries to fight small wars. . . . The possibility of fighting at low levels is not a bad price

to pay for the impossibility of fighting at high levels. This impossibility becomes obvious, since in the presence of nuclear weapons no one can score major gains, and all can lose catastrophically.

### 8.) The Stability-Instability Paradox

Finally, the "stability-instability" paradox, originally introduced by Snyder (1961), has been suggested to create a tendency toward instability in nuclear security relationships. Essentially, it suggests conventional war could erupt between nuclear armed opponents because "two states armed with mutual assured destruction capabilities may resort to conventional warfare with each other because they do not fear escalation" (Posen 2004, 355). Actors develop a "false sense of security" based upon their belief the possession of nuclear weapons, and the extreme levels of destruction that would result, make it impossible for either their opponents or themselves to escalate conventional hostilities beyond a certain point. Obviously, the concern is that escalation might take on a life of its own and outpace the best intentions of policy makers. While India and Pakistan are often used as examples by pessimists of a likely arena for the stability-instability paradox to become manifest, optimists like Hagerty (1998, 180) question the assumption that nuclear capabilities increase the likelihood of ramped-up conventional conflict, noting "the evidence from South Asia strongly rebuts the notion that there is any inevitability to preemptive nuclear escalation during crises between states with small, crude nuclear capabilities."

## BUILDING AN ANALYTICAL FRAMEWORK

The analytical framework presented in this chapter assumes the impact of nuclear proliferation upon crisis stability and the nature of interstate security relationships is contingent upon three basic factors. These three factors combine to define a state's security relationships with others and involves: (1) the *nuclear capabilities of states* (i.e., the size, differentiation, range, and interceptability characteristics of their force structures); (2) the *survivability of state nuclear arsenals* (i.e., the redundancy, mobility, site defense, and subterfuge characteristics of forces); and (3) the *credibility of a state's deterrent threats to opposing decision makers* (i.e., the psychological perceptions of policy makers regarding their situations, their opponent's capabilities, their control over the situation, and the nature of the threat posed by various actions to the central or peripheral security interests of both sides). The new framework also highlights the *evolving and highly contingent nature of state security relationships across several distinct phases*, ranging from nonnuclear security up to nascent, regional, or great power nuclear status. These differing phases in the security relationships between states will be shown to have significant ramifications for interstate deterrence, crisis stability, and the military options available to both challengers and defenders across a wide range of contexts. Finally, this approach will seek to bridge the existing gap between security scholars over the impact of proliferation by illustrating both optimist and pessimist assumptions are correct, but only under certain conditions.

## THE NUCLEAR CAPABILITIES OF STATES

The first dimension of interstate security relationships—the nuclear capabilities of the state—provide analysts with both a characterization of the objective nuclear capabilities possessed by states and the potential scope of their nuclear targeting strategies. Important elements comprising a nation's nuclear capabilities include: the size of its nuclear force structure, the range of its delivery systems, the degree of differentiation within that force structure, and the interceptability by opponents of its delivery systems (see table 2.1).

By delineating the nuclear capabilities of states using this basic set of indicators affecting potential usage/employment only, one avoids the common trap of Cold War security studies of engaging in irrelevant "bean counting" of missile numbers to define the power or likely strategies of nations. Further, one avoids using only the *numerical size* of forces to define terms such as "great power" or "small power," when a more useful definition involves considering a complex mixture of capabilities along with the requirements for accomplishing certain deterrence tasks—a measure that obviously varies greatly across differing country contexts. Indeed, as table 2.1 illustrates, differences in the size, differentiation, range and accuracy of delivery systems, and the interceptability of a state's delivery systems by opponents greatly shape the *nature and scope of the deterrent abilities* a state will possess (i.e., that of only nascent or local power, a regional power, or a great power).

## THE SURVIVABILITY OF STATE NUCLEAR CAPABILITIES

The second basic dimension of interstate security relationships—the survivability of state nuclear capabilities—applies to *both* nuclear arsenals *and* the infrastructure comprising the nuclear research and production programs of these states. As numerous analysts have observed, the nuclear weapons programs

**Table 2.1. Breakdown of Indicators of State Nuclear Capability**

| Overall Character of State Nuclear Capabilities | Size of Nuclear Force Structure | Differentiation within Nuclear Force Structure | Range and Accuracy of Delivery System Capabilities | Interceptability by Opponent of Delivery Systems |
|---|---|---|---|---|
| **Nascent or Local Deterrence Ability** | **Nascent Nuclear Force Structure** | **No Differentiation within Force Structure** | **Short-Range Delivery Systems** | **High Interceptability of Delivery Systems** |
| | Very small force structure; few available warheads (e.g., 1–20). | Possesses only one primary design type of nuclear weapon (i.e., first-generation fission). | Possesses only short-range delivery systems (e.g., 50–1000 km range). | Existing delivery systems are highly vulnerable to interception by enemy countermeasures (i.e., preemptive attack, antimissile defenses, interception by fighter aircraft, etc.). |
| | Nuclear arsenal consists of either component parts for disassembled warheads or relatively few assembled ones. | Lacks variation in deployed warhead designs (i.e., cruise missile, SLBM, ALCM, low-yield tactical, high-yield strategic, etc.). | Delivery systems are characterized by serious vulnerabilities, such as low accuracy (i.e., short-range missiles) and difficulty in penetrating enemy airspace (i.e., combat aircraft). | Short-range missiles, modified combat aircraft, or ground-based vehicles lack penetration aids to circumvent enemy defenses. |
| | Possesses mostly first-generation weapons with low yields (1–35 KT). | Does not possess different classes of nuclear weapons (i.e., boosted-fission; thermonuclear). | Delivery systems permit only local or tactical delivery of weapons. | |
| | Possesses delivery systems physically capable of delivering warhead-size payload (e.g., 500+ kg) to enemy targets. | | | |

| | Force Structure | Differentiation within Force Structure | Range Delivery Systems | Interceptability of Delivery Systems |
|---|---|---|---|---|
| **Regional Deterrence Ability** | **Moderate Nuclear Force Structure**<br><br>Moderately sized force structure (e.g., 20–100 warheads).<br><br>Nuclear arsenal consists of assembled warheads which are coupled to delivery systems and actively deployed.<br><br>Size of force structure allows for attacks on multiple enemy targets with single warheads with varying warhead yields (1KT–1MT)<br><br>Possesses delivery systems physically capable of delivering warhead-size payload (e.g., 500+ kg) to enemy targets. | **Moderate Differentiation within Force Structure**<br><br>Possesses multiple design types of nuclear weapons— mostly first- and second-generation fission weapons (i.e., fission and boosted fission)—but also possibly some thermonuclear weapons (i.e., hydrogen bombs).<br><br>Has deployed multiple types of warhead designs (i.e., cruise missile, SLBM, ALCM, low-yield tactical, high-yield strategic. | **Short- to Intermediate-Range Delivery Systems**<br><br>Possesses short-range to medium-range (1,000–3,000 km), and possibly intermediate-range delivery systems (e.g., 3,000–5,500 km).<br><br>Multiple delivery systems allow for both local and regional use.<br><br>Moderate accuracy (allows for countercity strategy only). | **Low to Moderate Interceptability of Delivery Systems**<br><br>Existing delivery systems have moderate to low vulnerable to interception by enemy countermeasures (i.e., preemptive attack, antimissile defenses, interception by fighter aircraft, etc.).<br><br>Larger numbers of weapons, more reliable delivery system technologies, and faster delivery greatly increases penetration abilities. |
| **Great Power Deterrence Ability** | **Large Nuclear Force Structure**<br><br>Large force structures (e.g., 100–1000+ warheads).<br><br>Size of force and accuracy of deployed delivery systems allow attacks on multiple targets with multiple warheads, providing either countercity or counterforce capabilities. | **Differentiation within Force Structure**<br><br>Maximum differentiation: tactical to high yield strategic weapons allows multiple targeting strategies.<br><br>Multiple delivery systems for local, regional, and global employment. | **Intercontinental-Range Delivery Systems**<br><br>Worldwide delivery ability (5,500+ km range).<br><br>High accuracy (allowing counterforce vs. hardened targets) or assured countercity capabilities. | **Low Interceptability of Delivery System**<br><br>Existing delivery systems (ICBMs, SLBMs, cruise missiles, strategic bombers) have low vulnerability to interception and assure some penetration of enemy defenses. |

of many countries are largely invulnerable to military preemption due to the hidden, dispersed nature of their facilities and the strategies employed which duplicate the individual components of such programs across scattered sites (Albright and Hibbs 1992; Blackwill and Carter 1993; Mazarr 1995a, 1995b; Preston 1997). In addition, states like North Korea have taken additional countermeasures against outside military attack by hardening or burying their facilities deep underground (Mazarr 1995a, 113–14). Such measures, if employed effectively, dramatically limit the preemptive options available to outside nations and increase the risks of nuclear retaliation if military actions are not completely successful. As Desert Storm illustrated, even prolonged, extensive bombing campaigns were unable to effectively locate or destroy Iraq's program (Albright and Hibbs 1992; Zelikow 1993; *Gulf War Air Power Survey* 1993). Since most nuclear states are unlikely to provide a pretext for outside opponents to completely defeat and occupy their territories, thereby allowing on-site inspections, the Iraqi experience would seem to suggest serious limitations to the present ability of great powers to militarily preempt nuclear programs.

However, even more critical than the preservation of nuclear infrastructure is the survivability of nuclear arsenals (see table 2.2). Without arsenal survivability, a state would be unable to effectively employ its nuclear capabilities or deterrent strategies during a crisis—leading to deterrence failure and crisis instability. An opponent, recognizing such weakness, could conceivably risk a preemptive attack in the belief a retaliatory strike could be prevented or substantially reduced. Further, vulnerable nuclear force structures provide weak platforms for making deterrent threats and require more unstable "launch-on-warning" approaches by states. Indeed, as Waltz argues, there are three specific requirements for effective deterrence: "First, at least a part of a state's nuclear forces must appear to be able to survive an attack and launch one of its own; second, survival of forces must not require early firing in response to what may be false alarms; and [third] command and control must be reliably maintained; weapons must not be susceptible to accidental or unauthorized use" (Sagan and Waltz 2003, 20).

As illustrated in table 2.2, the survivability of nuclear arsenals are primarily affected by: redundancy and mobility of available delivery systems, use of hardening or site defenses, robust C3I capabilities, and effective efforts at subterfuge. Advanced combat aircraft and ballistic missiles, particularly mobile ones, as well as cruise missiles, provide both effective and redundant means of weapons delivery (Spector 1986; Fetter 1991; Harvey 1992; Gormley 1998). And, as Iraq's effective use of subterfuge and mobile missiles during the First Gulf War demonstrated, even in the face of overwhelmingly superior great power opponents and lack of air superiority, small states are capable of effectively concealing and launching ballistic weapons (Postol

**Table 2.2. Survivability of State Nuclear Capability**

| Survivability of State Nuclear Capability | Characteristics of State Nuclear Arsenal |
|---|---|
| Low Survivability | **Limited or No Redundancy of Delivery Systems** (i.e., only one or two effective delivery systems employed). **Delivery Systems Characterized by High Vulnerability to Preemption** (i.e., dependency upon existing airfields and fixed-site missile launchers; lack of mobile launching systems; use of liquid-fueled rather than solid-fueled missiles; inadequate C3I capabilities; inadequate air or site defenses; lack of invulnerable launching platforms, like submarines, etc.). **Heavy Dependence upon Subterfuge to Prevent Preemption** (i.e., dummy missiles or missile sites in effort to counter heavy fixed-based assets and lack of mobile, survivable systems). **Limited C3I Capabilities** (i.e., lack of early-warning radars or satellite reconnaissance, EMP-vulnerable communications networks or delivery systems, nonfiber-optic communications networks, vulnerable command-and-control sites). |
| Moderate Survivability | **Limited to Moderate Redundancy of Delivery Systems** (i.e., at least two or three delivery systems employed, one of which is a mobile missile, cruise missile, or submarine-based system). **Delivery Systems Characterized by Moderate to Low Vulnerability to Preemption** (i.e., use of mobile launching systems; existence of hardened, fixed-site positions, like reinforced silos and bunkers capable of withstanding nearby conventional air strikes; existence of significant air or site defenses; use of some solid-fueled rather than reliance upon liquid-fueled missiles; etc.). **Adequate C3I Capabilities** (i.e., possesses early-warning radars or satellite reconnaissance, has some fiber-optic communications networks, possesses hardened command-and-control sites, has taken some steps to reduce EMP vulnerability of communications networks or delivery systems). **Limited Site Defense** (i.e., SAMs, aircraft capable of significant interdiction/creation of air superiority). **Sophisticated Use of Subterfuge** (i.e., decoys, mobile systems, shell games, hidden systems, denial of capability, etc.). |
| High Survivability | **High Redundancy of Delivery Systems** (i.e., multiple means of delivery employed: missiles, aircraft, bombers, submarines, etc.). **Hardened Fixed-Site Positions** (i.e., reinforced silos and bunkers capable of withstanding nearby nuclear strikes). **Use of Multiple Mobile Delivery Systems** (i.e., mobile missiles, SLBMs, bombers). **Advanced C3I Capabilities** (i.e., extensive early-warning radars or satellite reconnaissance, fiber-optic communications networks, hardened command-and-control sites, reduction of EMP vulnerability of communications networks or delivery systems). **Robust Site Defense Capability** (i.e., SAMs, aircraft capable of significant interdiction/creation of air superiority, strategic defense, etc.). **Sophisticated Use of Subterfuge** (i.e., decoys, mobile systems, shell games, hidden systems, denial of capability, etc.). |

1991/1992, 1992; *Gulf War Air Power Survey* 1993). Moreover, U.S. government studies suggest preemptively destroying rogue state or terror group WMD facilities or weapons will be extraordinarily difficult—especially given the extensive resort to deeply buried bunkers for protecting these assets (Ochmanek 2003, 28).

## CREDIBILITY OF THE THREAT TO OPPOSING DECISION MAKERS

The final dimension of interstate security relationships—the credibility of nuclear threats to opposing decision makers—involves the need to understand deterrence as a psychological relationship between individual policy makers. It requires us to recognize the *constraints* placed upon psychological variables by the *simplicity of the strategic situations* created by nuclear weapons across various contexts. It is an area that has often received only cursory attention within the security studies literature, and one previously utilized only by deterrence skeptics to criticize the concept. However, a more nuanced application of political psychology to the issue of deterrence can be equally useful in fleshing out the possible interactional dynamics within nuclear security relationships between states—especially since policy maker perceptions (regarding the nature of the situation, the type of interests [central or peripheral] at stake, their view of how opponents perceive their threats, etc.) are likely to be key to whether deterrence relationships will be effective or not.

As suggested earlier, the debate between deterrence advocates and skeptics often centers on epistemological disagreements between scholars over their rival's chosen theories or methodological approaches for studying deterrence. Critics pointed to the less than satisfactory treatment of psychological factors relating to deterrence within the security literature (Jervis 1976; Lebow and Stein 1989, 1990), which was primarily due to the dominance of rational-choice and game-theory approaches in this scholarship (e.g., Zagare and Kilgour 1993). Others note the dependence of much of the rational deterrence theory literature upon neorealist, system-level arguments that tend to leave out subsystem or psychological factors—leading critics to note that a more useful theory would incorporate both systemic and subsystemic factors (Feaver 1992/1993, 179).

In fact, real-life behavior by decision makers varies greatly from the rational model, and is neither as consistent nor predictable as implied by game-theory approaches. Indeed, a typical definition of *perception of threat* as "the product of the estimated capability of the opponent's forces multiplied by the estimated probability that he will use them" fits nicely into rational-choice or game-theory models, but is a poor approach to understanding or defining policy maker perceptions (cf. Singer 1958; Legault and Lindsey 1974). In order to understand the behavior of policy makers, one must develop an understanding of the psychological factors affecting the ways in which individuals perceive the world, process information, respond to stress, and make decisions (e.g., Jervis 1976; Hermann 1980; Vertzberger 1990; Burke and Greenstein 1991; Khong 1992; 't Hart, Stern, and Sundelius 1997; Preston 2001). Only through understanding the subjective perceptions of decision makers does it become possible to determine both the effectiveness of deterrent threats and ascertain the nature of security relationships between states. As Johnson et al. (2002, 12) observe:

> Deterrence, like all coercion, occurs in the mind of the adversary. Reality matters in deterrence only insofar as it affects the perceptions of those who will choose whether or not to be deterred. . . . [Thus] assessments of the adversary's capabilities are of only limited predictive value unless accompanied by sound understanding of what the enemy values, how it perceives the conflict, and how it makes decisions—to name but a few of the critical variables.

But, since this involves exploring the complex realm of decision-maker perceptions, characterized by substantial interplay between objective and subjective reality, much of the security studies literature has been content to avoid the issue, assume rationality, and emphasize bean-counting approaches instead. As a result, the primary focus was mistakenly placed on the "objective" characteristics of the situation (i.e., size of forces, actual military balance, political situation, etc.) as seen by observers, rather than upon the "subjective" characteristics of the situation as perceived by the decision makers themselves—which actually governs their behavior. These "subjective" perceptions of reality held by leaders provide the basis for strategic decisions and shape their beliefs regarding the credibility of opponent's nuclear threats or forces. And, despite Lebow and Stein's (1989, 224) contention that rational deterrence theories are theories "about nonexistent decision makers operating in nonexistent environments," and other epistemological critiques made by political psychologists regarding rational choice, neorealist, or game-theory approaches, *it is important to note that one can make very strong psychological arguments IN FAVOR OF deterrence and why it should work as well.*

For example, Tetlock et al. (1991) provide a useful overview of many of the psychological factors bearing on the issue of nuclear deterrence and find that their impact upon deterrence effectiveness or success is variable, and not predictably negative in all contexts. Moreover, one does not need to adopt the same conception of "rationality" employed in rational choice models for deterrence to remain a valid concept. As Johnson et al. (2002, 17–18) note:

> Because coercion depends on the adversary weighing the expected results of several courses of action and then choosing the more attractive one, it presumes that policy decisions are made with some degree of rationality. However, the adversary need not behave with perfect rationality for coercion to be applicable, its behavior simply must not be totally irrational. . . . In practice, no state acts perfectly rational, stemming from such factors as incomplete information, limited time to make decisions, bureaucratic politics and organizational processes, and leaders' personalities. Yet states (and significant non-state political entities) rarely act in ways that appear truly unreasoning on close analysis. It is far more common for states' actions to be branded as irrational when they are actually being driven by logical and consistent sets of preferences, but these are not well understood by others.

In fact, deterrence is best understood as a *psychological relationship* (between deterrer and deterree), in which notions like the "credibility of the threat," "attentiveness to signaling," "resolve," "willingness to take risks," "degree to which central or peripheral interests are challenged," or even the basic "awareness of the overall security environment (or military situation) in a given situational context" *are almost completely dependent upon the individual psychologies of the rival policy makers.* As such, deterrence becomes a contingent variable, whose effectiveness is dependent upon both the psychological characteristics of the policy makers involved *AND the structural clarity of the situation created by the absolute nature of the destructiveness of nuclear weapons.* This latter element serves as a constraint upon the impact of individual psychologies upon decision making and serves to clearly distinguish nuclear from conventional deterrence contexts.

Thus, while nuclear deterrence relationships, if properly structured, can be expected to be highly robust and reliable in preventing conflicts—because it is a *psychological* relationship between human beings, it can never be expected to function perfectly across all situational contexts. But, rather than use this argument, as many political psychologists have done, to suggest deterrence to be an unsound or ineffectual policy approach, we need to place this concept into its proper perspective. Just because something *could* potentially fail doesn't mean that it will, especially with any frequency, and in the case of nuclear deterrence, the empirical evidence to date suggests a highly reliable and robust system. The same psychological problems or malfunctions routinely associated by deterrence critics apply equally to any other policy approach one could imagine (e.g., conventional deterrence, diplomacy, sanctions, etc.), all of which have been linked in the last century alone to recourse to very costly wars.[5] Yet, human beings do *generally* make reasonably sound, reasonably rational decisions—especially when the stakes are high and there is little room for ambiguity regarding situational outcomes. In this regard, *nuclear deterrence relationships represent special cases that are not easily compared to fundamentally different kinds of policy contexts* (such as conventional deterrence). Indeed, extrapolating conventional deterrence processes and outcomes to hypothetical nuclear ones (as many deterrence skeptics have done) is as useful for determining the taste of an orange as eating an apple. Instead of placing unrealistic and unfair performance standards upon deterrence, we should recognize that it is like any other policy or strategy—dependent upon the perceptions of policy makers and the constraints on their actions for its success.

On a practical level, one reason why the importance of the psychological characteristics of *individual* policy makers upon determining the effectiveness of deterrence (or other types of security relationships) has been given short attention by scholars is the fact that one cannot (in the absence of unrealistic assumptions about "rational-choice"-type actors) develop broad, general security frameworks that apply to all possible decision makers across all country and cultural contexts. Though it is laudable to seek grand, general theories on security and simple formulations of deterrence relationships, this is—given the central importance of *individual* policy makers in the process—simply unworkable and inappropriate in this context. We are working with social science, not natural science—and the *psychology of individual decision makers*, within or across nations, and how they perceive their security environments, vary drastically from one another. It would be foolish indeed, for example, to assume that Kim Jong-Il, Saddam Hussein, George W. Bush, Bill Clinton, Ayatollah Khameini, or any number of other world leaders perceive the world, process information, possess belief systems, face political constraints, or make decisions in the same manner (Hermann 1999; Preston 2001). Who the leader is and what they are like as individuals makes a tremendous difference in determining what a nation's security policies will be, how they will perceive risk and threat, and what limitations they might believe exist in either their own capabilities or in the environment itself.

In figure 2.1, the importance of these individual policy maker filters are emphasized, along with the notion that *the actual security relationships between states rest in the nexus between the objective capabilities/characteristics of the arsenals and the subjective perceptions of this reality by the policy makers*. Although the overall analytical framework proposed in this book does place heavy emphasis upon the objective characteristics of state or nonstate actor capabilities in creating at least the potential for a wide variety of security relationships and strategic options, this is principally because this is

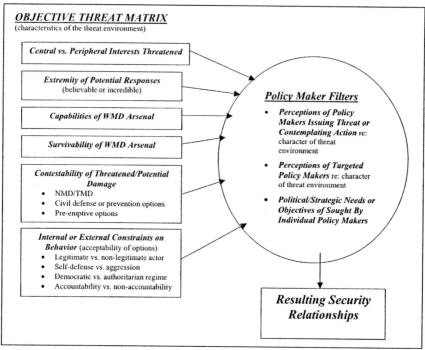

**Figure 2.1.  Objective Threat Matrix**

the only part of the analysis that is open to generalization. What must be kept in mind is that this represents *only the starting point for proper analysis of security relationships.* Practitioners (whether government officials or analysts) must consider the psychological elements of the individual (or group of) policy makers involved in *any* given deterrence or security context—and assess the likelihood of "their policy makers" accurately perceiving the "threat matrix" and how their individual psychological "filters" might assist or impede the process. In other words, for analysts seeking to predict behavior, one must gauge how the specific leader (or leaders) perceive the world, filter information about their own (and others) capabilities and motivations, and how their own individual personal or political contexts may be driving behavior. The proper use of the analytical framework in this book is to apply the assessed "objective" security contexts (characteristics of state capabilities, nature of opponents, etc.) arrived at for given countries to an individualized assessment of the "personal" security context of the leaders themselves, in which the analyst must consider how the psychological characteristics of relevant leaders serve as filters or constraints on the strategic behavior deemed possible by the framework.

## THE NATURE OF CONSTRAINTS
## ON POLICY MAKER PSYCHOLOGY

Just because the personalities of policy makers may sometimes matter with regards to outcomes, it would be a mistake to argue that they *always* matter. Indeed, it is generally accepted among scholars who work in the fields of personality or leadership that *context* (or situation) matters more (Greenstein 1969; George 1980; Preston and 't Hart 1999; Hermann 1999; Preston 2001). It is the situational context that provides the stage upon which the leader will interact with his or her environment, providing both opportunities for action and constraint upon it. In his classic book, *Personality and Politics*, Greenstein observed that while leader personality is often unimportant in terms of either political behavior or policy outcomes, the likelihood of personal impact: (1) increases to the degree that the environment allows restructuring; (2) varies with the actor's location in the environment; and (3) varies with the personal strengths and weaknesses of the actor (Greenstein 1969, 42). In nuclear deterrence contexts, the policy maker's perception of "the degree to which the security environment allows restructuring" is key. Do policy makers facing an opponent's nuclear threats believe there is a way to mitigate or avoid altogether their actual delivery (i.e., through missile defense, preemptive strikes, etc.)? Do they believe rising public pressure or weakness on the part of their opponent's political leadership might prevent them from carrying out their threats? Or do they believe that by engaging in an arms race, they might build up military capabilities that would enable them to offset their opponent's deterrent? All are examples of the varying ways an actor might perceive the existing security environment to allow "restructuring." At the same time, do well-established nuclear deterrence relationships (and the clear-cut consequences of an exchange) really provide the level of ambiguity normally associated with "flights of fancy"—or leader beliefs they can radically restructure the environment?

For Greenstein (1969, 40–62), it is largely *ambiguous situations* that provide the most room for the psychological characteristics of policy makers to make a difference. Completely new situations, for example, where people lack "socially standardized mental sets (i.e., shared bodies of professional knowledge, common stereotypes, etc.) to help them structure their perceptions and resolve ambiguities." Situations that lack social or political sanctions (or consequences) attached to various courses of action, that require large investments of personal effort to accomplish, that do not require policy makers to have intense needs to take cues from others, or ones that involve group contexts in which their decisions are largely invisible to others would all be expected to *increase* the impact of the psychology of policy makers on their decision making. Yet, how many of these should one expect to exist in the context of two (or more) opponents locked into a set of stable nuclear deterrent relationships (invulnerable forces, clear second-strike retaliatory capabilities, etc.), where any recourse to war risks activating their opponent's assured destruction capabilities against them? Is this really an *ambiguous* situation—or more to the point, the kind of ambiguous situation that policy makers would be inclined to be inordinately risk taking in their behavior toward? Is it really one in which there exists no "socially standardized mental sets" regarding the consequences or likely outcomes of their actions? Is it really a situation in which one would expect there to be few social or political sanctions attached to courses of action, a low visibility for any decisions taken, and little need to take cues from others?

Research into *accountability* by Tetlock (1985) suggests when individuals are held accountable by a higher authority for their decisions (a voting public, supreme leader, etc.), or cannot avoid personal accountability for the consequences of their actions, they will tend to be more risk averse, and vice versa. Though supporting elements of the "democratic peace" hypothesis, the implications of accountability research also suggest this psychological dynamic would pose a serious constraint on *any* policy makers considering a challenge to an existing nuclear deterrence relationship. Moreover, research into *prospect theory* suggests choices are strongly influenced by whether the policy problem is "framed" in terms of potential gains or losses, with people being more risk averse in the domain of gains and more risk accepting in the domain of losses (Kahneman and Tversky 1979; Kahneman, Slovic, and Tversky 1982). In the nuclear deterrence context, prospect theory suggests policy makers placed in the position of obtaining potential gains (i.e., conquering a neighboring province or country, making a preemptive strike to disarm the retaliatory forces of their opponent, etc.), at the potential cost of the loss of their own current resources (i.e., national survival, military and economic capabilities, etc.), would be expected to be highly *risk averse*. In contrast, policy makers facing a situation framed as one in which they were facing potential losses (such as being invaded and conquered by another state, or facing destruction of their political regime or economic capabilities), would be expected to be highly *risk acceptant*. Psychological research in prospect theory clearly shows people are more willing to take risks to avoid losses than they are to obtain potential gains (e.g., Kramer 1988).

Thus, in the nuclear context, the advantage in "credibility of the threat" clearly rests with the deterrer (defender) seeking to prevent losses rather than with the aggressor (deterree) seeking to achieve gains. Further, unlike the calculations surrounding conventional deterrence, where the calculation (or perception) of the likely costs and losses involved are likely to be unclear due to the inherent "contestability" of the effectiveness and costs of conventional warfare (Harknett 1994, 1998), the nuclear deterrence context removes much of the ambiguity surrounding the framing of alternative policy options in terms of costs or losses. Given the unavoidable costs attached to nuclear war, and the lack of "contestability" involved for states facing robust nuclear arsenals, policy makers in aggressor states challenging a neighbor's deterrent forces would be hard-pressed to misperceive the situation. While the domains of gains and losses are easier to miscalculate or misperceive in the conventional realm, once the context shifts to the incontestability of nuclear arms, the domains of gains and losses become clear. Policy makers assume immense, unacceptable levels of destruction and costs from the beginning, and structure their thinking accordingly.

Many political psychologists have also emphasized the degree to which policy makers vary in terms of their sensitivity (or attentiveness) toward their external policy environments when considering options and making decisions (e.g., Hermann 1980, Preston 2001). Indeed, the individual trait of complexity has long been linked to how attentive or sensitive leaders are to information from (or nuances within) their surrounding political or policy environments, and the extent to which they require (or need) information when making decisions. The more sensitive leaders are to information from the decision environment, the more receptive they are to the views of colleagues or constituents, the views of outside actors, and the value of alternative viewpoints and discrepant information. In contrast, leaders with a low sensitivity to contextual information will be less receptive to feedback from the outside environment, will operate from a previously established and strongly held set of beliefs, will selectively perceive and process incoming information in order to support or bolster this prior framework, and will be unreceptive or close minded toward alternative viewpoints and discrepant information. Low complexity individuals also tend to show symptoms of dogmatism, view and judge issues in black-and-white terms, ignore information threatening to their existing closed belief systems, and have limited ability to adjust their beliefs to new information.

What are the implications of policy maker *sensitivity to context* for deterrence? Firstly, it clearly relates to how receptive policy makers will be to threats made by opponents. For example, De Rivera (1968, 53) suggests that the signal-to-noise ratio (the strength of the signal relative to the strength of confusing background stimuli), the rewards and costs associated with recognizing (or not) the signals, and the general expectations of the observer play a role in whether initiator or defender threats are heard by the other. Secondly, for sensitive leaders (those high in complexity), they are highly unlikely to make rapid, impulsive decisions in even a conventional crisis, let alone a nuclear one. Such leaders are known for having extremely slow, deliberative, and cautious decision processes that seek out tremendous amounts of information for consideration prior to making decisions (Preston 2001). As a result, such policy makers would be exceedingly unlikely to "rush to judgment" and misperceive the relatively simple cost/loss equation created by nuclear weapons. They also would be highly attentive to signaling from potential adversaries in such a nuclear deterrence environment. In contrast, for insensitive leaders (those low in complexity), they would be far more likely to "rush to judgment," miss warning signals from potential adversaries, and pay little attention to information or feedback from the external environment. Such leaders would be far more vulnerable to the psychological malfunctions of selective perception, use of stereotypes and faulty analogies, and groupthink-type malfunctions (see Janis 1972; Janis and Mann 1977; 't Hart 1994; 't Hart, Stern, and Sundelius 1997). Hence, the risk of miscalculation or challenges to deterrence from such leaders would undoubtedly be greater than would be the case for sensitive leaders. At the same time, the fact that such leaders also view the world in simple, black-and-white terms and do not necessarily tune into nuances suggests they would be far more likely to accept the quite simplistic, black-and-white cost/loss benefit equation nuclear weapons thrust upon security relationships. Historically, American presidents scoring both high and low in complexity, sensitive ones like Eisenhower and Kennedy, as well as less sensitive ones such as Truman, Johnson, and Reagan, have all (despite their rhetoric) shown great caution when making foreign policy decisions that could in any way provoke a true nuclear response from an opponent. Indeed, Truman and Johnson (in Korea and Vietnam respectively) both recognized the serious constraints which the Soviet possession of nuclear weapons posed on the unlimited exercise of American power in both conflicts (see Preston 2001).

The reactions of policy makers under the immense stress of nuclear crises has also been pointed to by deterrence skeptics as likely leading to greater chances for decisional pathologies (e.g., misperception, motivated misperceptions, avoidance of value trade-offs, groupthink) to impact decision making and lead to deterrence failure (Janis 1972; Janis and Mann 1977; Jervis 1976; Lebow 1981, 1987; Lebow and Stein 1989, 1990). And while such dangers are clearly of concern, their application to nuclear confrontations has historically not resulted in these kinds of malfunctions. In fact, it is only in cases of *conventional* deterrence relationships—characterized by far less clear-cut and ambiguous cost/benefit equations—that one routinely sees these kinds of decisional pathologies. Even Janis (1972) cites the handling of the Cuban Missile Crisis, his lone nuclear crisis, as being an example of good group decision making and avoidance of groupthink. Similarly, George (1991) describes the Cuban Missile Crisis as an example of excellent crisis management (see also Preston 2001). And Blight (1992) notes that for policy makers, the fear of nuclear war (a "shattered crystal ball") served as an "adaptive device" preventing JFK and the ExComm from taking reckless actions and seeking every possible means to avoid a nuclear exchange. Nevertheless, a substantial literature in political psychology (Janis and Mann 1977; Hermann 1979; Hermann and Hermann 1990; 't Hart 1994) warns that policy makers reactions and decision making patterns under intense stress deteriorate and become less effective as the levels increase—an element that can never be fully removed from considerations of the resilience of nuclear deterrence under severe crises conditions.

## CREDIBILITY OF THE THREAT

Although the basic notion of deterrence can be expressed quite formally in rational choice, game-theoretic terms (as payoffs and value calculations, etc.), the concept itself long predates such epistemology and should be understood to represent a relatively simple psychological and security relationship between actors. Simply put, deterrence involves one actor seeking to influence (or shape) the motivations or intentions of another (in order to prevent aggression toward them) by raising the "perceived" costs of aggression to unacceptable levels for the aggressor. This "raising of the costs of aggression" is accomplished by: (1) the defender actually possessing the *physical military capabilities* to destroy (or seriously damage) assets their aggressor deeply values; (2) the defender making *credible threats of retaliation* (that they are really willing to destroy assets valued by the aggressor, regardless of what the attacker might do in retaliation) because of the magnitude of the threat posed by the aggressor to the defender's core central security interests (its national, economic, or political regime survival; territorial integrity; etc.); and (3) through the defender's ability to shape their opponent's perceptions of the existing security environment and convince them that *under no conceivable scenario* could they succeed in successfully carrying out their aggressions (and benefiting from it) without incurring unacceptably high levels of loss (or costs) to themselves.

Powell (2003, 89) correctly points out that at the heart of most critiques of deterrence theory rests a "fundamental credibility problem," specifically, how states with assured destructive capabilities vis-à-vis one another can credibly threaten to take a suicidal retaliatory action in response to the other's aggressive actions? The solution proposed within the deterrence literature by Schelling (1960; 1966) was to rely upon making *threats that leave something to chance*, the notion that while suicidal retaliatory threats might not be rational under normal conditions, policy makers would be faced with the possibility (during escalation of a crisis, or even limited initial uses of tactical nuclear forces) that control over the situation (and therefore the response) *could* be lost by their opponents. This is similar to Rhodes' (1989, 184–86) conception of the "contingently unsafe actor." The terror created by the threat of nuclear devastation was, therefore, the key to preventing the outbreak of war. Indeed, as Cimbala (1998, 18) noted, during the Cold War, it was not the certainty of threats, but the uncertainty of control over potential escalation that influenced policy makers and helped avoid conflicts during the Cuban Missile Crisis and other crises of the era.

Factors affecting the credibility of a nation's nuclear threats to opposing decision makers include leaders' perceptions of the deterring nation's nuclear capability, arsenal survivability, and command-and-control capabilities relative to the situation (i.e., are they in danger of loosing positive control over their forces and becoming an "unsafe" actor) (Powell 1990; Goldstein 1992). Perceptions of the opponents themselves are also very important. The threat to use nuclear weapons is more convincing when accompanied with images of an "irrational" enemy motivated by ideological or religious zeal than when paired with images of a "rational," pragmatic opponent (Cottam 1977). Indeed, much of the current premise about so-called rogue states is that their leaders will act irrationally and will be "undeterrable" by the United States, as illustrated by Joseph and Reichart (1999, 19):

> Many of the assumptions on which U.S.–Soviet deterrence was founded may not hold true today. For example, the United States ascribed a basic and shared rationality to Soviet leaders. . . . [it] assumed that the Kremlin would act in its own best interests and could be deterred if the United States held at risk assets of value to the Soviet regime. . . . Such "logic" may not apply . . . [to] regional states motivated by messianic anti-Western zealots or by regime survival . . . [who may be] more willing to risk annihilation for outcomes the United States would not consider "rational."

A more objective definition of a rogue state is provided by Powell (2003, 102–5), who focuses upon the relative characteristics of such actors, describing rogues as those states "willing to run a greater risk of suffering this retaliatory outcome than another state would be," in other words, they are simply states that "are more determined to prevail" and "more resolute than ordinary states." Interestingly, Powell's (2003, 106) analysis of interactional dynamics between the U.S. and a rogue state suggests that it is definitely in the best interests of America's opponents to be *perceived* by U.S. policy makers as rogues in terms of their ability to make irrational threats credible and obtain deterrence. Moreover, the value obtained by *any* nuclear state by *appearing* to "go rogue" (in terms of increasing its perceived resolve and the credibility of its threats to opponents) is not limited to small states. Indeed, when one looks at the nuclear alert ordered by President Nixon in October 1969, which he conceived of as a way to coerce the North Vietnamese and the Soviets to the bargaining table over Vietnam, one sees Nixon purposefully adopt the visage of a dangerous, perhaps irrational, rogue actor to lend credibility to his threat (see Sagan and Suri 2003).

## THREATS TO CENTRAL VERSUS PERIPHERAL INTERESTS

The perceptions of opposing decision makers regarding whether their actions threaten their opponent's central or peripheral interests greatly affect the credibility of nuclear threats made by that state. For the purposes of this discussion, the central (vital) interests of the state would include: it's national or economic survival, territorial integrity, or the survival of the nation's political leaders/elite—in other words, threats so central to the well-being of the state as to be a justification for war. On the other hand, the peripheral interests of the state would involve political, economic, or security issues which do not threaten the survival or significant well-being of the nation, and therefore do not constitute a justification for war. For example, during the Cold War, a Soviet invasion of western Europe or Alaska would have been seen as a threat to the central, national interests of the United States, whereas Soviet arms shipments to Vietnam, Angola, and the Middle East were threats to American peripheral interests and not cause to begin a hot war.

This emphasis upon the impact of central vs. peripheral interest activation upon state relationships is hardly unique in security studies. For example, George (1988, 644–46) developed a useful typology describing incentives for superpower security cooperation in different security issue areas utilizing both the degree of central-peripheral interest activation and the degree of "mutual dependence" between states. George considered mutual dependency to be "tight" when the magnitude of potential damage states were capable of inflicting upon each other's interests was substantial and "loose" when the potential for damage was more modest (George 1988, 644). It was the degree of perceived vulnerability in particular issue areas that influenced the severity of risk that was perceived and the strength of the incentives states had to cooperate and avoid it (George 1988, 645). However, the incentives for cooperation were influenced not only by the degree of mutual dependency between two states on a particular security issue area, but also by how "central" (or important) the issue area was to the fundamental security interests of the states (George 1988, 646).

If this definition appears quite general, it is because it can be nothing else given the dependence of the concept upon the perceptions of decision makers. Although everyone can list actions affecting the central interests of their nation that would justify the extreme use of force against the perpetrator, as well as actions affecting peripheral interests, this list varies across individuals. Indeed, wars have often been the result of misperception by decision makers in one country, who did not realize that their opponent would interpret their actions as a threat to their central rather than peripheral interests (De Rivera 1968; Lebow 1981; George 1991). Since these perceptions regarding central and peripheral interest activation vary from case to case, this factor must be assessed by analysts in each specific case. However, in terms of nuclear threat credibility, it is argued that these threats will be more believable to opposing decision makers when they believe that their actions are seriously threatening the nuclear state's central interests, and will be less credible if perceived to involve only peripheral interests. Only when a state's central interests are threatened can nuclear threats appear "rational" to opponents. This psychological "caveat" should be used to add greater predictive power to the theoretical framework. As Gallois (1961, 149) observed, "the greater the disparity of forces, the more critical the situation of the threatened nation would have to be, so that recourse to the nuclear arsenal would not appear irrational."

Likewise, Powell (2003, 90) notes the credibility of a state's nuclear threats depends on *what is at stake in the political conflict*, and "the higher the stakes, the more risk a state could credibly threaten to run." But, how much risk can nuclear states credibly take (either in their retaliatory threats or in their coercive pressure tactics) on nuclear opponents? A useful way of thinking about this dilemma was suggested by Aron (1965), who remarked that while opponents were enemies in combat, they were "brother enemies" in their desire to avoid annihilation. As Waltz observes: "No country will press a nuclear nation to the point of decisive defeat. In the desperation of defeat, desperate measures may be taken, and the last thing anyone wants to do is to make a nuclear nation desperate. The unconditional surrender of a nuclear nation cannot be demanded. Nuclear weapons affect the deterrer as well as the deterred" (Sagan and Waltz 2003, 29). As a Center for Counterproliferation Research (2001) study noted: "the stakes in regional conflicts . . . may well be asymmetrical. An adversary with higher stakes . . . is more likely to run greater risks and absorb higher costs in challenging the United States through NBC escalation. Particularly if the conflict jeopardizes the adversary's regime or survival as a nation-state, deterring its NBC use through even the most dire threats could prove difficult" (*Center for Counterproliferation Research* 2001, 50).

*Stability* in any ongoing nuclear security relationship between states hinges upon the clarity with which they view the "balance of resolve" between them. Indeed, as Powell (2003, 92–93) observes:

> Resolve is the reason why two adversaries' nuclear forces do not simply cancel each other out in brinkmanship, and why one side may have an advantage over the other. The more a state values prevailing, the more risk it would be willing to run in order to do so and the greater its resolve. Similarly, the higher the cost of acquiescing, the more risk it would be willing to tolerate in order to avoid losing and the greater its resolve. And the more catastrophic the outcome if events go out of control, the less risk a state would be willing to accept and the lower its resolve. . . . the less resolute state never escalates if there is no uncertainty about the states' levels of resolve. . . . As long as the balance of resolve is clear, the less resolute state still knows that the more resolute state is willing to push the crisis harder and run more risk. . . . Brinkmanship crises occur only if the balance of resolve is uncertain. If each state believes that it is likely to be more resolute than the other state, then each may escalate in the expectation that the other will back down.

In figure 2.2, the likely perceptions of challengers regarding the credibility of defender nuclear deterrent threats are considered based upon the challenger's perception of how their actions have affected the defender's risk domain (gains or losses), whether the challenger perceives the defenders central or peripheral interests being challenged by their actions, and finally, the challenger's perception of the defender's nuclear capabilities (nascent/local power, regional power, or great power). Whether the challenger's perceptions are accurate with regard to the objective situation is irrelevant in determining their behavior. Moreover, through the application of prospect theory and George's notions of centrality of issue, this framework suggests whether challengers will be likely to believe in the credibility of a defender's deterrent threats. As Brodie (1966, 43) once observed, "estimating probabilities of escalation is essentially an exercise in predicting the behavior of those leaders (as well as our own) under various kinds of crisis situations."

## NUCLEAR DETERRENCE AND ASYMMETRICAL SECURITY RELATIONSHIPS: CAN THE WEAK DETER THE STRONG?

Among the early proponents of the view that it was indeed possible for smaller nuclear states to deter larger ones, perhaps the most influential, was French air force general Pierre Gallois (1961), who argued for "proportional deterrence"—the notion that a small power could deter by threatening retaliation

| | | | Challenger Perception of Defender's Nuclear Capability | | |
| --- | --- | --- | --- | --- | --- |
| | | | **Low** (Nascent or Local Capability) | **Moderate** (Regional Capability) | **High** (Global Capability) |
| **GAINS** — *Challenger's Perception of Defender Interests Challenged by Action* | *Challenger's Perception of Defender Interests Challenged by Action* | **Central** | Defender deterrent threats limited credibility. Challenger & Defender will be risk averse (Crisis Stability) | Defender deterrent threats credible Challenger & Defender will be risk averse (Crisis Stability) | Defender deterrent threats credible Challenger & Defender will be risk averse (Crisis Stability) |
| **Challenger's Perception of What Defender's Risk Domain** | | **Peripheral** | Defender deterrent threats lack credibility. Challenger will be risk acceptant; Defender will be risk averse (Crisis Instability) | Defender deterrent threats lack credibility. Challenger will be risk acceptant; Defender will be risk averse (Crisis Instability) | Defender deterrent threats lack credibility. Challenger will be risk acceptant; Defender will be risk averse (Crisis Instability) |
| **Will Be in Response to Given Strategic Action** | *Challenger's Perception of Defender Interests Challenged by Action* | **Central** | Defender deterrent threats highly credible Challenger will be highly risk averse Defender will be risk acceptant (Crisis Stability) | Defender deterrent threats highly credible Challenger will be highly risk averse Defender will be risk acceptant (Crisis Stability) | Defender deterrent threats highly credible Challenger will be highly risk averse Defender will be risk acceptant (Crisis Stability) |
| **LOSSES** | | **Peripheral** | Defender deterrent threats lack credibility. Challenger & Defender will be risk acceptant (Crisis Instability) | Defender deterrent threats limited credibility. Challenger & Defender will be risk acceptant (Crisis Instability) | Defender deterrent threats limited credibility. Challenger & Defender will be risk acceptant (Crisis Instability) |

**Figure 2.2.** Likely Challenger Perceptions of Credibility of Defender's Nuclear Deterrent Threats

that would exceed the limited value that a small state might represent to a larger power (Legault and Lindsey 1974, 161). This later became the basis for the French nuclear doctrine of the *force de frappe*. However, Gallois (1961, 8) observed that for a state's nuclear threats to be credible, "a nation's very existence would have to be threatened." Indeed, as Mack (1975, 181) observes, weak states win asymmetric conflicts with more powerful states because their survival is only guaranteed by victory—in other words, they are more vulnerable, less powerful than their opponents, but they are also more likely to have their vital security interests more absolutely threatened. It is because of this differential in the degree to which state central interests are threatened that Gallois (1961, 9–10) suggests small states can obtain defensive capabilities vis-à-vis larger states, irrespective of their relative conventional military capabilities, which make aggression against them unattractive for a great power—"who would dare attack this small country, if, in order to depose its government and invade its territory, the aggressor would have to run the risk, in return, of seeing a dozen of his own major urban centers destroyed?"

However, in less central areas, where national survival isn't at stake, military officers in new nuclear states recognize nuclear deterrence cannot be expected to prevent all conflict. As former Indian army chief of staff Sundarji (1996, 183) observed, "in a wide range of low-level conflict situations—ranging from inspired insurgencies and border violations through 'salami slice' capture of disputed territory—the very presence of nuclear stability and mutual minimum deterrence will make nuclear use not credible in most situations. Only in extreme situations would the use of nuclear weapons be credible. Therefore, to deter such low-level situations, conventional forces would still be required." Indeed, even classic deterrence theorists like Gallois (1961, 12) did not suppose that nuclear weapons would end all conflicts between states so armed, but rather that it would limit them to more peripheral or indirect competitions:

> This is why the *coup d'etat*, the palace revolution, and subversion are henceforth to be substituted for the old open hostilities. If the new explosive cannot impose total peace, at least it limits the intensity of the conflict and condemns pitched battle as it condemns yesterday's wars of position and movement.

Even in the case of India, which has a far larger nuclear arsenal than Pakistan, military officers are aware of the reality that the smaller force deters the larger force. As Sundarji (1996, 185) admitted, "no Indian disarming first strike against Pakistan can succeed to the extent of preventing a Pakistani riposte causing unacceptable damage to India." Moreover, Sundarji argues that:

> The very term "disarming first strike" is misleading. Even when nuclear arsenals on both sides are quite small, to expect totally to disarm the other side's nuclear retaliatory capability by going "firstest with the mostest" is a pipe-dream of the think-tank theoretician; any practical military or political planner must reckon on the survival of a retaliatory capability with a high probability of inflicting unacceptable damage in the second strike. It is such unrealistic fears of successful disarming first strikes, especially in the case of small nuclear powers,

that produce theories of the instability of deterrence in their cases. . . . . in a situation where one is only talking of deterrence, and minimum deterrence at that, with a value-target oriented second strike, decapitation will not benefit the initiator to the extent expected, even if it succeeds. A hair-trigger response is not required for launching the second strike: response can be some hours after receipt of the first strike. A very highly sophisticated, highly responsive C3 system that functions in real time is not necessary. . . . Even a very successful decapitating attack by the adversary cannot give him any assurance of the non-launch of the surviving second strike. . . . there is no compulsion to react within minutes. This is an aspect that has been ignored by many Western analysts.

The problem faced by smaller states trapped in asymmetric power relationships with larger states has long been noted as a rationale for the pursuit of WMD capabilities. For example, Betts (1993) has suggested three small-state types that are likely to pursue nuclear weapons to enhance their security: *pygmies* (states threatened by much larger neighbors, like Pakistan); *paranoids* (states facing unpredictable, perhaps irrational opponents, like South Korea); and *pariahs* (states who face hostility from regional neighbors and isolation from most of the world, like South Africa). Similarly, Goldstein (2000, 2) notes that: "The Cold War security policies of China, Britain, and France reflected a common strategic logic. Each ultimately embraced a policy that had as its top priority the deployment of national nuclear forces sufficient to dissuade threats against vital interests, a priority that led all three to rely on a distinctive strategy of deterrence of the strong by the weak. While each also supplemented this policy by forming alliances with others and by procuring non-nuclear forces, each viewed its national nuclear deterrent as the indispensable core."

Further, many scholars have noted that nuclear weapons clearly provide smaller states with a deterrence capability versus larger states that is far more attainable and less expensive than would be *comparable levels* obtained through developing conventional military capabilities (Betts 1993; Goldstein 1992). For example, Goldstein (2000, 52–54), citing the experiences of France, Britain, and China, argues that nuclear deterrence not only provides for more robustness in strategies of dissuasion for smaller nuclear states than do conventional capabilities, but that while deploying nuclear arsenals is not cheap, "the relevant assessment of cost-effectiveness . . . is not the absolute amount spent on nuclear forces, but rather the amount that would have to be spent on conventional forces to achieve comparable levels of security." Indeed, for states facing powerful opponents, if they are unable to offset the conventional military might of their enemies, "dissuasion by deterrence may be the most practical alternative."

Thus, while the United States currently enjoys the benefits of RMA (Revolution in Military Affairs) and will undoubtedly increase the technological lead it possesses over other states in conventional military capabilities, nuclear weapons provide smaller states with a means of avoiding this kind of conventional weapons technology race. As Goldstein (2000, 55) observes:

> The enduring ability of the most basic nuclear weapons quickly to annihilate military forces or inflict catastrophic damage on society, even in the teeth of massive deployments of technologically sophisticated defenses, remains unchallenged. Until this changes, nuclear weapons will be an economical hedge against obsolescence for states seeking an affordable way to fulfill the requirements of strategies for dissuading highly capable adversaries.

Obviously, the degree to which small states might be able to deter larger ones, in the final analysis, comes down to how "contestable" their opponent believes the damage they might inflict upon them will be, as well as the extent to which the smaller state believes its retaliation might be blunted (Harknett 1994; 1998). Although this notion of "contestability" was originally used to distinguish between conventional and nuclear deterrence, it is equally useful when thinking about asymmetric security relationships between WMD states with differing levels of capabilities and defense. As Harknett (1994, 88–89) explains:

> Conventional deterrence is hampered by the nature of the weapons upon which it is based. The ability of conventional forces to inflict pain on an opponent is highly dependent on the skill shown in their application, on the capabilities possessed, and on the counter-capabilities employed by an opponent. The destructiveness of conventional weapons, and thus the cost that can be threatened, will only be felt over time after achieving military victory. . . . In the mind of a potential challenger, therefore, conventional weapons and their attendant costs hold out the *prospect* of technical, tactical, or operational solution, and it is this prospect that makes them less effective deterrents to war. The fundamental point that strategists devising a *conventional deterrence approach must recognize is that conventional deterrents represent contestable costs.*

Nuclear weapons produce a "reliability of effect" with regard to the immense damage they are likely to inflict, which unlike more contestable conventional weapons, "overshadow small differences," making potential gaps in power that in a conventional environment might translate into relative advantage, not sufficient in a nuclear one to provide military opportunity (Harknett 1998, 61). Similarly, Feldman (1997, 16–17) agrees that "nuclear weapons provide states with far more robust deterrence than conventional arms" because they leave far less room for misperceptions about the damage they cause, they provide states with nearly unlimited capability to inflict punishment, and are (unlike conventional weapons) not vulnerable to variations in states' sensitivity to costs. In almost every historical case they examined, George and Smoke (1974, 527) found "the initiator tried to satisfy himself before acting that the risks of the particular option he chose could be calculated and, perhaps even more importantly, controlled by him so as to give his choice of action the character of a rationally calculated, acceptable risk." Rather than focusing upon credibility, resolve, or signaling, George and Smoke argue the single factor of greatest importance for deterrence given their historical research was nearly always "the initiator's possession of multiple options" (1974, 532). Clearly, the nuclear realm provides far fewer of those than the conventional one.

But exactly what type of nuclear capability is required to achieve this effect? As Gallois (1961, 137) observed, "the thermonuclear force" fielded by the weaker state only need be "proportional to the value of the stake it is defending." For this task, destructive capability comparable to that possessed by great powers during the Cold War is unnecessary, since all that is required of weaker states is to obtain a "sufficient quantity of destruction." Similarly, Waltz (1988, 685) suggests deterrence for small states is not achieved through an ability to defend themselves militarily from interventions by great powers, but through the ability to punish aggressors by inflicting unacceptable levels of damage upon them. It is the ability of the small state to resort to what Schelling (1966) referred to as the "diplomacy of violence," or the "power to hurt," that characterizes the shift to a new set of interstate security relationships (Schelling 1988, 4). For unlike the "power to defend," the "power to hurt" is distinct and not dependent upon the relative strength of opponents:

> Opposing strengths may cancel each other, pain and grief do not. The willingness to hurt, the credibility of a threat, and the ability to exploit the power to hurt will indeed depend upon how much the adversary can hurt in return; but there is little or nothing about an adversary's pain or grief that directly reduces one's own. (Schelling 1988, 4)

Goldstein (1992), in an examination of the nuclear strategies adopted by small nuclear nations found they were able to deter superpowers because they possessed secure second-strike forces with enough assured destructive power that their opponents feared the "threat that left something to chance." In other words, what Bundy (1984, 8–10) described as "existential" deterrence operated upon the superpowers, who were deterred because of what *could happen*, not by any specific nuclear threat made by the smaller states. As Bundy explained:

As long as we assume that each side has very large numbers of thermonuclear weapons which *could* be used against the opponent, even after the strongest possible pre-emptive attack, existential deterrence is strong. It rests on uncertainty about what *could happen*, not in what has been asserted. Existential deterrence had a powerful day-to-day effect on both governments in the course of the Cuban missile crisis. Neither side had any desire to expose itself to the uncertainties. . . . The uncertainties which make existential deterrence so powerful have the further consequence that what either government says it might do, or even believes it might do, in the event of open conflict cannot be relied on either by friends or by opponents as a certain predicter of what it would actually do. Neither promises of restraint . . . nor threats of . . . retribution . . . could be confidently relied on. No one knows when or how such a crisis would arise, or who would be in charge at the moment on either side. No one knows what would happen, or how big any first strike would be, or what would happen next. The limits placed by these uncertainties on all kinds of plans and all kinds of expectations are inescapably tight. . . . responses would be full of unpredictables. All would be open to catastrophic misinterpretation. None could be confidently expected to lead to a good result.

Moreover, Bundy (1982, 10) argues existential deterrence "deters quite impersonally; no provocative threats are needed to support its power. It deters both sides at once, since the unpredictable risk of catastrophe is essentially symmetrical." Thus, fear from the point of view of existential deterrence is *not* bad. It was the possibility of facing what Rhodes (1989, 78–81) defined as a "contingently unsafe" actor, whose central interests were threatened to such an extreme it could loose control over its nuclear forces and unleash what would normally be considered an irrational response. Smaller nuclear arsenals become effective against superpowers, despite their nuclear superiority and arguments small states would be *self-deterred*, because of the existence of "autonomous risk"—risk genuinely beyond the control of the parties involved (Powell 1990, 487–88). Fear that the situation might spin out of the positive control of either side during a crisis, of what *might happen* in that event, created among decision makers a reluctance to take risky actions in the nuclear realm, thereby creating deterrence for smaller powers. As Goldstein (1992, 496) observes, "nuclear deterrence of the strong by the weak rests on the *possibility* that the latter will have at its disposal a deliverable devastating nuclear force *and* may prove to be an unsafe actor." Although small states will continue to lack the ability to *defend* against great power attacks, they *will* have the power to *destroy value*. Indeed, as Schelling (1966, 4) observes, "the power to hurt is bargaining power" and in security relationships with new nuclear states possessing a credible ability to strike back, great powers will be motivated to bargain and avoid threats to central interests. This represents a significant shift away from the logic of traditional power politics and toward the logic of deterrence in interstate security relationships.

That being said, discussions of credibility often lead to the somewhat questionable conclusion that against great powers, small states would be "self-deterred" due to the overwhelming superiority of their opponents (Waltz 1988, 698–701). This ignores the fact that such security relationships are *unaffected* by the number of weapons possessed by each side, at least beyond the point where each possesses survivable retaliatory forces and the ability to inflict unacceptable levels of damage upon the other. On this point, Waltz (1988, 700) correctly observes that overemphasizing the defending state's possible inhibitions against using WMD focuses on the wrong question and ignores entirely the likely unwillingness of great power aggressors to run extreme risks in areas not related to their central interests. But how impressive would a small nuclear state's potential attack need to be to deter? Gallois (1961, 198), for example, suggests small states would have to adopt countervalue targeting doctrines with their more limited forces to enter into deterrence relationships with more powerful states. Waltz (1988, 698), observes that during the Cold War, China's small force structure only needed to attack the USSR's top ten cities to destroy over a quarter of that nation's population and industrial capacity. Assuming no missile defenses degraded the attack and all missiles functioned correctly, carrying two warheads to each target, this attack required only twenty nuclear weapons. The essential point is that large nuclear force structures are not required (when adequate delivery systems are available) to inflict unacceptable levels of damage upon opponents. Force structures of forty to fifty warheads are not unreachable given proper motivation for new nuclear states and, in the absence of national missile defense (NMD) systems, would certainly be capable of immense destruction if unleashed.

It should also be noted that even the extensive requirements for *assured destruction* originally proposed by McNamara (one-fourth of a population and two-thirds of industrial capacity) would in many cases require *far fewer weapons* for today's small state actors. An analysis by the Natural Resources Defense Council shows that only fifty-one nuclear warheads (475-kiloton, W88 warheads) would achieve McNamara's level of "assured destruction" in Russia (McKinzie et al. 2001, 114). More importantly, the number of 475-kiloton warheads required to achieve McNamara levels of destruction decline dramatically when applied to smaller nations, Germany (33), Italy (21), France (25), Britain (19), Iran (10), North Korea (4), Iraq (4), Syria (2), and Libya (2). Clearly, it is difficult to argue such force levels are "beyond the reach" of medium nuclear powers (after all, France currently has 350 warheads) (NRDC Nuclear Notebook 2001, 70). Further, it is very difficult to imagine so many warheads would be required to *deter* as opposed to *destroy* these nations—even the chance of a couple warheads landing on U.S. cities would likely deter even the most bellicose administration from taking precipitate actions, much less 124 bombs!

As illustrated in table 2.3, when a state's nuclear capability and survivability of its forces improve, deterrence and crisis stability are enhanced. However, the reverse is also true. States possessing low capability and survivability of forces, a condition common to most newly nuclearized powers, achieve a security relationship with others which is initially more dangerous to them than the preexisting nonnuclear relationship with other powers. Preemption of their nascent nuclear abilities becomes a pretext for attack by surrounding states anxious to derail the development of more advanced nuclear security relationships. This lesson was aptly demonstrated by the preemptive attacks against Iraq by both Israel in 1981 and the U.S. in 2003. Further, the capabilities achieved by a state at this point are usable only in very limited ways. Local battlefield or demonstration use of weapons might signal a slightly different security relationship with other states, but is unlikely to create a strong deterrent against vastly superior nuclear powers with the opportunity to preempt a state's fledgling nuclear potential. As a result, a pragmatic strategy for new nuclear states is to conceal their programs and engage in covert programs to develop capabilities that create more advanced security relationships before revealing them to other powers.

In the case of new nuclear state arsenals, differentiating between strategic and tactical weapons systems or strategies is highly problematic. Not only are these states in close proximity to one another due to shared borders, but the smaller arsenals themselves are likely to lack the clear distinction between large and small yield weapons used to make this distinction between the superpowers. Even then, it was never an easy task to define what exactly were tactical nuclear weapons (TNW). As Van Cleave and Cohen (1978, 13) observed, "defining a tactical nuclear weapon is a thankless task. . . . it seems virtually impossible to define which systems" characteristics are critical to a tactical nuclear capability and what distinguishes TNW weapons and operations from non-TNW." The *key consideration*, according to Van Cleave and Cohen (1978, 14–15), separating tactical from strategic nuclear systems is their use, in which "the term tactical nuclear weapons in the closest approximation refers to battlefield nuclear weapons, for battlefield use, and with deployment, ranges, and yields consistent with such use and confined essentially in each respect to the area of localized military operations." Yet, when one considers that the U.S. Honest John tactical nuclear weapons system had a twenty-five-mile range and a warhead yield equivalent to the Hiroshima bomb (15 kilotons), one is forced to recognize that for a country like Pakistan

Table 2.3. Employment Options and Crisis Stability Characteristics Achieved by Differing Levels of Nuclear Force Survivability and Capability

|  | Nuclear Force Survivability | | |
|---|---|---|---|
|  | *High* | *Moderate* | *Low* |
| **Great Power Deterrent Ability (High)** | **Employment Options**<br>Tactical/local battlefield *and* regional countercity and counterforce use.<br>Global countercity and counterforce use.<br>Overt possession.<br>No need for "launch-on-warning" or early-use nuclear doctrine.<br>(**Crisis Stability**) | **Employment Options**<br>Tactical/local battlefield *and* regional countercity and counterforce use.<br>Global countercity and counterforce use.<br>Overt possession.<br>No need for "launch-on-warning" or early-use nuclear doctrine.<br>(**Crisis Stability**) | **Employment Options**<br>Tactical/local battlefield *and* regional countercity and counterforce use.<br>Global countercity and counterforce use.<br>Overt possession.<br>Need for "launch-on-warning" or early-use nuclear doctrine.<br>(**Crisis Instability**) |
| **Regional Deterrent Ability (Moderate)** | **Employment Options**<br>Tactical/local *and* regional countercity use.<br>Limited regional counterforce use.<br>May prefer *either* opaque or overt possession.<br>No need for "launch-on-warning" or early-use nuclear doctrine.<br>Preference for *minimal deterrent* doctrine.<br>(**Crisis Stability**) | **Employment Options**<br>Tactical/local *and* regional countercity use.<br>Limited regional counterforce use.<br>May prefer *either* opaque or overt possession.<br>No need for "launch-on-warning" or early-use nuclear doctrine.<br>Preference for *minimal deterrent* doctrine.<br>(**Crisis Stability**) | **Employment Options**<br>Tactical/local *and* regional countercity use.<br>May prefer *either* opaque or overt possession.<br>High need for "launch-on-warning" or early-use nuclear doctrine.<br>Preference for *minimal deterrent* doctrine.<br>(**Crisis Instability**) |

**Nuclear Force Capability**

| Nascent or Local Deterrent Ability | Employment Options | Employment Options | Employment Options |
|---|---|---|---|
| (Low) | Tactical/local battlefield use only. Potential ability to threaten neighboring state's cities if within range of delivery systems. May prefer *either* opaque possession or formally acknowledge nuclear capability. Reliance upon both *overt* and *existential* deterrence. Limited need for "launch-on-warning" or early-use nuclear doctrine. **(Crisis Instability)** | Tactical/local battlefield use only. Potential ability to threaten neighboring state's cities if within range of delivery systems. May prefer *either* opaque possession or formally acknowledge nuclear capability. Reliance upon both *overt* and *existential* deterrence. Limited need for "launch-on-warning" or early-use nuclear doctrine. **(Crisis Instability)** | Tactical/local battlefield use only. Potential ability to threaten neighboring state's cities if within range of delivery systems. Preference for *opaque possession* (no formal acknowledgement of nuclear capability). Heavy reliance upon *existential* deterrence. High need for "launch-on-warning" or early-use nuclear doctrine. **(Crisis Instability)** |

or North Korea, a weapon with similar range and yield could serve both strategic and tactical purposes (Van Cleave and Cohen 1978, 31 and 50). Other deployed U.S. tactical missile systems during the Cold War had similar or greater warhead yields and even greater ranges, like the *Lance* (75–80 miles), *Sergeant* (85 miles), or *Pershing* (425 miles) (Van Cleave and Cohen 1978, 50).

In addition, short-range systems potentially provide important de-escalation and deterrence bolstering effects. Bernard Brodie, one of the leading strategic thinkers of the Cold War, noted the threat to use tactical weapons was appropriate for deterrence, or failing that, could serve as a "de-escalating device" if used in a "limited and essentially tightly controlled manner." Brodie (1966, 28) noted that with the limited use of tactical weapons, "the possibility of further escalation will, to be sure, be unavoidably but also usefully present. It will tend to induce caution on both sides, but it will especially tend to dissuade the aggressor from testing very far the efficacy of a *resolute* local defense."

## HOW CAN THE COSTS BE CONTESTED?

For states faced by nuclear-armed adversaries, there exist principally four means of "contesting" the costs of a nuclear attack: (1) Engaging in offensive strategies of military preemption (whether conventional or nuclear) against an opponent's nuclear force structures; (2) Deployment of effective missile defense systems to interdict the weapons once fired; (3) Possession of strong antiaircraft defenses, surveillance and tracking technologies, and interceptor aircraft capable of interdicting enemy cruise missiles, unmanned aerial vehicles (UAVs), or nuclear-armed aircraft; and (4) Hardening of one's strategic facilities, dispersal of military and leadership assets, and civil defense. All of these options face extreme limitations in terms of what is going to be technically and operationally possible under battlefield conditions, what is economically and politically feasible strategies for states to adopt, and which (if any) approach is likely to result in the flawless (or at least nearly perfect) performance required to allow policy makers to believe they can avoid the consequences of actions they take against a nuclear state's central interests.

The last option will be discussed first, primarily because it is the least plausible and unlikely to be adopted (or accepted) by a state's policy makers as a feasible way to minimize an opponent's nuclear threats. While it is conceivably possible to harden at least some of almost any nation's strategic military assets (e.g., command centers, missile silos, military base facilities), this is primarily useful against opponents who might be tempted to try a disarming counterforce or decapitation attack. However, given that for most new nuclear states, countervalue (city-based) targeting would be a far more likely strategy, notions of relying upon civil defense and other measures would hardly be likely to reduce civilian casualties enough not to deter the opposing policy makers from taking undue risks.

In terms of developing strong antiaircraft defenses, surveillance and tracking technologies, and combat airpower capable of intercepting an enemy's aircraft, UAVs, and cruise missiles, a defending state would face the problem that no defense could be perfect—a notion as old as Clausewitz's admonitions about the "fogs of war" and "friction." This would be the case, even for the most technologically and militarily advanced great power. Although capable of monitoring the battlefield as no other power (through satellites, reconnaissance aircraft, and sophisticated radars) and possessing air power capable of maintaining complete air superiority over most targets, the U.S. would be hard-pressed to stop a new nuclear state with the capabilities of a Pakistan, India, Israel, or North Korea from effectively delivering *any weapon* (at least over short distances) using advanced combat aircraft, UAVs, or cruise missiles. Although interdiction rates might be quite high, only one failure would result in the loss of a carrier battle group, a large military base, or a city like Seoul or New Delhi. Further, for states with lesser technical and military capabilities (practically everyone else), the leakage from attacks would increase in both magnitude and cost—making deterrent threats even less likely to be tested.

Finally, among the most commonly cited options for both the United States and others facing nuclear opponents are to build and deploy active missile defenses or to adopt policies of military preemption to disarm an opponent before they can strike. Though frequently cited, both have severe limitations in terms of feasibility, practicality, and their likely impact upon deterrence and stability.

## THE IMPACT OF NATIONAL MISSILE DEFENSE ON DETERRENCE AND STABILITY

The debate over missile defense, whether in the form of national missile defense (NMD) or theater missile defense (TMD), centers around questions of cost, feasibility, and likely effectiveness (Lewis et al., 1999/2000; Deutch et al., 2000; Cirincione 2000; Garwin 2000; Moore 2000; Preston et al., 2002; Postol 2002).[6] Although an overview of this contentious debate is beyond the scope of this book, the likely effectiveness of missile defenses and their potential impact upon small state deterrence will be discussed briefly.

The most recent U.S. Nuclear Posture Review (2002) emphasized that a multiple-layered missile defense system was a fundamental component of the overall U.S. nuclear posture (Du Preez 2002, 68–70). This mirrors the view of others within the Bush administration, such as Hass (1999, 129), who argue that for the U.S. to maintain its strategic options against states possessing WMDs, it is necessary for it to pursue TMD capabilities. In contrast, scholars like Waltz (2004, 347–48) argue NMD poses a greater danger than the slow spread of nuclear weapons and generally dismisses the impact of NMD on the ability of small states to deter larger ones:

> According to Rumsfeld, it does not matter if defenses do not work well. Deploying them will make would-be attackers uncertain about how many of their weapons will "slip past the shield," and uncertainty will deter them. . . . Missile defenses would be the most complicated systems ever deployed, and they would have to work with near perfection in meeting their first realistic test—the test of enemy fire. No president will rely on such systems but will instead avoid actions that might provoke an attack. With or without defenses, the constraints on American actions are the same.

Which viewpoint is the correct one? Again the answer is dependent upon context—which countries we are talking about, the operational capabilities of any deployed ballistic missile defense (BMD) system, the countermeasures available to the attacker state, and, in the most fundamental sense, how much leakage (or risk of leakage) policy makers in any nation will accept from even a small state nuclear opponent without being deterred? Instructive to this discussion is the Cold War–era literature addressing the impact of missile defenses, which routinely argued that BMD around cities would undercut, but BMD around offensive missile sites would increase, deterrence and stability (Legault and Lindsey 1974, 190–92; Quester 1986, 236–37). For example, in a comment which could be seen to equally apply to current U.S. strategic thinking regarding North Korea, Legault and Lindsey (1974, 191) suggested that "if a state of stable unilateral deterrence applies because of the overwhelming superiority of one of the two adversaries, but strengthening of the weaker side threatens to make the situation unstable, it is possible that the stronger power can keep it stable by deploying BMD around his cities." A number of scholars have also agreed that BMD, whether based on a NMD format (Joseph and Reichart 1999; Cropsey 1994; Waltz 2004) or a TMD format (Mahnken 1993; Joseph and Reichart 1999), would serve to reduce constraints on American foreign policy that could otherwise be created by small state nuclear forces.

However, as Powell (2003, 88) observes, while NMD might provide more freedom of action for great powers, and make some rogue states more likely to back down from a confrontation, these effects would be modest unless missile defenses were *extremely* effective. Noting the technical effectiveness of NMD is likely to be less than on the test range, he warns that if "defenses are no more than moderately effective, then the balance of resolve remains relatively clear and in favor of the other state." Basically, NMD has to be "virtually flawless before the probability of an attack drops below what it would have been without NMD." Of course, this presumes NMD would become *increasingly effective* over time (a far from proven position), be able to remedy its substantial technical shortcomings, and overcome an adversary's increasingly sophisticated countermeasures. Indeed, as Glaser and Fetter (2001, 69) note, limited NMD would have little value in protecting U.S. foreign policy in the face of the danger of nuclear escalation "unless U.S. leaders believed that the NMD system was almost perfectly effective."

Yet, even the most wildly optimistic assessments of NMD seldom suggest a 100 percent effective system, with most reputable analysis suggesting interception rates (at best) only in the 80 to 90 percent ranges. Even the 1999 National Intelligence Council acknowledges simple, rudimentary countermeasures currently available would be sufficient to defeat planned U.S. missile defenses, and be available to states like North Korea and Iran "by the time they flight test their missiles" (Cirincione 2000, 129).

But, far more worrisome is the likelihood U.S. missile defense systems currently under development will never perform as advertised due to the politically biased and "rigged" nature of the component tests thus far—which have sacrificed realism and rigor in tests in order to demonstrate for Congress and BMD skeptics "successful" test results (with surprisingly limited success).[7] The systems are *never* tested under realistic battle conditions, operators are given forewarning of the launch of individual missiles to be intercepted, and these have sometimes even been equipped with transponders to assist in tracking. To assist the system in discriminating between warheads and decoys (its primary technical challenge), tests have "simplified" the targeting environment to artificially increase its chances. Early tests, with even rudimentary countermeasures and a variety of realistic decoys, easily defeated the defense systems, so future tests were "dumbed down" to remove all but a few, readily distinguishable balloon decoys from the mix. Realistic testing environments, which would have included substantial numbers of decoys of different types (i.e., balloons of varying sizes that could conceal warheads and decoys, the use of small batteries to provide heat signatures to decoys [to mimic live warheads], the use of coolant to make the live warheads appear as decoys, etc.) and other types of readily available countermeasures (e.g., radar absorbing materials, chaff, low-power jammers, spin-stabilized reentry vehicles, use of reentry vehicle reorientation), were completely avoided (Garwin 2000; Cirincione 2000; Postol 2002; Taubes 2002). When combined with the serious time constraints on operators surrounding the window of response to any hypothetical attack, and the basic Clausewitzian reality of "fogs of war" and "friction" in any complex military situation, the lack of full-blown tests calls into question how reliable any NMD system will be in practice.

As for "boost phase interception" of ballistic missiles, seen as a key component of any effective NMD or TMD system, a July 2003 study by the American Physical Society (the largest U.S. association of physicists) strongly called into question the ability of current technology to accomplish the task. The report warned boost-phase missile defense "is virtually impossible in all but a few limited circumstances" and concluded that "when all factors are considered none of the boost-phase defense concepts studied would be viable for the foreseeable future to defend the nation against even first-generation solid-propellant ICBMs" (Dawson 2003, 26). In June 2003, the General Accounting Office (GAO) also issued a report critical of the push to deploy NMD in 2004, stating the system was "hampered by immature technology and limited testing, raising the risk of failure" and noted the administration has refrained "from making long-term cost estimates for many elements of the planned system, clouding decisions about what technologies to pursue" (Graham 2003). The GAO report also criticized the Pentagon for "combining 10 crucial technologies into a missile defense system without knowing if they can handle the task" (Broad 2003; U.S. General Accounting Office 2003). These concerns do not even raise the potentially serious question of exactly how reliable a deployed NMD system could be given the organizational and operational problems surrounding the use (and dependence upon) such immensely complex, technologically complicated, "tightly coupled" systems (Perrow 1984; Sagan 1993, 1994; Feaver 1992/1993).

Clearly, it is hard to make the argument, regardless of "official test" results, that U.S. missile defense systems have been shown to work or have been tested under realistic battlefield conditions. It is apparent the Bush administration is rushing ahead to deploy unproven BMD systems that have not been demonstrated to function as advertised, but which are hoped will provide the "illusion of missile defense." The obvious danger would be if any future American president actually believed the rhetoric and relied upon it against real-world opponents, who are unlikely to be as generous in formulating their attacks as NMD test designers.

## DIFFICULTIES OF PREEMPTIVE STRATEGIES

The other option for states facing nuclear-armed opponents is to attempt preemptive attacks aimed at either completely disarming their nuclear forces before they can be used (the classic "counterforce" attack) or depleting their numbers sufficiently (even if the counterforce attack fails) to reduce the resulting damage on cities and strategic assets (hopefully weakening the attack enough to allow even imperfect BMD systems to reduce the blow). Preemptive strategies have also been proposed for eliminating budding nuclear weapons programs in "rogue states" or taking down nascent nuclear force structures in their most vulnerable developmental stage (Zelikow 1993). Indeed, the Bush administration's emphasis upon developing earth-penetrating tactical weapons for use against deeply buried bunkers of new nuclear states (like North Korea) illustrates the interest preemptive strategies stir among great powers.

Yet, while preemptive strategies have some history of success (e.g., Israel's attack on the Osirak reactor in 1981), they also have serious limitations—especially when directed against states already possessing some deliverable nuclear capabilities and well-hidden production facilities. Although great powers might conceivably intervene at such a late stage, by then, the potential costs would have risen beyond the traditional, conventional power politics-type equation. Further, many new nuclear states (North Korea, India, Pakistan) have substantial conventional military forces and large standing armies, making any preemptive attack a costly proposition for great powers, even when excluding their nascent nuclear capabilities. WMD infrastructures could be built deep within their territories, complicating the targeting problem for opponents seeking to launch preemptive attacks (Karl 1996/1997, 109). Some, like North Korea, are in tremendously strong, defensive positions requiring a major war to dislodge them, and which could not conceivably be accomplished by any great power before terrible retribution (conventional or WMD) would be unleashed upon vulnerable allies in South Korea or Japan. Hardened, deeply buried bunkers carefully dispersed and hidden throughout new nuclear states would also be extremely difficult to locate and destroy, as would the potential delivery systems (such as mobile missiles) available to these states. As Hass (1999, 130) observes, preventive attacks are easier to imagine than effectively carry out and "are attractive options only in rare circumstances."

Obviously, just as the first ballistic missiles possessed by the superpowers (in the early stages of arsenal development) were liquid-fueled systems requiring lengthy preparation time prior to firing, increasing their vulnerability to an opponent's first strike and the appeal of "launch-on-warning" doctrines, new nuclear states often share a similar vulnerability (Wohlstetter 1959). But, as Legault and Lindsey (1974, 150) observe, the superpowers took steps to rectify this early vulnerability by dispersing bombers to more bases, improving early warning systems, developing solid fuels for missiles (increasing their response times), and developing submarine-based forces. New nuclear states will also take steps to improve their arsenal's survivability through increased use of dispersal and concealment of launchers, the development of multiple means of delivery (i.e., greater differentiation of delivery systems), and the use of mobile systems. For example, some "low tech" options for states would be to deploy, as the Chinese have, their strategic forces in small, dispersed groupings (with as few as two missiles per launcher), store missiles/launchers in hidden caves or tunnels, and deploy the systems in concealed or camouflaged sites (such as valleys, mountainous terrain, etc.) (Karl 1996/1997, 109; Goldstein 2000, 127).

Even the use of tactical nuclear weapons, despite optimistic claims by the Bush administration, are viewed by the vast majority of the scientific community to be unworkable and impractical for a number of technical reasons (e.g., inability to construct warheads capable of surviving impact to burrow deeply enough to contain the fallout from nuclear blasts; the fragility of nuclear as composed to conventional warheads components; low-yield warheads at conceivable burrowing depths would be unable to destroy most deeply buried bunkers possessed by "rogue" states; fallout from high-yield weapons used to compensate for this would not be containable, etc.). Indeed, an excellent study by Nelson (2002, 18) notes that detailed technical analyses suggest preemptive attacks against hardened sites would be ineffective without use of sizable warheads (at least 100-kiloton yields), resulting in a substantial release of radioactive fallout—calling into question the entire technical feasibility or practicality of successfully employing any conceivable low-yield, earth-penetrating nuclear weapons against deeply buried targets.

In addition, Feldman (1997) notes that the size of a state's territory "has little bearing on its ability to protect its nuclear weapons from an adversary's first strike." New nuclear states with large territories (like China, India, or Pakistan) have the option of reducing the vulnerability of their forces by dispersal throughout their territories. Those with small territories (like Israel) can achieve similar invulnerability through what Feldman (1997, 22) describes as "a combination of concealment, variation, mobility and dispersal"— which for more advanced states can be accomplished, as Israel has likely done, by placing nuclear weapons aboard submarines or surface ships at sea. As Arnett (1990, 155) notes: "Diesel submarines with nuclear-armed heavy torpedoes could provide a secure retaliatory force, analogous in many ways to the superpowers' ballistic missile submarines (SSBNs), for countries whose principal adversaries had important coastal cities or installations." Moreover, torpedoes which could be fitted with small nuclear weapons are already widely proliferated, as are diesel submarines (Arnett 1990, 155).

The case of the First Gulf War (1991) also demonstrates the difficulties involved in eliminating through military means a small state's covert nuclear weapons program. Even with the advantage of advanced satellite intelligence, and extensive bombing of strategic sites throughout the war, Allied efforts to completely destroy Iraq's nuclear program were ineffective and large portions escaped destruction. In fact, after the war, UN inspections uncovered three times more nuclear sites than had been predicted by U.S. estimates (*Gulf War Air Power Survey* 1993, 224–27). Indeed, as the official U.S. military survey of the conflict observed, Iraqi subterfuge tactics made its nuclear program both "relocatable" and less vulnerable to Allied bombing "no matter how accurate." The report concluded that the end result of the massive bombing campaign had been only to "inconvenience" the Iraqi program, not destroy it (*Gulf War Air Power Survey* 1993, 328–30). Thus, without its complete military defeat and subsequent acceptance of on-site UN inspections after the war, Iraq would have been able to preserve major portions of its nuclear weapons program. This calls into question the ability of preemptive military strikes to effectively eliminate, not just delay, covert nuclear weapons programs undertaken by small states.

Another lesson of the Gulf War is that small states have begun to develop survivable means of retaliation against militarily superior opponents. The U.S. inability to successfully eliminate the Iraqi Scud threat, even after six weeks of extensive bombing and complete air superiority, clearly illustrates how even a small state with an antiquated mobile launch system can frustrate preemption efforts and maintain a credible retaliatory capability. Utilizing a strategy of "hide-and-seek," Iraq scattered its mobile Scuds throughout the countryside, deployed wooden decoys to confuse Allied reconnaissance efforts, and continued to launch missile attacks on Israel and Saudi Arabia for six weeks after the beginning of the air war. The Iraqis were able to launch forty-nine Scuds during the first ten days of the war, and continued to launch thirty-nine more during the final thirty days of the conflict. As the *Gulf War Air Power Survey* (1993, 334) observed:

> In sum, Iraq's operational approach and employment tactics meant that *the probability of finding Iraq's mobile launchers and destroying them from the air before they fired was very close to nil at the outset of the conflict.* Nor did the chances of finding mobile Scuds before they fired improve appreciably as the campaign unfolded. Even with the use of platforms like JSTARS and special forces on the ground, Coalition forces had little success either detecting mobile launchers moving from their hide sites or catching them while they were setting up to fire from pre-surveyed launch points. (emphasis added)

Had Iraqi Scuds been carrying nuclear warheads, dozens would have gotten through despite the unparalleled air campaign. Would the U.S. have been willing to trust that Saddam Hussein would not have dared strike its conventional military forces in the Saudi/Kuwaiti desert if a ground war began which actually threatened his regime's survival? Would any U.S. president trust that American nuclear superiority would deter such a leader to the extent that a risky policy, like the liberation of Kuwait or the overthrow of Saddam, would be attempted given the clear political risks of high U.S. casualties? Further, would the Saudis (like the Western Europeans during the Cold War) have been willing to serve as a nuclear battlefield in order to support U.S. policy in Kuwait or Iraq? Clearly, it is difficult to imagine a scenario in which a nuclear-armed Iraq would not have significantly altered the course of recent events in the Gulf (whether in 1991 or 2003).

Finally, although the Iraqi air force failed to play a significant role during the Gulf War, it still provides an important lesson which should not be overlooked by analysts. Specifically, the successful escape of over one hundred Iraqi aircraft into Iran, despite Allied air superiority and efforts to prevent it, demonstrated that although the Iraqi air force lacked the ability to directly engage Coalition air power, it still possessed some ability to escape interdiction and penetrate defenses (Freedman and Karsh 1991, 28). Had Iraq possessed nuclear weapons and the will to use them, a concerted effort to use its advanced strike aircraft, flying low to avoid radar, would have provided it with an effective and difficult-to-interdict delivery system. It should also be noted that in future great power–small state confrontations, the kind of overwhelming air superiority enjoyed by the Allies over Iraq is unlikely to be replicated in such a way as to render small state strike aircraft completely ineffective. Combined with the potential of mobile ballistic missiles, the possibility that only a few nuclear-armed aircraft could evade interception provides small nuclear states with the ability to develop redundant and survivable force structures capable of providing some degree of credible deterrence.

Now, with this chapter's theoretical framework presented, we move on to examples illustrating its application in the real world. In chapter 3, the implications of current trends in nuclear proliferation are discussed, as well as how new nuclear states might utilize their capabilities to ensure their security. As states like North Korea, India, Pakistan, and Israel further develop their nuclear arsenals, potential opponents will have no recourse but to take seriously the potential of their retaliatory forces when responding with any acts of aggression against their central interests. For, as Bundy observed regarding the requirements for minimum deterrence: "In the real world of real political leaders . . . a decision that would bring even one hydrogen bomb on one city of one's own country would be recognized in advance as a catastrophic blunder; ten bombs on ten cities would be a disaster beyond history; and a hundred bombs on a hundred cities are unthinkable" (Kaysen, McNamara, and Rathjens 1991, 106–107).

## NOTES

1. See "Nuclear Posture Review" [excerpts] on the GlobalSecurity.org website at www.globalsecurity.org/wmd/library/policy/dod/npr.htm.

2. Chinese assistance has helped Israel convert its *Delilah* UAV (unmanned aerial vehicle) into an ALCM (air launched cruise missile). Gormley, "Cruise-Missile Threat," 99.

3. For illustrations of the immense cost of conventional warfare regarding casualties, see Gilbert 1994; Mueller and Mueller 1999; Washington Headquarters Services, "Korean War—Casualty Summary" 2004; Washington Headquarters Services, "Vietnam Conflict—Casualty Summary" 2004; Schwarz 2001, 2004; Kelly 2002; "Casualties in World War II"; "Casualty Figures, United Nations Forces"; "Casualties—US vs. NVA/VC."

4. It should be noted that, while the Normal Accidents Theory (NAT) espoused by Perrow (1984) and Sagan (1993) has dominated the pessimist school of nuclear proliferation, there exists substantial debate in the organizations literature between it and what is known as High Reliability Theory (HRT), which suggests that while accidents can happen, it is also possible for organizations facing the problem of dealing with a complex, tightly coupled, hazardous task to have at least the potential for greatly limiting their chances of catastrophic failures (see La Porte and Consolini 1991; Rochlin 1993; La Porte 1994; Rochlin et al. 1987). The notion that failure is inevitable in complex, tightly coupled organizations should not be seen in the absolute, automatic way in which normal accidents scholars like Perrow and Sagan suggest—especially given the high stakes involved with control over nuclear arsenals (which almost guarantee substantial oversight of command and control issues and which, despite some minor bumps, has not resulted in an accidental launch or detonation of any weapon over a sixty-year period across a total of nine nuclear weapon states total).

5. Some of the critics of nuclear deterrence using political psychological arguments at times seem to be using a logic that would equally suggest one shouldn't fly on passenger airplanes (because of the potential for catastrophic failure), but rather drive cars everywhere (since the potential for large loss of life in any one incident is smaller). Yet, as we know, flying is by far and away the statistically safer means of travel—despite its technical and organizational complexity and potential for catastrophic failure. Indeed, the fatalities from automobile accidents each year dwarfs even the very worst years for aviation crashes. Nuclear deterrence (no wars or use at all over the last fifty years) versus conventional deterrence (sixty to seventy million killed over the last fifty years) are empirically even more dissimilar.

6. For those interested in abashedly pro-BMD sources (accentuating the positive and usually completely ignoring the negative), I suggest you examine the main

government website promoting NMD, the Ballistic Missile Defense Organization (BMDO)—www.acq.osd.mil/bmdolink/html/nmd.html—as well as any materials on the topic on the Heritage Foundation website (www.heritage.org).

7. For a detailed discussion, see both Postol 2002 and Cirincione 2000. Also see Coyle 2002 for discussion of attempts by the Pentagon to shield NMD tests from public (and political) scrutiny through unwarranted classification of the details of the tests and its withholding of data from *its own* independent review offices, such as the director of operational test and evaluation.

# 3

## Nuclear Security Relationships: Options and Constraints on New Nuclear States

Alone among potential WMDs available to state and nonstate actors, nuclear weapons provide the *purest combination* of both destructive capability and reduced ability for defenders to "contest" the damage inflicted upon them through their use. Even for states with relatively small arsenals, the basic physical characteristics of nuclear weapons and their effects mean only a few are required (if they are survivable and can be effectively delivered to target) to create levels of cost *far beyond* what any "rational" aggressor would be willing to pay. For a state like North Korea, the calculation need go no further than creating enough capability for destruction that neither the U.S. nor South Korea would deem it worth the risk to threaten the survival of the regime. In fact, it is difficult to conceive of any South Korean or American administration being willing to risk the damage likely to result from even *limited* North Korean nuclear attacks against countervalue targets throughout the region. For small states, the task is to create nuclear forces with robust capabilities and survivability that have clear credibility to threaten extensive harm to any belligerent who threatens their key central interests. And for a number of new nuclear states—Israel, Pakistan, India, and North Korea—these more robust nuclear capabilities are now at hand, fundamentally transforming the nature of their security relationships with potential opponents. They have, in all likelihood, now successfully passed through the more dangerous and vulnerable phases of nuclear possession (where the potential for successful opponent preemption is high) to the more stable phase III security relationships characterized by strong local and regional deterrence.

# EXPECTED NUCLEAR WEAPONS CAPABILITIES
# AMONG NEW NUCLEAR STATES

In this chapter, it is assumed all new nuclear states would be able to develop "first generation" atomic weapons at least equivalent to those possessed by the United States at the end of World War II (roughly fifteen to twenty kilotons in yield). Further, given the declassified knowledge available regarding bomb designs, the yields from the first nuclear tests of states like Pakistan, India, and China, and the technical advances that have occurred over the past five decades, it is also reasonable to assume most states would be capable of developing weapons of considerably greater yield without much difficulty. A report by the U.S. Office of Technology Assessment noted "a first-generation fission weapon developed by a state without much experience at nuclear weapon design would most likely have a yield in the range of 1 to 50 kilotons" (U.S. Congress Office of Technology Assessment 1993, 174). Therefore, "initial nuclear capabilities" of small states (like India, Pakistan, and North Korea) will be assumed to include the ability to produce arsenals in the fifteen-to-fifty-kiloton range.

For states with more long-standing programs, like Israel (and potentially India), it is reasonable to assume "mature nuclear capabilities"—which allow development of "boosted-fission" weapons (with yields between 50 and 300 kilotons) and for "thermonuclear" (or hydrogen) weapons with yields in the multimegaton range. Indeed, both Israel and India have been suspected of working on thermonuclear weapons, with Israel likely already mastering both "boosted" and "thermonuclear" designs. At the outer limits of its current capability, some analysts have speculated "Israel might have the capacity to manufacture 20-megaton (MT) hydrogen bombs" (Feldman 1982, 45). More significant, however, is the example of China, which as a new nuclear state in the 1960s rapidly developed and deployed both fission and thermonuclear weapons in its arsenal, with its first atomic bomb test in 1964 followed by a hydrogen bomb test (with a multimegaton yield) only three years later in 1967 (Goldstein 2000, 72). By 1971, China had deployed a 3.3-megaton warhead on the DF-3A land-based missile and by 1981 had deployed a four-to-five-megaton warhead onboard the DF-5A intercontinental missile (NRDC Nuclear Notebook September/October 2001, 71). Clearly, it cannot be assumed new nuclear states will be limited to first-generation weapons for long, and weapon yields in the 100-kiloton to one-megaton range should be easily within reach for many states during the first five to ten years of their programs. It is also likely such states would be able to design first-generation warheads "small and light enough to be carried by Scud-class missiles or small aircraft" (Office of Technology Assessment 1993, 5).

## THE PHYSICAL EFFECTS OF NUCLEAR WEAPONS ON POTENTIAL COUNTERVALUE TARGETS

How do the capabilities of new nuclear states translate into potential for inflicting harm on opponents? To answer this question, the physical characteristics of nuclear weapons will be discussed, along with various available employment strategies. As will become obvious, even limited nuclear capabilities, if deliverable, are capable of inflicting levels of damage far beyond what would be tolerable for any realistically conceivable aggressor. Indeed, for many who became acclimatized during the Cold War to thinking about requirements for effective deterrence being dependent upon massive numbers of weapons, or who remain fixated upon "bean-counting" notions of nuclear superiority, understanding the true nature of the security relationships posed by states with small arsenals to great powers requires a fundamental shift of analysis. Yet, even during the Cold War, realistic requirements for deterrence (believed to be an arsenal of a few hundred weapons by McNamara) were vastly different from the odd political dynamics that led to ever increasing (and unnecessary) numbers of warheads. During that time, France, Britain, and China understood that robust, minimal deterrent forces were all that was required to assure their central interests from superpower threats—and ridiculously large forces were never pursued or developed. New nuclear states, like Israel, India, Pakistan, and North Korea, similarly understand the logic of minimal deterrence. They will develop robust, moderate force structures (emphasizing survivability) to provide enough capabilities versus opponents to deter, while avoiding self-defeating arms races that attempt to match numerical capability for capability. When small state nuclear capabilities are more fully considered, it becomes obvious the "rules of the game" for these Melians have changed.

## NUCLEAR ATTACK SCENARIOS

A number of previous studies provide useful insights into the likely effects of either small state or terror group nuclear attacks on opponents. One study examined the effects of twenty-kiloton airbursts on overseas ports and airbases used by American forces (such as the port of Ad-Dammām or the air bases at Dhahran) and found such attacks able to effectively destroy or render inoperable either type of facility for U.S. military operations (Weaver and Glaes 1997, 28–50). This is of particular interest given the necessity of bases in Japan or South Korea for U.S. military operations on the Korean peninsula, and illustrates the desirability for North Korea of being able to strike such sites with nuclear weapons.

Similarly, the U.S. Office of Technology Assessment (OTA) (May 1979) provides a number of interesting scenarios (involving various types of nuclear attacks on cities and infrastructure targets) that, despite its Cold War–era nature, can be adapted to modern-day scenarios involving limited nuclear attacks by opponents. Scenarios included attacks on a single city (Detroit or Leningrad) with either a single one-megaton weapon or ten smaller weapons. Such an attack upon the U.S. would conceivably be within reach of a new nuclear state with either regional or great power capabilities using clandestine or missile means of delivery respectively. It should also be noted that none of the OTA scenarios incorporate the likely destruction and deaths that would be caused by firestorms in these cities, which would vastly increase both figures. In one Detroit scenario, a one-megaton thermonuclear weapon was detonated on the surface within the population of 4.3 million, resulting in seventy square miles of property destruction, 250,000 deaths, and 500,000 injuries (Office of Technology Assessment 1979, 27–35). In a second Detroit scenario, the same one-megaton bomb was airburst over the city at an altitude of 6,000 feet, resulting in 470,000 deaths and 630,000 injured on the ground along with far greater property destruction (Office of Technology Assessment 1979, 35–37). For Leningrad, given the more densely populated area, adjacent residential areas, and older buildings within the city, the toll from the same one-megaton airburst was predicted to be 390,000 killed and 1.26 million injured (Office of Technology Assessment 1979, 37–45). Further, a scenario involving ten forty-kiloton airbursts over Leningrad was expected to result in 1.02 million dead and 1 million injured (Office of Technology Assessment 1979, 37–45).

A 2001 study produced by the Natural Resources Defense Council (NRDC), employing a suite of nuclear war analysis models, argues a nuclear arsenal of about 1,300 warheads would provide the U.S. with the ability to destroy most of Russia's nuclear capabilities while inflicting 8 to 12 million casualties (McKinzie et al. 2001, x). Moreover, a limited countervalue attack using less than 3 percent of the current U.S. arsenal was found to be capable of inflicting well over 50 million casualties (McKinzie et al. 2001, x). Their study found approximately one-third of Russia's population (between 30 and 60 million people) would become casualties from an attack by only 150 to 200 warheads (the number carried aboard a single Trident missile submarine) (McKinzie et al. 2001, 130). The NRDC study also modeled a number of nuclear war scenarios involving primitive, first-generation Hiroshima-type atomic bombs (fifteen-kiloton yield) on ten major Indian and Pakistani cities, superimposing the Hiroshima casualty rates by distance to these cities. The results are impressive, and demonstrate that even with first-generation weapons, the higher population densities in these cities would likely result in casualties two or three times higher than Hiroshima (McKinzie et al. 2001, 29).[1]

What should be emphasized is that these *immense* casualty rates (a total of 2.863 million dead—1.691 million in India and 1.172 million in Pakistan) were produced by *only five first-generation nuclear weapons* identical to the 1945 Hiroshima bomb (fifteen kilotons) launched by each side! Arsenals of between five and ten first-generation weapons are easily obtainable by new nuclear states, and would provide immense destructive capabilities. Further, these figures only take into account blast effects, and do not take into account the use of higher-yield weapons or the impact of the massive firestorms likely produced by such weapons that would easily double or triple these casualty figures. For example, the NRDC study estimates (using U.S. Defense Department blast effects calculations) that a one-megaton airburst over New York City would kill 1.25 million people and injure at least 2.65 million (McKinzie et al. 2001, 31). However, MIT physicist Theodore Postol's firestorm model greatly increases (by three-and-a-half times) the number of fatalities to be expected in such an attack on New York to well over 4.39 million! (McKinzie et al. 2001, 30–31)

The magnifying effects of firestorms on the potential destructiveness of nuclear weapons on cities is described in great depth by Eden (2004, 33). Noting that U.S. government estimates have consistently underestimated the damage inflicted by nuclear attacks due to their reliance purely upon blast damage calculations that ignore fire effects, Eden describes a 300-kiloton near-surface airburst (1,500 feet) over the Pentagon in Washington, D.C. As she observes:

> By the time the fireball approached its maximum size, it would be more than a mile in diameter. . . . Vast amounts of thermal energy would ignite extensive fires over urban and suburban areas . . . the blast wave and high-speed winds would crush many structures and tear them apart . . . exposing ignitable surfaces, releasing flammable materials, and dispersing burning materials. Within minutes of a detonation, fire would be everywhere. Numerous fires and firebrands— burning materials that set more fires—would coalesce into a mass fire. . . . This fire would engulf tens of square miles and begin to heat enormous volumes of air that would rise, while cool air from the fire's periphery would be pulled in. Within tens of minutes after the detonation, the pumping action from rising hot air would generate superheated ground winds of hurricane force, further intensifying the fire. Virtually no one in an area of about 40–65 square miles would survive. (Eden 2004, 35)

All combustible materials in line of sight of the fireball (i.e., curtains and interior furniture in buildings and houses, interiors of cars or aircraft, rubber tires and fuel hoses, grass and trees) would explode into flames up to three miles from ground zero (Eden 2004, 36). The initial blast wave (300–400 mph at 1.6 miles and over 100 mph at 3 miles distance) would further damage structures, rupture gas lines, and spread burning embers (Eden 2004, 37). All told, Eden suggests "fires would be ignited to a distance of about 4.6 miles from the detonation—over an area of approximately 65 square miles" (2004, 37). The hurricane force winds would bring with them average air temperatures far above the boiling point of water (Eden 2004, 37). The firestorm would continue unabated over the city for three to six hours and "eliminate all life in the fire zone," even among those who were sheltered from the initial nuclear weapon effects (Eden 2004, 43).

The results would be similar to firestorms created by U.S. and British conventional bombings of German and Japanese cities during World War II. Over Hamburg, for example, between 60,000 and 100,000 civilians died in a five-square-mile area of the city where air temperatures reached 400 to 500 degrees Fahrenheit (Eden 2004, 40). In modern cities, the consequences would be enormous. In its analysis of the potential impact of a clandestine nuclear weapon attack on an American seaport, Abt Associates (2003, 1–2) notes:

> If terrorists smuggled a Hiroshima-sized bomb (15 kilotons) into a port and set it off, the attack would destroy buildings out to a mile or two; start fires, especially in a port that handled petroleum and chemicals; spread fallout over many square miles; disrupt commerce; and kill many people. By one estimate, a 10- to 20-kiloton weapon detonated in a major seaport or Washington, D.C. would kill 50,000 to 1 million people and would result in direct property damage of $50 to $500 billion, losses due to trade disruption of $100 billion to $200 billion, and indirect costs of $300 billion to $1.2 trillion.

The electromagnetic pulse (EMP) effects (to be discussed later) would also reduce the ability of surviving emergency response units to respond to the resulting mass fires. Indeed, water distribution systems in most cities include electrical pumps controlled by microprocessors vulnerable to EMP disruption, as are communications and diagnostic equipment routinely used by emergency fire, police, and medical response teams (U.S. Congress, *Prepared Testimony of Mr. Gordon K. Soper* 1999).

## THE DETONATION OF A ONE-MEGATON
## WEAPON IN THE PORT OF SEATTLE

One potential strategy for attacking a great power would be to place nuclear weapons on freighters in cargo containers, launch them using short-range missiles, or conceal them within the holds of commercial aircraft. To illustrate the potential for a small-state actor to employ clandestine delivery means, an attack upon the city of Seattle, Washington, is useful for laying out the possibilities.

Immense amounts of cargo are received by the Port of Seattle each year, with freighters routinely plying the waters of Elliot Bay along the coast of the city itself. The port facilities in Seattle are located on the southern end of the city, and a would-be attacker could decide to detonate their weapon once the ship reached its berth, or choose to detonate it closer to the city proper as it passed by en route. If the attacker relied purely upon a concealment strategy, placing the one-megaton warhead within the cargo of one of the many nondescript freighters passing perhaps one-half mile off the shoreline of the city of Seattle, the result would be destruction as effective as if it had been delivered by a long-range missile. Were a short-range missile used to launch the warhead, at one-mile distance, an individual would need to have the protection of four feet of concrete or twelve inches of steel to be relatively safe from the effects of the initial radiation from an airburst of a one-megaton nuclear weapon (Department of Defense 1964, 10). Or put another way, most people within one mile of a one-megaton explosion would receive fatal doses of radiation even if surrounded by twenty-four inches of concrete (Department of Defense 1964, 370).

Assuming the device (concealed in a cargo container) was exploded as it passed opposite the city center, halfway between the Seattle Center and Harbor Island, the initial flash from the explosion and the thermal radiation released would result in everyone within line-of-sight of the blast across the entire city and surrounding suburbs receiving third-degree burns at a distance of 4.75 miles and second-degree burns out to 5.5 miles. Within a four-and-a-half mile radius, all combustible items exposed to the flash would explode into flames (curtains and furnishing in buildings, wood structures, the interiors of cars and buses). The fireball itself would be more than one mile in diameter, incinerating everything within its reach with temperatures many times that of the surface of the sun. The shock wave from the blast (with winds between 300 and 400 mph at 1.6 miles distant) would completely destroy many of the older, brick masonry buildings within the city itself, causing severe damage to wall-bearing, masonry (apartment-house-type) buildings for a 2.6 mile radius from ground zero, and moderate damage out to 4.1 miles. Even the more modern, reinforced-concrete structures of many of the office buildings would be shattered, with severe damage being inflicted out to 1.875 miles and moderate damage at 2.55 miles from ground zero.

While the earthquake resistant Space Needle would (barely) avoid becoming engulfed within the fireball itself, the entire interior of the upper-level restaurants within its saucer section would be completely engulfed in flames as its furnishings were exposed to the thermal effects of the flash, its windows would be shattered by the blast wave, and immense structural damage (if not an actual collapse) would occur to a structure designed to withstand extreme earthquake stresses, but not the quite different ones resulting from such a large nuclear blast. Wood-frame, residential housing in the surrounding suburbs would be destroyed in a 4.1-mile radius and severely damaged out to 4.95 miles. The initial thermal and blast damage from a one-megaton weapon would completely cover the entire city of Seattle and substantial amounts of its surrounding suburbs. Given the close quarters and tightly packed nature of construction within the city, the resulting firestorm would engulf the entire city out to at least 4.5 miles, completely destroying what was left of the city proper and killing nearly everyone within the fire zone. Also requiring consideration are the casualties which would result from the plume of radioactive fallout, measuring at least twelve miles wide and seventy-four miles long, that would deliver lethal doses of radiation (between 300 and 3,000 roentgens per hour) across significant areas of the surrounding suburbs. According to the 2002 census, the city of Seattle itself has a population of 570,426, with the surrounding metro area adding a further 3 million residents. Were the attack to occur during business hours on a weekday, when the city would be full of workers and tourists alike, the likely fatalities could far exceed 600,000, with millions more injured or sickened from radiation exposure.

Other U.S. port cities would provide equally tempting targets for such unconventional delivery of nuclear weapons. Any number of U.S. port cities would provide an attacker with the ability to inflict massive casualties from a bomb exploded in or near the cities' port facilities. The illustration using an attack on Seattle is a fairly conservative one given the much larger casualties which similar attacks on more populous cities, like San Francisco, Los Angeles, or New York might produce. Indeed, while the average population density in Hiroshima was 8,400 per square mile in 1945, by the early 1960s, the population densities of U.S. cities like New York were already 24,700 per square mile (with Manhattan alone having a density of 74,800 per square mile) (Department of Defense 1964, 550–51). These growing population densities across major American cities, densities which increase greatly during the working day, mean that the casualty totals that would be produced even by one Hiroshima-type bomb would be substantially higher than those inflicted in 1945.

Other possibilities would include the launching of short-range ballistic missiles from freighters to produce more destructive airbursts over cities. This would allow for the possibility of multiple warhead detonations over a city with airbursts, with either several first-generation (fifteen to fifty kiloton) weapons or several large weapons in the megaton range. The damages associated with airbursts are considerably greater than those of ground bursts and would greatly increase the ability of an attacker to generate even larger casualty figures (Department of Defense 1964, 10, 91, 370, 564). Imagine, for example, the launching of two short-range missiles carrying one-megaton warheads from an approaching freighter over the city of New York or Los Angeles. The death toll in either event would easily be in the millions—all from only one attack by two weapons.

Depending upon how many weapons were employed (and their respective yields), additional casualties might be produced great distances from the initial city targets. Explosions at or near the surface can create substantial contamination from radioactive fallout, as was illustrated by the fifteen-megaton thermonuclear device tested at Bikini Atoll (March 1, 1954—the BRAVO experiment of Operation Castle), in which an area of more than 7,000 square miles (a cigar-shaped region 60 miles in width at its maximum and 20 statute miles long upwind and over 320 miles long downwind) was severely affected (Department of Defense 1964, 40). Over 100 miles from the explosion, an exposed individual would have received 3,300 roentgens of radiation during the first ninety-six hours (many times over a lethal dosage) (Department of Defense 1964, 463). Indeed, in an area 170 miles long by 35 miles wide, exposed individuals would likely have received lethal doses of radiation from fallout (Department of Defense 1964, 461). Any radiation dose over 1,000 rems is usually considered to be a fatal dose, with many dying who receive anything over 600 rems (Department of Defense 1964, 591–95).

## EMP LAY-DOWN STRATEGIES

One useful strategy for small states seeking to offset superior great power military and reconnaissance capabilities would be to employ a few of their nuclear weapons to create strong EMP (electromagnetic pulse) effects against these assets. Created by any nuclear explosion, EMP effects (particularly those occurring at high altitudes) can provide defenders with a wide range of possible options, for both local and long-range disruption of enemy forces. Five types of EMP tactics could be employed: (1) warning shot; (2) disruption of local military operations; (3) destroying value and creating economic-social disruption; (4) crippling NMD or air defenses of opponents; and (5) use as a defense to cripple an opponent's long-range attacks. The military or strategic utility of such tactics would vary in important respects.

For example, the "warning shot" tactic would involve a high-altitude detonation over either a regional battlefield or above great power territory itself as a "nonlethal" demonstration of nuclear capability and resolve during a crisis. The "disruption of local military operations" tactic, on the other hand, would employ a detonation over a local or regional battlefield to blind/cripple enemy reconnaissance, communications, and GPS satellites. The goal would be to effectively counter U.S. precision-guided munitions, surveillance, and communications advantages. This tactic could also be used during opening stages of massive air and ground operations by opponents to disable, damage, or disorient the attacking forces vulnerable military equipment.

The "destroying value and creating economic-social disruption" tactic would utilize a detonation over either regional or great power opponent territory to *destroy* the civilian satellites that form the basis of modern, high-tech societies (telecommunications, GPS, weather, etc.). This also could be used to inflict massive physical and economic damage to power grids and other vulnerable electronic equipment over wide area. Such a tactic would be particularly useful for nonstate terror groups seeking to inflict substantial economic damage or societal disruption.

The "crippling NMD or air defenses of opponents" tactic would employ a detonation over either regional or great power opponents to "blind" satellites and radars necessary for operation of missile defense systems or traditional air defense systems. The goal with this EMP tactic would be to improve ability of new nuclear state retaliatory capabilities (aircraft, cruise missiles, or ballistic missiles) to penetrate an opponent's defenses.

Finally, the "use as a defense to cripple an opponent's long-range attacks" EMP tactic would make use of a detonation above one's own territory *or* over regional/great power territory to destroy or seriously damage vulnerable components in either ballistic missiles or nuclear warheads during flight. The goal would be to obtain some limited interdiction ability of an opponent's strategic WMD attacks, even in the absence of a dedicated missile defense program.

While providing a clear demonstration of small-state resolve to escalate to more direct nuclear use if necessary, "warning shot" EMP attacks could inflict significant damage on enemy assets while avoiding the inescapable escalation that would result from inflicting mass casualties directly on opponents. In effect, it is a limited, tactical use of nuclear weapons that nevertheless foreshadows the "greater threat that is to come" if the provocative actions of the great power continues. In this sense, such limited nuclear use, which will greatly disrupt the GPS-guided conventional military capabilities of great powers (like PGM and cruise missile guidance systems) might serve (by making conventional operations more difficult) as a potential crisis de-escalation device for the small state. Furthermore, even if it does not prevent conflict, EMP lay-down attacks provide small states with a potent means for offsetting U.S. military superiority and complicating any planned offensive operations. As Dr. Lowell Wood warned during Congressional testimony in 1999, EMP attacks provide opponents with "unique opportunities for defeating both advanced U.S. forces abroad and the American Nation itself" by countering the ongoing revolution in military affairs (RMA) through attacks on the "classic Achilles heel which EMP poses to any information-intensive military force completely dependent for its electronic data flows on EMP fragile integrated circuits" (U.S. Congress, *Electromagnetic Pulse Threats* 1999). Indeed, as Gray (1999, 168–69) observes, if U.S. space-based assets were compromised (whether by EMP or antisatellite weapons), the advantages provided by information-led RMA would no longer work and enemies would "have found a notable equalizer to the military effectiveness" of the American military.

The creation of significant EMP effects in the upper atmosphere *does not* require large weapon yields to accomplish. In fact, because of saturation effects in the atmosphere caused by radiation-induced ionization, EMP fields are not fully dependent on yield and, as a result, small yield nuclear weapons often produce *comparable disruptions* to those produced by large ones (Grace 1994, 97). Even the use of one weapon in the ten-to-twenty-kiloton range can create quite wide-ranging and severe effects. As Dr. William Graham, president and CEO of National Security Research, warned during Congressional testimony in 1999, U.S. space-based systems (especially low-altitude assets used to support military forces in a theater) would be highly vulnerable to EMP effects:

> The detonation of a nuclear explosion outside the atmosphere, even if it were a small nuclear weapon, perhaps a few tens of kilotons, could produce sufficient direct and delayed radiation to degrade or destroy satellites in line of sight of the burst, as well as a second effect; that is, producing EMP near the Earth's surface, which could interfere with, among other things, the satellite ground stations on the Earth (U.S. Congress, *Electromagnetic Pulse Threats* 1999).

The wide-ranging potential effects of EMP from nuclear detonations on satellites were aptly demonstrated during American nuclear tests in the 1950s and 1960s. The 1962 *Starfish* nuclear test, which detonated a 1.4-megaton weapon at an altitude of 325 miles above the earth, resulted in the destruction from radiation exposure of seven satellites within seven months (Morris 2001, 1). During one high-altitude test over the Johnston Island area in 1962, the EMP effect caused communications and street light failures over 750 miles away on the Hawaiian island of Oahu (Department of Defense, *Radiological Defense Textbook* 1974, 49). Given the survivability of even "hardened" military satellites is questionable given many of the attack scenarios possible using high-altitude nuclear bursts, it is clear that the far more numerous, commercial satellites of today would be highly vulnerable to destruction by EMP and exposure to nuclear radiation (Morris 2001). As Dr. Lowell Wood explained during Congressional testimony, most existing U.S. satellites are extremely vulnerable to this kind of EMP attack:

> The satellites would die promptly due to gamma ray effects, so-called system-generated EMP, and other satellites that were not necessarily even in the line of sight of the blast would die at a timescale of hours to weeks due to the so-called pumping up of the Van Allen Belts, the radiation belts surrounding the Earth, by the beta decay products from the fission products of the explosion. . . . it was demonstrated by the U.S. in the Argus test series in the late 1950s that even very modest nuclear explosives detonated in the Van Allen Belts created large and enduring fluxes of radiation which are confidently expected to be of magnitude such that they would destroy satellites at low- to medium-level Earth orbits. (U.S. Congress, *Electromagnetic Pulse Threats* 1999)

Furthermore, the use of low-yield nuclear weapons in exoatmospheric bursts (at an altitude of least forty kilometers [or twenty-five miles] in height) to produce EMP effects to disable U.S. satellites is actually quite feasible for new nuclear states with only moderate missile delivery system capabilities. In fact, all of the recent small nuclear states (Israel, Pakistan, India, and North Korea) possess ballistic missiles capable of reaching the forty-to-seventy-mile altitude range required for optimal EMP effects (Department of Defense, *Effects of Nuclear Weapons* 1964, 514–15). For example, Iran's Shahab-3 is believed capable of reaching an altitude of 155 miles carrying a 2,000-pound warhead (Barletta et al. 1999, 162). Even the North Korean Scud-B or Scud-C is capable of carrying a 1,000 kilogram (2,200 pound) payload to a height of 300 kilometers (186 miles) (Cirincione 2002, 94). As Dr. Graham warned in testimony before Congress in 1999:

> One possible use of EMP against U.S. forces . . . might be against forces stationed overseas; for example, on the Korean peninsula or in the Persian Gulf. Even if an adversary had only a very few nuclear weapons, by launching even as primitive a missile as a SCUD and exploding a nuclear weapon above the atmosphere, the ability of the U.S. and Allied Forces to make full use of their electronics systems, including communications, fire control, radar systems, missiles and certainly network systems envisioned for our 21st century forces could be degraded to some degree. (U.S. Congress, *Electromagnetic Pulse Threats* 1999)

Further, the tactic of EMP lay down as a precursor to nuclear attacks has long been an integral part of *both* U.S. and Soviet (now Russian) strategic nuclear doctrines. Indeed, as one senior government scientist observed, "in all of the war games in which I have been present and all the ones which I have studied when I have not been present, the attack, the red attack, always begins with an EMP lay down on blue, that is to say a Soviet lay down on the continental United States by multiple megaton high-altitude bursts (U.S. Congress, *Electromagnetic Pulse Threats* 1999). Yet, as was repeatedly noted by experts during Congressional hearings on EMP in 1999, the EMP yield of any warhead is "very weakly dependent on its energy yield," and that "it doesn't take a megaton to do an awful lot of damage. You can do an awful lot of damage in ten kilotons or less" (U.S. Congress, *Electromagnetic Pulse Threats* 1999).

But, exactly how wide-ranging and damaging would these effects likely be? According to one study by the U.S. Defense Nuclear Agency (DNA), "a single high-altitude low-yield nuclear weapon could destroy $14 billion worth of low-earth-orbit satellites that would transit through the enhanced radiation belts produced by such a nuclear event" (U.S. Congress, *Prepared Testimony of Mr. Gordon K. Soper* 1999). But, as Gordon Soper, group vice president of Defense Group, Inc., noted in Congressional testimony, the potential damage to satellites would likely be far greater now than it was at the time of the original DNA study—which assumed decreased life expectancies for Iridium satellites (only twenty-four months rather than seventy-two) and for Globalstar satellites (surviving only one month instead of ninety) (U.S. Congress, *Prepared Testimony of Mr. Gordon K. Soper* 1999). As Zimmerman and Ferguson (2003, 58–59) explain:

> Even comparatively low-yield devices in the 50-kiloton range would inject so much radiation into the Van Allen belts that most satellites, including those on which U.S. armed forces rely for communications, navigation, and intelligence collection, would be destroyed—not immediately but over a few months. An April 2001 Defense Threat Reduction Agency report provides estimates of the anticipated damage from high-altitude nuclear detonations by other countries over their own territory or near their territory. If North Korea, for example, detonated a 50-kiloton device at 120 kilometers above its own territory, the estimated lifetime of a National Oceanic and Atmospheric Administration weather satellite in an 850-kilometer altitude orbit . . . would be reduced from 48 months to 0.8 months; an Orbcomm communications satellite at a 775-kilometer altitude . . . would see its lifetime degraded from 84 months to 0.5 months. By 55 days after such a detonation, the number of commercial satellites surviving in low-Earth orbit (LEO) would decline from about 450 (as of 2002) to zero. An Indian detonation of a similar device 250 kilometers above the Bay of Bengal would have similar results. We assume similar results would be found for detonations at other combinations of latitude and longitude.

Centered over Europe, a single airburst at 400 kilometers above the surface would disrupt power and communications systems across the entire continent, from Moscow to Iceland (Grace 1994, 97). A similar explosion at 100 kilometers over Europe would cause disruptions from southern England to the tip of Italy, across all of Eastern Europe, France, and Germany, extending into Belarus and the Baltic states (Grace 1994, 97). Very large areas can be affected by high-altitude detonations since the "lateral extent of the 'interaction region' is generally limited only by the curvature of the earth" (U.S. Congress, *Radiological Defense Textbook* 1974). Thus, a high-altitude burst over Omaha, Nebraska, would result in a circle passing through Dallas, Texas, (within which the EMP hazard would be greatest) and an outer circle denoting potential damage from EMP effects over much of the United States (U.S. Congress, *Radiological Defense Textbook* 1974).

Electronic equipment is at risk over enormous distances (out to the visible horizon as viewed from the burst point), so if "the burst height is 400 km [248 miles] the affected area extends out to 2,200 km [1,364 miles] in all directions from GZ, so one high-altitude burst can damage electrical and electronic systems over a whole continent" (Grace 1994, 96). In fact, Dr. Michael Bernardin, provost for Theoretical Institute of Thermonuclear Studies at the Los Alamos National Laboratory, warns "a high-altitude nuclear detonation would produce an electromagnetic pulse that would cover from one to several million square miles, depending on the height of the burst, with electric fields larger than those typically associated with lightning." As he notes, "the peak field ranges [of EMP within these regions] ranges from 12 to about 25 kilovolts per meter." Given that even optimistic assessments of EMP effects suggest that in the seven-to-twenty kilovolts-per-meter range, some equipment will be damaged, and above twenty kilovolts extensive damage is "most likely probable," U.S. vulnerability to EMP attack certainly exists to some degree (U.S. Congress, *Electromagnetic Pulse Threats* 1999).[2] Further, so-called system-generated EMP (SGEMP) poses a threat to military and communications satellites beyond that posed by normal EMP:

[W]e have been concerned with EMP generated by weapon gamma rays interacting with the atmosphere. Very similar effects may occur if . . . equipment is itself exposed to an intense pulse of nuclear radiation. It interacts with the structural materials of the equipment by ejecting electrons, so giving rise to charge separation and the creation of intense and potentially damaging electric and magnetic fields within the equipment. These are called system-generated EMP (SGEMP). The situation most likely to produce serious SGEMP is an exoatmospheric burst and a target such as a satellite or missile which is also above the atmosphere. . . . Since there is little absorption, radiation intensities are high enough to produce serious SGEMP problems even at ranges of several tens of kilometers. (Grace 1994, 98)

Even sophisticated U.S. military MILTSTAR satellites, deployed at higher altitudes than most commercial satellites and hardened against EMP effects, are not guaranteed to survive a high-altitude nuclear burst (U.S. Congress, *Electromagnetic Pulse Threats* 1999). In addition, a single high-altitude burst would produce EMP that would severely disrupt systems such as the entire national power distribution grid or its communications systems (Grace 1994, 96–97). As Graham notes, since EMP can produce electronic system failures simultaneously at many widely distributed points, system operators would have to try to recover from such failures at the time they occurred! (U.S. Congress, *Electromagnetic Pulse Threats* 1999) This would be a tall order in the absence of special nuclear EMP recovery preparation and training. As Graham observes, "I know of no training in U.S. commercial systems focused on multiple, widely spread, simultaneous failures of highly reliable equipment." Moreover, findings from U.S. government studies during the 1970s of the postnuclear attack recovery process (PONAST) suggested that after a hypothetical Soviet lay-down EMP attack, "essentially nothing electrical or electronic could be relied upon to work even in rural areas far from nuclear blasts," and that a period of months, perhaps up to a year, might be required to restore many services (such as electricity, telephones, etc.). As Dr. Wood explained:

> When the most vulnerable portions of a power system die, and these are usually the very high-powered transformers in major switching stations, when they go out, the time scale to replace them, if only one is lost, is about 90 days. If you lost 100 of them or 300 of them or whatever, it might be as long as a year or more before you could reconstitute a large portion of the major interconnect points that switch and convey electric power in this country. It is certainly true that the type of EMP levels that the Soviet Union, or nowadays the Russian Federation, could lay down on this country without killing anybody would be easily sufficient to bring down the entire power grid. (U.S. Congress, *Electromagnetic Pulse Threats* 1999)

Although there have been some concerns expressed about the effects of EMP upon nuclear power plants, and whether the type of electrical and control system disruptions produced might result in core melts, the U.S. Nuclear Regulatory Commission has stated its own research suggests any system failures would "likely be only momentary" and not threaten containment (Nuclear Regulatory Commission 2003). Of course, like much of the U.S. civilian technical infrastructure, no substantial studies or research have been conducted to conclusively test all of these components survivability against large EMP effects, leaving the assurance that control system disruption in nuclear facilities would be "momentary" unproven and potentially inaccurate (U.S. Congress, *Prepared Testimony of Mr. Gordon K. Soper* 1999; U.S. Congress, *Electromagnetic Pulse Threats* 1999).

So concerned was the U.S. government about potential EMP effects that the entire topic of EMP was (and remains) highly classified. But, recently, the Nuclear Technology Branch of the Defense Threat Reduction Agency (DTRA) developed a $100 million Decade Radiation Test Facility (DRTF) at Arnold Air Force Base in Tennessee to test the survivability of satellites and missile defense system equipment against nuclear weapon effects, including EMP and X-rays (Morris 2001). Yet, as Dr. Lowell Wood, a member of the director's technical staff at the Lawrence Livermore National Laboratory, observes, while parts of the U.S. military were significantly hardened against EMP, the protection was uneven:

> A number of important military systems were quite incompletely defended, and some were defended only on paper. . . . military hardware and systems, especially those not considered vital to the conduct of strategic war, weren't hardened against EMP very much at all . . . I know of major military systems, some very important to the Nation's war fighting capabilities, which were documented to have failed at EMP levels in order of magnitude and more below [7 to 20 kilovolt-per-meter fields]. . . . [Our] vulnerability to EMP attack is highly uneven, with large parts of our military machine and virtually all of the equipment undergirding modern American civilization being EMP-vulnerable. (U.S. Congress, *Electromagnetic Pulse Threats* 1999)

In a regional context, small nuclear states could make use of local EMP effects to blind the radar tracking capabilities of opponents—thereby disrupting air defense radars so strategic bombers (or converted fighter-bombers) and cruise missiles could go undetected (Department of Defense 1964). EMP effects could disrupt tracking radars of modern BMD systems, allowing even antiquated Scuds to serve as high reliability delivery systems. This would be particularly worrisome for distant great powers, like the U.S., since a small state possessing a handful of long-range systems could use EMP to blind any missile defenses that might be constructed, thereby facilitating nuclear countercity attacks. Since theater missile defense (TMD) systems would also be affected by EMP, states lacking long-range ballistic missile capabilities could compensate by smuggling shorter-range systems near U.S. shores prior to the beginning of hostilities. As Graham notes, for an adversary with long-range, relatively inaccurate missiles or short-range ones launched from platforms (like ships or submarines) that engender some inaccuracy itself, if they possess only low-yield weapons, they "could be more confidently used for an EMP attack than a direct attack, because . . . accuracy would not be required" for an EMP attack (U.S. Congress, *Electromagnetic Pulse Threats* 1999).

Even with a working national missile defense (NMD) or TMD system, trying to intercept an enemies' use of EMP effects would be highly problematic. As Graham observes, "one of the ways an offensive nuclear weapon on a missile can be armed is in what is called a sympathetic or a salvage fusing mode, so that even if you intercepted above the atmosphere before it reaches its target, once the offensive nuclear warhead knows it is being attacked, its fusing system may choose to detonate itself there to get at least the EMP and space radiation effect of the weapon" (U.S. Congress, *Electromagnetic Pulse Threats* 1999). Combined with the more obvious effects of nuclear weapons, EMP represents an often overlooked element in the arsenal of new nuclear states which could substantially magnify the threat faced by the U.S. (or other opponents of these states) in any future conflict. For the U.S. in particular, with its heavy reliance upon high technology on the battlefield, it represents a point of weakness that could be exploited by a new nuclear state mindful of that fact.[3]

## THE VALUE OF OPAQUE PROLIFERATION STRATEGIES

There has been a tremendous amount of scholarship on the concept of "opaque proliferation" as a strategy used by states to develop rudimentary nuclear weapons capabilities and obtain some *existential deterrence* value from them, without publicly admitting their existence and incurring negative sanctions from the nonproliferation regime. Cohen and Frankel (1990, 21–23), for instance, have laid out seven elements of an opaque proliferation strategy: (1) denial of possession; (2) no weapon tests; (3) no direct threats of use; (4) no elaborated military doctrine; (5) no military deployment of weapons; (6) no open debate about weapons or their role within the country; and (7) organizational insulation of the weapon program by labeling it R&D efforts. In terms of these criteria, Israel's nuclear weapons development program has often been described as following the classic "opaque" strategy (Evron 1990; Cohen 1998). Similarly, the development of India and Pakistan's nuclear weapons programs, at least prior to 1998, were also described as following "opaque" strategies to conceal both development and possession (Joeck 1990; Kampani 1998).

## MOVING BEYOND OPAQUE STRATEGIES

Historically, traditional opaque proliferation strategies have characterized only the earliest (most vulnerable) stages of a state's nuclear development. As the nuclear capabilities of states have grown, most have moved away from *opaque nuclear procurement strategies* and adopted more explicit postures, albeit ones that sought to preserve as many elements from their former opaque postures as possible. This limited preservation by states of opaque elements serves two purposes. First, it maintains uncertainty among opponents regarding their nuclear doctrines, deployment modes, and what might happen should a crisis escalate (thereby enhancing existential deterrence). Secondly, it serves to *slowly* introduce any overt changes to their existing security postures (like weapons tests or the beginnings of weaponization or deployment of standing arsenals), thereby avoiding the appearance of precipitate actions that might antagonize the international community and bring down military preemption or sanctions on nascent programs.

While opaque strategies result in only minimal or recessed arsenals, like those possessed by India and Pakistan prior to 1998, the reality is that when one observes the overall pattern of nuclear development over time across additional states (like Israel, North Korea, and Iran), it is more accurate to describe them as pursuing *opaque nuclear procurement strategies*—ones which adopt traditional opaque proliferation elements early on, but slowly move toward a combination of overt/opaque strategies as their capabilities grow. For most states, opaque postures appear to essentially be "rest stops" on the road toward more overt nuclear capabilities. And, as India and Pakistan discovered, even in the aftermath of overt tests, the preservation of some elements of the opaque strategy continued to shield their programs from the full intensity of outside scrutiny (and more importantly) from sanctions. Similarly, Israel is hardly considered in 2005 to be a nonnuclear state, or one with even a minimal or recessed arsenal, just because it has publicly followed most of the seven tenets of an opaque proliferation strategy. Rather, Israel adopted a clear opaque nuclear procurement strategy in the early stages of its program, but later pursued a combination overt/opaque posture as its nuclear capabilities became well established and it desired to gain the greater deterrence options available to it with an implied, but overt, nuclear status (Cohen 1998; Steinberg 2000). By maintaining some degree of opacity (i.e., avoidance of weapons tests, lack of public discussion of capabilities/doctrine, etc.), Israel gained (at little cost) substantial nuclear capabilities, avoided sanctions, and obtained the benefits (both in terms of security and prestige) of being a de facto nuclear power.

Over the coming decades, there will be a continuing benefit for nuclear weapon states (or those pursuing such capabilities) to adopt *opaque nuclear procurement strategies*—which provide protection for the early stages of vulnerable programs, yet increasingly overt status as their capabilities mature. As the Israeli, Pakistani, and Indian experiences demonstrate, such an approach provides the most unencumbered route toward the goal of becoming a full-fledged nuclear weapon state. In the following sections, I discuss the options/possibilities that exist for states that have decided, as North Korea, Israel, India, and Pakistan have done in recent years, to pursue increasingly overt nuclear postures. But first, we will discuss *prenuclear powers* (Iraq and Iran), which serve to illustrate the extreme vulnerability of such states in their early stages of nuclear development—prior to the advent of actual nuclear weapons capabilities. Next, we will discuss the nuclear strategies and options available to states of increasingly robust nuclear capabilities, beginning with *nascent nuclear power* North Korea. Afterward, the more impressive capabilities of *regional nuclear powers*—Israel, India, and Pakistan—will be analyzed.

## THE PRENUCLEAR POWERS (IRAQ AND IRAN)

Of course, the most vulnerable period for any would-be nuclear state is the span during which it attempts to develop a substantial nuclear infrastructure or viable weapons program, but lacks *operational* and *deliverable* weapons capabilities. For these states, the vulnerability to preemption of their programs by neighboring (or great power) states is enormous—as the experiences of Iraq in 1981, 1991, and 2003 illustrate. For prenuclear states, the traditional logic of power politics still applies—the strong do as they will and the weak suffer what they must. As a result, an *opaque nuclear procurement strategy* is best for these states, wherein their actual weapons-related efforts are concealed behind the facade of a civilian energy program, thereby avoiding both international nonproliferation regime sanctions and preemptive attacks from states threatened by the activity. All of the current *regional* nuclear powers (Israel, India, and Pakistan) have pursued exactly this kind of "opaque nuclear procurement strategy" until they were far enough along with their capabilities to rule out any realistic hope of effective military preemption of their programs by opponents. But, as prenuclear Iraq discovered, one must behave differently when one is a lamb rather than a lion.

### The Case of Prenuclear Iraq

Iraq must be considered the "poster child" for the dangers of a poorly implemented opaque nuclear procurement strategy. Not only were Baghdad's nuclear ambitions an open secret in the region, but Saddam Hussein's own reckless foreign policies provided opponents with ample opportunities to justify taking preemptive measures against Iraq's prenascent weapons programs. In 1981, recognizing the clear threat a nuclear-armed Iraq would pose to its security,

Israel launched a preemptive air strike against the Iraqi nuclear power plant at Osirak—effectively derailing the Iraqi nuclear weapons program for many years. Later, Hussein's invasion of Kuwait in 1990 led to the First Gulf War, and the effective dismantling of his nuclear, chemical, and biological weapons programs by UNSCOM inspectors. Indeed, the great success of the UNSCOM inspections in eliminating the existing Iraqi WMD capabilities, and deterring the resumption of large scale WMD efforts, were only fully appreciated after the end of the Second Gulf War in 2003—when U.S. inspectors (who had not believed the reports of the international inspectors that Iraq possessed little in the way of WMD capabilities) discovered to their surprise no actual WMDs! Instead, they found a weapons program mired in such massive corruption and disarray it was unlikely even Hussein himself realized the extent to which his old WMD programs were mostly a mirage (Burns 2002; Duffy 2004; Barry and Hosenball 2004).

As David Kay, the U.S. weapons inspector who led the WMD search in post-Saddam Iraq acknowledged, American intelligence suggesting active Iraqi WMD programs and large stockpiles of weapons had been almost completely wrong (Risen and Miller 2003, A1 and A12). Iraq's scientists mislead Saddam about their weapon's progress and diverted the money into their own pockets. And Iraq did not possess any significant WMD development programs—with the nuclear program "rudimentary at best" after having been abandoned in the 1990s and limited biological efforts centering principally around ricin production at the time of the 2003 war (Risen 2004). Even prior to 1991, there is evidence suggesting Iraqi scientists misled Hussein regarding the progress of his nuclear weapons program and exaggerated how much fissile material was being produced. As Imad Khadduri, one of Iraq's leading nuclear scientists noted, even had the First Gulf War and subsequent UN inspections not intervened, Iraq had, in reality, been several years from any weapons capability—not the six months claimed by U.S. sources (Hanley 2003).

Yet, while Saddam's perceptions of his own country's military capabilities were no doubt seriously distorted, he could have been under no illusion that he still possessed the extensive WMD capabilities and arsenals he enjoyed pre-1991. Indeed, it is known that he gave orders to dismantle and destroy much of his surviving bioarsenal after the First Gulf War to avoid its discovery by inspectors. The UNSCOM teams uncovered and destroyed massive quantities of chemical munitions, dismantled facilities, and destroyed equipment that could be used to produce chemical or biological weapons, and eliminated Iraq's nuclear infrastructure (United Nations 1999; McCarthy and Tucker 2000, 47–78). These actions were so extensive, and Iraqi efforts to conceal and preserve the remaining elements so dogged, that it is difficult to credit the argument that Saddam was not aware of the resulting massive roll-back of Iraqi WMD capabilities. Instead, what Saddam sought was the perpetuation of the "myth" of Iraqi WMD capabilities—not just for deterrence reasons (where its credibility was now extremely dubious), but for the far more important task of maintaining his own personal prestige and status in the region.

For Saddam, who had long styled himself as the next Nasser of the Arab world, only the continued view of Iraq as militarily potent—and more critically, still in possession of WMDs—would allow it to be seen as a credible counterbalance to Israel and the United States in the Middle East. For both adversaries and friends alike, the myth of Iraqi WMD allowed Saddam to cling to the strategy of appearing, at least to his domestic and regional audiences, to be a lion (rather than a lamb). Unfortunately, less than credible "myths" regarding WMD capabilities do not provide effective military deterrence against opponents who believe the costs are contestable. And, while U.S. officials worried about the potential for Iraqi chemical (and possibly biological) attacks during the Second Gulf War, all of the potential scenarios involved contestable costs (Harknett 1994) that failed to effectively threaten consequences dire enough to deter an American invasion. Unlike the First Gulf War, Saddam's military strength had eroded substantially, and Iraq lacked the large arsenals of chemical munitions and mobile ballistic missiles (e.g., Scuds and Al-Husseyns) that could effectively threaten reprisals against neighboring states or invading armies. More importantly, absent a credible and deliverable nuclear capability in either war, Baghdad lacked the ability to hold substantial countervalue assets in the region at risk—a capability that (had it existed) would likely have seriously constrained (or prevented) U.S. military action in both wars. But, in the absence of *credible, deliverable,* and *survivable* WMD arsenals, deterrence cannot function. As a result, Saddam's great WMD bluff proved to be the death knell for his regime, and a warning to all future prenuclear/biological states of the need to pursue opaque development strategies and avoid provocations that could justify preemptive military actions by opponents.[4] As Saddam discovered to his cost, only "real" lions can roar.

## The Case of Prenuclear Iran

Iran's pursuit of nuclear weapons capabilities, in contrast to Iraq's, have been far more clandestine and less visible, with Tehran closely mimicking the successful *opaque nuclear procurement strategies* of Israel, India, and Pakistan. However, unlike these other states, Tehran signed the Nuclear Non-Proliferation Treaty (NPT) and placed its existing civilian nuclear power industry under

IAEA (International Atomic Energy Agency) inspection. As a result, Iran found itself not only under greater scrutiny from the IAEA, but also subject to substantial supplier state restrictions on the importation of technology for its declared civilian nuclear power industry. By treaty, Iran is obligated to report all nuclear activities to the IAEA, and when rumors surfaced regarding a hidden program, Tehran (after intense outside pressure) was eventually forced to allow inspectors into the country in October 2003. Unfortunately for Tehran, these inspections revealed a long-running Iranian nuclear program that had effectively concealed itself from outside scrutiny for decades, and which unmolested, would have produced substantial nuclear weapons capabilities over the coming years. A crisis ensued with the U.S. and Israel suggesting possible preemptive military action and European-sponsored negotiations over Iran's uranium-enrichment activities eventually stalling in September 2005. With new efforts to report it to the UN Security Council for sanctions, Iran's new hard-line president, Mahmoud Ahmadinejad warns his country will never give up its rights to peaceful nuclear power and will retaliate economically against any state imposing sanctions upon it (Brinkley 2005).

Estimates within the U.S. intelligence community about the Iranian nuclear program have varied widely (in some ways, mirroring the worst-case assumptions found in prewar Iraqi WMD estimates). For example, the CIA reported in January 2000 that Iran might *at that time* be able to make a nuclear weapon—a claim hotly disputed by other intelligence agencies (Risen and Miller 2003, A1 and A8). Estimates of Iranian nuclear capabilities routinely overestimated the speed with which Tehran was progressing, with U.S. and Israeli intelligence in 1992–1993 predicting an Iranian nuclear bomb by 2002, and by 1995, a bomb within "7–15 years" (Cirincione 2002, 257).[5] Although a presidential commission in March 2005 reported U.S. "intelligence on Iran is inadequate to allow firm judgments about Iran's weapons programs," an August 2005 National Intelligence Council report concluded Iran was "determined to build nuclear weapons," but unlikely to possess them until 2010–2015 (Jehl and Schmitt 2005; Weisman and Jehl 2005).[6] But, while the speed and scope of the program is subject to much conjecture and debate, Cirincione (2002, 255) notes intelligence services in Israel, Germany, Britain, and the U.S. all agree on the fundamental point that Tehran has "a long-term program to manufacture nuclear weapons."[7] In the view of many experts, Iran already possesses the basic nuclear technology, infrastructure, and expertise to build weapons—and lacks only adequate stockpiles of fissile material to become a nuclear state (Cirincione 2002, 255).

The Iranian nuclear program began during the mid-1970s under the Shah, who embarked on an ambitious effort involving the establishment of a nuclear weapon design team, covert efforts to obtain the know-how and materials required, as well as plans to construct twenty-three nuclear power reactors (Hersh 2001; Sciolino 2003). The Shah openly remarked Iran would have nuclear weapons "without a doubt and sooner than one would think" (Sciolino 2003). Documents found after the Iranian revolution revealed the Shah's government and Israel discussed plans to adapt an Israeli surface-to-surface missile to carry nuclear warheads for use by Tehran (Sciolino 2003). During the mid-1980s, with Ayatollah Khomeini in power, between 15,000 and 17,000 Iranian students were sent abroad to study nuclear-related subjects. Iran actively recruited nuclear technicians from the former Soviet Union and other countries during the 1990s, offering salaries of up to $5,000 a month for skilled (but impoverished) nuclear scientists (Henry 2003, 45). More recently, there are reports of Russian scientists working in the Iranian program for fees of up to $20,000 per month (Boureston and Ferguson 2004). Moreover, Iran has sent engineers to Russia to receive university training in rocket-related technologies at the Baltic State Technical University, led by one of Russia's leading missile scientists, Yuri P. Savelyev (Tyler 2000). As a result, Tehran developed a substantial base of technical expertise and, along with the development of its civilian nuclear power industry, a large nuclear infrastructure. Basically, Iran's interest in nuclear weapons has continued, regardless of the nature of the regime.[8] As CIA director George Tenet observed in 2003, "no Iranian government, regardless of its ideological leanings, is likely to abandon [WMD programs] that are seen as guaranteeing Iran's security" (Sciolino 2003).

Under increasing pressure from the U.S., which received reports of extensive clandestine nuclear facilities, Iran accepted a European plan in October 2003 to open its suspect facilities to IAEA inspection and pledged to cease production of enriched uranium for an "interim period" (Sciolino 2003). The subsequent IAEA report on Iran's activities found:

Iran's nuclear programme . . . consists of a practically complete front end of a nuclear fuel cycle, including uranium mining and milling, conversion, enrichment, fuel fabrication, heavy water production, a light water reactor, a heavy water research reactor and associated research and development facilities. Iran has now acknowledged that it has been developing, for 18 years, a uranium centrifuge enrichment programme, and, for 12 years, a laser enrichment programme. In that context, Iran has admitted that it produced small amounts of LEU using both centrifuge and laser enrichment processes, and that it had failed to report a large number of conversion, fabrication and irradiation activities involving nuclear material, including the separation of a small amount of plutonium. (International Atomic Energy Agency 2003)

The ability of states to develop clandestine programs without detection is well illustrated by Iran's efforts to produce highly enriched uranium (HEU) and separate plutonium using hidden enrichment and reprocessing facilities. (Broad May 2004, D1 and D4)[9] In addition to building a gas centrifuge uranium enrichment program at Natanz, which IAEA director general El Baradei described as "sophisticated," Iran acknowledged it intends to build both a forty-megawatt thermal heavy water reactor at Arak and a fuel-fabrication plant for the reactor at Esfahan. The pilot plant at Natanz was designed to hold about 1,000 centrifuges and produce between ten and twelve kilograms of weapons-grade uranium per year (Albright and Hinderstein September/October 2003, 54–56). The main enrichment facility at Natanz, set to open in 2005, was envisaged to hold up to 50,000 centrifuges and produce about 500 kilograms of weapons-grade uranium annually (enough for twenty-five to thirty nuclear weapons per year). As Albright and Hinderstein (September/October 2003, 57) warn, this facility, if operated at full capacity, could "produce enough weapons-grade uranium for a nuclear weapon in a few days." In addition, Pakistan (through the illegal smuggling network of Iran's Dr. Abdul Qadeer Khan) provided Iran not only with advanced centrifuge technology and advice, but also with essential data on bomb design (Hersh 2001, 50). In total, this infrastructure has the capability (if completed) of rapidly transforming Iran not only into a nuclear weapon state, but one with a substantial arsenal by the end of decade.

In the absence of Iranian willingness to cease development of these facilities, analysts also have warned military strikes against the sites would be "unlikely to succeed given the dispersed and advanced nature of the Iranian program" (Albright and Hinderstein September/October 2003, 58). The Iranians clearly considered the potential for outside preemptive attack in designing the Natanz facility, which includes huge buildings buried 75 feet underground to withstand aerial attacks (Albright and Hinderstein May/June 2003, 15). Noting "extensive digging," a former senior Pentagon official noted that "they're going deep and clandestine," apparently spreading hidden sites widely across the country to avoid providing easy targets for Israeli or American air strikes (Hersh 2001, 43). Of course, this dispersal of hidden facilities raises the question of whether the full extent of the Iranian nuclear program was revealed to IAEA inspectors, and whether there might still be substantial facilities that have remained clandestine (Traub 2004).

Indeed, the discovery of Khan's nuclear black market operations led to the discovery Iran had received plans not only for the first generation (Pak-1) centrifuge used in Pakistan's nuclear weapons program, but also the more advanced, second generation (Pak-2) centrifuge design (Sanger and Broad 2004; Broad and Sanger 2004). Given Khan provided Libya with Pakistan's atomic bomb designs (along with centrifuges), there exists the distinct possibility Iran (which did far more extensive business with Khan) also received the designs (Sanger and Broad 25 May 2004). Dr. Khan's chief lieutenant, B. S. A. Tahir, arrested in 2004, admitted Iran not only received shipments from Pakistan during the 1980s, but also paid Khan's network $3 million for parts to manufacture additional centrifuges between 1994 and 1995 (Sanger 2004).

In terms of delivery systems, Iran has the indigenous equipment and technical capability to develop its own long-range missiles of mid- to late 1950s vintage, with the pacing technology no longer appearing to be propulsion or guidance, but instead "warheads and re-entry vehicles" (Karp 1998). Indeed, as Karp notes, "if minimal performance characteristics are acceptable, there may no longer be a hardware barrier to IRBM deployment" by Iran, although missiles of longer range may be further off:

> Unless Iran has a foreign-developed re-entry system, the range of its first IRBMs will be limited to approximately 1,000 to 1,200 km. Greater ranges involve higher re-entry speeds and concomitant heating and instability, necessitating more advanced RVs, which Iran is not capable of creating rapidly by itself.

According to Hersh (2001, 46), U.S. and Israeli intelligence observed a Russian military team (apparently working on its own initiative) dismantling a mothballed SS-4 missile production facility and shipping it "piece by piece" to Iran—a facility that was likely the source for the Shahab-4 missile program, which *Jane's Defence Weekly* described as an upgraded version of the SS-4 missile. Further, Iran has already begun production and deployment of the Shahab-3 mobile missile (810-to-930-mile range) (Barringer 2003; Fathi 2003). As one Israeli government spokesman noted after the Shahab-3's final test flight in July 2003, "We are very concerned. . . . the combination of the Shahab-3 and the nuclear weapon would be a very serious threat on the stability of the region" (Fathi 2003). In November 2003, Iran announced a halt to development of the Shahab-4 missile (Vick 2003). However, the Shahab-3 missile still provides Iran with a delivery system capable of striking Israel. It has also been reported Iran has worked to extend the range of its Chinese HY-1 Silkworm and Russian Styx cruise missiles from 80 kilometers to 400 kilometers or more, and on development of a new generation of cruise missile (based on stretched Silkworm/Styx designs) that might have ranges of between 600 and 800 kilometers (Karp 1998). In terms of shorter-range systems that could be effective in the tactical delivery of weapons against local targets, Karp notes: "Iran today is a world leader in the development of large artillery rockets, with ranges of 40 to 200 km. These might not individually be very effective delivery systems, but any technical weaknesses could be compensated by their low cost. Deploying large numbers or arming them with chemical or biological agents could compensate for any technical weakness and saturate any defensive system" (Karp 1998).

Even if Tehran actually submitted to IAEA inspections that slowed the pace of Iran's drive toward weapon capabilities, whether this would effectively derail these efforts is questionable. It is highly unlikely Iran would lose control of all the technical blueprints and designs it obtained from outside sources. And the probability of Tehran retaining some clandestine facilities and materials (given the historical experiences with Iraqi inspections) is considerable. Given the main barrier to development is the acquisition of enough fissile material to construct weapons, Iran's recent announcement that it would continue assembling centrifuges and convert thirty-seven tons of yellowcake into uranium hexafluoride—enough to produce five or six nuclear weapons—suggests materials may not be as unattainable as often supposed (Sanger 2004; Broad and Sanger 2004; "Iran Says It Will Not Give Up Uranium Enrichment Program" 2004).

## A Hypothetical Iranian Retaliatory Strike on Saudi Arabia

Apart from strikes against invading U.S. ground forces or carrier battle groups, a nuclear Iran would have a wide variety of countervalue targets available to it in the Middle East. In addition to obvious targets in Israel, another potentially lucrative target for retaliation might be Abqaiq. It is the world's largest oil processing facility, located only twenty-four miles inland from the northern end of the Gulf of Bahrain in Saudi Arabia—a target easily reachable by either ballistic missiles (launched from land or ship) or by aircraft (Baer 2003). As Baer (2003, 53) points out, only a "moderate to severe" strike against Abqaiq would reduce the oil flowing from Saudi Arabia over the following months to one million barrels a day (down from its normal average of 6.8 million barrels), an amount "equivalent to one third of America's daily consumption of crude oil." Further, over the following seven months, daily production would be at least 4 million barrels below normal, "a reduction roughly equal to what *all* of the OPEC partners were able to effect during their 1973 embargo" (Baer 2003). Importantly, Baer's scenario involved only *highly destructive terrorist attacks*, not the far more destructive consequences of a *nuclear attack*, which would completely destroy the facilities and eliminate 6.8 million barrels of oil per day from being processed. The oil normally pumped from Abqaiq is sent to yet another potential target, loading terminals at Ras Tanura and Ju'aymah, handling 4.5 million and 4.3 million barrels per day respectively. These facilities are highly vulnerable to even conventional attacks, and present a choke point allowing Iran to eliminate 8.8 million barrels of oil per day with only two nuclear strikes. If an attack were made on Pump Station No. 1, which sends oil overland through pipelines to the Red Sea port of Yanbu, 900,000 barrels of oil per day would be lost. Baer (2003, 54) observes, "if Saudi Arabia's contribution to the world's oil supply were cut off, crude petroleum could quite realistically rise from around $40 a barrel today to as much as $150 a barrel. It wouldn't take long for other economic and social calamities to follow." With the development of nuclear capabilities, coupled with survivable short-range systems, Iran will attain countervalue strike capabilities that would give *any* outside great power pause.

## A NASCENT NUCLEAR POWER (NORTH KOREA)

Unlike Israel, Pakistan, and India—which have substantial nuclear capabilities within their regions—North Korea is only in the early, or *nascent*, stages of being a nuclear power (as illustrated by its efforts at a nuclear test in October 2006). Although it certainly has the capability to expand its capabilities over the coming decade, at the moment, it likely possesses a very small nuclear force structure comprised of a few first-generation atomic weapons. There is little or no differentiation within this force structure, with North Korea lacking sea-based systems, reasonably survivable modern combat aircraft, or, in all probability, boosted-fission or thermonuclear weapons. At the same time, however, Pyongyang possesses highly survivable, "short-range" nuclear strike capability due to its emphasis upon mobile short-range ballistic missile (SRBM) and medium-range ballistic missile (MRBM) systems (like the Scud or No-Dong missile systems), as well as a multitude of elaborately hardened, reinforced launch sites (often buried deep within mountainsides). The North Koreans are masters of camouflage and subterfuge, and have studied well (and incorporated into their planning) lessons learned in Iraq and Kosovo regarding the requirements for evading strikes by U.S. air power. The expert use of mobile systems, dispersion, camouflage and decoys would undoubtedly provide enough survivability for North Korean missile systems to ensure their ability to launch a devastating attack on the South—regardless of the extent to which U.S. airpower were applied (Millot 1994). Of course, even in the absence of nuclear attacks, one estimate cited by GlobalSecurity.org found 4.56 million of Seoul's 12 million population could be killed by a North Korean nerve gas attack using only fifty ballistic missiles (Wiseman 2003).

Though North Korea is often credited with a large intermediate-range ballistic missile (IRBM) capability by U.S. sources, the reality is Pyongyang lacks both secure, survivable IRBM launch sites or significant numbers of deployable IRBMs to pose any large-scale threat.[10] At best, Pyongyang may possess some limited ability to target nearby Japan with a handful of missiles in the event of hostilities—although prepreparation of the launch sites would give away their intentions. In contrast, it possesses highly survivable and mobile SRBM and MRBM forces clearly capable of holding all of neighboring South Korea at risk with little chance they could be preempted successfully. Given the geographic proximity of major population centers in South Korea (including Seoul) to the deeply buried, reinforced North Korean artillery and rocket-launcher emplacements just north of the DMZ—Pyongyang can effectively hold a large proportion of the South Korean population hostage not only to conventional bombardment, but to potential nuclear, chemical, or biological bombardment as well. And, as U.S. military officials reluctantly acknowledge, there is little that can be done to prevent it (Defense Intelligence Agency 2000, 19).

As table 3.1 illustrates, North Korea currently possesses only a *nascent* local/minimal regional capability. However, this still provides the North with substantial deterrent potential.

North Korea is also credited by the analytical framework (see table 3.2) with possessing a *moderate to highly survivable nuclear capability* (i.e., limited to moderate redundancy of delivery systems, use of multiple types of mobile systems; extremely hardened fixed-site positions, strong site defense capabilities, and sophisticated use of subterfuge). The survivability of North Korea's nuclear arsenal will continue to improve markedly over the next ten years, as additional mobile delivery systems and a larger, deliverable arsenal render the already slim chances of successful preemption almost nonexistent.

### North Korea's Nuclear Capabilities

Prior to the 1994 Agreed Framework, U.S. intelligence suspected North Korea had produced around 12 kilograms (26 pounds) of weapons-grade plutonium from spent fuel taken from its Yongbyon reactor (Risen 2000). This led to the CIA's first warning, in late 1993, that North Korea might already possess one or two nuclear weapons—a finding subject to some dispute within the government (in particular, among dissenters at the State Department) which was based purely upon the amount of fissile materials Pyongyang *might* have been able to reprocess covertly from its spent reactor fuel (Engelberg and Gordon 1993). In June 2003, the CIA reported they believed North Korea capable of making nuclear warheads small and light enough to fit Pyongyang's arsenal of medium- and long-range ballistic missiles (Sanger July 2003). Later, the CIA reported to the Senate Select Committee on Intelligence

**Table 3.1.  North Korea's Nascent/Local Nuclear Capability**

North Korean Nuclear Capability
(Nascent/Local Power)

| Nuclear Force Structure | Differentiation Within Nuclear Force Structure | Composition, Range, and Accuracy of Delivery System Capabilities | Interceptability by Opponent of Delivery Systems |
|---|---|---|---|
| Estimated by various sources as likely consisting of between **8 and 18 nuclear weapons.** | **No Significant Differentiation Within Force Structure** **Possesses only first-generation nuclear weapons.** **Is working to deploy multiple types of warhead designs** (i.e., ballistic missile warheads (for Scud, No Dong, and Taepo Dong missiles); possibly for artillery or aircraft delivery. | **Land-Based Ballistic Missiles:** **Scud-B** (mobile SRBM; 300-km range/1,000-kg payload) **Scud-C** (mobile SRBM; 500-km range/600–700-kg payload) **No Dong** (mobile MRBM; 1,300-km range/1,000-kg payload) **Taepo Dong 1** (mobile MRBM; 1,500–2,000-km range/1,000-kg payload) **Taepo Dong II** (IRBM; 3,500–5,500-km range/1,000-kg payload—under development/not deployed) **Nuclear Capable Artillery and Rocket Launchers:** Potential for short-range (30–50 km) delivery of weapons by long-range artillery and rocket launcher systems. **Nuclear Capable Aircraft:** **MiG-23P/ML** fighter (1,800-km range/3,000-kg payload) **Su-25** fighter (650–900-km range/4,400-kg payload) **MiG-29K** fighter (1,500-km range/3,000-kg payload) | **Moderate Interceptability of Delivery Systems** Existing delivery systems and basing modes (i.e., road-mobile missiles, fixed missiles dispersed in hardened underground bunkers, artillery/rocket launcher sin hardened mountain sites, etc.) limit vulnerability to preemptive attacks. Small size of nuclear force structure poses some danger of preemption, however, reliable and rapid mobile delivery system technologies greatly increase penetration capabilities and survivability. |

*Sources:* Cirincione, *Deadly Arsenals* 2002; Department of Defense, *Proliferation: Threat and Response* 2001; www.globalaircraft.org/planes; www.aerospaceweb.org/aircraft; www.globalsecurity.org/military/world/dprk/airforce.htm; www.fas.org/man/dod-101/sys/ac/row/su-25.htm.

**Table 3.2. Survivability Characteristics of North Korea's Nuclear Capability**

| | Survivability of North Korean Nuclear Capability (Moderate) | | |
|---|---|---|---|
| *Redundancy of Delivery Systems* | *Vulnerability of Delivery Systems to Preemption* | *C3I Capabilities* | *Use of Subterfuge & Site Defense Capabilities* |
| **Moderate Redundancy of Delivery Systems** (i.e., multiple means of delivery employed: short- and medium-range mobile missiles, several different nuclear-capable aircraft, potentially artillery and rocket-launchers). | **Use of Multiple Mobile Delivery Systems** (i.e., both SRBM and MRBM are on mobile platforms). **No Dong and Taepo Dong 1 MRBMs are both road mobile systems. Scud-B and Scud-C SRBMs are both road mobile systems. Several modern fighter-bomber platforms** (i.e., MiG-29, MiG-23). | **Adequate C3I Capabilities** (i.e., early-warning radars; fiber-optic communications networks; dispersed and hardened command-and-control sites). | **Limited Site Defense Capability Surface-to-air missile capabilities.** **Sophisticated Use of Subterfuge** (i.e., use of advanced road-mobile ballistic missile systems to complicate and confuse an opponent's efforts to target strategic forces; extensive use of decoys and hidden bases, concealed and hardened underground mountain launching sites, dispersal of nuclear capable aircraft, etc.). |

*Sources:* Cirincione, *Deadly Arsenals* 2002; Department of Defense. *Proliferation: Threat and Response* 2001; www.globalaircraft.org/planes; www.aerospaceweb.org/aircraft; www.globalsecurity.org/military/world/dprk/airforce.htm; www.fas.org/man/dod-101/sys/ac/row/su-25.htm.

that North Korea had not only mastered the technology of turning its nuclear fuel into functioning weapons, but it's technology was advanced enough that a highly visible, "yield-producing" nuclear test was unnecessary (Sanger November 2003). The CIA also reported Pyongyang was working on designs to produce a miniaturized warhead to fit onto its ballistic missiles at a nuclear testing site called Youngdoktong (Sanger November 2003). And by October 2003, the IAEA suggested North Korea had probably produced enough plutonium to make two more weapons, in addition to the one or two weapons the CIA estimated Pyongyang produced in the early 1990s (Sanger October 2003). With the disclosure in January 2004 that North Korea had removed its 8,000 stored spent fuel rods from the Yongbyon facility and reprocessed them to obtain still more plutonium, Western analysts and governments alike were forced to consider the possibility North Korea possessed between three and twelve nuclear weapons. Moreover, in April 2004, Abdul Qadeer Khan reportedly told interrogators that during a visit to North Korea in 1999, he had been taken to an underground nuclear plant and shown three completed nuclear devices (Sanger April 2004).

Pyongyang is generally believed to be technically capable of producing first-generation, Hiroshima-type uranium bombs. And the possible collaboration of Pakistani nuclear scientists with the North's program also raises the distinct possibility North Korea might have workable, implosion bomb designs based on Chinese and Pakistani nuclear weapons (which would be necessary for utilizing their separated plutonium as weapons). As a result, actual nuclear tests may be unnecessary for Pyongyang to field weapons, especially if they obtained a stockpile of HEU, and analyses of its potential nuclear capability must rely upon assessments based on its overall available fissile stockpile. However, without some testing of the implosion-type warhead design, which likely resulted in the fizzle test in October 2006, Pyongyang would not likely have high confidence in the performance characteristics of its plutonium-based weapons stockpile. Given the collapse of the Agreed Framework and restart of the Yongbyon reactor (as well as the possible existence of a clandestine HEU program), Pyongyang over the coming decade will progressively increase its fissile stockpile and size of its nuclear arsenal.

In terms of delivery systems, North Korea possesses a wide array of short- to medium-range, mobile missiles that could strike targets throughout the Korean peninsula. In fact, North Korea possesses "the largest ballistic missile force in the developing world" including some thirty-six launchers and at least 700 missiles. Moreover, a 1995 Defense Intelligence Agency (DIA) report notes North Korea also has the ability to produce between fifty and 100 Scud missiles annually (as evidenced by its export of at least 250 of these missiles between 1987 and 1992) (*Theater Missile Defenses in the Asia-Pacific*

*Region* 2000). These Scuds and No-Dong missiles are dispersed in both fortified mountain tunnels (shielded by blast doors) and as mobile systems deployed in heavily defended, wooded valleys where they are easily concealed (Elliott and Barry 1994, 37). It is also highly likely the North Koreans have adopted the tactics used by the Iraqis and deployed large numbers of dummy missiles to confuse U.S. forces and draw their fire away from real systems (Shanker May 2003). Seeking to develop another reliable delivery system, North Korea also has developed a new cruise missile (dubbed the AG-1 by the Pentagon) by modifying and increasing the range of its Chinese HY-2 Silkworm missiles from sixty to just under 100 miles (Gertz 2003).

Further, by August 2004, North Korea reportedly was close to deploying a new mobile missile, based on designs from a Soviet-era SLBM (the SSN6), which may have a range of over 2,600 miles. This corroborated an earlier U.S. disclosure about the North's development of an SSN6-variant and other reports suggesting Russian missile experts from Chelyabinsk had worked on the program (Shanker 2004; Watts 2004). South Korean sources reported that perhaps ten of these new mobile missiles would be ready for deployment by September 2004 (Shanker 2004). If the reports prove accurate, it would provide Pyongyang with a medium-range mobile missile capable of targeting U.S. forces in Okinawa and Guam, as well as all of Japan and the Korean peninsula. Also of interest are reports the North has been attempting to refurbish twelve decommissioned Soviet-era Foxtrot and Golf II class submarines, sold to them by a Japanese trading firm in 1993 as scrap (though they still contained launch tubes and stabilizing subsystems), for use in launching a sea-based version of the SSN6 (with a 1,500 mile range) (Watts 2004). Though it is highly unlikely North Korea is close to successfully deploying this kind of submarine-based missile force, it provides yet another example of Pyongyang's efforts to diversify its means of WMD delivery to enhance its survivability and utility.

At present, North Korea apparently has no survivable ability to launch long-range missiles from well-prepared or hardened positions. Its only facility, the Rodong test site, has minimal infrastructure (it lacks rail links, paved roads, fuel tanks) and would be capable of launching only very limited missile attacks (which would be highly visible in advance and vulnerable to preemption) (Broad 2000). However, there have been reports by South Korean intelligence (later confirmed by a South Korean presidential spokesman) that North Korea has constructed more survivable, underground missile bases for its Taepodong I and II ballistic missiles in the mountainous region of Yeongjeodong, only twelve miles south of the Chinese border. In an apparent effort to complicate U.S. and South Korean targeting of the site, the facility (reportedly housing ten launching pads) has been built into a mountainside facing

China. This missile base at Yeongjeo-dong is one of three underground bases being constructed by Pyongyang to support its existing ten above-ground bases (Sullivan and Jordan 1999).

Unlike India, Pakistan, or Israel, Pyongyang does not possess advanced, nuclear-capable combat aircraft capable of reliable penetration of enemy airspace. In fact, the North Korean air force is mostly comprised of antiquated MiG fighters that have limited survivability against modern air forces. That being said, they *could* be employed in one-way nuclear missions as part of a surprise attack on targets just across the border, although delivery via ballistic missile would be far more reliable. There is also the potential for an even more surreptitious route for North Korea to deliver nuclear weapons into the South—namely, through a network of underground, infiltration tunnels that probably extend many miles past the border. These tunnels are large enough for jeeps or small trucks to traverse, and could be used to carry not only special forces and other military units behind Allied lines in the event of war, but also WMDs. Though four of these infiltration tunnels have been discovered, the U.S. military command in South Korea estimates there may be as many as thirty that have not been found (Diamond 2003). Still, these means of delivery are decidedly unreliable and risky. As a result, it is likely North Korea's short- to medium-range ballistic missiles, and its heavy artillery and rocket launchers, would be the likely delivery vehicles for nuclear or biological weapons in the event of war. Indeed, one 1998 air force analysis suggested that during a conflict, North Korea might launch extensively from underground facilities, disperse mobile launchers into the field, or employ a combination of the two (which was considered most likely) (Kristensen 2002).

Although the Pentagon hopes to develop the ability to link advanced reconnaissance systems to artillery and combat aircraft to "drench the North's artillery with fire during the magic minute" in which batteries of rocket artillery appear from behind their blast doors in mountain tunnel hideaways— the likelihood of this successfully preventing withering fire being directed against Seoul is practically zero.[11] Not only could North Korea easily employ subterfuge (i.e., create multiple openings in the sides of mountains to pose a "shell game" for attackers), the immense hardening of the artillery emplacements and the limited opening for attacks would greatly complicate any type of preemptive action. This analysis was supported by testimony before the Senate Armed Services Committee by General Thomas Schwartz, commander in chief of the United Nations Command, Combined Forces Command, and U.S. Forces in Korea (USFK):

North Korea fields an artillery force of over 12,000 self-propelled and towed weapon systems. Without moving any artillery pieces, the North could sustain up to 500,000 rounds an hour against Combined Forces Command defenses for several hours. The artillery force includes 500 long-range systems deployed over the past decade. The proximity of these long-range systems to the DMZ threatens all of Seoul with devastating attacks. Realizing they cannot match Combined Forces Command's technologically advanced war-fighting capabilities, the North's leadership focuses on developing asymmetrical capabilities such as ballistic missiles, over 100,000 special operations forces, and WMD designed to preclude alliance force options and offset U.S. conventional military superiority. The North's asymmetric forces are formidable, heavily funded, and the cause for concern. (*Theater Missile Defenses in the Asia-Pacific Region* 2000, 15–16)

The North Koreans lack advanced satellite reconnaissance or electronic surveillance technologies, but do possess an extensive early-warning radar network. Though this could be quickly blinded by U.S. forces, it is doubtful overall command-and-control could be disrupted given the emphasis placed by Pyongyang upon creating redundancy of facilities and its heavy use of fiber-optic cables to carry its sensitive military communications. Not only does this increase the survivability of North Korea's critical command-and-control functions in the event of war, but also reduces their vulnerability to American electronic eavesdropping (the interception of radio or microwave signals), resulting in U.S intelligence yielding "less and less" useful information (Diamond 2003).

## North Korea's Available Fissile Materials and Future Arsenal Potential

In December 2002, North Korea announced it would restart work at two unfinished nuclear power plants at Yongbyon and Taechon (with 50 and 200 megawatt capacities respectively) that had been 80 to 90 percent finished when construction stopped as part of the Agreed Framework (Struck 2002). These are the same facilities experts previously warned could have produced enough fissile material for at least 150–200 nuclear weapons by now had they been completed in 1994 (Saunders 2003). However, Dr. Sigfried Hecker of the Los Alamos Laboratory, a member of the U.S. delegation invited to visit the Yongbyon site in January 2004, observed that no new construction had been started at the fifty-megawatt-electric reactor facility and, given its immense state of disrepair, he believed it questionable how much of the current structure could be salvaged. In his view, this put the fifty-megawatt-electric reactor at *much more* than the one year away from completion it had been when construction was frozen in 1994 (U.S. Congress 2004). However, none of the American team actually observed the 200-megawatt-electric Taechon facility. Though it may take some time to reconstitute both facilities, it is likely well within Pyongyang's capabilities to complete them over the coming decade if the decision to do so is taken.

But, even in the absence of these two large facilities, North Korea will greatly increase its stockpile of fissile materials—not only from production of plutonium at the existing Yongbyon reactor, but also from the clandestine uranium-enrichment program the North has embarked upon. In fact, a July 2003 analysis by Jon Wolfsthal of the Carnegie Endowment for International Peace provides some sobering estimates of North Korea's "unchecked" nuclear weapons production potential. His analysis suggests that given Pyongyang's current (and future) plutonium production capabilities, as well as its future HEU output, it could be expected by 2010 to possess somewhere between 112 and 253 nuclear weapons (Wolfsthal 2003). Looking at his low-end estimate of 112 total weapons, Wolfsthal assumes late completion of the Yongbyon and Taechon reactors, no increase in North Korea's reprocessing capabilities, and late completion of its HEU production program—resulting by 2010 in a total fissile material production of 483 kilograms of plutonium (enough for ninety-seven weapons) and 300 kilograms of HEU (enough for fifteen weapons).

Experts who visited the five-megawatt-electric reactor at Yongbyon in January 2004 testified it had been restarted and was operating smoothly, resulting in the production of approximately six kilograms of plutonium annually in spent fuel (with another six kilograms of plutonium likely already existing in the fuel rods currently in use at the facility). Not only have all 8,000 spent fuel rods been removed from their storage ponds, Dr. Hecker was shown the main reprocessing facility at the Radiochemical Laboratory at Yongbyon, which was in good repair (U.S. Congress 2004). This was a serious finding given earlier estimates predicting these spent fuel rods would yield between twenty-five and thirty kilograms of plutonium metal—or enough for five to seven nuclear weapons.[12] Lending credibility to Pyongyang's claims about having reprocessed the rods, Hecker noted the North Koreans had "demonstrated the requisite facilities, equipment, and technical expertise required for reprocessing plutonium at the scale in question." The U.S. delegation was shown plutonium metal (which the North Koreans claimed to be scrap from a casting from the reprocessing of the fuel rods) as well as plutonium oxide powder. As Hecker noted in his January 2004 Senate testimony:

In the foreseeable future, the DPRK can produce 6 kg of plutonium per year in its 5 MWe reactor. It easily has the capacity to reprocess the spent fuel at any time to extract the plutonium. It also has the capacity to reload the reactor with fresh fuel for a second and subsequent reloading. It is not, however, in a position to increase the rate of plutonium production much beyond 6 kg per year without a major construction project at the 50 MWe or 200 MWe reactor sites, something that would be difficult to do clandestinely. (U.S. Congress 2004)

However, North Korea is also pursuing a parallel, uranium-bomb program that could compensate for these constraints on its plutonium production. In fact, a 2002 CIA report stated that North Korea's centrifuge-related materials acquisitions appeared to have the goal of establishing "a plant that could produce enough weapons-grade uranium for two or more nuclear weapons per year when fully operational" (Central Intelligence Agency 1 January Through 30 June 2002). Although a senior North Korean official admitted in October 2002 to U.S. officials (including Assistant Secretary of State James Kelly) that Pyongyang possessed a clandestine program to enrich uranium, North Korea later denied the existence of any such program (Kessler 2004). Yet, within the U.S. intelligence community, there is little doubt about the existence of a clandestine uranium enrichment program, especially given new evidence revealed in 2004 by an investigation into the dealings by Pakistan's lead nuclear scientist, Dr. Abdul Qadeer Khan, with Pyongyang.

What eventually came to light (and later confirmed by Pakistani President Musharraf) were transfers of advanced high-speed centrifuge designs, parts, and at least "a dozen" complete centrifuges, uranium hexaflouride, and technical advice needed to jump start a substantial enriched-uranium bomb-making program (Masood and Rohde 2005). Indeed, the only active dispute within the intelligence community by 2005 centered around the question of when the program would actually begin producing substantial amounts of material (estimates have ranged from the end of 2004 to 2007) (Kessler 2004). Of course, this assumes U.S. intelligence knows exactly when North Korean efforts began and how extensive the enrichment facilities are—both very dubious assumptions.

In June 2003, U.S. satellites and sensors collected air samples containing krypton-85 over North Korea, raising the possibility that hidden plutonium reprocessing facilities might exist in the mountains near the Chinese border in underground tunnels (Sanger October 2003; Shanker and Sanger 2003). Since that time, however, the intelligence community has been unable to reproduce those samples, leaving U.S. officials with what they describe as "a lot of suspicions, but zippo evidence" (Sanger October 2003). Yet, as Shanker and Sanger (2003) observe:

> North Korea has an estimated 11,000 to 15,000 deep underground military-industrial sites. . . . and the nation's leadership has a history of constructing duplicate facilities for such important capabilities as tank production or command-and-communications systems. "If you follow their logic, if we find a second reprocessing location, maybe there are more," said one American official. "It is a reasonable assessment given North Korea's proclivity to have multiple facilities for every critical aspect of its national security infrastructure."

The immensely difficult task of finding North Korea's hidden nuclear facilities was well illustrated by the embarrassing case of Kumchangri, an underground site U.S. intelligence suspected of concealing a clandestine nuclear reactor or reprocessing facility, which upon inspection was found to be a completely empty, if extensive, tunnel complex (Shenon 1999). Similarly, the DIA reportedly identified at least ten underground sites it suspected were part of North Korea's nuclear program in the late 1990s—but hard evidence was lacking, making it hard to assess if any of these are actually part of the program (Risen 2000). Further, though the operation of plutonium-reprocessing facilities may allow for the detection of the krypton gas byproduct in the atmosphere, if facilities operate at a low level or are carefully sealed to trap emissions, it is possible they may go undetected (as would all uranium enrichment activities, which give off no detectable signature) (Sanger and French 2003).

In table 3.3, an extremely conservative estimate is made of North Korea's available (and potential) stockpile of fissile materials over the coming decade. It assumes North Korea used the twelve kilograms of pre-1994 reprocessed plutonium in weapons and added an additional thirty kilograms worth from the reprocessing of 8,000 spent fuel rods in 2003 and 2004. This gave Pyongyang an initial fissile stockpile of forty-two kilograms of plutonium, enough for roughly a dozen nuclear weapons by mid-2004. Assuming North Korea possesses no hidden plutonium-producing reactors, it is limited to the six kilograms produced annually at the Yongbyon five-megawatt-electric reactor. Although we don't know how long the North's clandestine uranium-enrichment program has been at work, or how extensive it is, we can assume the CIA posited goal of producing enough HEU for two bombs per year (thirty-two kilograms) as an initial starting point. If we make the exceedingly conservative estimate the North Koreans are content with this level of clandestine production and do not expand upon it, this results in an additional two bombs per year of material from the HEU program. Obviously, this likely substantially underestimates the scale of the North Korean HEU program. However, it should serve to illustrate that even with the most conservative of estimates, North Korea quickly obtains enough fissile materials for a rather substantial nuclear arsenal—certainly one large enough to give potential invaders pause given the level of destruction which could be visited on the South.

It should also be noted that if North Korea were to use a "composite-core design" (a smaller plutonium sphere encased in a shell of highly enriched uranium), it would be capable of making far more bombs than if it stuck to using only purely plutonium- or uranium-based designs (NRDC Notebook 2003, 76).

**Table 3.3. Extremely Conservative Estimate of North Korea's Available (and Potential) Stockpile of Nuclear Materials over the Next Decade from Its HEU—and Plutonium—Production Facilities**

| | Estimate of Annual WGPu Production at Yongbyon Reactor (6.0 kg) | Potential Warhead Stockpile (4.0 kg each) | Conservative Estimate of Annual HEU Production from Clandestine Program (32.0 kg) | Potential Warhead Stockpile (16.0 kg each) |
|---|---|---|---|---|
| **Pre-1994** | 12 kg | 3 | 0 | 0 |
| **2001** | 42 kg | 11 | 0 | 0 |
| | (pre-1994 material plus material from 8,000 fuel rods) | | | |
| **2003–2004** | 48 kg | 12 | 32 kg | 2 |
| | (reprocessed spent fuel; Yongbyon reactor restarted) | | | |
| **2005** | 54 kg | 14 | 64 kg | 4 |
| **2006** | 60 kg | 15 | 96 kg | 6 |
| **2007** | 66 kg | 17 | 128 kg | 8 |
| **2008** | 72 kg | 18 | 160 kg | 10 |
| **2009** | 78 kg | 20 | 192 kg | 12 |
| **2010** | 84 kg | 21 | 224 kg | 14 |
| **2011** | 90 kg | 23 | 256 kg | 16 |
| **2012** | 96 kg | 24 | 288 kg | 18 |
| **2013** | 102 kg | 26 | 320 kg | 20 |
| **2014** | 108 kg | 27 | 352 kg | 22 |
| **2015** | 114 kg | 29 | 384 kg | 24 |

*Note:* Table assumes that North Korea possesed 12 kg plutonium from reprocessing Yongbyon spent fuel prior to 1994 Agreed Framework and was able to reprocess 30 kg of plutonium from 8,000 spent fuel rods in late 2003 and early 2004. Presumes North Korea only fashioned weapons from original pre-1994 material until 2003–2004, when it began utilizing its material to produce additional weapons. This calculates 6 kg annual production of plutonium at Yongbyon reactor (beginning 2003) and 32 kg of HEU at clandestine facilities (enough for two weapons annually). This does not include any material from the 50 or 200 MWe reactors, hidden plutonium-production facilities, or any expansion of HEU facilities.

## The Perceptions of North Korean Policy Makers
## Regarding Nuclear Weapons and Deterrence

The actual motivations and decision processes surrounding North Korea's leadership, in particular Kim Jong-Il, are difficult to assess with certainty given the shroud of secrecy and near impenetrability of the regime. As a result, U.S. and South Korean policy makers and analysts have long debated the rationale for North Korea's pursuit of nuclear weapons—with some seeing security as paramount, while others view it as driven by the need for bargaining chips to trade for economic or political benefits, or as merely part of their traditionally aggressive bargaining style (cf. Bracken 1993; Mazaar 1995b; Sigal 1998; Snyder 1999; Oh and Hassig 2000; Bermudez 2000). However, as the nuclear dispute with North Korea evolved over the past few years, it has become apparent that while all of these suggested motivations may play a part, security concerns are likely to be the *paramount* concern driving Pyongyang toward developing its nuclear capabilities. Indeed, given Pyongyang is suspicious (bordering on paranoid) regarding U.S. and South Korean intentions toward it at the best of times, the election of George W. Bush to the White House in 2001 and subsequent hardening of American policy unquestionably aggravated their concerns. Bush's use of the North as the poster child supporting the need for missile defense, his cessation of all Clinton-era diplomatic initiatives aimed at easing tensions, his lack of support for South Korean president Kim Dae Jung's "sunshine policies," and the listing of Pyongyang prominently among the "axis of evil"—convinced Kim Jong-Il that his regime was now truly in American crosshairs.

This was reinforced even more fully by the new preemptive war doctrine espoused by the administration, which was then implemented in the military invasion of Iraq and the explicit targeting of the Iraqi leadership by American bombs in the opening hours of the war in an effort at decapitation. Given similar calls for "regime change" in North Korea by the administration and other conservative figures in the U.S., it is hardly surprising Kim Jong-Il took the threat of a surprise, decapitation attack quite seriously. Indeed, as bombs began to fall on Baghdad, Kim broke a seven-year tradition by failing to appear at the appointed time and place to inaugurate the annual session of North Korea's Supreme People's Assembly, and continued to maintain a low profile over the next six months, avoiding appearances at any scheduled public events (Brooke 2003). As one senior Bush administration official remarked, "Clearly our willingness to attack leadership targets from the get-go has probably made Kim a lot more apprehensive" (Shanker 2003). Indeed, Pentagon officials, noting North Korea's military carefully studied U.S. war-fighting techniques after the 1991 Gulf War, observed that "we saw adjustments in the way they did things after that, especially in the areas of camouflage and concealment . . . suspect they are doing that again . . . [with Kim's decision to stay out of public view being] one of those adjustments" (Shanker 2003). But while it undoubtedly had this effect, it also spurred on Pyongyang's perception that it needed to fully develop its nuclear capabilities to deter a similar attack upon itself.

For example, during a meeting with a U.S. congressional delegation led by Representative Curt Weldon in 2003, North Korean officials stated nuclear weapons were being developed as "a response to what they saw happened in Iraq, with the U.S. removing Saddam Hussein from power" ("North Korea Makes New Bomb Boasts" 2003). As the Foreign Ministry stated in announcing Pyongyang had begun reprocessing its spent fuel rods in April 2003, "The Iraqi war teaches a lesson that in order to prevent a war and defend the security of a country and the sovereignty of a nation, it is necessary to have a powerful physical deterrent force" (Struck 2003). As a result, Pyongyang "would continue to boost its nuclear deterrent" because of the United States' continuing hostility to the North (Nesirky 2003). Similarly, during the September 2005 Six-Party Talks in Beijing, the North Korean spokesman, Hyun Hak Bong, noted Pyongyang had required nuclear weapons to defend itself from the U.S. because it had been singled out for a "preemptive strike." He noted the U.S. was "demanding that we give up our nuclear deterrent facilities first . . . I think this is such a naïve request. Our response is: Don't even dream about it" (Kahn 2005). North Korea also described its decision to build a nuclear deterrent as a way to reduce the costs of maintaining its large conventional army (1.1 million troops, the fifth largest in the world) and allow it to channel the funds back into its economy. As North Korea's official government news agency explained, given the U.S. threat, there was "no option but to build up a nuclear deterrent force," but that it did not seek "to possess a nuclear deterrent in order to blackmail others, but . . . to reduce conventional weapons and divert our human and monetary resources to economic development and improve the living standards of the people" (Reeves 2003).

Responding to dubious Bush administration claims that North Korea would transfer nuclear materials to other states or terrorist organizations, just as it had its other WMD capabilities, Choe Su Hon, North Korea's deputy foreign minister, emphasized Pyongyang had "no intention of transferring any means of . . . nuclear deterrence to other countries" (Brooke 2003). And despite alarmist assertions by the administration, the actual record of North Korean behavior does not support claims Pyongyang has widely exported its existing WMD capabilities. In fact, North Korea has only exported *conventional* ballistic missiles and weaponry to other states to raise hard currency (these ballistic missile exports account for perhaps $250 to $300 million annually). And though possessing chemical and biological weapons programs for decades, North Korea has never been shown to have transferred *any* true WMD to any other country! The questionable logic of exporting its extremely limited quantities of fissile materials or completed nuclear weapons to other actors, when its own basic security requirements have yet to be met, further undermines the validity of this worst-case thinking. Though not impossible, it is *far more unlikely* than would-be scenarios involving the smuggling of nuclear materials out of the former Soviet Union or Pakistan to terrorists—something the Bush administration has paid scant attention to in its budget reductions for the Cooperative Threat Reduction Program and other counterproliferation initiatives.

During a November 17, 2003, visit to Seoul, Defense Secretary Donald Rumsfeld stated the U.S. was committed to South Korea's defense and would use nuclear weapons if necessary—an explicit statement of nuclear threat directed at Pyongyang (Gertz 2003). However, despite such heated rhetoric from Washington, and Bush's statements that the U.S. would not accept a nuclear North Korea, it is apparent the North's ability to inflict catastrophic damage upon the South in the event of war (whether through conventional or nuclear means) have forced even the most conservative hawks to consider the deterring effects of even a small North Korean nuclear arsenal. It has also dampened any support the U.S. might have expected from South Korea for preemptive strikes on the North's nuclear facilities or leadership targets.[13] For South Korea, there is no choice but to take seriously the consequences of threatening Pyongyang's central interests or survival. According to one senior Bush official, South Korean president Roh "has made it clear he won't consider military action of any kind" (Sanger January 2003). This South Korean reluctance to consider military action reflects the realization in Seoul (which, after all, is only thirty kilometers from the DMZ and within easy range of North Korean artillery) that the costs of taking any aggressive action far outweighs any potential benefit.

So, despite the North recently agreeing to "end" its nuclear program in return for a rich package of payoffs, including normalized relations and nonaggression assurances from the U.S., substantial new economic aid, a future light-water nuclear reactor, and recognition of its right to peaceful uses of nuclear energy—the agreement was little more than window dressing (Sanger 2005; Cody 2005). It was a broad, immensely vague collection of points that avoided all the details guaranteed to scuttle it down the road (e.g., specifics for intrusive verification of the North, the sequence of aid versus disarmament, etc.). And most significantly, the tentative agreement fails to specifically mention the uranium-based nuclear program, and despite U.S. protestations to the contrary, only requires Pyongyang to rejoin NPT and open

Yongbyon to IAEA inspections/safeguards. In its present form, it provides North Korea with political cover for refusing to give up its program later (given the "poison-pill" nature of the intrusive verification requirements demanded by the U.S. or its calls for dismantlement *before* political/economic payoffs begin). Further, Pyongyang need only deny the existence of its uranium program, and comply on the plutonium-side, to garner enough political support to preserve part of its capability. It would be remarkable in the extreme if this tentative agreement survives.

## North Korea's Nuclear Options and Potential Strategies through 2015

For Pyongyang, restarting its reactor at Yongbyon and reprocessing its spent fuel greatly expanded its potential nuclear options and strategies. As of 2005, extremely conservative estimates (see table 3.3) suggest North Korea may have produced enough fissile material to build up to eighteen nuclear weapons, though the number actually constructed would probably be lower (around eight to twelve weapons). But, regardless of the number, the central point is Pyongyang possesses a small (but growing) arsenal that could be employed against local targets in South Korea. Until North Korea's stockpile of fissile materials grows sufficiently to allow construction of a larger arsenal (along the lines of Pakistan, India, or Israel's) and more extensive IRBM capabilities, it will remain purely a local, *nascent* (rather than *regional*) nuclear power. Yet, assuming only an arsenal of eight to twelve warheads, North Korea still has a wide variety of potential nuclear options it could pursue (see table 3.4).

It is extremely likely North Korea will seek to expand, as quickly as possible, its ability to generate additional stockpiles of fissile materials. Given the difficulties in completing the Taechon and Yongbyon (200- and 50- megawatt-electric) reactors, which may take much of the next decade to accomplish, it is probable Pyongyang will focus instead upon further expansion of its clandestine uranium-enrichment program. HEU-production facilities are capable of being effectively concealed in North Korea's labyrinthine system of underground tunnels and mountain bunkers. Moreover, even if North Korea agreed to some form of limited international inspections of its nuclear program, inspections which Pyongyang would never allow to be *truly* intrusive, it is practically assured of being able to successfully hide its HEU program. Unlike plutonium reprocessing, HEU production does not emit telltale chemical signatures into the atmosphere, nor does it require extensive facilities beyond those housing small cascades of centrifuges. As a result, detection of even a large-scale HEU weapons program would be extremely unlikely. Further, as more and more cascades are added to the initial centrifuge facili-

**Table 3.4. Available North Korean Nuclear Targeting and Employment Options**

| | North Korean Nuclear Targeting and Employment Options | | |
|---|---|---|---|
| Local Theater | Regional Theater | Global | Explicit/Implicit Nuclear Doctrine |
| **Tactical, Local Battlefield Use** **To blunt an opponent's military offensive by targeting conventional forces** (i.e., armored columns, troop concentrations, forward bases and air fields, supply lines, naval forces, etc.). **Use as a "demonstration" or "warning shot"** to signal nuclear resolve, encourage outside intervention, or warn of the need for conflict de-escalation. | **Regional Battlefield & Counterforce Use** **Conventional military counterforce usage** (i.e., targeting opponent's military forces, operational bases, command and control sites, supply lines, naval forces). **Regional Countervalue Use** **Countervalue targeting of population centers in neighboring states** (major cities and metropolitan areas). **Countervalue targeting of critical economic infrastructure in neighboring states** (i.e., oil installations—like pipeline pumping stations, refineries, loading terminals—sea ports, heavy industry factories, etc.). **EMP/antisatellite attacks.** **Countervalue targeting of sites of religious or cultural significance to opponents.** **Leadership decapitation or C3I disruption strikes.** | **Extremely Limited Unconventional Delivery of Countervalue or EMP attacks** (i.e., using commercial ships or aircraft). | **Has Invoked Rudimentary Deterrence Logic, But No Clear Statement of Doctrine** Overt nuclear possession strategy. |

ties, North Korea would see a rapid growth in its available HEU stockpile within only a few years (see the example of Pakistan's HEU production). The dual-track nature of North Korea's nuclear program will allow it to achieve a relatively sizable stockpile of fissile material in only five years. So by 2010, it could have material to construct between 35 and 253 nuclear weapons.[14]

However, even if North Korea currently possesses only a dozen weapons, it is clearly reasonable to assume (given its technical proficiency and experience in the design and production of ballistic missiles) that it has succeeded in mating existing warheads to both their short- and medium-range ballistic missiles. Over the coming decade, Pyongyang would be expected to continue expanding its mobile, ballistic missile forces so a wider array of South Korean (and eventually, regional) targets can be held at risk. Given the antiquated nature of the North's air force, it is probable other nuclear delivery systems would be considered, including modifications to existing Silkworm missiles (for potential use against U.S. naval forces at sea), as well as development of nuclear artillery rounds—both of which are considered within North Korea's technical capabilities. Pyongyang should also be considered to have the ability to stage clandestine nuclear attacks, using weapons concealed in either commercial ships or aircraft, or perhaps the ability to stage an effective EMP attack (either in region or over the U.S. using a nuclear-capable Scud fired from a converted freighter at sea). Combined with its ability to launch either conventional or chemical/biological munitions on major South Korean cities with existing artillery or ballistic missile forces, North Korea's nuclear capability provides a strong additional deterrent against large-scale attacks on its central interests.

## A Hypothetical North Korean Retaliatory Strike on South Korea

How difficult would it be for Pyongyang to inflict immense casualties on South Korea with even a limited nuclear arsenal? The answer is not difficult at all, and this capability serves to illustrate how seriously any North Korean nuclear threat to retaliate would have to be taken by the South. Unlike Iran, which has long distances between itself and the most attractive targets of retribution, North Korea benefits from incredibly close geographic proximity to many high-value targets. This proximity becomes even more critical given that *any* hope of interdiction (using air or missile defenses) would require defending not only a broad geographic area replete with potential targets, but also with practically no warning time whatsoever for defenders. Even assuming first-generation nuclear weapons (15–20 kilotons), within only fifty kilometers of the border (or roughly thirty miles) there exist a large number of targets (South Korean cities, military bases, etc.) which a small arsenal of only eight to twelve warheads (carried aboard short-range ballistic missiles) could target. This small number of warheads is chosen as an example since it represents the number of weapons U.S. intelligence suggests North Korea might already possess. It should be further noted that North Korea currently possesses four different fielded and tested short- to medium-range ballistic missile systems easily capable to carrying out such strikes: the Scud-B (300 km/186 m range); the Scud-C (500 km/310 m range); the No Dong (1,300 km/806 m range); and the Taepo Dong (1,500–2,000 km/930–1,240 m range) (Cirincione 2002, 94). North Korean artillery could also conceivably be used to attack this fifty-kilometer-deep area in South Korea, using nuclear shells (if developed) or more likely, chemical or biological munitions. Indeed, it has been widely reported that North Korea is capable of delivering over half a million artillery rounds per hour on the South Korean capital of Seoul (18.6 km or 30 m distant from the border). There can be little doubt that North Korea, even in its fairly early stages of nuclear development, has a highly credible capability to deliver WMD on a range of South Korean targets.

South Korea's vulnerability to North Korean attack is a result of its rapid postwar development. Nearly half of the country's population lives within a three-minute flight of the DMZ (Demick 2003). Thus, even in the case of conventional war, the costs would be immense for South Korea (estimated at 1 million dead), as former defense minister Lee Yang Ho noted:

> It is assumed that if the United States were to strike North Korea that the North Koreans would fight back . . . All industry would be destroyed, gas stations, power plants. This is such a densely populated area that even if North Korean artillery were not very accurate, anyplace you would hit there would be huge numbers of casualties. (Demick 2003)

Of course, the recent redeployment of U.S. forces further South, away from the DMZ and Seoul, removes 14,000 troops who could have easily been targeted by North Korean artillery—but this does not prevent them from remaining targets of a North Korean nuclear riposte (Brooke 2003). Indeed, the redeployment envisions creating "hub bases" south of Seoul that would be roughly seventy-five miles from the DMZ, a location out of range of North Korean artillery, but certainly not beyond the reach of its ballistic missiles (French 2003).

Assuming that North Korea effectively develops even a small arsenal of twelve first-generation atomic warheads (15–20 kilotons) carried aboard short-range missile systems (Scud-Bs or Scud-Cs with 300–500 kilometer ranges), this would allow them to effectively target over 16 million South Korean civilians in eight cities no further than thirty-one miles distant from the

DMZ.[15] Given the extremely high population densities in these cities, it is certain the detonation of Hiroshima-strength bombs across these eight South Korean cities would produce far more than the 120,000 fatalities in each of these cities than occurred from the 1945 attacks on Japan. Indeed, if one only assumed each weapon produced the same casualties as Hiroshima, the result of these airbursts would produce a minimum of 1,440,000 dead! In reality, the death toll in these densely populated cities could easily double or triple this amount. As indicated above, these casualties could be further inflated by targeting multiple weapons on the heavily populated cities of Seoul and Incheon. Would this be too high a price for South Korea to pay to support either its own or an American-led invasion of North Korea? Undoubtedly. Further, the North Korean nuclear capability extends far beyond these very short-range attacks, since its medium-range ballistic missiles would allow delivery of weapons throughout the entire Korean peninsula and its Taepo-Dong systems are even capable of striking neighboring Japan.[16] It currently possesses the ability to launch nuclear strikes against U.S. military bases on the peninsula and hit any large concentrations of U.S. forces in ports or at sea. Over the coming decade, as North Korea vastly expands its deliverable nuclear arsenal to *at least* fifty warheads (by the most optimistic projections), it will further increase its ability to destroy dozens of additional cities (and millions of additional civilians) throughout the region in retaliation for any regime-threatening aggression. North Korea should be expected to become a full-fledged *regional* nuclear power by 2015, with a survivable, regional nuclear strike capability that will severely constrain the military options of the U.S., Japan, and South Korea.

## THE REGIONAL NUCLEAR POWERS
## (ISRAEL, INDIA, AND PAKISTAN)

As described in chapter 2, regional nuclear powers are those with moderately sized and differentiated nuclear force structures, short- to intermediate-range delivery systems, and only low to moderate delivery system interceptability by opponents (see table 2.2). By these criteria, Israel, India, and Pakistan are full-fledged regional nuclear powers. In this section, the current and future development of these state's nuclear arsenals will be discussed, as will the perceptions of these nation's decision makers regarding the utility of nuclear weapons and their impact upon deterrence. As will become clear, across all three of these new nuclear lions, most senior policy makers share the belief that nuclear capabilities not only provide for their national security interests, but preserve peace and stability in their regions.

## The Case of Nuclear Israel

Israel has been a nuclear state since the late 1960s and developed its capabilities through use of a carefully crafted "opaque possession" strategy, wherein Israel concealed its nuclear program, never conducted visible tests, and at first denied, but later merely refused to publicly acknowledge whether or not it possessed nuclear weapons (Hersh 1991; Feldman 1997; Cohen 1998).[17] This very successful approach allowed Israel to obtain substantial nuclear capabilities without provoking international sanctions. Further, it allowed Israel to protect its key central interests (i.e., national survival) through either *active defense* (if invaded) or *existential deterrence* (during peacetime) of neighboring Arab states (who despite Israel's official "no comment" position on nuclear weapons, were never disabused by Tel Aviv of their belief that Israeli nuclear capability did indeed exist).

As of 2005, Israel would be classified (according to the analytical framework presented in chapter 2) as a *regional nuclear power* (i.e., possessing a moderately sized and differentiated nuclear force structure; medium- to intermediate-range delivery systems with moderate to low vulnerability of interception). Moreover, Israel's probable nuclear capabilities are at the extreme edge of a regional power and border on those characterizing great powers — with only the lack of intercontinental delivery systems or advanced submarine (SLBM) forces separating it from joining the ranks of states like Britain and France.

Israel would also be credited by the analytical framework with possessing a *highly survivable nuclear capability* (i.e., high redundancy of delivery systems, as well as use of multiple types of mobile systems; advanced C3I capability, hardening of fixed-site positions, strong site defense capabilities, and sophisticated use of subterfuge). In fact, with the newly operational status of its Arrow antimissile defense system, Israel becomes the first nuclear state in the world with a functioning national missile defense system (Cirincione 2002, 230). This combination of capability and survivability results in a regional deterrent capability with strong crisis stability characteristics, low need for "launch-on-warning" postures, and great flexibility in targeting options (ranging from local battlefield use to regional countervalue or counterforce missions).

### Israel's Nuclear Capabilities

Since Israel has never publicly acknowledged or provided information on its nuclear program, any assessments of its current program "must rely entirely on non-Israeli sources," as well as some degree of informed conjecture

(Feldman 1982, 45). In the open literature, estimates regarding the size of Israel's nuclear arsenal have varied greatly, ranging anywhere from between 75 and 200 weapons (NRDC Nuclear Notebook 2002, 73). Recently, however, Israeli Arab legislator Issam Makhul, who pushed for the only open session of the Israeli Parliament since the early 1960s to discuss Israeli nuclear policy in February 2003, not only condemned the secrecy surrounding the program, but stated during the session that Israel's nuclear arsenal consisted of some 200 to 300 warheads and that "the whole world knows that Israel is a large warehouse of nuclear, chemical and biological weapons" (Sontag 2000). Given Israeli legislators are briefed about the nuclear program in closed sessions, the fact that such specific numbers were used during the heat of discussions may well be suggestive of the size of Israel's current arsenal. Indeed, these numbers would not appear to be unrealistic given the data provided by Mordechai Vanunu, the former Dimona technician, who fled to London in 1985 and suggested Israel (at that time) had an arsenal of over 200 warheads, including boosted devices, neutron weapons, and warheads deliverable by F-16 or Jericho missile (Farr 1999, 17). In fact, it has been suggested after the 1973 October War, Israel fielded low-yield, tactical nuclear artillery rounds for its American 175 millimeter and 203 millimeter self-propelled howitzers capable of at least a twenty-five-mile range (Farr 1999, 15). At the outer limits of its current capability, some analysts have speculated "Israel might have the capacity to manufacture 20-megaton (MT) hydrogen bombs."[18] Despite a lack of nuclear testing, it is thought Israel obtained data from France's first nuclear test, and may have obtained data from U.S. nuclear tests from the 1950s and early 1960s, including the results from tests of boosted and thermonuclear weapons (Cirincione 2002, 225–26). If this is correct, Israel may have enough confidence in these designs to avoid the necessity of tests.

In terms of delivery systems, Israel recently completed development of the final "sea-based" leg of its strategic nuclear triad by deploying nuclear-armed cruise missiles aboard its small submarine fleet (and potentially onboard some of its surface vessels as well). Senior Bush administration and Israeli defense officials acknowledged in October 2003 that Israel had modified U.S.-supplied Harpoon cruise missiles to carry nuclear warheads for use aboard three specially designed German Dolphin-class submarines purchased during the late 1990s. The diesel-powered vessels can remain at sea for up to a month, have a range of several thousand miles, and are deployed so that at least one remains at sea at all times—thereby ensuring Israel of a survivable retaliatory force. The Harpoon has a normal range of eighty miles (129 kilometers), but analysts have suggested Israel is quite capable of further extending its range, perhaps to as much as 217 miles (350 kilometers) (Frantz 2003). Israel also possesses a large, modern air force with aircraft well suited to nuclear strike roles, such as its U.S.-supplied F-16 (1,600-kilometer range) and F-15 (4,450-kilometer range) fighter-bombers (NRDC Nuclear Notebook September/October 2002, 73).[19] Israel also has deployed two different advanced, solid-fueled, nuclear-capable, mobile ballistic missiles, the Jericho I (1,200-kilometer range) and Jericho II (1,800-kilometer range) (NRDC Nuclear Notebook September/October 2002, 73).[20] To increase the survivability of its missile fleet, Israel incorporated a combination of hardened storage facilities and system mobility for its Jericho I and II missiles. As the *Bulletin of the Atomic Scientists* (September/October 2002, 74) notes: "There are about 50 Jericho II missiles [which]. . . . appear to be stored in caves. Upon warning, they would probably be dispersed on their transporter-erector launchers (TELs) so as not to be destroyed. The shorter-range Jericho I is deployed nearby in approximately equal numbers."

Israel also possesses an extensive UAV and cruise missile development program, which produced at least three different land-attack cruise missile (LACM) platforms: the Popeye 1 (100-km range/350-kg payload); the Delilah (400-km range/450-kg payload); and Popeye 3 (350-km range/350-kg payload). Israel is also reported to have tested a new ALCM (possibly a variant on the Popeye Turbo design) off the coast of Sri Lanka in May 2000 which hit targets at a range of 1,500 miles (Cirincione 2002, 231). Israel has the technical capability, but perhaps not the motivation at present, to take the next step to great power nuclear status through development and deployment of operational ICBMs. But, as analysts have observed, Israel's current satellite launching missile system, the Shavit, could readily be converted into a ICBM with a range of up to 7,000 kilometers (NRDC Nuclear Notebook September/October 2002, 75).

*Israel's Available Fissile Materials and Future Arsenal Potential*

Israel possesses enough fissile materials and production facilities to greatly expand its nuclear arsenal if a decision were made to do so. In addition to the underground plutonium reprocessing facility at Dimona, reportedly producing forty kilograms of plutonium annually, Vanunu's 1986 photographs showed sophisticated designs experts believe would enable Israel to build bombs with as little as four kilograms of plutonium (Farr 1999, 17). Israel reportedly developed a laser uranium-enrichment technique in 1972 allowing it to enrich seven grams of uranium-235, 60 percent in one day (Farr 1999, 15). However, as Cirincione (2002) observes, Western analysts have varied in their calculations of what Israel is likely to have produced, estimates which do not completely match Vanunu's. According to Albright, Berkhout, and Walker (1997), the Dimona reactor could have produced (depending upon its operating power level) between 370 and 650 kilograms of weapons-grade plutonium by the end of 1999 (Cirincione 2002, 224; Albright, Berkhout, and Walker 1997, 263). This would only be enough material for between 74 and 130 nuclear weapons (if one assumes five kilograms of plutonium per warhead) (Cirincione 2002, 224). Given the estimate the Dimona reactor produces roughly 10.6 to 18.6 kilograms of plutonium annually, Cirincione calculated by the end of 2001, it would have produced 391 to 687 kilograms of weapons-grade plutonium since it began operations in early 1964 (enough for 98 to 172 nuclear weapons at four kilograms apiece) (Cirincione 2002, 221–24).[21] By these calculations, the annual production at Dimona is sufficient for Israel to increase its nuclear stockpile by two to four bombs per year (Cirincione 2002, 224). This means that by 2015, Israel's Dimona reactor will have produced between 539 and 947 kilograms of weapons-grade plutonium, enough for between 135 and 237 bombs at four kilograms of weapons-grade plutonium each.

What is quickly apparent is that estimates of the size of Israel's arsenal vary greatly across analysts, who differ in terms of how much fissile material they calculate may have been produced and how much of it will have been used per individual warhead (four kilograms or five kilograms of plutonium in the Cirincione vs. Albright assessments respectively). However, fixating upon such numbers misses the essential point—once we begin talking of arsenals in excess of fifty deliverable weapons for new nuclear states, it is highly likely a credible minimum deterrence threshold has already been amply crossed. Further, though analysts can divide up a total amount of likely fissile material produced by the smallest possible amount required for a weapon to inflate the numbers and excite us about the size of these potential arsenals—why would any new nuclear state construct an arsenal in this fashion?

Yes, it is possible to construct a nuclear weapon with four kilograms of plutonium, but this would result in a relatively low-yield weapon (probably no more than 12–15 kilotons). Given that city-busting, countervalue targeting is the most likely option for small nuclear states with minimal deterrence doctrines, it is far more probable they would choose to use more than the minimum amount of fissile material (once sizeable stockpiles were available) to increase the yield of their warheads—especially if they (like Israel) possess the ability to produce the tritium and lithium deuteride needed for either boosted-fission or thermonuclear weapons. Also, all of these numbers and estimates regarding the size of Israel's nuclear arsenal assumes Israel has not (unlike *all* of the other new nuclear states—India, Pakistan, and North Korea) diversified its nuclear weapons program beyond the sole site at Dimona, and has not pursued development of an easily concealed, uranium-enrichment capability to further expand its stockpile of fissile materials.[22] Although clearly in the realm of conjecture, it would be surprising indeed if Israel—given its historically volatile relationships with its neighbors—had placed all of its nuclear eggs in one basket at Dimona. Given Israel's technical sophistication and nuclear infrastructure, the possibility it also possesses an extensive uranium-based weapons program (in addition to its plutonium one) cannot be discounted out of hand.

### The Perceptions of Israeli Policy Makers Regarding the Need for Nuclear Weapons and Their Impact on Deterrence

Israel's first prime minister, David Ben Gurion, perceived nuclear weapons as a "great equalizer" to counter the numerical superiority of the surrounding Arab states in populations, armies, and conventional weapons. As Feldman (1997, 96) observes, nuclear weapons became a central element of Ben Gurion's notion of "cumulative deterrence": "that an evolving Israeli track record of defeating the efforts of Arab states to destroy the Jewish state would eventually lead them to understand that Israel cannot be defeated militarily and must be accommodated politically. Implicitly, the development of Israel's nuclear potential was intended to contribute to such a track record and thus to become part of its peace policy." As Cohen (1998, 1) notes: "Israel began its nuclear program in earnest about four decades ago, when it constructed the core of its nuclear infrastructure in Dimona. In 1966–67 Israel completed the development stage of its first nuclear weapon, and on the eve of the Six-Day War it already had a rudimentary, but operational, nuclear weapons capability."

Yet, Cohen (1998, 274–76) observes that while Israel faced a crisis threatening its survival in the period leading up to the Six Days' War in 1967—and was, in reality, a nuclear state at the time—the war had "no direct nuclear dimension."[23] Apparently, neither U.S. policy makers nor Israel's Arab opponents considered (or believed) that Israel had nuclear weapons. And for Israeli leaders, announcing a nuclear capability would have had political consequences (damaging U.S.–Israeli relations, provoking international sanctions, etc.) and military consequences (provoked an umbrella pledge of protection by the Soviets for the Arab states that might make it difficult for Israel to militarily preempt the Arab armies conventionally, etc.). Nevertheless, had the war not gone well for the Israelis, the notion the 1967 war had no nuclear dimension could very well have been premature and history might well now tell a different tale. As Cohen (1998, 274–75) notes: "it would have been unthinkable for those in charge not to have placed Israel's most fateful weapons system on operational alert. In a crisis that, for Israelis, evoked memories of

the Holocaust, prudence required taking such a step." Moreover, it is fairly
clear there was at least some discussion of the nuclear option among Israeli
policy makers in the run-up to the 1967 war:

> There were individuals in Israel, particularly Shimon Peres, who thought, and
> even proposed, that under the circumstances Israel should make use of its nu-
> clear capability for coercive or deterrent purposes. In his 1995 *Memoirs* he
> wrote: "My contribution during that dramatic period was something that I still
> cannot write about openly for reasons of state security. After Dayan was ap-
> pointed defense minister I submitted to him a certain proposal which . . . would
> have deterred the Arabs and prevented the war." This remark was interpreted as
> a suggestion that a demonstrative test of a nuclear device might have deterred
> war and also established Israel's nuclear status. (Cohen 1998, 275)

During the 1973 war, though it is impossible to know for sure, it has been
suggested by some scholars that Israeli prime minister Golda Meir authorized
assembly of thirteen twenty-kiloton atomic bombs as a last-ditch effort to halt
the rapidly advancing Arab armies (Hersh 1991, 225–40; Farr 1999, 12). As
it turned out, Israel's nuclear option was not required and the conventional
tide of battle turned in their favor prior to the need to use WMDs. However,
had the situation continued to deteriorate, there can be little doubt nuclear
weapons would have been employed to preserve Israel's survival and blunt
the Arab attacks. Moreover, after discovering it was on the Soviet nuclear target list, it has been suggested the satellite-imaging data of the Soviet Union
stolen by Jonathan Pollard (the American-born Israeli spy) was taken to allow
more accurate targeting by Israel's nuclear arsenal of Soviet cities to create a
deterrent capability vis-à-vis Moscow (Farr 1999, 16). Indeed, Israel's nuclear-capable Jericho II missile has an operational range that placed the Soviet capital within striking distance.

Leading up to the First Gulf War, in response to Hussein's threats to "burn
half of Israel" with chemical munitions, Israeli defense minister Itzhak Rabin
warned that Israel had the means for a devastating response and would retaliate "tenfold" if Iraq used chemical weapons:

> One of our fears is that the Arab world and its leaders might be deluded to be-
> lieve that the lack of international reaction to the use of missiles and gases gives
> them some kind of legitimization to use them. They know they should not be de-
> luded to believe that, because it is a whole different ball game when it comes to
> us. If they are, God forbid, they should know we will hit them back 100 times
> harder. (Steinberg 2000, 52; Feldman 1982, 102)

During the Gulf War, Lieutenant General Dan Shomron, Israel's chief of
staff, announced Israel would not be the first state to "use" nuclear weapons

in the conflict, a tacit admission of Israeli nuclear capability and a wording confirmed by former Israeli officials as intentionally designed to deter Iraqi WMD use (Baram 2001, 33). Thus, thinly veiled Israeli threats of possible nuclear retaliation against Iraq in the event of any unconventional attack, media speculation regarding this possibility, and Israel's long-standing policy of retaliating against attackers is quite likely to have had a substantial deterring effect on Saddam—who despite the possession of chemical and biological warheads for his Scuds, fired none against the Jewish state during the war. Later, Israel's deputy defense minister, Mordechai (Motta) Gur, during a June 1993 seminar at the Tel Aviv University's Jaffee Center for Strategic Studies, remarked:

> Any Arab leader of a country hostile to Israel must carefully weigh what he stands to win or lose if he decides to drop a nuclear bomb on Israel. Each and every Arab leader knows full well that we will not sit idly by, that [Israel] has an active defense, and that it will not be worth his while to expose his country to the risk of an Israeli retaliation. As far as Israel is concerned, we are capable of turning the situation around in such a way as to make it too costly for anybody to wage a nuclear war against us here in the Middle East. The damage Israel will inflict on the nuclear aggressor will far outweigh the so-called profits they may be able to reap. They will never catch us in a moment of weakness, because Israel is capable of dealing a devastating blow which will make a nuclear war not worth their while. (Feldman 1982, 103)

Obviously, there is little question among Israeli policy makers regarding the value and deterrent effects of their nuclear weapons (Peres 1993; Cohen 1998, 2000; Steinberg 2000). Among Arab political and military analysts, there is also general agreement Israel's nuclear weapons place severe limits on the degree to which Arab states can challenge Israel's security. In fact, just before the 1967 war, Syrian Left-Ba'athists called for an immediate Arab attack on Israel before it could obtain nuclear weapons because "none of the Arab armies, however strong by then, would even consider the idea of liberating Palestine at the risk of nuclear destruction" (Rosen 1977, 1372). Similarly, other Arab commentaries, such as one in the pro-Arab London monthly, the *Middle East*, noted in 1977 that "since [nuclear weapons] were developed [by Israel] at the end of the 1960s, there has never been the realistic possibility of a total Arab victory. The Arab states simply could not afford to win to the extent of overrunning the heavily populated heartland of Israel" (Rosen 1977, 1372). As Israeli Defense Forces chief of staff Dan Shomron noted in 1988, "during the Yom Kippur war [1973], the Arab countries possessed gas. . . . But they never used it, and there is a reason for this. This type of weapon invites very harsh reaction" (Steinberg Fall/Winter 2000, 52). As

Rosen (1977, 1372) observes, Arab military strategists have little doubt Israel would use nuclear weapons in the event of a large-scale Arab conventional attack that broke down its conventional defenses and threatened its survival (Sayed 1997). Indeed, as former Israeli prime minister Ehud Barak suggested in 1999, "Israel's nuclear policy, as it is perceived in the eyes of the Arabs, has not changed, will not change and cannot change, because it is a fundamental stand on a matter of survival which impacts all the generations to come" (Steinberg Fall/Winter 2000, 48–49). Or as other Israeli leaders noted, in explaining their negative response to calls for Israel to join the NPT: "The main reason is that Israel is the only country in the world threatened by other countries with destruction. . . . Their fear, or their suspicion, is our deterrent" (Steinberg Fall/Winter 2000, 48).

Those who have argued Israeli nuclear proliferation most likely strengthens deterrence in the Middle East (e.g., Rosen 1977; Feldman 1982; Evron 1990; Steinberg 2000) have long outnumbered proliferation pessimists—especially among Israeli scholars.[24] At the far end of the spectrum, only Maoz (2003) argues Israel's nuclear deterrence has *failed completely* because Arab states never wanted to destroy Israel in the first place, and it hasn't resulted in no armed conflict or Palestinian uprisings, nor in success at peace talks. His argument parallels those of Cold War "nuclear peace" skeptics, and basically argues the absence of major wars during the period do not prove the intent of their opponents to conduct them had weapons been absent. Unfortunately, Maoz's argument is an example of the "Kumbaya Effect" expected by many nuclear deterrence skeptics (i.e., that it is a silver bullet that should solve all disputes, whether central or peripheral) between parties, and that failing to remove even low-level skirmishes or move forward peace talks, should be seen as failure. It is a wholly unrealistic position. To suggest Israel's nuclear weapons have been ineffectual in creating stability because peace talks with the Palestinians have not been successfully concluded, or because Israel had skirmishes in Lebanon during the 1980s (or had Scuds fired at it by Iraq in 1991), is to severely miss the point about what nuclear deterrence can be expected (or was intended) to accomplish. Further, the immensely benign interpretation of Arab intentions during 1967 and 1973 by Maoz definitely would be a minority view among scholars of the region. In fact, the overwhelming majority of scholarly works suggests Israeli nuclear deterrence had an impact on Arab behavior (Freedman and Karsh 1991; Preston 1997; Steinberg 2000).

In reality, the U.S. has long turned a blind eye toward Israel's nuclear program, and Israel is routinely omitted from reports by the intelligence community to Congress identifying nations pursuing WMDs, in order to avoid triggering otherwise required economic and military sanctions (Frantz 2003).

To a great extent, this is due to the implicit acknowledgement—which is never explicitly made by U.S. officials due to the negative impact it would have on American counterproliferation policies—that in the case of Israel, nuclear weapons have brought stability and prevented major wars between Israel and her neighbors for thirty years.[25] As one senior Bush administration official explained, "We tolerate nuclear weapons in Israel for the same reason we tolerate them in Britain and France. . . . We don't regard Israel as a threat" (Frantz 2003).

## Israel's Nuclear Options and Potential Strategies through 2015

Over the coming decade, Israel will likely continue its current pattern of significantly improving and expanding its *regional* nuclear strike capabilities. For example, it should be assumed Israel will continue to outfit its three Dolphin-class strategic submarines with a substantial force of nuclear-tipped cruise missiles (currently modified Harpoon SLCMs, but eventually to include Israeli-produced systems). Each Dolphin-class submarine is equipped with ten twenty-one-inch tubes capable of launching cruise missiles, which would eventually provide Israel with a submarine-based nuclear force of at least thirty warheads (and perhaps more if these cruise missiles are also placed aboard other Israeli surface naval vessels) (NRDC Nuclear Notebook September/October 2002, 75). The development of an extensive, sea-based nuclear deterrent is a logical one for a geographically small state seeking survivable, retaliatory nuclear forces difficult for an opponent to preempt. Moreover, it would provide Israel with a highly flexible, mobile launching platform that could conceivably be used not only against neighboring states, but also against far more distant opponents (e.g., scenarios involving a nuclear or near-nuclear Iran, or hypothetical threats arising from a radical new Islamist regime in Pakistan). Along with the likely development and deployment of the new Jericho III MRBM (2,500-km range/1,000-kg payload) and a new Popeye-variant ALCM (1,500-km range), which could be employed as a stand-off weapon from long-range aircraft platforms, Israel will obtain from its submarine and ballistic missile based forces the ability to strike any realistically foreseeable adversary within the Middle East and South Asia (Cirincione 2002, 221–36).

Israel will also undoubtedly continue to work on improving its ability to launch and deploy military surveillance satellites, enhance its missile and guidance system technologies, and proceed with efforts to improve the design (and yield) of its nuclear weapons arsenal. It is highly likely Israel will continue production of weapons-grade fissile materials (mostly plutonium, but possibly also highly enriched uranium)—a step necessary to ensure the development of a fissile materials stockpile large enough to allow Israel to respond (if necessary) to any new strategic developments or threats in the region.

What Israel is unlikely to do, however, is proceed toward developing *great power* nuclear capabilities, especially those involving long-range ballistic missiles. While Israel is more than capable, technically, of converting its three-stage *Shavit* (Comet) space-launch rockets (7,000-km range) into an ICBM, it lacks any kind of realistic strategic motivation to go down this path (NRDC Nuclear Notebook September/October 2002, 75). Israel enjoys regional military superiority over its potential opponents, and its currently deployed (and envisioned) nuclear force structure is well suited to dealing with the kinds of regional nuclear threats it might face. In contrast, Israel faces no strategic opponents requiring it to develop great power delivery capabilities, nor is it likely to divert its limited economic resources away from development of its regional nuclear forces to pursue strategically unnecessary ones. It is also unlikely Israel will choose to conduct nuclear weapons tests, since these would provoke a great deal of unwanted political and economic sanctions, as well as undercut her long-held policy of officially denying nuclear capabilities. Given the substantial size of the Israeli nuclear arsenal, and the reality that first-generation fission weapons do not require testing to have confidence they will function, there is no overriding rationale for Tel Aviv to test. While thermonuclear weapon designs do generally require testing, if Israel succeeded in obtaining validated U.S. weapons designs (as some analysts suspect), then even the development and deployment of hydrogen bombs would not be limited by a lack of testing. Moreover, as the most advanced of the new nuclear weapon states, Israel clearly has substantial strategic targeting and employment options as the predominant regional nuclear power of the Middle East.

## A Hypothetical Israeli Retaliatory Strike on Iran

In order to illustrate the magnitude of Israel's potential retaliatory capabilities against opponents, let us imagine a scenario in which a nuclear-armed Iran launched a first strike on Tel Aviv and other Israeli targets. Although Israel possesses a substantial nuclear arsenal (108–190 warheads in 2005; 135–237 by 2015), any retaliation would likely involve only a fraction of this arsenal—since some might have been destroyed, delivery systems capable of reaching Iranian targets might be limited, and there would be the need to hold back a significant reserve arsenal to maintain future retaliatory capabilities. For simplicities sake, it will be assumed that Israel does not possess thermonuclear or boosted-fission weapons and does not employ any aircraft delivered weapons (such as ALCMs, gravity bombs, etc.). Obviously, these are debatable assumptions that may be highly unlikely given what analysts generally suspect about the depth of the Israeli nuclear program. Nevertheless, even with these extremely artificial constraints on Israeli retaliation, an immensely destructive attack on Iran would be possible. Using only half of Israel's fifty mobile Jericho II MRBMs and two of the three Dolphin-class strategic nuclear submarines to be deployed over the next few years—an attack of only forty-five, 15–20 kiloton warheads—would hold at risk more than 16 million Iranians in cities across the country. Given this number of warheads still allows Tehran to be targeted with ten warheads, and most other cities with two to three warheads apiece, it is likely that well over 10 million civilians would be killed (perhaps many more), by this attack. Moreover, these numbers could be inflated even more if more weapons were used (i.e., more Jericho IIs, ALCMs) or we assumed that boosted-fission or thermonuclear weapons were employed. But the fundamental point is that even with a limited nuclear attack using forty-five first-generation warheads, Israel is still capable of causing far more damage and casualties to the people and cities of Iran than any leadership in Tehran is likely to ever find acceptable.

## The Cases of Nuclear India and Pakistan

With their twin series of tests conducted in May 1998, both India and Pakistan cast aside their opaque proliferation disguises and formally adopted the mantles of declared nuclear states. By doing so, they openly (and successfully) challenged what they deemed to be an immensely hypocritical counterproliferation regime which merely preserved the ability of the great powers to hold onto weapons denied to other states. Both nations had long-running nuclear programs, extending back into the late 1960s and early 1970s, with India actually testing a "device" in 1974. However, the highly visible, formal demonstration of nuclear capability provided by the 1998 tests thrust both India and Pakistan into a new, overt posture that forced them to move toward developing explicit nuclear doctrines and (in all likelihood) standing nuclear forces. It also brought the "reality" of nuclear weapons more explicitly into discussions surrounding any flare-ups of the long-simmering Kashmiri border dispute—with crises in 1999 and 2002 bringing many alarmed pessimists to begin digging personal fallout shelters.

However, the actual record of the interactions between India and Pakistan over the past several decades, and the clear recognition shown by policy makers on both sides regarding the constraints imposed on their actions by nuclear weapons, provides for a much more comforting interpretation. Across both nations, policy makers share the belief that nuclear weapons have not

only provided a guarantee of their own state's central national security interests, but have also brought welcome deterrence and stability to a region that
has traditionally been one of the most dangerous and unstable in the world. In
this, their nuclear experience has mirrored that of the Israelis, who have long
inhabited a similarly treacherous region.

As of 2005, both India and Pakistan would be classified as *regional nuclear
powers* (i.e., possessed of moderately sized and differentiated nuclear force
structures; medium-range delivery systems, with only moderate vulnerability
to interception). Indeed, as a 2003 Congressional Research Service (CRS) report to Congress noted: "India and Pakistan have the ability to strike and destroy military and civilian targets outside of their respective countries by
means of nuclear weapons, ballistic missiles, and aircraft. These forces, associated readiness postures, command and control, and missile defense constitute a strategic capability on a regional scale" (Feickert and Kronstadt 2003).
While neither India nor Pakistan possess the full-range of capabilities exhib-
ited by the Israeli nuclear force structure, both are clearly formidable regional
nuclear powers who share the ability to rapidly improve and develop their capabilities over the coming decade (see table 3.5).

India would also be credited by the analytical framework (see table 3.6)
with possessing a *moderate to highly survivable nuclear capability* (i.e., moderate redundancy of delivery systems, as well as use of multiple types of mobile systems; adequate C3I capability, hardening of fixed-site positions,
strong site defense capabilities, and sophisticated use of subterfuge). The survivability of India's nuclear arsenal will continue to improve markedly over
the next ten years, as additional mobile delivery systems and a larger, deliverable arsenal render the already slim chances of successful preemption almost nonexistent.

Taken together, the current level of Indian nuclear capability and survivability results in a strong regional deterrent capability with strong crisis stability characteristics, low need for "launch-on-warning" postures, and great
flexibility in targeting options (ranging from local battlefield use to regional
countervalue strikes).

### India's Nuclear Capabilities, Available Fissile
### Materials, and Future Arsenal Potential

Although difficult to separate bluster from fact in the dueling pronounce-
ments by Indian and Pakistani governments following their tests, A. P. J. Abdul Kalam, scientific adviser to the Indian defense minister, noted the tests
provided "critical data for validation of our capability in the design of nuclear
weapons of different yields for different applications and different delivery

**Table 3.5. India's Regional Nuclear Capability**

| | Indian Nuclear Capability (Regional Power) | |
|---|---|---|
| Nuclear Force Structure | Differentiation Within Nuclear Force Structure | Composition, Range, and Accuracy of Delivery System Capabilities | Interceptability by Opponent of Delivery Systems |

| Nuclear Force Structure | Differentiation Within Nuclear Force Structure | Composition, Range, and Accuracy of Delivery System Capabilities | Low to Moderate Interceptability of Delivery Systems |
|---|---|---|---|
| Estimated by various sources as likely consisting of between 35 and 178 nuclear weapons. | **Moderate Differentiation Within Force Structure** Possesses **multiple types of nuclear weapons** (likely first- and second-generation fission and boosted-fission weapons). **Is working to deploy multiple types of warhead designs** (i.e., SLBM, SLCM warhead for the Dhanush, SLCM warhead for Sagarika, gravity bombs (for aircraft delivery), ballistic missile warheads (for Prithvi and Agni missiles), possibly high-yield boosted-fission or (less likely) thermonuclear strategic warheads). | **Nascent Nuclear Triad** **Land-Based Ballistic Missiles:** **Prithvi I** (mobile SRBM; 150-km range/ 800-kg payload). **Prithvi II** (mobile SRBM; 250-km range/ 500-kg payload). **Prithvi III** (mobile SRBM; 350-km range/ 500-kg payload). **Agni II** (rail- and road-mobile MRBM; 2,000-km range/1,000-kg payload). **Agni III** (under development; road- and rail-mobile IRBM; 3,000-km range/ unknown payload). **Nuclear Capable Aircraft:** **Jaguar IS/IB** fighter-bomber (1,600-km range/4,775-kg payload). **MiG-27** fighter-bomber (800-km range/4,000-kg payload). **Mig-29** fighter (630-km range/3000-kg payload). **Su-30K** fighter-bomber (3000-km range/ 8,000-kg payload; 5200-km range w/refueling). **Mirage 2000H** fighter-bomber (700-km range/6300-kg payload). **Sea-Based Capabilities:** **Dhanush** (SLBM; Prithvi-variant; 250-km range/500-kg payload). **Sagarika** (SLCM; 350-km range/ 500-kg payload). | Existing delivery systems and basing modes (i.e., road- and rail-mobile missiles, sea-launched systems, aircraft widely dispersed in hardened hangers, etc.) limit vulnerability to countermeasures (i.e., preemptive attack; antimissile defenses. interception by fighter aircraft, etc.). Large size of nuclear force structure, reliable and rapid delivery system technologies greatly increases penetration capabilities. |

*Sources: Bulletin of the Atomic Scientists* March/April 2002, 70–72; Cirincione, *Deadly Arsenals* 2002; Feickert and Kronstadt 2003, 26–33; Department of Defense, *Proliferation: Threat and Response* 2001; www.globalaircraft.org/planes; www.aerospaceweb.org/aircraft.

**Table 3.6. Survivability Characteristics of India's Nuclear Capability**

| | Survivability of Indian Nuclear Capability (Moderate to High) | | |
|---|---|---|---|
| Redundancy of Delivery Systems | Vulnerability of Delivery Systems to Preemption | C3I Capabilities | Use of Subterfuge and Site Defense Capabilities |
| **Moderate to High Redundancy of Delivery Systems** (i.e., multiple means of delivery employed: short- and medium-range mobile missiles, several different nuclear-capable aircraft, naval launching platforms). India seeks to possess an operational strategic nuclear triad by adding a submarine-based component over the next decade. | **Use of Multiple Mobile Delivery Systems** (i.e., both SRBM and MRBM are on mobile platforms). **Agni II MRBMs are both road and rail mobile. Prithvi I, II, & III SRBMs are both road mobile. Dhanush sea-based SRBM for surface naval vessels.** (Seeking to develop submarine-based SLCM or SLBM capability over next decade). **Variety of advanced fighter-bomber platforms** (i.e., Jaguar IS/IB, Su-30K, Mirage 2000H, MiG-27, MiG-29, etc.). | **Adequate C3I Capabilities** (i.e., early-warning radars or satellite reconnaissance, fiber-optic communications networks, hardened command-and-control sites). **Some limited satellite reconnaissance capability. Israeli Greenpine radar system. Some hardened C3I sites with fiber-optic communications networks.** | **Site Defense Capability** (i.e., SAMs, large air force capable of significant interdiction/creation of air superiority). **Extensive surface-to-air missile capabilities and modern air superiority combat aircraft. Sophisticated Use of Subterfuge** (i.e., road- and rail-mobile missile systems to complicate and confuse an opponent's efforts to target strategic forces, placement of Dhanush SRBM aboard some naval vessels to conceal their location, scattering of nuclear aircraft at geographically distant bases, etc.). Current disassembled state of majority of Indian nuclear arsenal (with components at multiple locations) makes preemption exceedingly difficult. Allows leisurely retaliatory strategy. |

Sources: Bulletin of the Atomic Scientists March/April 2002, 70–72; Cirincione, Deadly Arsenals 2002.

systems." P. K. Iyengar, former chairman of India's Atomic Energy Commission (AEC), later noted the tests demonstrated India possessed three weapon designs (low-yield tactical, full-size fission, and thermonuclear) (Albright 1998, 22). Nevertheless, seismic readings and other evidence collected by Western governments cast doubt upon the reported yields and success of both Indian and Pakistani tests—which in all likelihood did not achieve yields much larger than fifteen kilotons (perhaps less) and are unlikely to have involved high-yield boosted or thermonuclear weapons (Tellis 2001; Cirincione 2002).[26] Among skeptics of India's claimed nuclear capabilities is Tellis (2001, 520), who argues that given the lack of a clear demonstration of ability to construct boosted or thermonuclear weapons, "it is reasonable to conclude that the Indian nuclear estate can primarily produce simple fission weapons capable of yields not much beyond 15 kt."[27] At the same time, however, Tellis does acknowledge that while it cannot be "credited with unambiguously demonstrating its capacity to produce such weapons," India does possess designs for "both boosted fission and thermonuclear weapons" (2001, 522).

Thus, whether one accepts Indian claims it can produce boosted-fission weapons in the twenty-kiloton range, or perhaps even thermonuclear ones, or only assume an arsenal based on what has been conclusively tested—it is important not to make the mistake of assuming a static situation unchanging over time. India may well have obtained technical expertise or designs from former nuclear weaponeers it decided not to test openly, but still use to build higher-yield weapons. Furthermore, India's nuclear tradition of opacity suggests it will not openly discuss *exactly* what capabilities it has, any more than it will discuss explicitly its nuclear doctrine. So while appropriate for security analysts to state that *technically* India has demonstrated no more than the ability to build Hiroshima-size atomic bombs to date, whether they *can*, in fact, build larger ones cannot be answered conclusively (one way or the other).

Estimates of the size of India's arsenal vary widely across analysts, who differ regarding how much usable weapons-grade material exists and how active New Delhi has been in constructing it. Obviously, since New Delhi, like Islamabad, has never provided hard figures regarding the size of their respective arsenals, the debate will likely continue. For example, according to a study by the Natural Resources Defense Council, India was estimated to have a small (but growing) stockpile of roughly thirty to thirty-five nuclear warheads (NRDC Nuclear Notebook March/April 2002, 70). Other analysts, like Raghavan (2001, 84) placed the number of warheads at closer to sixty-five, while the Institute for Science and International Security (ISIS) in 1998 stated India had 370 kilograms of weapons-grade plutonium, enough for seventy-four weapons (Barletta et al. 1998, 152).[28] Similarly, Cirincione (2002,

191) reports India produced between 225–370 kilograms of weapons-grade plutonium and an unknown amount of weapons-grade uranium. If these figures are correct, at four kilograms per warhead, this plutonium stockpile alone would be capable of producing between fifty-six and ninety-three weapons! Jones (2001, 8) suggested by 2000, India would have amassed sufficient plutonium from its Cirus and Dhruva reactors to produce 133 weapons, with projected annual increases in production from these facilities resulting in an additional 6.8 weapons per year. But, by reprocessing its spent fuel, India could eventually obtain enough material for an additional 475 weapons (resulting in a total figure of nearly 700 potential weapons). Suggesting a smaller current capability, Tellis (2001, 492–94) argues unless there were vast expansion of weapons-grade plutonium production capability to boost fissile stockpiles, India would be able to produce an arsenal of only 100–150 weapons by 2010. In contrast, Albright (1998, 24–25) suggests an arsenal of 100 warheads was obtainable by 2005 given the stock of 370 kilograms of weapons-grade plutonium previously generated by the Cirus and Dhruva reactors (enough for seventy-four weapons) and ongoing plutonium production of twenty kilograms per year (enough for four weapons) from the Dhruva reactor alone.

However, attempting to estimate how many weapons India *could have* produced given assessments of its currently existing stockpiles of *weapons-grade plutonium* becomes far more difficult when one includes the possibility of Indian reprocessing of additional material from spent fuel rods (from its many nuclear reactors), the possible use of nonweapons-grade plutonium in warheads, or the impact of a hidden uranium-enrichment program on the amount of available fissile materials. For example, Tellis (2001, 498) observes that should India choose to extract over 3,000 kilograms of plutonium from its spent fuel rods, it would obtain enough material to produce an additional 500 weapons (on top of those produced using the already existing weapons-grade plutonium stockpiles). Others, like Heisbourg (1998/1999, 79), suggest:

> India may have produced some 400 kilograms of plutonium reprocessed from fuel irradiated in Cirus and Dhruva reactors, from which 70–80 nuclear devices could have been manufactured. Given the age, breadth and depth of the Indian nuclear programme, this should be considered a minimum, rather than a maximum figure. Other sources suggest that India may dispose up to 1.95 tonnes of plutonium derived from its six unsafeguarded CANDU-type nuclear reactors— in other words, enough to produce more than 400 warheads. . . . India also has a tritium-production capability for hydrogen bombs.[29]

Indeed, estimates of India's available fissile stockpile would greatly increase should it make use of it's large stockpile (over 700 kilograms) of less desirable, reactor-grade plutonium—which would require either: (a) obtaining the foreign technical expertise needed to design high-yield fission weapons using reactor-grade plutonium; or (b) obtaining atomic vapor laser isotope separation (AVLIS) technology needed to convert it to weapons-grade material (Tellis 2001, 497–98). Significantly, Perkovich (1999) suggests one of India's low-yield tests in 1998 involved the use of nonweapons-grade plutonium (65–70 percent PU-239, compared to the 93 percent concentration in weapons-grade material), and while the use of reactor-grade materials has downsides, these can be resolved:

> The use of non-weapon-grade plutonium in weapons has several potential liabilities. For example, the higher concentrations of isotopes other than plutonium-239—particularly plutonium-240 and plutonium-238—increase the risks that a weapon will explode with less than its designed yield. These isotopes have high rates of spontaneous fission that produces neutrons that could initiate the neutron chain reaction prematurely, that is, before the plutonium core has been fully compressed by the surrounding conventional high explosive. As a result, most of the plutonium will remain unfissioned by the time thermal expansion of the core causes the chain reaction to terminate. Isotopes other than plutonium-239 also have higher rates of alpha particle emission and electromagnetic radiation. This may cause the high explosive to degrade and raise radiation exposure to workers during weapon fabrication, respectively. Despite these difficulties, nuclear weapon designers in the United States and elsewhere learned how to make effective weapons from non-weapon-grade plutonium. (Perkovich 1999, 428–29)

Further, as Perkovich (1999, 429) notes, Indian nuclear scientists are well aware of techniques for addressing the problems arising from the use of reactor-grade plutonium, and as the U.S. Department of Energy notes, "reactor-grade plutonium can be used to make nuclear weapons at all levels of technical sophistication."[30] According to Tellis (2001, 17), "India today is probably at the point where it faces no *technological* constraints on its ability to produce any level of weapons-usable (including weapons-grade) plutonium it desires for the purposes of fabricating nuclear weaponry" (Chow, Speier, and Jones 1995). In fact, Ramana and Nayyar (2001, 79) estimate India's three main nuclear reactors produce between 26.6 and 42.9 kilograms of plutonium annually (Cirus reactor 6.6–10.5 kg; Dhruva 16–26 kg; and Kalpakkam 4–6.4 kg), in addition to the unknown amount of highly enriched uranium produced at the Rattehalli facility. This facility is likely involved in the long-suspected (from 1988 onward) Indian conversion and stockpiling of uranium-233 (an artificial type of uranium produced by transmuting it with thorium), which can also be utilized for making weapons (Barletta et al. 1998, 152). If India's 1998 nuclear tests included one validating the use of nonweapons (reactor) grade plutonium, as Perkovich suggests, the addition of this material could vastly increase the size of India's arsenal. Indeed, as Perkovich (1999, 430) notes, "if the plutonium was reactor-grade, then India's entire stockpile of this material . . . could be used directly in weapons." Further, if this plutonium were of "intermediate composition," Perkovich suggests "a large amount of such material could be created by mixing the stockpiles of weapon- and reactor-grade plutonium." With the completion of two new 500-megawatt-electric nuclear power reactors at Tarapur (estimated in 2005 and 2006), and the construction of a massive 500-megawatt-electric Prototype Fast Breeder Reactor (PFBR) at Kalpakkam (scheduled for completion in 2009)—which will produce immense amounts of additional plutonium—India is set to vastly expand its available fissile material production in the very near future (Cirincione 2001, 201–3).

As table 3.7 illustrates, considering *only* the potential weapons-grade plutonium (WGPu) production from the existing Cirus, Dhruva, and Kalpakkam reactors over the next decade, India will accumulate enough material (roughly 848.8 kg to 1142.2 kg) to produce between 212 and 286 nuclear weapons. These calculations do *not* include any weapons that might be produced from using the 3,000 kilograms of reactor-grade plutonium residing in spent fuel rods from other Indian nuclear facilities, material generated by newly constructed reactors, nor does it include any weapons utilizing highly enriched uranium or U-233 produced by India's extensive uranium-processing and enrichment facilities (Cirincione 2001, 202–4). Obviously, including these would add potentially hundreds of weapons to India's arsenal beyond those listed in the table.

In terms of delivery systems, India currently possesses both short- and medium-range ballistic missiles capable of carrying nuclear payloads, as well as a large number of nuclear-capable combat aircraft. Further, India is developing both intermediate-range ballistic missile and sea-launched cruise and ballistic missile platforms. Although many of these are still in the testing, pre-deployment stage, as of 2006 India clearly possesses a robust nuclear delivery capability which will only improve over time as other delivery systems come on line.

Foremost among India's nuclear-capable delivery systems are its land-based ballistic missiles (both short- and medium-range), with new air- and sea-launched cruise missiles, sea-launched ballistic missiles, and a new intermediate-range missile likely to be deployed over the next decade. Importantly, India has emphasized mobility in these systems, something critical for ensuring the survivability of its retaliatory forces and reducing the likelihood of preemption. For example, India's short-range Prithvi (I, II, and III) mobile missile series are nuclear capable and possess ranges of between 150

Table 3.7.  India's Available (and Potential) Stockpile of Nuclear Materials over the Next Decade from Its Three Main Reactors (Cirus, Khruva, and Kalpakkam)

| Albright Estimate of Existing Indian Stockpile of WGPu (1997) | Low-End Annual Production Estimate of 26.6 kg WGPu | Potential Warhead Stockpile (4.0 kg each) | High-End Annual Production Estimate of 42.9 kg WGPu | Potential Warhead Stockpile (4.0 kg each) |
|---|---|---|---|---|
| | 370.0 kg | 93 | 370.0 kg | 93 |
| 1998 | 396.6 kg | 99 | 412.9 kg | 103 |
| 1999 | 423.2 kg | 106 | 455.8 kg | 114 |
| 2000 | 449.8 kg | 113 | 498.7 kg | 125 |
| 2001 | 476.4 kg | 119 | 541.6 kg | 135 |
| 2002 | 503.0 kg | 126 | 584.5 kg | 146 |
| 2003 | 529.6 kg | 132 | 627.4 kg | 157 |
| 2004 | 556.2 kg | 139 | 670.3 kg | 168 |
| 2005 | 582.8 kg | 146 | 713.2 kg | 178 |
| 2006 | 609.4 kg | 152 | 756.1 kg | 189 |
| 2007 | 636.0 kg | 159 | 799.0 kg | 200 |
| 2008 | 662.6 kg | 166 | 841.9 kg | 211 |
| 2009 | 689.2 kg | 172 | 884.8 kg | 221 |
| 2010 | 715.8 kg | 179 | 927.7 kg | 232 |
| 2011 | 742.4 kg | 186 | 970.6 kg | 243 |
| 2012 | 769.0 kg | 192 | 1013.5 kg | 253 |
| 2013 | 795.6 kg | 199 | 1056.4 kg | 264 |
| 2014 | 822.2 kg | 206 | 1099.3 kg | 275 |
| 2015 | 848.8 kg | 212 | 1142.2 kg | 286 |

Sources: Bulletin of the Atomic Scientists March/April 2002, 70–72; Cirincione, Deadly Arsenals 2002, 191; Albright 1998, 24–25; Ramana and Nayyar 2001, 79; Tellis 2001, 498.
Note: Assumes Albright calculation of Indian WGPu stockpile of 370 kg in 1997 and applies Ramana and Nayyar calculation of annual production of WGPu from the three main Indian nuclear reactors (Cirus 6.6–10.5 kg, Dhruva 16–26 kg, and Kalpakkam 4.0–6.4 kg).

to 350 kilometers (93 to 217 miles)—enough to threaten most of Pakistan's major cities from launch sites near the border (Cirincione 2001, 93–94). The Dhanush sea-launched ballistic missile (SLBM), which India will presumably deploy aboard its surface ships, is a naval version of the Prithvi II (250-km range/1,000-kg payload) (NRDC Nuclear Notebook March/April 2002, 72). Moreover, India has also deployed a medium-range ballistic missile (MRBM), the Agni II (2,000-km range/1,000-kg payload), which is solid-fueled, both road- and rail-mobile, and has the range to target all of Pakistan and large parts of southern China (Salik 2002, 49). India is reportedly developing a follow-on missile to the Agni II (variously described as the Agni III or IV) which would have a range of between 3,700 and 5,000 kilometers and be capable of striking Chinese targets as far away as Beijing, Shanghai, and Hong Kong (Cordesman 2002, 6; NRDC Nuclear Notebook March/April 2002, 72; Cirincione 2001, 197–98; Karp 2000, 112). To assist in this task, the Agni missile systems have incorporated into their reentry vehicles (RVs) altitude control systems and aerodynamic maneuver fins designed to assist their penetration of any potential missile defenses (Feickert and Kronstadt 2003, 27).

Also on the development front, India is working on the Sagarika sea-launched ballistic missile (SLBM), which is intended to have a range of at least 350 kilometers and be launched from a new class of Indian-built nuclear-powered submarines (Koch and Sidhu 1998, 49; Cirincione 2001, 94). The Sagarika is expected to be deployed aboard Indian submarines sometime after 2010. However, construction of India's nuclear-powered submarine, the Advanced Technology Vessel (or ATV), has been plagued by delays, and while it began in 1997 with an estimated launch date scheduled for 2007, most assessments expect technical problems to delay completion beyond that time frame (NRDC Nuclear Notebooks March/April 2002, 72).

India has also sought to develop cruise missile capabilities, although conversion of these systems into nuclear delivery vehicles may prove challenging. Even so, the Indians have installed Russian Klub cruise missiles (300-km range/450-kg payload) onboard its Kilo-class submarines and some of its surface vessels (Salik 2002, 49). There have been reports India obtained Russian technology for firing a missile from underwater, which would be applicable to either SLBMs or SLCMs, and greatly improve their chances of successfully developing the Sagarika system on schedule (Koch and Sidhu 1998, 49). Russia and India are jointly developing the BrahMos antiship cruise missile (185-m range/440-lb payload) which travels at supersonic speed (over 1,400 mph; three times faster than a U.S. Tomahawk cruise missile) and incorporates stealth technology that could make it virtually impossible to intercept (Feickert and Kronstadt 2003, 29). Some of these technical improvements may find their way into the Indian nuclear program, even if the BrahMos cannot be converted to nuclear roles.

Although India does not appear to be pursuing an ICBM-capability at present, it is well positioned to develop such a system in the future given its advanced, civilian space-launch industry and current level of rocket technology. In fact, a January 2002 U.S. National Intelligence Estimate report stated India's Polar Satellite Launch Vehicle (PSLV) could easily be modified into an ICBM within a couple of years (Central Intelligence Agency "Foreign Missile Developments" 2001). Similarly, the National Resources Defense Council noted "most components needed for an ICBM are available from India's indigenous space program," and "conversion of its polar space launch vehicle (PSLV) to an ICBM would take a year or two after a decision to do so" (NRDC Nuclear Notebook March/April 2001, 72). But, while India's civilian space program has often been pointed to as providing India with a rapid capability to develop and produce ICBMs, analysts like Tellis (2001, 97–99) argue that India's current launch vehicles, though doubtlessly providing some assistance to an ICBM program, are just too heavy to serve as ICBMs and too fragile to be easily converted into mobile systems. However, while Tellis suggests many of India's missile programs are unlikely to actually be developed (or be appropriate for strategic missions), another noted missile expert, Karp (2000, 112–13), warns not to underestimate India's programs. Karp (2000, 112) notes the solid-fueled Agni-2 (2,000-km range/1,000-kg warhead), flight tested in April 1999, is an "extensively improved design" far more reliable and better suited to military operations than the earlier, liquid-fueled Agni-1. Further, India is currently developing (and clearly capable of producing) missiles appropriate for strategic missions, as illustrated by the Agni-3 MRBM, with a range of over 3,500 kilometers, and the early R&D work on the Surya ICBM program (Karp 2000, 112). As Karp notes:

> Only vague speculation surrounds the Indian ICBM program, the Surya. Indian officials do not deny the existence of the project, which they say could use the massive solid first-stage sustainer engine of the Polar Space Launch Vehicle created by the civilian Indian Space Research Organization. . . . progress on such a weapon is likely to be slow. Nevertheless, a project like the Surya deserves to be taken seriously, if only because of the unusual tenacity of Indian weapons procurement; *in 45 years of military research and development (R&D), India has never failed to complete a major weapons system program.* (2000, 112) (emphasis added)

In terms of other delivery systems, India possesses modern combat aircraft that could easily be configured for nuclear missions (e.g., MiG-27, MiG-29, Su-30, Jaguar, and Mirage fighter-bombers) (Heisbourg 1998/1999, 80). However, it is generally assumed the most likely aircraft to be so adapted are its MiG-27 (800 km/4,000 kg) and Jaguar IS/IB (1,600 km/4,775 kg) fighter-bombers, both of which served nuclear delivery roles for the Soviet and

British/French air forces respectively. India's growing fleet of Russian Su-30K and Mirage 2000H aircraft are also capable of being converted into nuclear delivery vehicles, with a Mirage 2000H possibly being used in the test drop of a mock nuclear weapon in May 1994 (NRDC Nuclear Notebook March/April 2001, 721). Moreover, the Su-30MK-1 and Su-30K fighter-bombers provide an effective long-range delivery platform (3,000-km range, 5,200-km range with refueling/8,000-kg payload) for delivering nuclear weapons on targets not only throughout Pakistan, but deep into China as well.[31]

Finally, India has obtained some elements of an early warning defense system by acquiring the Israeli Greenpine radar system (used onboard Israeli PHALCON AEW aircraft), and has sought to acquire three Israeli PHALCON airborne early warning (AEW) aircraft for $1 billion (Central Intelligence Agency 1 July Through 31 December 2001). The CIA also reports Israel sold the Harpy unmanned aerial vehicle (UAV) to India (which could conceivably be of aid to its ongoing cruise missile development program), and was engaged in negotiations to sell the Arrow-2 antitactical ballistic missile system to New Delhi (Central Intelligence Agency 1 July Through 31 December 2001).

*Pakistan's Nuclear Capabilities, Available
Fissile Materials, and Future Arsenal Potential*

As of 2005, Pakistan would be classified as a *regional nuclear power* (i.e., possessed of moderately sized and differentiated nuclear force structures; medium-range delivery systems, with only moderate vulnerability to interception (see table 3.8).

Pakistan also would be credited by the framework (see table 3.9) with a *moderate to highly survivable nuclear capability* (i.e., moderate redundancy of delivery systems, as well as use of multiple types of mobile systems, adequate C3I capability, hardening of fixed-site positions, strong site defense capabilities, and sophisticated use of subterfuge). The survivability of Pakistan's arsenal will continue to improve markedly over the next decade, as additional mobile systems and a larger arsenal render the already slim chances of successful preemption almost nonexistent.

Estimates of Pakistan's arsenal and available fissile materials also vary greatly. According to the *Bulletin of the Atomic Scientists* (January/February 2002, 70), the most reliable estimates regarding Pakistan's nuclear capabilities by 2001 were that it possessed somewhere between twenty-four and forty-eight weapons and had "produced enough fissile material for 30–52 nuclear weapons." Raghavan (2001, 84), on the other hand, estimated Pakistan

**Table 3.8. Pakistan's Regional Nuclear Capability**

| | Pakistani Nuclear Capability (Regional Power) | | |
|---|---|---|---|
| Nuclear Force Structure | Differentiation Within Nuclear Force Structure | Composition, Range, and Accuracy of Delivery System Capabilities | Interceptability by Opponent of Delivery Systems |
| Estimated by various sources as likely consisting of between **48 and 111 nuclear weapons.** | **Moderate Differentiation Within Force Structure**<br><br>Possesses **multiple types of nuclear weapons** (likely first- and second-generation fission and boosted-fission weapons).<br><br>**Is working to deploy multiple types of warhead designs** (i.e., gravity bombs (for aircraft delivery), ballistic missile warheads (for Haft, Ghauri, and Shaheen missiles), possibly high-yield boosted-fission. | **Land-Based Ballistic Missiles:**<br>**Haft I** (mobile SRBM; 80-km range/500-kg payload).<br>**Haft II** (mobile SRBM; 300-km range/500-kg payload).<br>**Haft III/M-11** (mobile SRBM; 600-km range/500-kg payload).<br>**Shaheen 1** (mobile SRBM; 750-km range/1,000-kg payload).<br>**Ghauri/No Dong** (mobile MRBM; 1,300-km range/750-kg payload).<br>**Ghauri II** (mobile MRBM; 2,300-km range/1,000-kg payload).<br>**Shaheen II** (mobile MRBM; 2,500-km range/1,000-kg payload).<br>**Nuclear Capable Aircraft:**<br>**F-16A/B** fighter-bomber (3,900-km range; 7,800-kg payload).<br>**Mirage IV** fighter-bomber (2,400-km range/4,000-kg payload).<br>**A-5 fighter** (1,380-km range/500-kg payload). | **Low to Moderate Interceptability of Delivery Systems**<br><br>Existing delivery systems and basing modes (i.e., road-mobile missiles, aircraft widely dispersed in hardened hangers, etc.) limit vulnerability to countermeasures (i.e., preemptive attack, antimissile defenses, interception by fighter aircraft, etc.).<br><br>Large size of nuclear force structure, reliable and rapid delivery system technologies greatly increases penetration capabilities. |

*Sources: Bulletin of the Atomic Scientists* January/February 2002, 70–71; Cirincione, *Deadly Arsenals* 2002; Feickert and Kronstadt 2003, 26–33; Department of Defense, *Proliferation: Threat and Response* 2001; www.globalaircraft.org/planes; www.aerospaceweb.org/aircraft.

**Table 3.9. Survivability Characteristics of Pakistan's Nuclear Capability**

| | Survivability of Pakistani Nuclear Capability (Moderate to High) | | |
| --- | --- | --- | --- |
| Redundancy of Delivery Systems | Vulnerability of Delivery Systems to Preemption | C3I Capabilities | Use of Subterfuge and Site Defense Capabilities |
| **Moderate to High Redundancy of Delivery Systems** (i.e., multiple means of delivery employed: short- and medium-range mobile missiles, several different nuclear-capable aircraft). | **Use of Multiple Mobile Delivery Systems** (i.e., both SRBM and MRBM are on mobile platforms). **Ghauri I & II, Shaheen II MRBMs are all road-mobile systems. Haft I, II, & III, Shaheen I SRBMs are all road-mobile systems. Variety of advanced fighter-bomber platforms** (i.e., F-16A/B, Mirage IV). | **Limited C3I Capabilities** (i.e., early-warning radars, some fiber-optic communications networks, some hardened command-and-control sites). | **Moderate Site Defense Capability** (i.e., SAMs, large air force capable of significant interdiction). **Surface-to-air missile capabilities and modern air superiority combat aircraft. Sophisticated Use of Subterfuge** i.e., use of advanced road- (mobile ballistic missile systems to complicate and confuse an opponent's efforts to target strategic forces, scattering of nuclear-capable aircraft at geographically distant or hidden bases, etc.). **Current disassembled state of majority of Pakistani nuclear arsenal** (with components at multiple locations) makes preemption exceedingly difficult. Allows leisurely retaliatory strategy. |

*Sources: Bulletin of the Atomic Scientists* January/February 2002, 70–71; Cirincione, *Deadly Arsenals* 2002.

possessed roughly forty nuclear weapons by 2001. In contrast, Heisbourg (1998/1999, 79–80) suggested Pakistan may have produced between 400–600 kilograms of enriched uranium, enough for twenty to thirty weapons, and will soon be able to extract weapons-grade plutonium from its Chasma reprocessing facility.[32] Other analysts like Jones (2001, 8) estimate Pakistan had enough HEU by 2000 to produce forty-three weapons, with estimated production increases from its nuclear facilities (both HEU and WGPu) resulting in another seven weapons annually. Similarly, Cirincione (2002, 207), suggests the amount of HEU produced by Pakistan has now risen to between 585 and 800 kilograms. Though Pakistan's program was originally a uranium-based program, in recent years, plutonium reprocessing capabilities have been added allowing Islamabad, like New Delhi, to pursue a dual-track (HEU and WGPu) program. For example, Ramana and Nayyar (2001, 78) estimate Pakistan's Khushab reactor produces between 6.6 and 18 kilograms of plutonium annually, along with 57–93 kilograms of highly HEU annually at the Kahuta facility. The reprocessing facility at Rawalpindi is estimated to produce an additional 10–20 kilograms of plutonium annually (Ramana and Nayyar 2001, 78). As table 3.10 illustrates, these facilities combine to provide Pakistan a growing stockpile of weapons-grade materials by 2015 and allow for a substantial expansion of its arsenal.

As these calculations demonstrate, Pakistan's probable fissile stockpile in 2005 includes between 66.4 and 152 kilograms of WGPu (enough to produce seventeen to thirty-eight bombs), as well as between 813 and 1,172 kilograms of HEU (enough for roughly fifty-one to seventy-three warheads). Thus, given this stockpile, Pakistan possesses a hypothetical nuclear capability in 2005 of anywhere between 68 and 111 weapons. Within a decade, at current production levels, this projects to a Pakistani capability of between 144 and 264 total weapons.

In terms of delivery systems, China and North Korea have been instrumental in assisting Pakistan's development of ballistic missile capability. For example, Chinese assistance is suspected in the development of Pakistan's first indigenous missiles (the Hatf-1 and Hatf-2), and more overtly, in the sale in 1992 of at least thirty-four M-11 ballistic missiles (with 300-km range/800-kg payload or 250-km range/1000-kg payload). Later, China actually provided Pakistan with the blueprints and machine tools allowing for the construction of a missile production complex at Tarnawa outside Rawalpindi that allowed it to domestically produce the M-11 (or Hatf-3 by the Pakistani designation). North Korea, on the other hand, exported Nodong missiles to Pakistan during the 1990s, which Pakistan designated the Ghauri, a liquid-fueled, 1,500-kilometer delivery system capable of striking deep into India (Tellis 2001, 47–49). Further, Karp (2000, 113) notes that while the Ghauri was

Table 3.10.   Pakistan's Available (and Potential) Stockpile of Nuclear Materials over the Next Decade from Its HEU—and Plutonium—Production Facilities

| | Low-End Estimate of Annual WGPu Production (16.6 kg) | Warhead Potential Stockpile (4.0 kg each) | High-End Estimate of Annual WGPu Production (38.0 kg) | Potential Warhead Stockpile (4.0 kg each) | Low-End Estimate of Annual HEU Production (57.0 kg) | Potential Warhead Stockpile (16.0 kg each) | High-End Estimate of Annual HEU Production (93.0 kg) | Potential Warhead Stockpile (16.0 kg each) |
|---|---|---|---|---|---|---|---|---|
| 2001 | 0 | 0 | 0 | 0 | 585 kg | 37 | 800 kg | 50 |
| 2005 | 66.4 kg | 17 | 152 kg | 38 | 813 kg | 51 | 1,172 kg | 73 |
| 2006 | 83.0 kg | 21 | 190 kg | 48 | 870 kg | 54 | 1,265 kg | 79 |
| 2007 | 99.6 kg | 25 | 228 kg | 57 | 927 kg | 58 | 1,358 kg | 85 |
| 2008 | 116.2 kg | 29 | 266 kg | 67 | 984 kg | 62 | 1,451 kg | 91 |
| 2009 | 132.8 kg | 33 | 304 kg | 76 | 1,041 kg | 65 | 1,544 kg | 97 |
| 2010 | 149.4 kg | 37 | 342 kg | 86 | 1,098 kg | 69 | 1,637 kg | 102 |
| 2011 | 166.0 kg | 42 | 380 kg | 95 | 1,155 kg | 72 | 1,730 kg | 108 |
| 2012 | 182.6 kg | 46 | 418 kg | 105 | 1,212 kg | 76 | 1,823 kg | 114 |
| 2013 | 199.2 kg | 50 | 456 kg | 114 | 1,269 kg | 79 | 1,916 kg | 120 |
| 2014 | 215.8 kg | 54 | 494 kg | 124 | 1,326 kg | 83 | 2,009 kg | 126 |
| 2015 | 232.4 kg | 58 | 532 kg | 133 | 1,383 kg | 86 | 2,102 kg | 131 |

Sources: Cirincione, Deadly Arsenals 2002, 207–19; Ramana and Nayyar 2001, 79; Cochran and Paine 1995, 9.

Note: Assumes Ramana and Nayyar calculations of annual production of WGPu from the Khushab reactor runs between 6.6 and 18.0 kg per year and the spent fuel reprocessing facility at Rawalpindi produces an additional 10–20 kg annually. It also assumes their calculation of the Kahuta enrichment facility of 57–93 kg HEU annually is correct. Uses Cirincione's estimate of 2001 stockpile of HEU at between 585 and 800 kg. Also employs Paine's assessment that states vary in how much HEU they need to produce a 20-kt nuclear weapon based upon their technical capability (high = 5 kg, medium = 9 kg, and low = 16 kg). In this table, Pakistan is credited with only low technical capability, although it may well be the case that this significantly underestimates that capability given the possession of validated Chinese nuclear weapon designs. Also, since there are no reliable estimates of the existing stockpile of Pakistani WGPu available in open sources, the calculations in this table begin at zero in 2001.

based on the Nodong, "there are small but important differences which suggest that Pakistan has refined the North Korean design to better serve its own requirements." This cooperation led to the Ghauri-2, successfully test fired in April 1999, which has a maximum range of 2,300 kilometers. Also of note is Pakistan's solid-fueled rocket program, which successfully tested the nuclear-capable, Shaheen-1 SRBM (750-kilometer range) in early 1999.

Pakistan further increased the survivability of its forces by developing the Shaheen-2 medium-range missile (2,500-km range/1,000-kg payload), deployed on a sixteen-wheel mobile launcher. Similarly, the Gharui-2 (2,300-km range/1,000-kg payload) also employs a mobile launcher (NRDC Nuclear Notebook March/April 2001, 70). In fact, Pakistan's ability to quickly respond to any Indian attack is sometimes underestimated by analysts. Its road-mobile, solid-fueled Shaheen I missile requires limited launch preparations, allowing it to be launched upon arrival at presurveyed launch sites within five to ten minutes (Feickert and Kronstadt 2003, 31). Pakistan possesses aircraft easily configured for nuclear missions (like its F-16A/B or 15 Mirage IIIEP fighter-bombers) (Heisbourg 1998/1990, 80). The U.S.-supplied F-16A/Bs (1,600-km range/5,450-kg payload) is the most likely aircraft to be used to deliver weapons, although it also possesses French Mirage V or Chinese A-5s that could be used as well (NRDC Nuclear Notebook March/April 2001, 70).

U.S. intelligence suggests Pakistan based the warhead design used in its weapons program from the fourth Chinese nuclear test (October 1966) which used an enriched uranium fission core producing a yield of 20–25 kilotons (Koch and Sidhu 1998, 44; Kampani 1998, 17; Tellis 2001, 47). Western experts believe its design is light enough to be carried by Pakistan's F-16 fighter-bombers (Koch and Sidhu 1998, 44). This is in addition to the ring magnets, special furnaces, heavy water, HEU, tritium, and integrated nuclear facilities (like the Khushab research reactor) China also provided to Pakistan (Tellis 2001, 46–47).[33] Following India's lead in seeking antimissile defenses, Pakistan reportedly sought to buy the outdated U.S. Hawk and Nike-Hercules antiaircraft systems for use in defending its nuclear and missile-production facilities (Feickert and Kronstadt 2003, 46–47). As Tellis (2001, 4,546) observes:

Pakistan's nuclear potential, as exemplified both by its weaponry and by the plethora of delivery systems it is developing or has already acquired, is certainly problematic in that for the first time in India's post-independence history, its immediate—and weaker—rival has acquired the ability to hold at risk significant national assets such as major population and industrial centers, critical military facilities, and strategic infrastructure assets located great distances from the frontier. This new vulnerability to standoff attack by weapons of mass destruction represents a dramatic change in the strategic balance vis-à-vis Pakistan. . . . In effect, then, Pakistan—the traditionally weaker adversary—has now neutralized India's conventional and geostrategic advantages.

## The Perceptions of Indian and Pakistani Policy Makers Regarding Nuclear Weapons and Deterrence

There is sharp debate between those who believe nuclear weapons provide a deterrent, stabilizing relationship between India and Pakistan (Sundarji 1996; Hagerty 1998; Ganguly 1999; Jones and Ganguly 2000; Waltz 2004) and those who believe they will destabilize South Asia and make war more likely (Poulose 1998; Carranza 1999; Bowen and Wolven 1999; Chari 2000; Raghavan 2001; Khan 2003; Sagan 2004).[34] Among potentially destabilizing problems, scholars have focused on the difficulties of command and control and suggested their vulnerability and the need for extensive delegation of authority lead toward instability (Bowen and Wolven 1999). Others suggest the possession of weapons by both sides leads to policy makers believing they are immune to the worst consequences of conventional escalation (due to the enormous costs involved if it leads to a nuclear exchange), thereby increasing the chances of low intensity combat operations like those in Kargil in the spring of 1999 (Tellis et al., 2001).

Yet ironically, as Tellis (2001, 27) observes, those closest to the conflict (Indian and Pakistani policy makers) appear to disagree with the nuclear pessimists, with "most Indian policy makers today" noting that in addition to condoning their own nuclear arsenal, "Pakistan's acquisition of nuclear weapons should also be condoned by the United States as a means for enhancing strategic stability in South Asia." During the 1980s, Pakistani president Zia once noted regarding India's nuclear capabilities: "If they create ambiguity, that ambiguity is the essence of deterrence. The present programs of India and Pakistan have a lot of ambiguities, and therefore in the eyes of each other, they have reached a particular level, and that level is good enough to create an impression of deterrence" (Spector 1988, 145). Similarly, in a March 2000 interview, Indian prime minister Vajpayee asserted that India was more secure in the aftermath of its nuclear tests and establishment of a minimum credible deterrent (Raghavan 2001, 85). At the same time, Pakistani president Musharraf was quoted by CNN as suggesting the chances of "open conflagration" between India and Pakistan over Kashmir had been reduced by nuclear weapons. In other interviews, Musharraf stated he didn't think the tensions over Kashmir with India would get out of hand because India knows "there is a deterrent in place on our side." Indeed, while Vajpayee pointedly ruled out the possibility of nuclear war with Pakistan, Musharraf noted that nuclear deterrence would constrain India and prevent war over Kashmir.

But, as would be expected, in low-level conflicts, nuclear capabilities do not prevent opponents from considering at least limited military options. For example, after statements by Musharraf suggesting that Pakistan's nuclear deterrence would prevent India from taking military action in Jammu or Kashmir, both India's defense Minister and chief of army staff asserted India's readiness to fight a limited war, despite Pakistan's nuclear capabilities (Raghavan 2001, 85). Indeed, as K. Subrahmanyam suggested, "the main purpose of a third world arsenal is deterrence against blackmail" (Tellis 2001, 262).[35]

Although neither India nor Pakistan have explicitly laid out their nuclear doctrines in detail, leading Western analysts to suggest their strategic thinking is not as advanced as it was for the Cold War superpowers, this conclusion is unwarranted. Firstly, it is not self-evident that a U.S.-style, openly laid out, detailed nuclear doctrine is required for effective deterrence—especially given the opaque evolution of the Indian and Pakistani nuclear programs and their emphasis upon existential deterrence. Second, by not spelling out every last detail, India and Pakistan increase the uncertainty on their opponent's part about how they might react under certain conditions—something not necessarily undesirable (Tellis 2001, 271). This position is not unlike that taken by Israel, which also refuses to explicitly state its nuclear doctrine or targeting philosophies, in order to obtain the maximum deterrence benefit possible from such ambiguity and uncertainty for opponents. Lt. General V. R. Raghavan, India's director general of military operations from 1992 to 1994, noting "neither side would accept the risks of nonweaponized deterrence," argued "it can be safely said that weaponization is complete and under continuing refinement in both India and Pakistan" (Raghavan 2001, 84). Yet, as he explained:

> It also seems reasonable to anticipate that warheads, triggers, cores, and missiles have not been mated, in keeping with the non-deployment assurances given by the two governments. This approach helps ensure that the risk of accidents is reduced and effective command and control is retained, until the absolute necessity arises of using nuclear weapons. In this sense, the nuclear deterrent forces of India and Pakistan are not deployed. (Raghavan 2001, 84)

Still, the fairly explicit statements by both Indian and Pakistani leaders about the "red line" issues that would call for a nuclear response are more than likely sufficient to prevent any serious miscalculation on the part of New Delhi or Islamabad during a confrontation. The simple reality that each side has a deliverable nuclear deterrent and would use it under certain conditions is readily apparent to both countries, and does not require much more detail than that to deter. As Tellis (2001, 269) observes:

> Since India's preferred outcome is thus defined solely in terms of deterrence . . . the possession of even a few survivable nuclear weapons capable of being delivered on target, together with an adequate command system, is seen as sufficient to preserve the country's security. Preserving safety in the face of blackmail and coercion does not, however, require any additional *pronouncements* about the

size of the nuclear stockpile, theories of deterrence, use doctrines, targeting philosophy, or operational posture. As one highly placed manager associated with India's nuclear program pointed out, "We don't fall into the standard pattern of declared doctrines, specific weapons, delivery capabilities or force postures," since the very recognition that India possesses nuclear weapons suffices to ensure that all "aggressive acts" would be adequately deterred even without the promulgation of any particular doctrine of deterrence.

Indeed, given existential deterrence operated for both countries during their opaque nuclear stage (when even less was explicitly stated about their nuclear plans or strategies), one can only note that the nuclear equations for both have become clearer and more defined as each have moved to explicit nuclear force structures and statements of philosophy regarding their use.[36] As leading Indian strategic analyst K. Subrahmanyam wrote:

> Those against India being a nuclear weapon state and those conditioned by U.S. nuclear strategic theology . . . raise the question of what minimum nuclear deterrent the Indian Government has adopted as its declaratory policy. [This] is an arcane question and cannot be answered in precise numerical terms like 30, 300, 3,000 or 30,000. The very idea that there must be a precise numerical value to the deterrent arsenal is part of the sedulously fostered nuclear theology of former U.S. defense secretary Robert McNamara, who has now abjured it. . . . Minimum deterrence is not a numerical definition but a strategic approach. If a country is in a position to have a survivable arsenal, which is seen as capable of exacting an unacceptable penalty in retaliation, it has a minimum deterrence [as] opposed to an open-ended one aimed at matching the adversary's arsenals in numerical terms. (Subrahmanyam 1998, 1)

In India, the August 1999 "Draft Report of [the] National Security Advisory Board on Indian Nuclear Doctrine" remains the most well-publicized statement regarding its nuclear doctrine, although Tellis (2001, 253–56) correctly observes it does not represent the "official" Indian nuclear policy, is somewhat contradictory at times, and is purely a set of nonbinding recommendations by India's leading security experts submitted for consideration by the National Security Council. In outlining India's current thinking about nuclear doctrine, Tellis (2001, 261–475) notes the following elements: (1) The view that India's weapons serve purely as political instruments of deterrence and have no usable role as military tools; (2) A rejection of notions of defense (e.g., preemption; limited or war-fighting nuclear options; robust strategic defenses); (3) A statement of "no first use" weapons policy; (4) View that if weapons are employed, they will be used for punishment alone; (5) That immediate responsiveness of retaliatory forces is not required since "delayed— but assured—retaliation" by India in response to an attack (even if it takes days, weeks, or months) will be sufficient to deter; (6) Development of retaliatory forces capable of both "massive" and "graduated" nuclear responses; (7) Emphasis upon countervalue targeting; (8) An arsenal limited in size to that required for a minimum, credible nuclear deterrence; (9) Force structure differentiated across a variety of survivable delivery systems; and (10) Civilian control over nuclear forces. In 2002, Admiral Madhvendra Singh, the navy chief, while refusing to confirm or deny the presence of nuclear weapons aboard his ships, observed that "those who have been at the nuclear game for a long time have the most powerful leg of the triad in their navy, hidden, moving, under the water" (Dugger 2002).

As India's president Narayanan noted, "nuclear weapons are useful only when they are not used. They can only be a deterrent in the hands of a nation" (Tellis 2001, 261). Similarly, K. Subrahmanyam, one of India's leading strategic thinkers, observed that, "India does not subscribe to the outmoded warfighting doctrine [followed by the United States and the USSR], and [in contrast to the doctrines upheld by these states] . . . Indian nuclear weapons are meant solely for deterrence."[37] Prime Minister Vajpayee stated that India would not build an arsenal beyond that required for a "minimum, but credible, nuclear deterrent" (Tellis 2001, 261–62). As Tellis (2001, 323–24) observes, India's doctrine is similar to China's in that it stresses "certitude rather than alacrity of retaliation" if attacked, explained by one Cold War–era Chinese strategist in the following terms:

Chinese deterrent strategy is based on "launch at any uncertain time" . . . the Soviets—who cannot preempt all of China's nuclear missiles, which are carefully stored in caves or otherwise protected and camouflaged—would have to continue to worry about Chinese retaliation "perhaps hours, days, weeks, months or even years later." Even if China's leadership is destroyed in a decapitating nuclear attack, "the Chinese people would not lose confidence. . . . the Chinese people can wait until a new leadership is capable of ordering retaliation. Orders could even be sent by foot. The Soviet Union cannot help but be uncertain . . . "China does not need an invulnerable C3 system" to ensure the viability of its nuclear deterrent.

In the aftermath of India's nuclear tests, Vajpayee defended his decision before a rally of supporters by referencing NATO's "naked aggression" in Yugoslavia and declaring, "Who is safe in this world? . . . In this situation, we cannot let our defenses slip. Nuclear weapons are the only way to maintain peace" ("Indian Prime Minister Defends Nuclear Test Decision" 1999).

Pakistan's nuclear doctrine refuses to rule out "first-use" of nuclear weapons, a position to be expected from a country vastly inferior in conventional military terms to its neighbor. Indeed, it is no different from the stated

U.S./NATO position during the Cold War calling for use of tactical weapons against vastly superior Soviet/Warsaw Pact conventional forces to prevent the overrunning of Western Europe. Moreover, Pakistani officials, including Foreign Minister Sattar, have actually enunciated the "red line" that would trigger a Pakistani nuclear strike: (1) if India launched a general war and undertook a piercing attack threatening to occupy large territory or communication junctions in Pakistan; or (2) if during a conventional conflict, the military situation deteriorated to the point India would likely (or had) pierced Pakistan's main defense line causing losses that could not be restored by conventional means and threatened collapse of Pakistan's overall defenses (Raghavan 2001, 93). In an April 2002 interview, Musharraf stated that while "nuclear weapons are the last resort" in a crisis with India, "if Pakistan is threatened with extinction, then the pressure of our countrymen would be so big that this option, too, would have to be considered" ("Pakistan: Musharraf Says Nuclear Weapons Are an Option" 2002).

Tellis (2001, 746–47) argues both India and Pakistan's nuclear force structures will be "heavily biased in support of crisis stability" due to their minimal deterrent footings, countervalue targeting, survivable deployment patterns, and slow strike or retaliation response times. Further, counterforce targeting by India of Pakistan's forces is unlikely because "mobile ballistic missiles will be largely undetectable in a conflict" (Tellis 2001, 358). As Tellis notes:

> The fact that the nuclear capabilities of all three states—India, Pakistan, and China—are not structured for the conduct of prompt operations seems to have eluded many commentators in the United States, who, especially in the aftermath of the nuclear tests of May 1998, spewed forth several assertions that one scholar correctly described as "more visceral than thoughtful." Examples of such assertions include claims that both sides "would . . . have weapons on aircraft or missiles capable of striking with as little as 3 minutes warning" and that "India and Pakistan might opt to Launch on Warning of attack." Not only are such assertions misleading, but the evidence that ought to underwrite them simply does not exist. Consequently, the alarmist conclusions often derived about stability from raw geographic or technical facts are usually dubious and, more dangerously, could skew U.S. policy in directions that are either fruitless or counterproductive. (Tellis 2001, 747)

Indeed, as Indian general Sundarji (1996, 175) observed, it is inappropriate for Western analysts to use the norms and yardsticks that applied to the nuclear doctrines of Cold War superpowers and apply these unchanged to third world situations between two small nuclear powers. Instead, Sundarji (1996, 176–77) notes that small states adopting a simple minimum deterrence posture geared toward providing second-strike, countervalue capabilities require:

(1) No adoption of a first-strike doctrine;
(2) A focus on strategic, countervalue targeting;
(3) Finite requirements for numbers of weapons in arsenal needed to achieve a minimal deterrent capability;
(4) No launch-on-warning posture, but delayed retaliatory response with second-strike forces to any first strike;
(5) No requirement for high state of availability or reliability of arsenal (i.e., limited testing requirements, no need for immediate ability to launch weapons, etc.)
(6) No need to develop explicitly tactical weapons systems.

Contrary to pessimist concerns, Sundarji (1996, 177) notes small nuclear states do not require adopting "launch-on-warning" postures to preserve their retaliatory capabilities, nor highly sophisticated command, control and communication (C3) systems that function in real time, since "even a very successful decapitating first-strike attack by the adversary cannot give him any assurance that the recipient will not launch its surviving second-strike capacity." Instead, the "standard operating procedures may well stipulate the launch of the second strike against predetermined targets, say after $x$ hours of receipt of the first strike, if no countermanding orders are received by that time."[38] Sundarji suggests a *new nuclear state might find limited need for actual testing of its arsenal* since only area, or countervalue, targets are envisioned in any retaliatory strike by simple, first-generation weapons. Further, Sundarji (1996, 178) observes the history of India and Pakistan suggests that when considering small nuclear states, Western analysts need to understand that:

(1) The absence of a visible strategic nuclear force, or an articulated doctrine, and elaborate C3 does not mean that a force capable of carrying out a first or second strike is not yet ready on the minimum deterrent scale;
(2) The fact that no massive reorganization of conventional forces has taken place or no revised doctrine for conventional war has been articulated does not mean that nuclear weapons have not yet been fielded;
(3) The fact that no physical testing has gone on does not mean that nuclear weapons are not yet ready to be fielded, or that they would be ineffective or too unreliable if fielded.

## How Much Capability Is Perceived to Be Required for Deterrence?

How many weapons are necessary for a minimum deterrent force? Throughout the Indian military and security communities, there are a wide range of estimates. For example, Sundarji was widely cited as proposing thirty to forty weapons as sufficient for minimum deterrence, while another former chief of army staff, General V. N. Sharma argued fifty warheads should be sufficient (Albright 1998, 21).[39] Elsewhere, Sundarji suggested that against Pakistan, fifty twenty-kiloton weapons would suffice for deterrence, whereas against *both* Pakistan and China, a minimal deterrence capability would be obtained by targeting five Pakistani and ten Chinese cities with "three fission warheads of 20 kt each, detonated as low airbursts"—which would require a *survivable* Indian nuclear arsenal of forty-five warheads. Later, Sundarji reduced the absolute number of weapons required for deterring a small to medium-sized country to twenty, 20-kiloton weapons, and argued around fifty were needed to deter a larger country (Tellis 2001, 386–87). All told, Sundarji suggested a force of between 90 and 135 weapons would be reasonable number (if properly mobile) to provide India with a survivable, retaliatory deterrent force. On the other hand, Subrahmanyam, another leading strategist, suggested a force of sixty deliverable warheads would be required (Tellis 2001, 387). At the far end of the spectrum, Bharat Karnad argues for a stockpile of around 330 weapons by the year 2030, including tactical atomic demolition munitions and thermonuclear weapons (Tellis 2001, 268).

Interestingly, Indian commentator Vijai Nair suggests that India's arsenal should be capable of targeting in Pakistan "six metropolitan centers including port facilities; one corps-sized offensive formation in its concentration area; three sets of bottlenecks in the strategic communications network; five nuclear-capable military airfields; [and] two hydroelectric water storage dams" with a total of seventeen nuclear weapons (Tellis 2001, 170). With regard to China, Nair calls for the ability to target five or six major industrial centers, as well as two ports, with eight high-yield thermonuclear weapons (Tellis 2001, 385–86; Nair 1992, 170). According to Nair, this deterrent capability requires (after allowing for two weapons on each target, twenty-five designated targets, and a 20 percent strategic reserve) an arsenal of 132 nuclear weapons, including high-yield city-busting thermonuclear weapons (Tellis 2001, 386; Nair 1992, 181). As Tellis (2001, 386) points out, absent hydrogen bombs (which India cannot be confirmed to possess at this point), destroying Nair's targets would require "upwards of 800 20-kt-size weapons"—a vastly inflated total which does not take into account the destructive power of even these smaller-yield weapons on cities or populations, relies solely on building blast effects damage estimates to determine the necessary number of weapons to destroy a city, and ignores the deterrent effect a potential large-scale strike of twenty-kiloton weapons (even with an arsenal of 132) on Chinese cities would have on China's leaders!

Obviously, one of the problems is the assumptions used by analysts. Wedded to Cold War–era notions of what is required for nuclear weapons to be effective—notions that are inherently arbitrary, focused solely upon blast damage effects on vehicles rather than the total range of nuclear effects, and biased by ridiculously inflated estimates of the kinds of capabilities required for deterrence—some analysts have arrived at force requirements suggesting only massive numbers of warheads could be effective in the Indian–Pakistani context. For example, Tellis (2001, 133) suggests that for Pakistan to destroy a *single* Indian armored division (i.e., 50 percent of the armored vehicles within a fifteen by twenty-five kilometer space), it would take "between 436 and 257 nuclear weapons of 15-kt yield, depending on the hardness estimates selected for armored vehicles." A mind-numbing quantity likely exceeding the entire U.S. nuclear arsenal during the 1940s and early 1950s! Even when calculating how many weapons Pakistan would require to kill 50 percent of the personnel in that Indian armored division (if total destruction of the armored vehicles themselves were abandoned), a total of thirty-seven warheads of fifteen-kiloton yield was said to be required!!! That these estimates are wildly overinflated should be beyond doubt, as should be the assumptions that any *sane* nuclear state would employ its strategic arsenal in this fashion! Would Pakistan even need to stop an Indian armored division if it credibly threatened to use those 257–436 (or even thirty-seven) Hiroshima-size weapons on nearby Indian cities instead?!? It strains credulity to assume any leadership in New Delhi would continue an armored attack into Pakistan under such circumstances. In fairness to Tellis, he also notes that while the contingency of Pakistan using nuclear weapons to prevent a battlefield defeat was plausible, "there are no political reasons today—and few that can be envisaged for the future—why New Delhi would want to place Islamabad in a position where, fearing for its very survival, it must use nuclear weapons to prevent strategic defeat. . . . this would be all the more true if Pakistan was known to have nuclear capabilities" (2001, 134–35).

## India and Pakistan's Nuclear Options and Potential Strategies through 2015

Given their official statements and directions of their weapons programs, both India and Pakistan appear intent upon developing robust, standing nuclear force structures and diversifying their arsenals to improve survivability. In the case of India, this movement appears directed toward development of an operational nuclear triad (land-based missiles, nuclear-capable aircraft, and submarine-launched weapons). Although clearly not as advanced as Israel's sea-based capabilities, India already has tested and begun deployment of the

Dhanush (a naval version of the Prithvi SRBM) aboard several surface ships in its navy. Though this provides India with some sea-based nuclear strike capability against coastal targets (and potentially against an opponent's naval forces at sea), these surface ships, while mobile, will still be highly visible and at risk of preemption. The short range of the Dhanush system (only about 250 kilometers/155 miles) means it provides India with only limited (though substantial) retaliatory capabilities against Pakistan. In a conflict with China (or some other great power), it would be exceedingly difficult for India to get close enough to coastal targets with its surface naval forces to ensure a reliable retaliatory capability.

Thus, for India to achieve a truly survivable nuclear triad, it will need to achieve success over the coming decade in developing its new strategic submarine, the Advanced Technology Vessel (ATV). Though analysts question how quickly India will be able to successfully complete and deploy this submarine, it is clear that India is placing a great deal of emphasis upon this system. Given the likelihood India has obtained significant Russian assistance in submarine, cruise missile, and sea-launched ballistic missile technology, it is reasonable to assume India will have deployed an operational ATV equipped with either a modified, extended-range Dhanush SLBM or Sagarika SLCMs by 2015. Once it has possession of this more stealthy, survivable sea-based deterrent force, India will have obtained the same kind of *operational* nuclear triad fielded by Israel and greatly broaden its possible nuclear employment strategies. Coupled with the likely addition of the Agni III (an IRBM with a range of over 3,000 kilometers and the ability to hold important targets like Beijing in neighboring China at risk), India will have obtained a credible nuclear deterrent force against the great power next door as well.

At the same time, given resource limitations and no driving need to expand its nuclear forces beyond those required to solidify its regional nuclear power status, it is unlikely India will make any substantial effort to join the nuclear great power club by developing ICBM-capabilities. While such long-range missiles are certainly well within India's technical competence (as its civilian space program demonstrates), there is no compelling strategic rationale (at present) for New Delhi to divert resources toward deterrence of the United States. Indeed, given the clear need to improve its regional nuclear capabilities against traditional opponents (Pakistan and China), it is anticipated that India will be content through 2015 in cementing its strong, regional nuclear power status. In table 3.11, the wide range of available nuclear targeting and employment options currently available for India (as of 2005) are listed at the local, regional, and global levels. As the discussion above indicates, advancements in Indian capabilities over the coming decade will likely expand this list significantly.

**Table 3.11. Available Indian Nuclear Targeting and Employment Options**

| Indian Nuclear Targeting and Employment Options | | | |
|---|---|---|---|
| Local Theater | Regional Theater | Global | Explicit/Implicit Nuclear Doctrine |
| **Tactical, Local Battlefield Use** To blunt an opponent's military offensive by targeting conventional forces (i.e., armored columns, troop concentrations, forward bases and air fields, supply lines, naval forces, etc.). Use as a "demonstration" or "warning shot" to signal nuclear resolve, encourage outside intervention, or warn of the need for conflict de-escalation. | **Regional Battlefield and Counterforce Use** Conventional military counterforce usage (i.e., targeting opponent's military forces, operational bases, command and control sites, supply lines, naval forces). **Limited nuclear counterforce usage** (i.e., targeting opponent's deployed nuclear forces or infrastructure to potentially weaken any subsequent attack). **Regional Countervalue Use** Countervalue targeting of population centers in neighboring states (major cities and metropolitan areas). Countervalue targeting of critical economic infrastructure in neighboring states (i.e., oil installations—like pipeline pumping stations, refineries, loading terminals—sea ports, heavy industry factories, etc.). EMP/antisatellite attacks. Countervalue targeting of sites of religious or cultural significance to opponents. Leadership decapitation or C3I disruption strikes. | **Extremely Limited** Unconventional delivery of countervalue or EMP attacks (i.e., using commercial ships or aircraft). | **Minimal Deterrence Nuclear Doctrine** (Explicit) **Overt nuclear possession strategy.** **Emphasizes survivable, assured destruction retaliatory capability** (i.e., goal is deployment of operational nuclear triad). **Declared "No First Use" Nuclear Policy** (i.e., relies on conventional military capabilities to blunt any initial attack by China or Pakistan). |

With regard to Pakistan, it is clear Islamabad will not be able to match either the size or diversification of India's nuclear weapons program. However, this does not mean Pakistan will lack regional nuclear power status. Indeed, lacking the need for longer-range systems to target a more distant opponent (as India does to deter China), Islamabad can focus its more limited development and deployment efforts toward ensuring possession of a credible and survivable deterrent against New Delhi. Although Pakistan has suggested it would like to follow India's lead in developing a nuclear triad, given resource limitations, Islamabad simply lacks the ability to effectively establish a submarine-based deterrent in the coming decade. At best, Pakistan would be able to deploy SRBMs aboard naval surface ships (or clandestinely aboard civilian freighters) to mimic what India has done with the Dhanush. However, given the advanced state of Pakistan's land-based missile program, it would probably be a better investment of resources to focus upon production of mobile MRBM/IRBM systems that could be concealed throughout the country, yet hold all of India's territory at risk. This is a survivable force that could not be reliably preempted by India and ensures that Pakistan will retain a retaliatory capability regardless of any actions by New Delhi. Strategically, Pakistan simply lacks the rationale for investing in either expensive sea-based or long-range missile delivery systems, and should be content to emphasize the development of its regional nuclear capabilities between now and 2015.

In table 3.12, the wide range of available nuclear targeting and employment options currently available for Pakistan (as of 2005) are listed at local, regional, and global levels.

It should be noted that while it is likely both India and Pakistan exaggerated the results (and yields) of their 1998 nuclear tests, what matters from the analytical standpoint is that while neither may possess boosted-fission or thermonuclear warheads (at least, not yet), both do undoubtedly possess first-generation nuclear capabilities at the very least. As the next section demonstrates, large arsenals of effective (yet simple) first-generation 15–20 kiloton weapons are clearly capable of creating enough destruction to give rival policy makers pause about escalating conflicts with nuclear neighbors. It should also be recognized that it is possible (and I believe highly likely) India and Pakistan do possess boosted-fission weapon capabilities, or will shortly attain them. It is quite conceivable, given India's technical expertise, that it would be able to design (though not test) a workable thermonuclear weapon that might be produced in small numbers. If any of these scenarios (especially regarding the possession of second-generation, "boosted" weapons) proved to be the case, the amount of potential destruction to civilian populations in both countries would be greatly magnified.

**Table 3.12. Available Pakistani Nuclear Targeting and Employment Options**

| | Pakistani Nuclear Targeting and Employment Options | | |
|---|---|---|---|
| Local Theater | Regional Theater | Global | Explicit/Implicit Nuclear Doctrine |
| **Tactical, Local Battlefield Use** **To blunt an opponent's military offensive by targeting conventional forces** (i.e., armored columns, troop concentrations, forward bases and air fields, supply lines, naval forces, etc.). Use as a **"demonstration"** or **"warning shot"** to signal nuclear resolve, encourage outside intervention, or warn of the need for conflict de-escalation. | **Regional Battlefield and Counterforce Use** **Conventional military counterforce usage** (i.e., targeting opponent's military forces, operational bases, command and control sites, supply lines, naval forces). *Limited nuclear counterforce usage* (i.e., targeting opponent's deployed nuclear forces or infrastructure to potentially weaken any subsequent attack) **Regional Countervalue Use** **Countervalue targeting of population centers in neighboring states** (major cities and metropolitan areas). **Countervalue targeting of critical economic infrastructure in neighboring states** (i.e., oil installations—like pipeline pumping stations, refineries, loading terminals—sea ports, heavy industry factories, etc.). **EMP/antisatellite attacks.** **Countervalue targeting of sites of religious or cultural significance to opponents.** **Leadership decapitation or C3I disruption strikes.** | **Extremely Limited** **Unconventional delivery of countervalue or EMP attacks** (i.e. using commercial ships or aircraft). | **Minimal Deterrence Nuclear Doctrine** (Explicit) **Overt nuclear possession strategy.** **Emphasizes survivable, assured destruction retaliatory capability** (i.e., goal is deployment of operational nuclear triad). **Explicit nuclear utilization doctrine** (i.e., envisions tactical use to stop conventional Indian military offensive). |

## Hypothetical Retaliatory Strikes by India and Pakistan

To illustrate the potential destructiveness of current Indian and Pakistani nuclear capabilities, a hypothetical retaliatory exchange will now be described which takes into account the size of both nation's potential arsenals (as of 2005) and the likely types (and ranges) of delivery systems available to each. I assume each side loses one-quarter of their forces in a preemptive strike by their opponent (which may be overly optimistic given the highly mobile and dispersed nature of each side's standing or deployable forces). I also assume both sides would retain one-quarter of their existing forces as a strategic reserve to deter further attacks. I select a number of civilian population (countervalue) targets, describe the number of first-generation (15–20 kiloton) nuclear warheads airburst above them, and the type of delivery system that could be employed. I only consider ballistic missiles in these hypothetical attacks, but the reader should recognize that both sides also possess nuclear-capable aircraft that could be used to target these sites. I have focused upon missiles since these are the more reliable (in terms of penetration of enemy air defenses) of the two types of delivery systems. This leaves each side with one-half of their arsenals for use against their opponents, a total of eighty-nine warheads for India and fifty-six for Pakistan. First, a Pakistani nuclear strike against India.

Given the range capabilities of Pakistan's short- and medium-range missiles, substantial Indian populations centers could be held at risk. Using just seventeen warheads delivered against four cities (Delhi, Ahmadabad, Jaipur, and Vadodara), Pakistan could effectively target 17.1 million Indian civilians.[40] Thirty-nine additional warheads delivered by medium-range missiles could target twelve additional Indian cities (Bombay, Pune, Kanpur, Surat, Lucknow, Indore, Bhopal, Calcutta, Bangalore, Hyderabad, Chennai, and Nagpur) holding a combined population of 55.4 million (Brinkhoff City Population). Thus, a Pakistani attack utilizing only half of its maximum potential total of warheads by 2005 would theoretically hold 72.5 million Indian civilians across sixteen cities subject to nuclear retaliation.

I have made no attempt to estimate the types of casualties produced by these attacks (dead vs. wounded). For the purposes of deterrence, the exact numbers are less important than the reality that this kind of attack on densely populated Indian cities would undoubtedly kill tens of millions of civilians and injure millions more. Imagining a series of eight airbursts using Hiroshima-size weapons (15–20 kilotons) scattered across various parts of New Delhi (population 9.8 million) should leave little doubt of this basic truth. Further, even this casualty figure of 72.5 million Indian civilians could be increased by targeting more existing weapons on cities or factoring in the potential growth of the Pakistani arsenal by 2015. Taking into account the likely size of fissile stockpiles available to Pakistan by the end of the decade, it is conceivable Islamabad could build a total of 264 warheads by 2015, which would mean a strike on India using only half of Pakistan's arsenal would result in 132 weapons (rather than fifty-six) being employed—an addition of seventy-six warheads for use in either saturating the cities listed above or targeting new ones. Without question, this credible, nuclear capability could not possibly be ignored by New Delhi, or its horrific implications minimized by Indian policy makers faced by a crisis with Pakistan.

For Pakistan, the proposition of a nuclear exchange with India would be just as bleak. Assuming India used only half of its existing nuclear arsenal (2005), eighty-nine nuclear warheads would descend upon countervalue targets across Pakistan. While the total Pakistani population held at risk of death or injury from the Indian attack is far lower than the number from an attack on India by Pakistan (primarily due to smaller populations and fewer major urban areas), in terms of proportion of the total population, it is just as dire. All major Pakistani cities would be leveled, and over 26.7 million civilians would be targeted with nuclear retaliation. Just imagining the casualty totals that could be produced in Karachi (2001 population, 9.3 million), Lahore (2001 population, 5.1 million), and Faisalabad (2001 population, 2 million) were eight to twelve Hiroshima-size atomic weapons dropped on each of them should illustrate that only a fraction of India's retaliatory forces would need to strike home to inflict immense casualties on Pakistan (Brinkhoff City Population; Cirincione 2002). As was the case in the last example, the totals could be further inflated by using more weapons or realizing that by 2015, India will have the fissile materials (produced by just three of its main reactors) to produce 286 nuclear warheads—meaning an attack by half of this arsenal would be 143 weapons (rather than eighty-nine), or fifty-four more than the one described above.

Needless to say, given these possibilities, it is difficult to imagine either Indian or Pakistani leaders wishing to peer into Blight's (1992) "shattered crystal ball" during a potential crisis. Rather, given the inescapable destruction that would occur from even far more limited attacks than those described above, it is little wonder both Indian and Pakistani leaders have expressed the belief that major war is now unthinkable and that neither now dare take actions fundamentally threatening the other. Each side is clearly aware of the implications— just as U.S. and Soviet decision makers were during the Cold War.

## THE TERROR USE OF NUCLEAR WEAPONS

Up to this point, our emphasis has been upon potential nuclear strategies available to *state* actors seeking such capabilities primarily to ensure their own central interests using a strategy of deterrence. For such actors, whether it be the U.S., India, Israel, or North Korea, the decision to use nuclear weapons against an opponent would not be made lightly. Even if the opponent were unable to retaliate in-kind, there would be no concealing the identity of the attacker—that they had broken the nuclear taboo, released radiation into the atmosphere (to float over others), and directly killed multitudes of people. Such a decision, regardless of the context, would forever be controversial, just as Truman's August 1945 decision has been to this day. Undoubtedly, even in the absence of direct physical retaliation, there would be sanctions (both economic and political) leveled against the perpetrator by the international community. In countries were public opinion matters, political leaders would likely face harsh questioning and a volatile electorate. And, were retaliation in-kind possible from the victim, as it would be if the attacked were either India or Pakistan, then the long-term consequences of the physical destruction (of both people and property) would be keenly felt.

As a result, though proliferation pessimists warn of the "irrationality" of many state actors, it is far more likely that state actors—not immune to concerns for their own well-being—would behave in a more considered, rational manner regarding resort to such weapons. Although miscalculation and misperception will always be with us, and often play a role in political leaders making decisions not in their best interests, the monumental levels of destruction and the high costs (political, economic, personal) accompanying any use of nuclear weapons would likely "focus" policy makers on the extreme costs rather than the limited benefits of taking aggressive actions. As prospect theory suggests, this should result in less risk-taking behavior on their part. Only outside threats to a state's *key central interests* (sovereignty, regime survival, etc.), where policy makers faced the prospect of losing everything, would the situation likely be dire enough to take such extreme risks and engage in WMD warfare. This returns us to the notion of "credibility of the threat" which is key for deterrence relationships. It is not only the WMD capabilities of a state that matters, but the nature of the threat posed to their national interests that make their threats of use either believable or incredible to opponents. For state actors, a variety of security relationships—including those centered around deterrence—are possible.

Unfortunately, for *nonstate* actors (like terror groups, millennial cults, fanatical religious sects, etc.), these considerations are far less valid. These groups are unlikely to be worried about political legitimacy, and often see the infliction of mass casualties and destruction upon opponents as supported by either their religious or political beliefs. As Hoffman (1998, 94) warns, religion can serve as a "legitimizing force" that lowers the inhibitions a terrorist group might normally have against inflicting indiscriminate, mass casualties on an opponent. Moreover, terror groups like Al Qaeda do not have "return mailing addresses" and therefore are unlikely to be overly concerned about the threat of retaliation from victims. Unlike states, it is difficult to target nonstate actors for direct retaliation since they lack the kind of "fixed targets of high value" possessed by states (e.g., cities, monuments, industries, economic assets controlled by the ruling elites, etc.). Although economic assets and fundraising efforts can be targeted for disruption—as the U.S. has sought to do since 9/11—it will never be possible to eliminate half of a population and a third of an economy with the push of a button as it is for state opponents. Indeed, since deterrence requires the ability of a victim to retaliate and inflict unacceptable levels of damage against an attacker's valued assets, the amorphous nature of nonstate actors makes such deterrence efforts by states impossible.

Because of these difficulties, state actors seldom (if ever) enter into deterrent security relationships with nonstate actors. Instead, they face the kind of "irrational" opponent long feared by pessimists—one uninterested in negotiation, unconcerned about consequences or, in many cases survival, who seeks only to inflict as much harm as possible upon the victim whenever possible. And, unlike state opponents, who are viewed as less threatening when only their peripheral interests are at stake or they possess only rudimentary WMD capabilities, *nonstate actors can credibly threaten WMD use regardless of their level of capability* and they do not have interests easy decompiled into central vs. peripheral areas. As a result, *the state vs. nonstate actor security relationship is the most unstable, most prone to conflict, and least susceptible to notions of deterrence of any that exist.* As noted terrorism expert Jessica Stern observes:

> It is difficult to preempt or deter adversaries whose identities, motivations, and likely responses are unknown. It is also difficult to preempt or deter adversaries whose responses are not rational. . . . For ad hoc groups seeking revenge, acts of violence are likely to be expressive rather than instrumental. They do not measure success by political changes but by a horrified and hurt audience and a humiliated target government. Ad hoc groups have little to lose and are therefore hard to deter. Religious extremists, similarly, may be actively aiming for chaos or, in some cases, for martyrdom. . . . State sponsors, in contrast, may be possible to deter. (Stern 1999, 130–31)

## POTENTIAL FOR STEALTHY NUCLEAR ATTACKS BY NONSTATE ACTORS

The most likely form of nuclear attack upon the U.S. itself (both today and in the future) lies not in the threat of ICBMs fired from distant shores, but from nuclear devices smuggled into the country through its porous borders or fired from just offshore. National missile defenses, even if possible, would not be able to prevent this most probable kind of nuclear threat. Sea-skimming cruise missiles, fired from just offshore, could easily evade detection and strike coastal city targets so rapidly that little could be done to intercept them even if spotted. And, weapons concealed inside shipping containers entering ports or arriving by truck across land borders, could not be intercepted through missile defenses. Further, as Francesco Calogero, chairman of the Pugwash Council, observes:

> [A] device need not be transportable: An easier option would be to build it in a rented garage or apartment near the center of the target city, to be set off by a timer allowing ample time for the perpetrators to get away. It would be easy to smuggle to such a destination a half dozen or so half-liter parcels of highly enriched uranium. A Hiroshima-type nuclear explosive device weapon could then be manufactured rather easily, using openly available information. All the other materials necessary to complete the project could be bought in place without difficulty, presumably without any need to use black market suppliers (except, possibly, to purchase some conventional explosives). (Calogero 2002, 5)

Even a small weapon of only one-kiloton yield could cause immense casualties in a major city if detonated by terrorists. Based on a computer simulation of a one-kiloton explosion in Times Square, New York, during a normal work day, Matthew McKinzie, a staff scientist at the Natural Resources Defense Council, found over 20,000 people would be killed instantly, and that up to a quarter-mile away, all those exposed to a direct view of the fireball would receive fatal doses of radiation. Up to a quarter-million workers would be affected by the attack to some degree, and radioactive fallout would spread at least five to ten miles from ground zero (Keller 2002, 57). As Spiers (2000, 80) observes:

> The potential effects of nuclear terrorism have always been formidable: if a group with sufficient skills was able to obtain about 30 pounds of highly enriched uranium, which is easily carried in a briefcase, or a small amount of plutonium (baseball size), and then spent some $200,000 acquiring readily available materials and equipment, it could build a nuclear device within a couple of months. Had such a nuclear device been in the mini van placed at the World Trade Center, it is estimated that "the lower part of Manhattan would have disappeared up to Gramercy Park, all of Wall Street."

Of course, the construction of a nuclear device by terror groups—either outside the U.S. or with components smuggled into the country—would be no simple task. But could it be accomplished, there is little question a group like

Al Qaeda would seek to use it against a target to produce a maximum level of casualties. And, as former UN weapons inspector David Albright observes, while the technical difficulties in assembling a working weapon should not be underestimated, it is also a mistake to overestimate the hurdles—especially if you are dealing with a well-organized terror group that has no interest in maintaining a reliable, safe arsenal and is willing to take the risk its jury-rigged weapon will either not achieve its full yield (or fail to explode at all). As Albright suggests, "as you get smarter, you realize you can get by with less . . . You can do it in facilities that look like barns, garages, with simple machine tools. You can do it with 10 to 15 people, not all Ph.D.'s, but some engineers, technicians. Our judgment is that a gun-type device is well within the capability of a terrorist organization" (Keller 2002, 28–29).

There are also legitimate concerns about the use by terror groups of stolen nuclear fuels created for use in nuclear power plants. For example, a study by Barnaby (2002, 1) found that "a terrorist organization could relatively easily extract the plutonium and fabricate a nuclear explosive having first acquired MOX fuel [containing a mixture of uranium oxide ($UO2$) and plutonium oxide ($PuO2$)]." As Barnaby warns:

> The procedures required for the chemical separation of plutonium from uranium in MOX fuel pellets would be simple and well within the technological capabilities of a moderately sophisticated terrorist organization. The preparation of Sarin for the attack on the Tokyo underground involved considerably more sophisticated chemistry and greater acute danger to the operators than that required for the separation of plutonium from MOX. The chemistry is less sophisticated than that required for the illicit preparation of designer drugs. (Barnaby 2002, 2)

Sophisticated terrorist groups, who successfully obtained MOX fuel through diversion or theft, would have "little difficulty in making a crude nuclear explosive" with yields of anywhere from a "few tens of tons of TNT" to perhaps even "one thousand tons or more." Even if the resulting explosion were minimal or nonexistent, a substantial radiological event would be produced due to the dispersal by conventional explosives of plutonium-oxide over a wide area. Once dispersed, plutonium-oxide (with a half-life of 24,400 years) is insoluble in rainwater, remains in surface dusts and soil for long periods of time, and renders a large part of any city "uninhabitable until decontaminated, a procedure which could take many months or years" (Barnaby 2002, 5).

It is also highly feasible to construct weapons using powdered plutonium or uranium oxide powder instead of the more difficult to obtain metallic plutonium. In fact, Stober (2003, 63) notes a group of well-known Los Alamos weapon designers concluded that oxide powder of either type "would seem to be the simplest and most rapid way to make a bomb." Moreover, terrorists could simply "pour the oxide into a container until it began producing neutrons," a level that would be close to a critical mass (and the amount required for a bomb whose yield could be from tens to hundreds of kilotons) (Stober 2003, 63). Indeed, as Barnaby (2002, 4–5) explains, the technical issues surrounding the use of plutonium-oxide for construction of crude nuclear weapons are not complex and certainly not beyond the technical ability of future terror groups:

A nuclear device could be constructed using either PuO2 or plutonium in metal form. But the critical mass of PuO2 is considerably greater than that of the metal. The critical mass of reactor-grade plutonium in the form of PuO2 crystals is about 35 kilograms, if in spherical shape; while that of reactor-grade plutonium metal is about 13 kilograms. A terrorist group prepared to convert the plutonium oxide to the metal would, therefore, need to acquire significantly less PuO2. A bare sphere of reactor-grade PuO2 having a critical mass would be about 18 centimeters in diameter; a bare sphere of plutonium metal having a critical mass would be about six centimeters in diameter. The sphere could be placed in the center of a mass of conventional high explosive to compress it to super-criticality. The critical mass can be reduced and the size of the explosion increased by using a "reflector/tamper": a shell of material, such as beryllium or uranium, that surrounds the plutonium sphere. The high explosive . . . it is more likely that a terrorist group would use . . . Semtex . . . is easier to handle and can be molded into a spherical shape around the plutonium sphere ensuring more even compression of the plutonium. About 400 kilograms of plastic explosive, molded around the reflector/tamper . . . should be sufficient to compress the plutonium enough. If PuO2 is used it could be contained in a spherical vessel, or it could be cast into two hemispheres by melting it at very high temperatures in suitable molds. The molded hemispheres of PuO2 would be placed on top of each other to make a sphere with their flat surfaces separated by one centimeter of a compressible material such as expanded polystyrene. The sphere would be surrounded by the reflector/tamper, and then surrounded by plastic explosives. The assembled device would have a radius of about 40 centimeters constructed from 18 kilograms of PuO2. If seven kilograms of Pu metal were used instead, and the Pu sphere (with a radius of just 4.8 centimeters) was surrounded by a five-centimeter shell of beryllium and 400-kilograms of plastic explosive, the radius of the total device would be just less than 40 centimeters. A large number of detonators (say, about 50) would be inserted symmetrically into the plastic explosive to give a roughly symmetrical shock wave to compress the plutonium sphere. The detonators would be fired simultaneously by an electronic circuit. A remote radio signal or timer would trigger the electronic circuit.

The danger would also be great were a terror group able to obtain reactor-grade plutonium—through either diversion or theft—since weapons may also be fashioned from such materials. As Matthew Bunn, former chairman of the U.S. National Academy of Sciences study of issues surrounding the disposal of plutonium removed from existing nuclear weapons, observed during a 1997 conference:

> For an unsophisticated proliferator, making a crude bomb with a reliable, assured yield of a kiloton or more—and hence a destructive radius about one-third to one-half that of the Hiroshima bomb—from reactor-grade plutonium would require no more sophistication than making a bomb from weapon-grade plutonium. And major weapon states like the United States and Russia could, if they chose to do so, make bombs with reactor-grade plutonium with yield, weight, and reliability characteristics similar to those made from weapon-grade plutonium. That they have not chosen to do so in the past has to do with convenience and a desire to avoid radiation doses to workers and military personnel, not the difficulty of accomplishing the job. Indeed, one Russian weapon-designer who has focused on this issue in detail criticized the information declassified by the US Department of Energy for failing to point out that in some respects it would actually be easier for an unsophisticated proliferator to make a bomb from reactor-grade plutonium (as no neutron generator would be required).

The same would undoubtedly hold true for a well-funded, sophisticated terror group able to obtain reactor-grade material. Robert Seldon, a former U.S. weapons designer, citing the test of a bomb using reactor-grade plutonium at the Nevada test site in 1962, warns that "all plutonium can be used directly in nuclear explosives. The concept of . . . plutonium which is not suited for explosives is fallacious" (Stober 2003, 62). Indeed, while the high percentage of plutonium-240 in reactor-grade material would pose more of a radiation risk, reduce the maximum yield of the weapon, and require the use of more fuel than would be required were weapons-grade plutonium used, Carson Mark, former head of the theoretical division at Los Alamos from 1947 to 1972, observed that "any group sophisticated enough to fabricate a bomb from weapons-grade plutonium could handle reactor plutonium as well" (Stober 2003, 63).

Yet, while much attention has been placed upon the possibility that terrorists might smuggle nuclear weapons or radiological bombs into the U.S., the reality is that just as the World Trade Center terrorists used airliners already in the country to stage their attacks, there are plenty of sources of nuclear materials domestically that pose a threat to security. Indeed, of the 103 nuclear power plants in the U.S., almost half have failed drills over the past decade simulating mock attacks by terrorists on these facilities (Pasternak 2001, 44–46; Wald 2001). Classified reports from Sandia National Laboratories suggest a significant release of radiation could be caused by well-placed truck bombs targeting spent fuel storage facilities (mostly soft targets) or external water or electrical supplies (Pasternak 2001, 46; Archibold 2001). After the September 11th terrorist attacks, the U.S. Nuclear Regulatory Commission began reviewing security at the nation's nuclear plants and noted that while a direct hit from a commercial airliner would not cause a nuclear explosion, "the danger would come from the release of high levels of radiation caused by a break in the protective barriers that seal in radiation produced by reactors" (Archibold 2001; Guterl 2001, 28).[41]

Similarly, the vulnerability of nuclear weapons laboratories and manufacturing plants are a growing concern. Like nuclear power plants, many of these U.S. facilities have failed security drills simulating terrorist attacks. In 1997, a drill conducted at the Los Alamos National Laboratory resulted in infiltrators, played by Navy Seals, obtaining enough weapons-grade uranium to construct a number of nuclear weapons and wheeling it out of the compound in a garden cart (Wald 2002). There is also the less likely possibility more sophisticated terrorists could infiltrate such facilities and assemble a crude nuclear device from the stored materials obtained and detonate it at the site, spreading radioactive material widely around the surrounding region. As Ron Timm, a former Energy Department security official, noted, in some cases, assembling a device without the use of explosives could be accomplished by manually bringing uranium parts together to start a chain reaction. At the far end of this potential threat spectrum, physicist Frank N. von Hippel notes that a 100-pound mass of uranium dropped from a height of six feet onto a second 100-pound mass would result in a blast of between five and ten kilotons, destroying an area five to ten square miles in diameter (Wald 2002). Indeed, as Nobel Laureate Luis Alvarez warns:

> With modern weapon-grade uranium, the background neutron rate is so low that terrorists, if they have such material, would have a good chance of setting off a high-yield explosion simply by dropping one half of the material onto the other half. . . . Most people seem unaware that if separated, highly enriched uranium is at hand, it's a trivial job to set off a nuclear explosion . . . even a high school kid could make a bomb in short order. (Stober 2003, 63)

Aside from bomb-grade materials, radioactive materials provide a tempting target for terrorists seeking to construct radiological devices using conventional explosives to cause contamination of a target. Though not true nuclear weapons, and hence, not a focus of this book, radiological weapons would be the easiest use by terrorists of radioactive materials since they do not require either the ability to fabricate a working nuclear device nor the amount (or purity) of fissile material required to create nuclear detonations (Keller 2002). Further, there have already been instances where terror groups have sought to employ such devices. For example, in November 1995, after Chechen separatists threatened to explode a radiological device in Moscow, Russian authorities discovered seventy pounds of cesium-137 at Ismailovsky Park—one of Moscow's most popular tourist spots (Smithson and Levy 200, 9).

## CONCLUSION

In this chapter, the potential nuclear capabilities of a variety of state actors (Iran, North Korea, Israel, India, and Pakistan) were evaluated. These capabilities were also projected into the future—ten to fifteen years—to illustrate how these changing nuclear capabilities will provide a variety of new nuclear "options" for these states and potentially alter existing interstate security relationships. Clearly, nuclear proliferation threatens to change the rules of the game, transforming conventional Melians into ones capable of devastating retaliation against opponents threatening their central interests. But, nuclear weapons are not the only WMD that threatens to alter existing state security relationships. Though most attention tends to be devoted to nuclear threats, the proliferation of biological weapons capabilities to state and nonstate actors also threatens to initiate substantial changes in security relationships in the coming decades. In the next two chapters, we turn to this growing bioweapons threat, and how these may also turn lambs into lions.

## NOTES

1. Another study estimated one 15-kiloton weapon dropped on Bombay would cause between 150,000 and 850,000 deaths. See Ramana and Nayyar 2001, 82.

2. There is substantial criticism of these test results due to lack of putting equipment through realistic test scenarios actually exposing equipment to the type and magnitude of EMP effects that would occur in real environments. In fact, there are strong reasons to believe a great deal of equipment would fail at substantially lower EMP levels. See comments of Dr. Graham and Dr. Wood in *Electromagnetic Pulse Threats*, 7 October 1999.

3. Obviously, the recent U.S. development of a deliverable EMP weapon, designed to make use of the disruptive effects of EMP on an opponent's power grids, communications, command and control, and missile and weapons components, requires new nuclear states to "harden" their strategic weapons sites to ensure survivability. This should not prove beyond the capabilities of new nuclear states. As Grace (1994, 100–1) explains: "The simplest as well as the most obvious way of protecting a system against EMP is to put it inside an electromagnetic shield, called a 'global shield.' This may be made of any reasonably good conductor such as steel, aluminum or copper, and need not be very thick—3 mm of steel is more than adequate. However, it is essential that it should be free of gaps and apertures through which EMP energy could

enter. . . . If one ensures that the shield is able to reduce the EMP fields inside to about 1 volt/metre, then within the shield no special precautions need to be taken. Indeed, ordinary commercial equipment, not hardened in any way against EMP, may be installed inside it."

4. There is some evidence to suggest, based on interviews with key Hussein associates, that Saddam did not believe the U.S. would actually go to war and invade the country in 2003. See Shanker 2004.

5. Indeed, a January 2005 briefing to the Israeli Knesset by Meir Dagan, head of the Mossad intelligence agency, warned Iran could build a bomb in less than three years, and if it successfully enriched uranium in 2005, could have a weapon two years later. See BBC News 2005. By August 2005, Israeli intelligence had adjusted its estimate to Iran having the bomb as early as 2008, "if all goes well for it," but probably by 2012. See Halpern 2005.

6. Agreeing with this assessment, London's International Institute for Strategic Studies concluded Iran would not be expected to build nuclear weapons before the next decade. See Cowell 2005.

7. The IAEA, after two years of inspections, has stated it has not found evidence of any weapons program. See Jehl and Schmitt 2005.

8. For a detailed discussion of Iran's post-revolution pursuit of nuclear, biological, and chemical weapons, see Giles 2000, 79–103.

9. Uranium ore can be converted into uranium hexafluoride, which when heated, turns into a gas that can be fed through centrifuges to obtain U-235.

10. For example, see the inflated projections of the infamous Rumsfeld Commission report of 1999.

11. As noted by Elliott and Barry (1994, 37), "Kim has batteries of rocket artillery housed in tunnels bored into hillsides, protected by blast doors. The rockets can be fired without leaving their lairs (the rocket launchers come up on elevators; the doors open; bang; the doors close; the launchers go down). So to destroy the launchers with conventional arms, you have about a minute while they are in the open."

12. This estimate is found in a book by Albright and O'Neill on the Korean Nuclear Puzzle, which was a report from the Department of State/Department of Energy Spent Fuel Canning Team, and was cited in "Visit to the Yongbyon" by Siegfried S. Hecker. How many weapons this material would translate into depends upon whether one assumes four or five kilograms of material per weapon.

13. During talks between cabinet-level delegations in Seoul in July 2003, North Korean envoys warned "our nation faces a stark situation as the black clouds of a nuclear war are coming toward the Korean peninsula minute by minute." See "North Korea 'Reprocessing Nuclear Fuel.'"

14. The lower estimate is generated by my own fairly conservative estimates of North Korean production. The high estimate is found in Wolfsthal (July 2003).

15. This example assumes targeting three warheads each on Seoul (2002 population, 10.2 million) and Incheon (2002 population, 2.6 million), and one warhead each on Goyang (840,000), Bucheon (821,000), Euijeongbu (380,500), Shibeung (359,000), Chuncheon (253,532), and Anyang (600,000). These cities lie as close as fifteen miles (Goyang) and eighteen miles (Bucheon) from the DMZ to only 30–31

miles away (Seoul, Chuncheon, Anyang). See Brinkhoff City Population and Cirincione 2002.

16. This was a key motivating factor in Japan's decision in December 2003 to begin building a missile defense system, as well as the realization that North Korea's 100 Rodong missiles could hit any point in Japan in roughly ten minutes. See McAvoy 2003.

17. In February 2000, the Israeli parliament actually held the first public discussion since the early 1960s on the subject of Israel's nuclear weapons program. The hearings ended after only fifty-two minutes and did not result in any significant discussion or airing of the subject. See Sontag 2000.

18. Feldman 1982, 45. Other analysts, such as Cirincione (2002, 224), assume Israel does not possess thermonuclear weapons due to a lack of past tests.

19. It should be noted the F-15E Strike Eagle has a nuclear role in the U.S. Air Force.

20. Israel has reportedly actively deployed at least fifty of both types of missile.

21. In describing how much fissile material is usually produced by reactors, Zimmerman (1993, 351), notes "the rule of thumb is for every one megawatt (thermal)-day of reactor operation one gram of plutonium is produced. If six kilograms of plutonium are needed to produce a bomb, the production reactor must be operated for 6,000 megawatt (thermal) days. A 100 MW(t) reactor would, therefore, have to operate around the clock for sixty days to produce the active material for one bomb. In order to reduce the content of 240 PU in the total plutonium inventory, one must frequently change the fuel rods in the reactor. As a result, the duty factor of a plutonium production reactor is probably only about 60–70 percent, extending the required number of calendar days to produce material for a bomb."

22. Israel does possess the nuclear infrastructure needed to jump-start an enriched-uranium program, including uranium phosphate mining operations in the Negev area, near Beersheeba; two yellowcake production plants; and a uranium purification, conversion, and fuel-fabrication facility at Dimona (and possibly a pilot-scale enrichment facility as well)—none of which are under IAEA inspection. See Cirincione 2002, 234.

23. Cohen reports on the eve of war, two "improvised" nuclear weapons were assembled.

24. The most authoritative account of the history of Israel's nuclear weapons program is found in Cohen's excellent book, *Israel and the Bomb* (1998), which was until very recently banned in Israel, with the author facing arrest if he returned to Israel.

25. Interviews by the author with a number of anonymous senior-level U.S. government officials.

26. See also NRDC Nuclear Notebook March/April 2002, 70–72 and NRDC Nuclear Notebook January/February 2002, 70–71.

27. For those interested in the details of this controversy surrounding India's nuclear tests, Tellis 2001 provides an excellent overview.

28. This assessment assumes five kilograms of plutonium per weapon to arrive at seventy-four warheads from 370 kilograms of material.

29. Note that Heisbourg's calculations assuming the ability to construct between seventy and eighty nuclear devices from 400 kilograms of plutonium assumes between 5.7 and 5.0 kilograms of plutonium per weapon respectively.

30. Canadian CANDU reactor design (used by most Indian nuclear power plants) produces spent fuel with fairly low concentrations of the troublesome, heat-producing Pu-238 isotope, thereby reducing the problems faced by Indian nuclear scientists in using these nonweapons-grade materials in warheads.

31. See www.bharat-rakshak.com/IAF/Aircraft/Specs/Su-30.html.

32. This calculation assumes Pakistan is using twenty kilograms of highly enriched uranium per weapon.

33. See also the materials available on the Sino-Pakistani nuclear relationship and South Asia security on the Center for Nonproliferation Studies, Monterey, California, website at http://cns.miis.edu.

34. There have been numerous, excellent overviews of the dynamics (both political and security-based) that motivated India to pursue a nuclear arsenal (see Sundarji 1996; Paul 1998; Kampani 1998; Ganguly 1999; Perkovich 1999, 2000). For example, Perkovich (1999, 6), in the most in-depth analysis of the history of India's nuclear weapons program, argues domestic political considerations have been the driving force behind the weapons program, and development efforts have "only vaguely responded to an ill-defined security threat." Similarly, there have also been numerous overviews of the dynamics (both political and security-based) that motivated Pakistan to pursue a nuclear arsenal (see Beg 1996, Ahmed 1999). All of these analyses differ with regards to the importance placed upon domestic versus bureaucratic versus security variables.

35. See also Subrahmanyam 1993, 7.

36. See, for example, Sidhu 2000, 125–57 and Cheema 2000, 158–81.

37. See also Subrahmanyam 1998, 1.

38. "*Weaponization* need not mean that the nuclear warhead has already been married to the bomb-casing or placed in the missile's warhead compartment. Likewise, *deployed* need not mean that the completely assembled missile has to be in or very near its launch pad. If the doctrine demands reaction within say 6 hours, the definition of 'weaponized' and 'deployed' would reflect the state of readiness which such doctrine demands."

39. Similarly, Ganguly (Spring 1999, 176), suggests that India's leadership and strategic community have "argued that a 'minimum deterrent' of some thirty to forty bombs that can be delivered by air would constitute a sufficient deterrent."

40. This assumes eight warheads targeting Delhi (2001 population, 9.8 million) and three warheads each for Ahmadabad (2001 population, 3.5 million), Jaipur (2001 population, 2.3 million), and Vadodara (2001 population, 1.5 million). See Brinkhoff City Population and Cirincione 2002.

41. See also Begley 2001, 32 and U.S. Congress, House of Representatives, Statement of Paul Leventhal 2001.

# 4

# Biological Proliferation and the Future of Warfare

People don't realize biological weapons could be the most sophisticated weapons. Biological weapons could be used covertly. There are a lot of different deployment scenarios. There are a lot of different techniques to manufacture biological weapons. And a lot of different agents could be used in biological weapons.

—Ken Alibek, 2001(Wolfinger "Interviews: Bill Patrick and Ken Alibek" 2001)

While the blinding flash and mushroom cloud of nuclear weapons have dominated security thinking over the past sixty years, a far less visible, but equally deadly menace has slipped beneath the radar screens of most analysts. It is an ancient form of warfare, and with the rapid advancements of scientific knowledge and biotechnology, now holds an *equal* potential for inflicting harm upon mankind. It is a form of warfare often misunderstood, underestimated, and dismissed as either "too difficult to effectively utilize" or "morally repugnant." Yet, as will be explained in the next two chapters, the first charge is wildly inaccurate, and growing increasingly so with each passing day, and the second, while accurate, has yet to slow the development or use of any weapon in human history. Whether or not we would wish that medical advancements and greater understandings of the human genome and immune system would lead to a world without disease or misery, the hard reality of the security environment which dawns at the beginning of the twenty-first century is one in which state and nonstate actors will increasingly have available biowarfare capabilities that easily rival or surpass the destructive potential obtained from splitting the atom. As Nobel Prize–winning scientist Joshua Lederberg (2001, 7) warns:

> Unlike nuclear weapons, the capability for BW is unlikely to be reliably contained by any degree of legal prohibition and formal verification. The facilities required for producing and dispensing BW agents are modest, easily concealable, and almost indistinguishable from licit production of pharmaceuticals and vaccines. The same holds for the underlying technical knowledge, which is part and parcel of medical research and education. The potential for grave enhancement of virulence and the intractability of pathogens for BW use go hand in hand with the advances of biotechnology for human life enhancement.

In this chapter, the ramifications of the proliferation of bioweapons technologies and capabilities throughout the international system are examined. Included are critical questions such as, Who might be able to achieve biowarfare capabilities? How difficult is it technically to acquire and develop bioweapons? What is the nature of the future threat spectrum, especially given the potential utility to bioweaponeers of rapid advancements currently being made in biotechnology and genetic engineering? What lessons might we learn from previous state-run BW programs? What strategies or tactics are available to bioweapon states, and how might these capabilities impact future security relationships? And finally, how great is the potential for terrorist organizations to make effective use of bioweapons to achieve their goals in the coming decades?

Unfortunately, the answers to these questions are not reassuring and suggest over the coming decades, *biological weapons will pose a far greater threat to U.S. security than will nuclear weapons*. Bioweapons will be more readily available to potential opponents technically, and more impossible to control using traditional counterproliferation policies. For terrorists as well as for states, bioweapons provide the ultimate in stealthy, asymmetrical warfare and are well suited to clandestine development and employment—a must for the weak seeking to strike at the strong. As a November 2001 report observes, not only is the "operational utility" of nuclear and biological weapons now becoming more widely acknowledged, but also the realization such weapons have strategic utility because "the credible capability to hold friendly cities and other important civilian assets at risk . . . could confer significant strategic advantages to a regional aggressor, even if its overall NBC capability was limited" (Center for Counterproliferation Research 200, 4–6).[1]

Indeed, just as the rapid spread of nuclear capabilities can radically alter the security relationships between states (described in chapters 2 and 3), so does proliferation of biowarfare technologies and capabilities throughout the international system. Dr. Matthew Meselson, a key adviser to President

Nixon when the U.S. renounced biowarfare in the 1972 treaty, in explaining the administration's rationale observed:

> First, it was understood that biological weapons could be as great a threat to large populations as nuclear weapons and that no reliable defense is likely. . . . Second, it was evident that biological weapons could be much simpler and less expensive than nuclear weapons to develop and produce. . . . Third, it was realized that our biological weapons program was pioneering an easily duplicated technology and that our program was likely to inspire others to follow suit. (Dando 1994, 11)

Meselson warned that the U.S. has a "major interest" in keeping other nations from acquiring bioweapon arsenals, because the existing balance of power could be upset by states possessing "germ weapons that could threaten a large city"—especially since these bioweapons "are much simpler and cheaper to acquire than the corresponding nuclear weapons." Moreover, while biotechnology advances and we gain more knowledge about the inner workings of disease pathogens—mapping out their genomes in intricate detail—the "dual-use" quality of all medical research increasingly comes into play. As Koblentz (2003/2004, 87) observes, "the offense-defense balance in biological warfare strongly favor the attacker because developing and using biological weapons to cause casualties is significantly easier and less expensive than developing and fielding defenses against them."

## WHO MIGHT BE ABLE TO ACQUIRE BIOWARFARE CAPABILITIES?

Discussions of "who" might actually possess biowarfare capabilities are sometimes contentious, and generally based upon assessments made by analysts within governmental intelligence communities or by outside academic experts. Official government publications and statements often produce lists of potential BW proliferants that read like the list of the "usual suspects" produced by the police chief in *Casablanca*. And though the wildly exaggerated claims by the Bush administration regarding the existence of WMDs in Iraq introduces a cautionary note against uncritical acceptance of such lists, it is nevertheless important to consider in our analyses both the "offensive" and "defensive" BW capabilities possessed by states (and nonstate actors), along with informed speculation by outside analysts regarding their potential. The reason for this is a simple one. No nation on earth freely acknowledges possession of "offensive" bioweapons programs, and those involved in BW-related areas of research invariably describe them as "defensive" programs allowed under the Biological Weapons Treaty, making it largely impossible using open sources to conclusively "prove" the biowarfare intentions of any particular country. Instead, *realistic threat analysis* requires a degree of supposition on the part of analysts along with a "reasonable" amount of worst-case thinking—which doesn't wildly exaggerate the possibilities (as occurred with Iraq), but at the same time, doesn't dismiss reasonable hypotheses regarding potentially viable threat scenarios either.

Unfortunately, the problem of generating realistic threat assessments is greatly complicated by the "dual-use" nature of all bioweapons-related research, since *all* "defensive" research also provides information valuable for improving the effectiveness or military viability of "offensive" biowarfare programs. The technical task of understanding how disease organisms infect their hosts, what causes their virulence, how easily they are disseminated, and detailed genetic mapping of their genomes all provide the basis for development of vaccines, new generations of antibiotics or antiviral drugs, ideas for boosting the human immune system, development of protective equipment, and the means for developing effective clinical diagnostic, detection, or field-testing kits. Yet, this same knowledge could also assist bioweaponeers by providing techniques for modifying existing pathogens (or creating novel ones) that could evade vaccines or existing antibiotics/antiviral drugs to more efficiently overwhelm the human immune system. It could provide guidance for developing techniques to deliver these agents so they could be disseminated more effectively and persist in the environment without degradation. Advances in the pharmaceutical industry to microencapsulate peptides to prevent degradation in the environment is a technique necessary for aerosol delivery of drugs and vaccines, but equally useful for BW purposes (Dando 1994, 110).

Inevitably, with biowarfare, what is "offensive" or "defensive" research is determined not so much by the actual nature of the work, but by the motivations and intentions of the scientists carrying it out. Indeed, as former Soviet bioweaponeer Sergei Popov observed, in the initial stages of *either* defensive or offensive bioweapons research, it's the "same process" with only the "intent of a bioprogram, not a technical or material difference, that separates defensive from offensive capability" (Kelley and Coghlan 2003, 27). In fact, if elements in the current "defensive" U.S. BW program were seen in other countries (say North Korea or Iran, for instance), Washington would no doubt view the activities with deep suspicion and as evidence of "offensive" intent. For example, work at the new Livermore BSL-3 biofacilities focusing on aerosolizing bioagents to conduct animal challenges (a key step toward weaponization) or its related work with genetically modified agents (Kelley and Coghlan 2003). Similarly, various "defensive" research efforts run by the CIA, Defense Department, and Department of Energy have sought to, among other things: (1) reconstruct the multiantibiotic resistant Russian super strain of anthrax to see if the U.S. vaccine is effective against it (due to fears it may have fallen into the hands of rogue states or terrorists); (2) constructing and testing Soviet-era biobomblets to see how efficiently they distribute agent (in case rogue states were to obtain them); and (3) assembling small laboratories using "off-the-shelf" materials capable of producing high quality bioagents (such as powdered anthrax) to see how detectable such facilities would be to U.S. surveillance methods and how difficult constructing hidden facilities would be for rogues or nonstate actors. As Wheelis and Dando (2003, 44) observe:

> [T]he investigation into the anthrax letter attacks revealed that the United States had an ongoing program to produce dried, weaponized anthrax spores for defensive testing. How much was made is unclear, but multiple production runs were apparently conducted over many years, and total production must have been in the 10s or 100s of grams of dried anthrax spores. Since a single gram of anthrax spores contains millions of lethal doses, the quantities produced seem unjustifiable for peaceful purposes under the bioweapons treaty. Whether excess spores were stockpiled or destroyed—or whether they can even be adequately accounted for—is unknown.

Obviously, were China or North Korea engaged in similar research, the U.S. would argue (as analysts such as Wheelis and Dando (2003, 44) have done regarding American efforts) that these actions violated the Biological Weapons Convention. Thus, while the same research can be justified as either "defensive" or "offensive," depending upon ones assumptions regarding the underlying motivations of those involved, it illustrates how difficult the task of ascertaining the nature of state BW programs is—especially in an era where if states do not "push the envelope" of defensive biotechnical research, they will be unable to defend themselves against opponents using these new technologies to augment their bioarsenals.

As a result, unlike the discussions of potential state *nuclear capabilities* likely to exist over the coming decades presented in the last chapter, there will be no substantial effort in the remaining chapters to conclusively demonstrate specific BW capabilities of various state or nonstate actors around the world over similar time frames. This would require access to highly classified intelligence and still, in all likelihood, require a substantial dose of supposition. Instead, the following chapters will refer briefly to what is publicly known or assumed about various state BW programs or capabilities, and direct most of the discussion on the more generic questions of "what is possible?" "how might it be done?" and "what would be the impact upon state security of various BW capabilities?" This focus should help provide analysts with a foundation for making assessments of individual cases should additional information come to light. Therefore, with these caveats in mind, what is the current state of biological proliferation or the quality of ongoing (potentially offensive) bioweapons programs today?

In November 2001, John Bolton, undersecretary for arms control and international security, charged at a biological weapons conference in Geneva that Iraq, North Korea, Libya, Syria, Iran, and Sudan were pursuing biological weapons. Bolton argued North Korea "likely has the capability to produce sufficient quantities of biological agents for military purposes within weeks of a decision to do so," and that Iran has probably produced and "weaponized" biological warfare agents (Mufson 2001). And while the intensely partisan Bolton's "objectivity" is open to question, as well as the accuracy of some of his more extreme claims regarding the BW programs purported to exist in Cuba and Iraq, his general claims about the widespread proliferation of BW programs across the globe finds more support.[2] For example, a classified 1998 CIA report concluded that clandestine stocks of smallpox probably remained in North Korea, Iraq, and Russia. In addition, China, Cuba, India, Iran, Israel, Pakistan, and the former Yugoslavia have also been suggested to have possibly retained smallpox samples from earlier periods when the disease was present in those nations (Begley "Unmasking Bioterror" 2001, 25). As Popov, a leading virologist, who worked in the Soviet BW program at the top secret Vector facility during the 1980s and 1990s observed, close cooperation existed among former Soviet Cold War allies in the biological field: "We had a nice collaboration with North Korea . . . they traveled to our facilities several times." Further, the North Korean program succeeded in obtaining large quantities of anthrax, cholera, and plague bacteria from a Japanese commercial firm during the 1970s (Begley "Tracking Anthrax" 2001, 38). Other countries often suggested by experts as possessing BW programs include Egypt, Algeria, and Taiwan (Mufson 2001).

## HOW DIFFICULT IS OBTAINING BW CAPABILITY?

How difficult is it for a state to acquire the requisite technology and knowledge needed for development of a strategic or tactical BW capability? Further, what is the likelihood of terrorist groups obtaining bioweapons knowhow or capabilities in the near future? To answer these questions, we must consider, firstly, how technically difficult (or accessible) the basic technical skills or materials needed to develop bioweapons capabilities are for state and nonstate actors. Secondly, it requires an understanding of just how difficult it would be for states or terror groups to obtain the knowledge or technical expertise to weaponize their BW agents from former scientists or technicians who had worked in state-run BW programs (the "brain drain" issue). For states, the hurdles are easily surmountable and the promise of bioweapons capabilities readily within reach. For terror groups, the obstacles are much greater, but not impossible to traverse.

A March 1997 DoD report to Congress noted: "For chemical and biological weapons in particular, the potential for proliferation is almost unlimited. Any state with a basic chemical, petrochemical, pharmaceutical, biotechnological, or related industry can produce basic chemical or biological agents (Technical Annex 1997). Similarly, a more recent U.S. Defense Department report from October 2001 noted that *any* country possessing a sufficient munitions-production infrastructure (like Iran, North Korea, or China) also possessed the ability to accomplish weaponization of BW agents (Department of Defense October 2001, 20–21). The report warns that while efficient weaponization of agents requires "design and production skills" normally found in countries with munitions development infrastructures, "crude agent dispersal devices could be fabricated by almost any nation or group" (Department of Defense October 2001, 25). Since "many of the technologies and processes used for weaponizing chemical warfare agents can be applied to biological warfare agents," it is exceedingly difficult to completely control the diffusion of technology for production of bomblets and sprayers to new proliferators. Moreover, the Pentagon warns "there is little to distinguish a vaccine or pharmaceutical plant from a biological agent facility" given "virtually all equipment, technology, and materials needed for biological agent production are dual use" (Department of Defense October 2001, 18). As former secretary of defense Cohen (2001, xii) observes:

> Virtually all the equipment, technology, and materials needed for biological agent production are dual use. . . . Very little differentiates a facility producing vaccines or antibiotics from one that produces lethal pathogens or toxins. Therefore, any facility being used for the good of mankind could also be used to produce these lethal agents, and could be disguised as a legitimate business.

There is also lively debate among bioterrorism specialists regarding the degree of knowledge or training required to effectively develop bioagents and weaponize them sufficiently to carry out attacks. Some argue terrorist groups would have to acquire teams of scientists with advanced degrees to stage such an attack, while others suggest only basic training or a background in microbiology would be sufficient.[3] Smithson and Levy (2000, 48) note the general consensus among professionals seemed to be that "higher skill levels are needed" to effectively carry out biological attacks. Thus, despite websites purporting to provide all the knowledge and recipes needed for would-be bioweaponeers to stage attacks (the oft-stated "kook in the basement" scenario), it is *extremely unlikely* terror groups composed of members with limited training in the biological sciences or relying upon Internet sources alone could actually carry off an effective, large-scale strike.

That being said, this *does not* rule out the ability of such groups to develop effective BW capabilities *if* they acquire individuals with graduate-level expertise (or higher) in the relevant biological sciences or, better yet, technical advice from those who once worked in state-run bioweapons programs. As former Soviet bioweaponeer Alibek notes, "It's not difficult. . . . Not everybody can do it. But if you have some knowledge, you can do it . . . (at a cost of) not millions, maybe thousands of dollars" (Broad and Miller 26 October 2001). Similarly, former U.S. bioweaponeer Bill Patrick warns if one is faced with "an honest-to-goodness terrorist who knows what he is doing, your probability of defeating him is very slim" (Miller, Engelberg, and Broad 2001, 163). In fact, Patrick suggests a knowledgeable terrorist who possessed a starter culture of Tularemia, could grow enough bacteria in thirty-six hours on a thousand agar plates to produce five liters of material, which could then be used to attack a large office building using no more than a blender, cheesecloth, a garden sprayer, and some widely available hospital supplies (Miller, Engelberg, and Broad 2001, 163).

Indeed, a growing number of analysts argue the technical and financial hurdles barring state or nonstate actors from developing substantial BW arsenals are not insurmountable (Cole 1997; Falkenrath et al. 1998). Patrick notes the potential culprit(s) in the U.S. anthrax mail attacks could easily be someone with specialized knowledge: "A disgruntled professor who didn't get tenure, he could do it . . . He wouldn't provide the ultimate, like we did. But he'd do all right" (Broad and Miller 26 October 2001). Moreover, according to Falkenrath et al. (1998, 112), a small team composed of individuals with "good skills in experimental microbiology and engineering, provided they are capable of carrying out a multistage research and development project," at least one "competent microbiologist (undergraduate-level training or higher), one experimental physicist or mechanical engineer able to work with aerosol technology," and a few hundred thousand dollars "for research, testing, production, and weaponization," should be able to effectively produce bioweapons in facilities that "would fit in a large apartment."

Illustrating this possibility, the U.S. Defense Department carried out a project in 1999 known as *Bacchus*, which sought to simulate the technical feasibility and degree of difficulty for a state or terrorist group seeking to assemble a clandestine bioweapons production facility. The results were not comforting. At a cost of $1.6 million, the team succeeded in equipping a mini-BW plant, using off-the-shelf technology ordered from commercial outlets, that produced two pounds of simulated anthrax (Begley, "Tracking Anthrax" 2001; Miller September 2001). As Dr. Craig Smith, an infectious-disease specialist, observes, "So many of these machines are dual-use . . . The same small, sealed milling unit used for producing pharmaceuticals can be used to weaponize anthrax. Fermenters can produce antibiotics as well as bioweapons. Culture media can grow bacteria for vaccines as well as weapons" (Begley "Tracking Anthrax" 2001). Obtaining growth media, and the laboratory and production equipment necessary to make bioweapons is relatively cheap and easy (Central Intelligence Agency 1996, 30). As Smithson warns:

> [T]errorists can buy the same equipment that commercial enterprises use to make beer, yogurt, vaccines, and antibiotics. A top-of-the-line biological production facility would include fermenters, centrifuges, freeze or spray driers, milling equipment, and such safety features as class II or III hoods and high-efficiency particulate air filters. These items are widely available. As many as 150 companies may manufacture fermenters, over eighty-five firms centrifugal separators, and over forty companies freeze driers. Costs for commercial facilities range from $50 million for a fully equipped vaccine plant to $10 million for a generic, no-frills fermentation plant. . . . The cost estimates for a bioterrorism facility vary quite widely, from $2 million to $200,000. For a truly small-scale operation, the price could be even lower (Smithson and Levy 2000, 45 and 48).

Further, Dando (2001, 110) notes "the equipment needed to produce a freeze-dried and milled agent would not differ greatly from that required to freeze-dry and mill pharmaceutical material for aerosol delivery. . . . Moreover, the quantities that can be milled are limited only by the dimensions of the collection vessel and feed hopper. Commercially available attrition mills range in size from those that can just mill gram-sized quantities up to manufacturing units capable of producing kilogram quantities." As Falkenrath et al. (1998, 118–19) observe:

> Personnel producing certain very deadly agents, including anthrax and some toxins, would face minimal health risks, provided they were careful to observe good laboratory technique and some simple protective practices. . . . certain biological warfare agents, such as anthrax, are not particularly infectious except by the aerosol route, and working with them does not require unusual equipment. Toxins, provided they are not ingested, injected, or inhaled, remain harmless. Gloves, filter masks, hoods, good ventilation, sound laboratory technique, and regular decontamination, perhaps supplemented with antibiotic prophylaxis or vaccination, would be adequate. Risks would rise sharply if agents were aerosolized and tested, or if agents were dried and milled into powders.

Of course, if the goal is to merely produce a liquid slurry of agent, it is possible to produce several kilograms of concentrated anthrax slurry in ninety-six hours or less, and for botulinal toxin, about five days (U.S. Congress December 1993; Smithson and Levy 2000, 49–51). When asked how complex the process of weaponizing bioagents was, former U.S. bioweaponeer Patrick replied:

> First, you've got to be able to mass-produce the organism on an industrial scale. Now, a lot of organisms grow well in the laboratory in very small containers, but you start having problems when you expand these organisms into a 3,000 or a 5,000 gallon fermenter. The conditions are entirely different. Then you've got to have industrial equipment like centrifuges and ion exchange resins to purify and concentrate the organism from its growth substrate. And then, finally, you've got to be able to stabilize the organism and freeze dry it, or dry it by some other means like spraying it. (Broad 21 December 2001)

But, as Col. David Franz, former commander of the U.S. Army Medical Research Institute of Infectious Diseases, notes: "Making a powder is a huge hurdle for the bad guys . . . It's hard to dry stuff without killing it. And the material needs other treatments as well" (Begley "Unmasking Terror" 2001). In fact, while drying germs is straightforward, the process creates a mix of particles that stick together in clumps far too large for use as an effective weapon. Former American and Soviet bioweaponeers observe that grinding material down to a small, uniform size without significantly damaging the pathogens is not easily done (Johnston and Mitchell 2001). Yet, as Major General John Parker, head of the U.S. Army's Medical Research and Material Command, warns in describing the anthrax from the letter sent to Senator Tom Daschle, it was "very light, uniform in size, highly concentrated and highly pure." (Parker, Sternberg, and Johnson 2001). Al Zelicoff, a biowarfare specialist at Sandia National Laboratory, upon examining the Daschle material, remarked: "I'm truly worried . . . they have the keys to the kingdom" (Haberman 2001).

## THE BRAIN DRAIN AND THE AVAILABILITY OF LOOSE MATERIALS/KNOWLEDGE

The availability of scientific and technical expertise in the form of individuals who worked in state-run bioweapons programs is an example of "loose" materials—a problem usually referred to as "brain drain" (Sanger December 2001). It is also a critical variable determining how difficult it would be for state or nonstate actors to develop viable bioweapons capabilities. Though information on producing rudimentary bioweapons exist in many places, the most dangerous sources are former bioweaponeers from state programs who possess production knowledge for sophisticated bioweapons (Overbye and Glanz 2001; Thomas 2001). During its zenith, the Soviet bioweapons program employed roughly 65,000 people, including 40,000 in Biopreparat (of whom 9,000 were key scientists and engineers) and around 10,000 to develop plant and animal pathogens for warfare (Smithson 1999, 9–10).[4] In comparison, the former Soviet nuclear weapons complex employed 50,000–60,000 workers (Smithson 1999, 9). The U.S. government *conservatively* estimates there are at least 7,000 former Soviet bioweapons scientists who pose a "critical proliferation risk"—who, in other words, have full-cycle knowledge of weapons production and dispersal techniques. Observing that many are unemployed or have disappeared, Dastan Eleukenov, head of the Monterey Institute office in Kazakstan, warns that "when you're talking about bioweapons, the brain drain is more important than the material" (Begley "Unmasking Terror" 2001). So, while U.S. intelligence reports a number of former bioweaponeers traveled to Afghanistan for job interviews with Al Qaeda, with many turning down offers because they found their employers "too creepy," this is not altogether comforting (Hosenball and Klaidman 2002, 6). It suggests *some* were able to deal with creepiness for cash, and U.S. intelligence reportedly found evidence within Afghanistan of Russian scientists helping Al Qaeda to develop anthrax (Bartholet 2001, 23).

Given salaries of former Soviet weapons scientists have fallen to $25 per month or less in many cases, it is not difficult to understand why some bioweaponeers might be tempted to sell their knowledge and expertise to outside bidders (Smithson 1999, 15–17). Iranian "recruiters" have offered salaries of up to $5,000 a month to lure ex-bioweaponeers with expertise in genetic engineering or agricultural-livestock pathogens to work in Iran or consult via computer.[5] Similar overtures to ex-Soviet bioweaponeers by North Korea, India, and China have been reported by U.S. intelligence agencies and defectors (Miller, Engelberg, and Broad 2001, 207).[6] Indeed, the Russian newspaper *Kommersant* reported Tehran obtained anticrop agents from a visiting Russian scientific delegation in January 1999, while at least five former bioweaponeers reportedly took well-paying jobs in Iran or consulted (via the Internet or other means) without leaving home (Smithson 1999, 17–18).[7] Given that Iranian president Ali Akbar Hashemi Rafsanjani once stated Iran "should at least consider biological weapons" for its defense, this movement of expertise to Tehran is clearly worrisome (Smithson 1999, 17). As Alibek notes:

The services of an ex-Biopreparat scientist would be a bargain at any price. The information he could provide would save months, perhaps years, of costly scientific research for any nation interested in developing, or improving, a biological warfare program. It is impossible to know how many Russians have been recruited abroad, but there is no doubt that their expertise has been attracting bidders. . . . I've heard that several went to . . . North Korea. A former colleague, now the director of a Biopreparat institute, told me that five of our scientists are in Iran. (Alibek 1999, 271)

Some ex-Soviet bioweaponeers established companies selling techniques to develop genetically engineered strains of pathogens, while Russian scientific journals routinely publish articles explaining how to manufacture very sophisticated, highly pathogenic agents. As Alibek observes, "ten years ago it would require several million dollars to get one or another technique. Now you can get this information just for the cost of a translator from Russian into English" (Wolfinger "Interviews: Bill Patrick and Ken Alibek" 2001). Indeed, with bioweapons, the ability to create dry powders lacking electrostatic charge so they aerosolize easily and float in the air requires extensive technical knowledge, knowledge possibly already circulating with these former weaponeers. Alibek notes that while the USSR's antistatic advances took a significant amount of research, rogue Soviet scientists might make this knowledge available to terrorists or states: "This knowledge is accessible . . . many people with this knowledge are wandering around the world now, and these people could be in demand" (Broad and Miller 26 October 2001). In fact, Alibek warns the acquisition of ex-bioweaponeers by would-be proliferators "could significantly improve the ability" of programs "overnight" and transform a country "with just a few changes in strains, just a few changes in production procedures" into a "very capable BW country" (Wolfinger "Interviews: Bill Patrick and Ken Alibek" 2001). And, as former Soviet bioweaponeer Popov remarked, "there were people [*other bioweaponeers*] I knew very well who were in Iraq or Iran and other Muslim countries" (Begley "Tracking Anthrax" 2001, 37).

But it is not just ex-Soviet bioweaponeers who pose a significant proliferation risk. South African bioweaponeers, who worked on the Project Coast program during apartheid, have also pursued business opportunities overseas. In fact, South African scientists report being approached by recruiters from foreign countries interested in their knowledge — yet no programs exist to prevent this *non-Soviet* brain drain (Warrick and Mintz 2003). Further, now that Saddam Hussein has been overthrown, there is no reliable data regarding the status or whereabouts of many of the scientists and technicians who worked in the Iraqi BW program during the late 1980s to early 1990s. Obviously, the number of individuals who could potentially provide production and weaponization knowledge to new clients has grown markedly over the past decade. Thus, while possession of sophisticated equipment and appropriate pathogens are needed for an effective BW program, Popov soberly notes: "The most important thing is knowledge—knowledge of how to make a specific biological agent, what is required to provide enough viability to that agent, and how to use that agent. All that was the subject of very intensive research in the Soviet Union" (Wolfinger "Interviews: Sergei Popov" 2001).[8]

Unfortunately, the enormous danger from brain drain rests in the fact that just one little bit of expert information can radically improve *any* actor's ability to weaponize a bioagent. For example, the main anthrax "battle strain" in the Soviet arsenal, which Alibek helped to weaponize during his time at Biopreparat, became fully operational in 1989.[9] However, due to the spread of ex-bioweaponeers to other countries, it is highly likely this secret anthrax formula (as well as master seed stocks and possibly samples of the finished product) were taken by these scientists who now work for new employers. In fact, Alibek notes the formula is a simple one which mixed two unrelated materials with pure powdered anthrax spores to produce an easily aerosolized agent (Preston 1998). Similarly, the deadly Marburg hemorraghic fever virus was weaponized by the Soviet BW program and the technique for producing the dry, powdered agent perfected. Unfortunately, the Marburg weaponization process was also a simple one, and when asked how many former bioweaponeers would have knowledge of it, Alibek replied "definitely thousands."[10] As Alibek observes: "What we need to keep in mind as time goes by, for example, twenty years ago, or ten years ago, you wouldn't find, for example, such a big number of people with knowledge of how to grow anthrax. Now the number of people with this knowledge is quite wide. Absolutely the same thing is happening with Marburg. Hundreds of people with the knowledge of how to grow Marburg and how to weaponize it."[11]

Because Russian scientific journals have published technical details of Marburg virus production, you don't even need access to a former bioweaponeer, "to develop Marburg, all you need to have are a couple of translators from Russian into Chinese or whatever."[12] When asked whether weaponized Marburg variant U virus might have been smuggled out of Russia in freeze-dried form, Alibek admitted that "from a technical standpoint, it's possible."[13] He warns:

> Marburg has been developed as a weapon and, unfortunately, the technique to develop Marburg weapon is very easy, and even more unfortunately, one of the Russian scientific journals has published an article describing how to manufacture high concentrations of Marburg virus using some of these techniques. It was published sometime in late 90s. Published by the scientist who I'm sure worked to develop this weapon.[14]

A more significant shortcut for states or terror groups seeking effective bioweapons would be to procure pathogens produced by sophisticated state-run programs. For example, it is impossible to know whether samples have been procured by stealth from the Soviet's primary open-air BW test range on Vozrozhdeniye (Renaissance) Island (in the middle of the Aral Sea between Kazakstan and Uzbekistan), which is the world's largest anthrax burial ground. In 1988, under orders from Soviet president Gorbachev to destroy evidence of the nation's BW program, between 100 and 200 tons of military grade anthrax was packed into steel drums filled with bleach and transported by train to Renaissance. Not wanting to waste the valuable steel drums, soldiers poured the pink sludge into burial pits on the island along with more bleach and buried the evidence (Alibek 1999; Lewis 1999). However, despite these efforts, between 1994 and 1998, U.S. military scientists and intelligence experts who traveled secretly to the site to collect soil samples repeatedly discovered spores that were still alive and viable (Miller June 1999). Indeed, "tests of the soil samples taken from six of eleven vast burial pits" on Renaissance showed "that although the anthrax was soaked in bleach at least twice, once inside 250-litre containers and again after it was dumped into the sandy pits and buried for a decade under a metre of sand, some of the spores are still alive—and deadly."

Moreover, the retreat of the Aral Sea has now effectively left a land bridge from Renaissance to the mainland, ending its status as an island, raising concern that anthrax (or other deadly microbes) might escape their confinement through animal vectors or as a result of state or terrorist agents obtaining samples from the site. The disposal method for the anthrax would certainly not pass U.S. EPA standards, with anthrax sludge reportedly now beginning to leach up through the sand covering some of the burial pits (Miller June 1999). Experts warn that many of the bioagents tested in open-air sites around the world during the Cold War resulted in continuing "reservoirs" of these pathogens, now endemic in the local wildlife around the old test sites (Choffnes 2001).

Some experts are concerned that an international black market in "hot strains" may exist in which pathogens stolen from the former Soviet BW program (such as engineered forms of anthrax, plague, and other agents) are being sold to states seeking BW capabilities (Preston November 1997). Indeed, there have been several instances of theft of pathogen cultures from former Soviet BW facilities or research centers in recent years. At the Institute of Experimental Pathology and Therapy in Sukhumi, Georgia, plague and cholera cultures were reportedly stolen from its collection. In 1995, at the Kazakh Antiplague Institute, plague, cholera, and anthrax cultures were reportedly stolen by individuals planning a terrorist attack on the city of Khabarovsk (Smithson 1999, 19).[15] Bakhyt Atshabar, director of a Kazakstani research center keeping at least eighty strains of anthrax, plague, and cholera at its main facility and eight satellite labs, noted that, "Just this year we built a concrete wall and were able to hire a guard who is actually a professional . . . We've put up bars and doors and strenghtened security. Of course, before, things were not so well controlled. People got in" (Begley "Unmasking Terror 2001, 25). During the late 1980s and early 1990s, the U.S. intelligence community asserted North Korea had obtained smallpox samples from the former Soviet Union, and there have been claims a company associated with the Kazakh Antiplague Institute sold plague bacteria to Indian militants who subsequently used it to cause the 1994 outbreak of pneumonic plague in Surat, India. Although Kazakh officials have denied these allegations, Indian officials have stated the strain of plague from the Surat outbreak was not endemic to the region, which certainly raises questions regarding whether this was a "natural" outbreak of the disease (Smithson 1999, 20).

Unfortunately, there are *hundreds* of germ banks and laboratories worldwide that lack adequate security. Although the World Federation for Culture Collections (WFCC), a loose association of 472 repositories of living microbial specimens in sixty-one countries, has urged its members to set up tighter rules for access to materials, there are no enforcement mechanisms in place and at least two-thirds of the over 1,500 germ banks worldwide are not members of the organization (Tucker October 2001). Barletta et al. (2002, 59) warn that of over 1,000 germ banks outside of the WFCC, many contain poorly secured or regulated collections. Thus, for states or groups interested in obtaining pathogens, there are plenty of facilities outside of the former USSR where agents could be procured (Schemo 2002). Moreover, even the strictest inventory and security procedures may be circumvented in practice. Indeed, the consensus opinion among former bioweaponeers is that smuggling "seed cultures" of pathogens out of bioresearch facilities is frighteningly easy since only small amounts are required as a starter to produce large quantities of agent (Smithson 1999, 83–85). As Dr. C. J. Peters, director of the Center for Biodefense at the University of Texas Medical Branch at Galveston observes, even with tight security, it would likely still be possible for a laboratory employee to steal microscopic cultures of anthrax (or by implication, many other types of pathogens) and escape without detection with a useful starter culture. As Peters notes, "I'd only need one spore to get all the anthrax I wanted. . . . It's not hard to grow . . . you could go from a smidgen to a hundred billion spores" (Johnston and Kocieniewski 2001).

Lastly, in addition to knowledge about pathogens and techniques for producing bioagents, technical expertise regarding the delivery or dissemination of BW agents is also highly dangerous. It represents the final hurdle BW actors have to cross to obtain a full-fledged capability to use such weapons. What is required? In the old Soviet BW program, strategic missiles were outfitted with specialized biowarheads to deliver the agent to U.S. cities in time of war. It required special shielding and cooling systems inside each warhead to keep the virus alive during the heat of atmospheric reentry. Parachutes were deployed to slow the warhead's descent and, at a certain altitude, more than a hundred oval bomblets the size of small cantaloupes would be released over the target in overlapping patterns and release a haze of bioparticles (Preston 1998). The Soviet program also utilized a spray technique using tanks installed on medium-range bombers and worked on modifying cruise missiles to disperse agent. Unfortunately, the technical constraints on terrorist use of BW have been eroding, as evidenced by a 1991 Office of Technology Assessment study that concluded for some BW scenarios, "the level of technological sophistication required . . . may be lower than was the case for some of the sophisticated bombs that have been used against civilian aircraft" (U.S. Congress 1991, 51–52).

Concerns about the potential spread of BW munitions capabilities were heightened by clear evidence gathered throughout the mid-1990s that several countries were running tests on what appeared to be biological munitions, as well as reports Soviet-style biobomblets (or the technical knowledge to guide in their manufacture) was becoming available on the international black market. These developments spurred on the CIA's super-secret Clear Vision project, which sought to understand future BW threats by examining how these technologies (if obtained by proliferators) might threaten U.S. security (Miller, Engelberg, and Broad 2001, 290–92). One of the Clear Vision projects involved replication of the Soviet biobomblet design that reportedly was available on the black market (or from the minds of former bioweaponeers hired as consultants) and tests of its performance characteristics (Miller, Engelberg, and Broad 2001, 290–95; Weiss and Warrick 2001). Similarly, Clear Vision also examined the threat of genetically modified, recombinant weapons, although its research was eventually halted and transferred to the Defense Intelligence Agency (DIA), where defensive work similar to that of Clear Vision is conducted.

In 1999, the Defense Threat Reduction Agency (DTRA) demonstrated in Project Bacchus that it was possible for proliferators to easily obtain, over the counter from retail suppliers in the U.S. and Europe, all of the dual-use equipment and materials needed to develop a working biological weapons production facility capable of producing pounds of lethal agents (in this case, anthrax) and milling the dried materials down to easily respirable size for around $1.6 million (Miller, Engelberg, and Broad 2001, 297–99). As Miller et al. (2001, 298) noted after visiting the small-scale BW facility set up by DTRA in the Nevada desert:

The project had proven its point—a nation or bioterrorist with the requisite expertise could easily assemble an anthrax factory from off-the-shelf materials. DTRA officials say the overseas purchases were not detected. The results suggested that with precious little money and off-the-shelf equipment, a state, or even a group of terrorists, could build and operate a small-scale germ weapons plant, probably without the intelligence agencies' knowledge.

It is reasonable to expect mobile, or at least transportable, BW production facilities to be used in state-run programs (and possibly in some terrorist organizations). This assumption is not based upon merely worst-case analysis, but by a review of not only what is possible, but also by what other state-run BW programs have done (or considered) in the past. For example, Alibek warns such mobile bioweapon production facilities are "very practical" and would be perfect for small states seeking to clandestinely manufacture relatively small amounts (not tons, but tens or hundreds of kilos) of agent.[16] Similarly, according to William Patrick, during the 1950s, U.S. scientists drew up plans for constructing mobile BW production units, capable of producing large amounts of weaponized anthrax to serve as a strategic reserve in the event the Soviets destroyed the country's existing BW plants in Arkansas and Maryland (Broad, Johnston, and Miller 2003). As former CIA director James Woolsey observes:

> Transportable is probably a better word than mobile, but trucks can be pretty large and production equipment for biologicals can be very small. In a lot of ways, it resembles equipment for microbrewery attached to a restaurant. You can load that up in two or three trucks probably. If they're big enough. So, transportable production facilities, especially for biologicals, are I think entirely feasible.[17]

In fact, in 2000, the DoD secretly constructed a mobile germ plant in just such a trailer, which was designed to be a trainer used to instruct Special Operations units on how to find and disarm such facilities in Iraq. The mobile BW lab consisted of a fermenter, centrifuge, and mill for grinding clumps of anthrax into a fine powder (Broad, Johnston, and Miller 2003). Thus, when one looks into the future, it is reasonable to assume state-run BW programs will not necessarily be housed in their entirety in massive buildings and plants (like the old Soviet or U.S. programs), but rather in small, well hidden and nondescript facilities (above or below ground) or aboard mobile facilities that could be moved about to prevent detection. And, just as mobility and concealment improve the survivability of a state's strategic nuclear forces, such dispersal and mobility also will enhance the survivability and concealment of a state's BW production facilities—making them incredibly difficult to preempt successfully or discover in the absence of extreme inspections. The ease of concealment and the low need for large technical infrastructures to produce bioweapons also raises the danger posed by nonstate terror groups, who may be able to construct crude but efficient production facilities and acquire enough agent to launch attacks.

## THE TRUE POTENTIAL OF BIOLOGICAL WEAPONS

The potential impact of a widespread release of highly virulent, contagious pathogen by either a state or bioterrorist could be enormous. As Lederberg warns, the appropriate model to describe what such an attack might look like would be the 1918 Spanish Flu pandemic, which spread worldwide and killed between 40 and 100 million people (Vergano 2000; Davies 2000, 46–48).[18] Indeed, a brief review of several estimates published in open-source literature should illustrate the immense destructive potential of bioweapons.

One 1993 study by the Office of Technology Assessment warned 100 kilograms of anthrax effectively released by aircraft as an aerosol cloud over Washington, D.C. on a calm, clear night, would kill somewhere between 1 and 3 million people (U.S. Congress August 1993, 54). Another study by the US Army at Dugway Proving Ground in 1983 found that under ideal conditions, a line-source release of only forty kilograms of anthrax would produce 50 percent fatalities in the population over a 900-square-kilometer area over Washington, D.C. (Dando 1994, 10–11). Perhaps the most oft-quoted series of estimates regarding bioweapon attacks against cities were provided by a 1970 World Health Organization (WHO) study. One example provided was of a small-scale, aerosol BW attack using anthrax on a city population of between 500,000 and 5 million using an aircraft to lay down a two-kilometer-long line-source release with the wind (World Health Organization 1970, 18). The predicted result was a death toll in the tens to hundreds of thousands (World Health Organization 1970, 19). In addition, it noted attacks "causing the secondary spread of epidemics of yellow fever, pneumonic plague, smallpox or influenza, might under certain conditions ultimately result in many millions of illnesses and deaths." Emphasizing the effectiveness of plague as a bioweapon, the WHO (1970, 74) report warns "if an initial infection with pneumonic plague were to involve about 50% of a population, it is likely that, unless precautions had been taken, up to about 90% of the rest of the population would be infected in 20–30 days with a case fatality rate of 60–70%" (World Health Organization 1970, 19). Even thirty-five years ago (prior to many of the recent medical advances increasing the potential of bioweapons), the WHO figures suggested a high level of vulnerability to bioattack.

These are not very large attacks and the statistics purposefully lower impact. The WHO figures assume agent was dispersed effectively and 50 percent of those exposed become ill, and then base fatalities on the normal fatality rate for that pathogen. Thus, if 500,000 people in city of 5 million are exposed to ID50 (infective dose 50 percent) attack, they calculate 250,000 clinical cases. But, "many more would probably occur because of the very large number of doses to which most of the population would be exposed" (World Health Organization 1970, 105).

Yet another simulation illustrating the potential threat posed by a smallpox bioweapon was the 2001 *Dark Winter* exercise involving a dozen former senior government officials playing key leadership roles during a fictional bioterrorist release of smallpox in Oklahoma City.[19] Although officials sought to contain the outbreak and seal borders, the scenario went from 3,000 total smallpox cases (with 1,000 deaths) on December 17th to 3 million cases worldwide (and 1 million deaths) by February 6th!

In addition to the human costs, Kaufmann et al. (1997) have developed an elaborate mathematical model predicting the economic impact of various bioterror attacks on the suburbs of a major city in which 100,000 people are exposed to aerosolized anthrax, brucellosis, or tularemia. Their findings warn of dire economic consequences from such attacks, ranging from $477.7 million per 100,000 people exposed to brucellosis, $5.5 billion per 100,000 exposed to tularemia, and $26.2 billion per 100,000 exposed to anthrax! (Kaufmann, Meltzer, and Schmid 1997, 83) This, in addition to the 413 brucellosis deaths, 6,188 tularemia deaths, and 32,875 anthrax deaths produced by their scenario. They also note that all of these figures represent "minimum estimates" of the costs (both economic and casualty wise) of the attacks since they "consistently used low estimates for all factors directly affecting costs" (Kaufmann, Meltzer, and Schmid 1997, 83–94).

And, only small amounts of agent are required to produce strategically significant effects. Indeed, if efficiently spread as an aerosol cloud, 200 kilograms (440 pounds) of tularemia would infect an area of sixty square miles (Carus 1991, 62). According to Russian bioweaponeers, tests to establish the effective range of aerosol bomblets at Vozrozhdeniye Island (the main Soviet open-air testing facility) demonstrated that BW agents can be disseminated using these delivery systems over a distance of up to twenty kilometers—easily enough to blanket a small city (Bozheyeva, Kunakbayev, and Yeleukenov 1999, 6). U.S. aerosol BW tests over the Pacific island of Eniwetok (part of the Marshall Islands chain in the central Pacific) in the summer of 1968 demonstrated the high effectiveness of jet aircraft dissemination of bioagents (in this case, staphylococcal enterotoxin B, or SEB) over large areas (Regis 1999, 205). The exercise, officially known as DTC Test 68-50, used F4 Phantom jet fighters to stage a line-source release of a liquid slurry of SEB (which would aerosolize due to the jet stream around the aircraft) to effectively cover a 2,400-square-kilometer (926.5-square-mile) area more than twice the size of metropolitan Los Angeles (Regis 1999, 205–6). As the unclassified final report on the DTC Test 68-50 concluded:

> Test 68-50 was a full-scale field test of the area coverage potential of the F4/AB45Y-4 incapacitant weapon system. The weapon system disseminated the aerosol over a 40–50 km downwind grid, encompassing a segment of the atoll and an array of five tugs. . . . The agent proved to be stable and did not deteriorate during storage, aerosolization, or downwind travel. A single weapon was calculated to have covered 2400 square km, producing 30 percent casualties for a susceptible population under the test conditions. No insurmountable problems were encountered in production-to-target sequence. (Regis 1999, 206)

Similarly, a series of open-air tests over the continental U.S. in 1958 dubbed "Operation LAC" dropped large quantities of zinc cadmium sulfide from aircraft to test the feasibility of contaminating large areas with biowarfare agents (Cole 1997, 19). Flight patterns during Operation LAC covered vast stretches of territory, with individual flights dropping simulant from Ohio to Texas, and from Michigan to Kansas, dispersing particles for hundreds of miles along these flight paths. The conclusions reported by these tests were that they had "proved the feasibility of covering large areas of a country with BW agents" (Cole 1997, 21). Other tests involving aircraft employing sprayers to disseminate liquid BW agents in 1955 illustrate what could prove feasible for nations capable of employing jet aircraft, or more preferably, cruise missiles over targets. These U.S. BW tests proved a "spray system could contaminate 50,000 square miles with BW aerosol in a single sortie. . . . [T]hree large aircraft, each carrying 4,000 gallons of liquid BW agent, and flying at a speed of 500 knots, could spray an area of 150,000 square miles, causing more than half the people in the area to become ill" (Cole 1997, 36–37).

Advanced bioagents can be even more economical in terms of the amounts needed for significant military effects. For example, Alibek notes Anthrax 836, the formulation he developed at Stepnogorsk, was capable of infecting half the people living in a square kilometer of territory using only five kilograms of agent! (Alibek 1999, 105) During the early 1960s, the U.S. deployed biowarheads aboard a half-dozen Pershing, Regulus, and Sergeant missiles: "The payload for the Sergeant consisted of 720 bomblets, each three inches wide, holding seven ounces of disease agent. Released ten miles up, at the fringes of the atmosphere, the bomblets would scatter during their downward plunge to cover more than sixty square miles, spraying agent into the air as a fine spray" (Miller, Engelberg, and Broad 2001, 53).

The potential effectiveness of bioweapons was even more decisively demonstrated during four years of U.S. open-air tests over the Pacific near Johnston Atoll, culminating in a line-source lay-down test in 1968 using a marine Phantom jet equipped with a single pod filled with a weaponized biopowder (Preston 1998).[20] Flying low and in a straight line over the horizon, the jet released a small amount of biopowder for every mile of flight over a series of barges containing test monkeys, half of whom died as a result. As Patrick, who observed the tests, recalls: "When we saw those test results, we knew beyond a doubt that biological weapons are strategic weapons. We were surprised. Even we didn't think they would work that well" (Preston 1998). The implications of these tests are disturbing. Were a state or terrorist actor able to obtain a suitable agent and design for such a biopod, it would be possible to employ a line-source lay down of agent over a target (like a U.S. city or military forces deployed abroad) and potentially create immense levels of casualties! A modest amount of agent, properly disseminated, could easily kill half the population of a major U.S. city and, failing that, certainly cause massive disruptions and panic.

The U.S. bioweapons program conducted numerous open-air tests over civilian targets to ascertain the effectiveness and dispersal characteristics of agents (Cole 1988/1997; Miller, Engelberg, and Broad 2001, 53). For example, Project Saint Jo involved 173 releases of simulant aerosols over Saint Louis, Minneapolis, and Winnipeg (cities chosen to represent Soviet targets like Kiev, Leningrad, and Moscow due to their comparable sizes and climates) using a cluster bomb that carried 536 bomblets, each of which emitting an ounce of simulated anthrax mist (Miller, Engelberg, and Broad 2001, 42; Cole 1997, 17–76). Conducted under ideal winter conditions with a strong heat inversion covering the site, the Minneapolis test showed the simulated anthrax traveled nearly a mile from the release point and the effective "dosage area" was "unusually large" (Miller, Engelberg, and Broad 2001, 43). Once smallpox had been converted into a dry agent by U.S. bioweaponeers, tests were conducted using simulants to study the ease with which the disease could be clandestinely spread to the civilian population:

Tiny aerosol generators, or atomizers, that could be hidden in everyday objects were developed. In May 1965, experts from Detrick's special-operations unit took the system on the road, using men's briefcases to spray mock smallpox germs in Washington National Airport. . . . The lengthy report on the secret test, which was done to gauge America's vulnerability to enemy smallpox attacks, concluded that one in every twelve travelers would have become infected, quickly producing an epidemic as the disease spread across the country. (Miller, Engelberg, and Broad 2001, 60)

In 1950, the army conducted tests using aerosol generators aboard ships to release clouds of the simulants *Bacillus globigii* and *Serratia marcescens* off the Virginia coast over the cities of Norfolk, Hampton, and Newport News (Smithson and Levy 2000, 56).[21] Similar tests conducted over San Francisco covered the city and spread twenty-three miles inland, with an estimated 800,000 people inhaling a minimum of five thousand fluorescent particles. In 1966, the army staged tests in the New York City subway system using an open container of an anthrax simulant placed on the subway tracks and pushed through the tunnels by the pneumatic pressure of the trains (Smithson and Levy 2000, 56). U.S. tests in central Alaska during the mid-1960s also demonstrated the agents had reduced biodecay in the cold and would spread better under such conditions (Mangold and Goldberg 1999, 40). Overall, the Pentagon acknowledged, during Senate hearings in 1977, that between 1949 and 1969, it conducted 239 open-air biowarfare tests over American cities including San Francisco, Minneapolis, St. Louis, Key West, and Panama City, Florida, as well as tests in the New York City subway, the Washington, D.C., National Airport terminal, and the Pennsylvania Turnpike (Cole 1997, 18).

A number of other nations also conducted covert exercises over populated areas using biosimulants. The Soviet program, for example, conducted many open-air tests (often over civilian targets) using simulants to study the characteristics of likely BW agents and how differing methods of dissemination worked in practice. Between 1979 and 1989, large-scale tests of aerosol simulant occurred over the Novosibirsk region using planes carrying civilian markings, as well as similar tests over military proving grounds in the Caucasus and the Kara Kalpak Republic. There also were a series of tests using missiles carrying simulants conducted over the Pacific between 1960 and 1980, and several tests of simulants inside the Moscow Metro system during the 1980s (Alibek 1999, 42–43).

Similarly, Britain carried out a series of simulated bioweapons tests during the 1960s in the London subway system, in various government buildings, and over cities such as Salisbury and Norwich (Moore 2002, 66–67). The British also carried out a series of tests in the Caribbean during the late 1940s and early 1950s on a variety of bioagents, ranging from anthrax, brucellosis, and tularemia in 1948 off Antigua, to aerosol sprays of Venezuelan equine encephalitis off the shores of the Bahamas between 1954 and 1955. In addition to the well-known tests of anthrax during World War II off Scotland, Britain also tested prototype plague bombs off the Isle of Lewis in 1952–1953 (Moore 2002, 67).[22]

But, regardless of country, it was readily apparent to all after these tests that bioweapons could be effectively dispersed over populated areas and cause substantial casualties—that they were, in fact, potentially highly effective weapons of war. None of the parties to these tests abandoned their work on developing bioarsenals because of these tests, and until their accession to the Biological Weapons Convention in 1972, all continued work to further hone their existing BW arsenals and improve upon the agents they were weaponizing. Moreover, the Soviet Union, seeing the tremendous potential of bioweapons, proceeded to sign the BWC and then cheat—creating the largest BW program in history over the coming decades. Further, many analysts contend that despite some degree of openness and dismantling of facilities after the fall of the Soviet Union, the offensive BW program continues to this day in Russia under the auspices of the Russian military (Alibek 1999; Davis 1999). As a March 1997 DoD report to Congress notes:

> Key components of the former Soviet program remain largely intact and may support a possible future mobilization capability for the production of biological agents and delivery systems. Moreover, work outside the scope of legitimate biological defense activity may be occurring now at selected facilities within Russia. Such activity, if offensive in nature, would contravene the Biological and Toxin Weapons Convention of 1972, to which the former Soviet government is a signatory. It would also contradict statements by top Russian political leaders that offensive activity has ceased. (Department of Defense 1997)

Far from viewing bioweapons as ineffective, the Pentagon described such agents as a "strategic as well as operational threat," and noted they could be "effectively employed against military targets such as headquarters, ship or aircraft crews, and troop concentrations, as well as civilian population centers" (Department of Defense October 2001, 17). In fact, Pentagon reports note that bioweapons "aimed at certain critical nodes in the military infrastructure of the United States, either domestically or abroad . . . could disrupt the execution of military objectives." The four categories of targets listed by the Pentagon as being most vulnerable to BW attack include: (1) *High-value, large-area facilities/targets within or outside of theater*—leadership, diplomatic, military headquarters, industrial, commercial, population centers susceptible to infectious agents that have relatively slow onset of effect, but large area coverage; (2) *Theater support military facilities*—command and control, troop barracks, air bases, missile launch sites, naval ports, logistical transfer/storage facilities; (3) *Military assets near engagement areas*—troop convoys, staging areas, drop zones, airstrips, air defense systems, artillery support bases, naval task forces; (4) *Forces in engagement*—infantry, amphibious, mechanized/armor, especially from agents with relatively rapid onset of effect but smaller area of coverage per unit weight of agent (Department of Defense October 2001, 6).

And this does not address an even more likely occurrence, namely the use of bioweapons by terror groups against domestic U.S. targets. In fact, many senior analysts argue the threat posed to the U.S. from covert delivery by terror groups is "significantly higher than is commonly assumed." Falkenrath, Newman, and Thayer (1998, 1) note "the defining element of a covert attack is that the weapon is delivered against its target in a manner that cannot readily be distinguished from normal background traffic and activity." For a terrorist, hoping for the element of surprise in delivering a bioattack to maximize casualties and increase their ease of escape afterward, bioagents make perfect terror weapons. And, though no one can predict the likelihood of such an attack, an NBC (nuclear-biological-chemical) attack against the U.S. must at the very least be considered the "quintessential low-probability, high-consequence event" (Falkenrath, Newman, and Thayer 1998, 2). The stealthy characteristics of a bioweapons attack are also not limited to providing delayed effects in a populace to allow the perpetrators to leave the area. As Chyba (2001, 96) observes, "the early symptoms of a biological warfare agent most likely will resemble those of the flu," so that "sufficiently covert or widely dispersed attacks could, at least initially, be difficult to distinguish from . . . naturally occurring outbreaks." This would dramatically increase the number of fatalities arising from a bioagent's release, since victims would not receive medical treatment early in the course of the disease—often a lethal delay when considering many potential bioweapon pathogens such as anthrax or smallpox.

## THE PAST UNDERESTIMATION OF THE POTENTIAL OF BIOLOGICAL WEAPONS

In the fourteenth century, Tartars hurled the corpses of plague victims into the Ukrainian city of Kaffa to cause an epidemic among the defenders (Manning 1997). During the French and Indian War (1754–1767), British soldiers distributed blankets used by smallpox victims to Native Americans, resulting in many tribes loosing up to 50 percent of their populations ("The First Defence" 2001; Broad 1999). In the sixteenth century, the Aztecs were defeated by the Spaniards largely due to the inadvertent introduction of smallpox into their population by the invaders, a disease that would kill more than 500 million people in the twentieth century alone, a total far greater than all that era's wars combined (Brownlee 2001; Broad 9 October 2001). Throughout history, there have been those who have made use of the natural occurrence of disease for military purposes. In the twentieth century, however, states began to develop dedicated bioweapons programs for use against their enemies. Some programs, like the Japanese BW efforts of the 1930s and 1940s, actually unleashed bioweapons against civilian population centers and against opposing military units in China and Russia. During the Cold War, the superpowers developed massive bioweapons programs and actively weaponized agents into arsenals that would have held destructive potential easily rivaling those of their nuclear ones. By the 1990s, even terror groups had joined the game, with the Japanese Aum Shinrikyo cult's unsuccessful attempts to release anthrax onto downtown Tokyo and nearby U.S. military bases. With each passing decade, the "genie" appears more decidedly "out of the bottle" as more and more obtain the technology and know-how to develop biowarfare capabilities.

Although no state admits to possessing "offensive" BW programs, it is clear from the rapid expansion of countries with dedicated "defensive" BW programs, that interest and concern about biowarfare is increasing rather than ebbing in the international system. As Cirincione (2002, 49) notes, the "dirty dozen" of potential bioproliferators include:

> Iran, [Iraq], Israel, North Korea, Syria, Libya, Russia, and possibly India, Pakistan, China, Egypt, and Sudan. Almost all the programs are research programs. Only three nations (Iraq, Iran, and Russia) are believed to have produced and stockpiled agents; three others (Israel, North Korea, and China) may have done so. Other countries that have been of concern include South Africa, which had a bioweapon program that the new unity government says it ended in 1992, and Taiwan, which is now rarely mentioned in either official or expert reviews.

Unfortunately, the trends are clear. Rather than an ebbing of interest or decline in the number of states engaged in bioweapons-related research, the movement has been toward *increasing* numbers of states establishing "defensive" BW programs, growing numbers of countries who are suspected of having hidden "offensive" programs, and an accelerating threat posed by non-state actors (like Al Qaeda) seeking to obtain the biological "Holy Grail."

## FUTURE LESSONS FROM PAST AND CURRENT STATE BW PROGRAMS

From the early bioweapons programs of Japan, the U.S., and USSR, we can learn many lessons about what kinds of BW capabilities are possible, even with the antiquated technologies of the 1940s through the 1980s that are now easily available to any would-be proliferator. Indeed, when postulating about the current potential of even small BW facilities, it should be remembered the U.S. "Marshall Plan" strategy against Cuba could easily be supplied with enough bioagent using just one small production facility at Pine Bluffs, Arkansas. Certainly, this scale of facility would be within reach of most would-be bioweapon states today! Given the current state of medical and technical knowledge, and advancements in the necessary equipment since that time, a new bioweapon state would not need to repeat the failings of the early programs and would find the path toward a robust biowarfare capability much less strewn with obstacles.

The massive Japanese BW program from 1932 to 1945 is a good example of the scale of production possible for new bioweapon states using even antiquated technology (Harris 2002; Blumenthal and Miller 1999). Ping Fan, Japan's main BW production facility in Manchuria, was capable of producing between thirty and forty kilograms of pathogenic bacteria in only three to four days—and it was only the largest of dozens of BW facilities scattered throughout China (Harris 2002, 68–69). As Maj. Gen. Kawashima Kiyoshi noted in 1949, when Ping Fan was operating at full capacity, it could "manufacture as much as 300 kilograms of plague bacteria monthly," and its production divisions could similarly produce "500–600 kilograms of anthrax germs, or 800–900 kilograms of typhoid, paratyphoid or dysentery germs, or as much as 1000 kilograms of cholera germs" (Harris 2002, 69–70). The Changchun BW facility, which focused principally on animal/plant pathogens, also produced at least 1,000 kilograms of anthrax, over 500 kilos of nose bacteria, and perhaps as much as 100 kilos of glanders annually during the early 1940s (Harris 2002, 114–18). The Nanking BW production facility, which produced extensive amounts of plague bacteria (and fleas), was capable of producing ten kilograms every three-to-four-day production cycle (Harris 2002, 143). All told, Unit 731 worked on several dozen diseases simultaneously, including both human and animal/plant pathogens (Harris 2002, 69–70, 77–80, 115–18; Mangold and Goldberg 1999, 14–28). Although the Japanese employed crude delivery systems (e.g., typhoid or cholera poured into wells; drops of plague, flea-infested sacks of grain, animal vectors), the resulting outbreaks of disease among the Chinese population resulted in the deaths of tens (if not hundreds) of thousands of people—both during the decade of active use by the Japanese and for many years after the war due to outbreaks springing from the residue of these attacks (which had taken up residence in local animal reservoirs) (Harris 2002, 68–104). Between 1932 and 1945, Japan killed over 260,000 Chinese civilians with bioweapons (chiefly plague), a toll far greater than that wrought by the use of chemical munitions in the First World War (which caused 1.3 million injuries, but only 100,000 deaths) (Simons 2002, 16).

During the 1940s, the British BW production technology used to grow anthrax consisted of 50-liter (13-gallon) stainless steel milk churns normally used for making butter. As Regis (1999, 42–43) notes:

There were four of them ganged together in a line, each connected to the next with flexible tubing. All the cans had stainless steel lids that were held in place by metal clamps. The first can in the sequence was for media preparation. The last can was for disinfecting the slurry at the end and was equipped with a verticle pipe as an exhaust flue. The two middle cans were the actual growth vessels, and they had spigots in the bottom for drawing off the contents: turn the tap and out poured a slurry of fresh-grown anthrax bacteria. That . . . had been their entire production works. . . . All you needed, basically, was a starter culture, a growth medium, and a container. And if what you were growing was *Bacillus anthracis*, the anthrax microbe, then you'd also have to pump air through the broth in order to get the bacteria to sporulate, for *Bacillus anthracis* was an aerobic bacterium and required air to reproduce. The anthrax growth medium . . . had been a typically British mixture of marmite (a commercial brewer's yeast), West Indian molasses, and distilled water, plus a few chemical herbs and spices. The growth cycle had taken some thirty-six hours from start to finish. They put a primer culture into the two culture churns, bubbled air through perforated aeration heads at the bottom, and let it sit for the next day or so. At the end of it they had simply drained off the liquid from the spigots. The final yield of a single growth cycle was a one-liter glass bottle of anthrax suspension.

Moreover, a cursory look at the early years of the U.S. BW program demonstrates that nations do not necessarily require the immense facilities that typified the Soviet program to produce significant quantities of agent (cf. Regis 1999; Tucker 2002; Miller et al., 2001). For example, at Fort Detrick during the early 1950s, the virus pilot plant in Building 434 employed thirty-four technicians who processed about one thousand eggs per day to obtain quarts of Q-fever slurries for testing (Miller, Engelberg, and Broad 2001, 46–47). The more elaborate Pine Bluff virus plant (known as X1002) built during the late 1950s, using technology clearly within reach of current proliferators, used a mechanized conveyor belt process to infect and harvest thousands of eggs for Venezuelan equine encephalitis (VEE) and Q fever virus:

> In a week, workers at X1002 could infect and process about 120,000 eggs, which . . . produced 120 gallons of agent [Q fever] . . . The pace of production was even higher for the virus that caused Venezuelan equine encephalitis, or VEE. In a week, workers on the mechanized line could infect and harvest about 300,000 eggs, which . . . produced nearly 500 gallons of . . . agent. (Miller, Engelberg, and Broad 2001, 49–50)

The U.S. program at Fort Detrick during the early 1940s adopted the British production approach, but replaced the four 13-gallon milk churns with four 100-gallon reactor tanks, surrounded by an external water jacket allowing for sterilization of the equipment and growth medium using pressurized steam generated by a wood-burning furnace and steam boiler. The "Black Maria" facility also included paddles within the reactor tanks (to stir the mixture before the start of the growth process) and a closed plumbing system (which drained the tanks directly into settling tanks below them) (Regis 1999, 44). Assigned the task of producing three kilograms of dried botullin toxin for the British, the Fort Detrick facility used the following simple procedure:

> The production cycle in "Black Maria" began with . . . sending steam through the water jackets of the empty 100-gallon fermenter tanks, then filling the tanks with the corn steep liquor and heating it almost to the boiling point. That sterilized the medium. After a prescribed time, they sent cold water through the jackets, cooling it down again. Then they were ready to inoculate the tank. There was a six-inch-wide hand hole in the top of each fermenter, and they removed the stopper, poured in a flask of the prepared starter culture, and replaced the stopper. They turned the hand cranks on the top of each fermenter, and the agitator paddles blended the mixture into a smooth broth. . . . For the next two days, the tanks simply sat there quietly while the bacteria inside them propagated, multiplied, and exuded toxin. At the end . . . each tank held a hundred gallons worth of extremely diluted botulinum. The . . . slurry [was drained] into the settling tanks on the ground floor of "Black Maria" and then . . . a coagulating agent [was added] to the mixture. The toxin molecules clotted together into bigger clumps that settled out at the bottom of the tank. The . . . consolidated mix [was then transferred] to a second and final settling tank. The final settling tank was long and slender, with a conical base that terminated in a short vertical pipe, the outflow from which was controlled by a value. . . . a five-gallon glass bottle [was then connected] to the outflow pipe, and at the end of the settling period they opened the valve and drew off the doubly-concentrated toxin. (Regis 1999, 45)

Patrick recalls that although the American BW program weaponized anthrax early on, "our favorite weapon was freeze-dried tularemia" because "we could modify or change the biological decay of tularemia from a high rate of decay to a much lower rate of decay" (Broad "Interviews: Bill Patrick" 2001). Patrick noted that while U.S. bioweaponeers studied plague "very hard" as a weapon, they had been unable to keep the organism virulent in a weaponized form, a puzzle the Soviet program later solved. While dry smallpox could remain viable as a weapon for years after manufacture, as a rule this was difficult to achieve with most viruses, which must have their storage stability factors increased by the use of chemicals (Broad "Interviews: Bill Patrick" 2001).

Given what we now know about the old Soviet BW program, if Russia continued its offensive program to the present day (which appears likely), a substantial number of pathogens will have been weaponized. Alibek (1999, 2) notes that by the early 1990s, the Soviet program had developed antibiotic-resistant strains of plague, anthrax, tularemia, and glanders, had developed smallpox and plague as *strategic biological weapons*, tularemia, glanders, and VEE as *operational biological weapons*, and anthrax, Q fever, and Marburg virus as *strategic-operational weapons*. In the decade since Alibek's defection, it is reasonable to assume other pathogens being developed during the last years of his tenure at Biopreparat (Lassa fever, Ebola, Machupo virus, Bolivian and Argentine hemorrhagic fevers, and Russia spring-summer encephalitis) have also been effectively weaponized by the Russian military's BW program (Alibek 1999, 2). Indeed, Alibek warns the Russian military is likely still running an offensive BW program (Alibek 1998, 1999, 267–69).[23] Despite Yeltsin's April 1992 decree calling for an end to any offensive work, Russia is suspected by the U.S. of continuing to develop its offensive BW program (especially in the area of genetic engineering) and of maintaining clandestine production facilities (Moodie 2001). There is great suspicion that Russia's BW program continues at its four leading military labs—at Zagorsk (Sergiyev Posad), Kirov, Sverdlovsk (Yekaterinburg), and Strizhi—all of which remain closed and inaccessible to Western inspection (Miller, Engelberg, and Broad 2001, 229).

China also has long been suspected of having an active "offensive" bioweapons program. A January 2001 DoD report warns: "China continues to maintain some elements of an offensive biological warfare program it is believed to have started in the 1950s. China possesses a sufficiently advanced biotechnology infrastructure to allow it to develop and produce biological agents. Its munitions industry is sufficient to allow it to weaponize any such agents, and it has a variety of delivery means that could be used for biological agent delivery. China is believed to possess an offensive biological warfare capability based on technology developed prior to its accession to the BWC in 1984" (Department of Defense January 2001, 14–15). Similarly, Taiwanese sources also suggest the existence of a Chinese BW program. Still, Croddy (2002, 26) questions whether Alibek's (1999) claim that a Crimean-Congo hemorrhagic fever outbreak during the late 1980s in the Xinjiang province near Lop Nor was the result of a release from a clandestine BW facility instead of a natural outbreak. While acknowledging China possesses considerable expertise in aerobiology, has the ability to mass-produce most traditional BW agents (including those it has already done extensive "defensive" research on, such as Q fever, tularemia, anthrax, plague, and eastern equine encephalitis), and has conducted laboratory scale aerosolization experiments on potential BW pathogens, Croddy argues it is impossible to accurately assess whether China has either conducted field tests of agents or has the technology to effectively deliver BW agents (Croddy 2002, 26).

However, given the efficient technologies employed by the U.S. and Soviet programs during the 1950s and 1960s to deliver slurries of agent using the jet streams of aircraft, for example, it seems rather optimistic to argue China lacks delivery capability for its agents. Given the extensive size of China's biological production base (which by 1994 made it the world's largest vaccine-producing nation, able to produce over 1.2 billion doses annually), its potential to develop clandestine facilities or convert civilian facilities to BW production are considerable. Indeed, according to U.S. intelligence, China possesses the indigenous ability to manufacture all of the components for an advanced BW production program, including large-scale fermenters, and freeze-driers. As Croddy (2002, 28) acknowledges, there have been reports of a much larger Chinese effort, allegedly involving large-scale R&D, cultivation, experimentation, and some weaponization work conducted at large biological facilities in Yan'an, Dalian, and Changchun, as well as extensive BW research and cultivation of agents at another nine facilities scattered across China (including ones in Beijing, Shanghai, Wuchang, and Chongqing).

The current Israeli BW program operates under the guise of the Israel Institute for Biological Research and was established at Ness Ziona in 1952 (Cohen 2001, 33). The Israeli BW program focuses on plague, typhus, rabies, and mosquito, flea, and tick-borne diseases, various toxins (among these, SEB), as well as numerous anti-livestock agents (Cohen 2001, 38). Cordesman (2002, 17) notes U.S. experts privately state that Israel is "one of the nations included in U.S. lists of nations with biological and chemical weapons." Not only is Israel believed to have stockpiled anthrax at Ness Ziona, but is also rumored to provide toxins to Israeli intelligence for covert operations and assassinations (Cordesman 2002, 17). Though opinion differs as to whether they are actively loaded and deployed aboard Israeli Defense Forces F-16s, U.S. experts believe Israel has "fully developed bombs and warheads capable of effectively disseminating dry, storable bioagents in micropowder form and has agents considerably more advanced than anthrax (Cordesman 2002, 17). Further, Cohen (2001, 31) suggests there is "little doubt" about an incident during the 1948 war where Israeli soldiers attempted to contaminate artesian wells in Gaza with canteens filled with dysentery and typhoid—an early biowarfare effort. Yet, in the absence of a Mordechai Vanunu–style whistle-blower, it is impossible to know for certain whether Israel's BW program is primarily defensive or offensive in orientation.

As for Iran, the CIA reported in late 2002 that "Iran probably maintains an offensive BW program" supported through procurement (primarily from Eastern Europe) of "dual-use biotechnical materials, equipment, and expertise" providing Tehran with the ability "to produce small quantities of BW agents" (Central Intelligence Agency 1 July through 31 December 2001).

Similarly, a January 2001 DoD report noted Iran was considered to possess the "overall infrastructure and expertise to support a biological warfare program." In fact, the report later explains:

> Iran has a growing biotechnology industry, significant pharmaceutical experience and the overall infrastructure to support its biological warfare program. Tehran has expanded its efforts to seek considerable dual-use biotechnical materials and expertise from entities in Russia and elsewhere, ostensibly for civilian reasons . . . . Iran's biological warfare program began during the Iran-Iraq war. Iran is believed to be pursuing offensive biological warfare capabilities and its effort may have evolved beyond agent research and development to the capacity to produce small quantities of agent.

In 2003, an Iranian exile group, Mujaheddin-e Khalq, which exposed Iran's secret nuclear enrichment program, also made unconfirmed claims Iran had begun production of weaponized anthrax, and was working with aflatoxin, typhus, plague, cholera, and smallpox in an effort to buildup a bioarsenal. The group reported that foreign experts from North Korea, Russia, China, and India had been recruited to assist the Iranian bioprogram. Although such reports are impossible to confirm, Albright notes that "often their information is correct, in part because they have reliable human sources well-placed in the Iranian government," and William Potter, director of the Center for Nonproliferation Studies at the Monterey Institute of International Studies, warns that "it can't be dismissed out of hand. . . . there is no doubt the Iranians have been very interested in such weapons. We know they left their calling cards at various institutes in the former Soviet Union seeking to recruit experts in the field" (Warrick 2003). In fact, in 1997, Iran approached Gen. Nikolai N. Urakov, director of the Obolensk Institute in Russia, once part of the Soviet BW program and currently repository to the world's largest collection of over 3,000 anthrax strains, with a request to share his center's biological expertise with Tehran—an overture which was rejected (Miller 2000). In summing up the Iranian BW program, Cordesman (2002, 39) observes:

> Iran has conducted research on more lethal active agents like Anthrax, hoof and mouth disease, and biotoxins. In addition, Iranian groups have repeatedly approached various European firms for the equipment and technology necessary to work with these diseases and toxins. . . . reports by U.S. experts indicate that Iran has begun to stockpile anthrax and Botulinum in a facility near Tabriz, can now mass manufacture such agents, and has them in an aerosol form. . . . Iran may have the production technology to make dry storable and aerosol weapons. . . . Iran is believed to have weaponized live agents and toxins for artillery and bombs and may be pursuing biological warheads for its missiles. The CIA reported in 1996 that . . . Iran holds some stocks of biological agents and weapons

. . . probably has investigated both toxins and live organisms as biological warfare agents. . . . [and] has the technical infrastructure to support a significant biological weapons program with little foreign assistance.

Further, Cordesman (2002, 30) notes that Iran has built numerous hardened shelters and tunnels along its coast to protect its ballistic and cruise missile forces. He suggests that "a U.S. examination of Iran's dispersal, sheltering, and hardening programs for its anti-ship missiles and other missile systems indicate Iran has developed effective programs to ensure they would survive a limited number of air strikes." Such steps would be necessary for the development of a regional deterrent force, whether based around nuclear or biological weapon force structures.

As for the North Korean BW program, some intelligence sources allege the North has an advanced BW program, modeled on the old Soviet program, that has not only developed anthrax, botulinum, and plague bioweapons, but also succeeded in producing anthrax particles in the four to five micron range and microencapsulated them to enhance their persistence after release (Mangold and Goldberg 1999, 329–30). An October 2001 DoD publication noted "in the early 1990s, an open press release by a foreign government referred to applied military biotechnology work at numerous North Korean medical institutes and universities dealing with the anthrax, cholera, plague and smallpox pathogens" (Department of Defense October 2001, 20). Obviously, these are bioagents routinely associated by most government assessments with the thrust of any active North Korean bioweapons program. As Tucker (2001, 203) notes:

In 1993, the Russian Foreign Intelligence Service. . . . published an unclassified report titled *A New Challenge After the Cold War: Proliferation of Weapons of Mass Destruction*. The entry for North Korea stated that Pyongyang was "performing applied military-biological research at a whole series of universities, medical institutes, and specialized research institutes. Work is being performed at these research centers with pathogens for malignant anthrax, cholera, bubonic plague, and smallpox." Supporting this allegation . . . was the fact that blood samples drawn from North Korean soldiers who had defected to the South contained antibodies to smallpox vaccine, and some of the vaccinations appeared fresh. Pyongyang could have acquired strains of variola virus from several sources: seed cultures transferred from the former Soviet Union or China, indigenous stocks dating back to the Korean War, or samples collected during smallpox epidemics in other developing countries during the 1960s and 1970s.

In fact, a 1998 South Korean Defense White Paper reported that North Korea had succeeded in producing bacterial and viral agents, engaged in live experiments with these weaponized agents in the late 1980s, and maintained several facilities suspected of producing bioweapons (Ministry of National Defense 1999, 65). Moreover, as Preston (2002, 95) warns:

The Russians themselves have told us that they lost control of their smallpox. They aren't sure where it went, but they think it migrated to North Korea. They haven't said when they lost control of it, but we think it happened around 1991, right when the Soviet Union was busting up. A master-seed strain of smallpox virus could be a freeze-dried bit of variola the size of a toast crumb, or it could be a liquid droplet the size of a teardrop. If a teardrop of India-1 smallpox disappeared from a storage container the size of a gasoline tanker truck, it would not be missed.

More recent intelligence analyses reinforce these suspicions and underscore at least the technical "potential" of North Korea to develop an advanced bioarsenal. For example, a January 2001 DoD publication noted their ongoing "research and development into biological agents and toxins suggest North Korea may have a biological weapons capability. (Department of Defense January 2001, 9). Similarly, an October 2001 DoD publication warned "North Korea does possess a sufficient munitions production infrastructure to accomplish weaponization of BW agents" (Department of Defense October 2001). Later, the CIA reported Pyongyang had acquired dual-use biotechnical equipment, supplies, and reagents that could be used to support BW efforts. As of late 2002, North Korea is believed to possess a munitions production infrastructure that would allow it to weaponize BW agents and may have such weapons available for use (Central Intelligence Agency 1 July through December 2001).

As for India and Pakistan, only the former is assumed to have an extensive bioweapons research program, which is generally assumed to be "defensive" in nature. According to a January 2001 DoD report: "India has many well-qualified scientists, numerous biological and pharmaceutical production facilities, and biocontainment facilities suitable for research and development of dangerous pathogens. At least some of these facilities are being used to support research and development for biological warfare defense work." This is in contrast to Pakistan, which was assessed to only "have the resources and capabilities to support a limited biological warfare research and development effort" (Department of Defense January 2001, 28). For the present, it would seem both of these states are focusing most of their energies upon nuclear weapons–related research and production rather than efforts in the biological realm.

Finally, the Iraqi BW program serves as an example of what even rudimentary technical capabilities were capable of providing a would-be biostate during the early 1990s—a deliverable bioweapons capability. The Iraqis developed relatively unsophisticated gravity bombs and spraying equipment to disperse their liquid anthrax weapon, developed botulinum toxin and aflatoxin biowarheads, and conducted extensive research into other potential bioagents (such as camelpox, ricin, and T2 mycotoxins) (Department of Defense October 2001). The most comprehensive report on Iraq's BW activities (pre–Gulf War and postwar disarmament) is Richard Butler's to the UN secretary general in January 1999.[24] Although the Iraqi BW program (along with its nuclear efforts) were brought to a halt by the First Gulf War and subsequent UNSCOM inspections, which uncovered and destroyed most of Iraq's capabilities, the progress Baghdad made prior to this serves to illustrate how far a new biostate could progress using only the technology and capabilities possessed by Iraq more than a decade ago. In fact, the lead-up to the Gulf War is an example of what is likely to be a recurring problem for policy makers dealing future security scenarios involving biologically armed states, namely a lack of clear understanding regarding their opponent's "use doctrine" regarding its bioweapons. Indeed, General Schwarzkopf's analysts admited there were "significant intelligence gaps" in their understanding of Iraq's "use doctrine" and the DIA, while reporting estimates of the size of the Iraqi BW arsenal, was still forced to acknowledge it had "no reliable information on how Iraq might use" its BW weapons. This problem is to be expected given the obvious lack of interest most states have in even acknowledging they *possess* a BW program, let alone communicating "use doctrines" to opponents. One of the few firm predictions came from the CIA, which warned ominously in November 1990 that: "If Saddam concluded his personal position was becoming hopeless . . . this could convince him to use biological weapons to shock the coalition into a cease-fire. In such a situation, the use of anthrax against a coalition military installation or major Saudi oil facility might seem an attractive option" (Miller, Engelberg, and Broad 2001, 113).

Among the scenarios that worried Pentagon planners was the potential Saddam could threaten retaliation against civilian populations in Coalition countries if attacks did not cease, or even more worrisome, that he could imply terrorists (against his wishes) were plotting a BW attack unless the bombing halted (Miller, Engelberg, and Broad 2001, 156). Concerns about civilian casualties caused by American preemptive strikes on likely germ factories or weapons stockpiles also were a concern. Though bioweapons experts suggested the amount of spores released from incendiary bombing of such sites would be quite low, perhaps between 0.001 and 0.1 percent, this would still result in potentially thousands of Iraqi civilians being killed by inhalation anthrax (Miller, Engelberg, and Broad 2001, 114–15). If not destroyed, scientists warned Pentagon officials Iraq's bioweapons could be "easily disseminated from aerosol sprayers used to apply pesticides." Highlighting the problem posed by dual-use technology, Iraq had earlier obtained forty modern aerosol generators from an Italian company compact enough to fit in the back of a pickup truck, a small boat, or a single-engine aircraft and capable of dispersing 800 gallons of liquid or dry agent per hour (Miller, Engelberg, and Broad 2001, 110). While their assessment prior to the war predicted Iraq would use BW "only as a last resort," a report by the Armed Forces Medical Intelligence staff noted numerous delivery systems were at Baghdad's disposal, including aircraft, artillery, missiles, and aerosol generators that could be carried on trucks, boats, or helicopters. In fact, the navy sent its commanders a warning on August 6, 1990, that Iraq could potentially possess bioweapons effective against ships at a distance of up to twenty-five miles and "would deploy these agents if needed" (Miller, Engelberg, and Broad 2001, 101–2).

## WHY BIOLOGICAL WEAPONS?

Countries choosing to pursue BW capabilities could be motivated by a number of different factors: (1) They may be facing either a much stronger, conventionally armed opponent or one possessing WMDs of their own, in which case, the threat of biowarfare might serve as an effective deterrent against their use; (2) They may be a nation in active pursuit of nuclear capabilities, but in their absence utilize bioweapons as an "interim" WMD to provide a stop-gap deterrent until their nuclear systems come online; (3) Bioweapons could be "coupled" with a nuclear arsenal to create a much more robust, versatile, and effective WMD deterrent or war-fighting capability, much like the Soviet Union's *strategic* thinking regarding BW during the Cold War; (4) Bioweapons could provide a variety of *tactical* military applications to augment the defensive or offensive missions of conventional forces; or (5) Bioweapons could provide *clandestine*, stealthy weapons of blackmail, disruption, or terrorism if used by a state or transferred to nonstate actors for use against opponents. All of these uses, however, depend upon the ability of state or nonstate actors to effectively deliver their bioagents onto target and disseminate them using one of two methods: *point-source* or *line-source* release.

*Point-source* release of bioagents involves any kind of delivery technique that limits the dispersal of material to a given, specific location. For example, state-run programs developed small bombs that dispersed agent using conventional explosives (Iraq) or more advanced bomblets that would nonexplosively release agent as they descended on parachutes toward targets (the U.S., Soviet Union).[25] The 2001 anthrax postal attacks in the U.S. employed small packages or envelopes in point-source attacks. Sending infected individuals into crowded areas, such as airports—the oft-suggested (but unlikely) terrorist approach to releasing smallpox—contamination of food or water supplies, or the introduction of agent into the ventilation systems of buildings would also be considered point-source attacks.[26] The advantage of such delivery is that it is generally capable of saturating a given area heavily with agent if successful. The downside, at least in terms of producing mass casualties, is that the area of release will be quite limited and these releases often "give away" the fact an attack has taken place—allowing medical treatment of those exposed.

In contrast, *line-source* releases involve delivery systems capable of widely dispersing a given material outdoors over a large geographic area in sufficient quantity to produce substantial effects on a target population. Using delivery systems like strategic bombers, modified fighter jets, cruise missiles, UAVs, or even crop dusters, an agent is released in a straight line upwind of the target. Given suitable weather conditions (e.g., nighttime release during an inversion), the agent would then slowly drift over a large area downwind of the release point, heavily contaminating any exposed population.[27] Moreover, it is a form of release which, in the absence of active monitoring of air samples for bioagents or discovery of the attackers by the authorities, would not provide defenders any telltale signs of attack (such as explosions, parachuting bomblets, or powder-laden packages). This prevents authorities from issuing preventative prophylactics or taking other defensive steps, since the attack would remain unrecognized until the first wave of clinical cases of disease appeared in medical facilities across the region. For producing mass casualties in a large urban area, the line-source release of a suitably virulent agent is ideal. And, as the U.S. open-range tests of bioagents using line-source releases demonstrated, hundreds of square miles could be effectively contaminated using a single aircraft.

However, either form of attack (point source or line source) still relies upon the ability to effectively disseminate a bioagent in aerosol form producing particles small enough (one to five microns in size) to be inhaled deeply into the lungs and cause infection. This obviously poses a critical question: How might bioagents be disseminated as aerosols? As Peters (2000, 202–3) notes:

> Only a limited number of viruses or bacteria are highly aerosol infectious; stabilization and dissemination of aerosolized organisms require special expertise; the particles must be of a small, discrete size to avoid settling out and to be able to deposit deep in the lung to efficiently initiate infection; and weather or wind conditions may confound delivery of an aerosol. Although these objections are all valid, aerosols have powerful advantages when they can be overcome. . . . Theoretically, airborne viruses can be disseminated silently and clandestinely over very wide areas to achieve infections of large numbers of people. Many in-

cidents of aerosol infections in the laboratory attest to the insidious way in which coworkers and passers-by have been infected by the low intensity aerosols generated in laboratory procedures.

In fact, Patrick (1996, 208–10) observes that aerosolization of either liquid or dry powder forms of agents into particles small enough to be easily respirated can be accomplished by a variety of means—some of which are easier than others. For example, although crude liquid slurries of agents can be effectively disseminated as aerosols by explosive energy from devices, the slipstream energy of high performance aircraft and missiles, or gaseous energy from self-contained devices (such as compressors using nozzles)—these techniques tend to be quite difficult and posed a challenge to even state-run BW programs like Iraq's (Patrick 1996, 208–10). The primary problem with employing liquid BW agents is that many of the aerosolization techniques result in high levels of mortality for the agents themselves (even when these are hardy anthrax spores). For example, explosive charges creating aerosols of the appropriate particle size of one to five microns also tend to kill all but 1 percent of the spores and all but 0.1 percent of vegetative cells! One effective means of disseminating liquid BW agents would be to use the slipstream energy of high performance aircraft or missiles. But, while state programs might be able to master the technique, the use of the turbulent energy created by aircraft, missiles, or turbojet engines is deemed to be beyond the abilities of even the most sophisticated terrorist groups (Patrick 1996, 208).

Probably of greater use would be the gaseous energy produced by compressors that push liquid agent through a narrow nozzle at high pressure to produce a small particle aerosol (something of use for outfitting cruise missiles or crop dusters to release agent). For example, a two-fluid nozzle and assembly composed of quality grade stainless steel produces an aerosol recovery of about 10 percent when a standard *Bacillus subtilis* liquid is used, and requires only the use of a first-rate machine shop to produce if a terrorist possesses the basic technical knowledge. Less effective would be a simple single-fluid nozzle using high-pressure gas, which only produces an aerosol recovery of around 1 percent—a small number, but still potentially effective for a terrorist attacking a small site. A problem common to all of these methods of dispensing liquid agent is the small orifices in sprayer nozzles become easily plugged, especially if the liquid has not been extensively processed to eliminate any extraneous materials from the slurry or the liquid itself is too viscous to effectively flow through the nozzles without causing blockages (Patrick 1996, 209). Mechanical stresses created by the pressure from the fine nozzles required to obtain the appropriate particle size also has the downside that up to 95 percent of the pathogens in liquid agent are killed by the spraying process. Liquid aerosols also do not tend to remain airborne for long distances, reducing the area downwind affected by a release (Smithson and Levy 2000, 55).

In contrast, advanced dry powders (characterized by high agent concentration, small particle size, and absence of electrostatic charge) are easily disseminated from any number of devices, require only small amounts of energy to produce an aerosol, and preserve a high proportion of viable particles upon release. This, in addition to their ease of storage and enhanced shelf life, is why powdered agents are the weapon of choice for advanced BW programs. Even an ABC fire extinguisher filled with a standard *Bacillus subtilis var niger* powder achieves a greater than 40 percent aerosol recovery of viable particles using roughly twenty psi, compared to only 10 percent recovery for a well-made two-fluid nozzle device! (Patrick 1996, 208–10) Thus, dry powders are the most versatile and easily disseminated agent (Patrick 1996, 209).

Cruise missiles could provide an immensely effective delivery system for either form of bioagent. In the Soviet BW program, special twenty-liter canisters for carrying liquid or dry agent were developed for release from cruise missiles as they passed over successive targets, canisters which would break apart upon impact with the air to release their contents (Alibek 1999, 140). As Alibek recalled, harnessing cruise missiles would "dramatically improve the strategic effectiveness of biological warfare":

> Cruise missiles would require far smaller quantities of biological agents than intercontinental missiles and would do just as much damage. And they would increase our capacity for surprise. Multiwarhead intercontinental missiles can be detected by electronic surveillance minutes after they are launched. Planes can be detected by ground observers, giving civil defense and medical teams time to ascertain that an attack has occurred, determine what kind of agent was used, and mobilize for treatment. A cruise missile would offer little advance warning. (Alibek 1999, 141)

Cruise missiles adapted to release bioagents from aerosol sprayers in their wings could be made even more efficient though the use of built-in meteorological sensors allowing guidance computers to alter the missiles flight profiles and "release a line source of BW agent tailored to the local topography, micrometeorlogical conditions, and shape of the target, thus maximizing the resultant lethal area of the BW payload" (Kiziah 2003). Cruise missiles with biowarheads could be launched with little warning near coastlines or just off the territorial waters of the U.S. from normal cargo freighters. Launched from such locations, it would be difficult to intercept such missiles, even in the unlikely event they were detected in the first place. And because of the small size, low radar, infrared, and visual signatures, LACMs (land-attack cruise missiles) would have high survivability in penetrating air defenses and reaching their targets, even were nominally effective theater missile defense (TMD) systems in place. Moreover, small state opponents could easily complicate the efforts of any air defense network by treating their cruise missiles with radar-absorbing coatings, constructing airframes using radar-absorbing polymers or nonmetallic composites, or by incorporating infrared (IR) reduction cones around their engines to reduce IR signatures (Kiziah 2003). Cruise missiles could also be equipped with simple, but highly effective countermeasures—such as chaff ejectors and decoy flares—to further complicate the task of interceptor missiles.[28]

As a result of the proliferation of technology and know-how, Kiziah (2000, 29) warns "commercial availability of accurate satellite navigation updates has allowed Third World countries to leapfrog probably 15 years of development for long-range, fairly accurate LACMs." Rather than starting from scratch with highly expensive R&D programs, as most great powers were forced to do, new states can rapidly acquire the technology to produce cruise missile systems. And, in the unlikely event the U.S. developed reasonably effective national missile defense (NMD) systems to upgrade its air defenses, an opponent still may be able to overwhelm these defenses if they coupled the launching of theater or long-range ballistic missiles with the clandestine launching of cruise missiles scheduled to reach their targets simultaneously. Such an attack, or even a more limited one in a given region using only short- to medium-range missiles coupled with cruise missiles, would create substantial problems for the defender. As one specialist warns, "the different characteristics of these two approaching missiles—the high-altitude, supersonic ballistic trajectory of the ballistic missiles and the low-altitude, subsonic flight of the cruise missiles—could overwhelm the capabilities of even the most sophisticated air defense systems" (Kiziah 2003).

Interestingly, Kiziah (2000, 49–50) notes a study conducted by a team of scientists and engineers tasked with ascertaining how difficult it would be for a third world state (like Iran or Syria) to convert existing Chinese HY-4 Silkworm ASCMs (antiship cruise missiles) into LACMs capable of delivering BW agents at 500-, 700-, and 1,000-kilometer ranges.[29] The results illustrate the ease with which ASCMs can be converted to serve as biocruise missiles:

The conversion of the HY-4 into a 300-kg payload, 500-km range LACM/BW (or biocruise) weapon system, which will be called the Biocruise-500, required four modifications: (1) replacement of the autopilot and radar subsystems with a land-attack navigation system costing only an estimated $40,000 and constructed from commercially available GPS-GLONASS integrated receivers, radar altimeter, inertial measurement unit, flight management computer, electronic servos, and DC power system with alternator; (2) installation of extra internal fuel tanks for additional fuel; (3) installation of wing tip sprayers for BW liquid agent release; and (4) development of guidance software for the most efficient dispersal of the agents. The 1,000-km range LACM, the Biocruise-1000, required reduction of the BW payload to 120 kg and the additional and more complicated modification of lengthening the existing HY-4 fuselage to carry more fuel. This paper study led to the conclusion that China, Iran, Iraq, North Korea, and Pakistan possess the ability to convert the HY-4 into Biocruise-500s or 1000s. Furthermore, with limited outside assistance, a resourceful and creative proliferant like Iran could probably produce the Biocruise-1000 within 7 to 10 years. If the outside assistance were more substantial, including experienced technicians, senior engineers, and advanced production equipment, the time might be halved to four or five years. The cost of the Biocruise-1000 was estimated to be $250,000–$350,000, substantially less than the $500,000–$1,000,000 price tag for the Iraqi Al Hussein ballistic missile. (Kiziah 2003, 50)

The example of the fictional Biocruise 500s and 1000s is that such systems, if employing low-observable technologies and simple countermeasures (like chaff and decoys), have a good chance of penetrating air defenses and delivering their payloads. Indeed, Kiziah warns that by 2005, one or more states may possess biocruise systems capable of delivering bioagents in a highly effective manner against military or civilian targets in regional conflicts (Kiziah 2003, 51–52).

Among other BW delivery systems that could easily be developed by states are the use of naval mines for clandestine delivery of agent. For example, the U.S. developed the E-4 marine mine for just such a purpose:

It was designed to be fired from a submarine's torpedo tube, but instead of speeding toward an enemy ship it would remain motionless under water for a specified period of up to two hours. Then it would rise to the surface. At that point, the mine's C generators would poke out above the waves and disseminate into the prevailing wind some forty-five quarts of a biological agent, a particular strain of virus or bacteria that would waft toward the enemy ship, and, depending on the species of microbe used, would either kill or incapacitate the crew. The mine would then scuttle itself and sink to the bottom forevermore. (Regis 1999, 4)

It is useful to remember also that by 1958, the U.S. had developed a BW warhead for its 762-millimeter Honest John rocket capable of delivering 356 4.5-inch spherical bomblets onto targets sixteen miles distant, and by the 1960s had developed a warhead for the Sergeant missile able to deliver 720 bomblets at ranges up to seventy-five miles (Mangold and Goldberg 1999, 37–38). New biostates with ballistic missile programs of at least early 1960s U.S. technical capabilities should equally be considered capable of developing similar types of delivery systems.

The *strategic* use of bioweapons, for either deterrence or war-fighting purposes, has long been seen as perhaps the primary reason for states to develop such capabilities. Indeed, countries facing extreme threats from external opponents could seek bioweapons to act as "a poor man's atomic bomb" to deter aggression against them. As Carus (1991, 38–39) notes, "given that biological weapons are most suitable for attacks on large areas, and for use against unprotected populations, BW programs seem well suited as weapons of mass destruction." In fact, during WWII, British military strategists developed plans for a mass strategic bombing campaign over six German cities (Berlin, Hamburg, Stuttgart, Frankfurt, Aachen, and Wilhelmshaven) using four-pound anthrax bomblets which Churchill's staff estimated would wipe out half of these cities populations and render them contaminated for years (Mangold and Goldberg 1999, 33–34). However, the war ended before the necessary weapons could be produced. Yet, the long-term effects of the strategic use of BW could have been quite startling. Given the British BW testing site at Gruinard Island, off the coast of Scotland, was still contaminated with anthrax spores more than *forty years* after the original tests, had anthrax bombs been used on Berlin during World War II, the city would still be contaminated to this day (Cole 1998, 6).

By the 1970s, the Soviets "had managed to harness single-warhead intercontinental ballistic missiles for use in the delivery of biological agents." One of the biggest hurdles overcome in developing true strategic BW capability had been the problem of producing agent in enough quantity to fill a large number of missile warheads in a relatively brief period of time. As Alibek recalls, 400 kilograms of dry powdered anthrax was required to arm the ten biowarheads aboard a single SS-18 ICBM (roughly forty kilograms per warhead)—a substantial amount (Alibek 1999, 5–6). In fact, it took a single twenty-ton fermenter working at full capacity for one or two days to produce enough spores to fill one strategic missile, which even given massive Soviet BW production facilities, required ten to fourteen days to produce enough material for its rocket forces (Alibek 1999, 6–7). Yet each one of these biowarheads were fearsome strategic weapons, easily the equivalent of a nuclear warhead in terms of the potential casualties they could deliver on a major U.S. city. Delivering a payload of "a hundred kilograms of anthrax spores would, in optimal atmospheric conditions, kill up to three million people in any of the densely populated metropolitan areas of the United States. A single SS-18 could wipe out the population of a city as large as New York." Of course, anthrax was not the only agent the Soviets weaponized for delivery aboard their SS-18s. Smallpox and bubonic plague were also developed for use inside strategic biowarheads, and research was underway to develop the prototype for a strategic biowarhead using the Marburg virus (a close relative of Ebola) (Alibek 1999, 8). An elaborate production system was established with six biowarfare facilities around the country that could be mobilized as special production units in the event of war, when agents would be poured into bomblets and spray tanks for transport to military sites for placement aboard bombers or ballistic missiles (Alibek 1999, 89).

Clearly, the most advanced modes of attack remain limited to states possessing sophisticated BW programs. For example, during the Soviet-era, bioweaponeers succeeded in modifying pathogens to survive delivery by warhead and engineers succeeded in developing platforms that could release canisters of liquid or dry pathogens (such as anthrax, smallpox, plague, etc.) as the missile moved over successive targets" (Brownlee 2001). To amplify the effectiveness of their bioagents and maximize civilian casualties and disruption, Soviet strategic targeting of U.S. and British cities in the event of total war would have employed "cocktails" of between three to five agents per attack— usually involving combinations of weapons-grade anthrax, plague, tularemia, smallpox, and Marburg weapons (Mangold and Goldberg 1999, 182–83). According to Alibek (1999, 2), Soviet military doctrine divided bioweapons into three main categories—*strategic*, *operational*, and *strategic-operational*. Strategic bioweapons utilized highly lethal and contagious pathogens (such as smallpox or plague) which could be delivered by ICBM to distant countervalue (city) targets in the U.S. to inflict maximum casualties upon the population and undermine the ability of the society to continue military operations. In contrast, operational bioweapons would employ less lethal, incapacitating pathogens (such as tularemia, brucellosis, glanders, and Venezuelan equine encephalitis) against deep military targets 100 to 150 kilometers behind an opponent's front lines in order to degrade defenses and disrupt rear area support and reinforcement operations. Strategic-operational bioweapons were those that could be used against either strategic or operational targets using agents such as anthrax, Marburg, or Q fever (Alibek 1999, 2).

Skeptics regarding the *tactical* military value of bioweapons usually point to the many factors limiting their effectiveness on the battlefield or when deployed against cities. There is the problem of time lag for many agents between time of release and the onset of symptoms in a target population. For tactical use on a battlefield, this could be a problem if one is depending upon bioweapons to immediately impact combat operations by incapacitating personnel. On the other hand, if one is interested in disrupting command-and-control, logistics, and supply lines in rear areas prior to the start of combat operations, bioagents could be ideal. And, as Dando (2001, 19) notes, a more rapid effect can be accomplished through the use of toxins in aerosol form (examples would be botulinum toxin and staphylococcal enterotoxin B, or SEB), which do not require incubation periods. Moreover, if one is looking to inflict *mass casualties* upon soft, civilian targets, such as urban or residential areas, strategic bioweapons, though suffering from a time lag, would still more than compensate for this delay through the immense level of damage inflicted upon an opponent. Additional problems for bioweapons include the fact aerosol dissemination of agents can be greatly impacted by temperature and weather conditions, with heavy rain or snow, wind currents, or high humidity impeding effective delivery, and ultraviolet radiation from sunlight quickly killing most viruses or bacteria (Alibek 1999, 20–21). There is also the danger of immense civilian casualties (or collateral damage) from attempts to use such weapons tactically against an opponent's military forces, as well as the danger of "blow back" (or contamination of one's own military forces or population centers due to a shift in wind direction or the contagious nature of some microbes). However, as experienced bioweaponeers like Alibek note:

Such obstacles complicate the planning of a biological attack, but they are not insurmountable. A bioweaponeer will know to strike at dusk, during periods when a blanket of cool air covers a warmer layer over the ground—a weather condition called an inversion, which keeps particles from being blown away by wind currents. We packed our biological agents in small melon-sized metal balls, called bomblets, set to explode several miles upwind from the target city. Meticulous calculation would be required to hit several cities at the same time with maximum effectiveness, but a single attack launched from a plane or from a single sprayer perched on a rooftop requires minimal skill. (Alibek 1999, 21)

In fact, concern about "blow-back" effects is why many of the agents weaponized by the U.S. BW program during the 1950s and 1960s involved either *incapacitating* agents, like VEE or SEB (pathogens producing low mortality rates, but high prostration effects), or *lethal* agents, like anthrax or tularemia, that were *not communicable*. Prevaccination of one's own military personnel (or even the civilian populace) against a bioagent that might be used, or the active stockpiling of vaccines, antidotes, or antibiotics, also provide protection against blow-back. Thus, while the *tactical* utility of bioweapons has often been dismissed due to a lack of immediacy of effects for most (but not all) such weapons, this overemphasis on the time lag between employment and effects misses the point. An "adaptive" enemy could easily use such weapons to disrupt an opponent's conventional military support operations. As Carus (1991, 36–37) observes:

Forces stationed in rear areas are obvious targets. This could include reserve combat units, formations massing behind the lines in preparation for an offensive, or air force squadrons. Biological weapons might also be aimed at rear area support units. The benefits of incapacitating command and control, intelligence, and logistics units are clear. Without such units, the fighting effectiveness of any modern military force would be significantly reduced.

Prior to the First Gulf War, U.S. military planners were very concerned about the battlefield potential of Iraq's stocks of botulinum toxin weapons against Coalition frontline troops, who could be affected by this fast-acting poison within hours of exposure and suffer substantial casualties (Miller, Engelberg, and Broad 2001, 119). While Bush secretly made a decision not to threaten Iraq with nuclear retaliation for any chemical or biological strike, Pentagon planners still developed contingency plans for nuclear strikes in the event of a particularly lethal biostrike. But, chemical weapons had little potential to cause the kind of apocalyptic casualty levels on American forces to make the threat of U.S. nuclear retaliation credible. Only bioweapons could inflict those kind of mass casualties, whether on U.S. forces or against civilians in neighboring states. But, this begs the question of whether Iraqi use of BW during the war was really a credible threat in that context, or whether that credibility would only apply if Coalition forces invaded Iraq proper to overthrow the regime? Koblentz (2003/2004, 103–6) argues bioweapons are not "well-suited to serving as a strategic deterrent" because they do not provide assured destruction capability against opponents (since defensive measures can be taken to mitigate their destructive potential). Instead, Koblentz argues bioweapons only have the potential to serve as an "in-kind deterrent or contribute to a state's general deterrence posture" (Koblentz 2003/2004, 104). But, while this may be true regarding states *lacking* survivable, deliverable BW (or nuclear) capabilities, will this always be the case? Given the increasing proliferation of advanced BW-relevant technologies and delivery capabilities, as well as the potential for developing novel, designer pathogens that could circumvent existing medical defenses, these conclusions are quite suspect if applied to the future.[30]

The potential tactical value of bioweapons can be illustrated by the impact of natural outbreaks of disease on military campaigns. For example, during World War I, the debilitating effects of the Spanish flu was cited by German commander Erich von Ludendorff as largely to blame for the failure of his great summer offensive of 1918 (which might have won the war for Germany had it succeeded, but guaranteed its defeat with its failure) (Davies 2000, 58–59; Kolata 1999, 11). The British grand fleet was unable to put to sea for three weeks in May 1918 because over 10,000 sailors were afflicted, and the British army's Twenty-Ninth Division had to cancel an attack at La Becque in June 1918 for the same reason (Kolata 1999, 11). Over 25 percent of the U.S. population came down with the illness and, perhaps unsurprisingly given the strain's predilection for striking young healthy males, the American military suffered greatly (36 percent of army personnel and 40 percent of navy personnel were afflicted) (Kolata 1999, 6–7).

There have also been claims the Soviets employed tularemia as a bioweapon against the Germans during the summer of 1942 near Stalingrad. For example, Alibek makes the case that a tularemia weapon, developed at a secret facility in Kirov in 1941, had likely been sprayed at the Germans during the Battle of Stalingrad, resulting in significant casualties and a slowing of the momentum of the German offensive. In addition to the confirming testimony of former Soviet BW officers of the time, Alibek points to epidemiological studies of the 1942 outbreak showing over 100,000 cases of the illness, first centering directly around the German military forces and a week later spreading to Soviet soldiers and civilians in the surrounding areas. This outbreak looks even more suspicious considering it occurred only on the German side initially (despite the close proximity of Soviet forces), that 70 percent of the German casualties came down with pneumonic forms of the disease (a rare form unlikely to be caused in such numbers in the absence of aerosol dissemination), and that the average number of tularemia cases across the entire Soviet Union on either side of the Stalingrad outbreak (1941 and 1943) consisted of only 10,000 cases annually (Alibek 1999, 30–31). Given the German offensive at Stalingrad threatened the very survival of the Soviet Union, it is not surprising bioweapons (if available) would have been used against the invaders—just as nuclear weapons would in a later age. A similar, suspicious outbreak of Q fever among German forces in the Crimea in 1943 (a disease practically unheard of before or after in the Soviet Union) has also been suggested to have been the result of a deliberate Soviet BW attack (Alibek 1999, 35–36). More recently, it was suggested the Soviets employed a glanders bioweapon in Afghanistan between 1982 and 1984, outbreaks noted by U.S. intelligence at the time.[31]

Yet, whether Alibek's claims are true or not, the fact remains that bioweapons hold some promise for weaker states facing major strategic challenges from stronger opponents or intractable low-intensity conflicts. Although the context Alibek describes will be different for new bioweapon states, the underlying logic might not be:

> Russia is interested in maintaining its offensive biological potential because biological weapons have unique capabilities. Imagine the situation in a mountainous region like Chechnya or Afghanistan. It's very difficult to fight in the mountains using conventional weapons. But a single plane or cruise missile armed with biological weapons could kill absolutely everybody in any deep valley in the mountains. That's unfortunately a good application of biological warfare. So these weapons can be considered highly effective for certain types of low-intensity or high-intensity conflict. Especially, in my opinion, for a country

that is losing its conventional military potential and becoming weaker practically every single day. (Alibek 1999, 9)

The U.S., though never employing BW in wartime, still developed elaborate plans for the tactical use of agents during the 1960s. Of particular interest is the Marshall Plan, which unlike its economic counterpart, was actually a plan calling for a massive BW strike against the Cuban military and civilian population as a precursor to an American invasion. The Pentagon estimated that of a potential 180,000 strong invasion force, it was likely in the first ten days of battle, U.S. casualties would reach 18,500 dead or wounded (Miller, Engelberg, and Broad 2001, 54). While the Marshall Plan was never considered for use by Kennedy or his inner circle during the Cuban Missile Crisis, it is noteworthy for elaborating the military utility of BW in support of U.S. conventional operations.

Relying upon a special "cocktail" of two different incapacitating pathogens (Venezuelan equine encephalitis virus, known as VEE, and Q fever virus) and one biological toxin (staphylococcal enterotoxin B, known as SEB, which causes food poisoning) to incapacitate the Cubans within hours for up to three weeks, specially equipped American jets would release the agent over Cuban cities, military bases, moving east to west into the trade winds (Miller, Engelberg, and Broad 2001, 55–57). VEE has long been utilized as a bioweapon by state-run BW programs. Although it has a mortality rate of less than 1 percent, it produces an incapacitating illness in humans within two to five days that can last weeks (Weaver and Glaes 1997, 151). If released as an aerosol in a bioattack, especially during the warmer times of the year when mosquitoes were present, it is likely a second wave of infection would occur by this vector—potentially creating a source of endemic infection. There exists no licensed vaccine or effective antiviral treatment for VEE in humans (Weaver and Glaes 1997, 164). The Pentagon estimated that of Cuba's population of 7 million, around 70,000 people (roughly 1 percent of the population) would die from the agent, far less than the casualties resulting to both U.S. forces and the Cuban population in a full-blown conventional military assault. Moreover, since the diseases in the "cocktail" are not contagious, there would be no threat to U.S. forces once the mist had dissipated (Miller, Engelberg, and Broad 2001, 57). As Riley D. Housewright, Fort Detrick's scientific director at the time, later recalled, employing the incapacitating agents (instead of lethal ones) "showed that there was a humane aspect to the whole situation. It was not the same as putting an atomic bomb down their throat, which would have been just as easy or easier to deliver. It was a humane act" (Miller, Engelberg, and Broad 2001, 55–56).

Similarly, commenting upon the Marshall Plan in 1999, Patrick argued the tactical use of incapacitating, low-lethality bioweapons could be viewed as *morally superior* to the use of conventional explosives:

> I can make a very good case for biological warfare as a more humane way of fighting war than with the atom bomb and chemical warfare. We can incapacitate a population with less than 1 percent of the people becoming ill and dying. And then we take over facilities that are intact. When you bomb a country, you not only kill people but you destroy the very facilities that are needed to treat them—the electricity, water, all the infrastructure is gone when you bomb. So, to my way of thinking, if you must have warfare, if you use incapacitating agents, it is more humane than what we refer to now as "conventional warfare" with bombs and conventional weapons. (Broad "Interviews: Bill Patrick" 2001)[32]

Interestingly, on a practical level, UNSCOM inspectors found videotape of an Iraqi remote-controlled Phantom jet drone doing a line-source lay down over the desert in a technique that looked precisely like those used by the U.S. in its BW tests over the Pacific during the 1960s (Preston 1998, 52–65). Moreover, during the fall of 1989, Iraq developed a biobomb (by modifying existing R-400 aerial bombs) which could be aircraft delivered and employed parachutes to slow them sufficiently to allow better dispersal of their ninety liters of anthrax or botulinum (Miller, Engelberg, and Broad 2001, 186–87).[33] According to UN inspectors, Iraq's BW program, originally only able to produce a wet anthrax slurry for its missiles and bombs, later acquired the ability to produce high-grade, dry anthrax of the appropriate particle size needed for aerosol distribution (Johnston and Mitchell 2001). Iraq developed 2,000-liter tanks to spray anthrax or botulinum from jet aircraft and modified chemical warheads for their Scud missiles to carry 145 liters of anthrax, botulinum, or aflatoxin.[34] While conventional explosives would have destroyed much of the agent in these bomb munitions, the aerosol generators and spray tanks would have allowed a significant attack had they evaded Coalition air defenses (Miller, Engelberg, and Broad 2001, 186–87). In fact, Baghdad purchased specialized nozzles for its fleet of crop dusters to allow widespread dispersal of powdered anthrax agent (Johnston and Mitchell 2001). Though these missile and bomb delivery systems were crude by U.S. or Soviet standards, experts who examined them noted, "this would have worked" (Miller, Engelberg, and Broad 2001, 186).

Clearly, the lesson to be learned from these examples is not only do bioweapons have tactical military utility, but this potential has historically been considered by states possessing BW capabilities in their planning. Were an opponent (whether a state or nonstate actor) able to obtain large quantities of the type of dried anthrax powder used in the U.S. bioattacks, it would clearly be possible to stage a credible, mass-casualty attack on a city itself (were crop dusters or other aerosol generators employed) or on enclosed public facilities (such as office buildings, malls, or subway systems). Although crop dusters would have to be fitted with specialized nozzles to disperse such agent, it is a technical hurdle that could be circumvented were expert advice available (in the form of former bioweapons scientists) or enough resources devoted to the task by a state actor.

As for the *clandestine* use of bioweapons to support blackmail, disruption, or terrorism, there is a long history of exactly these kinds of uses. For example, South Africa possessed an advanced BW program, known as *Project Coast*, during the apartheid era which was primarily used to assassinate black opponents of the regime (Burgess and Purkitt 2001). Similarly, the Soviet BW program during the Cold War was known to have had a substantial "wet works" project providing bioweapons and toxins for use in assassinations of opponents (Alibek 1999), the most famous of which was the killing in London of a prominent dissident using an umbrella-tip injection of deadly ricin pellets. Noting the ease with which bioweapons might be produced, the CIA warned that bioweapons were far more likely to be used by terrorists than nuclear weapons (Central Intelligence Agency 1996). Indeed, Richard Butler, the former head of UNSCOM, remarked that, "Everyone wonders what kinds of delivery systems Iraq may have for biological weapons, but it seems to me that the best delivery system would be a suitcase left in a Washington subway" (Preston 1998, 52–65). Indeed, a DoD study in 1949 demonstrated that a BW simulant introduced into a single air-conditioning unit in the Pentagon effectively distributed the agent throughout the entire building, demonstrating the ease with which a knowledgable attacker could stage a serious bioattack.[35] And, as Alibek warns, the extent of the Soviet BW program "shouldn't lead anyone to assume that biological warfare is beyond the grasp of poorer nations" (Alibek 1999, 276). The same could be said for large, well-funded terror organizations.

Moreover, stealth attacks could leave people unaware and allow no early medical intervention—a lethal combination. As C. J. Peters, director of the Center for Biodefense at the University of Texas at Galveston, observed, someone capable of producing the quality of material sent in the Daschle letter could easily manufacture larger quantities, but even the two grams from the letter could be devastating: "With two grams of finely milled anthrax, if you can disseminate it in a closed system like a subway or building, you could infect hundreds of thousands of people." Further, the infectious dose of anthrax might be quite small, with one Office of Technology Assessment (OTA) report suggesting "1,000 spores or less can produce fatal pulmonary anthrax" in some people (Powell and Connolly 2001). After the 1995 Tokyo sarin subway attacks by the Aum Shinrikyo cult (which killed twelve and injured 5,500), and various U.S. studies done in New York, Washington, D.C., and other city subways during the 1950s and 1960s, it has generally been accepted by experts that a well carried out attack using high-grade BW agents could produce mass casualties (Begley "Mass Transit" 2001, 36–37). A surreptitious release of anthrax, or worse, a contagious pathogen like smallpox, into a city's subway system would also make it extraordinarily difficult for authorities to later trace where the attack had occurred or who among the general public might need medical treatment or isolation to prevent the spread of the disease. When considering the potential of bioweapons, it is useful to bear in mind the distinction many former bioweaponeers make regarding how to think about them:

The most effective biological weapons go on killing long after they are used. Some viruses, such as Marburg, are so hazardous that casually inhaling as few as three microscopic viral particles several days after an attack would be enough to kill you. Biowarfare strategists often look beyond the immediate target to focus on the epidemic behavior of disease-causing agents. Unlike nuclear weapons, which pulverize everything in their target area, biological weapons leave buildings, transportation systems, and other infrastructure intact. They should properly be called *mass casualty weapons*, not weapons of mass destruction. (Alibek 1999, 22) [emphasis added]

In fact, viruses have long been considered "among the most valuable munitions" in the arsenals of BW states because of their ability to infect vast numbers of people with smaller amounts of material than required by bacteriologically based agents. As Alibek notes:

Fewer than five viral particles of smallpox were sufficient to infect 50 percent of the animals exposed to aerosols in our testing labs. To infect the same percentage of humans with anthrax would require ten thousand to twenty thousand spores. For plague, the comparable figure is fifteen hundred cells. The differences in quantity are too minute to be discernible to the naked eye, but they are significant if you are planning attacks on a large scale. Smallpox requires almost no concentration process. (Alibek 1999, 115)

But, any discussion of the *clandestine use* of bioweapons involves an assessment of how likely any nonstate terror group (like Al Qaeda) would be to make use of such pathogens to stage an attack.

## THE DEBATE OVER LIKELIHOOD

Terrorism experts had long argued, at least prior to the events of and following September 11th, that the historical record did *not* suggest terrorists would
want to use WMDs or seek to cause mass civilian casualties in future attacks,
noting as Brian Jenkin's had, "[t]errorists want a lot of people *watching*, not
a lot of people *dead*" (Jenkins 1985, 511).[36] The logic of the argument was
that historically, terrorists wanted to legitimize their political grievances or
achieve certain political goals through the use of mainly symbolic acts of violence targeting limited numbers of people. To do otherwise, and engage in
nonconventional attacks causing massive, indiscriminate civilian casualties,
would only create popular revulsion (among both their own supporters and
the victimized populace), delegitimize their political agenda, and likely result
in an overwhelmingly harsh response from government authorities.[37] These
factors were seen as sufficient to deter terrorists from adopting WMDs and
mass-casualty strategies in the foreseeable future. Moreover, the uncritical
overreliance upon simplistic, if sophisticated, data sets of historical terrorism
incidents led many to unwarranted beliefs that "past would be prologue" and
that statistical trends of the 1970s and 1980s would hold into the coming
decades and predict future terrorist behavior. A good example of this under-
estimation of the threat posed by terrorism was a piece by Larry Johnson in
the *New York Times* on July 10, 2001 entitled, "The Declining Terrorist
Threat," which made the case that based upon statistical analyses of global
terrorism patterns, the threat was vastly overdrawn and that the frequency of
attacks was actually going down and would continue to do so in the coming
decade (Johnson 2001).

Unfortunately, concealed beneath the surface methodological sophistication of these data sets was the unwelcome reality that these were inevitably
*small-n* sets that could not in any sense be argued to capture with certainty the
entire range of the variables (i.e., the breadth of the universe of possible terrorist groups or constellations of capability) that would allow meaningful pre-
diction. More critically, these data sets are ahistorical because they place historical events they catalog "out of context," do not take into account that
terror group motivations and capabilities have changed dramatically over the
decades (with the rise of religious extremist groups), and fail completely to
recognize that changes brought about by the increasing proliferation of WMD
technology and know-how provides opportunities impossible for past terror
groups to even consider. As a result, no matter how sophisticated the data set,
comparisons of data from the 1970s and 1980s, or perhaps even the 1990s,
offer no reliable guide to the likely behavior of terror groups of the twenty-
first century. The historical periods are just too dissimilar to allow for mean-

ingful comparison. Illustrating the danger of uncritical overreliance upon statistical data of historical events, former CIA director James Woolsey remarked:

> A lot of people like to put their heads in the sand. We had one, I won't name him, we had one nationally famous expert, so-called, on terrorism testify to the terrorism commission that I was on in 2000, that terrorism had never been really more than a nuisance. And I said, that may be right and if you had said on December 6th, 1941 that the Japanese navy had never been more than a nuisance, you would have been right too!"[38]

At least prior to the U.S. anthrax attacks of 2001, many security analysts also tended to mostly discount the possibility terrorists would be able to either obtain or effectively employ bioagents, especially in any sort of large-scale or mass-casualty attack (Chevrier 1996; Pilat 1996; Hoffman 2001, 137–39). Others, while still emphasizing the small probabilities of such an attack and the immense technical obstacles standing in the way, argued it was only certain "types" of terrorists (e.g., those motivated by religious or racial fanaticism, or driven by cults) who would likely break the taboo against using WMDs to produce mass civilian casualties (Tucker 1996; Pearson 1996, 210–12; Roberts 1996; Smithson and Levy 2000, xiii). However, not all terrorism scholars accepted these more benign predictions of the future.

For example, long before September 11th, well-known terrorism expert Bruce Hoffman (1998, 205) warned the conventional wisdom holding that terrorists will not want to kill large numbers of people using WMDs was likely to be "dangerously anachronistic." Similarly, Carus (2001, 11), in his study of *Bioterrorism and Biocrimes*, which tracked the illicit use of BW agents statistically since 1900, acknowledged that "Aum Shinrikyo demonstrated that terrorist groups now exist with resources comparable to some governments," and as a result, "it seems increasingly likely that some group will become capable of using biological agents to cause massive casualties." Others, criticizing the overconfidence of many security analysts and terrorism scholars in their conclusions (all drawn from a "paucity of hard data" and an all-to-brief historical record), warned that as capabilities to obtain and use WMDs increased, the potential for terrorist groups (as well as nations) to employ them also increased dramatically! (Falkenrath 1996; Shoham 1996; Zilinskas 1996) Unfortunately, as Falkenrath (1996) remarked in a rather presentient observation:

> Although U.S. vulnerability to C/B terrorism probably merits vigorous corrective action . . . the uncertain nature of the threat and the absence of a powerful bureaucratic patron suggest that C/B terrorism is likely to remain at the margins of U.S. national security planning until there is a major domestic incident.

One of the developments leading analysts to reconsider the likelihood of terrorists using WMDs was the rise of religiously motivated terrorism over the past decade. While responsible for only 25 percent of all terrorist acts in 1995, religiously motivated groups caused over 58 percent of all fatalities (and all of the cases where eight or more were killed) and comprised nearly half of the fifty-six identifiable international terrorist groups in the world (Hoffman 1998, 90–94). Such groups are generally regarded as more dangerous because their religious beliefs sanction (or legitimize) violence against nonbelievers or enemies, with perpetrators relatively unconcerned about earthly consequences of their actions in light of the rewards they will receive in heaven. Other types of terrorists willing to consider the WMD option include apocolyptic cults, extreme single-issue groups, fanatical nationalists, right-wing militias, as well as the FBI's favorite suspect, the individual psychopath (Smithson and Levy 2000, 24; Stern 1999). As Smithson and Levy (2000, 22) observe:

> Terrorists may resort to weapons of mass destruction for one or more reasons: 1) to massacre as many people as possible; 2) to incite the type of widespread panic that could bring down a government; 3) to establish a position of strength from which to negotiate their demands; 4) to enhance their ability to execute attacks anonymously; 5) to disrupt and significantly damage a society or an economy; 6) to copy state behavior; or, 7) to copy other terrorists.

And, WMD terrorism may be increasingly useful for groups not only seeking to employ bioagents as weapons of mass destruction, but also those seeking "weapons of mass impact" or disruption (Stern 1996).

So, whatever the past historical record may suggest, *the past will not be prologue* regarding the willingness of terrorists to engage in mass-casualty attacks. The attacks of September 11th, which killed thousands of civilians, the bombings of the embassies in Kenya and Tanzania in 1998, which killed hundreds, along with various plots to destroy the World Trade Center with a bomb in 1993, blow up eleven U.S. jetliners over the Pacific in 1995, and the Tokyo sarin attack of 1995—all vividly demonstrate (whatever the past pattern might have been) that many modern terrorists seek to cause mass casualties (the more the better). And, while some point to the RAND–St. Andrews database of terrorism incidents to argue the overall number of attacks declined between 1991 and 1998, this same data also shows the number of nonfatal casualties tripling from the earlier two decades! (Hoffman 1999) Similarly, the State Department's database shows fatal terrorist incidents increased by nearly 23 percent from 1990 to 1996 (U.S. Department of State 2000).[39] As Danzig and Berkowsky (2001, 11) observe, "the assumption that biological weapons will not be used in the future because they have not been used in the past is based on an error of fact. History is replete with examples in which biological weapons have been used."

## THE CASE OF AUM SHINRIKYO

The first major effort by a nonstate actor to develop and deploy bioweapons to produce mass casualties were a series of ineffectual strikes by the Japanese Aum Shinrikyo cult, which carried out at least ten chemical and nine biological attacks between 1990 and 1995 (Smithson and Levy 2000, 103). Although best known for unleashing sarin into the Tokyo subway in 1995, Aum also attempted to use a liquid anthrax slurry (sprayed both from specially constructed vans and a high-rise downtown building) and unsuccessfully sought to acquire other dangerous pathogens (like Ebola) to weaponize. Lacking any scientists with true expertise in BW production, Aum's efforts to produce bioweapons (despite state-of-the-art laboratory equipment) became a comedy of errors. This included the cultivation and release over Tokyo of a nonlethal, veterinary vaccine strain of anthrax (which if anything vaccinated people *against* anthrax) and several attempts to dispense botulinum toxin in several locations (e.g., Tokyo, the U.S. naval bases at Yokohama and Yokosuka, and the international airport at Narita) using trucks with compressors and hidden vents (Smithson and Levy 2000, 77–78).[40] In the streets below the eight-story building in downtown Tokyo, where Aum spent four days in moon suits pouring their anthrax into a steam generator attached to a sprayer and fan system, pedestrians only noted "clots of jellyfish-like material in the street" due to clogging problems during the spraying (Smithson and Levy 2000, 78–79). Two further attempts to disperse anthrax using their compressor truck in downtown Tokyo also failed in July 1993 (Smithson and Levy 2000, 79).

However, had they actually possessed *viable* agents, some of Aum's efforts might have been productive. For example, they "assembled three briefcases with side vents, battery-powered fans, and vinyl tubes to hold biological agents," which were tested in the Kasumigaseki subway station (Smithson and Levy 2000, 80). They procurred a Russian helicopter and two remote control drones, which they intended to equip with a sprayer. Aum was also able to set up a production laboratory containing fermentation and concentration tanks, systems to turn slurry into solid cakes for milling into powder form, as well as advanced incubators and electron microscopes (Smithson and Levy 2000, 75–76, 80). Thus, while some analysts point to the dismal failure of Aum, who despite technicians with graduate degrees and massive investments in laboratory and production facilities, failed to produce effective bioweapons, this misses the point! What the case illustrates is that the lack of *specific kinds* of technical expertise (or knowledge) is perhaps the most important component to any BW effort. A similar observation about the correct interpretation of the Aum Shinrikyo's BW efforts was made by Dr. D. A. Henderson in testimony before the Senate Foreign Relations Committee in 2001: "Some have argued that preparing a biological weapon is complicated and have been mistakenly reassured by the failure of Aum Shinrikyo's efforts to aerosolize anthrax throughout Tokyo. In fact, although the sect did include some with experience in microbiology, those who actually worked on the project were not well-trained microbiologists. Nonetheless, they came very close to succeeding" (U.S. Congress 5 September 2001).

An interesting counterfactual to consider is this: What if Aum had actually managed to obtain the services of a former bioweaponeer, could they have succeeded? Given the technical facilities possessed, all that was really lacking was someone with the technical expertise to select a viable pathogen and weaponize it properly, clearly skills a former bioweaponeer would possess. Had Aum been able to produce a powdered form of anthrax (like that used in the 2001 U.S. attacks), its spraying of agent from large trucks using a compressor system and hidden vents through the streets of Tokyo and around the U.S. naval bases at Yokohama and Yokosuka might not have ended so uneventfully. Similarly, their efforts in June and July 1993 to spray anthrax from an industrial sprayer on top of an eight-story building in downtown Tokyo, with the presence of a true technical expert and powdered agent, might have resulted in more than "clots of jellyfish-like material" littering the streets at the base of the building (Smithson and Levy 2000, 78–79). With an effective agent, the cult's assembly of briefcases with side vents, and battery powered fans might not have been ineffective in attempted attacks on the Kasumigaseki subway station on March 15, 1995 (only five days before the infamous sarin attack). Further, their Russian helicopter and remote control drones, equipped with sprayers, might have provided a line-source dispersal capability (Smithson and Levy 2000, 80). So, while it is true, as Smithson and Levy suggest, that Aum's actual BW efforts—a series of at least nine failed biological attacks over a five-year period—was "from start to finish, a serial flop," it is important we not discount how great a difference the input of even one former bioweaponeer would have made to the outcome (Smithson and Levy 2000, 80 and 106).

Another major hurdle for states or terrorists seeking bioweapons is finding the pathogen itself. For while many organisms useful for bioweapons are found in nature, selecting the right one to weaponize is no easy task. Indeed, as Aum discovered, after attempting to weaponize a nonlethal strain of anthrax, the right bug *makes* the weapon. As former U.S.-bioweaponeer Patrick notes, nature evolved dozens of different strains, or subspecies, of anthrax, some of which are deadlier than others:

> We went through 22 or 23 of them, a large number, before we got the right one [*for the U.S. anthrax weapon*] . . . The probability of going out in nature and getting a virulent strain on the first try would be about 50–50. . . . You'd pick the one that killed the most species with the lowest dose . . . and that takes facilities and hard work. (Broad 10 October 2001)

## THE 2001 U.S. POSTAL ANTHRAX CASE

Of course, as the U.S. anthrax attacks of 2001 demonstrated, high-tech delivery systems are not required to carry out immensely disruptive (and potentially lethal) attacks. Though two sets of studies by Canadian researchers in 2000 clearly demonstrated mailed letters could effectively deliver anthrax, these results never registered with U.S. officials until long after the actual postal attacks. Using "weapons-grade" spores of an anthrax simulant (*Bacillus globigii*) obtained from the U.S. Army, the Canadians tested how letter envelopes containing such materials would disperse their contents upon opening, counting the spores in units called LD-50s (lethal dose 50 percent), in which the given dose has a 50/50 chance of infecting and killing an individual (Brown 2002). Noting people can become infected by doses smaller than a single LD-50 (or avoid infection entirely), the researchers discovered that a person opening a letter and remaining in its vicinity for ten minutes "would inhale 480 to 3,080 LD-50s" and a dose as high as 9,000 LD-50s if breathing heavily—both doses virtually certain to kill the victim in the absence of preventative antibiotics. In their final report, they observed "*passive* dissemination of anthrax spores from an envelop presents a far more serious threat than had been previously assumed." In other tests, dispersal patterns of anthrax from such a letter (unopened) which was simply carried around an office were examined. The findings were a clear harbinger of what would happen to envelopes sent through the U.S. mail and its sorting machines a year later:

> Contamination was present on the desk, papers, file folders and pen prior to opening the envelope (contamination was concentrated at the corners of the envelope where it was leaking out). . . . Potentially contaminated persons are not limited to those in direct contact with the envelope and/or its contents. (Brown 2002)

It is ironic U.S. experts generally discounted the potential for mail-borne dissemination of bioagents given the U.S. BW program during the 1940s considered weaponizing an Asian strain of smallpox by grinding it into a fine powder to dust over letters (Alibek 1999, 115). Still, the letter sent to Senator Daschle's office marked the first time in history such a sophisticated form of anthrax had ever been used in warfare or bioterrorism (Engelberg and Miller 2001). Observing that the army's Medical Research and Material Command at Fort Detrick described the Daschle sample as "pure spores" (or highly concentrated), Dr. David R. Franz, former commander of the army's germ defense laboratory remarked that: "It suggests it wasn't a kitchen or garage operation, or if it was, someone knew how to purify spores . . . The cleaner the preparation, the more likely it is that it was someone who knew what they were doing" (Broad and Miller 18 October 2001). Using the additive silica to reduce the electrostatic charge of the anthrax, the sender of the Daschle letter achieved particle sizes much smaller than three microns in diameter (only 1.5 to 3 microns in diameter)—ideal for inhalation (Weiss and Warrick 2001; Weiss and Eggen 2001).

At the same time, there has been concern expressed by several BW experts after Mohammed Atta, one of the September 11th terrorists, was found to have asked a local pharmacist for something to soothe an inflamation of his hands resembling that caused by contact with caustic detergents or bleach—materials that can be used to weaponize anthrax by breaking up clumps of spores into smaller, deadlier particles (Begley and Isikoff 2001). Downplaying the possibility of a rogue, domestic "bio-bomber," Richard Spertzel noted in testimony to the House Committee on International Relations (December 5, 2001): "The quality of the product contained in the letter to Senator Daschle was better than that found in the Soviet, U.S., or Iraqi program, certainly in terms of the purity and concentration of spore particles" (Weiss and Warrick 2001). Interestingly, the U.S. BW program also used silica to help aerosolize bacteria such as tularemia and anthrax for weapons use (Weiss 2001). As Zelicoff observed: "The evidence is patent on its face . . . the amount of energy needed to disperse the spores [by merely opening an envelope] was trivial, which is virtually diagnostic of achieving the appropriate coating" (Weiss and Eggen 2001). Indeed, a month after the spores were released in Daschle's office, researchers were able to stir up the spores and disperse them into the air just by simulating normal activity in the office—yet another indication of the high quality of the agent (Altman 2001).[41]

Even more worrisome was the concentration level of spores achieved by whoever sent the Daschle and Leahy letters was equivalent to that produced at the height of the U.S. BW program, and far beyond what experts assumed most rogue state or terrorist actors could achieve (Broad 3 December 2001). These letters contained 2.5 grams of powdered anthrax with as many as one trillion spores per gram, a concentration scientists say is near to the theoretical limit of how many spores could be packed into a given space, and a feat that requires substantial sophistication. By comparison, according to Alibek, the Soviet BW program routinely produced dry anthrax containing 100 billion spores per gram, and with some effort, 500 billion was sometimes attained (Broad 3 December 2001). Yet this latter figure is just half the concentration attained by both the U.S. program and the sender of the anthrax letters. The high-quality, weaponized anthrax powder used in the 2001 incidents not only employed a highly virulent strain (the Ames), it also had been finely milled, treated to reduce its electrostatic charge (thereby making it aerosolize more readily), and highly refined to create extremely high-spore concentrations (Engelberg and Miller 2001; Johnston and Mitchell 2001). Given that weaponized anthrax powder is so dangerous to handle, it suggests not only that scientific expertise was required to produce the material, but also that protective equipment or facilities were required to handle it safely. However, for the bioterrorist(s) involved in the U.S. postal attacks, this obviously was not too high a hurdle to pass. Indeed, agreeing with the notion that a "bullet was dodged" during the 2001 anthrax attacks, Alibek observed "if this more sophisticated product is used someplace else, for example the Metro system, the number of casualties would be enormous."[42]

## AN ANALYTICAL FRAMEWORK FOR BIOLOGICAL WEAPONS AND SECURITY RELATIONSHIPS

Unlike nuclear weapons, where a given level of destructive effects can be assumed with use, bioweapons are highly variable in their effects and behavior once employed. As a result, it is necessary to take a number of additional factors into account when considering the impact of bioweapons on security relationships and the strategies they allow state or nonstate actors to pursue. First, one must take into account the actual *characteristics or properties of the bioagent* used in the bioweapon: Has it been engineered or modified, or is it in its natural/unaltered form? What is the bioagent's lethality, communicability, treatability, and incubation period? Next, one must take into account the nature of the *weaponized form of the bioagent* present in the bioweapons — that is, Does it exist in liquid or dry powder form? Has the liquid been effectively concentrated or the powder properly milled? Was the powder microencapsulated or electrostatically treated to improve its aerosol properties? Thirdly, what *delivery system capability exists for disseminating the bioagent*? Are we dealing with a terror group limited to "crude point-source delivery" (i.e., handheld sprayers, packages/letters, human biobombers, direct contamination of food stuffs or water supplies, or dispersal using conventional explosives)? Or is it a state actor capable of more "sophisticated point-source delivery" of bioagent, using carefully designed biobomblets able to release their contents without destroying most of it through the blast and heat of conventional explosives? Might it be a state actor with "advanced area-effect or line-source delivery" capabilities (e.g., "jet stream" delivery of liquid or powder agents, bio–cruise missiles, modified aircraft, or missile delivery of biobomblets)? Fourthly, what is the *militarily relevant context surrounding bioagent use*? For example, what target has been selected (i.e., military, civilian, agricultural/economic)? What is the motivation of the actor and the employment strategy adopted (i.e., attempting to develop a mass-casualty weapon for strategic/deterrence purposes, seeking a pure terror weapon, or looking for an applied battlefield weapon)? What are the meteorological and seasonal conditions present at the time? These four factors form an analytical foundation for assessing the potential use and effectiveness of various bioweapons vis-à-vis different kinds of sought-after security relationships.

## 1.) The Characteristics or Properties of the Bioagent

In theorizing about the potential applications and effectiveness of bioweapons across a variety of contexts, a number of factors must be considered. Firstly, what are the *characteristics* of the bioagent itself? Indeed, the nature of the bioagent possessed by a state or nonstate actor greatly influences the types of employment strategies that will be available.[43] For example, possession of a highly lethal and communicable pathogen, such as smallpox or plague, would permit the holder to either threaten or actually cause mass casualties in an opponent's civilian population, whereas possession of only a mild strain of salmonella would limit the holder to strategies of only incapacitating or disrupting an opponent. A pathogen susceptible to all standard antibiotics would pose less of a threat if released than would a multiresistant strain immune to most drugs, just as one that was highly contagious would pose a greater risk to the broader population than a noncontagious strain. But, while there are a large number of characteristics that vary across potential bioagents, five in particular stand out as being of crucial importance for determining their effectiveness or strategy for employment: (1) Has the bioagent been engineered or modified, or is it in its natural/unaltered form? (2) What is the lethality of the bioagent? (3)What is the communicability (or transmissibility) of the bioagent person to person? (4) What is the treatability of the bioagent? and (5) How long is the incubation period of the bioagent prior to onset of symptoms?

## Has the Bioagent Been Engineered/Modified?

One of the most crucial characteristics of a bioagent is whether or not it has been bioengineered or modified to possess traits (such as antibiotic or antiviral drug resistance, vaccine immunity, enhanced virulence, or other factors) not present in its natural/unaltered form. For example, the Soviet plague "battle strain" weaponized for use in biowarheads aboard ICBMs was not only an extremely virulent strain, but one enhanced to possess resistance to at least eight different antibiotics—including all of the ones typically used to treat this disease. As a result, most medical treatments would have proved ineffective, the mortality rate would have skyrocketed to levels associated with the untreated fatality rate for the disease, and the ability of the medical community to contain further spread of the virus significantly hampered. In effect, because of the bioengineering, this bioagent would not have behaved or responded to treatment in the same fashion as its naturally occurring, unmodified cousins. And, the potential for modifying bioagents through genetic engineering techniques is practically limitless and can radically alter the normal characteristics of any bioagent. Therefore, the most important characteristic of bioagents, and one that may alter all subsequent qualities of a given agent, is whether or not it has been modified through genetic engineering or is present only in its natural/unaltered form. Increasingly over the coming decades, the bioweapons threatening our security will take the form of enhanced, engineered types that will complicate our defensive planning and expand their potential as either military or terror weapons for opponents.

## Lethality

Another important characteristic of bioagents is their lethality. For example, some possible bioagents, like Venezuelan equine encephalitis (VEE) and Q fever, have very low mortality rates (of 4 percent and 1 percent respectively). Because of their low mortality rates and the high degree of incapacitation they cause, the U.S. BW program developed these bioagents for tactical battlefield use to incapacitate rather than kill an enemy's troops and support personnel, as well as for incapacitating an opponent's civilian population to reduce their ability to resist occupation by U.S. forces (e.g., Marshall Plan). Such a bioweapon would not cause mass casualties and be ineffective as a terror or strategic weapon that required mass casualties. For that purpose, the selected bioagents need to (at a minimum) possess moderate mortality rates, with the most highly weaponized being those of exceptionally high lethality. For example, pathogens generally considered to have "moderate" mortality rates associated with them would include typhoid (10–20 percent untreated), smallpox (20–40 percent unvaccinated), and tularemia (30–60 percent untreated). Naturally occuring pathogens with exceptionally high mortality rates would include pneumonic plague (100 percent untreated), inhalation anthrax (over 90 percent untreated), and Ebola (over 90 percent). However, the behavior of various pathogens in nature is not necessarily a guide to their lethality if employed as a bioweapon. For example, the lethality of a given pathogen can be affected by the infective dose received by an individual. And given that the infective dose of a weaponized bioagent received by an individual in aerosol form can be hundreds or thousands of times higher than a naturally occurring dose, even pathogens with only moderate lethality may turn highly lethal and massively overwhelm an individual's immune system. Further, a genetically modified pathogen may prove more lethal due to enhancements in its virulence or ability to evade treatment. Chimeras combining the characteristics of multiple disease pathogens or toxins, such as those developed by the Soviet BW program, also are of unpredictable lethality.

### Communicability

The person-to-person transmissibility of bioagents also affects how they may be applied by states. For example, if the goal is to have an incapacitating or lethal effect on an opponent's military forces or civilian centers, yet not risk "blow-back" that would infect one's own troops or population, a noncommunicable bioagent (or at least one with minimal transmissibility) would be preferred. On the other hand, were the goal purely to create mass casualties for the purposes of terror or for strategic retaliation, the more communicable the agent, the greater its potential effect on the target population. Bioagents that are not communicable person to person include anthrax, tularemia, SEB, and botulinum toxin. Those which have low transmissibility are bioagents such as cholera, Q fever, VEE, and cutaneous anthrax. Moderately communicable pathogens, such as viral hemorraghic fever viruses like Ebola or Marburg, are not airborne, but are passed on only through contact with contaminated body fluids like blood. Finally, highly communicable bioagents are those which are easily passed to others through airborne transmission, like pneumonic plague, smallpox, and influenza.

### Treatability

The degree to which bioagents respond to medical treatment greatly affects their ability to incapacitate or cause fatalities in a target population. This characteristic is affected not only by the natural qualities of the pathogen or toxin, but also whether or not they have been engineered or modified to evade existing treatments. For example, though pneumonic plague can be treated effectively and mortality greatly reduced through the administration of antibiotics within the first twenty-four hours after exposure, untreated cases approach 100 percent mortality. The Soviet plague bioweapon was modified to have multispectrum antibiotic resistance, meaning this particular strain would not respond to early administration of antibiotics and those exposed would likely progress clinically the same way as if they had received no treatment at all. Obviously, the less treatable a given bioagent, the greater the fatalities it will cause and the more effective it would be as a terror weapon. Imagine if the 2001 anthrax postal attacks, in which over 30,000 people received preventative courses of antibiotics (such as cipro or penicillin), was carried out using an anthrax strain engineered to be resistant to all of these standard antibiotics. In such an event, it is possible that even the mailing of a few letters would have caused hundreds or possibly thousands of people to come down with clinical cases of anthrax, since the preventative courses of antibiotics would have been ineffective. Also, the infective dose can also affect treatability in that it is commonly known that high-challenge doses of infectious particles can overwhelm the normal immunity conferred by many vaccines (such as the ones for smallpox or anthrax). As a result, vaccination using vaccines proven effective against given pathogens cannot be guaranteed to provide protection under biowarfare contexts. Moreover, the high-infectious dose received could potentially overwhelm a patient's immune system so rapidly that other treatments (with antibiotics or antiviral drugs) would be too late.

Even with pathogens that have not been engineered or modified, timely warning that an attack has taken place is often essential for medical treatments to prove effective. For example, while inhalation anthrax can be treated successfully using antibiotics prior to the occurrence of symptoms (usually during the first one to three days after exposure), once symptoms occur, the illness has a high mortality rate and requires a high degree of intensive care in medical facilities that would be overwhelmed and unavailable after a large-scale attack. Similarly, vaccines against smallpox must be administered prior to the occurrence of symptoms (usually during the first four days after exposure) to prevent the disease or at least reduce its severity. Were authorities unaware a bioattack had occurred and treatment delayed, many vaccines or drugs would prove worthless in preventing mass casualties even when treating unmodified, natural strains of many diseases. In fact, were the rabies virus weaponized as an aerosol, for example, a population not receiving the vaccine prior to clinical symptoms would experience a 100 percent mortality rate.

For the purposes of analysis, bioagents with low treatability would include those for which there currently exist no vaccines or effective drug treatments (such as Ebola and Marburg), as well as those based upon bioregulatory compounds and genetically engineered agents specifically designed to evade prophylaxis. Such bioagents make highly effective strategic mass casuality or terror weapons. Those with moderate treatability are those agents for which treatments are nominally effective at preventing disease or at least greatly reducing the mortality rate associated with it. However, these agents also tend to be ones (like smallpox, anthrax, rabies, etc.) that are moderately treatable *only* if treatment occurs prior to onset of clinical symptoms. Once these occur, they become bioagents with low treatability. Finally, bioagents with high treatability would be any pathogens generally highly responsive to antibiotic or antiviral treatment, or for which a vaccine is highly effective. Such agents tend to be less effective as mass-casualty weapons because they respond well to treatment.

### Incubation Period

Obviously, the time it takes for a given bioagent to cause effects in people also has implications for how it can be used. Bioagents with long incubation periods tend not to be used as strategic weapons or for tactical military purposes because they have no effect within a reasonable time frame. One of the few examples of a "long incubation period" weapon developed as a strategic system to target mass populations (whether Kurdish or Israeli) was Iraq's aflatoxin (which over decades causes liver cancer from exposure). However, such weapons, while less useful for state BW programs, could prove *highly useful* as terror weapons. For example, were a prion-based bioagent used against a civilian population (either in aerosol form or through contamination of food supplies), a terror group could raise the fear that mad cow disease (or vCJD) would have infected large numbers of people without their knowledge. More useful for military purposes are agents with moderate incubation periods, such as smallpox (7–17 days), Ebola (4–16 days), or tularemia (1–21 days). Used against civilian targets as a mass-casualty weapon or against rear military areas, the incubation period of these agents would not prove to be an unacceptable problem since strategies employing stealth attacks and clandestine releases could easily be adopted. Finally, bioagents with short incubation periods have the most application for tactical military use, and also remain valuable for attacking civilian and rear area targets as well. Such agents would include pneumonic plague (1–3 days), VEE (1–6 days), SEB (1–6 hours), inhalation anthrax (1–7 days), and any number of bioregulatory compounds and toxin weapons that have immediate effects. Moreover, even agents normally assumed to have moderate incubation periods could be made to take affect sooner were subjects exposed to high-challenge doses through an aerosol bioweapon, which would be more likely to overwhelm the immune response and cause disease more rapidly than naturally occurring forms.

### Four Types of Bioweapons Based on Properties of Bioagents

As table 4.1 illustrates, these differing characteristics (or properties) of bioagents combine analytically into four useful "ideal" types of potential bioweapons (*strategic/retaliatory, tactical counterforce, tactical counterforce disruptive,* and *terror*). For example, *strategic/retaliatory* bioweapons are those capable of producing mass casualties in the populace of a targeted state, whether for the purpose of actual retaliation for an attack or to achieve a threatened level of mass destruction required to obtain a deterrence security relationship with an opponent. It is also possible to conceive of strategic/retaliatory bioweapons geared toward creating mass casualties or enormous economic losses on agricultural targets (either animal or crop). Mass-casualty weapons tend to use bioagents of high-moderate lethality (e.g., smallpox, plague, viral hemorraghic fever viruses, anthrax), the more virulent the better. The agents also tend to be ones (excepting anthrax) that are highly communicable amongst the target population and have limited treatability (either preventative or postexposure). Incubation periods tend to be less important for such weapons given these other characteristics and the nature of the goal, which is purely retalitatory/mass-casualty oriented. Ideally, such bioagents will also have been genetically engineered or modified to have enhanced virulence, produce broad-ranging or novel clinical effects, or possess broad resistance to antibiotics, antiviral drugs, or vaccines. In essence, any steps that could be taken to increase the killing efficiency of a bioagent used for a *strategic/retaliatory* bioweapon serve to enhance its effectiveness in accomplishing its goal—namely, to produce mass casualties. Past historical examples of such bioweapons would include the genetically modified "battle strains" of viruses (such as smallpox and Marburg) and bacteria (such as plague and anthrax) weaponized by the Soviet Union for use in biowarheads aboard ICBMs. Not only were all of these agents selected for their immense initial virulence, but the "battle strains" also underwent selective modifications to further increase their virulence, as well as engineering to create broad spectrum resistance to antibiotics and vaccines. The result of these efforts were true, mass-casualty strategic bioweapons that were the equal of any WMD—including nuclear weapons—in terms of their ability to take life.

*Tactical counterforce* bioweapons are those designed to produce significant effects on current battlefield conditions in order to shape outcomes of ongoing

**Table 4.1. Types of Bioweapons Based upon the Characteristics (Properties) of Bioagents**

| Strategic/Retaliatory Bioweapon (Mass Casualty) | Tactical Counterforce Bioweapon (Affecting Battlefield Conditions) | Tactical Counterforce Disruptive Bioweapon (Incapacitating Military Rear Areas & Support Infrastructure) | Terror Bioweapon (Mass Casualty or Social-Economic Disruption) |
|---|---|---|---|
| **Bioagent Characteristics:**<br>High-Moderate Lethality<br>High-Moderate Communicability<br>Low/No Treatability<br>Variable Incubation Period | **Bioagent Characteristics:**<br>High-Moderate Lethality<br>Low/No Communicability<br>Low/No Treatability<br>Short/No Incubation Period | **Bioagent Characteristics:**<br>Variable Lethality<br>Low/No Communicability<br>Variable Treatability<br>Moderate-Short Incubation Period | **Bioagent Characteristics:**<br>Variable Lethality<br>Variable Communicability<br>Variable Treatability<br>Variable Incubation Period |
| **Ex's**<br>USSR (smallpox, plague, Marburg bioweapons for ICBM delivery) | **Ex's**<br>U.S./USSR (botulinum toxin)<br>Future (bioregulatory compounds, bioengineered novel pathogens) | **Ex's**<br>USSR (tularemia, anthrax)<br>U.S. (VEE/SEB cocktails, anthrax) | **Ex's**<br>Rajneeshies (salmonella)<br>Aum Shinrikyo (anthrax)<br>Unknown (anthrax postal attacks of 2001)<br>Future (mass casualty or agricultural bioagents) |

engagements. Such bioagents need to have either short or no incubation periods, since rapidity of effect is a highly critical variable for influencing an existing battle. The bioagent should also have high-moderate lethality, low or no communicability, and limited or no treatability (either pre- or postexposure). The reasons for this are fairly obvious. Unless an agent possesses suitably high lethality, military personnel might be able to continue to perform their combat missions (even if with reduced efficiency). Further, if prewar vaccination or prophylactic antibiotic treatments will prevent meaningful battlefield effects, the value of a given bioagent is reduced and is less likely to produce the desired military results. Also, given the close proximity of opposing military units on a wartime battlefield, only bioagents with low or no communicability can be reliably used in order to avoid the debilitating effects of "blow-back" upon ones own forces. Generally, bioagents have not historically been relied upon for tactical counterforce roles, with militaries traditionally viewing chemical or nerve agent weapons as superior due to their immediacy of effect and lethality. However, some toxin-based bioagents, such as botulinum toxin, were weaponized and stockpiled by states such as the U.S. and Soviet Union for tactical use on the battlefield. As Hansen (1990, 49) observes:

> It is possible to speak of four broad categories of toxins which have some potential application for use in warfare: 1) toxins derived from genetically engineered living organisms or from ordinary organisms such as fungi, molds, and bacteria; 2) toxins synthesized from inorganic chemicals; 3) endogenous bioregulator proteins genetically engineered for specific pathophysiological effect; and 4) virus particles, parts of viral coat proteins, portions of their DNA or RNA, and compounds derived from them. Beyond the better known bacteriological weapons, it is the potential to create novel toxins through genetic engineering techniques that is of particular concern to security officials.

Thus, in the future, with biotechnology providing motivated states the ability to produce *bioregulatory* agents for use as bioweapons (combining immense lethality and immediacy of effect with a lack of treatability), it is likely the tactical counterforce uses of these weapons will be greatly enhanced.

*Tactical counterforce disruptive* bioweapons, on the other hand, do not require the ability to take immediate effect on a battlefield in order to affect outcomes. Instead, such bioweapons are targeted (either preemptively or during wartime) on an opponent's rear support areas, disrupting reserve forces, command and control, and maintenance and supply efforts. As a result, bioagents may be used with variable lethality, since it is not necessarily as important to kill personnel in rear areas as it is to incapacitate them and disrupt their support functions for frontline units. Similarly, the treatability of the bioagent employed for such purposes can be variable as well, since in many cases, it is actually preferable from a military standpoint to incapacitate rather than kill such personnel. Indeed, far greater disruption may be caused by overloading (or overwhelming) the medical support services of an opponent in rear areas through widespread incapacitating illness—since unaffected personnel are forced to care for the afflicted instead of carrying out their normal tasks. To avoid "blow-back" onto friendly forces, bioagents with low to no communicability are generally used, although Soviet bioplanning did envision employing some moderately communicable bioagents against an opponent's more distant rear areas (e.g., viral hemorraghic fever viruses). Historical examples of *tactical counterforce disruptive* bioweapons include the planned use by the Soviets of modified tularemia "battle strains," as well as the proposed U.S. use of a line-source spray release of a liquid VEE-SEB cocktail bioagent over Cuba during the late 1950s and early 1960s to incapacitate the population and ease the way for an American invasion of the island.

Finally, pure *terror* bioweapons employed by either state or nonstate actors (like Al Qaeda) can take widely varied forms, matching the widely varied goals for use likely to be held by such groups. In essence, terror bioweapons can take any of the three forms previously mentioned (strategic/retaliatory, tactical counterforce, or tactical counterforce disruptive). Some applications of bioweapons could envision producing mass casualties to civilians in urban areas or to deployed military forces in the field, thereby requiring many of the characteristics present in either strategic/retaliatory or tactical counterforce bioweapons. A historical example, albeit an abortive one, of a nonstate actor's attempt at such a weapon would be the Aum Shinrikyo cult's efforts to attack Tokyo with anthrax. Alternatively, some terror applications of bioweapons could seek primarily to cause social or economic disruption in the target state, such as through the point-source delivery of bioagents against either people or agricultural targets. For example, attempts by the Rajneeshi cult in the U.S. to influence a local election in Oregon through salmonella contamination of salad bars in local restaurants and the U.S. postal anthrax attacks illustrate such bioweapons use. Of course, the future potential of bioweapons and the proliferation of technical capabilities means that increasingly sophisticated and more large-scale attacks by nonstate actors using *terror* bioweapons of various kinds will become ever more likely.

### 2.) Weaponized Form of the Bioagent

Obviously, the higher the "quality" of the weaponized form of any bioagent, the greater its potential for effective dissemination and creation of desired effects. The lowest quality bioagent tends to be liquid slurries that have not been concentrated and purified to contain high proportions of organisms without contaminants. Such agents require considerable effort to aerosolize (using sprayers or jet-stream dispersion techniques) and pose problems for their users like clogging of spray nozzles and the uneven quality of the liquid agent. An example would be Aum's abortive anthrax attack in which liquid anthrax slurry clogged sprayer nozzles and expelled clumps rather than a mist. Such crude weaponization of bioagents is not conducive to good aerosolization and greatly reduces their effectiveness. Of course, liquid bioagent can be made highly effective if it is properly concentrated and the suspension largely free of contaminants—like the Soviet smallpox bioagent during the Cold War, which was always produced in liquid form for dispersal from biobomblets delivered by ballistic missile.

However, it is the dry powder forms of bioagent, especially if they have been milled properly to create one-to-five-micron size particles easily respirated, which tend to be the most effective bioweapons. Even more so if the particles have been microencapsulated to prevent environmental degradation (from sunlight, moisture, etc.) and electrostatically treated to prevent them from clumping (thereby increasing their ability to float through the air, or re-float if previously settled). Such powders are easily disseminated, float long distances in the air, and are highly effective at infecting an exposed population. These dry powder agents are also more easily preserved and have longer shelf lives in storage than liquid agents. Of course, not all dry powder forms of bioagent are created equal, as illustrated by the initial anthrax packages sent in 2001 to the American Media office building, which were not as well milled or electrostatically treated as the later material in the Daschle and Leahy letters. However, when properly prepared, dry powder weaponization of bioagents represent the most versatile and ideal form for bioweapons.

### 3.) Delivery System Capability for Disseminating the Bioagent

Of course, the effectiveness of bioweapons is not only determined by the characteristics of the bioagents and the form of weaponization adopted, but also by the type of delivery system available for dissemination of the agent over a target. State BW programs are likely to have more sophisticated delivery systems available to them than would nonstate actors like Al Qaeda, however, this may not always remain the case—especially with the increasing proliferation of delivery-system technology around the world. For the purposes of our analysis, we will consider essentially three forms of bioweapon delivery systems: (1) crude point source; (2) sophisticated point source; and (3) advanced area effect or line source.

*Crude point-source* delivery systems denote any of the many types of low-tech, simple modes of delivery easily within reach of both terror groups and state actors. These means of delivery are not generally capable of producing mass-casualty attacks (although a suitably creative terrorist could employ some of these modes of delivery to accomplish this—like releasing a container of anthrax powder of similar quality to the Daschle letter in front of a speeding Metro train during rush hour in Washington, D.C.). Mostly, however, this delivery is only capable of contaminating a limited area around the point of release. Techniques could include handheld or battery-powered sprayers; the use of letters or packages; individuals serving as biobombers who are infected with communicable diseases; direct contamination of food, cosmetics, or medical supplies; or the dispersal of agent using high explosives. Such delivery could provide effective means of attack, and multiple points of attack across a city (or cities) could mimic the spread provided by more advanced delivery systems. However, it would generally be the case that such crude point-source attacks would be effective only over limited areas and would be most suited to terrorist use (by state or nonstate actors).

*Sophisticated point-source* delivery systems use means of dispersal more advanced than the use of simple conventional explosives to release agent. For example, the U.S. and Soviet BW programs perfected biobomblets for use aboard ballistic missiles and gravity bombs which released the agent not by high explosives, but by dispersal as a mist as bomblets floated toward the ground via parachute. These were highly effective at saturating a location with a high infective dose of agent and reducing the impact of meteorological effects like wind upon the dispersion of agent over the target. Other examples include the biomines developed by the U.S. that remain concealed until activated, float to the surface, and release a fine mist of bioagent produced from an aerosol generator. These point-source delivery systems were deemed to be effective at striking enemy naval forces or ports within a limited area around the mine. These types of delivery systems allowed state-run BW programs to envision more sophisticated military employment of their bioweapons and increased their confidence that the bioagent would be effectively disseminated over the target.

*Advanced area-effect or line-source* delivery systems include those capable of producing effects over large geographical areas and causing mass casualties. To date, such bioweapon delivery has been completely in the purview of advanced biostates (like the Soviet Union, Unites States, Britain, etc.), but the capability for future bioweapon states to achieve such abilities is enormous and unlikely to prove a substantial hurdle. Indeed, given the aforementioned bioweapon states possessed such advanced area-effect or line-source delivery capabilities by the late 1950s and early 1960s, it is reasonable to assume developing bioweapon states of the twenty-first century will be able to match technology now forty years old! These means of delivery can be as simple as they are devastating. For example, the release of liquid or powder agent into the slip stream of a jet aircraft has been demonstrated to effectively aerosolize material over a wide geographical area (see the U.S. tests over the South Pacific during the 1960s). Bio–cruise missiles could be equipped to release bioagent in a line-source attack against cities or regions, as could normal aircraft equipped with spray release tanks. The epitome of city-busting bioweapons were the Soviet smallpox, plague, or anthrax biowarheads of the Cold War, which could release hundreds of biobomblets to saturate entire cities with agent.

## 4.) Militarily Relevant Context Surrounding Bioagent Use

Finally, several factors surrounding the existing military context are relevant when considering the effectiveness or use of bioagents: (a) The *target selected* (i.e., military, civilian, agricultural/economic); (b) The *employment strategy adopted* (i.e., counterforce, such as war-fighting, tactical, or strategic applications; countervalue, such as deterrence/retaliation; or purely terror); and (c) The *meteorological or other relevant conditions associated with the target* (i.e., night/day usage, existence of inversion, season, air circulation within buildings/subways/malls, etc.).

In terms of the *target selected*, the characteristics of the bioagent, its weaponized form, and delivery system available for dissemination greatly affect the likelihood of success. For agricultural targets, for example, highly weaponized forms of bioagent (such as foot-and-mouth disease) are not required, and simple delivery methods (such as individual biobombers spreading infectious material at numerous livestock sites) would be sufficient to spark an epidemic. On the other hand, mass-casualty attacks against military and civilian human targets require far more advanced delivery systems, more lethal bioagents, and are enhanced through the use of more highly weaponized forms of the bioagent (i.e., dry powdered anthrax microencapsulated and electrostatically treated). Purely terrorist operations are the least demanding of all, and while creating mass casualties does require more advanced capabilities and materials, strategies causing social disruption and fear require little sophistication.

The *employment strategy adopted* by the biostate or bioterrorist are also influenced by the characteristics of the bioagent, its weaponized form, and the available delivery system available for dissemination—as well as by the goals sought from their use. For example, bioterrorists seeking to unleash mass-casualty attacks against military or civilian populations (e.g., counterforce or countervalue), may simply try to stage disruptive attacks designed to sow fear amongst a populace (e.g., spreading prion bioagents into food supplies, sending anthrax letters through the post, staging limited strikes using bioagents against people across numerous locations), or may seek only to harm a na-

| | Delivery System Employed for Dissemination of Bio-Agent | | |
|---|---|---|---|
| **Weaponized Form of Bio-Agent** | **Advanced Area Effect or Line-Source** | **Sophisticated Point-Source** | **Crude Point-Source** |
| **High-Sophisticated** (i.e., concentrated liquid or dry powder; micro-encapsulation; electrostatic treatment, etc.) | **Potential Bioweapon Applications –** (*Strategic–Retaliatory, Tactical Counterforce, Tactical Counterforce Disruptive, or Terror bioweapons*). Capable of producing mass casualties over large geographic areas (cities or regions) in either human or agricultural targets. Counter-value or counter-force application. Produces bioweapons with greatest offensive capabilities for effective dispersal after dissemination and the ability to deliver the highest possible infective dose to targets. Provides bioweapons with long shelf-lives that may be stockpiled in arsenals for long periods without degradation. Deliverable by wide variety of dispersal systems (e.g., aircraft, cruise or ballistic missiles, bomblets, sprayers, etc.) | **Potential Bioweapon Applications –** (*Strategic–Retaliatory, Tactical Counterforce, Tactical Counterforce Disruptive, or Terror bioweapons*). Capable of producing mass casualties over small geographic areas (like cities or agricultural areas) and in concentrated military forces, but only by using clustered delivery of bio-bomblets by aircraft or missile. Counter-value or counter-force application. Provides bioweapons with long shelf-lives that may be stockpiled in arsenals for long periods without degradation. Deliverable by wide variety of dispersal systems (e.g., bio-bomblets, sprayers & aerosol generators, etc.). | **Potential Bioweapon Applications –** (*Tactical Counterforce Disruptive or Terror bioweapons*). Able to produce large numbers of casualties only in small areas (like subway stations, enclosed arenas or malls, or inside buildings). Counter-value application only. Provides bioweapons with long shelf-lives that may be stockpiled for long periods without degradation. Deliverable by wide variety of dispersal systems (e.g., hand-held or battery powered sprayers, letters or packages, bio-bombers infected with communicable disease, direct contamination of food, cosmetics, or medical supplies, or the dispersal of agent using high explosives). |
| **Low-Unsophisticated** (i.e., unconcentrated liquid or unrefined, clumpy powder; lacks micro-encapsulation or electrostatic treatment.) | **Potential Bioweapon Applications –** (*Tactical Counterforce Disruptive or Terror bioweapons*). Limited ability to produce mass casualties, affecting only small geographic areas due to inability of bio-agent to remain airborne for any length of time, its inability to remain aerosolized in effective respirable particle size (1-5 microns), and its vulnerability to degradation by sunlight & other meteorological conditions. Provides bioweapons with short shelf-lives that cannot be stockpiled in arsenals for long periods without degradation & must be constantly replenished with new agent. Difficult to deliver or effectively disseminate. | **Potential Bioweapon Applications –** (*Tactical Counterforce Disruptive or Terror bioweapons*). Limited ability to produce casualties in a given locale due to inability of bio-agent to remain airborne for any length of time, its inability to remain aerosolized in effective respirable particle size (1-5 microns), and its vulnerability to degradation by sunlight & other meteorological conditions. Provides bioweapons with short shelf-lives that cannot be stockpiled in arsenals for long periods without degradation & must be constantly replenished with new agent. Difficult to deliver or effectively disseminate. | **Potential Bioweapon Applications –** (*Terror bioweapons*) Limited ability to produce large numbers of casualties. Provides bioweapons with short shelf-lives that cannot be stockpiled for long periods without degradation & must be constantly replenished with new agent. Difficult to deliver or effectively disseminate. |

Figure 4.1.  Potential Bioweapon Applications of Bioagent Given Different Weaponized Forms and Employed Delivery Systems

tion's economic well-being (e.g., release of agricultural bioagents, contamination of export products, etc.). For all of these employment strategies, the bioagent possessed, its weaponized form, and the available delivery capabilities all influence the likely effectiveness of a given application. Similarly, the requirements for significant biostate efforts at counterforce strategies (actual tactical application to affect battlefield conditions or substantial strikes against rear areas) or the development of deterrent/retaliatory biocapabilities capable of countervalue strikes (producing mass casualties in civilian populations) require substantially different types of biowarfare abilities.

Finally, the *meteorological or other relevant conditions associated with the target* play a role because they have the potential to affect whether or not a given attack is successful or achieves nominal effects. For example, if an attacker does not possess sophisticated point-source delivery capabilities (e.g., advanced biobomblets delivered with precision by aircraft or missile—that are less affected by existing weather conditions), meteorological conditions will greatly shape how less sophisticated biowarfare capabilities can be employed. Crude point-source delivery against outdoor targets would not prove nearly as effective if conducted during daylight hours, during rain or snow storms, or in the face of stiff winds. However, if the target is a building and access to ventilation systems can be obtained (or biobombers are able to release materials by other methods), crude point-source delivery under such conditions might prove highly effective. Obviously, regardless of delivery technique, it is ideal for most bioagents to be delivered during nighttime hours, during cold conditions with little or no wind, and during meteorological conditions known as heat inversions, which trap a layer of air over a target for lengthy periods of time. Such conditions increase the persistence of a given bioagent over the site (reducing degradation of the material), preserves high concentrations in the area (enhancing its ability to deliver infective doses to a populace), and allows larger geographic areas to be affected (through drift and limited dispersal of the agent). The inverse is also true, greatly reducing bioweapon effectiveness over targets. Here again, the bioagent possessed, its weaponized form, and the available delivery capabilities all influence the likely effectiveness of a given application across differing meteorological or target contexts.

## THE IMPACT OF BIOWEAPONS
## CAPABILITIES ON SECURITY RELATIONSHIPS

Although bioweapons are legitimately viewed as *weapons of mass destruction*—and do possess the potential to rival nuclear weapons in terms of casualties produced—their application to notions of deterrence are not nearly so straightforward. The reason for this is simply that if the essence of deterrence is to present opponents with the threat of inescapable, unavoidable levels of damage far exceeding any potential benefit they may receive from taking aggressive actions, then the degree to which this damage could be viewed as "contestable" (subject to preemption or limitation) seriously undermines the effectiveness of any deterrent threat. This notion of *contestability*, described by Harknett (1998) as the primary difference between conventional and nuclear deterrence, also distinguishes between deterrence built around biological as opposed to nuclear weapons. In terms of pure destructive power, nuclear weapons trump all other weapons since they destroy both people and property—a city attacked with nuclear weapons is utterly destroyed. Further, in the absence of a futuristic, functioning missile defense that could somehow prevent nuclear weapons from being delivered and detonated over cities, the ability of a nuclear opponent to inflict unacceptable levels of damage are for the foreseeable future uncontestable. This makes a deterrent threat based upon the assured destructive potential of nuclear weapons far more robust than ones based upon only conventional military threats.

In contrast, bioweapons do not cause the "physical destruction" of cities, though they may cause similar numbers of casualties as their nuclear cousins. This "lesser" level of destruction will always lack, at least in the minds of some opponents, the perceived "completeness" of destruction produced by nuclear attacks. Neither are bioweapons instantaneous in their effects, providing a defender with at least the possibility of protecting their populations or military forces against the agents through the use of antibiotics, vaccines, or quarantines. In other words, costs are potentially *contestable* when bioweapons are used. This results in a fundamentally different type of security relationship arising from these kinds of weapons, since the *assured* nature of the resulting destruction is often essential for the credibility of deterrent threats.

But, just because bioweapons do not possess the same raw destructive power of nuclear weapons, this does *not* mean they *cannot* be effective weapons on the battlefield or for deterrence. Indeed, all weapons—whether conventional or unconventional—have different characteristics, strengths, and limitations. The key to their effectiveness is not some simple measure of destructive power, but rather how they are employed, taking into account their strengths and weaknesses, and how they *could* be used against one's opponents. For deterrence, the issue is the ability to inflict "unacceptable levels of damage" on one's opponents (whether in terms of countervalue or counterforce strikes) with a degree of certainty that makes gambling with fate undesirable for the enemy. Although no weapon is 100 percent guaranteed to always reach target and function as expected—nuclear or not—the reality of the security environment of the twenty-first century is that the proliferation of BW-relevant technology and scientific know-how will steadily enhance the abilities of both state and nonstate actors to carry out sophisticated attacks using bioagents that could reliably target opponents.[44] Moreover, properly employed, bioweapons are unquestionably as effective at producing mass casualties as nuclear weapons and could quite easily hold substantial parts of an opponent's civilian population at risk. Thus, while nothing is certain, the high probability that a successful bioattack *could* be carried out is likely to produce deterrent effects on potential combatants whose policy makers feel uninclined to accept extreme risks that might produce mass casualties or economic loss to their nations.

## OPAQUE BIOWEAPONS POSSESSION STRATEGIES AND EXISTENTIAL DETERRENCE

Since few biostates will overtly announce either bioweapons capabilities or link them formally to deterrence strategies by stating their existing targeting philosophies governing their bioarsenals, the security relationships *likely* to develop between states in the biological realm will be of the *existential deterrence* variety (Bundy 1982). Opponents will be aware of their rival's unacknowledged BW programs and understand that were war to erupt, their rivals would potentially be capable of effectively employing bioweapons against them. This "bugs in the basement" posture would resemble the "bombs in the basement" existential deterrence postures adopted by India and Pakistan prior to their overt testing of nuclear weapons in 1998.

Unfortunately, such opaque deterrence postures are not as stable as overt, above-the-board nuclear postures and leave open considerable room for misperception and miscalculation by opponents regarding their opponent's bioforces. For example, a lack of understanding about an enemy's motivations or willingness to take risks to defend areas of central interest could lead to misperceptions regarding the will of opponents to actually use their bioarsenals. Similarly, mistaken beliefs about the technical capabilities, or the complexities of launching a mass-casualty attack, might lead opponents to entertain unjustified notions about the "contestability" of an enemy's bioweapons potential. In either case, these misperceptions or miscalculations serve to undermine the credibility of a state's implicit biological deterrent threats.

Indeed, if states do develop bioarsenals in the coming decades, deterrence would be much better served by *overt* postures and declaratory policies reducing the dangers of miscalculation and better communicating the nature of deterrent threats to opponents. Yet, given the strong existing taboo against acknowledging "offensive" BW capabilities, and the extremely negative sanctions that would be visited upon the offending biostate by the international community, it is probable new biostates will adopt opaque possession strategies and rely upon existential rather than overt deterrent threats to enhance their security. But whether overtly or covertly held, bioarsenals will provide their possessors concrete ability to inflict massive damage upon their enemies (whether their opponents know it or not) and potentially provide some degree of deterrence against threats to their central interests by states wary of their capabilities—even if they never achieve the clear-cut deterrence provided by nuclear forces.

It is also likely states will pursue a *coupled WMD strategy*, with the more easily acquired bioweapons providing an initial WMD-type capability serving as a stopgap until nuclear capabilities are acquired. Once nuclear weapons are obtained, bioarsenals *augment* these capabilities, increasing the confidence of planners that combined WMD arsenals could achieve the requisite levels of destruction required to defend their nations and establish credible deterrent threats. This would be much like how the Soviet BW arsenal was coupled to its nuclear arsenal for joint strategic use during the Cold War. Further, for new biostates, these combined arsenals would provide redundancy of WMDs *and* employment flexibility—since nuclear weapons could be held in reserve as the ultimate deterrent to prevent retaliation for the use of bioweapons on the battlefield or in limited use against civilian targets.

Since the use of bioweapons carries such a stigma and evokes such negative sanctions, it is likely new biostates will view all bioweapon use as "strategic"—*only to be considered to defend against the most critical threats to their central interests*. For less central, peripheral interests, the use of bioweapons would be too costly (in terms of likely repercussions and sanctions that would result) and not very credible for backing up a deterrent threat. On the other hand, if a state's very survival and independence were at stake, and an opponent were aware of its potential possession of a substantial bioarsenal, the threat (either explicit or implicit) they might be used would surely create some degree of existential deterrence. For new biostates like North Korea, the use of its bioarsenal to undermine or repel a U.S.–South Korean invasion, or punish one via retaliation against population centers in South Korea, would not likely be a "tactical" use by Pyongyang, but a "strategic" one. Further, the general awareness of opponents, like the U.S. or South Korea, of a potentially robust North Korean bioarsenal would serve a strategic purpose as well, by potentially creating an existential deterrence relationship to deter such an invasion in the first place.

But, beyond their use for strategic deterrence or threats of retaliation, it is accurate to say that most bioweapons have limited ability to instantly produce militarily significant effects on the battlefield. The only bioweapons that could have the same immediacy of effect of nerve agents would be various toxins or bioregulatory agents—which could combine immediate effects with limited blow-back potential. Yet, for most bioweapons, which lack such immediate effects, such application is just not feasible. However, if the goal is not immediate incapacitation or destruction of military forces, but disruption of an opponent's ability to maintain military operations, bioweapons hold immense tactical value. Dispersed into rear areas, bioagents could create mass casualties in reserve forces and disrupt command-and-control and logistics/supply functions. Deployed against ports or airfields, personnel critical for unloading supplies from ships and planes, for maintaining equipment, for transporting food, ammunition, and fuel to the front lines would suffer serious attrition. Employed in this manner, bioweapons could prove immensely effective for affecting events on the battlefield.

An example of the potential tactical effectiveness of BW against U.S. forces in the Korean theater was demonstrated by a top secret 1995 Pentagon war game called Global 95, which assumed North Korean use of anthrax, disseminated by stealth speedboats offshore and special forces teams arriving via hidden tunnels under the DMZ, resulting in the complete, catastrophic disruption of American military operations and ability to reinforce or resupply its forces in the field (Mangold and Goldberg 1999, 325–27). The exercise ended with at least 50,000 U.S. troops infected with anthrax and the inability of U.S. forces to stage an effective overland counterinvasion of North Korea due to the disruption of its staging areas and the continuing ability of Pyongyang to stage further BW attacks that would contaminate invasion routes. As Mangold and Goldberg (1999, 326) observe, the postgame analysis of Global 95 found "air bases and ports in host countries (like Korea and Saudi Arabia) are particularly vulnerable to biological attack because the vital workers there are civilians, contractors, and third-country nationals who are unprotected and untrained in biowarfare defence" and that "once this crucial support staff is contaminated, incapacitated, or killed in an attack, it will drastically erode the ability to supply and reinforce the friendly 'guest' troops."

Finally, in terms of nonstate actors, such as terror groups, the security relationships resulting from obtaining biowarfare capabilities vis-à-vis state actors is comparable to that arising from their acquisition of nuclear capabilities. Essentially, such nonstate, terror group actors are *undeterrable* in the classical sense by state actors, regardless of whether these states are able to

Deterrence Security Relationship Sought

| Nature of State/Non-State Actor — Interests Activated | Bioweapons Capabilities | Ability of Targeted Opponent to Directly Retaliate | *Existential Deterrence* (Use of Implied Threat Based Upon Opponent's Awareness of Potential BW Capabilities) | *Existential Deterrence* (Use of Explicit Threat Coupled With Opponent's Awareness of Potential BW Capabilities) | *Classical Deterrence* (Explicit Threat Based Upon Demonstrated Use or Possession of BW Capabilities) |
|---|---|---|---|---|---|
| (Central Interests) | (Sophisticated/High Deliverability) | (High) | Low-Moderate Deterrence Possible. High Credibility of Bio-threats. Deterrence favors actor whose security most directly threatened. Likely state vs. state actor pattern. | Probable Mutual Deterrence. High Credibility of Bio-threats. Deterrence favors actor whose security most directly threatened. Likely state vs. state actor pattern. | Probable Mutual Deterrence. High Credibility of Bio-threats. Deterrence favors actor whose security most directly threatened. Likely state vs. state actor pattern. |
| (Central Interests) | (Sophisticated/High Deliverability) | (Low) | Challenger May Be Deterred (i.e., one-way deterrence relationship). High Credibility of Bio-threats. Likely non-state vs. state actor pattern. | Challenger May Be Deterred (i.e., one-way deterrence relationship). High Credibility of Bio-threats. Likely non-state vs. state actor pattern. | Challenger Likely Deterred (i.e., one-way deterrence relationship). High Credibility of Bio-threats. Likely non-state vs. state actor pattern. |
| (Central Interests) | (Unsophisticated/Low Deliverability) | (High) | Deterrence Unlikely. Bio-threats Lack Credibility. Likely state vs. state actor pattern. | Deterrence Unlikely. Bio-threats Lack Credibility. Likely state vs. state actor pattern. | Deterrence Unlikely. Bio-threats Credible. Likely state vs. state actor pattern. |
| (Central Interests) | (Unsophisticated/Low Deliverability) | (Low) | Deterrence Unlikely. Bio-threats Somewhat Credible. Likely non-state vs. state actor pattern. | Weak Deterrence Possible. Bio-threats Somewhat Credible. Likely non-state vs. state actor pattern. | Challenger Possibly Deterred (i.e., one-way deterrence relationship). Bio-threats Credible. Likely non-state vs. state actor pattern. |
| (Peripheral Interests) | (Sophisticated/High Deliverability) | (High) | Deterrence Unlikely. Bio-threats Lack Credibility. Likely state vs. state actor pattern. | Deterrence Unlikely. Bio-threats Lack Credibility. Likely state vs. state actor pattern. | Weak Deterrence Possible. Bio-threats Lack Credibility. Likely state vs. state actor pattern. |
| (Peripheral Interests) | (Sophisticated/High Deliverability) | (Low) | Weak Deterrence Possible. Bio-threats Credible. Likely non-state vs. state actor pattern. | Challenger May Be Deterred (i.e., one-way deterrence relationship). Bio-threats Credible. Likely non-state vs. state actor pattern. | Challenger May Be Deterred (i.e., one-way deterrence relationship). Bio-threats Credible. Likely non-state vs. state actor pattern. |
| (Peripheral Interests) | (Unsophisticated/Low Deliverability) | (High) | Deterrence Unlikely. Bio-threats Lack Credibility. Likely state vs. state actor pattern. | Deterrence Unlikely. Bio-threats Lack Credibility. Likely state vs. state actor pattern. | Deterrence Unlikely. Bio-threats Lack Credibility. Likely state vs. state actor pattern. |
| (Peripheral Interests) | (Unsophisticated/Low Deliverability) | (Low) | Deterrence Unlikely. Bio-threats Somewhat Credible. Likely non-state vs. state actor pattern. | Deterrence Unlikely. Bio-threats Somewhat Credible. Likely non-state vs. state actor pattern. | Weak Deterrence Possible. Bio-threats Somewhat Credible. Likely non-state vs. state actor pattern. |

Figure 4.2.   Nature of Potential Biodeterrence Security Relationships

threaten conventional or unconventional retaliation. Unlike a nation-state launching an attack, a terror group provides no "return address" against which retaliation can be launched. They are clandestine by nature and often widely dispersed, making targeting efforts against them extremely problematic to say the least. Since deterrence relationships require the ability to deliver an *assured* retaliatory response to any attack that would inflict unacceptable levels of damage on the opponent (thereby affecting their calculations of the value to be gained from the attack), it is plain that terror groups would seldom provide a state with any viable targets for such retribution. Also, many of the types of terror groups believed most likely to employ nuclear or bioweapons against states (religious fundamentalist, millennial cults, etc.) are also the least likely to worry about the impact of such attacks upon their political legitimacy or aspirations. For states, the unfortunate reality is that if deterrence is likely to exist at all, it will probably exist as a "one-way street"—where terror groups will be able to issue extremely credible threats of bioweapons use against civilian targets unless their demands are met and effectively deter state actors—regardless of how powerful they are.

For instance, were Al Qaeda to develop the ability to produce fairly advanced bioweapons—like an antibiotic-resistant anthrax powder or a high-quality liquid or dry weapon employing a lethal, communicable pathogen like smallpox or plague—it would take only a demonstration usage against a civilian target to conclusively demonstrate both their *capability* and the *credibility* of subsequent threats. State actors might have some ability to interdict or preempt some of these potential bioattacks, but if Al Qaeda demonstrated a robust, survivable capability to deliver attacks regardless of these measures—states would face the quandary of dealing with a nonstate opponent who could deliver an assured destructive capability on their civilian centers at will. Were this to occur, state actors would be forced into a one-sided deterrence relationship with these terror group opponents, in which continued U.S. economic support for Israel or troop presence in Iraq, could be met with potential mass-casualty biological attacks on their cities. Consider the following counterfactual: Had Al Qaeda previously demonstrated a survivable, robust ability to deliver bioweapons attacks on U.S. civilian targets, would the U.S. have continued military efforts to overthrow the Taliban in Afghanistan in 2001 if Al Qaeda promised to respond with mass-casualty attacks in the U.S. or against regional allies? Without question, the gravity of the threat and the credibility of the group's ability to carry it out would have to be strongly considered by American policy makers, regardless of their decision. Any number of potential blackmail or retaliatory scenarios can be envisioned involving nuclear-armed or bioarmed nonstate actors over the coming decades, with most demonstrating the decidedly one-way nature of the deterrence security relationships likely to exist between these state and nonstate actors.

## CONCLUSION

In this chapter, the nature of the current threat posed by bioweapons was explored, as were existing trends making proliferation of bioweapons capabilities and technologies more likely to both state and nonstate actors. Examples of past BW programs provided hints to the future direction of new biostate programs, and an analytical framework for assessing the impact of such developments upon existing (and future) security relationships was proposed. In the next chapter, the nature of various bioagents will be discussed, as will the enormous potential of biotechnology and genetic engineering to radically alter the threat spectrum we face from future bioweapons. Several illustrations will be provided to demonstrate how such agents might be employed by either state or nonstate actors across several threat scenarios. WMDs could be used (or threatened to be used) for the goal of undermining U.S. domestic political support for a military intervention (by threatening large numbers of military or civilian casualties), disrupting or undermining U.S. or allied military operations abroad, or undermining allied support for or participation in operations. And with greater capabilities, new biostates could pose U.S. policy makers with the risk that true mass-casualty strikes—comparable to the fatalities resulting from a nuclear attack—could be directed against American territory or military forces abroad if actions threatening their central interests were continued. Even for bioterror groups, the potential for inflicting damage and altering security relationships brought about by the proliferation of bioweapons know-how is immense. We now move to a more in-depth discussion of the "nature of the evolving bioweapons threat" and what form the "grey rider" may take if unleashed.

## NOTES

1. The National Defense University report (p. 50) also warns U.S. nuclear threats might not deter BW use if the calculus of deterrence were altered by the asymmetrical nature of the stakes involved for the two states (e.g., the adversary having higher stakes and greater willingness to run risks/absorb costs in defending its central interests than the U.S.).

2. The most comprehensive report on Iraq's BW activities is found in the report by Richard Butler to the UN secretary general in January 1999 (see full report at www.un.org/Depts/unscom/s99-94.htm).

3. Arguing high-skill levels are required are experts like Selden (1997) and Carus (2001). Those suggesting less skill is required include the CIA (1996). See Smithson and Levy (2000) for an in-depth discussion.

4. The Soviet BW program explored the military application of over fifty pathogens lethal to humans and collected over two hundred antianimal strains for their weapons research.

5. Interview with anonymous government official, March 2000, who suggested Iranian success at getting former Biopreparat scientists to provide information by computer was far more extensive than reported in the press. Also see Miller, Engelberg, and Broad 2001, 206–7; Warrick 2002; Miller and Broad 1998; Smithson 1999, 15–17.

6. See also Smithson 1999.

7. This information about the movement of ex-Soviet bioweaponeers to Iran was also confirmed to me during an interview with a senior U.S. government official.

8. For more detailed discussion of the manufacturing process surrounding BW agents, see Alibek 1999, 96–99.

9. This weapons-grade anthrax was described as "an amber-gray powder, finer than bath talc, with smooth, creamy particles that tend to fly apart and vanish in the air, becoming invisible and drifting for miles." (Preston 1998, 52–65)

10. Interview by author with Ken Alibek.

11. Interview by author with Ken Alibek.

12. Interview by author with Ken Alibek.

13. Interview by author with Ken Alibek.

14. Interview by author with Ken Alibek.

15. See also Rimmington 1999, 100.

16. Interview by author with Ken Alibek.

17. Interview by author with James Woolsey.

18. Davies (2000, 46–48), notes the death toll of the 1918 flu pandemic was undoubtedly far higher than the very conservative figure of 20 million that was adopted by scientists in the 1920s. Given the inaccurate/incomplete reporting from rural areas worldwide, and no consideration of the toll the virus took in Africa, China, Latin America, and Russia in this early estimate, Davies suggests the Spanish flu likely killed at least double the official estimate (or 40 million people worldwide). Indeed, some historians place the death toll in India alone from the 1918 influenza at over 17 million victims and nearly 100 million worldwide!

19. All *Dark Winter* simulation materials can be found at the University of Pittsburgh Medical Center's Center for Biosecurity website at www.upmc-biosecurity.org.

20. Large-scale, open-air tests of live agents were run at Johnston Atoll from 1963 to 1969 involving trials of liquid Q fever and tularemia bioweapons released from spray tanks aboard F-105 navy jets. Mangold and Goldberg 1999, 39.

21. For more detailed discussions of these tests, see Cole (1988) and Department of the Army (1977).

22. See also Balmer 2001.

23. Former British weapons inspector Christopher Davis, who was among the team inspecting the Biopreparat facilities during the 1990s, agrees with Alibek and suggests the Russian Ministry of Defense BW sites may still be engaged in offensive BW work (Davis 1999, 511).

24. See the full Butler report at www.un.org/Depts/unscom/s99-94.htm.

25. Countries capable of producing aerial bombs or ballistic missile warheads containing bomblets to deliver their biological agents will generally pass through two distinct stages: (1) "first generation" crude, rough delivery and (2) "second-generation" advanced, highly effective point-source delivery. The first stage represents the type of delivery systems employed by the United States and the Soviet Union during the 1950s, in which liquid or dry agent was placed in bombs or warheads laden with explosives—resulting in relatively ineffective delivery of the agents since 98–99 percent of the agent in each weapon was destroyed upon detonation. Second-generation delivery systems eventually eliminated this problem, with the U.S. creating bomblets filled with freon for cooling and the Soviets surrounding the material in their bomblets with plastic pellets to deflect the pressure and heat of the chemical explosion away from the agents. See Miller, Engelberg, and Broad 2001, 291.

26. Most smallpox experts dismiss this mode of release because by the time people were contagious with the disease, they would likely be so sick and weak (prostrated) that they would lack the mobility to stage an attack. In the unlikely event they did move about, they would not do so undetected as they would be clearly manifesting symptoms of serious illness (and smallpox pustules).

27. Inversions are meteorological conditions in which a layer of cold area hugs the ground and warmer air at higher altitudes holds it down. This prevents air circulation and holds the pocket of air over a given location, thereby trapping any pollutants (or bioagents) within it. Such heat inversions are most typically found at dawn, dusk, or during nighttime hours and represent ideal conditions for a bioweapons release (Department of Defense October 2001, 18).

28. "A LACM can also avoid detection by following programmed flight paths on which the missile approaches the target at extremely low altitudes, blending with the ground clutter while simultaneously taking advantage of terrain masking. Technologies that enable 'terrain hugging' flight. . . . are becoming increasingly available from commercial sources at affordable costs. These technologies allow longer-range LACMs to fly lengthy and circuitous routes to the target, thus minimizing or eliminating their exposure to air defense systems" (Kiziah 2003).

29. Included on this team were a small number of aeronautical and propulsion engineers, proliferation analysts, and aerosol dispenser and weapons effects specialists (Kiziah 2000, 49–50).

30. Moreover, other analysts have argued that U.S. nuclear weapons are neither credible nor effective in deterring states possessing bioweapons and that only conventional responses should be considered. See Sagan 2000, 85–115.

31. "[Glanders] is not usually lethal to humans, but we considered it an excellent battlefield weapon. Sprayed from a single airplane flying over enemy lines, it could immobilize an entire division or incapacitate guerrilla forces hiding in rugged terrain otherwise inaccessible to regular army troops—precisely the kind of terrain our soldiers faced in Afghanistan" (Alibek 1999, 268–69).

32. He also notes that tactical use degrades a society's ability to counter external attacks because "[It] takes more support people to take care of sick people—maybe 5

or 10 people to administer to the needs of someone who is sick. With a lethal agent that kills, it only takes two people to bury you, and then that is the end of that."

33. Iraq made 100 bombs with botulinum and fifty with anthrax according to UN-SCOM inspectors. For a detailed discussion of Iraq's BW program and possible means of delivery prior to the Gulf War, see Tucker 1993, 229–71.

34. Iraq filled twenty-five warheads: sixteen with botulinum, five with anthrax, and four with aflatoxin.

35. Special Report, No. 117, "Study of the Vulnerability of the Pentagon to Sabotage with BW Agents Via the Air-Conditioning System," 12 October 1949, cited by Mangold and Goldberg 1999, 36.

36. The database prepared by the Center for Nonproliferation Studies at Monterey covering terrorist cases using chemical or biological substances is also often interpreted in this fashion by scholars downplaying the threat posed by terrorist use of WMDs. For a discussion, see Cameron et al. 2000, 157–74; Tucker 1999, 498–504; and Smithson and Levy 2000, 57–69.

37. For examples of this argument, see Mullen 1978, 63–89; Jenkins 1985, 507–15; Wohlstetter 1978; and Tucker and Sands 1999. There is even a similar argument made regarding agricultural bioterrorism; see Pate and Cameron 2001.

38. Interview with James Woolsey by author.

39. U.S. Department of State, Office of the Coordinator for Counterterrorism, *Patterns of Global Terrorism 1999* (Washington, D.C.: U.S. Department of State, 2000). See also *First Annual Report to the President and the Congress of the Advisory Panel to Assess Domestic Response Capabilities for Terrorism Involving Weapons of Mass Destruction* 1999—usually referred to as the 1999 Gilmore panel report.

40. The botulinum toxin was deployed *despite* the fact it had not made any of their laboratory rats ill in tests prior to the attack! (Smithson and Levy 2000, 77–78).

41. As Dr. Richard Spertzel, a microbiologist and former head of biological inspection teams in Iraq, observed, the removal of electrostatic charges was as important as particle size in creating an effective anthrax weapon: "If you don't have small particles, you can't get them into the lungs . . . If they're not slippery, it's hard to get them airborne" (Broad and Miller 18 October 2001).

42. Interview by author with Ken Alibek.

43. The term bioagent is used in this book to denote the actual pathogen, toxin, or bioregulatory compound used in a biological weapon.

44. Skeptics who point to the "blow-back" potential of biological weapons to suggest that they are not usable weapons ignore the fact that nuclear weapons have "blow-back" problems as well, such as fallout or the potential for "nuclear winter" in a large-scale exchange.

# 5

## Biological Security Relationships: Options and Constraints on New Bioweapon States

New biotechnological methods could be developed to overcome many of the deficiencies in older, recognized biological agents, such as low environmental stability, slow onset times, low infectivity, and difficulty in production of some virus and toxin materials. Recombinant DNA techniques could be employed to produce more stable biological and viral agents, splice more rapid acting components into known agents, or even alter the infectivity of recognized agents. Probably of greater importance is the possibility of adapting small continuous culture production technology to produce large quantities of highly infectious materials in a short period of time starting only with a vial of frozen seed stock. Simple purification of the culture using state-of-the-art large scale chromatography, now in place for large scale commercial enzyme and pharmaceutical production, could follow. Thus, the large refrigerated storage vaults, time consuming large batch fermenters for production, and high speed centrifugation equipment which were signatures of such efforts in the past are now no longer required, making detection of such activities even more difficult.

—Dashiell (1990, 88)

The impact of bioweapons varies greatly depending upon the nature of the bioagent and degree to which advancements in biotechnology and genetic engineering have been employed to enhance their characteristics. In this chapter, various bioagents that could serve as future bioweapons for state or non-state actors are examined, including those targeting not just humans, but also agricultural targets (such as crops and animals). In particular, the potential impact of the biotechnology revolution and genetic engineering upon the nature of this threat is explored. Finally, a number of employment scenarios are provided to illustrate how bioagents might be used in the future. As will quickly become apparent, the potential threat spectrum we face is virtually limitless, posing a unique challenge to our efforts to develop defenses or counter the impact of bioweapons capabilities on our security relationships.

## A ROGUE'S GALLERY OF POTENTIAL BIOAGENTS

Many pathogens are suitable for use as bioweapons (see table 5.1). At least seventy different types of bacteria, viruses, rickettsia, and fungi can be effectively weaponized, with treatments available for no more than 20 to 30 percent of these diseases (Alibek 1999, 281). Japanese encephalitis, with a fatality rate of 20 to 30 percent, is "easily reproduced in tissue culture" and has been successfully dispersed in aerosol form in laboratory settings (World Health Organization 1970, 64). Similarly, tick-borne, Far Eastern encephalitis, can also be easily grown in the lab and is highly infective and lethal through aerosol routes (25 percent fatality rate). Yellow fever, with 30 to 40 percent fatality rates among unvaccinated populations, grows well in eggs or tissue cultures, is readily freeze-dried, and transmissible via aerosol form (World Health Organization 1970, 62–64). Moreover, for many of the viral diseases (such as Ebola, Marburg, etc.) there are no vaccines available and some existing vaccines (such as for plague) have been shown in laboratory studies to possibly be ineffective against aerosol dissemination (Alibek 1999, 286). Indeed, Dashiell (1990, 86) warns that given an aerosol attack is considered the most likely method of BW release against U.S. forces, it is important to recognize "current vaccines probably will not effectively protect against an aerosol challenge or will require long time periods and multiple immunizations to reach effective protective levels." Further, Alibek (1999, 10) notes there are "dozens of natural disease agents" that "could be used as biological weapons, and if we add genetically engineered agents, hundreds."

Despite post-9/11 efforts to improve U.S. biodefense, the nation remains tremendously vulnerable to sophisticated bioweapons attack. Commenting on this vulnerability, Dr. Tara O'Toole, deputy director of the Johns Hopkins Center for Civilian Biodefense Studies, warns that "the worst-case attack is a concerted campaign against the United States, in which you do a little anthrax attack here, a little plague here, and . . . a little smallpox there, and a little anthrax again, and then we have chaos. The vulnerability of our health care and medical system is not well appreciated. The capacity to really cause disruption and civil disorder here is terrific" (D'Esopo 2000/2001, 1). The Pentagon, in a study of the 2001 anthrax attacks, concluded the U.S. is "woefully ill-prepared to detect and respond to a bioterrorist assault" (Miller March 2004; Heyman 2002). Indeed, a study by the Partnership for Public Service, a public service advocacy group, suggested that were a large-scale infectious disease attack staged on the U.S., the government would quickly be overwhelmed by serious shortages of skilled medical and scientific personnel needed to contain and respond to the outbreak (Johnston 2003). In fact, a 2003 government simulation of the simultaneous release of anthrax in aerosol form across several American cities, code named Scarlet Cloud, found that antibiotics still would not be distributed quickly enough to prevent thousands of fatalities (Miller 2003).

The challenge of finding enough medical personnel either vaccinated against a potential pathogen, or more critically, willing to risk their own health to treat contagious victims of a BW attack, were well illustrated by the difficulty in finding enough staff to treat one ten-year-old girl who contracted monkeypox from her infected prairie dog in 2003 (Reynolds 2004). A large-scale outbreak would rapidly overwhelm most medical systems. Further, as the U.S. Army Medical Research Institute of Infectious Diseases (USAMRIID) warns, "many diseases caused by weaponized biological agents present with nonspecific clinical features that could be difficult to diagnose and recognize as a biological attack" (U.S. Army Medical Research Institute 2001, 6).

But, even in the face of less extreme bioterror events, in which mass casualties have not occurred, the costs (in terms of time and resources) incurred by authorities would be extensive. During the 2001 anthrax attacks, police and health services were innundated during the first weeks with false alarms and practical jokes, with the FBI and other agencies responding to over 2,300 incidents alone! (Whitworth 2001) The cost in man-hours and other resources across the nation were easily in the millions of dollars, stretched the ability of authorities to respond to real incidents, and contributed to a growing sense of panic among the general public.

## Smallpox

Perhaps the most feared of all classical biological weapons is smallpox—a virus which until eradicated in 1980 had killed tens of millions worldwide and hideously scarred countless more survivors. Moreover, were smallpox unleashed upon the world again, it is unlikely to ever be returned to the hibernation of frozen test tubes in Atlanta and Siberia. Instead, with millions unable to be vaccinated due to compromised immune systems, the virus would likely reestablish a foothold in the developing world and periodically produce renewed epidemics. The spector of smallpox loose amongst us once again understandably arouses great concern. Unfortunately, it is the great killing power of the disease, its ease of transmission, and the horrible lingering

**Table 5.1. Examples of Potential BW Agents and Their Characteristics**

| Potential Bioagent | Untreated Mortality Rate | Incubation Period | Duration of Illness | Infective Aerosol Dose | Transmit Person to Person | Effective Treatment? (Aerosol Dissemination) | Previously Weaponized in State BW Programs? |
|---|---|---|---|---|---|---|---|
| **Anthrax** (inhalation) | 90% (or more) | 1–7 days | 3–5 days | 1–3 to 8,000 spores | No | Yes. Vaccine & antibiotics (presymptom only) | Widely. Soviet BW program engineered vaccine and multispectrum antibiotic resistant strains. |
| **Pneumonic Plague** | 100% | 2–3 days | 1–6 days | 100–500 organisms | Yes | Yes. Antibiotics (presymptom only) | Yes. Soviet BW program engineered "Super" strain resistant to 16 antibiotics. |
| **Smallpox** | 30% (or more) | 7–17 days (average 12) | 4 weeks | 10–100 organisms | Yes | Yes. Vaccine (presymptom only) | Yes. Soviet BW program. |
| **Ebola** | 50%–90% (varies by strain) | 2–21 days | 7–16 days | 1–10 organisms | Yes | None | Yes. Soviet BW program. |
| **Marburg** | 23%–70% | 2–14 days | 7–16 days | 1–10 organisms | Yes | None | Yes. Soviet BW program developed dry powder |

| Tularemia | 30%–60% | 2–10 days | Weeks to Months | 10 organisms (or less) | No | Yes. Antibiotics & vaccine | Widely. Both U.S. & Soviet BW programs developed vaccine & antibiotic resistant strains. |
|---|---|---|---|---|---|---|---|
| **Rickettsia** (Q fever; Rocky Mountain spotted fever; typhus, etc.) | 20%–25% (RMSF) to 10%–60% (epidemic typhus) to 1% (Q fever). | 6–14 days (average 12) | Weeks to Months | 1–10 organisms | No | Yes. Antibiotics & vaccines for some Rickettsia (but not for all) | Yes. U.S. & Soviet programs developed Q fever weapons. Others likely weaponized as well. |
| **Glanders** | 50% (or more) | 3–5 days | 7–10 days | 1–10 organisms | No | None | Yes. U.S. & Soviet programs. |
| **Venezuelan Equine Encephalitis** | 4% | 2–6 days | Days to Weeks | 10–100 organisms | No | Yes. Vaccine | Widely. U.S. BW program developed as main incapacitating bioweapon. |

*Sources:* Jane's Chem-Bio Handbook, 2nd ed 2002; Cirincione, Deadly Arsenals 2002; Inglesby et al. 2002; Inglesby et al. 2000; Henderson et al. 1999; Dennis et al. 2001; Walker 2003; Peters 2000; Borio et al. 2002; U.S. Army Medical Research Institute of Infectious Diseases 2001.

effects it produces that make it ideal as a bioweapon, especially for terrorist or apocalyptic groups, or for states seeking ultimate "strategic" weapons. In fact, smallpox already has (along with plague) a long history of use as a bioweapon over the centuries.

Although inadvertently introduced by the Spanish, smallpox proved an immensely effective bioweapon against both the Aztecs and Incas, eliminating both empires' ability to resist conquest by the relatively small expeditionary forces of the conquistadors (Tucker 2001). Not only were the Aztec and Inca populations decimated, the North American native population was reduced from perhaps 72 million prior to 1492 to only 600,000 by 1800 as a result of both warfare and diseases introduced by Europeans (smallpox, measles, etc.) (Tucker 2001, 9–12).[1] A smallpox epidemic wiped out nearly nine-tenths of the native population in the Massachusetts Bay area prior to the Pilgrim's landing in 1620, facilitating the colonization of the area—a pattern repeated across the continent (Tucker 2001, 11). The British used smallpox as a weapon against Ottawa chief Pontiac's allied Indian tribes in 1763 when Sir Jeffrey Amherst, the British commander in chief in North America, suggested to the defenders of Fort Pitt, "Could it not be Contrived to Send the *Small Pox* among those Disaffected Tribes of Indians? . . . We must, on this occasion, Use Every Stratagem in our power to Reduce them." A delegation of Delaware Indians, visiting Fort Pitt to recommend British surrender, were given, according to the diary of William Trent, commander of the local militia, "two Blankets and a Handkerchief out of the Small Pox Hospital. I hope it will have the desired effect" (Tucker 2001, 19–20). A severe smallpox epidemic soon engulfed the surrounding Indian forces.

For the British, the use of smallpox as a bioweapon had the added advantage of providing a weapon against which their opponents were vulnerable, but to which their own military forces were largely immune. As Tucker (2001, 20–21) observes, British troops who had not already experienced smallpox were "routinely variolated" (or inoculated) to provide immunity, whereas American colonists (as well as the Indian tribes) were not—providing all the ingredients for a "virgin-soil epidemic." During the Revolutionary War, British forces were also believed to have deliberately spread smallpox, with two notable cases occurring in December 1775. The first involved the inoculation of civilian refugees fleeing Boston with smallpox, who then met up with surrounding American forces, starting an epidemic. During the American siege of Quebec, the British fort commander also had civilians variolated and set out to mingle with the surrounding troops, resulting in a major smallpox epidemic afflicting half of the ten thousand troops and causing the army's eventual retreat (Tucker 2001, 17).[2]

During the Cold War, both the U.S. and Soviet Union weaponized smallpox, though the Soviets are the only ones known to have actually produced smallpox biowarheads for use aboard ICBMs (Alibek 1999; Tucker 2001; Miller et al. 2001). The Soviet biobomblets, delivering either dry powder or liquid agents, resembled "oblong grapefruit" and "consisted of two agent-filled aluminum hemispheres surrounding a small, egg-shaped explosive charge" (Tucker 2001, 156). In their final descent stage, the biowarheads deployed parachutes to slow their velocity and "at the appropriate altitude, the warhead would break open, releasing its payload of bomblets to disperse a deadly cloud of aerosolized virus over the target area."[3] Each tiny bomblet held approximately two hundred grams of liquid smallpox and likely used pressurized $CO_2$ to produce a mist of agent as it descended toward the ground (Preston 2002, 92). As Tucker (2001, 144) observes:

> Smallpox biological weapons were intended for use against U.S. cities in a war of total mutual annihilation, with the aim of killing the survivors in the aftermath of a nuclear exchange. Although smallpox normally had a two-week incubation period, individuals exposed to a cloud of aerosolized virus released by a weapon would receive many times the dose encountered under natural conditions. It was believed that this concentrated exposure would accelerate the infection process so that the incubation period might be as short as one to five days, depending on the dose and the immune status of the host. It was also likely that people infected with smallpox by secondary spread would rapidly develop acute illness because radioactive fallout from nuclear explosions would suppress the immune system and reduce the body's ability to fight infection.

By 1965, U.S. bioweaponeers developed a dry powder smallpox, encapsulating the particles in a protective coating to improve their persistence in the environment (Tucker 2001, 139). The freeze-drying process used was particularly effective at preserving smallpox. Once converted to a dry agent, it was capable of being stored years without refrigeration, while still maintaining its viability and virulence (Miller, Engelberg, and Broad 2001, 59–60). Microencapsulation of agents using protective coatings of cellulose and gelatin, or the use of colloidal silica, ultraviolet-resistant pigments, or other compounds to improve the stability and dissemination effectiveness of agents greatly increases their military versatility—but requires substantial expertise (Smithson and Levy 2000, 50). Indeed, the Soviet BW program did not develop a dry powder smallpox weapon, since "the liquid smallpox formulation retained its viability for months when deep-frozen and was extremely stable in aerosol form" (Tucker 2001, 141). Still, given liquid *variola* suspensions had a limited shelf life in refrigerated storage of six months to one year, it wasn't possible to store it for long periods of time (Alibek 1999, 3; Tucker 2001, 147). As a result, the Soviets needed ongoing production of both smallpox and plague liquid agent (Alibek 1999, 3).[4] State programs not wishing to maintain continuous production of agents like smallpox to maintain their arsenals will gravitate, wherever possible, toward production of dry, powder agents.

Other states no doubt followed suit. According to a secret 1998 U.S. intelligence report, North Korea and Russia were viewed as likely to be concealing smallpox for military use (Broad 9 October 2001; Calabresi and August 2004, 16). Moreover, based on his knowledge of previous contacts between the Soviet BW program and other states, Lev Sandakhchiev, director of Russia's State Research Center of Virology and Biotechnology (known as Vector), warned U.S. officials that North Korea, among other countries, is secretly keeping smallpox stocks (Miller November 2001).[5] There is deep suspicion within government circles, fueled by warnings from former scientists and officials from the old Soviet BW program, that offensive bioresearch involving smallpox continues in Russia to this day, carried out behind the walls of off-limits, ultrasecret laboratories controlled by the Russian military (Alibek 1999).

One of the more interesting assumptions often made, lacking *any* empirical evidence (beyond a belief in the honesty of state governments), is that all countries have completely given up their smallpox stocks. Though many countries declared they had transferred their variolla samples to one of two WHO depositories (CDC or Vector) or destroyed their samples (e.g., China), there can be no definitive proof that any (or all) of the prior holders eliminated every last vial. Though many probably did, and refrained from keeping any for a *rainy day*, it is difficult to believe (given the normal willingness of states to secretly follow policies of pure self-interest) that *all* of them were completely honest in this regard. If the final decision were ever taken to destroy the last "official" samples held at CDC and Vector—how believable is it that Russian military BW centers (which never admitted having *variola* in the first place) will be clean—or that somewhere at the highest levels of secrecy, U.S. research centers haven't preserved some samples as a hedge against future security threats?

Since inspections would never (even if attempted) be able to verify the ultimate, final destruction of every sample of smallpox in every nation, top secret laboratory, or freezer, its final fate will forever be an open question—regardless of the disposition of WHO's two *official* stockpiles. Given human nature, and the potential power contained within the smallpox virus, only the completely unskeptical could take *any* government's assurances regarding its fate at face value. Indeed, given the danger of undeclared smallpox stocks, the

Bush administration decided in November 2001 to forego destruction of the U.S. samples in Atlanta and allow continued defensive research and work on improved medical treatments for the disease.[6] Further, advances in biotechnology and the genomic mapping of many strains of smallpox means it may be possible to reconstitute the virus "from scratch" in the lab in the *absence* of actual seedstocks. As Tucker (2001, 158) notes, one of the tasks pursued by Soviet bioweaponeers "was to clone fragments of India-1967 in bacteria so that the viral DNA would be available to Soviet researchers even after the stocks of live variola virus were destroyed, perhaps making it possible to reconstitute the virus in the laboratory."

Not only are major BW facilities run by the Russian military completely closed to outside inspection (such as those at Zagorsk or Pokrov), but there was never conclusive evidence Moscow actually destroyed the tons of frozen smallpox it had produced in its earlier weapons program or eliminated the biowarheads that would have carried it aboard either aircraft or ballistic missiles. As Preston (2002, 94–95) warns, many outside analysts and government officials believe the Russians have clandestine smallpox stockpiles at Zagorsk and are continuing offensive BW research. Also suggestive is the fact the Russian government refuses to share the India-1 strain used in its bioweapons with any outside researchers or governments, a refusal that would preserve any unique qualities of that particular strain from research that might undercut its effectiveness on the battlefield (Preston 2002, 143). In fact, analysis of the clinical manifestations among the population during a 1971 outbreak of smallpox in Aralsk, Kazakstan—the result of an open-air Soviet test of a smallpox weapon on Vozrozhdeniye Island that floated out to sea, contaminating a research vessel fifteen kilometers offshore—suggests the "battle-strain" being tested was not only a highly virulent strain that produced hemorrhagic smallpox in unvaccinated individuals, but was one which was also able to evade previous vaccination to cause disease. Of the ten cases of smallpox in Aralsk, *all three individuals* who were unvaccinated developed the rare (and nearly always fatal) hemorrhagic form of the disease, while seven others (who had all been previously vaccinated) still contracted smallpox, but tended to suffer only a modified or typical discrete form of the disease (Zelicoff 2002). Indeed as Zelicoff (2002, 17) notes, since "the efficacy of the smallpox vaccine . . . is usually described as being in excess of 90 percent," the data from the Aralsk case suggests "the variola virus strain involved in the epidemic may have been somewhat vaccine-resistant."

Continuing research published over the past decade by former Soviet bioweaponeers (e.g., creation of libraries of cloned fragments of *variola* DNA, mapping of *variola* genomes and identification of virulence genes, genetic engineering of a wide range of pox viruses, etc.) have led many analysts to worry such "dual-use" BW research continues to support an offensive Russian BW program (Tucker 2001, 218–19). Among the foreign genes Russian scientists inserted into vaccinia are those from various hemorrhagic fevers (like Ebola), Venezuelan equine encephalititis (VEE), beta-endorphin and dynorphin (two morphinelike brain peptides), and various toxins produced by shellfish, among others (Tucker 2001, 158–59). Coupled with related research on pox viruses openly published in Western medical journals, the "know-how" to use or manipulate pox-type bioweapons will only increase. For example, the complete genomes for a number of different strains of *variola major* have been completed in recent years, including those for the Bangladesh-1975 and India-1967 strains (Massung et al. 1994; Shchelkunov et al. 1995). Other research into virulence factors of smallpox virus has highlighted which *variola* proteins are most effective at overcoming human immunity (Rosengard et al. 2002; Dunlop et al. 2003). Similar work has also been done analyzing the genome of monkeypox (Shchelkunov et al. 2002) and camelpox (Gubser and Smith 2002). Obviously, while such work is important for treatment and vaccine development, it is also potentially useful for bioengineering pox strains to evade human immunity.

It also opens up the possibility of manufacturing a pseudo-smallpox virus from a modified, related pox virus (such as camelpox or monkeypox). This is why UNSCOM inspectors were so concerned to discover the Iraqis had been researching camelpox. Although natural camelpox does not cause disease in humans, comparative analysis of the CMPV and VAR genomes show that camelpox is more closely related to smallpox than to any other virus and could prove dangerous if modified (Gubser and Smith 2002, 856). Indeed, as Gubser and Smith (2002, 869) warn:

> [I]t is unclear whether all, only a few, or just one of the differences between the CMPV and VAR genomes are responsible for the inability of CMPV to cause human disease. Consequently, genetic modification of CMPV to delete genes that are present in CMPV but absent in VAR might be unwise. It might also be unwise to insert into CMPV genes encoding Th2 cytokines, which caused a dramatic change in ectromelia virus virulence. (Jackson et al. 2001)

Similarly, while Shchelkunov et al. (2001) found that monkeypox is not a direct ancestor of variolla, and is unlikely to *naturally* acquire all of its properties, this does not eliminate the potential for bioengineering monkeypox to *artificially* produce a pathogen with the characteristics of variolla major. Given monkeypox virus (MPV) does cause disease in humans resembling smallpox, albeit with lower person-to-person transmission rates, genetic modification of this pathogen would also seem a reasonable route for bioweaponeers who lack access to *variola major* to take in developing a pseudo-smallpox weapon

(Shchelkunov et al. 2001, 66). As one former Soviet bioweaponeer warns, by conducting genetic manipulations, it is certainly possible to make monkeypox virus as contagious as smallpox (Alibek 1999, 8).

Were smallpox to reemerge, either through the natural evolution of a related pox virus or from a purposeful release by man, it might prove extraordinarily difficult to prevent a global pandemic. As D. A. Henderson observes, "if smallpox were to appear anywhere in the world today, the way airplane travel is now, about six weeks would be enough time to seed cases around the world. . . . Dropping an atomic bomb could cause casualties in a specific area, but dropping smallpox could engulf the world" (Preston 2002, 103). Similarly, John Huggins, director of antiviral drug development at USAMRIID at Fort Detrick, warns that in a highly susceptible population like the U.S. (lacking extensive prior vaccination or herd immunity in the populace), a single case of smallpox might infect twenty others, each of whom would similarly infect twenty others, resulting in a "wild-fire" type spread of the disease. Not only does Huggins fear such an outbreak would far exceed the capacity of traditional ring vaccination strategies to contain, but because there would be a substantial time lag before authorities were aware of the exposure, hundreds or thousands of people would be acutely ill (and beyond the help of vaccination) before smallpox was detected (Tucker 2001, 199–200). O'Toole (1999, 541), in her analysis of various smallpox attack scenarios, notes initial symptoms from a release could easily be mistaken for chicken pox by medical personnel, delaying response.

More ominously, the *Dark Winter* simulation of 2001, involving a fictional bioterrorist release of smallpox in Oklahoma City, found that while steps were rapidly taken to contain the outbreak and seal state/national borders, 3,000 total smallpox cases (with 1,000 deaths) on December 17th of the scenario quickly escalated to *over 3 million cases worldwide* (and 1 million deaths) by February 6th![7] As Henderson et al. (1999, 2128) warns, "aerosol release of variola virus would disseminate widely, given the considerable stability of the orthopoxviruses in aerosol form and the likelihood that the infectious dose is very small." Further, experts have suggested *variola* would likely persist in the environment for twenty-four hours or longer as an aerosol if not exposed to UV light, and in cooler temperatures (10 degrees Celsius) and lower humidity (20 percent) (Henderson et al. 1999, 2135). Although these figures were originally provided by Henderson et al. (1999, 2136) to illustrate the viability of aerosolized *vaccinia virus* under various temperature and humidity conditions, these same figures are expected to be accurate for *variola major* as well.

This suggests smallpox would be at its most effective if released at night during the winter months, where the cold would allow it to survive longer in the air and the flu season help mask its arrival. Of course, other means of release could also widely spread the disease. For example, one U.S. BW experiment at Washington's National Airport in May 1965 demonstrated that briefcases containing small aerosol generators spraying a smallpox simulant infected one out of every twelve airport passengers, resulting in a widespread distribution of the virus across the country (Tucker 2001, 232). This has led critics of existing plans to respond to a bioterrorist release of smallpox using the traditional targeted, ring-style vaccination strategy (so successful in eradicating natural smallpox) to argue that unlike a natural outbreak, a bioterrorist incident would not allow for isolation of patient contacts for vaccination (since a release in an airport or elsewhere would seed the infection over large areas). Further, unlike the 1960s and 1970s, there are no preexisting levels of "herd immunity" from prior smallpox vaccinations in the population. As a result, were multiple attacks launched simultaneously, the spread of the disease would rapidly outpace efforts by officials to contain it through traditional vaccination strategies.

Some mathematical studies of hypothetical smallpox outbreaks have attempted to model how quickly the virus would spread and what containment strategies would be most effective. Meltzer et al. (2001, 959) produced a model in which 100 people are initially infected and arrive at the conclusion a combined vaccine and quarantine campaign would result in approximately 4,200 cases before the outbreak was stopped after 365 days. Since historical data suggests an average of 2,155 smallpox vaccine doses per case were given to stop past outbreaks, Meltzer et al. (2001, 959) suggest a stockpile of 40 million doses would be adequate to deal with this level of bioterror release. Of course, this scenario is confined geographically and does not take into account the spread and logistical problems created if smallpox were released on the same 100 individuals at a busy regional or international airport. In contrast, Kaplan et al. (2002) demonstrate that mass vaccinations after an attack would be far more effective in mitigating casualties than the traditional, targeted vaccinations currently planned. In their scenario, a large attack of 1,000 initial cases in a population of 10 million is assumed, which is responded to by authorities with either mass or targeted vaccination approaches. The results are disturbing. The targeted vaccination strategy results in 367,000 active smallpox cases and results in 110,000 deaths over 350 days; whereas mass vaccination leads to 1,830 cases and 560 deaths over 115 days (Kaplan, Craft, and Wein 2002, 10936). But, as Jahrling et al. (2000, 187) warn, "the factors that facilitate the spread of naturally occurring microbes would also contribute to the potential for even a small, deliberate introduction of smallpox virus to develop into a global pandemic." In fact, they note that "given the remarkable contagiousness of smallpox virus, a terrorist could initiate a massive epidemic by exposing a modest number of individuals in a small group. If the exposure occurred at a transportation hub, such as an airport, smallpox virus would be effectively disseminated to a wide geographic area during the incubation period and before the first cases had appeared."

Further, though the historical lethality of smallpox was high, it would be even more lethal (and produce a higher mortality rate) in a population lacking resistance. As one expert warns, if someone were to unleash smallpox against us now, "we are all Indians" (Miller, Engelberg, and Broad 2001, 252). Indeed, Henderson et al. (1999, 2129) note "typical variola major epidemics such as those that occurred in Asia resulted in case-fatality rates of 30% or higher among the unvaccinated, whereas variola minor case-fatality rates were customarily 1% or less." While 90 percent of smallpox cases present clinically in a classical manner, the remaining 10 percent take one of two forms—hemorrhagic or malignant smallpox:

Hemorrhagic cases are uniformly fatal and occur among all ages and in both sexes, but pregnant women appear to be unusually susceptible. Illness usually begins with a somewhat shorter incubation period and is characterized by a severely prostrating prodromal illness with high fever and head, back, and abdominal pain. Soon thereafter, a dusky erythema develops, followed by petechiae and frank hemorrhages into the skin and mucous membranes. Death usually occurs by the fifth or sixth day after onset of rash. In the frequently fatal malignant form, the abrupt onset and prostrating constitutional symptoms are similar. The confluent lesions develop slowly, never progressing to the pustular stage but remaining soft, flattened, and velvety to the touch. The skin has the appearance of a fine-grained, reddish-colored crepe rubber, sometimes with hemorrhages. If the patient survives, the lesions gradually disappear without forming scabs or, in severe cases, large amounts of epidermis might peel away.

The seasonal occurance of smallpox was highest during winter and early spring, since orthopoxviruses in aerosolized form have a duration of survival "inversely proportional to both temperature and humidity." Also, smallpox was historically transmitted through populations slower than diseases like measles and chicken pox:

Patients spread smallpox primarily to household members and friends; large outbreaks in schools, for example, were uncommon. This finding was accounted for in part by the fact that transmission of smallpox virus did not occur until onset of rash. By then, many patients had been confined to bed because of the high fever and malaise of the prodromal illness. Secondary cases were thus usually restricted to those who came into contact with patients, usually in the household or hospital. (Henderson et al. 1999, 2129)

As Gubser and Smith (2002, 868) observe, "highly infectious diseases, such as measles and smallpox, require human populations of between 100,000 and 300,000 to retain transmission between susceptible (non-immune) hosts." In fact, epidemiologists have discovered smallpox requires, in order to keep its life cycle going and not burn out, a human population of around two hundred thousand people living within fourteen days of travel from one another (Preston 2002, 53). Because of how highly contagious smallpox is in hospital settings, experts recommend isolating patients at home or in other hospital facilities solely dedicated to treating smallpox victims if possible, with all family members and contacts being immediately inoculated with vaccine to prevent their coming down with the disease as well. Henderson et al. (1999, 2129) explain that because "smallpox spreads from person to person primarily by droplet nuclei or aerosols expelled from the oropharynx of infected persons and by direct contact. Contaminated clothing or bed linens can also spread the virus." But, they note "vaccination administered within the first few days after exposure and perhaps as late as 4 days may prevent or significantly ameliorate subsequent illness." Even if these newly vaccinated individuals do come down with smallpox, they have "significant protection against a fatal outcome" (Henderson et al. 1999, 2129).

Until recently, it was assumed past smallpox immunizations would be of limited use against any renewed exposure. But, recent research shows that, while protection does wane, a degree of "residual immunity" still exists that might prevent infection, or at least reduce the severity of the disease, even if the vaccinations occurred fifty years earlier (Rubin 2001; Brown 2003). Still, Henderson et al. warn "an unnaturally heavy dose of smallpox virus, as might occur in a bioterrorism attack, could overwhelm whatever immunity may remain from a decades-old vaccination" (Brown 2003). Indeed, though commercially available vaccines (Wyeth Dryvax) are known to be effective against natural exposures to smallpox, there is *no data* on their effectiveness against much higher doses of virus delivered during a bioattack. Jahrling et al. (2000, 194), in an experiment using a monkeypox-monkey model, demonstrated the two existing *vaccinia virus* vaccines (Dryvax and TSI-GSD-241) both immunized test monkeys at high levels of aerosol exposure, leading them to conclude the vaccines would likely protect humans against a similar aerosol bioattack. But this is no certainty, especially given unknowns about the dose.

While current U.S. biodefense efforts focus upon building up new stockpiles of smallpox vaccine, recombinant research done by Australian scientists on mousepox virus warn of the limits of such defenses (Jackson et al. 2001). Just as the modified-mousepox strain killed even mice who had been vaccinated against mousepox in their experiments, it is equally possible a new, genetically enhanced smallpox (one that had spliced to it the interleukin-4 gene from the Australian experiments) *could* defeat the current human vaccine (which was designed to defeat only "normal" smallpox) (Miller, Engelberg, and Broad 2001, 311–12). Although subsequent research suggests recent vaccination (only weeks old) might still protect against an IL-4 *variola*, the engineered smallpox would still blow through people whose immunizations were older, which would make the task of immunizing a large population effectively exceedingly difficult—especially since only *very* recent vaccinations would protect against the engineered pox (Preston 2002, 226–27). Defenses against such new pathogens would require either advanced gene-based vaccines or new, more powerful antiviral drugs, both of which are yet to be developed (Miller, Engelberg, and Broad 2001, 306 and 312).

Of existing antiviral drugs, Cidofovir shows the most promise in potentially treating smallpox, having been demonstrated to protect mice from aerosol cowpox virus and monkeys from MPOX. However, Cidofovir requires intravenous administration, a factor which limits its utility in any attack involving mass numbers of people (Jahrling, Zaucha, and Huggins 2000, 196–99). Moreover, as recent research by Smee et al. (2002, 1334) demonstrates, numerous pox viruses (including camelpox, cowpox, monkeypox, and *vaccinia virus*) develop resistance to Cidofovir after prolonged usage. In fact, these researchers developed Cidofovir-resistant forms of all four of these viruses that were eight to twenty-seven times as resistant as wild-type viruses (Smee et al. 2002, 1329). Though the research seeks to understand what mutations in viral DNA polymerase of orthopoxviruses leads to resistance to Cidofovir (an important task given this antibiotic is one of the few possible treatments for smallpox), it could also be used to engineer more resistant viruses without harming their virulence. Indeed, while a number of Cidofovir-resistant poxviruses showed some decline in their virulence, one resistant monkeypox virus isolate actually demonstrated *enhanced* virulence over its wild-type counterpart (Smee et al. 2002, 1334).

## Plague

Another pathogen particularly well suited for use as a bioweapon is plague bacteria. From the first recorded plague pandemic in 541 AD (which killed 50 to 60 percent of the populations of Europe, North Africa, and central/southern Asia) to the Black Death of fourteenth-century Europe (which killed 20 to 30 million people—or one-third of the entire European population), to the third great pandemic of 1855 (which killed more than 12 million in India and China alone)—plague has truly been a pathogen of mass destruction (Inglesby et al. 2000, 2282). The immense virulence of plague and its high communicability during natural outbreaks made it even more desirable to bioweaponeers of the twentieth century. The Japanese BW program sought to harness plague using insect vectors, dropping infected fleas in porcelain containers onto Chinese villages to start epidemics (Harris 2002). Several other state-run BW programs also attempted to develop plague bioweapons with varying degrees of success (including the U.S. program). However, it was the Soviet BW program whose bioweaponeers made the breakthrough, allowing them to create a dry powder form of plague that could be effectively disseminated and avoiding the disadvantages of relying upon insect vectors or liquid agents. This plague bioweapon was enhanced by Soviet bioweaponeers to have resistance to a broad range of antibiotics, making it even deadlier to an exposed population and more difficult to treat. Along with smallpox, tularemia, and Marburg, the Soviets developed biowarheads that could be filled with plague for use aboard their ICBMs (Alibek 1999).

Unfortunately, the advent of modern genetic engineering and proliferation of advanced biotech equipment and knowledge may once again make plague the "bioweapon of choice" in the strategic arsenals of states. As our understanding of the plague bacterium expands (through research exploring [and modifying] the factors causing virulence and antibiotic resistance in plague, along with the decoding of its entire genomic sequence), there exists growing potential for development of modified "super plague" bioweapons (with enhanced virulence and resistance factors) almost impossible to defend against. And, unlike the Soviet "super plague" strains of the Cold War–era, genetic engineering of new plague bioweapons could produce *recombinant* strains containing genes from other pathogens or ones specifically designed to produce toxins or bioregulatory peptides. Such developments could make plague, which is far more obtainable to potential bioweaponeers than more exotic pathogens like smallpox or Marburg, an agent likely to pose a serious future threat to U.S. security.

The consequences of any release of plague on civilian populations could be quite dire, even if only "classic," unmodified plague were used in the attack. For example, a simulated bioterrorist release of aerosolized plague at the Denver Performing Arts Center formed the basis of the May 2000 TOPOFF exercise conducted by the Department of Justice to see how effectively top U.S. officials (hence the TOPOFF name) would respond to such an incident. The results showed both officials and medical resources would be overwhelmed by the influx of patients, the difficulties in distributing antibiotics, the problems associated with placing a quarantine around the city (or state), locating asymptomatics, and the rapid spread of the illness (Inglesby et al. 2001). By the end of the simulation, cases of pneumonic plague had spread beyond the U.S. to other countries, with nearly 4,000 known cases and between 950 and 2,000 deaths from the disease (Inglesby, Grossman, and O'-Toole 2001). And this assumed a plague strain susceptible to antibiotics and unmodified in any way. A large-scale release over an entire city—rather than the point-source attack in the TOPOFF scenario—using either a line-source release from an aircraft or cruise missile, or dispersal by biowarheads aboard missiles, would be a different matter altogether. Modeling by Soviet planners during the Cold War suggested plague would be highly effective as a strategic weapon against urban targets, spreading rapidly throughout the civilian populations producing a high mortality rate (Alibek 1999). Delivered in clandestine fashion during the cold and flu season, without warning or knowledge of its release by local authorities, a plague bioweapon modified to possess high virulence and broad spectrum resistance to antibiotics would cut a broad swath through a civilian population and cause high levels of fatalities before effective countermeasures could be taken.

An aerosolized plague weapon would produce symptoms consistent with severe pneumonia (fever, cough, chest pain, hemoptysis) one to six days after exposure, with rapid deterioration of patients in two to four days after symptom onset due to septic shock. Inglesby et al. (2000, 2284) describe how the appearance of plague after a bioterror release might manifest itself:

> Inhaled aerosolized *Y pestis* bacilli would cause primary pneumonic plague. The time from exposure to aerosolized plague bacilli until the development of first symptoms in humans . . . has been found to be 1 to 6 days and most often, 2 to 4 days. The first sign of illness would be . . . fever with cough and dyspnea, sometimes with the production of bloody, watery, or less commonly, purulent sputum. Prominent gastrointestinal symptoms, including nausea, vomiting, abdominal pain, and diarrhea, might be present. The ensuing clinical findings of primary pneumonic plague are similar to those of any severe rapidly progressive pneumonia. . . . In contrast to secondary pneumonic plague, features of primary pneumonic plague would include absence of buboes (except, rarely, servical buboes) and, on pathologic examination, pulmonary disease with areas of profound lobular exudation and bacillary aggregation. Chest radiographic findings are variable but bilateral infiltrates or consolidation are common. . . . The time from respiratory exposure to death in humans is reported to have been between 2 to 6 days in epidemics during the preantibiotic era, with a mean of 2 to 4 days in most epidemics.

Rapid diagnostic tests for plague are not widely available (usually these are found only at the CDC and military laboratories), and many tests take days to weeks to yield results—by which time the initial wave of victims would be dead. And time is of the essence with pneumonic plague. As Inglesby et al. (2000, 2286) warn, "the fatality rate of patients with pneumonic plague when treatment is delayed more than 24 hours after symptom onset is extremely high." Complicating matters further is the fact no currently existing vaccine is effective in preventing or ameliorating development of primary pneumonic plague. The one existing vaccine (discontinued in 1999 and no longer available) was effective only against the bubonic form of the disease, and would be useless against a deliberate aerosol release (Inglesby et al. 2000, 2285).

It is recommended that once a pneumonic plague outbreak is underway, anyone with symptoms of fever or cough should be treated with antibiotics, as should all those asymptomatics in close contact with these individuals, since any delay in therapy dramatically decreases survival (Inglesby et al. 2000, 2287–88). Since pneumonic plague is primarily spread person to person via respiratory droplets (and previous epidemics have shown transmission to close contacts has been prevented by wearing masks), the use of disposable surgical masks by the public and medical workers should largely prevent exposure. However, in a large-scale attack, the local medical facilities would easily be overwhelmed and result in a high fatality rate among those exposed. As Inglesby et al. (2000, 2287) note: "Patients with pneumonic plague will require substantial advanced medical supportive care in addition to antimicrobial therapy. Complications of gram-negative sepsis would be expected, including adult respiratory distress syndrome, disseminated intravascular coagulation, shock, and multiorgan failure."

The recent completion of the genome sequence for *Yersinia pestis* (plague) provides future bioweaponeers with a useful roadmap for modifying the bacteria to enhance its pathogenic qualities (Parkhill et al. 2001). As Inglesby et al. (2000, 2281) warn, given "the availability of *Y. pestis* around the world, capacity for its mass production and aerosol dissemination, difficulty in preventing such activities, high fatality rate of pneumonic plague, and potential for secondary spread of cases during an epidemic, the potential use of plague as a biological weapon is of great concern." In addition, preventing access to the pathogen itself would prove next to impossible given it is a common "infection of rats, ground squirrels, prairie dogs, and other rodents on every populated continent except Australia." More worrisome still were findings by Galimand et al. (1997), who isolated multidrug resistance genes in a Madagascan-strain of *Yersinia pestis* located in a plasmid (pIP1202) that likely originated in enterobacteria (like *E. coli*) and was somehow transferred into the plague bacterium. The researchers found "the multidrug-resistant plasmid was highly transferable in vitro to other strains of Y. pestis, where it was stable," a finding that means not only could other strains obtain similar resistance under natural conditions, but bioweaponeers could easily transfer such resistance to other plague strains artificially.

Normally, plague is treated with streptomycin (an antibiotic now infrequently used in the U.S. and in short supply), but it may also be treated with gentamicin, tetracycline, doxycycline, and (though not FDA approved for this purpose) the fluoroquinolone family of antibiotics that includes ciprofloxacin (Inglesby et al. 2000, 2286). Unfortunately, the Madagascar (17/95) strain "was resistant not only to all the antibiotics recommended for therapy (chloramphenicol, streptomycin, and tetracycline) and prophylaxis (sulfonamides and tetracycline) but also to drugs that may represent alternatives to classic therapy, such as ampicillin, kanamycin, spectinomycin, and minocycline" (Galimand et al. 1997, 680).[8] Although it remained susceptible to cephalosporins and quinolones, this last line of defense is also a shaky one. Russian scientists recently published research on quinolone-resistant *Y. pestis*, something not occurring in nature, raising serious questions about the underlying intent of their work (Ryzhko et al. 1994).

## Anthrax

The most prevalent and frequently weaponized bioagent in state-run programs has long been anthrax. For the U.S., anthrax was seen as an immensely desirable bioweapon because it, like tularemia, posed no danger of person-to-person transmission (Inglesby et al. 2002, 2248). It could be used tactically without posing the risk of epidemics that could "blow-back" on American military forces or cities. In fact, because of its advantages as a biowarfare agent, *every* known state-run BW program—both historically and in recent years—has sought to develop and stockpile anthrax as one of its primary biowarfare agents. It is also widely thought to be one of the most "sought-after" agents for bioterrorists. But, what makes anthrax so powerful a bioweapon?

First, anthrax is extraordinarily lethal when inhaled, often resulting in mortality rates of well over 90 percent in those left untreated, or in individuals when antibiotics are administered only after clinical symptoms have already manifested themselves. It is easily grown, and when shocked into its nongermanitive state, anthrax produces hardy, resilient spores that survive prolonged periods of exposure to sunlight and other elements that would quickly destroy other, nonspore forming pathogens like plague or smallpox. Further, weaponized anthrax (in liquid slurry or dry powder forms) is easily disseminated using aircraft, cruise missiles, or bomblets, and is capable of traveling great distances upon release, making it highly effective against large urban targets. It is readily modified to increase its resistance to a broad range of antibiotics and can potentially be modified to evade existing vaccines through genetic engineering—steps which the Soviet BW program took to enhance the effectiveness of its own anthrax bioweapons. And, for bioterrorists, anthrax is one of the easiest pathogens to obtain and use, despite the dreadful incompetence shown by the Japanese Aum Shinrikyo cult in its attempts to use the agent in 1995.

Far from demonstrating anthrax is too difficult to weaponize to pose a significant threat, Aum illustrates how close even a group without bioweapons expertise can come to producing and disseminating substantial quantities of agent—and serves as a warning about future groups who might be able to obtain the needed expertise to avoid Aum's failures.[9] Indeed, responding to suggestions by some scholars that Aum's experience demonstrated terror groups did not pose a serious BW threat, Alibek replied, "the biggest problem that we've got here is ignorance."[10] Similarly, when Sergei Popov was asked whether the same argument was reasonable given just one individual with experience (like he or Alibek) would have likely changed the outcome, he replied: "No. Of course not. Of course not. I agree with you. Sometimes it just sounds silly! (laughs)"[11]

Since the postal attacks of 2001, anthrax has been the bioagent most synonymous in the minds of the American public with the growing danger posed by bioterrorism.[12] At least 10,000 people may have been exposed to anthrax during these attacks, in addition to more than a dozen others who were sickened and five who died (Stolberg 8 January 2002). Perhaps even more worrisome is that all of these exposures, illnesses, and deaths were the result of only *two* mailings (on September 18th and October 9th)—with the quality of the agent and the dispersion provided by running letters through postal equipment doing the rest (Wade November 2001). Independent sources estimated in November 2001, long before the final costs would become known, that the total expense of reacting to the anthrax emergency and terror attacks within the U.S. could reach $8 billion (DePalma and Deutsch 2001; Stolberg November 2001). Traces of anthrax were found in more than twenty postal facilities in Florida, Indiana, New Jersey, New York, and Washington, D.C.; the offices of media companies; as well as in government mail-sorting facilities handling mail for the White House, the Supreme Court, the CIA, and the Justice, Defense, and State departments. More than 10,000 postal workers were tested for anthrax and over 30,000 people were given preventative antibiotics as a result of these attacks (Miller November 2001). Further, the degree of contamination produced by only a couple of anthrax-laced letters, resulting in cases of both cutaneous and inhalation anthrax, was significant (Lipton 2001).

The anthrax used in the postal attacks was the highly virulent Ames strain, discovered in Iowa in 1980, which is even more dangerous than the type of anthrax weaponized by the U.S. BW program during the 1950s and 1960s (Broad 21 October 2001). How dangerous? It should be noted that *even with* prior warning about the release of the agent available in all but two initial cases, and the full availability of intensive medical care, 45 percent of those infected with inhalational anthrax in the fall of 2001 died (five of eleven)! (Fennelly et al. 2004. 996) In a large-scale release without warning, in the

Washington Metro during rush hour or by a line-source release from an aircraft at night over the city, the casualties would have been enormous and the city's medical facilities rapidly overwhelmed.

Illustrating this potential danger are several studies estimating the effects of an anthrax release in a large U.S. city. Employing an elaborate statistical model, Wein et al. (2003, 4346) demonstrated the need to respond to any large-scale release of anthrax extremely aggressively through "timely use of oral antibiotics by all asymptomatics in the exposure region, distributed either preattack or by nonprofessionals postattack, and the creation of surge capacity for supportive hospital care via expanded training of nonemergency care workers at the local level and the use of federal and military resources and nationwide medical volunteers." In the Wein et al. (2003) study, an aerial, line-source release of 2.2 pounds of anthrax produced a cloud which floated over an urban area of 11.5 million people (infecting 1.5 million) in a region stretching 120 miles long and 11 miles wide downwind of the release site (Weiss 2003). Without warning an attack has occurred, Wein et al. assume at least forty-eight hours pass before the first anthrax cases appear symptomatic in hospital emergency rooms and authorities begin trying to distribute antibiotics—although they would be hampered by not knowing exactly who needs them at this point. Current CDC plans call for the flying of antibiotics (such as doxycycline or ciprofloxacin) to any U.S. city within seven hours, but distribution plans for actually delivering the medicines to the public are likely to take days (Weiss 2003).

The Wein study suggests if the CDC plan were implemented, it would likely take four days for antibiotics to be distributed, resulting in 123,400 deaths (or 8.3 percent of those infected) (Wein, Craft, and Kaplan 2003, 4346). Significantly, Wein et al. (2003, 4350) note a forty-eight-hour delay in detecting the anthrax release is *very* optimistic, and that were a longer delay included (a more realistic 2 to 4.8 days), the fatality rate doubles to 246,800.[13] If authorities respond more slowly and provide antibiotics only to symptomatics, or have difficulty in distribution of antibiotics to the nonsymptomatic population who are waiting in hastily established queues, they estimate 660,000 people (or 44 percent of those infected) would die of anthrax (Wein, Craft, and Kaplan 2003, 4346). And this study presumes the use of an unaltered, antibiotic-susceptible strain that could be effectively treated with antibiotics. Were a genetically engineered strain used in this scenario, one resistant to doxycycline and cirpofloxacin for example, the fatality rate among the 1.5 million exposed during the attack would no doubt be even higher! Indeed, even without assuming any modified or antibiotic resistant anthrax is released, a U.S. Office of Technology Assessment (OTA) report in August 1993 estimated the release of 100 kilograms of anthrax over a large city, like

Washington, D.C., would cause between 130,000 and 3 million fatalities (U.S. Congress August 1993). But, how difficult would it be to develop effective anthrax weapons or to modify the anthrax to produce magnified effects? Unfortunately, the experience of the Soviet BW program and recent experimental research involving anthrax suggests it may not prove too difficult at all.

Although anthrax vaccines could provide some protection for civilians against attacks, the U.S. military has long been warned "as with all vaccines, the degree of protection depends upon the magnitude of the challenge dose," and "vaccine-induced protection could presumably be overwhelmed by extremely high spore challenge" (U.S. Army Medical Research Institute 2001, 17). The U.S. anthrax attacks forced experts to revise downward the level of spore exposure likely to cause infection, greatly increasing the potential effectiveness of anthrax as a bioweapon. Though estimates based upon U.S. and Soviet BW programs, as well as animal studies, had long suggested exposure to roughly 8,000 to 10,000 spores would be sufficient to create pulmonary anthrax, the exposures of postal workers in New Jersey and Washington, as well as the mysterious deaths of Kathy Nguyen and Ottilie Lundgren (a ninety-four-year-old woman in rural Connecticut) from very minor exposures possibly contracted through letters, strongly suggest far smaller amounts of spores can bring on fatal illness than previously believed (Engelberg and Altman 2001; Revkin and Altman 2001).[14] Indeed, Inglesby et al. (2002, 2239) report that while extrapolations from animal data have suggested the dose required to kill 50 percent of those exposed is 2,500 to 55,000 inhaled spores, other data derived from primate data suggest the dose could be as low as one to three spores (Peters and Hartley 2002). As David Franz observed, "We don't have much data on humans . . . Most of what we know is based on 3,000 monkeys" (Engelberg and Altman 2001). Similarly, using mathematical models of airborne infection, Fennelly et al. (2004, 996) studied the likely dynamics surrounding the mail release of anthrax spores during the 2001 U.S. case. Their findings suggest "a small number of cases of inhalation anthrax can be expected when large numbers of persons are exposed to low concentrations of B. anthracis."

Due to the rapid onset of severe illness from inhalational anthrax, it is currently recommended antibiotic treatment begin immediately, since any delay (especially to the point where victims become symptomatic) may substantially decrease their chances for survival. Yet, future attacks might well involve anthrax strains genetically modified to resist the three main antibiotics currently approved by the FDA for inhalational anthrax—penicillin, doxycycline, and ciprofloxacin (Inglesby et al. 2002, 2245). Indeed, recent research by Russian scientists could be viewed as suggestive of not only the potential for engineering anthrax into a more fearsome bioweapon, but also call into question the belief "offensive" Russian BW work has ceased. Stepanov et al. (1996), for example, despite the fact no natural anthrax strain possesses these properties, felt the need to improve upon the Russian vaccine strain STI-1 (used for over forty years) by creating a new vaccine strain resistant to six different classes of antibiotics! (Stepanov et al. 1996, 156) The argument made by Stepanov et al. was there are currently an "incompatibility of live vaccines with antibiotics on simultaneous administration," which "gave rise to the idea of developing a vaccine strain, resistant to antibiotics, which would allow one to conduct simultaneous prophylaxis and immunization in case of emergency." Of course, given it is widely known the Russian BW program developed anthrax strains resistant to multiple antibiotics, it is understandable skeptics would question what "emergency" would require a vaccine strain resistant to tetracycline, penicillin, rifampicine, chloramphenicole, macrolydes, and lyncomicine-classes of drugs except the release of a "battle-strain"? (Stepanov et al. 1996, 157)

Similarly, other studies have shown anthrax can develop in vitro resistance to ofloxacin (a fluoroquinolone class antibiotic closely related to ciprofloxacin), suggesting engineering a strain resistant to *all* currently recommended antibiotics would be easily accomplished by technically competent bioweaponeers (Choe et al. 2000). In fact, a Johns Hopkins working group on biowarfare recently argued the post-2001 CDC guideline of recommending combination therapy of two to three antibiotics, though not shown by the 2001 incident to have increased survival, should be continued because of "the possibility that an engineered strain of *B anthracis* resistant to 1 or more antibiotics might be used in a future attack" (Inglesby et al. 2002, 2245). Other research identifying the plasmids responsible for the virulence of anthrax strains could also potentially provide bioweaponeers (using genetic modification techniques) the ability to artificially enhance many times over the virulence of a given strain by increasing the number of pX02 plasmids in each bacterial cell and potentially overwhelming vaccine protection (Coker et al. 2003). Indeed, strains with only one pX02 plasmid killed just 25 percent of prevaccinated guinea pigs, but a strain with thirty-two copies of the pX02 plasmid killed all of the test animals (Broad March 2003). Reengineering of anthrax bacteria itself is also a possibility. For example, recent analysis of tissue samples from victims of the April 1979 Sverdlovsk accident in the Soviet Union revealed the weaponized anthrax released contained a *blend of at least four different anthrax strains*—which raises the question of whether this recombinant battle-strain could evade existing U.S. anthrax vaccines (Jackson et al. 1998).

Then again, there has always been considerable uncertainty regarding how effective U.S. vaccines would be against massive inhalation doses of anthrax (such as would occur on the battlefield or during a terror attack) given the vaccine has only been tested in people for protection against cutaneous anthrax. In fact, much of the evidence it will provide protection against inhalation anthrax comes only from animal studies involving monkeys (which doesn't necessarily mean it will work in humans) (Wade March 1998). Although the U.S. Food and Drug Administration (FDA) did issue a controversial ruling in December 2003 that the current anthrax vaccine (Anthrax Vaccine Absorbed) was safe and effective for preventing anthrax infection "regardless of the route of exposure" (which would include inhalational anthrax), this still does not *prove* it would actually be effective given the far higher challenge doses that would occur in a BW attack (Shanker December 2003; Barbaro 2004). In reality, the only way to prove it would be to test it against human subjects at high challenge doses, something medically unethical given the extreme lethality of anthrax. As a result, it would only be after an actual attack of aerosolized anthrax against vaccinated individuals who received a high-spore dose that the matter could be conclusively decided.

Given reports Russian scientists have developed a genetically modified anthrax strain producing additional toxins (not normally associated with anthrax), this also calls into question whether the American vaccine would prove effective (Wade March 1998). So concerned were U.S. officials about this potential *super anthrax strain*, the Pentagon embarked on a secret program to duplicate it to see if U.S. vaccines would be effective (Loeb 2001). Indeed, as former U.S.-bioweaponeer Bill Patrick told American military officers in February 1999 he had taught personnel at Dugway Proving Grounds how to turn wet anthrax into powders, and while the process had been more crude than during the U.S. BW program, "We made about a pound of material in little less than a day. . . . It's a good product" (Broad and Miller December 2001).

The countries with BW programs who made anthrax all developed different techniques for drying, milling, and chemically preparing the spores for optimal aerosolization. For example, instead of using the more traditional method of grinding down (milling) clusters of anthrax into a fine powder, Iraq employed industrial dryers and chemical additives to make dry, static-free material (Broad and Miller 18 October 2001; Broad and Miller 26 October 2001). As former UN weapons inspector Tim Trevan noted, Iraq "perfected the technique of one-step drying of bacterial culture to produce dried spores" using bentonite to produce the necessary small particle sizes (Broad and Miller 26 October 2001). Further, using "sequential filters" in devices about the size of coffins, particle size was further reduced to ideal respirable levels by the Iraqis in a technique nearly identical to that used in the U.S. bioweapons program at Fort Detrick during the 1950s (Begley "Tracking Anthrax" 2001, 37). Although highly classified, the fact that U.S. bioweaponeers had perfected drying processes for agents by the 1950s suggests technically modern, reasonably advanced proliferator states could replicate these techniques after either trial-or-error or by obtaining a "technical expertise shortcut" via ex-bioweaponeers from state programs. And, more recent techniques for "freeze-drying" microbes could be applied not only to anthrax, but to other potential biowarfare pathogens (like smallpox, plague or Marburg) to enhance their ability to be effectively stored and disseminated. As Miller et al. (2001, 59) note:

> When microbes are frozen in exactly the right way (surrounded by sugar and protein, cooled quickly, and put under high vacuum to remove ice in a process known as sublimation), they can enter a dormant state in which they behave like vegetative spores. This process is known as lyophilization, or freeze-drying. Once dormant, the germ remains asleep even when returned to room temperature, staying that way for years or even decades. Industry uses the trick to make dry yeast for baking. It is only when such hibernating organisms are doused with water that they revive and multiply, in effect rising from the dead.

## Tularemia

Requiring inhalation of as few as ten organisms, tularemia is one of the most infectious pathogenic bacteria known and has frequently been weaponized by state-run BW programs due to its extreme infectivity, substantial capacity to cause illness, and ease of dissemination (Dennis et al. 2001, 2763–64). Both the U.S. and Soviet BW programs stocked tularemia as a tactical bioweapon that was noncommunicable, but capable of incapacitating large numbers of military personnel. The initial symptoms of tularemia would be difficult to distinguish from an outbreak of influenza or atypical pneumonias, with acute, nonspecific febrile illness occurring three to five days after exposure and pleuropneumonitis developing in a large number of cases in the following days and weeks. Further, the symptoms of untreated tularemia could last for several weeks or months (Dennis et al. 2001, 2765–67).

Prior to the use of antibiotics, which have now cut the death rate to less than 2 percent in the U.S., type A strains of tularemia resulted in overall mortality of 5 to 15 percent, with mortality rising to 30 to 60 percent in pneumonic or severe systemic forms of the disease. Further, as Dennis et al. (2001, 2766) observe, both the U.S. and Soviets developed virulent, streptomycin-resistant tularemia strains in their BW programs—a modification that doesn't pose much difficulty for a new generation of bioweaponeers. Indeed, Pavlov et al. (1996) already have engineered plasmids in tularemia to express chloramphenicol and tetracycline resistance (Dennis et al. 2001, 2765–67). In addition, current vaccines have shown incomplete protection against inhalational tularemia. The CDC estimates the economic impact of a tularemia aerosol release in the U.S. at $5.4 billion for every 100,000 people exposed (Dennis et al. 2001, 2764).

## Rickettsia

Another potential biowarfare pathogen available to states are several members of the Rickettsiaceae family, which includes Rocky Mountain spotted fever, epidemic typhus, and Q fever. Although not often mentioned in the same breath as more well-known BW agents like smallpox or plague, Walker (2003) argues *Rickettsia*, like *R. prowazekii* (epidemic typhus), *R. rickettsii* (Rocky Mountain spotted fever) and *R. typhi* should be considered as having important potential as bioweapons. In fact, a tetracycline-resistant strain of epidemic typhus was developed in the Soviet BW program and, as Walker (2003, 740) notes, "the possibility exists that an *R. prowazekii* weapon has been developed that is completely resistant to all antibiotics." Given many antibiotics, including the new class of fluoroquinolones, macrolides, and rifamprin, have not been proven effective against Rocky Mountain spotted fever or epidemic typhus, Walker (2003, 739–42) notes: "In theory, it would be simple to transform any *Rickettsia* to resistance to tetracyclines and chloramphenicol. . . . It is possible that this has already been done in one or more of the laboratories developing bioweapons around the world."

Although *Rickettsia* are not transmissible person to person, the high mortality rate of selected agents, their high infectivity at low dose, ease of aerosolization, and potential to be engineered for antibiotic resistance make them potentially serious threats. As Walker (2003, 739–42) warns:

> A naturally occurring form of *R. prowazekii* in dried louse feces and of *R. typhi* in dried flea feces is stable and infectious for long periods. It is highly probable that the investigation and understanding of this stable, dormant, infectious form of *R. prowazekii* was achieved in military microbiology laboratories in the USSR. *Rickettsia* can also be preserved stably in a lyophilized state which, in theory, can be milled to 1–5 um particles and treated to prevent electrostatic clumping for aerosol dispersal. Rocky Mountain spotted fever (20–25% mortality) and epidemic typhus (10–60% mortality) are among the most severe infectious diseases of humans, manifesting as diseases clinically similar to the severe viral hemorrhagic fevers.

## Viral Hemorrhagic Fever Viruses

Of all potential bioagents, viral hemorrhagic fever (VHF) viruses (like Ebola and Marburg) evoke a particular dread in people (equaled perhaps only by smallpox) due to their high lethality, communicability, and the manner in which they kill—with victims hemorrhaging blood from every body orifice. Hollywood movies like *Outbreak*, and books, like Richard Preston's *The Cobra Event*, depict the horrors of VHF infection, and the actual release of such an agent on a civilian population would—from the standpoint of a bioterror-ist—likely produce disruption and upset exceeding the effects of any other possible bioweapon. Fortunately, into the foreseeable future, VHF viruses (as well as smallpox) will likely exceed the reach of most terror groups. However, over time, this too will change. And for state actors, VHFs, which are already available, will become increasingly so as new research expands our basic understanding of these viruses and genetic engineering allows bioweaponeers to modify these agents into even more fearsome weapons, or even potentially create them from scratch. As Peters (2000, 207–8) notes:

The severe dramatic disease [VHF] produce, with its attendant need for inten-sive supportive care, would increase their impact. VHF lack the simplicity and stability of an agent such as anthrax, but they have other interesting features. There would be little need to enhance virulence or look for antigenic variants to evade vaccines; they are stable in aerosol; and their manufacture requires no un-usual equipment beyond that needed for large-scale production of other intra-cellular pathogens. Specific treatment does not exist or is not likely to be avail-able in the quantities needed. If the industrial requirements for stabilization of powdered aerosol weapons were met, VHF could be developed as weapons of mass destruction.

In fact, such development of VHFs into deliverable WMDs have already occurred. For example, the Marburg virus was successfully weaponized by the Soviet BW program during the 1980s into a dry powder form that could be carried aboard ICBMs (Preston 1998, 52–65). Not only did the Soviet pro-gram succeed in developing weaponized Marburg virus (known as Variant U), the powdered agent was mass-produced and coated with special materi-als to protect it from degradation in the air upon release, thereby allowing it to drift for miles as an effective weapon. Marburg was extremely potent in airborne form and, by the fall of 1991, was on the verge of becoming a strate-gic/operational bioweapon—although this deployment decision was not made at that time (Preston 1998, 52–65). But, as former U.S.-bioweaponeer Bill Patrick remarked regarding Marburg's potential as a bioagent:

They [the Soviets] weaponized Marburg virus. They grew it to high concentra-tions in guinea pigs. Now it takes a lot of guinea pigs to produce the amount of dry powder they had on hand when supposedly their program came to an end. They produced a very, very scary product with Marburg virus . . . It only takes one to two virus particles to cause an infection of the respiratory tract. There is not a vaccine. And once you contract the disease, there is only one way to go, and that's death. So it is very scary. (Broad "Interviews: Bill Patrick" 2001)

Further, given the large stocks of freeze-dried Variant U believed to be on hand by the early 1990s, some analysts have suggested the possibility samples of this agent (as well as samples of battle-strain anthrax) may have been taken out of the former Soviet Union by ex-bioweaponeers who left to work for other countries (Preston 1998, 52–65). And, as former Vector virologist Popov notes, producing Marburg bioagent is not exceedingly difficult:

> Well, because the procedure is primitive. The procedure is just enormously primitive because you know the whole animals will just dissolve because of the disease and becomes biological substance from the animal. It just needs to be prepared and stabilized. . . . All relatively simple, but it could be done with Ph.D. knowledge. I would doubt if Al Qaeda could be capable of doing something like this, but if someone was a country.[15]

Alibek, warning of the dangers posed by such proliferation, observes Marburg became one of the most effective weapons in the Soviet bioarsenal, and was as important as smallpox in their program (Alibek 1999, 124). It was considered a true strategic weapon, with a killing power equivalent to their other strategic bioweapons like plague, anthrax, and smallpox. Moreover, like Popov, Alibek believes it is entirely possible samples of this dry-powdered Marburg agent (or, even more worrisome, the secrets of its manufacture) may have escaped to other countries.[16] If this has indeed happened, it raises the disturbing possibility advanced Marburg bioweapons in dry powder form may come into the possession of a new generation of bioweapon states (and possibly even terrorist groups). For states, such proliferation provides an immense "jump-start" to their development of effective strategic bioweapons capable of producing mass casualties. And for terrorist groups, the possession of dry-powder Marburg would provide an ability to launch devastatingly lethal attacks against civilian targets. Unfortunately, at this point, the proliferation of Marburg has likely already reached state actors and steps to prevent the spread of this knowledge have limited chances for success.

But Marburg is not the only VHF weapon produced by state-run bioweapons programs. For example, the U.S. program produced less lethal VHF weapons (using Rift Valley and yellow fever viruses) during the 1960s, demonstrating that states possessing technology equivalent to America of the mid-1960s should also be capable of weaponizing such agents. The Soviet program worked on weaponizing the Ebola virus and combining its genes with smallpox to produce a so-called, Black Pox weapon capable of producing hemorrhagic smallpox (Alibek 1999). Indeed, as Borio et al. (2002, 2393) note:

Hemorrhagic fever viruses have been weaponized by the former Soviet Union, Russia, and the United States. There are reports that yellow fever may have been weaponized by North Korea. The former Soviet Union and Russia produced large quantities of Marburg, Ebola, Lassa, and New World arenaviruses (specifically, Junin and Machupo) until 1992. Soviet Union researchers quantified the aerosol infectivity of Marburg virus for monkeys, determining that no more than a few virions are required to cause infection. Yellow fever and Rift Valley fever viruses were developed as weapons by the U.S. offensive biological weapons program prior to its termination in 1969. . . . Several studies have demonstrated successful infection of nonhuman primates by aerosol preparations of Ebola, Marburg, Lassa, and New World arenaviruses.

Used as either a strategic or terror weapon, VHFs like Ebola or Marburg could easily produce high levels of casualties in a civilian population because of their high mortality rates and the lack of effective prophylactics or vaccines to respond to outbreaks. For example, in previous Ebola outbreaks, such as the one in the Democratic Republic of the Congo in 1995, fatality rates and the age of victims were associated, with 97 percent of patients older than fifty-nine years of age dying, compared to 69 percent of those fifteen to twenty-nine years old. Although the mortality rate is high, patients surviving at least one week after onset of symptoms had a probability of survival of 30 percent, while those surviving at least two weeks had a 70 percent chance of survival (Sadek et al. 1999, S26–27). The overall mortality rates during 1976 and 1995 outbreaks of Ebola in the Democratic Republic of the Congo ranged from 80 to 90 percent (Rodriguez et al. 1999, S170) As Peters (2000, 204–5) notes:

None of these diseases is highly transmissible from patients under ordinary circumstances, so epidemics of disease would not be expected to spread. The fact that the viruses are highly infectious in small particle aerosol suspensions does not necessarily imply that patients will generate significant aerosols to pose a hazard. Nevertheless, a patient's blood does contain virus, and nosocomial transmission has been observed with Machupo and Marburg viruses.

Yet, the use of VHF bioweapons would not cause these diseases to manifest themselves in the same manner as in natural outbreaks. Though secondary transmission after an attack would be of concern, an aerosol delivery exposing hundreds of thousands or millions of people to a Marburg or Ebola bioweapon could conceivably kill 80 to 90 percent of these individuals in the first wave alone. In a natural setting, it has been noted the "transmission of Ebola and Marburg virus rarely, if ever, occurs before the onset of signs and symptoms," which is a helpful factor in controlling the spread of these illnesses beyond the initial victims (Borio et al. 2002, 2394). In many respects, this is similar to smallpox, which also is unlikely to be transmitted prior to the onset of clinical symptoms such as rash and fever. But, used as bioweapons, this will not aid in preventing the initial wave of victims from developing the illnesses and dying. Instead, it will prove valuable primarily for containment of any second wave of infection spreading from the site of attack through the use of quarantines. And the likelihood medical personnel would be aware that an attack using VHFs has occurred in the early stages of the illnesses—before many victims may have traveled elsewhere around the country or world—is unlikely because of the manner in which these diseases present themselves clinically. As Borio et al. (2002, 2397) observe:

> There are a variety of potential clinical manifestations following infection with these viruses, and not all patients develop the classic VHF syndrome. Clinical manifestations are nonspecific and may include fever, myalgias, rash, and encephalitis. The propensity to cause the classic VHF syndrome also differs among agents. Therefore, in the event of a bioterrorist attack with one of these agents, infected patients may have a variety of clinical presentations, complicating early detection and management. It may not be possible to differentiate among these diseases on clinical grounds alone. . . . The overall incubation period for HFVs range from 2 to 21 days.

And while large numbers of similar cases might arouse suspicions, Peters (2000, 207) warns "if an attack were to occur, it is unclear whether clinicians would initially recognize VHF." As Bray (2003, 55) observes:

> If terrorists were to secretly release a filovirus in an urban area, a week or more would elapse before the first cases of illness appeared. For each infected individual, the incubation period would depend largely on the quantity of virus inhaled; those closest to the course of the aerosol would tend to become ill first. It is very unlikely that the first patients to show up at medical facilities would be recognized as suffering from a filovirus infection. The diagnostic difficulty lies both in the non-specific nature of the early signs of illness and in the extreme improbability that a case of Marburg or Ebola infection would be seen anywhere outside of central Africa.

Although natural Ebola and Marburg outbreaks are characterized primarily by person-to-person transmission through contact with infected body fluids, especially blood, Peters and LeDuc (1999, xi) warn "data on formal aerosol experiments leave no doubt that Ebola and Marburg viruses are stable and infectious in small-particle aerosols, and the experience of transmission between experimental animals in the laboratory support this." These stability characteristics of Ebola and Marburg no doubt led to the successful development of these pathogens into bioweapons capable of aerosol dispersion. As

Peters (2000, 201) notes, both viruses are "assigned to biosafety level (BSL) 4 because of their aerosol infectivity and the serious disease they cause in humans." Further, he warns the aerosol stability of VHFs are impressive:

> Marburg virus, for example, is as stable in aerosol as are Venezuelan equine encephalitis virus, a notorious aerosol biological warfare agent and laboratory hazard, and influenza viruses. Note also that the persistence of the Marburg virus aerosol is markedly enhanced by the simple addition of glycerol, demonstrating that appropriate additives have the ability to enhance aerosol stability. (Peters 2000, 203)

That VHF viruses like Marburg and Machupo have aerosol properties similar to Venezuelan equine encephalitis (VEE), regarded as one of the easiest biowarfare agents to disseminate, is worrisome. Further, the percentage of infectivity decreasing each minute within an aerosol cloud of various pathogens in laboratory chambers show Marburg virus in a +10 percent glycerin formulation only declines 1.5 percent per minute, compared with *vaccinia virus* (0.3 percent per minute), influenza virus (1.9 percent per minute), and Venezuelan equine encephalitis virus (3.0 percent per minute) (Peters 2000, 204). And, while a great deal of progress has been made in development of an Ebola vaccine, it has to this point showed its effectiveness only in primates (Sullivan et al. 2003). There are currently no antiviral drugs for the treatment of hemorrhagic fever viruses (HFVs) approved by the U.S. Food and Drug Administration (FDA) (Borio et al. 2002, 2399).

Postattack challenges posed by either Ebola or Marburg would also include a lengthy period in which the virus would remain present in patients who had recovered from the illness. As Rodriguez et al. (1999, S170) note, "Marburg virus has been isolated from seminal fluid and from the anterior chamber of the eye of convalescent patients recovering from hemorrhagic fever up to 80 days after onset of disease," while Ebola was found in seminal fluid sixty-one days after disease onset. Other studies have found Ebola in seminal fluid up to 101 days after disease onset, and eighty-three days after onset for Marburg (Borio et al. 2002, 2394). And, while the natural animal reservoir for Ebola and Marburg are unknown, Peters (2000,205) warns were a VHF to be released, it is possible it could become established in various local wild and domestic animal species, potentially leading to further epidemics (as happened in Egypt when Rift Valley fever was introduced into that country in 1977).[17]

Finally, like the research on other potential biowarfare agents, recent work exploring Ebola and Marburg viruses show great promise in expanding our understanding of these pathogens and possibly speeding the development of vaccines or antiviral drugs for their treatment. However, as with all modern medical research, these results also provide bioweaponeers opportunities.

Illustrating the dual nature of such work, Volchkov et al. (1999), by determining the nucleotide sequences of the L gene and 5' trailer region of Ebola, completed the sequence of the Ebola virus genome. However, the implications of this research means a roadmap for reconstructing this virus is now available to state-run BW programs. As Volchkov et al. (1999, 361) explain, "the completion of the genomic sequence and the availability of a full-length clone of the L gene will now allow reverse genetic systems to be established which will enable studies of transcription and replication of Ebola virus." In another study, utilizing genetic engineering, Volchkov et al. (2001, 1965) recovered infectious Ebola virus from cloned cDNA, eliminated the editing site of the gene encoding envelop glycoprotein (GP), and created a recombinant mutant virus far more cytotoxic than the wild-type virus. While such work does advance our understanding of the determinants of pathogenicity in Ebola, it also provides guidance for state-sponsored BW programs on how to increase the virulence of their "battle-strains" of Ebola. Also of potential use to bioweaponeers is work done by Muhlberger et al. (1999), who used genetic engineering to create chimeras combining *vaccinia virus* with DNA from both Ebola and Marburg viruses. Though this research was designed to compare the replication and transcription strategies for both viruses, it also illustrates the potential for creating dangerous chimera from two lethal viruses (smallpox and VHF).

Sanger et al. (2001) conducted research on the inner workings of the Marburg virus, to better understand its processes for infecting cells. Similar work has also been done examining the genetic makeup of Crimean-Congo hemorrhagic fever virus, a disease with a mortality rate of 10 to 50 percent, by Russian scientists exploring the genetic variability of the pathogen in southern regions of European Russia, Kazakhstan, Tajikistan, and Uzbekistan (Yashina et al. 2003). That both of these particular pathogens were weaponized by the old Soviet BW program means this research has potential offensive application. Other research by Russian scientists that has potential biowarfare application are studies demonstrating how to calculate the infective aspiration dose of aerosolized agents, in this case, Q fever (Vorobeychikov et al. 2003). Clearly, ongoing research into VHFs provide a classic example of the "dual-use" problem of biological research.

## THE GENETIC ENGINEERING OF BW PATHOGENS

In their "natural" unaltered forms, so-called classical BW agents (such as smallpox, plague, anthrax, etc.) were always considered fearsome and deadly potential weapons of war. State-run BW programs in the U.S. and Soviet

Union (and countless other countries) worked feverishly to obtain the most lethal strains of disease organisms and weaponize them into forms (both liquid and powder) that could provide advantage against opponents. The science of the bioweaponeer advanced as the decades passed, and though the U.S. program changed course toward a more "defensive" form after the 1972 treaty, advances in the "dark arts" of biowarfare continued inside the massive Soviet program—including the beginnings of what would become a *revolution in military affairs* in the BW field, namely, genetic engineering.

New biowarfare work made possible by advances in biotechnology provided the ability to create novel, "designer" pathogens (unknown to nature) that would couple antibiotic resistance with characteristics of multiple disease organisms. Such work involved creation of frightening chimeras (recombinant organisms) merging the deadly smallpox and Ebola viruses, creating "super-plague" strains resistant to sixteen different antibiotics, engineering antibiotic resistant anthrax capable of overwhelming all known vaccines, combining Legionnaires' disease with a myelin toxin gene (causing fatal multiple sclerosis–type symptoms), and many others still shrouded in secrecy in Russia's military laboratories. Yet, as disturbing as this work was, it merely foreshadowed a far more sinister future stage in biowarfare research—one in which advances in biotechnology and genetic engineering will provide current and future bioweaponeers the ability to make bioweapons either highly effective and limited in scope (for tactical applications) or potentially unstoppable (for strategic use) (Dando 1994, 41). Looking into this future, a recent CIA report warned, "the biotechnology underlying the development of advanced biological agents is likely to advance very rapidly, causing a diverse and elusive threat spectrum. The resulting diversity of new BW agents could enable such a broad range of attack scenarios that it would be virtually impossible to anticipate and defend against" them all (Central Intelligence Agency 2003). Unfortunately, this "revolution in biowarfare" renders all previous calculations about the viability or effectiveness of bioweapons in war dangerously outdated and obsolete.

Indeed, observing the tremendous advances made by medical science in genetic engineering, Block (1999, 42) warns of the creation of bioweapons "endowed with unprecedented power to destroy." In fact, as one DoD report warns:

Biological weapons have the greatest potential for lethality of any weapon. Biological weapons are accessible to all countries; there are few barriers to developing such weapons with a modest level of effort. The current level of sophistication for many biological agents is low, but there is enormous potential—based on advances in modern molecular biology, fermentation, and drug delivery technology—for making more sophisticated weapons. . . . Advances in biotechnology and genetic engineering may facilitate the development of potentially new and more deadly biological warfare agents. The ability to modify microbial agents at a molecular level has existed since the 1960s, when revolutionary new genetic engineering techniques were introduced, but the enterprise tended to be slow and unpredictable. With today's more powerful techniques, infectious organisms can be modified to bring about disease in different ways. Many bioengineering companies (both U.S. and foreign) now sell all-in-one kits to enable even high school-level students to perform recombinant DNA experiments. The availability of free on-line gene sequence databases and analytic software over the Internet further simplifies and disseminates this capability. It is now possible to transform relatively benign organisms to cause harmful effects. Genetic engineering gives biological warfare developers powerful tools with which to pursue agents that defeat the protective and treatment protocols of the prospective adversary. Genetically engineered micro-organisms also raise the technological hurdle that must be overcome to provide for effective detection, identification, and early warning of biological warfare attacks. (Department of Defense January 2001)

The possibility of genetically engineering old, or even new, pathogens through biotechnology is rapidly growing, opening up many potential avenues for future opponents. For example, some experts fear sophisticated opponents may one day be able to manufacture their own versions of the smallpox virus from scratch, eliminating the need to obtain it from the vaults of state-run BW programs. Since the complete genome sequence for smallpox is freely available on the Internet, the theoretical possibility exists genetic engineers could use this blueprint to transform a related virus, such as camelpox or mousepox, into smallpox itself.[18] Similarly, the full genome for pneumonic plague was decoded in 2001, providing a roadmap for future bioweaponeers (Wade October 2001).

Genetic engineering could also be used to modify existing or created viruses to avoid standard treatments, a danger well illustrated by the inadvertent finding of several Australian scientists in 2001 who, in transferring an immune system gene into the mousepox virus while attempting to design a contraceptive, instead created a new, highly lethal version of the virus that even killed mice previously vaccinated (Pollack "With Biotechnology" 2001; Pollack "Scientists Ponder" 2001). This finding was particularly worrisome to many experts because it suggested unethical biologists might adopt similar methods to strengthen other human viruses, potentially rendering a newly weaponized smallpox immune to vaccines or even turn the common cold into a killer (Broad January 2001; Cookson 2001). Similarly, scientists at Stanford University, who have studied the potential uses of biotechnology in warfare, suggest "stealth" pathogens may also be a possibility, which would infect people but not produce symptoms until activated later by some chemical or food. Of course, the use of genetically engineered or altered prions, which are responsible in their natural forms for mad cow and Creutzfeldt-Jakob disease in humans, could be employed as the "ultimate stealth terror weapon" if introduced into food supplies by terrorists.

Other possibilities include transferring genes responsible for producing toxins or antibiotic resistance from one microbe to another. For example, American scientists in the 1980s made *E. coli* more virulent by transferring a gene from a relative of the plague bacterium into it, while other scientists created strains of *E. coli* bacteria 32,000 times more resistant to antibiotics than the natural strain. During the same period, Soviet bioweaponeers succeeded in placing a virus inside bacteria, so the virus would be activated when the bacteria were killed by antibiotics—thereby creating combination pathogens (or chimera) that would combine the lethality of one pathogen with the infectiousness of another (Pollack "With Biotechnology" 2001). In another experiment, a strain of bubonic plague resistant to all antibiotics was discovered in 1997 which was able to easily transfer its resistant genetic material to other strains of the bacteria in the laboratory ("Plague Strain Found Immune" 1997). Indeed, the promise of biotechnology is such that the National Defense University recently decided not to publish a report on how new techniques could make bioweapons more dangerous because the implications were so ominous (Pollack "Scientists Ponder" 2001).

Genetic engineering is also capable of enhancing the ability of BW agents to survive under hostile environmental conditions (e.g., UV radiation from sunlight, humidity, heat, etc.) that would normally rapidly destroy agent and render it ineffective. For example, modifying an agent through "splicing a gene from a toxin or other lethal agent with an otherwise non-lethal spore forming bacteria," allows the bacteria's spore to provide increased protection from environmental degradation. Microencapsulating an agent by surrounding it with substances to shield it from environmental effects that will degrade and release the agent once a particle is inhaled increases the survivability and potential effectiveness of such weapons (Office of Counterproliferation 1996, 6). Any steps to reduce a BW agent's rate aerobiological decay (or half-life) increases its offensive potential by allowing an agent to remain lethal over target for longer periods of time, create lengthier disruption of military operations, and allow for effective employment of weapons under what would normally be poor environmental conditions (such as daytime). The length of time over a target can increase dramatically using such techniques.

## WHAT DESIGNER WEAPONS ARE POSSIBLE?

The possibilities are seemingly endless, limited only by the imaginations of bioweaponeers. The technical annex to the 1997 DoD publication,

*Proliferation: Threat and Response*, describes new types of potential agents that might be produced through the application of genetic engineering:

- Benign microorganisms, genetically altered to produce a toxin, venom, or bioregulator;
- Microorganisms resistant to antibiotics, standard vaccines, and therapeutics;
- Microorganisms with enhanced aerosol and environmental stability;
- Immunologically altered microorganisms able to defeat standard identification, detection, and diagnostic methods;
- Combinations of the above four types with improved delivery systems. (Department of Defense January 2001)

A sampling of recently published findings from genetic engineering or genome research projects illustrates how obtaining knowledge about pathogens, how they evade the immune system, what affects their virulence, and so forth can be of "dual-use" to a bioweaponeer. For example, American university researchers in the mid-1980s were able to move the gene from *Yersinia pseudotuberculosis*, a less virulent cousin of *Yersinia pestis* (which causes plague) into *E. coli* microbes, a normally harmless bacteria of the human gut, in a technique which clearly could be applied to creating a super-plague pathogen. Similarly, U.S. military researchers reported success in modifying the genetic makeup of harmless bacteria (such as *E. coli*) to produce any "level of pathogenicity" (Miller, Engelberg, and Broad 2001, 83). An example of this was work by Dr. Willem Stemmer on *E. coli* using polymerase chain reaction (or PCR). Using PCR, Stemmer was able to "direct evolution" and select strains of *E. coli* that were "32,000 times as resistant to a given antibiotic" than the original *E. coli* starter strain (Cohen 2002, 123). The concern generated by the potential to genetically modify pathogens is illustrated by an analysis of Pentagon defensive bioresearch between 1980 and 1986, which lists fifty-one projects examining development of novel pathogens, thirty-two at boosting toxin production from organisms, twenty-three involving research to defeat existing vaccines, fourteen to inhibit diagnosis, and three studies of the ability to outwit protective drugs (Miller, Engelberg, and Broad 2001, 84).

As numerous studies examining the genetic makeup of the 1918 influenza are published, Popov notes that genetically modified influenza was on the list of potential agents being researched by the old Soviet BW program (Cohen 2002, 123). Indeed, Mark Gibbs of Australian National University, who conducted research on the 1918 flu, is puzzled by the lack of focus upon influenza as a possible bioweapon and warns of the dangers of publishing the entire genetic sequence of the 1918 strain: "That is really dangerous stuff . . . It is totally feasible to reconstruct that virus. And we know that if we got the sequence right, it would go" (Cohen 2002, 123).

In 1995, Russian researchers Andrei Pomerantsev and Nikolai A. Staritsin announced at a scientific conference in Winchester, England, they had produced a genetically engineered, more virulent strain of anthrax (a "super anthrax") by inserting the virulence genes from *Bacillus cereus*, a bacterium that attacks blood cells, but usually without producing human disease (Miller, Engelberg, and Broad 2001, 208; Miller 2000). More alarming to U.S. officials was the fact Russia's own powerful anthrax vaccine was useless against this new super strain of anthrax , eventually leading to current Defense Intelligence Agency (DIA) efforts, known as Project Jefferson, to replicate it to determine whether American vaccines would be similarly impotent and design some defense against it (Miller, Engelberg, and Broad 2001, 308–9). The power of this genetically altered strain, so-called invisible anthrax, is that it evades the body's natural defenses through the introduction of an alien gene that altered the bacterium's immunological properties—resulting in a superbug against which existing vaccines proved ineffective (Pomerantsev et al. 1997).

It is also known Russian scientists at Obolensk used genetic engineering to splice the diphtheria toxin gene into a highly virulent strain of plague bacteria (Miller, Engelberg, and Broad 2001, 303). More importantly, Soviet bioweaponeers discovered that recombinant work with plague and smallpox was possible because these agent's virulence and stability stayed essentially the same in the new versions.[19] As a result, work was conducted to actually insert viruses inside plague bacteria—creating essentially a "double-barreled" bioweapon—a development Popov views as "very troublesome" because "it's so easy, and it could be so devastating!"[20] Research also explored a large range of combinations of different viruses and bacteria, including one version combining plague and encephalomyelitis virus (Wolfinger "Interviews: Sergei Popov" 2001). As Popov explains:

Imagine a bacterial agent which contains inside its cells a virus. The virus stays silent until the bacterial cells get treated. So, if the bacterial disease gets recognized and treated with an antibiotic, there would be a release of virus. After the initial bacterial disease was completely cured, there would be an outbreak of a viral disease on top of this . . . A good example would be plague bacteria, which is relatively easy to treat with antibiotics, and viral encephalomyelitis inside. So, in case of biological attack, people would be treated against plague, and after that they would be sick with this viral disease of choice. It could be encephalomyelitis. It could be smallpox. It could be ebola. Those viruses were on the list of potential agents.

When asked how likely it was that countries or groups pursing these programs could obtain the ability to put viruses into bacteria, and do these combinations with things like plague, Popov replied:

> You see, it's like this mousepox and interleuken 4, it could be a single step. Because what they are talking about copy of the virus, the copy is available everywhere in the scientific world. So you just take a piece of DNA and the procedure itself takes overnight to transform it to put it in, say, plague.[21]

Alibek (1999, 8–9) notes recently published Russian research involving genetic manipulation of *vaccinia virus* (by inserting some genes from the Ebola virus) is worrisome because, even though *vaccinia virus* is only used to make vaccines:

> The genome of the smallpox virus, *Variola major*, is 95 percent homologous with the vaccinia virus. So if you are able to conduct some genetic engineering manipulations and insert some genes into the vaccinia virus, it is just a technical problem to do the same with smallpox. In 1988, we realized it wouldn't be possible in the future to work intensively with smallpox because of the political implications. . . . So we developed a special program to determine what "model" viruses could be used instead of human smallpox. We tested vaccinia virus, mousepox virus, rabbitpox virus, and monkeypox virus as models for smallpox. The idea was that all research and development work would be conducted using these model viruses. Once we obtained a set of positive results, it would take just two weeks to conduct the same manipulations with smallpox virus and to stockpile the warfare agent. We would have in our arsenal a genetically altered smallpox virus that could replace the previous one. So everything was prepared for conducting further development work under strict observation from the international community.

In 2002, researchers (Rosengard et al. 2002) modified the *vaccinia virus* to produce a protein normally produced by the related *variola major virus*—producing a genetically engineered pathogen 100 times as potent as the original *vaccinia* version (Stern 2002/2003, 111). Indeed, as Popov warns regarding the wide availability of scientific research useful to bioweaponeers:

> You reminded me of one more example, published data on cowpox in the United States and they found the same mutation that considerably increased the virulence of cowpox. So in this case, what could be done with a single mutation, a single substitution, one nucleotide in smallpox virus and essentially no modification is necessary to get more virulent virus. Essentially, the cause, the essence of all of those genetic engineering programs to create more virulent biological agents, something like this, increased virulence essentially there is little modification. And they published this, and nobody pays attention! I don't know! (laughs).[22]

Thus, a disturbingly real possibility is that bioweaponeers, even if they were unable to obtain a "wild-type" strain of a given pathogen, might be able to modify similar viruses to mimic them or even create one from scratch using its published genome as a recipe. After the long, successful struggle to eradicate smallpox from the planet, the remaining "official" stocks of the virus exist in only two locations—the CDC in Atlanta and at the Vector facility in Russia. And while a bioterrorist release of smallpox continues to be one of the biggest fears of security analysts, it has largely been considered a remote possibility given the difficulty of access to the existing stocks of the virus. Even for state-run BW programs, it was thought to be nearly impossible to obtain samples of smallpox unless they had clandestinely preserved some from earlier outbreaks before eradication of the disease in 1980—as Iran and North Korea may have done. Now, however, the possibility exists to re-create smallpox (or at least a pseudo-smallpox) from related pox viruses using genetic engineering—and in the future, the potential to perhaps re-create the actual virus using its published genome. Agreeing that genetic manipulation of related-pox viruses could be used as a surrogate to the more difficult to obtain smallpox, Alibek observes:

> Yeah, I would say it's credible, but not from the standpoint that it is smallpox, it would be genetically engineered monkeypox. Because you cannot say it would be smallpox. It would be monkeypox with maybe some additional genetic modifications, for example, to increase virulence and increase contagiousness. Assumes you know what genes are responsible for virulence and what are genetic differences between monkeypox virus and variola major smallpox virus. And we know, for example, and now we know techniques. . . . it's very simple. To infect with corresponding genes from variola major into monkeypox virus. . . . At least the Soviet Union had something like this in mind. Just one of the projects was to determine whether or not it was possible to develop new type of viruses, based on monkeypox, because in this case you wouldn't do any prohibited work in terms of.[23]

Although Alibek notes such work is "not something you can do in a couple of days or easy," he nevertheless warns that "if you do some thoughtful work, I'm sure it would be possible to increase virulence of monkeypox for humans and it would be possible . . . to insert genes that would be responsible for contagiousness."[24] Further, Alibek observes the Australian mousepox experiments strongly suggest a similarly small modification in smallpox would allow it to evade current vaccines.[25] Similarly, Popov, a virologist who once worked at Vector, agrees that a simple modification of smallpox, such as occurred in the Australian mousepox experiment, would create a new strain that would not only be more virulent, but evade all current vaccines.[26] And it is not only mousepox or monkeypox that could be modified, but other related pox viruses as well. As Popov notes, it is purely a matter of determining what modifications need to be made in a given pox virus to make it more similar to natural smallpox:

> People sequenced different viruses than smallpox only, you know. You remind them to see where they are different and where they are the same. And that give you a clearer idea of what has to be replaced in camelpox in order to become smallpox. It becomes smallpox. The cowpox-type vaccinia, compare genomes and you will see what is missing, what has to be removed, and what has to be replaced. It's not very difficult at all, it's just, maybe, you know, not very productive way to do it. [However] it could be multiplied indefinitely, you know, because it's virus. It would be no problem keeping it multiplying and to produce much quantity. But I think it's not been done simply because it's easier to isolate good virus from nature that would work. Except for smallpox. [But] if it's necessary, it can be done.[27]

Although current biotechnology can replicate only simple viruses from scratch, with the large smallpox virus (for the moment) being out of reach, Popov warns against assuming this will always remain the case: "technically we can create again smallpox, we can make it chemically. It's a big virus. But it's well known. It's a complete sequence. So if it's a complete sequence, its just a matter of time."[28] Similarly, Van Aken and Hammond (2003, 59) add that while "the method for creating polio virus artificially cannot be directly transferred to smallpox virus" yet due to the large size of the *variola* genome (over 200,000 base pairs), there still might be other ways to accomplish the same goal:

> It would, for example, be possible to start with a closely related virus, such as monkeypox or mousepox, and to alter specifically those bases and sequences that differ from human smallpox. Some months ago, researchers documented for the first time that the sequence of a pathogenicity-related gene from the vaccinia virus could be transformed through the targeted mutation of 13 base pairs into the sequence of the corresponding smallpox gene (Rosengard et al. 2002). It is probably only a matter of time before this technique is applicable to full genomes, and then we shall have to reconsider our current assessment of the smallpox threat. (Van Aken and Hammond 2003, 59)

As the lead Australian mousepox-experiment scientist, Bob Seamark, later noted, "We now have the capacity to approach the creation of new pathogens in a Lego-type way—mixing and matching. . . . If the purpose is for biological weapons, for evil purposes, we can be as evil as you bloody well like. Be warned" (Cohen 2002, 118). Similarly, Van Aken and Hammond (2003, 57) suggest "the introduction of antibiotic resistance into bacterial pathogens" today is "routine work in almost any microbiology laboratory." Popov also observes that while this required a large infrastructure for the Soviet Union, the task of creating antibiotic resistance is not particularly difficult.[29] Agreeing that antibiotic-resistant anthrax would be a disaster, Popov warns the technical knowledge to develop it "does not require very sophisticated knowledge," only "PhD knowledge."[30] Moreover, the simple step of creating antibiotic resistance in anthrax or some other bioagent would markedly increase its value as a weapon. For example, had penicillin and cipro-resistant anthrax been spread in the U.S. postal attacks, the death toll for those exposed would no doubt have been much higher and the difficulty of providing effective prophylactic treatment (considering 30,000 were given preventative antibiotics due to potential exposure) would have increased enormously! Popov warns even without resort to genetic engineering, a pathogen with antibiotic resistance could be produced that would be "very difficult" for us to counter.[31] As Dennis (2001, 232–33) observes:

> Perhaps the simplest way to "enhance" a bacterial bioweapon is to make it resistant to antibiotics. . . . Some of the genes that convey this antibiotic resistance lie in the bacteria's genomes. But others can be carried on plasmids, circular pieces of DNA that replicate themselves independently—and the same is true of genes for other important traits such as virulence and infectivity. Plasmids can move between bacteria, and genes carried on plasmids can be incorporated into the genome, which means that genes conferring antibiotic resistance, or any other advantageous trait, can spread rapidly. . . . So splicing genes for antibiotic resistance into plasmids and introducing them into a bacterium being developed as a biological weapon would, by the standards of today's top biology labs, be child's play. Anthrax, for instance, is typically treated using derivatives of penicillin, but they could be rendered ineffective by introducing a gene for the enzyme B-lactamase, which disables the antibiotics, into the anthrax pathogen, *Bacillus anthracis*.

Perhaps one of the most disturbing Soviet BW efforts was the Hunter Program, which focused upon combining whole genomes of different viruses to produce completely new hybrid viruses, or chimeras, combining two microorganisms (such as encephalomyelitis and smallpox viruses) into one new pathogen with the properties of both (Wolfinger "Interviews: Sergei Popov" 2002). As Popov observes:

> There could be numerous advantages. First of all, it is a completely artificial agent with new symptoms, probably with no known ways to treat it. Essentially, the major feature would be a kind of surprise effect. Nobody would recognize it. Nobody would know how to deal with it.

One of the hurdles in producing chimera viruses is that researchers must find (as Vector scientists did after many years of research) more than one place in the smallpox DNA where new genes could be inserted without decreasing smallpox's virulence. This research led to the successful creation of a recombinant smallpox-VEE (Venezuelan equine encephalitis) chimera during the early 1990s (Preston 1998; Alibek 1999, 259–60). Further, Alibek warns Vector researchers may have created a recombinant Ebola-smallpox chimera (or Ebolapox) through grafting the disease-causing DNA parts of Ebola onto the smallpox virus (Alibek 1999, 261; Preston 1998, 52–65). Alibek believes the Ebolapox virus, which would likely produce a hemorrhagic form of smallpox called blackpox, is stable and would reproduce itself in both the laboratory and in people. The natural form of blackpox is nearly 100 percent fatal, but "as a weapon, the Ebolapox would give the hemorrhages and high mortality rate of Ebola virus. . . . plus the very high contagiousness of smallpox." Further, there is no effective vaccine or treatment for Ebola. In addition, program costs would not be high to create genetically engineered smallpox (if you had the pathogen). Indeed, Alibek notes it cost the Soviets only a few million dollars to produce the smallpox-VEE chimera at Vector in the early 1990s (Preston 1998, 52–65).[32] And, in terms of difficulty, creating chimeras of different viruses, say smallpox-Ebola, is unproblematic according to Popov:

> In my opinion, the combination is not a problem at all. To combine two viruses in one is not a problem. The major problem would be what kind of biological properties would it have? How stable will it be? Will it be of interest in military terms? Because again, military requirements are very strict. If you do not improve virulence, if your load is heavier than it was before, etc. . . . In my opinion, these kind of requirements become more important and to fulfill these kind of requirements will take more time than to create a pattern.[33]

Interestingly, if someone did create a recombinant agent, say for example an Ebola-smallpox chimera, it would only clinically manifest itself as that combined agent among the first wave of infected. It would not be able to self-replicate as the chimera, but instead, would replicate as either smallpox or Ebola alone.[34] And, if one were to develop a combined bioweapon with a bacteria carrying a virus through genetic engineering, or one carrying a foreign gene, the new agent would not be able to reproduce itself from seed stocks you might obtain clandestinely.[35] Still, when asked how difficult it would be for other countries, down the road, to produce chimeras and other recombinant pathogens for offensive BW purposes, Alibek replied:

> Well, let me put it this way. In 1979, when we started talking about genetic engineering. . . . various techniques were considered hard, mostly hard for science.

But now time is passing by. Now, for example, many recombinant techniques are very easy to do and, even sometimes its undergraduate students could do recombinant work. In this case, zero doubt in my opinion. It wouldn't be very difficult for many of these countries to develop new microorganisms, even though I'm not talking about something in ten or twenty years. It's now. We shouldn't, in my opinion, underestimate their capabilities. Their smart, of course, and we shouldn't be very arrogant and say, "okay, they're not very smart and they wouldn't do this." Cuba is capable, Iran is capable, in my opinion. When some scientists say it's not possible, they are somehow doubtful—what I'm saying is, guys, in all cases before you say it's impossible, you need to read a little bit more than you do now.[36]

Another significant area within the Soviet BW program involved production of synthetic genes (constructs that do not exist in nature) that could be incorporated into bacterial agents and viruses so they would develop completely new properties. As Popov, one of the top genetic scientists in the Soviet program, explains:

A virus could produce something absolutely difficult to imagine in natural circumstances, like peptides which destroy the immune system in a very special way. . . . My most successful research was the finding that a bacteria called *Legionella* could be modified in such a way that it could induce severe nervous system disease. And the symptoms of nervous disorders [similar to those of multiple sclerosis] would appear several days after the bacterial disease was completely "cured." So there would be no bacterial agent, but symptoms—new and unusual symptoms—would appear several days later. . . . Imagine a new weapon which is difficult to diagnose initially and then which is impossible to treat with conventional antibiotics. That would be [a good weapon] from the point of view of [masking] who originated the problem. (Wolfinger "Interviews: Sergei Popov" 2002)

This work on myelin toxin (which destroys the myelin sheaths allowing transmission of nerve impulses in the human nervous system) proceeded to the point that a bacterial host (*yersinia pseudotuberculosis*) was found for the myelin toxin. As Alibek notes, it is a "short step from inserting a gene of myelin toxin into *Yersinia pseudotuberculosis* to inserting it into *Yersinia pestis*, or plague," thereby creating a new "toxin-plague" chimera weapon. More importantly, such research demonstrates the potential for placing genes for other toxins (such as botulinum, various venoms, etc.) into bacteria for use as weapons (1999 163–67). In addition to the *Legionella*-myelin toxin gene combination, Popov notes this technique was applied to other viruses as well:

You know *vaccinia* smallpox has been done. I am not exactly saying smallpox. *Vaccinia virus. Vaccinia virus* has been created with the same genes as with myelin gene. Because I initiated this work at Vector with viruses. And the primary purpose was to put it in smallpox and other viruses. So the initial experiments was *vaccinia* viruses, showed that it was very successful. The virulence went up to 90 percent from initial. . . . in the particular conditions of the experiment the initial virus virulence was about 40 percent and it went up more than twofold. Twofold. Just because of the insertion of this myelin gene. And it is one more step from *vaccinia* to smallpox. So, if you talk about possibility, it's not even a question. It's been done, it's well known, and the virulence of this smallpox strain will be at least twofold higher.[37]

Indeed, Popov notes that because the myelin toxin produces paralytic disease on top of the symptoms of the main virus vector, a smallpox-myelin recombinant would leave very little in the way of possible medical treatment for victims:

No. You see multiple sclerosis and similar diseases could be treated with relatively limited success. And the treatment right now is not very simple. It's a treatment that is very sophisticated. They are very expensive. And in case of multiple sclerosis, people get sometimes substantial relief, sometimes it does not help at all. But on this scale, on the scale of thousands, or how many people, it's absolutely impossible. [The] initial infectious process could be treated. But it's quite probable that this treatment won't cure the second wave of autoimmune disease. Autoimmune disease is very difficult to treat, and even if you stop it somehow, it usually relapses. It's the nature of these kind of diseases. They come and go, they come and go.[38]

Although to Popov's knowledge, his new pathogen was never made into munitions or deployed, the *Legionella* bacteria carrying the myelin toxin gene is a particularly insidious weapon that might be replicated by other state BW programs possessing biotechnical expertise (Miller, Engelberg, and Broad 2001, 302). It is also an incredibly lethal and virulent one. Laboratory tests of Popov's recombinant *Legionella* showed it not only produced a mortality rate of close to 100 percent (from brain damage and paralysis) in guinea pigs exposed to the pathogen, but required only a few cells to infect victims (compared to the thousands normally required of normal *Legionella*). Doctors responding to an attack by this agent would see patients with pneumonia symptoms treatable by antibiotics, but within days, new symptoms of neurological disease would rapidly appear, causing brain damage, paralysis, and death—leaving no trace in the body of the agent that caused the damage. As Popov notes:

It's a very powerful technique. . . . If somebody wants to employ genetic engineering in creating weapons, the most exciting discoveries are still ahead. I think it opens—every day it opens—more and more possibilities to create something dangerous, to create a new kind of weapon. (Miller, Engelberg, and Broad 2001, 303–4)

The technique of using a virus to deliver a gene producing, for example, myelin toxin, is a form of "gene therapy." As Block (1999, 60) explains, in normal medical contexts "the goal of gene therapy is to effect a change in the genetic makeup of an individual by introducing new information designed to replace or repair a faulty gene." Gene therapy has great potential for treating genetic diseases in humans (such as the famous "bubble-boy" disease) and has shown some promise in the directed treatment of cancer. However, what bioweaponeers seek to accomplish is essentially "bad gene therapy," whereby viruses are used to deliver genes (such as those producing various toxins or bioregulatory peptides) into the cells of targeted individuals to produce debilitating or lethal effects.

Thus, the potential of biotechnology involves more than merely modifying the antibiotic resistance of agents, but includes the possible use of DNA shuffling to promote more rapid, directed evolution of enhanced pathogens or the insertion of toxin producing genes into preexisting agents (Dando 1994; Crameri et al. 1998; Hamilton 1998; Coffield et al. 1994).[39] Although in the past, it was difficult to alter the characteristics of pathogens to increase their effectiveness as a BW agent (such as enhancing its virulence) without inadvertently altering other properties of the agent in the process that simultaneously reduced its effectiveness, genetic engineering now promises to allow bioweaponeers to make more precise changes to pathogens without such tradeoffs (Dando 1999, appendix 13A, 1–16). As Popov observes:

You know, several years ago, the major argument would be that any interference with natural virus or bacteria would lead to decreased virulence. But now we know from experimental data that this is not the case. And its published. I always had this kind of data, you know, based on my own experimental work, so we found that *Legionella* became considerably more virulent because of the insertion of relatively small piece of foreign DNA. So, from my point of view, its still difficult to find that particular approach to make pathogens more virulent. But if somebody has written on it, pay considerable attention to it. It may be very successful in my opinion.[40]

Some viruses previously not weaponized may suddenly have potential as reengineered strains created to be spread in aerosol form. For example, rabies (an incurable viral encephalitis usually transmitted by contact with an infected animal) has a 100 percent mortality rate once symptoms have occurred, regardless of any attempts at aggressive medical therapy (Jackson et al.

2003). Only administration of rabies vaccine prior to development of symptoms prevents the fatal disease from developing, which means if rabies were converted into a bioweapon and distributed in aerosol form onto a population without warning, it is probable every individual who suddenly came down with symptoms (which at first would go unrecognized as rabies) would die. Given the long incubation period (up to six weeks) and mild nature of the initial symptoms (i.e., drowsiness, chronic headache, and malaise), it is highly unlikely authorities would recognize the nature of the BW attack until it was far too late to save the afflicted (Osvold-Doppelhauer et al. 2004). Moreover, as Lederberg (2001, 326) warns, the use of a pathogen like rabies could have unforeseeable consequences were it to undergo an evolutionary change and adapt to a new form after having been deployed as an aerosol bioweapon:

> Recent reports of airborne or pneumonic rabies, a terrible disease, which is normally spread by the bite of an infected dog or animal, illustrate this possibility. There is then the danger that, if a large nucleus of people is attacked in this way, further evolution of the virus will occur to give rise to a new form of the disease that does spread from person to person, contrary to the calculations of the attacker. The Black Death itself underwent a similar evolution from the original bubonic flea-born plague to outbreaks of the far more contagious pneumonic variety.

Further, when pathogens jump species to infect humans, the results can be deadly. For example, the avian virus responsible for the bird flu outbreak in Hong Kong in 1997 was not only lethal to its normal prey, but killed six of the eighteen people who contracted it, a 33 percent mortality rate! (Kolata 2001) Research on this particular virus later revealed its transformation from a noninfectious pathogen to a dangerously lethal one to humans involved changes to only a few genes. Indeed, scientists at the University of Wisconsin were able to change a nonlethal strain of bird virus into one that would be lethal to humans by altering only one base in the gene responsible for allowing the virus to produce the protein hemagglutinin (used by the virus to enter and infect cells) (Kolata 2001). This raises the possibility that genetic engineering may allow bioweaponeers to create new flu viruses. For a discussion of other emerging viral diseases (such as Nipah, Hendra, Barmah Forest, Ross River, and Australian Bat Lyssavirus) that might also hold potential for future bioweaponeers, see Mackenzie et al. (2001). One virus that particularly worries veteran virologists is the Nipah virus, a distant relative of the measles virus, against which there is no vaccine or treatment to prevent fatal brain infections (Zuger 2001).

Another disturbing possibility created by the spread of biotechnology is the widespread accessibility of peptide synthesizers, now widely found throughout research and medical communities, as well as in companies specializing in providing custom-order peptides for researchers (e.g., for use in generating antibodies, screening drug targets, or purification of proteins, or for use as drugs). As Kwik (2002, 4) notes regarding a recent journal article entitled, "Engineering the Prion Protein Using Chemical Synthesis" by Ball et al. (2001) in the *Journal of Peptide Research*:

> The title is alarming—after all, prions are infectious particles of protein that don't provoke an immune response, aren't destroyed by extreme heat or cold, and are responsible for such diseases as scrapie, bovine encephalopathy (mad cow disease), kuru, and Creutzfeldt-Jakob disease. . . . The peptide synthesizers and chemicals the authors used for this research have many uses that are important for biological and medical research. However, the results from this kind of research (which are available on the Internet), and the use of this kind of equipment (which is commonly available and relatively inexpensive) do hold potential for negative downstream consequences, including the synthesis and use of a prion as a biological weapon.

Indeed, for terrorists, slower acting genetically modified or engineered pathogens would be ideal (e.g., prions carrying mad cow disease). Bovine spongiform encephalopathy (BSE) is on the Homeland Security list of pathogens that terrorists might weaponize, so the ability to synthesize such prions artificially in the laboratory is a concern (Blakeslee January 2004). Further, developing the primative prions in the laboratory required to weaponize mad cow disease is a simple task that Popov describes as only "PhD level."[41] As Popov notes:

> It would be much more useful to terrorists, rather than on the battlefield. The symptoms, I think, they would produce very strong psychological effect. . . . like mad cow disease . . . only a few people are exposed to mad cow disease, but its very scary. Because you never know your fate. You could be infected. So, it's not really in my opinion a battlefield weapon, but for terrorist purposes, that would be almost ideal.[42]

In fact, researchers by July 2004 had successfully created an "artificial prion" that was effective in causing mice to develop spongiform degeneration in their brains, like that in people with variant Creutzfeldt-Jakob disease (Blakeslee July 2004). The potential for biowarfare applications of prion-based weapons is enormous.

Moreover, as Stern (2002/2003, 110–1) warns, the growing number of pathogens whose genomes have been decoded and published on the Internet in microbial genome databases, combined with the demonstrated ability of researchers to create viruses "from scratch" using these codes and mail-order

DNA, leads to an increasing danger in the coming decades that either bioweaponeers or bioterrorists will take the gene sequences for Ebola, influenza, smallpox, or other viruses (already published), and replicate them in the lab (see www.tigr.org). In fact, recent research into the chemical synthesis of life artificially in the laboratory, using PCR amplification and DNA sequencing to generate synthetic genomes of existing or novel pathogens, is showing enough promise to warrant serious concern. As Smith et al. (2003, 15445) note:

> We have demonstrated the rapid, accurate synthesis of a large DNA molecule based only on its published genetic code. The accuracy of our final product was demonstrated by DNA sequencing and phage infectivity. Our methods will permit serial synthesis of gene cassettes containing four to seven genes in a highly robust manner. . . . Selection for infectivity, such as we have used, or for ORFs in single genes provides advantages for synthesizing viruses or short sequences. However, when our method of synthesis is coupled with DNA sequencing and site-directed mutagenesis, it will enable rapid production of accurate cassettes that can be assembled into larger genomes. . . . [and] will enable rapid, accurate synthesis of genomes of self-replicating organisms.

In August 2002, scientists were able to artificially create the polio virus in the laboratory using off-the-shelf chemicals and its published genome (Cello, Paul, and Wimmer 2002). As the researchers noted, "the synthetic virus had biochemical and pathogenic characteristics of poliovirus" in mice and these results "show that it is possible to synthesize an infectious agent by in vitro chemical-biochemical means solely by following instructions from a written sequence." The potential of synthetically created polio virus is noted by the team of researchers who pioneered the technique:

> As a result of the World Health Organization's vaccination campaign to eradicate poliovirus, the global population is better protected against poliomyelitis than ever before. Any threat from bioterrorism will arise only if mass vaccination stops and herd immunity against poliomyelitis is lost. There is no doubt that technical advances will permit the rapid synthesis of the poliovirus genome, given access to sophisticated resources. The potential for virus synthesis is an important additional factor for consideration in designing the closing strategies of the poliovirus eradication campaign. (Cello, Paul, and Wimmer 2002)

And, as Van Aken and Hammond (2003, 58) warn, the same technique employed to create the synthetic polio virus could be employed to produce other BW agents:

> In principle, this method could be used to synthesize other viruses with similarly short DNA sequences. This includes at least five viruses that are considered to

be potential biowarfare agents, among them Ebola virus, Marburg virus and Venezuelan equine encephalitis virus. The first two in particular are very rare viruses that might be difficult to acquire by potential bioweaponeers. . . . Using the method that has been published for polio . . . a group or an interested state could theoretically construct Ebola virus in the laboratory. However it should be noted that this method is complex, and probably only a few highly trained experts would be able to master this technique, at least for the time being.

Dr. Robert Lamb, president of the American Society for Virology, is among those concerned such techniques could be applied to creating dangerous viruses like Ebola (Pollack 2002). Indeed, using a variety of techniques, researchers have already successfully created a number of potential biowarfare viruses in the lab, ranging from polio and pandemic flu, to Ebola (Mullbacher and Lobigs 2001; Volchkov et al. 1999). Indeed, as Kwik et al. (2003, 4) warn:

Using such technologies, which have been utilized to investigate Ebola, pandemic flu, influenza, hantaviruses, lassa, rabies, and Marburg viruses, there is no need for a bioweaponeer to isolate the virus from an infected patient, acquire it from a germ bank, or culture it from nature. All the required starting materials, such as cell lines and DNA synthesizers, are widely available and used for many beneficent purposes. And the sequences for a growing variety of viruses that infect humans, animals and plants, including Ebola, pandemic influenza, and smallpox, are published in the open literature.

Of course, the biotechnical revolution offers possibilities for not only developing designer pathogens or toxin weapons, but also for developing new generations of chemical weapons (Wheelis 2002). As Wheelis (2002, 49) observes:

Currently, a single industrial research facility can screen several hundred thousand new compounds per day against several dozen different proteins. In aggregate, the pharmaceutical industry is screening several million new potential ligands [*compounds that bind to specific sites on protein surfaces in the human body*] per year, and the results are stored in proprietary databases. In the course of toxicity testing of ligands identified in this way, about 50,000 compounds are identified each year that are highly toxic. For the pharmaceutical company, such toxic compounds have little potential as drugs and further development is halted. However, any one of these is a potential lethal chemical weapon (CW) agent. (emphasis added)

Further, Wheelis (2002, 50) notes that as the human "genomic sequences are annotated (assigned a function), the number of potential targets for pharmaceutical development will skyrocket," as will the "potential targets for novel CW agents." Wheelis argues the momentum of this research is now "clearly unstoppable" and in the near future, a "very large number of new, highly toxic compounds with precisely understood and controllable physiological effects will soon be discovered," and be capable of being "synthesized from precursors that are not currently regulated under the CWC [Chemical Weapons Convention]." Such novel biochemical agents could be tailor-made to not only be highly toxic, but also to affect "perception, sensation, cognition, emotion, mood, volition, bodily control, or alertness." Similarly, another feasible use of recombinant DNA, according to Dando (2001, 36), would be to cheaply manufacture toxins using "newly created bacterial strains under controlled laboratory conditions." Although most toxins are unable to be absorbed directly through the skin, unlike classic chemical or nerve agents, and require their targets to either ingest them or inhale a respirable aerosol of the toxin to produce lethal effects, a great deal of current pharmaceutical research (e.g., aerosol delivery of drugs/vaccines, etc.) could be coupled to efforts to engineer more effective toxin weapons (Dando 1994, 51). In fact, given current advances in genetic engineering and sequencing of toxin genes, Dando (2001, 59–60) warns:

> If we assume that, potentially, the genes for any of the vast range of naturally produced toxins (and their vastly variable effects, by different mechanisms) might be introduced into a variety of environmentally hardy infectious organisms, the long-term future threat from toxin weapons could change quite radically. It would no longer be a case of worrying about the delivery of a relatively small number of reasonably well-characterized bacterial toxins. Imagine the problems for a defender, given even a few of the possible toxins and mechanisms of action that might be encountered.

Another refinement in the nature of future bioweapons might be the ability to create "safe" binary warheads individually storing harmless components for a bioagent and only mixing them to create more lethal material close to or after launch. The feasibility of such bioweapons becomes possible due to increasing knowledge of exactly what components of a bacterium produce virulence and new techniques for manipulating them. As Block (1999, 54) explains:

> Most pathogenic bacteria carry small circular DNA elements that coexist with their main chromosomes. These are called "plasmids" . . . Plasmids carry an autonomous origin of DNA replication and therefore can copy themselves independently of the chromosome itself. . . . Plasmid gene cassettes endow bacteria with specialized functions. . . . As it happens, the genes that cause virulence in bacteria are most often found on plasmids; this happens to be the case for plague (*Yersinia pestis*), anthrax (*Bacillus anthracis*), dysentery (*Shigella dysenteria*),

and other diseases. . . . plasmids can be transferred among different kinds of bacteria across species barriers. Bacterial cells can also be "cured" of their plasmids; i.e., caused to lose them altogether.

Thus, to create a functional binary bioweapon, it requires bioweaponeers to merely manipulate this process within an active warhead. For example, Block suggests that one approach to constructing such weapons would look much like this:

First, a virulence plasmid is isolated from a pathogenic parent strain and an antibiotic resistance gene is introduced into it using standard molecular biology techniques. The plasmid is then amplified directly, using biosynthetic-based methods, such as the polymerase chain reaction (PCR). Independently, the original parent strain is cured of its plasmid, and the resulting nonvirulent isolate is cloned and grown up. Both components are individually harmless, and can therefore be handled in significant quantities without risk. The final step comes just before the weapon is deployed, and consists of transforming the host strain back into a pathogen. In practice, there are many ways to accomplish such a transformation. Perhaps the simplest is to treat the bacteria briefly with a solution of calcium chloride, which makes their cell walls leaky. With small probability (roughly 1 in 100,000), the plasmid DNA is taken up by the cell. If treated cells are then grown up in a medium containing the right antibiotic, only those organisms that have been successfully transformed will propagate, since the virulence plasmid also confers antibiotic resistance. In actual practice, the final transformation (i.e., the combination of cells and plasmids) and subsequent regrowth phase would presumably take place inside a small bioreactor that constituted the weapon itself, perhaps the size of a beer can. . . . The deployer of the weapon need not even be present to initiate the final transformation/regrowth phase, which would be accomplished automatically upon triggering the device. . . . The key point is that a binary weapon makes it feasible to grow up kilogram quantities of reagents without posing an undue risk to its manufacturer.

Finally, another possibility would be to develop agents that do not attack the victim's body directly, but instead turns the victim's own autoimmune system against itself—either leaving their bodies vulnerable to infection or, more insidiously, destroying itself (Dando 2001). Bioregulators are natural substances produced in the human body which regulate metabolism and control physiological functions ranging from blood pressure, heart rate, breathing, and temperature to muscle contraction and immune responses. However, as our understanding of bioregulators has increased, genetic engineering will increasingly allow bioweaponeers to utilize them to create designer agents able to specifically target the body's metabolism, immune system, or physiological functions. Bioregulators could be used to cause pain, deprive individuals of sleep, cause hypotension or hypertension, bring on heart failure, paralysis, psychological disturbances, uncontrollable bleeding, or death. In fact, the sky is practically the limit for what could be possible using such bioregulatory peptides. Further, genetic engineering makes it possible not only to produce these substances, using bacteria or viruses, on large scales, but to incorporate genes expressing these regulators into pathogens that could then be spread to other organisms (plant, animal, or human) (Dando 1994, 69).

Also possible, and an area where the Soviet BW program made substantial advances, was in developing bioregulator agents having the ability to "take control of human functions like moods, heart rhythms and sleep patterns" (Miller and Broad 28 December 1998, 1). Suggesting science had progressed to the point where "it can be done," Dr. Igor V. Domaradskij, a longtime Soviet bioweaponeer, noted his scientists were searching for compounds that could "sharply change a person's behavior or emotions, such as causing fear or an ultra-rapid heartbeat" (Miller and Broad 28 December 1998). Obviously, if speedy results are required on the battlefield, the use of toxins or bioregulators would be much preferred over the more slower acting, classic BW pathogens. Indeed, a 1996 Pentagon study noted advances in biotechnology and genetic engineering increased the potential for opponents to successfully modify BW agents for use as "tactical battlefield weapons" (Office of Counterproliferation 1996, 5).

Weapons designers will increasingly be able to disrupt the natural bioregulatory systems of people by artificially creating vast increases in "the concentration (within the living organism) of a naturally occurring bioregulatory chemical, or by introducing large quantities of a substance that mimics its effects." As Dando (2001, 30) observes, "there is not a great deal of difference between attacking the nervous system with a chemical nerve agent and disrupting it with an excessive amount of a bioregulatory mimic." So-called mid-spectrum agents, which have characteristics of chemical and biological agents, are also increasingly possible as a result of advances in biotechnology, including such compounds as toxins, bioregulators, and physiologically active compounds (PACs) (Office of Counterproliferation 1996, 4). Although it is generally accepted that ethnic group-specific genetic weapons are beyond current or foreseeable technical capabilities, some experts still warn against assuming such weapons will be forever out of reach (Dando 1994, 14–15; Miller and Broad 1998, 42). As Alibek observed:

> One of the problems is biotechnology is moving fast. We see a lot of changes in biotechnology in general—in microbiology, genetic engineering. And all the developments will give more and more information about how to develop and manufacture sophisticated types of biological weapons. (Wolfinger "Interviews: Bill Patrick and Ken Alibek" 2001)

## THE POTENTIAL OF AGRICULTURAL BIOWEAPONS

When people think about biowarfare, they often tend to focus purely on attacks against people. However, a potentially devastating mode of asymmetrical warfare against the U.S. and other advanced industrial nations would be to strike not at their people, but their agriculture (Whitby 2002; Parker 2002). Although most agricultural BW attacks would not result in human fatalities, the potential damage to the economies of nations so targeted could be immense. In extreme cases, the devastation to the agricultural sector in nations could lead to their economic collapse. Moreover, the task of striking the agricultural sector—either crops or animals—is far easier than staging attacks against people. Often, the agents require no special preparation and require only dispersal across a number of different locations near major feedlots or production hubs to spark a major epidemic. And, unlike efforts at biopreparedness protecting civilian populations—where at least some resources have been spent and increased surveillance achieved—the agricultural sector, which is far more vulnerable, has received scant attention.

State-run BW programs have long recognized the potential value of attacking the agricultural sectors of opponents, and in many cases, extensively weaponized huge numbers of potential agricultural pathogens for delivery in wartime. During WWI, German agents laced sugar cubes with anthrax spores in an effort to sicken the pack mules and horses of the Allies to disrupt their ability to resupply their forces in the field. Although never deployed, during WWII, the British developed "cattle cakes" laced with anthrax to cripple the German beef industry (Chalk 2004, 30). During the apartheid years, South Africa weaponized both foot-and-mouth disease (FMD) and African swine fever (ASF). And during the Cold War, both the U.S. and Soviet BW programs undertook substantial efforts to develop and weaponize various plant and animal pathogens for use against one another. For example, the U.S. program field-tested classical swine fever (hog cholera), exotic Newcastle disease (END), rinderpest, glanders, as well as foot-and-mouth disease (FMD) (Chalk 2004, 30). In addition to a wide range of animal pathogens, the U.S. also developed an extensive array of anticrop weapons, including rice blast, rice brown spot disease, wheat blast fungus, wheat stem rust, and various potato blights (Whitby 2002). Similarly, the Soviet BW program weaponized cow and sheep pox, blue tongue, African swine and horse fevers, rinderpest, glanders, and foot-and-mouth disease (Miller September 1999; Chalk 2004, 30). As Ban (2000, 3) notes:

The former Soviet Union probably had the most innovative and wide-reaching offensive anti-crop and anti-animal BW programs, although the primary focus was on agents for targeting Amerian and Western European crops. On the anti-animal side, the Soviets experimented with FMD, rinderpest, African swine fever (ASF), vesicular stomatitis virus, contagious bovine pleuropneumonia, mutants of avian influenza, and contagious ecthyma of sheep. The Soviets successfully used ticks to transmit FMD, avian ticks to transmit the causative agent of ornithosis to chickens, and insects to transmit plant pathogens. On the anti-plant side, work was conducted on wheat and barley mosaic streak viruses, potato virus, tobacco mosaic virus, brown grass mosaic virus (for use against barley, maize, and thornapple), wheat fungal, and brown leaf rust. Viability testing in indoor chambers was conducted on FMD, and as early as 1935, tests were conducted to develop reliable methods of disseminating FMD in combat situations. Lycophilization and vacuum storage experiments were conducted on maize rust, and stabilization techniques for Newcastle disease virus were also discovered.

Similarly, Alibek reports the Soviet BW program focused extensively on antilivestock and anticrop weapons:

> Scientists at the agriculture ministry developed variants of foot-and-mouth disease and rinderpest for use against cows, African swine fever for pigs, and ornithosis and psittacosis to strike down chickens. Like anti-personnel biological weapons, these agents were designed to be sprayed from tanks attached to Ilyushin bombers and flown over a target area along a straight line for hundreds of miles. This "line source" method of dissemination could cover large stretches of farmland. Even if only a few animals were successfully infected, the contagious nature of the organisms ensured that the disease would wipe out agricultural activity over a wide area in a matter of months. (Alibek 1999, 37–38)

Much like the clandestine tests of bioagent simulants in cities and airports during the 1950s and 1960s, the U.S. program (and one presumes the Soviet one as well) staged numerous exercises simulating the intentional release of foot-and-mouth disease (FMD) at animal trade fairs across the country, successfully introducing mock versions of the virus at several locations without being detected. And, as Terry Wilson, a senior USDA liaison officer stationed at Fort Detrick's Armed Forces Medical Intelligence Center, warns, over the past forty or fifty years little has changed in terms of safeguards and similar (successful) intrusions are just as possible today (Chalk 2004, 10–11). Indeed, the greatest current U.S. vulnerability to attack lies not necessarily with people targets (though these are also of concern), but in the far easier area to strike—agriculture. And, just as advances in biotechnology increase the dangers of biological attacks against people, these same advances also expand the capabilities of numerous actors—both state and nonstate—to strike at a wide range of crops and animals with potentially devastating effect.

Agricultural BW has numerous advantages for asymmetric warfare, such as the relatively low technical barriers to obtaining nonhuman pathogens and the ease with which they can be employed to harm animals and crops, causing major economic disruptions for nations. Noting that even nonstate actors now have the ability to inflict severe damage on U.S. agriculture, Casagrande (2000, 93) suggests "a major act of agricultural terrorism, one that causes over a billion dollars in damage, could be produced by a series of limited infections triggered by pathogens delivered by simple methods." Unlike the technical hurdles facing actors seeking to weaponize agents for use against people, most agricultural BW agents do not require agents to be aerosolized. Instead, just spreading pathogenic fungi onto the crops themselves, or placing materials contaminated with foot-and-mouth disease where they could come into physical contact with animals, would be sufficient to create a major outbreak. Such attacks could be multifocal across regions to cause massive outbreaks, or be limited to natural ports of entry into a country in order to mimic a natural outbreak (Casagrande 2000, 95). And, as Chalk (2004, 15) notes, not only is foot-and-mouth disease (FMD) prevalent near American shores in South America (where clinical specimens could be readily acquired from infected animals), but the pathogen itself could be easily smuggled into the U.S. "in manure stuck to the bottom of a shoe . . . or via vesicular fluids absorbed onto a handkerchief."

But, however delivered, given the incredibly contagious nature of some potential animal and plant pathogens, determined actors could cause major economic harm with relative ease. As Casagrande (2000, 96) observes:

If current trends continue, by 2002 the 40 largest pig producers will provide 90 percent of pigs to the US market and by 2010 the largest 30 feedlots will generate 50 percent of the finished cattle. A typical poultry farm will have from 250 thousand to several million birds. Four meat packers process about 80 percent of the animals sent to slaughter. This concentration of animals, combined with the communicability of livestock diseases, suggests that a handful of attacks could cause widespread devastation to an important sector of the US economy.

A good illustration of the potential for damage is the 2001 outbreak of foot-and-mouth disease in Great Britain, which cost the British economy as much as $5.9 billion, necessitated the mass slaughter of millions of infected farm animals, and caused lasting harm to both tourism and meat exports (Houlder 2001; Lyall 2002). Not only did this epidemic force the British government to impose travel restrictions on much of the English countryside to prevent the spread of the disease, but it came dangerously close to requiring policy makers to begin widespread vaccination of farm animals to halt further infection. While seemingly innocuous, this action would have had severe economic consequences by eliminating Britain's disease-free status (since vaccinated animals not infected with foot-and-mouth would also test positive for the disease). Thus, even after the epidemic was over, extensive restrictions on meat exports would continue to be applied for many years, costing farmers additional billions of dollars. Though this was a natural outbreak, a man-made outbreak would have been no less damaging and could have been implemented using follow-on attacks to circumvent efforts by the authorities to contain the spread of the epidemic.

Further, according to disease transmission models developed by the USDA, foot-and-mouth (FMD) released into the U.S. would spread within five days to as many as twenty-five states through the normal, regulated movement of animals from farm to market, and as Chalk (2004) warns:

> If one takes into account that certain livestock consignments are unregulated (as either illegal shipments or re-selling or switching animals at market) and that in some cases the signs of clinical infection are not always immediately apparent (a pig afflicted with FMD, for instance, typically starts shedding vesicular droplets seven to ten days *prior* to symptoms becoming visibly evident), then the true rates of transmission could be even greater.

If an actor's goal is to cause economic harm to an enemy, agricultural BW provides an effective and difficult to prevent form of attack capable of producing significant damage. For the U.S., agriculture provides 13 percent of the Gross Domestic Product (GDP), provides jobs for over 15 percent of the public, and accounts for more than $50 billion in exports (Casagrande 2000, 92). Overall, food production alone constituted 9.7 percent of U.S. GDP in 2001, amounting to earnings of over $991 billion (Chalk 2004, 17). This is obviously not an insignificant part of the American economy. In the largest natural animal disease outbreak in recent American history, an epidemic of avian influenza struck the chicken industry in Pennsylvania in the mid-1980s, forcing U.S. agricultural officials to kill all exposed chickens at a cost of $63 million and caused poultry prices to rise by $349 million over the six-month crisis. Had this outbreak not been contained, economists estimate that the epidemic would have cost U.S. agriculture as much as $5.6 billion (Miller September 1999). But the costs of a successful attack could be far higher.

For example, Parker (2002, 15) notes the FMD outbreak in Taiwan in March 1997, which nearly destroyed its pork industry, cost that nation "at least $19 billion—$4 billion to diagnose and eradicate the disease and another $15 billion in indirect losses from trade embargoes." And how difficult had the delivery of this FMD pathogen been? After much investigation, it was determined this $19-billion outbreak had been caused by a *single pig* imported from Hong Kong! Similarly, the prion-based mad cow disease in Britain has already cost that nation between $9 billion and $14 billion in compensation costs to farmers and laid-off employees, as well as another $2.4 billion in lost export earnings (Parker 2002, 14–15). Given the cost of these "natural" outbreaks, the potential for economic harm to the U.S. economy from intentional BW attack is clear. The USDA estimated in 1994 that were a disease like African swine fever (ASF) successfully introduced into the United States, it would cost at least $5.4 billion over a ten-year period (roughly 2 percent of the agricultural sector's total annual revenues)—a figure which other experts suggest would probably be three to five times higher in today's dollars (Chalk 2004, 20). Similarly, a U.S. Department of Defense report in January 2001 warned:

> U.S. livestock markets would be vulnerable to the causative agents of diseases including anthrax, Q fever, brucellosis, FMD, Venezuelan equine encephalitis, hog cholera, African swine fever, avian influenza, Newcastle disease, Rift Valley fever, and rinderpest. Soybean rust, which can easily be introduced and spreads quickly, could cause U.S. soybean producers, processors, livestock producers, and consumers to lose up to $8 billion annually, according to USDA estimates. An outbreak of FMD, which is also easily introduced, highly contagious, and persistent, in the U.S. livestock industry could cost as much as $20 billion over 15 years in increased consumer costs, reduced livestock productivity, and restricted trade, according to the USDA. (Department of Defense January 2001)

Given the U.S. cattle and dairy farming industry earns between $50 and $54 billion annually through meat and milk sales, with another $50 billion in revenue generated through farm-related exports, it is obvious the costs of an attack would extend far beyond those involved in culling herds and compensating farmers (Chalk 2004, 4). Indeed, it is difficult to imagine these costs would not double or triple official estimates.

## HOW DIFFICULT WOULD AGRICULTURAL ATTACKS BE?

There are a number of factors increasing U.S. vulnerability to agricultural BW attack. For example, Chalk (2004, 7) notes the U.S. agricultural and food industry are highly vulnerable due to: (1) concentrated and intensive contemporary farming practices in the U.S.; (2) increased susceptibility of livestock to disease; (3) a general lack of farm/food-related security and surveillance; (4) an inefficient, passive disease-reporting system that is further hampered by a lack of trust between regulators and producers; (5) lack of training in foreign animal diseases (FADs) or large-scale husbandry in U.S. veterinarian training; and (6) the current focus on aggregate, rather than individual, livestock statistics (which make monitoring and tracking outbreaks difficult). Similarly, Parker (2002, x) warns:

American agriculture is often concentrated, highly accessible, vertically integrated, and of limited genetic diversity; historically it has been free of major disease outbreaks, so vaccines are not routinely used. Consequently, pathogens could be introduced easily and spread rapidly. Widespread use of antibiotics in livestock production makes U.S. animals vulnerable to antibiotic-resistant bacteria. Advances in genetic engineering have raised the prospect of transgenic pathogens and pests that are resistant to conventional control methods.

As a result, U.S. agriculture is vulnerable on many levels to the intentional release of a virulent animal or crop pathogen. An excellent overview of the technical and policy issues surrounding agricultural bioterrorism can be found in Parker (2002) and Whitby (2002). However, it is important to note not all agricultural biological attacks would be simple to carry out. Some are easily within the capability of terror groups, others require the technical sophistication of a state-run program. For example, while agricultural pathogens could easily be carried into the U.S. across customs checkpoints, unregulated border areas, or potentially through the international mail, Cameron et al. (2001) correctly point out:

Obtaining a strain of a virus or a fungus does not necessarily mean, however, that it can be used directly as a biological weapon. For example, different strains of the rinderpest virus are immunologically similar, but they vary widely in pathogenicity, lethality, ease of transmission, and host affinity. Such variations, which occur in all animal and plant pathogens, complicate the selection of a weapons-usable strain. In most cases, a terrorist would need the right strain to cause a significant disease outbreak. Some foreign animal pathogens, like foot-and-mouth disease virus, are highly infectious and would not need to be cultured—a vial of material might be enough to cause an epidemic. But that is not always the case. Depending on the pathogen, different infective doses would be needed. And infectivity varies even between different isolates of the same viral strain and for different routes of infection (ingestion versus inhalation). If widespread destruction is the goal, moderate or high levels of scientific expertise may be needed to grow, handle, and store larger quantities. (Cameron, Pate, and Vogel 2001, 42)

Thus, while some animal pathogens, like FMD, are environmentally hardy and highly infectious (and therefore require no special handling or preparation), many animal (and most plant) pathogens do require special processing (such as microencapsulation, milling, and drying) in order to be effectively weaponized. While this could pose a significant challenge for a terrorist organization, a state-level BW program would be more likely to not only successfully identify weapons-usable strains appropriate to their targets, but also effectively process the agents to enhance their ability to be disseminated (Cameron, Pate, and Vogel 2001, 42–43).

This being said, there exists no shortage of potential agricultural bioagents that could inflict serious harm on the U.S. without requiring tremendous technological sophistication on the part of opponents. For example, foot-and-mouth disease (FMD) is clearly one of the easiest agents for both state and nonstate actors to acquire and disseminate, is monumentally contagious, and carries with it the potential for immensely costly economic disruption. Indeed, a bioattack introducing FMD into cattle at multiple sites across the U.S. would be relatively easy to accomplish and almost assuredly trigger massive economic destabilization:

> The means for disseminating FMD could be as simple as scraping a viral sample directly onto a cow grazing in a remote field or merely introducing the agent into a silage bin or feedlot at an auction barn. Because the disease is highly contagious, and because contemporary U.S. farming practices are concentrated and intensive, a multifocal outbreak across several states would be virtually assured. (Chalk 2004, 31–32)

Further, as Parker (2002, 15) notes, FMD is "the most infectious virus known, capable of spreading as a wind-driven aerosol over 170 miles from its source." Its ease of delivery and high degree of infectiousness led one DoD report to warn that since FMD had not occurred naturally in the U.S. since the 1920s, it would pose a serious threat to American agriculture:

> This agent is somewhat unique, as the animal becomes infective shortly after exposure and prior to the onset of clinical symptoms. To disseminate the agent, the mere transport of sloughed nasal vesicular tissue and modest preservation in transport could easily start an epidemic. For example, a single infected cow, or particularly a pig, can generate enough viral particles to infect vast geographical areas in a short period of time. (Department of Defense January 2001)

Other potential agricultural BW agents which would have the ability to kill both animals *and* humans (zoonotic pathogens) are also readily available to a variety of actors and easy to disseminate. Chalk (2004, 31), for example, warns that one possible zoonotic agent that could be employed in a bioterror attack is screwworm myiasis:

> The parasite is endemic throughout the world, and it is a serious concern in areas close to American shores. Screwworm myiasis is caused by the Cochliomyia

hominivorax maggot, which feeds on the living tissue of any warm-blooded mammal. Cattle are easily infected with the agent because the female maggot is able to oviposit eggs (in excess of 400 in a single laying) in a wide range of wounds common to these animals, including tick bites and cuts or lesions resulting from dehorning and castration. An initial infestation has the potential to quickly spread to urban areas (adult flies can travel up to 200 miles on wind currents) where it would pose an immediate health risk to both domestic pets and humans.

The possible animal pathogens having bioweapons potential, in addition to screwworm myiasis, include: Lyassa viruses, Porcine Enteriovirus Type 9, rabies viruses, Teschen disease virus, and Venezuelan equine encephalitis (Parker 2002, 19).

## ILLUSTRATIONS OF FOUR TYPES OF BIOWEAPON USE (STRATEGIC/RETALIATORY, TACTICAL COUNTERFORCE, TACTICAL COUNTERFORCE DISRUPTIVE, AND TERROR)

### Scenario 1—Strategic/Retaliatory Bioweapon Use

The freighter with its cargo of metal shipping containers had arrived in the Port of Seattle several days earlier and, like dozens of others, was now anchored offshore awaiting its turn at the cranes on the loading docks. The crisis that had led to the U.S. preemptive air strikes on the military and leadership facilities of a key Asian nation had dominated the headlines for over a week and resulted in stepped-up border security, but the Panamanian-flagged freighter had raised no particular concern among port officials. Like so many of the freighters entering port, the nationalities of the ships and, more particularly, the origins of their cargo containers, were concealed by the long-standing practice of registering vessels in various third world countries and often nebulous bookkeeping practices. Liberian, Panamanian, and many other registries graced the ships in harbor that day, and whatever inspections were likely to occur would wait until the ship was actually unloaded at dockside, or perhaps when the containers were at their final destinations. Regardless, with only about 4 percent of containers ever inspected, there was little risk of discovery. Planned many years earlier in the event strategic retaliation would prove necessary against the U.S., one specific container had serruptiously been loaded aboard the freighter—its contents and point of origin carefully concealed.

As darkness descended that summer's evening, operatives onboard ship, intermingled with the crew, released the latches of the specially designed cargo container and revealed its contents to the cool night air. The modified land-attack cruise missile, like its counterpart being deployed simultanously in San Francisco Bay, had been equipped with a biowarhead and tanks that would spray a steady release of a dry powder bioagent in a line-source release after launch. The form of the modified, Chinese-designed Silkworm rose from the container, pointing toward the night sky shoreward, so that its flight path would cross over the main sections of the city of Seattle and its neighboring suburbs.

It was 10 p.m. on a busy Saturday evening, with throngs of tourists still walking along the sidewalks that skirted the restaurants and bars along the piers. A major league baseball game was in its final innings inside Safeco Field, a crowd of over 35,000 enjoying an evening's entertainment. And, in the suburbs, people enjoyed the breeze flowing from their open windows and rested from a busy work week. The noise of the launch would have been the first warning of an attack, a sound hardly likely to be recognized as such by anyone on shore. Perhaps a plane was flying toward Seattle's airport to the south? Observers, if any, since few were likely to be gazing into the middle of the harbor, would have seen the light from the rocket engines of the cruise missile streaking up from the water. How much suspicion this would have raised is uncertain—but whether observed or not, the attack had been accomplished. The bio–cruise missile, flying below radar level, began releasing its cargo seconds after launch—a fine powder dispersed into the evening air, floating in a straight line across the city and suburbs, carried by a slight summer breeze. After traveling nearly seventy-five miles, the cruise missile crashes into the trees of the Cascade Mountains, concealing its wreakage.

Two days later, thousands of people begin to feel ill with an abrupt onset of symptoms including high fever, headache, malaise accompanying nausea, abdominal pain and nonbloody diarrhea. Since people who had traveled into the city for dinner or other entertainment had also been exposed, these cases were dispersed throughout the surrounding region, including patients in neighboring states who had driven in to Seattle to enjoy the baseball game. For doctors in the area, the wave of abrupt illness drew their attention, as did the sizeable numbers of people being reported statewide as experiencing similar clinical symptoms. But, since the infected patients would present a variety of clinical symptoms that could be associated with any number of routine viral infections, the initial cases would in all likelihood go undiagnosed. Within a day or two, this initial confusion was replaced by the growing recognition that tens of thousands of people were now exhibiting symptoms of abrupt onset of extreme malaise, headache, and fever. Some of the original patients had now begun to develop cutaneous flushing and skin rashes. Blood samples are sent away to CDC for analysis and news of a similar outbreak in the San Francisco/Oakland, California, area lead some to suggest that an unusual flu or virus is the culprit. As Bray (2003, 56) notes:

> There are . . . no unique clinical findings by which Ebola or Marburg infection can be recognized. Specific virologic tests are required for diagnosis, as described below. Physicians will be most likely to suspect filovirus infection if a previously healthy person becomes abruptly ill with a high fever, and shows the following signs and symptoms: hemorrhagic manifestations, perhaps limited to the eyes and mucous membranes; a maculopapular rash, typically on the trunk, without other skin lesions; steady worsening of illness to intractable shock, with death within 1 week; absence of productive cough; absence of neurologic involvement, other than obtundation.

However, as patients begin to show signs of these kinds of hemorrhages in the skin, in the whites of their eyes and mucous membranes, and in their stools, the diagnosis returns from Atlanta—*Marburg virus!*

There is no question now that the U.S. has been attacked with bioweapons. Marburg is not indigenous to any location outside of Africa, there is no animal reservoir from which it could have sprung, and it is a virus normally transmitted through contact with contaminated body fluids, most especially blood. Yet, in two U.S. cities, tens of thousands of patients are now exhibiting early symptoms of Marburg infection. It was a pathogen known to have been weaponized in the old Soviet BW program. Moreover, the possibility samples of the virus (and the secrets surrounding its production and processing into a weapons-grade powder) might leak out to both state and terror group actors had concerned bioterror experts since the mid-1990s. Over the following one to two weeks, at least 70 percent of those showing clinical symptoms of Marburg die of hemorrhagic diathesis, shock, and multiorgan system failure (Borio et al. 2002, 2397). New cases continue to occur for nearly three weeks after the first one, with deaths continuing to mount for several weeks more. There are no vaccines or antiviral drugs that can be administered to treat Marburg. No antibiotics are effective against a virus. The regions medical facilities were overwhelmed, so that even advanced supportive treatments are unavailable to most. Although Marburg does not easily travel person to person through the air, the virus is extremely communicable from contact with a victim's blood or other bodily fluids (feces, vomit, sweat, urine)—something which would result in significant secondary transmission to family members and some medical personnel who, unaware of the nature of the pathogen, were caring for the initial first wave of patients (Bray 2003).

The horror of tens of thousands of Americans dying in both Seattle and San Francisco of a hemorrhagic fever like Marburg would forever traumatize the nation. Bodies of the victims would have to be burned or buried without preparation, since normal embalming practices could not be continued on corpses teaming with Marburg virus particles (Borio et al. 2002, 2402). It is also apparent that, even had the attack been discovered in progress, nothing could have been done to save those exposed to the aerosol—the Marburg bioagent was an untreatable death sentence. Indeed, Marburg is one of the most stable of all possible bioagents in aerosol form (roughly equivalent to Venezuelan equine encephalitis virus) (Peters 2000, 203–4). And, properly weaponized in dry powder form and encapsulated to enhance its aerosol properties, the 50–100 kilograms of material released by each bio–cruise missile was capable of infecting a sizable proportion of all those exposed to the bioagents release. Although an epidemic would not occur, and the Marburg outbreak would soon burn itself out, it is possible hundreds of thousands of victims would die as a result of these bioattacks.

This scenario reflects a strategic/retaliatory use of advanced bioweapons, although it substantially reduces the severity of the attack by using a non-communicable pathogen and a limited number of attacks. Were a bioengineered smallpox, plague, or combined chimera (such as an Ebola-*variola* virus) used in attacks on half a dozen U.S. cities—all of which could be carried out as easily as the one described above—not only would casualties be similarly immense, but a massive epidemic would also likely erupt as the contagion spread beyond the confines of the area attacked to strike across the rest of the nation. In the case of a bioengineered smallpox or influenza virus, the result could be a pandemic killing millions. Were the biostate opponent capable of launching large numbers of bio–cruise missiles, or even ballistic missiles with advanced biowarheads, the toll could be greater still. In regional contexts, in which a biostate opponent would not be required to effect a long-range delivery of bioagents onto vulnerable targets, true mass-casualty attacks would appear quite feasible. Consider the millions who live within fifty kilometers of the North Korean border in South Korea—just as these cities provide easily accessible targets for any future nuclear arsenal, they provide equally tempting targets for future bioweapons employments. In such cases, it is difficult to envisage any kind of theater missile defense system providing adequate protection to forestall devastating mass-casualty attacks on the South Korean populace. Obviously, the ultimate on this spectrum of strategic/retaliatory bioweapons would be represented by the ability of the Soviet Union during the Cold War to kill tens or hundreds of millions of people through the use of ICBM-delivered biowarheads against American cities.

## Scenario 2—Tactical Counterforce Disruptive Bioweapon Use

The crisis between China and Taiwan had been brewing for years, but with the declaration of independence from Taipei, the useful fiction of the "one-China" policy had been lost for diplomats. Since the late 1990s, China had been increasing its naval and air force capabilities so it would have military options in the event they were needed against Taiwan. Moreover, its missile forces facing the shores of Taiwan had been greatly expanded and Beijing warned Taipei there would be consequences for breaking away from China. Although military preparations were being detected in China by U.S. reconnaissance satellites and other intelligence sources, it was deemed unlikely they could overwhelm Taiwan's defenses or successfully invade the island.

After a number of weeks in which the crisis had not appeared to worsen and Chinese rhetoric had apparently toned down, 100 bio–cruise missiles were launched from below radar level by both aircraft and ships. Outfitted with specially designed tanks and sprayers, the cruise missiles began line-source releases of their contents over Taiwan, effectively covering the entire island with a fine cocktail of VEE (Venezuelan equine encephalitis) and SEB (staphylococcal enterotoxin B) bioagent. Within hours, the populace began to experience the debilitating symptoms of food poisoning, and over the coming days, the extreme malaise and headache of VEE. Though it was clearly no natural occurrence, there was little that Taiwan's military forces could do to restore the ranks of its drastically depleted units who were lying prostrate in their barracks. In fact, much of the nation was at a standstill, with medical facilities overwhelmed and much of the populace either sick or caring for ill family members. As a result, the Chinese airborne units faced little resistance in their initial landings and substantial elements of a Chinese expeditionary force were able to land on Taiwanese shores facing miminal opposition. Taiwanese military units deployed to the field lacked logistical support and began to run short of ammunition and other supplies. Without the normally strong support of the rear areas and the civilian populace, the severely depleted frontline Taiwanese troops faced a severe disadvantage in trying to stop the invading forces. Within days, the invasion was essentially complete.

Since the VEE-SEB cocktail is not communicable, the Chinese armed forces were not affected by the bioagent. Only those who had respirated particles of the cocktail were infected, and for days or weeks following the release, a large proportion of the island's population remained ill. With a mortality rate of under 3 percent, the bioagent had not only resulted in diminished losses to the invading Chinese forces, but had incapacitated the Taiwanese defenders without the high levels of casualties that would normally have been anticipated from an invasion. Taking a page from the hypothetical U.S. plans to invade Cuba during the 1960s using a similar biococktail, China's *tactical counterforce disruptive* use of bioweapons proves an effective complement to its conventional military forces in retaking the island.

## Scenario 3—Tactical Counterforce Bioweapon Use

The U.S.–South Korean armored columns had finally breached the heavily mined DMZ and allied units were moving into the valleys snaking up into the mountains of North Korea. Anticipating the possible use of chemical munitions, U.S. field commanders have their advancing troops in a high state of readiness for possible use of their biochem suits and nerve agent antidotes. Sensitive sensor equipment constantly samples the air for signs of mustard or VX gas, as well as for a number of classic BW agents like anthrax or botulinum toxin. North Korean artillery and rocket fire is often intense, and sometimes appears to be ill targeted, striking in front of the advancing U.S. units.

Suddenly, without warning and with no indication of attack from the chemical/biosensors deployed with the units, soldiers begin dropping dead with massive heart attacks. Others become incoherent, paranoid, and irrational, as if high on psychotropic drugs. Gas masks are doned, but personnel continue to become affected by one symptom or the other. The advance halts and the U.S.–South Korean forces come under withering artillery and rocket fire from the surrounding mountains. Unable to regroup, the columns have difficulty seeking cover and suffer heavy casualties. Still, there is no indication in any of the biochem sensors of any agent in the air that could be responsible for the effects visibly occurring among the troops. As soldiers continue to remain unresponsive to treatment, the advance is forced to halt and pull back—leaving thousands, perhaps tens of thousands, of soldiers littering the field.

Unbeknownst to the allies, North Korea had acquired the technical expertise and biotechnical equipment necessary to produce several novel *bioregulatory* agent compounds. Spread both by the artillery and rocket fire, and by aerosol generators hidden in the hillsides, the bioregulatory agents affected the autonomic nervous systems of their victims, instantly causing heart failure as if by massive heart attack. Other peptides upset the chemical balance of the brain, resulting in hallucinations, paranoia, and other psychological manifestations in the exposed troops. Combined, this genetically engineered bioweapons attack had severe and almost immediate effects on the battlefield, dramatically affecting ongoing operations. Moreover, the novel nature of these natural bioregulatory agents did not match the profiles of existing chemical or classic bioweapons agents. As a result, there was no warning and the attack remained undetected until it was too late.

This use of novel bioregulatory bioweapons in a *tactical counterforce* manner in this scenario builds upon how Soviet bioweaponeers envisaged such weapons being used by their own armed forces. Further, it illustrates the vast potential of such novel bioregulators—which might either be inhaled or absorbed through the skin—to take the place of nerve agents and other chemical munitions on future battlefields.

## Scenario 4—Terror Bioweapon Use

The Islamic terror group had issued its final demands for drastic changes in U.S. foreign policy and a withdrawal from the Middle East, but had received no positive response from Washington. Although the American intelligence community had expressed some concern over the years that the group had obtained bioweapons know-how and technology from former weapons scientists on the black market, their threats to unleash a "plague upon their foes" was difficult to quantify with any certainty. Seeking to create "credibility" for their future threats, the group decided to launch several mass-casualty attacks on U.S. or allied interests—thereby demonstrating their very real bioweapons capabilities. Over the following months, individual terrorists or strike teams proceeded to infiltrate major targets, like London and Washington, D.C. Smuggled along with them were small containers of fine powder, concealed within preprocessed food packages and disguised as seasoning pouches. Over time, the two strike teams—in London and Washington—had each managed to collect nearly a pound of the powdered seasoning pouches. Inside these packages was powdered anthrax, milled to one-to-three-micron-size particles and electrostatically treated so that it would disperse well once released into the air. More importantly, this particular strain of anthrax was not only highly virulent, but had also been engineered to possess broad-spectrum antibiotic resistance, especially to ciprofloxin and penicillin-class drugs.

Waiting until the morning rush hour, the strike teams dispersed to multiple subway stations carrying their powder-laden pouches. Unconcerned about personal exposure to the anthrax, the terrorists stand near the entry tunnel of the platform as the subway trains approach, await the telltale rush of wind preceeding the trains arrival, and (as surreptitiously as possible) tear open the packets and dump the powder onto the tracks and platform just as the train appears. Simultaneously, in Washington, D.C.'s Metro and in London's Underground, two pounds of weapons-grade anthrax powder is released into the air. It rapidly circulates throughout the entire system, pushed through the tunnels by the pneumatic pressure of the trains, and breathed in by the densely packed crowds of morning rush hour commuters packed like cattle along the platforms. The powder floats in the air, and because it has been electrostatically treated, continues to be stirred back up into the air and recirculated with each passing train or person. It remains in the air throughout the day and into the evening rush hour as well, since the spores are well protected from sunlight in the subway stations. In each city, tens of thousands of commuters inhale an infective dose of anthrax and begin incubating the disease. Within three days, the first patients with symptoms of inhalation anthrax flood into British and American hospitals in the two cities. Since the medical community has been on the lookout for anthrax since the U.S. postal attacks of 2001, patients are immediately recognized as likely suffering from anthrax, tests confirm the diagnosis, and antibiotics are administered.

Unfortunately, even if the anthrax attack were discovered within a day by biosensors concealed within Washington's Metro, the task of delivering prophylactic antibiotics to all those potentially infected through riding the subways would be derailed by the discovery that the strain was antibiotic resistant. And, were that discovery only made after the first wave of clinical cases arrived in the nation's hospitals, it still would not change the fact that this anthrax was not going to respond to most antibiotics—and certainly not those which had been stockpiled for this purpose. That means tens of thousands of patients would soon become symptomatic with inhalational anthrax with no possibility of providing the kind of intensive care medical support needed to give them even a remote chance of survival. Untreated inhalational anthrax, which is essentially what one faces when dealing with a strain immune to antibiotic intervention, historically had a mortality rate of 89 percent (based on cases of occupationally acquired inhalation anthrax prior to the advent of antibiotics and critical care units in the early twentieth century) (Inglesby et al. 2002, 2240). Since as few as one to three spores have been shown to be sufficient to cause infection according to some recent studies, assuming each gram of the terrorist's anthrax weapon had only half the spore content as the fall 2001 postal letters, that means over 500 million spores per gram were released in an enclosed space densely packed with commuters (Inglesby et al. 2002, 2239). Given the enormous numbers riding both the Metro and Underground each day (650,000 and 3 million respectively), the enormity of the potential casualties were quickly apparent to the respective governments.[43] Over the coming seven days, well over one hundred thousand people (and potentially far more) would die of inhalation anthrax. And, with the next warning from the terror group that further attacks would occur unless their demands were met, and given that effectively delivered, this bioagent was essentially untreatable, the respective governments were forced to acquiesce.

This nightmare scenario employing the terror use of bioweapons is hardly far-fetched. It is a reasonable possibility that many terror groups (whether state or nonstate based) could develop such capabilities over the coming decades. In such an event, the early efforts of groups like Aum Shinrikyo and the postal anthrax attacker will seem mild by comparison.

## CONCLUSION

As this chapter has shown, the potential for the offensive use of bioweapons, whether by states as strategic weapons, or by nonstate actors as terror weapons, is enormous. The only limitation at this point is "knowledge" about how to weaponize and manipulate agents, as well as deliver them effectively to their targets. Knowledge is the true WMD when considering the threat of bioweapons, and perhaps the most difficult element to control. It is knowledge that often has a "dual-purpose" nature—to both harm and heal. The remarkable advancements in biotechnology and genetic engineering hold potential for healing many of mankind's most perplexing and lethal diseases, extending life, and vastly increasing its quality. At the same time, this knowledge and technology can be used for the "dark arts" of biowarfare and hold equal potential for inflicting harm on opponents, upsetting security relationships and providing avenues of potential attack for terrorists and states alike.

## NOTES

1. Indeed, Cortés was able to conquer the millions within the Aztec empire with only five hundred soldiers, while Pizarro overwhelmed the Inca empire with a force of only 177 soldiers—accomplishments that would have plainly been impossible in the absence of the decimating effects of the smallpox epidemics unleashed on these societies.

2. Variolation was a form of smallpox inoculation practiced before Jenner's cowpox discovery and involved the removal of scabs or pus from smallpox patients with a minor form of the disease and its insertion into the skin of healthy people. As Tucker (2001, 15) notes, variolation provided lifelong immunity to smallpox, with the procedure having only a 1 percent fatality rate (compared to 30 percent for naturally acquired smallpox) and generally resulted in "only a few dozen pustules" appearing around the inoculation site, not full blown disease.

3. As Tucker (2001, 156) explained: "In wartime, bomblets filled with smallpox virus suspension would be loaded into cluster bombs for delivery by TU-95 long-range strategic bombers; a cluster bomb held roughly 110 bomblets. The other delivery systems for smallpox were intercontinental ballistic missiles (ICBMs). . . . In December 1988 . . . the Soviet Ministry of Defense decided to use the giant SS-18 ICBM . . . to carry biological agents. An SS-18 could deliver ten independently targetable warheads over a range of six thousand miles. Each smallpox warhead contained about 150 bomblets; at a predetermined altitude above the surface, the casing would break open and disperse the bomblets in a large "footprint" over the target. A fixed propeller would cause each bomblet to spin as it fell to earth; at about twenty-five to one hundred meters above the ground, the explosive charge would detonate, rupturing the thin aluminum walls and breaking up the liquid suspension into tiny droplets. The exploding bomblets would create multiple point sources over the target that would merge into a vast infectious cloud. One SS-18 missile could deliver a total of 375 kilograms of viral suspension, or enough to cover a target area of 75 to 150 square kilometers. Several other delivery systems for smallpox were studied but not implemented, including high-speed cruise missiles that disseminated the agent with various spraying techniques."

4. The standard method of producing smallpox in fertilized chicken eggs was developed by Soviet bioweaponeers: "This technique involved cutting a small window in the eggshell and using an extremely fine needle to inject a minute amount of the virus into the developing chick embryo. The infected egg was then sealed with paraffin and warmed in an incubator, allowing the virus to multiply prolifically. . . . After three or four days, the egg membranes were harvested and homogenated, yielding a liquid suspension so enriched in variola virus that it usually did not require further concentration" (Tucker 2001, 141).

5. See also, Miller, Engelberg, and Broad 2001, 252.

6. The Bush administration also ordered a large-scale smallpox vaccination program that by mid-June 2004 had vaccinated around 627,000 military personnel and 40,000 civilian first responders and health-care workers—but also produced nearly 1,000 adverse reactions and at least two deaths (Calabresi and August 2004, 16).

7. *Dark Winter* simulation materials, p.43. All *Dark Winter* simulation materials can be found at the University of Pittsburgh Medical Center's Center for Biosecurity website at www.upmc-biosecurity.org.

8. Naturally occurring resistance to tetracycline-class drugs is rare and would immediately raise suspicions of bioterrorism in any widespread outbreak in a Western city. See Inglesby et al. 2000, 2286.

9. Interviews by author with former bioweaponeers Ken Alibek and Sergei Popov and with former CIA director James Woolsey.

10. Interview by author with Ken Alibek.

11. Interview by author with Sergei Popov.

12. The origins of the 2001 anthrax mail attacks remains a mystery. One possibility, never adequately investigated by the FBI, was that one of the September 11 hijackers was reportedly treated for what an emergency-room physician describes as a black lesion on his lower left leg consistent with cutaneous anthrax. A leading expert on anthrax, Dr. Thomas W. McGovern of the American Academy of Dermatology's bioterrorism task force, noted it was "highly unlikely" someone could naturally contract cutaneous anthrax on their lower leg (Fainaru and Connolly 2002).

13. Wein, Craft, and Kaplan (2003, 4350), also note that even if detection of the anthrax release was reduced to only six hours, expanded hospital resources and pre-distribution of antibiotics would only reduced these fatalities to around 70,000 deaths.

14. See also Kleinfield 2001; Rosenbaum 2001; and Altman 12 December 2001.

15. Interview by author with Sergei Popov.

16. Interviews by author with Ken Alibek and Sergei Popov.

17. Researchers have begun to suspect various species of bats as the natural reservoir for both Ebola and Marburg viruses in the wild (Monath 1999).

18. Dr. J. Craig Venter, who has led efforts to sequence the smallpox virus genome, argues a synthesis of smallpox is doable, "though not by an amateur" (Pollack 2001).

19. Interview by author with Sergei Popov.

20. Interview by author with Sergei Popov.

21. Interview by author with Sergei Popov.

22. Interview by author with Sergei Popov.

23. Interview by author with Ken Alibek.

24. Interview by author with Ken Alibek.
25. Interview by author with Ken Alibek.
26. Interview by author with Sergei Popov.
27. Interview by author with Sergei Popov.
28. Interview by author with Sergei Popov.
29. Interview by author with Sergei Popov.
30. Interview by author with Sergei Popov.
31. Interview by author with Sergei Popov.
32. Interestingly, the threat of bioterrorism using chimera viruses was the focus of Preston's (1997) fictional account in *The Cobra Event*, which chronicled the release of an engineered pathogen reminiscent of the kind of smallpox-Ebola combination Alibek warned was developed in the Soviet BW program.
33. Interview by author with Sergei Popov.
34. Interview by author with Sergei Popov.
35. Interview by author with Ken Alibek.
36. Interview by author with Ken Alibek.
37. Interview by author with Sergei Popov.
38. Interview by author with Sergei Popov.
39. See Dando 1994; Crameri et al 1998; Hamilton 1998; Coffield et al 1994.
40. Interview by author with Sergei Popov.
41. Interview by author with Sergei Popov.
42. Interview by author with Sergei Popov.
43. For London Underground, see www.tfl.gov.uk/tfl/abt_tfl.shtml; for the Washington Metro, see www.wmata.com/about/MET_NEWS/PressReleaseDetail.cfm?ReleaseID=443.

# 6

## The Bionuclear Security Threat:
## Implications and Recommendations for Policy

> Too many times in the past we have failed to anticipate future develop-
> ments; refused to think the unthinkable and expect the unexpected. Too
> many times we have been out maneuvered by those who take the time to
> think and plan and do not simply rely on reacting to events. We must learn
> to think like our potential adversaries if we are to avoid conflict or blunt
> an attack, because only superior thinking and planning (not just better
> technology) will enable us to survive biological warfare.
>
> —Davis (1999, 509)

This warning, by former British weapons inspector Christopher Davis, criticizes what he describes as "nuclear blindness" or "tunnel vision suffered by
successive governments, brought on by the mistaken belief that it is only the
size of the bang that matters" (Davis 1999, 509). It is a criticism applying
equally well to those who dismiss the deterrence potential of small nuclear arsenals vis-à-vis other states, or to those who downplay the potential of
bioweapons because of their lack of the *absolute* physical destructiveness of
nuclear weapons. It is a criticism of any form of "tunnel vision" obscuring our
focus upon existing security threats due to dominant institutional thinking or
analytical biases—of not thinking "outside of the box" as an adaptive enemy
would in seeking to harm us. In many respects, this criticism serves as an in-
dictment of what has been an ongoing problem within the security and policy
communities as a whole—namely, the serious lack of attention to what the future security environment will look like given existing trends in bionuclear
proliferation.

Some of this lack of reflection is due to the strong normative and organizational biases existing in many institutional or scholarly communities

against considering any future *other than* one in which the controls of the counterproliferation regime have been successful. For those involved in the International Atomic Energy Agency (IAEA) or counterproliferation efforts in government, it is accepted "organizational wisdom" that *only* controls or elimination of WMD capabilities will lead to stability and security among states. Such analysts tend to accept these dominant institutional norms and values, which reflect the rationale not only for their own jobs, but also for the existence of their organizations as well. Unremarkably, the analyses and reports arising from such organizations generally provide nearly unqualified support for institutionally derived, control-oriented perspectives on most proliferation matters.

For many academic specialists as well, the strong proliferation pessimist tradition in the security studies field has fiercely resisted *any* consideration of optimist arguments modifying or conflicting with their intensely held theoretical or normative biases against the validity of any stabilizing or security-enhancing roles for WMDs between states. Of course, control-oriented perspectives *do* make important contributions by bringing greater awareness of the potential dangers and harmful consequences of proliferation to our attention. However, their dominance in the debate also creates a form of "proliferation blindness" that fails to take into account the *contingent* nature of how nuclear or biological weapons are likely to affect the wide range of security relationships possible between state and nonstate actors. Indeed, as the theoretical frameworks proposed in chapters 2 and 4 suggest, pessimists are probably correct about the nascent or early stages of WMD development—it does produce less stable, more dangerous security relationships for not only the new bionuclear states, but also for their neighbors as well. Stable, survivable deterrent force structures are often absent, command and control (as well as arsenal security) may be inadequate, and there is tremendous pressure on neighboring states (or external great powers) to attempt preemptive strikes to disarm the new WMD state. On the other hand, once stable, survivable force structures exist—and are known (or generally accepted) to exist by opponents—stability is enhanced and the likelihood of preemptive attack greatly reduced. The Israeli, Indian, and Pakistani experiences to date support this interpretation. These are contingent security relationships greatly affected by the nature of the WMD arsenals possessed, how survivable they are, and the motivations/perceptions of the states involved. By only accepting the "tunnel vision" perspective that all proliferation is bad or destabilizing, we bias our analyses and prematurely accept conclusions that may or may not reflect reality.

Unfortunately, this particular bias has forced less pessimistic scholars into a debate largely divorced from actual trends in the "real world," and instead centered around a "theoretical one" in which discussions focus upon what would "ideally" be the most stable and peaceful security environment. Optimists are placed in the untenable position of arguing a world with nuclear weapons is *always* more stable than one without them; or that the risks of accidental (or intentional) nuclear war are not decreased unless such weapons are completely removed from state control. Moreover, they are pushed by pessimists into discussions about "irrational" or "crazy" third world leaders compared to "rational" Western ones, along with demands they justify their "immoral" position of putting at risk the lives of millions of people to establish nuclear deterrence rather than just completely eliminating such weapons. The practicality of the pessimist prescriptions and validity of their assumptions are uncritically accepted—an ideal against which optimist arguments are set up to flounder. It is a fascinating philosophical argument—but it is one that largely misses the point if one is actually concerned about the real world, the motivations and behaviors of actual state actors, and how current trends in proliferation are likely to affect future security relationships. That discussion would require us to move our analysis away from how we might *wish* the world to be—an ideal in which the genie is returned to the bottle for good— toward a more realistic assessment of *how the world actually is*. It tasks us with asking why state or nonstate actors might seek WMDs, the likelihood that counterproliferation efforts (however constructed) can succeed absent changes in the motivations driving these actors toward WMDs, and what current trends suggest the future might hold. The focus of this book has been toward this latter approach.

## PROLIFERATION AND TWENTY-FIRST CENTURY SECURITY

As we look ahead over the next ten to fifteen years, a number of critical observations should form the basis of our thinking about the kinds of security threats the U.S. will face, the types of constraints that may limit our power abroad, and the policy requirements necessary to adequately improve our defenses at home, limit our vulnerabilities to attack, and better meet the challenges ahead. The more we fail to adapt to this new security environment, the greater will be our vulnerability to future September 11th–style attacks. It also requires us to accept that, while greater awareness and enhancing our defensive preparedness will reduce our vulnerabilities, nothing will provide us with "assured security." There is no "silver bullet" to provide us with a "perfect" security that cannot be threatened by the adaptive enemies we face. And it is unrealistic to expect there to be. But, given the *catastrophic* consequences of nuclear or biological attack, failing to recognize the changing nature of our security environment vis-à-vis other state or nonstate actors, and failing to take what precautions we can to limit or reduce our vulnerabilities is simply unacceptable.

## THE CHANGING NATURE OF FUTURE
## STATE SECURITY RELATIONSHIPS

The first essential element we *must* accept is that, despite all of our best efforts at counterproliferation or military preemption, *existing state security relationships are going to dramatically (though gradually) change over the coming decades.* New nuclear or biological states will obtain increasing abilities to deter or constrain the actions of great powers which threaten their critical central interests (like sovereignty or regime survival). Though this new deterrent will be limited to central rather than peripheral areas of interest (much as it has been for the great powers), this marks a monumental change. For the first time in history, pure power politics of the "strong doing what they will and the weak suffering what they must" will be altered by nuclear-armed or bioarmed Melians capable of exacting punishment upon their more powerful foes far disproportionate to their own conventional military capabilities and small state status. Deterrence will become not only the prerogative of the great nuclear powers, but for smaller bionuclear states as well. And the changing nature of these security relationships between states, reviewed in the analytical frameworks presented in chapters 2 and 4, bring with them *both* the potential for greater strategic stability *and* enhanced short-term instability for the international system.

It should be emphasized, however, that these security relationships between states are inherently *contingent* ones. How they develop and play out depend not only on the type of WMD involved (nuclear or biological), but also upon a number of critical variables reviewed in these analytical frameworks (e.g., which of the available employment options are chosen; the nature of the security problem; the means of delivery, and quality of available weapons, etc.). What is also clear for the U.S. is that we will increasingly come into contact with small states that will, through their explicit or implicit nuclear or biological capabilities, be able to seriously constrain our freedom of action abroad or threaten extensive levels of destruction on citizens at home or military forces abroad if provoked.

Similarly, the rise of nonstate actors armed with WMDs represents a historically unique security problem, especially given the near impossibility of developing effective state-based deterrence strategies against such opponents. In fact, *the rise of nonstate, bionuclear actors is unquestionably the most serious threat facing us in this future security environment.* It is a far more serious problem than the rise of bionuclear *state* actors, who can be effectively deterred by threats of retaliation against their vulnerable central interests. In contrast, nonstate actors (like Al Qaeda) lack such "centers of gravity" for retaliation and tend toward purely instrumental uses of violence geared to inflict the greatest levels of damage and fear on their opponents as possible without regard for consequences. Once such groups possess WMDs, they become the most unpredictable, undeterrable, and dangerous threats to any state's security. Indeed, the greatest future threat to U.S. security will take the form of nonstate opponents possessing advanced bioweapons capabilities, since this combination couples the actors *most likely* to employ such weapons against American interests with the *most technically accessible* of WMDs.

## THE INEVITABLE SPREAD OF TECHNICAL CAPABILITIES AND KNOW-HOW

Given the accelerating pace of technological development and spread of advanced industrial capabilities and know-how around the world, we have reached the point where counterproliferation strategies centered purely upon "denial" of materials or technology cannot prove effective at preventing development of nuclear or bioweapons capabilities *if* a state is sufficiently motivated to pursue them. This is particularly true with bioweapons, where production equipment and know-how are already widespread and completely dual use in nature. It is a program easily concealed by state or nonstate actors, doesn't require a large "footprint" in terms of research or production facilities, nor require unreasonable expenditures of money to support. In fact, the *knowledge* of how to effectively weaponize and deliver bioagents represents the true WMD at this point—and scientific knowledge has always been notoriously difficult to contain. Nuclear weapons technologies, in contrast, are arguably more esoteric and less easily obtained by state or nonstate actors, making control measures potentially more effective. However, new advances in centrifuge and laser-enrichment technologies, and a thriving black market, will make it less difficult for motivated actors to surreptitiously obtain fissile materials.

Moreover, the states discussed in this book as examples of "lambs being transformed into lions" over the coming decade (North Korea, Iran, India, Pakistan, and Israel) already possess the requisite technology and materials to pursue nuclear weapons and significantly expand their programs, regardless of what trade sanctions or import restrictions might be adopted. As states industrialize and develop technologically, they inevitably obtain dual-use capabilities that can be employed for civilian or military purposes. For well over sixty states in the world who currently possess the infrastructure and technical sophistication to develop nuclear weapons (e.g., Japan, Germany, South Korea, Taiwan, etc.), it is not lack of access to technology or equipment preventing their ascension to nuclear status, but merely a lack of motivation to do so. For state actors seeking WMD capabilities, counterproliferation measures serve, at best, as a brake slowing the momentum toward possession. They are unlikely to prevent it.

In contrast, counterproliferation measures may prove far more successful in restricting *nonstate* actor possession of nuclear capabilities, since access to specialized technology, materials, and technical training is easier to restrict for such groups than it is for state actors. This is not to say such groups might not be able to obtain through the black market or sympathetic elements within state-run programs the essentials to create a nuclear weapon. But, this will not be an easy route for terror groups to pursue and suggests that nuclear attacks will be the least likely of the potential nonstate actor threats faced in the coming decades. Far more likely, and more accessible in terms of materials, would be the terror use of radiological devices (dirty bombs) that spread radioactive contaminants using conventional explosives.

Unfortunately, a far more serious threat will arise from a different kind of WMD—biological weapons. While counterproliferation efforts may, for the reasons discussed above, limit the accessibility of the nuclear option to terror groups, they will prove unsuccessful in restricting the biological option. Indeed, the greatest threat to U.S. security in the coming years will flow from the growing potential of nonstate actors to obtain significant bioweapons capabilities, ones capable of producing mass casualties in a civilian population. Given the dual-use nature of the technologies involved and their widespread availability, the scientific know-how to harness microbes for terrorism will prove a far easier hurdle to jump for terrorists than the nuclear one. If a mass-casualty attack by terrorists occurs in the coming years, it will most probably take the form of a biological attack.

## THE NEED FOR A REALISTIC
## APPROACH TO COUNTERPROLIFERATION

If we are to reduce our vulnerabilities to nuclear or bioterrorism, and slow (or reverse) the momentum of WMD spread to state actors, we must adopt a more realistic counterproliferation approach. One cognizant of the realities we face and the decreasing likelihood traditional counterproliferation approaches (centering around control or preemption) will be successful. That we might "wish" the situation were not so does not change the matter, and wishful thinking or reliance on ineffective counterproliferation approaches will not avert the future we fear. Rather, we need to continue to pursue control efforts of proven effectiveness (like the Nunn-Lugar Cooperative Threat Reduction Program), but recognize the limitations of efforts centered purely around "control" or "denial" strategies.

The most effective counterproliferation "control" measures deal directly with a state's "motivations" for developing WMDs, not solely upon efforts to eliminate "capabilities" or control the spread of technology. This basic reality should be the main criteria for evaluating any U.S. or international counterproliferation policy. By meaningfully addressing the underlying motivations of states seeking WMDs (e.g., by providing "security guarantees," "economic or political payoffs," etc.), we increase the likelihood they will not feel the need to continue their programs. Indeed, the most successful examples of counterproliferation (e.g., South Africa, Ukraine, South Korea, Taiwan) were all cases in which the motivations driving their WMD aspirations (in this case, security) were relieved by either changing political conditions (South Africa, Ukraine) or provision of security guarantees by allies (South Korea and Taiwan from the U.S.).

In contrast, when such motivations are *not* adequately addressed by the counterproliferation regime, especially when states feel their fundamental security interests (like regime survival) are at stake—as with Israel, North Korea, Iran, and Pakistan—they will *not* cooperate with control efforts and fervently pursue WMDs to meet their perceived security needs. And while proposals to cut "deals" with proliferating states are often resisted by governments and academics as "rewarding misbehavior," the cold reality is we can either adhere to this principle (and accomplish no meaningful reversal of movement toward WMD capabilities) or we can deal with the "world as it is" and recognize that since we cannot unilaterally remove the ability of states to develop WMDs, it will require cooperation and compromise to accomplish our goals.

A good example of this problem is the current U.S. policy toward North Korea. The Bush administration insists Pyongyang surrender its plutonium reprocessing and uranium-enrichment capabilities prior to any meaningful U.S. actions (such as normalization of relations, a formal peace or nonaggression treaty, security guarantees, or lifting of economic sanctions). For North Korea, this is an absolute "nonstarter" since Pyongyang views its ability to create a viable nuclear deterrent as essential to guaranteeing its security against the threats it perceives from the U.S. and South Korea. The nuclear program is seen as a way to ensure regime survival (a key central interest) and prevent America attacking it like other, so-called rogue states (like Iraq) that lacked deterrent capabilities. In the absence of improved relations between

Washington and Pyongyang, or measures to address the North's intensely felt security concerns, it is utterly unrealistic and naive to expect Kim Jong-Il to relinquish his main means of defense.

Since military strikes would be ineffective at eliminating the North's nuclear program, and bring fearful conventional retaliation against the South, forcing Pyongyang to relinquish its arsenal through military means is not a viable option. What remains are two basic choices. To "not reward" the North, adopt a confrontational policy approach, and refuse to negotiate (the current U.S. strategy)—which will result in no meaningful change in Pyongyang's behavior and expansion of its WMD efforts. Or, "engagement" through negotiations and confidence-building measures addressing Pyongyang's main reasons for pursuing WMDs (its security concerns and desire to ensure the survival of Kim's regime). Providing a peace treaty or nonaggression pact, along with normalization of relations and lifting of sanctions, would be among the first steps required toward building the degree of trust and confidence necessary for Pyongyang to change its current course. And, whatever we might prefer, the bottom-line reality is that North Korea will *never* accept the kind of invasive, comprehensive weapons inspections throughout the entire country demanded by the U.S. to verify abandonment of its nuclear program in the *absence* of confidence-building measures that would build trust and adequately address its security concerns. If Washington is unwilling to pursue this policy path, it will have to get used to accepting North Korea as a nuclear state—because that will be the reality produced by any other course.

## THE EVOLVING CONSEQUENCES FOR
## U.S. FOREIGN AND DEFENSE POLICY

What are the implications of these changing security relationships for the United States? On a practical level, we must come to terms with the fact that, despite our unparalleled global conventional military superiority, *we will increasingly face limitations or constraints on our ability to apply that power abroad.* As the framework of chapter 2 suggests, such limitations will not take the form of serious constraints over policy areas within the *peripheral* interests of our new nuclear or biostate opponents. Traditional power politics, and the U.S. advantage, will remain unaltered in these areas. Rather, the evolving security context will take the shape of constraints on our ability to intervene directly or threaten the key *central* interests of new nuclear or biostates. Simply put, the difference is between invading a state lacking WMD retaliatory capabilities, like Iraq, to affect "regime change" and considering such actions against a state, like North Korea, Pakistan, or Israel, who possess credible retaliatory forces.

In the first case, the costs are calculated as they have been throughout history for great powers, in purely conventional military terms, with the far stronger power having the decided advantage. And while such interventions can prove enormously costly, both in terms of lives lost and monetary resources wasted, the smaller states (whether a Vietnam or Iraq) lack the ability to inflict enough harm instantaneously on their attackers to make the costs greater than the perceived benefits of intervention. In other words, they lack a credible deterrent capability that could visit an unacceptable level of assured destruction upon their attackers with certainty. For the U.S., liberating Kuwait in 1990 or overthrowing Saddam Hussein's regime in 2003, held the possibility of substantial military casualties and costs, but never of the magnitude that would assuredly deter policy makers. In contrast, seeking to effect "regime change" by force in North Korea would unquestionably result in massive conventional and unconventional retaliation upon not only South Korea, but possibly also against U.S. bases in Japan and Guam. As chapter 3 illustrated, using potential North Korean nuclear strike scenarios against the South, even small-force structures are capable of causing millions of deaths. It would be taking a risk of a completely different order of magnitude for policy makers—one in which the "contestability" of the costs would be less negotiable and the damage inflicted upon our interests easily beyond politically acceptable limits. Such realities force policy makers to accept certain limitations or constraints upon their actions.

Over the coming decades, American policy makers will increasingly face new bionuclear state opponents who possess the ability (if only within local or regional theater contexts) to massively retaliate with WMDs in response to U.S. aggression. The inability to deliver WMD strikes over intercontinental distances will not be a significant impediment to states seeking to deter U.S. military interventions in their countries, since Washington would doubtlessly be equally deterred by a survivable Iranian capability to strike and obliterate most major oil installations in Saudi Arabia or a North Korean ability to level South Korean or Japanese cities. Further, delivering nuclear or biological strikes against military forces based nearby, or defensively striking at deployed military units engaged in offensive operations, is not only credible (when undertaken in response to key central interest threats), but also does not require delivery capabilities beyond the reach of new bionuclear states. Moreover, a nuclear strike against a carrier battle group offshore or against large formations of U.S. troops would produce enormous casualties and greatly increase the costs (and risks) faced by policy makers weighing the desirability of military interventions. As a result, the U.S. *must* engage in a realistic reappraisal of its existing foreign and defense policies pertaining to regions affected by these evolving bionuclear security relationships. Only in this way will policy makers be prepared to adequately consider, during the formulation and implementation of U.S. policy, how the changing security context will constrain our policy options, limit our freedom of action, and affect the likelihood of success for any given initiative.

Another consequence of this changing security environment is the need to reassess current U.S. missile defense programs and the funding emphasis placed upon area defenses (national missile defense [NMD]) versus point defenses (theater missile defense [TMD]). First, despite the domestic political value to politicians of appearing "tough on defense" by providing a "national" missile defense to protect the entire country, the inescapable reality is NMD is unlikely to provide the degree of protection required to eliminate the WMD threat from missiles and is incapable of preventing "alternative" forms of delivery from being successful. Over the past ten years, numerous National Intelligence Estimates (NIEs) have concluded ICBM delivery of WMDs against the U.S. is the *least likely* mode of attack (Central Intelligence Agency "Foreign Missile Developments" 1999; Central Intelligence Agency "Foreign Missile Developments" 2001; Defense Intelligence Agency 2000; House National Security Committee 1996). Not only are such missiles traceable, giving a clear return address for overwhelming retaliation, but *none* of the states of immediate concern (like North Korea or Iran) possess (or are likely to over the next fifteen years) the ability to develop ICBMs or the warhead miniaturization technology required to create effective delivery systems (Cirincione 2000, 2002). To the extent we continue to spend $10 billion annually to deploy an inadequately tested NMD system unable to deal with the likely countermeasures that could be employed, the more we divert resources away from areas of far greater need (U.S. General Accounting Office 2003; Cirincione 2002). And a fully deployed NMD could cost between $500 billion and $1 trillion, funds that could have gone toward other critical homeland security needs addressing greater areas of potential WMD threat and vulnerability.

The *more likely* missile or cruise missile threat scenario involving WMDs would center upon local or regional use against U.S. military forces deployed abroad or instances targeting regional American allies. The far more pressing requirement to help reduce future U.S. vulnerabilities and constraints on power is development of viable *Theater Missile Defense (TMD) systems*, not NMD. Short- to medium-range delivery platforms are widely proliferated in the Middle and Far East, and would not pose a significant problem for new bionuclear states to employ effectively within region. And, assuming the proposition is true that U.S. policy makers would be equally deterred by massive retaliatory threats against either its military forces abroad or vulnerable allied targets, it becomes quite clear missile defense efforts should center upon the *most likely* rather than *least likely* modes of delivery! This requires a reemphasis upon theater missile defense.

That being said, it is also critically important to be realistic about the degree of protection we can expect, regardless of our redirection of missile defense efforts. Will it ever be possible to erect a "perfect" defense rendering all of our opponent's WMD delivery systems (whether cruise or ballistic missile, aircraft, or clandestine concealment within container ships or commercial aircraft) "impotent and obsolete"? Of course not. At best, such efforts will complicate the ability of opponents to target us with their WMD capabilities and reduce the magnitude (and destructiveness) of potential attacks. However, they will not eliminate them, nor is there a technological "silver bullet" on the horizon that will completely prevent a determined and adaptive opponent from delivering mass-casualty WMDs against us if they decide to do so. As earlier chapters on nuclear and biological employment strategies demonstrate, there are many ways to circumvent an opponent's defenses and deliver devastating attacks. What we must avoid is becoming prisoners of our own wishful security thinking. Missile defenses, efforts to enhance border controls, development of defensive BW programs, or any other conceivable steps to address our changing security environment may serve to reduce our vulnerability and the damage that will occur if (and when) an attack takes place. But, missile defenses must not become the "Maginot Line" of the twenty-first century, where we, like the French of the 1930s, become convinced of the superiority of a given defensive approach, only to be defeated by an adaptive enemy willing to attack our strategy rather than our defenses.

The limitations of missile defense are nowhere better illustrated than by the example of the other type of WMD actor we will face in the coming decades—the nonstate, terror group. Against this threat, it is missile defenses that prove "impotent and obsolete." For nonstate actors, ballistic missile delivery of WMDs over great distances is the least efficient, least practical, and most expensive option possible—and one difficult to credibly argue is likely to be adopted by groups like Al Qaeda. Instead, such groups are likely to prefer the far easier and less technically demanding *clandestine* modes of delivery. For example, options such as smuggling bomb components or bioagents into the country across porous borders, concealing weapons within cargo containers aboard ships or within the holds of commercial aircraft, or the use of more readily obtainable, short-range cruise missiles launched from ships just offshore (or in harbor). Equally, delivery of bioagents could be accomplished using human delivery systems, releasing sophisticated powdered bioweapons into subway systems or other enclosed facilities. As our discussions in preceding chapters illustrate, defenses against such clandestinely delivered nuclear or bioweapons will prove extraordinarily difficult and expensive to implement. And, against this *most likely* WMD threat, missile defenses are irrelevant.

Another likely consequence of this changing security environment is not only reduced U.S. freedom of action vis-à-vis new bionuclear states, but also an increased unwillingness of regional allies to cooperate with American policies that might make themselves a target. For example, were the U.S. to become involved in a conflict with a nuclear-capable North Korea or Iran, the price of providing military bases or port facilities to American forces in Kuwait, Bahrain, South Korea, or Japan could well be the targeting of those sites (as well as others) with nuclear weapons. And, if the price of cooperating with a muscular U.S. military policy were possible nuclear strikes on Seoul, Okinawa, or Kuwait City, it is easy to imagine a great reluctance on the part of these regional allies to take such enormous risks. Indeed, one already sees shadows of such reluctance in the case of South Korea today, which has shunned the Bush administration's confrontational strategies toward the North in favor of continuing the nonaggressive, engagement-style Sunshine policies of Kim Dae-Jung. The reality that Seoul is only thirty kilometers from the DMZ and within easy reach of North Korean artillery, let alone WMDs, produces a steely eyed realism often lacking among U.S. policy makers not facing a similar threat.[1] As the potential costs of supporting U.S. military policies become more apparent to allies as neighboring bionuclear state capabilities grow, this will result in further constraints on American political and military options. This should be anticipated in advance by policy makers, so realistic policy options can be designed that take into account the reluctance of U.S. allies staring down the barrel of a neighbor's WMD. Similarly, one should also anticipate greater difficulties in assembling "coalitions of the willing" in the face of such dangers, forcing the U.S. to "go it alone" if it insists upon confronting established bionuclear states.

## THE IMPLICATIONS FOR NEW BIONUCLEAR STATES

While credible, survivable WMD capabilities will provide new bionuclear states with the ability to deter (and absent that, massively punish) either great power or regional state enemies, this too has its limitations. Like the Cold War–era nuclear states, the credibility of deterrent threats (whether using nuclear or biological weapons) is only firm when dealing with direct threats to key central interests (e.g., regime survival, sovereignty, territorial integrity, etc.), not for peripheral policy areas (see chapter 2). Thus, while the traditional power politics security relationship will no longer apply in the fairly limited arena of central interests, new bionuclear states will still have to compete conventionally (and at a disadvantage) in all other areas of political and economic competition.

While this transformation is limited, it is nonetheless profound and historically unprecedented. New lions—like North Korea, Iran, Pakistan, India, and Israel—will be able to deter (or retaliate against) threats to their survival, eliminating the notion of "driving a people into the sea" or effecting "regime change" involuntarily. This will generally produce an initially more unstable, dangerous security relationship for the new bionuclear states vis-à-vis their neighbors and other great powers during their *nascent* phase of development. As of this writing, Iran is the most vulnerable (like Iraq before it) to preemption of its budding nuclear program by opponents seeking to prevent development of WMD capability. As proliferation pessimists correctly point out, this is a dangerous, volatile, and unstable period for any proliferant state. Indeed, only time will tell if Iran will join Israel, North Korea, Pakistan, and India in possessing WMD capabilities that are past the point of viable preemption by opponents and able to credibly threaten assured levels of destruction to any enemy foolish enough to threaten it.

Yet, so far, the examples of these new nuclear lions, much like the Cold War–era nuclear powers before them, suggest the likely outcome of these evolving security relationships will be greater strategic stability and an increased reluctance to go to war with similarly armed opponents. Could accidents or war still occur? Most certainly. But are policy makers more cognizant of the great costs and less likely to misperceive the contestability of these costs in such a conflict? Most certainly. It is the difference for American policy makers between attacking a country like Iraq, that is unlikely to be able to retaliate, versus risking a conflict with a nuclear-armed North Korea, unquestionably capable. It is a deterrent to adventurism by great powers and against resort to war between regional neighbors in all but the most-dire circumstances (involving the central interests of both parties).

## THE IMPLICATIONS FOR NEW BIONUCLEAR NONSTATE ACTORS

Unfortunately, the growing potential for nonstate, terror groups to obtain substantial WMD capabilities means that, for the first time in history, such actors will gain destructive abilities comparable to those possessed traditionally only by state actors. This is an immensely destabilizing and undesirable development which drastically decreases the security of all states in the international system, but most especially the security of great powers (like the U.S.). Indeed, for nuclear-armed states like Israel and the U.S., who are fully capable of deterring unprovoked WMD attacks by state actors across practically any realistic threat scenario, the primary consequence of facing bionuclear nonstate actors is to lose the deterrence protection of their arsenals.

Were Al Qaeda or some unnamed future terror group to obtain nuclear or advanced bioweapons and use them against an American or Israeli city, against whom could the overwhelming might of a retaliatory strike be directed? They are called *nonstate* actors for a reason, and it is highly unlikely such a terror group would provide an easily traceable return address for the retaliation. Further, since these groups often operate in countries without the knowledge or cooperation of national authorities, even were an Al Qaeda training camp discovered in the mountains of northern Pakistan, launching a nuclear response onto an ally's territory would not be a viable option. Since such groups are generally unconcerned with issues of political legitimacy, but employ mass-casualty attacks as a form of instrumental violence designed to inflict harm or terror on a given government/population, the use of WMDs would not be thought of in central vs. peripheral interest terms (as with state actors), but only in terms of doing it if possible.

Obviously, for nonstate actors, the increasing accessibility of WMDs dramatically increases their ability to inflict harm upon enemies on a massive scale. It is not a question of "if" such capabilities will come into the hands of terror groups, only a matter of "when"—with the consequence of this being a high probability such weapons will be used to cause the greatest number of civilian casualties possible. This is by far the most serious security threat posed by WMDs to states in the twenty-first century, and the one against which we are the *least prepared* or capable of defending against! If we are to reduce this vulnerability and limit the damage caused by what must be regarded as inevitable future attacks, it requires us to place less emphasis upon WMD threats from *state-based* opponents, and refocus our attention on the far graver threat of *nonstate* WMD adversaries. The nascent moves to focus upon "homeland security" are only a beginning. We must become far more serious in actually delivering meaningful reforms in this area if we are to skirt disaster.

## HOW SHOULD WE PREPARE? WHAT CAN BE DONE?

Existing counterproliferation programs should be embraced and supported with adequate funding. Although imperfect and incapable of completely preventing proliferation of technology, materials, and know-how to state or nonstate actors, they do serve as an effective brake to the pace of such spread. Further, it should be obvious that, to the extent we *can* complicate or make difficult the task of those seeking WMDs, the longer it will take for threats to materialize and the greater the chances political, economic, or military policies might have time to reshape the *motivations* driving proliferators to acquire weapons in the first place. For example, the highly successful, but chronically underfunded, Nunn-Lugar Cooperative Threat Reduction Program demonstrates how valuable counterproliferation programs can be in reducing the spread of materials, technology, and know-how (Nunn-Lugar Cooperative Threat Reduction Program 2004). It has worked to remove unsecured fissile and biological materials from the former Soviet Union, provided security upgrades for existing facilities housing such materials, provided alternative employment for scientists to combat "brain drain," and decommissioned many former weapons facilities themselves. Unfortunately, this program has not been adequately funded by the Bush administration, and actually threatened with funding cuts in recent years, illustrating how far policy makers still have to go in terms of recognizing how to combat WMD threats. Indeed, the entire Nunn-Lugar program is funded at only $2 billion a year, while NMD, defending against the *least likely* WMD threat, receives $10 billion in the most recent Bush administration budgets (Kristof August 2004). In the absence of such counterproliferation programs, or in the presence of only underfunded ones, the opportunity to staunch the flow of WMD-related materials and know-how to state and nonstate actors alike is lost. And, knowledge is the true weapon—and the one against which we have yet to dedicate ourselves properly.

We also need to perform a self-diagnostic, or "reality check," regarding many of our existing counterproliferation policy positions. For example, proliferation pessimists often rail against assisting proliferators in any fashion, especially in terms of improving their command-and-control or arsenal security measures, since this is viewed as "rewarding bad behavior"! This is utterly inconsistent with what must be our *main* concern of preventing unauthorized or accidental use of nuclear or biological weapons! It is counterproductive in the extreme to have such logically inconsistent policy. Bottom line: If it is impossible for the U.S. to change the views of governments in Islamabad, Tel Aviv, or New Delhi to abandon their nuclear weapons, it is nevertheless in our interests to provide them with permissive-action-lock (PAL) technology to prevent unauthorized use by rogue military or terrorist groups who might somehow obtain them. Taking steps to improve command-and-control helps to reduce the chances of miscommunication, misperception, or vulnerability to decapitating attacks that force nations to adopt "launch-on-warning" postures or extreme delegation of launching authority to subordinates. All of these actions reduce crisis instability and improve control and security over arsenals. We need to be less concerned about standing on "principle" and more interested in assuring greater stability and reducing likelihood of use—especially when these states are not going to adopt a nonnuclear posture. U.S. counterproliferation policy should be grounded in reality, not in how we "wish" reality would be—any other position merely increases our own danger and the risks of war.

It is perhaps also time to reevaluate our commitment to the Nuclear Non-Proliferation Treaty (NPT) framework as the centerpiece for counterproliferation efforts. Adopted in 1970, the NPT represented a grand compromise, with the nuclear states promising to move "in good faith" toward disarmament themselves while sharing peaceful uses of nuclear technology with non-weapon states. In return, these states opened themselves to IAEA inspection and foreswore the option of developing nuclear arsenals. In practice, it was the hypocrisy of the agreement, which has been repeatedly violated over the years by both nuclear and nonnuclear states alike, that led a number of the new nuclear lions (Israel, India, and Pakistan) to refuse to sign the NPT and assert their right to possess arsenals. Despite the NPT becoming "permanent" in 1995, it is clear that none of the existing nuclear states, especially the U.S., have *any* intention of eliminating their nuclear arms. Indeed, the Bush administration recently proposed developing a new class of tactical, "bunker-busting" weapons. The NPT has been reduced to a sham agreement—with the nuclear states never intending to hand in their weapons, yet using the treaty to justify attacking or placing sanctions on nonnuclear states who seek to emulate their nuclear capabilities or try to withdraw from the treaty (as is their right). Whatever moral authority the agreement might once have had in its early days has long since faded away. It is yet another example of the "strong do what they will and the weak suffer what they must."

Instead of basing U.S. counterproliferation policy on this hollow document, a far better approach would be to back UN proposals to internationalize the nuclear fuel cycle. In other words, only allow an international body to produce nuclear fuel (whether it be enriched uranium or plutonium), store, and distribute it. The cost might be subsidized or even covered by the international community—a new grand arrangement. The provision of free or cheap nuclear fuel for peaceful uses (power, medical, agricultural, etc.) in return for the absence of enrichment or reprocessing facilities in the states and lack of a military fuel cycle. States refusing to agree to only peaceful nuclear activities would not be allowed to purchase nuclear materials or equipment. Dropped would be the charade of demanding disarmament or nonnuclear status of states, which have proved in practice to be unenforceable by treaty. Obviously, this is not a perfect solution. However, it does address the most critical area for controlling the spread of nuclear capabilities—easy access to fissile materials. The less points of production worldwide, the less availability to state and nonstate actors alike. Coupled with enforcement policies, like the Bush administration's Proliferation Security Initiative (2003), which seeks to obtain multinational agreement to interdict *illegal* shipments of

WMD-related materials around the globe, the resulting counterproliferation policy might actually provide both the requisite carrots and sticks to be successful. Coupled with security guarantees and confidence-building measures, such an approach might reduce the nuclear motivations of states.

In terms of nonstate threats, improvements in U.S. border security and more extensive funding of programs using sensors and other devices to detect smuggled nuclear materials or weapons inside cargo containers, ships, or other vehicles might help to reduce an obvious area of vulnerability. Adequate funding and expansion of existing programs designed to secure fissile materials abroad and reduce "brain drain" would also help reduce the chances of terror groups obtaining the materials or knowledge necessary to manufacture weapons. Yet, despite all of these measures, it will likely prove impossible to completely prevent nonstate actors from sometimes obtaining these capabilities. The key, and the focus of our efforts, should be to take what steps are possible to *increase* the difficulties for groups seeking to successfully obtain materials and/or smuggle them across our borders. Counterproliferation programs, like Nunn-Lugar, which help secure and deny nuclear capabilities to proliferators, along with greater emphasis upon border control and surveillance measures are likely the best defense against nonstate nuclear attacks.

## THE NEED FOR EMPHASIZING BIODEFENSE EFFORTS

Far more difficult will be improving defenses against bioattacks. The reason is simple—the technologies underpinning biowarfare capabilities are generally dual use, widely available, easily concealed, and evolving at a dizzying pace. Unlike nuclear weapons, which require access to rare materials like highly enriched uranium or plutonium, bioweapons can be created using relatively easily acquired materials and equipment—the main limiting factor being relevant biowarfare *knowledge* rather than access to materials. Although states continue to have the advantage over nonstate actors regarding the ease with which bioweapons capabilities could be created (since dual-use facilities, access to trained scientists, and financial resources are more available to states) this represents no substantial hurdle. Indeed, as recent U.S. experiments creating models of clandestine BW facilities illustrate, substantial biowarfare capabilities can be created relatively inexpensively using readily available commercial equipment—all easily within the reach of most sophisticated nonstate actors.

The U.S. needs to place *far greater emphasis and sustained policy commitment toward serious biodefense efforts* than it currently does to reduce its growing vulnerability to attack. Given bioweapons are the easiest WMDs for actors to acquire, grow increasingly so with each passing year, and hold casualty potential on a par with nuclear weapons, it is fair to assume terror group BW use will be the *likeliest* form of WMD attack we will face in the future. For state actors, bioweapons capabilities would likely be held in reserve for dire strategic situations, where they could be used in conjunction with existing nuclear capabilities to provide either a "warning shot" to potential opponents or "augment" existing nuclear retaliatory capabilities. For nonstate actors, however, BW is more likely to serve as a "first-strike" weapon and is more likely to be employed against state targets as soon as an effective capability is developed. It is also the most difficult by far of WMDs to defend against. As the biowarfare discussions in previous chapters made clear, there are a wide range of potential applications of bioweapons against states and immense potential (using genetic engineering and biotechnology) to make more effective bioweapons for use against civilians or agricultural targets. This leaves us with the question: What should we do to reduce our vulnerability?

To begin with, we must be realistic about finding "perfect" defenses against future bioattacks. Bottom line: We will never completely eliminate our vulnerability, especially in the area of biowarfare, where the advantage generally lies with the attacker, who develops novel agents and determines when and where to attack. However, this is not to say *significant defensive measures* cannot be taken to *reduce* our obvious vulnerabilities, make the attacker's task more difficult, and limit the casualties that will result. Unfortunately, most of these proposed solutions are enormously expensive and would require sustained policy effort by political leaders to implement—a factor which explains the dismal current state of U.S. biodefenses. Yet, failing to take action can also be expensive, not only in lives lost, but economically as well. For example, after the anthrax mail attacks of 2001, the U.S. Postal Service was forced to ask Congress for $5 billion in aid—an immediate $2 billion to cover lost revenues and at least $3 billion in costs for cleaning up anthrax contaminated facilities, buying mail-sanitizing equipment, and taking other preventative measures ("Post Office Needs $5 Billion in Aid" 2001). This includes billions of dollars to install electron beam irradiation machinery at all of its more than 300 regional mail centers in order to kill anthrax spores and other pathogens in letters and packages (Feder and Revkin 2001). Similar to the irradiation machines proposed for use in sterilizing foodstuffs, each cost upward of $1 million a piece (Begley "Food Supplies" 2001). But the costs could be far higher. As noted in chapter 4, Kaufmann et al. (1997, 83) warn the economic consequences of a large-scale release of anthrax in a major U.S. city would likely run to $26.2 billion per 100,000 people exposed.

So the issue becomes, will our *rhetorical emphasis* on "homeland security" actually hold substance and result in serious attention to our areas of biovulnerability, or will politicians and the general public accept half-measures due to an unwillingness to spend significant amounts of money addressing a "hypothetical" rather than "demonstrated" security threat? Unfortunately, at present the answer is the latter. And this places the U.S. at immense risk of being caught by surprise by a new 9/11 and being unprepared to prevent (or deal with) threats which were reasonably predictable to analysts cataloging existing trends in proliferation and potential application of bioweapons. Waiting for a "demonstration" of the potential of mass-casualty bioweapons against U.S. citizens is an inexcusable policy approach to take, especially when the warning signs are so clear.

After the September 11th and postal anthrax attacks, homeland security measures were announced with great fanfare: a new department, increased security at airports, reinforced cockpit doors, irradiation machines at post offices, and so forth. All needed improvements and necessary to reduce obvious areas of vulnerability. But, our response was also analogous to the traditional criticism of military strategists, who always *prepare to fight the last war rather than the likely future one*. We responded based upon what had actually been done to us, and failed to seriously address threats not physically "demonstrated" by previous attacks. So, increased security in the passenger airline industry focuses on countering the specific means used by the 9/11 hijackers, and since bombs were not smuggled in nonpassenger-related packages and cargo (also carried aboard civilian airliners), these have still not been subjected to screening and search. The cargo airline industry has been largely ignored by the security upgrades that occurred on the passenger side. We took steps to reduce the vulnerability of the mail system since that was attacked, but failed to take steps required to reduce the vulnerability of other civilian targets or adequately increase our medical facilities to cope with large-scale attacks. We failed to adequately fund biodefense research that might provide better medical defenses against classic or novel bioagent threats. This *must* change. It is essential we begin to think "outside the box," recognize the growing warning signs signaling the increasing danger posed by bioterrorism, and take real and sustained policy actions to address this threat.

## IMPROVING U.S. BIODEFENSES AND PREPAREDNESS

A number of areas need to be addressed to improve U.S. biodefense and preparedness. Firstly, resources need to be directed toward improving existing laboratory and hospital facilities. For example, in 2001, the analysis of the anthrax letter sent to NBC in New York was delayed because of a power failure at the CDC in Atlanta, demonstrating a surprising lack of backup capability at the labs ("Responding to Anthrax Attacks" 2001).[2] But, given the lack of adequate funding provided by Congress to the CDC over the years, which prevented it from expanding its technical capabilities for responding to a large event or replacing deteriorating laboratory facilities, this was hardly surprising. And, while the rapid identification of the anthrax bacterium in the initial Florida case was encouraging, Mohammad Akhtar, executive director of the American Public Health Association, recalling the image of 770 people waiting for hours to be tested for exposure, observed: "What if it had been 50,000 people? . . . Would it have taken days to find out who was infected and provide treatment? This shows a real flaw in the system" ("The First Defence" 2001). Indeed, while the Bush administration proposed distributing more than $1 billion to assist states to improve their defenses against bioattack, this falls far short of the resources needed merely to update the nation's hospitals to meet such threats, estimated by the American Hospital Association at a minimum of $11 billion! (Stolberg 25 January 2002; Freudenheim 2001) There is a serious lack of intensive care units in most U.S. cities, and even those judged adequate under normal situations (say thirty or forty beds) would be quickly overwhelmed in the event of a mass-casualty bioweapon release. Although intensive and heroic medical treatments managed to save several of the 2001 inhalation anthrax patients from death—after weeks or months of care—it is obvious that similar care would be unavailable were thousands of patients to be infected.

Clearly, there is a need to dramatically increase our ability to provide intensive medical care for large numbers of patients exposed to virulent bioagents. Since it is unrealistic, on both a practical and economic level, to expect all American hospitals to develop massive ICU facilities capable of handling thousands or tens of thousands of victims, the solution will have to come from the government. Funding should be provided for development of a national "rapid response" ICU capability that could be deployed to U.S. cities targeted by a bioagent to augment existing medical facilities and cope with the thousands of patients produced by a mass-casualty attack. This will no doubt cost tens of billions of dollars to create and maintain. However, the alternative is to be unable to provide medical treatment to thousands or tens of thousands of American civilians, many of whom will die as a result.

In addition to improving hospital facilities and creating emergency "rapid response" capabilities, resources must also be committed to improving existing laboratory and biodefense-related facilities. The U.S. has taken a good first step toward dealing with this problem through the current construction of a number of additional biosafety level 4, or BSL-4, laboratories around the country (Broad June 2004).[3] These facilities are desperately needed and a useful augment to our only previously existing BSL-4 labs housed at Fort Detrick, Maryland, and the CDC in Atlanta. Although defensive biowarfare research may be viewed with concern by many critics, who correctly note the ambiguous line between offensive and defensive applications of such work, it is nevertheless an essential component to ongoing efforts to reduce our vulnerability to bioattacks, develop effective medical treatments, and design better detection capabilities against potential bioagents (Dasey 1990; Dashiell 1990). Additional labs may make all the difference in treating victims of bioattack by decreasing the time between a release and identification of the pathogen—something which is often critical for patient survival since many treatments are ineffective once victims are symptomatic.

Another area in need of improvement is the level of government support available to the pharmaceutical industry for developing and producing new antibiotics, vaccines, and other treatments to counter biowarfare agents. This is not an area where "market forces" can be relied upon to provide the proper incentives, since there will always be a limited civilian market for vaccines treating unusual pathogens like Ebola or Marburg—and certainly not one that would merit the enormous costs of research and development. Currently, it takes the pharmaceutical industry somewhere between $500 and $800 million, and anywhere from ten to fifteen years, to bring a new drug or vaccine onto the market (Smith, Inglesby, and O'Toole 2003, 197; Smithson and Levy 2000, xviii). Moreover, only 23 percent of all drugs entering clinical trials eventually gain FDA approval (Smith, Inglesby, and O'Toole 2003, 197). Overall funding of U.S. biotechnology and pharmaceutical research reached $40 billion in 2001 (funded by biotech and pharmaceutical companies themselves), $22 billion by the National Institutes of Health in 2002, as well as another $4 billion from other government agencies (Smith, Inglesby, and O'Toole 2003, 195). However, as many analysts observe, the U.S. lags behind in efforts to improve research and production of new vaccines, antiviral drugs, and other biologics needed to improve the effectiveness of any response to a biological attack (cf. Rettig and Brower 2003; Brower and Chalk 2003).

Some initial steps have been taken to address this problem. In 2004, Project Bioshield was established and set aside $5.6 billion over ten years to provide incentives for drug companies to develop new drugs, vaccines, diagnostic devices, and medical treatments for countering potential bioattacks (Lamb 2004). It was meant to spur on the pharmaceutical industry to engage in more research and development of drugs by providing a buyer in advance (the U.S. government) to make it more economically viable. Ideally, Bioshield would speed up procurement of drugs from companies by allowing them to be purchased (and used) prior to their gaining approval by the FDA and provide some protection (though not enough according to the drug industry) against liability from adverse reactions in those receiving the new drugs (Barbaro 2004).

Unfortunately, at present funding levels, Bioshield will never provide enough resources or guarantees to motivate the pharmaceutical industry to engage in the kind of R&D necessary to develop the wide range of drugs required to address the bioterror threat, nor will enough vaccines and antibiotics be purchased by the government to adequately prepare for an attack. For example, the Strategic National Stockpile is the repository of supplies for bioterrorism incidents (e.g., antibiotics, chemical antidotes, surgical items, respirators, and other medical supplies) which was put under the control of the Department of Homeland Security in 2002. That the stockpile needs to be better funded and supplied is obvious. In 2000, the Defense Science Board concluded there were fifty-seven countermeasures needed to protect the American public from known biothreats with only one being currently available. By 2004, only two were available—the anthrax and smallpox vaccines—and even these are useful only against unmodified agents (Lamb 2004). Given the development of new vaccines or antibiotics take between ten and fifteen years, and cost perhaps $500 to $800 million apiece, it is plain Bioshield—though well conceived—will remain seriously underfunded at current levels and fail to produce an ability to rapidly ramp up U.S. vaccine production in the face of any new biological threat (Brower and Chalk 2003, 98).

And, while the Bush administration called for stockpiling drugs to protect the civilian population against bioterror attacks in 2002, by late 2004 only enough anthrax vaccine had been set aside for civilian use to vaccinate 530 people. This compared to the million doses of vaccine, enough for more than 330,000 people, stockpiled by the Pentagon for military personnel (Miller 2004). Of course, even if *all* of this stockpile were instantly available and somehow immediately transported to the location of a major bioterrorist release of anthrax (an unlikely sequence of events), were the attack a large-scale one using a line-source delivery of high-quality agent against a sizable city, millions of people could potentially be infected and the entire stockpile would fall far short of what was needed to respond to the crisis. Far greater effort needs to be put into developing these defensive medical stockpiles that could be used with the earlier proposed rapid response ICU capability.

Another step that has been taken by the government has been the creation of a large stockpile of smallpox vaccine (up to 300 million doses by the end of 2002) (Stolberg October 2001), which is argued to serve not only a preventative, but a deterrence function (Ewald 2001). In other words, the more the potential costs of a smallpox attack are reduced through the existence of a vaccine stockpile or vaccinated population, the lower the benefit of initiating such an attack in the first place for the attacker. However, many biowarfare experts question the value of the vaccine approach as a safeguard against BW, since opponents who become aware of a vaccination program may well counter these defensive moves by switching to a different pathogen or genetically altering an existing one (Broad 15 June 1999). As former U.S. bioweaponeer Bill Patrick observed, "it takes 18 months to develop a weapons-grade agent and 10 more years to develop a good vaccine against it" (Broad and Miller 1998). This is yet another reason for engaging in robust biodefense research that works to improve detection and identification of pathogens (even novel ones) and seeks medical defenses or treatments against them. Maintaining an adequate strategic national stockpile of antibiotics, antivirals, and vaccines is important, but equally important is the coupling of such measures with well-funded defensive BW research. As Alibek observes:

> We need to keep in mind that for some time, we will still be dealing with natural strains. Not genetically engineered strains. If we see situations where biological terrorism is worse in the future, then we will start dealing with genetically engineered strains. But, at the same time, our strategy has to develop how to protect against natural strains. We need to invite all possible ways, including development of vaccines. . . . Antibiotics for bacterial agents, but it is absolutely important to understand that our immune system is a major protector and we need to find ways of how to stimulate, how to boost, how to stimulate a persistent response against specific pathogens. And protect against general spectrum of pathogens. It would be a solution for the future.

Dr. D. A. Henderson has suggested at least three areas of BW research and development are important for improving our preparedness: "(1) More definitive, rapid, automated means of diagnosing major pathogens, basically building microchips that could identify specific pathogens by deciphering the molecular genomes; (2) Mechanisms for being able to rapidly develop and produce new antibiotics and antiviral drugs for new and emergent diseases; (3) Mechanisms for enhancing the immune response generally, so as to get beyond the one organism–one drug approach" (U.S. Congress *Testimony of Donald A. Henderson* 2001). However, these steps will require greater levels of effort to carry out.

For example, high-tech detectors for use in public places need a great deal of further development and funding to be practical. Indeed, of the four current types of detection technology that could be employed versus anthrax (DNA-based detectors, mass spectrometry, antibody-based tests, and the "dog's nose" project) all have significant weaknesses (Begley and Isikoff 2001, 35). Though DNA-based detectors can identify virulent strains of anthrax by their DNA in as little as thirty minutes, they are not yet capable of continuously monitoring the air (something at least five years away at best), thereby limiting their utility as sentinels in public places. Mass spectrometry machines isolate submicroscopic samples and could spot anthrax's molecular profile, but the technology has not yet been successfully adapted to this task and would likely require years of work to do so. Antibody-based tests, utilizing strips of treated paper that change color upon contact with spores, is currently available and inexpensive, but far less sensitive than other methods. Finally, the "dog's nose" project uses synthetic compounds that instantly glow upon contact with distinctive particles in the air, but so far, this technique is used only to detect traces of TNT and would take at least five years to adapt for anthrax or other bioagents (Begley and Isikoff 2001, 35).

In terms of developing new treatments, it is important to remember that just as advances in biotechnology and genetic engineering provide means for enhancing bioweapons and making them more lethal, they also hold the potential for providing more effective drugs and treatments against such bioagents. For example, recent research has suggested the possibility of employing enzymes from bacterium-killing viruses to counter antibiotic-resistant strains of anthrax, since these enzymes work by destroying the bacterial cell wall (thereby killing the bacteria) and work by a different process than antibiotics (Rosovitz and Leppla 2002). Indeed, research by Schuch et al. (2002) into these bacteriophage enzymes, called lysins, suggests they could be used to treat anthrax in people and detect it in the environment—regardless of whether it is a wild-type or antibiotic-resistant strain. Further, they note "because the catalytic and binding targets of lysins are largely essential for viability, lysine resistance should be rare" and anthrax bacillus are unlikely to be easily modified to prevent lysine action (Schuch, Nelson, and Fischetti 2002). However, even enzyme therapy would have to be given to victims before the anthrax infections had proceeded to the point where lethal levels of toxin were present in their systems. These enzymes may one day be employed to create highly sensitive detection devices to pick up an anthrax release around urban targets, or as a deployable field test to quickly reveal the presence of bacterial spores in the environment (Rosovitz and Leppla 2002, 826).

Similarly, extremely promising work has been conducted by Riemenschneider et al. (2003), who tested a combined DNA vaccine for anthrax, Ebola, Marburg, and VEE in guinea pigs, that produced an immune response in laboratory animals *equally effective* as provided by individual vaccines. Such defensive research opens up a wide range of possibilities for prevaccination of military personnel or populations who might potentially become exposed to one or more bioagents.[4] More futuristic efforts might be to develop aerosol-based vaccines (which were commonly employed by the Soviets) to not only vaccinate individuals, but also to potentially respond to BW attacks against people or livestock with a cloud of vaccine sprayed over many square miles of infected territory (Miller, Engelberg, and Broad 2001). In the event of a mass-casualty attack over large geographical areas, such aerosol delivery of combined DNA vaccines might prove an effective weapon in the defensive bioarsenal.

Another possible measure to reduce the vulnerability of the population to *novel* BW agents involves developing means of boosting the "passive antibody" or "immediate immunity" of people by administering specific antibodies, either intravenously or intramuscularly (Casadevall 2002). Indeed, as Casadevall (2002, 836) notes, "an antibody-based defense strategy against biological warfare agents can be supported by a mature technology" given that:

[S]pecific antibody can be effective against some of the major biological warfare agents. In fact, antibody preparations in the form of serum therapy were used historically for the treatment of anthrax, tularemia, and plague . . . The major advantage of passive antibody immunization in defense against biological weapons is that it provides a state of immediate immunity that can last for weeks and possibly months. . . . Antibodies are natural products with minimal toxicity . . . If vaccines are available, simultaneous administration of vaccine and antibody may be possible to provide both immediate and long-lasting protection, as is done for rabies in postexposure prophylaxis. . . . With the exception of rabies antiserum, most antibody preparations in clinical use are given intravenously. The need for intravenous administration is a severe constraint for mass passive immunization and would likely limit this practice to a few recipients. However, this disadvantage may potentially be circumvented because Ig preparations can theoretically be administered intramuscularly.

Development of gene-based vaccines and techniques for identifying the composition of new microbes (even designer pathogens previously unknown to medical science) could also assist our efforts to develop effective drugs or vaccines against such agents much more rapidly than in the past (Miller, Engelberg, and Broad 2001). And, as Casadevall (2002, 838) notes, antibody therapies show particular promise:

Stockpiling antibody-based reagents that can be rapidly administered to exposed populations would substantially reduce the threat of many biological agents by providing a means of conferring immediate immunity to susceptible persons. For persistent threats for which vaccines are available, this measure would provide additional time for immunization, as well as reducing the threat. Development of antibody-based therapies may reduce the attractiveness of biological warfare as a weapon of terror by providing antidotes to help neutralize the threat. An aggressor could attempt to defeat a passive antibody defense by engineering the agent to express antigenic changes, proteases, or antibody-binding proteins. However, in this arms race the advantage may favor the defender, since it is technologically easier to generate a new antibody effective against the changed agent than to engineer a pathogen or agent to enhance virulence.

In addition, experienced bioweaponeers have long argued that building up *nonspecific immunity* in people would be a critical first step toward improving our biodefenses.[5] Unlike "specific immunity" (as produced against influenza by a flu shot), "nonspecific immunity" boosts the entire immune system to resist foreign invaders. As a result, when faced with modified, genetically engineered pathogens or novel bioagents, against whom existing antibiotics, vaccines, or antivirals may have little affect, techniques for boosting the nonspecific immune response in people could provide the only immediate or viable medical treatment available. It is also an area of medical research for which increased government funding would not only produce greater protections against bioagents, but in peacetime also improve our response to infectious diseases in the population as a whole.

This is an important point, especially given the need to justify substantial increases in biodefense spending to skeptical politicians or the general public. Unlike many areas of defense policy, defensive bioresearch is "dual use" and can be highly beneficial to society even in peacetime. For example, the worldwide problem of increasing antibiotic resistance has resulted in many previously treatable diseases (like malaria, tuberculosis, or staph infections) becoming difficult (if not impossible) to cure. The global pandemic threat posed by the avian influenza, which if unleashed could kill tens or hundreds of million people, or the emergence of new infectious diseases (like SARS and AIDS) greatly imperil public health. And yet, there are few effective antiviral drugs in existence for use in the treatment of viruses and limited resources to develop more. All of which results in greater levels of illness, suffering, and mortality worldwide.

To truly address our growing vulnerability to attack by bioweapons (including genetically engineered or novel ones), the government must undertake massive R&D funding to scientists and pharmaceutical manufacturers to develop viable treatments. Given the public health issues at stake, even in the absence of considerations about the bioterrorist threat, a "Marshall Plan" for biomedical R&D should be adopted. Initial funding for research efforts to produce new classes of antibiotics and antivirals, new and more effective vaccines, and techniques for enhancing both specific and nonspecific immunity in individuals should at a minimum approach the annual funding provided to combat one of the *least likely* security threats facing the nation—missile defense. Given the far-reaching benefits that would accrue to both society as a whole, and our biopreparedness efforts in particular, from such directed medical R&D spending, one could easily argue the eventual levels of spending should double or triple the amounts currently spent on missile defense.

Less expensive or grandiose measures that could also be adopted involve assisting in the financing (or merely requiring) businesses or public facilities to institute simple countermeasures. For example, a highly effective means of reducing the vulnerability of office buildings to bioattack is to attach high-efficiency particulate air filters (called HEPA) to ventilation systems. These filters are five to ten times as expensive as normal filters and require more powerful air circulation systems, but do remove 99.97 percent of airborne particles down to at least five microns in size in a single pass, greatly reducing the threat posed by bioagents. Unfortunately, due to their cost and system requirements, they are currently used on few buildings and most facilities ignore long-standing recommendations they keep the air pressure in office buildings at a slightly higher pressure than the outdoors and carefully monitor all intake vents to prevent unauthorized access to the ventilation system (Glanz and Rosenbaum 2001). However, while these steps reduce a site's vulnerability to attack, it doesn't completely eliminate it, as was illustrated by a 1997 experiment in which a quarter-cup of spore-filled aerosol was sprayed into the air-conditioner return vent of a large, convention-hall type building, an attack which, had it been conducted with real anthrax, would have within hours been capable of infecting thousands of occupants with inhalation anthrax (Begley "Skyscrapers" 2001, 36). Additional measures, such as the use of UV lighting in such buildings, could be used to augment enhanced air filtration systems. For example, research has shown that UV germicidal irradiation of upper-room air in buildings reduced *B. subtilis* spore concentrations by 46 to 80 percent, which suggests similar techniques might be modified to combat the spread of anthrax or other pathogenic agents if distributed in office buildings or other enclosed areas. (Fennelly et al. 2004, 998).[6]

Further, national and local authorities need to engage in greater planning regarding the logistics and legal issues surrounding the use of another traditional and highly effective means of containing contagious disease outbreaks—quarantines. Indeed, in the event of the release of a highly contagious pathogen, such as smallpox or plague, among the public, quarantine of individuals or entire cities and regions might prove the only effective means of preventing catastrophe. In an excellent overview of the many challenges facing authorities in imposing effective quarantines in the event of a large-scale BW attack, Barbera et al. (2001) note that in most recent BW simulations, participants quickly moved to invoke quarantines only to discover the lack of clear planning to implement such measures, murky jurisdictional issues, and a likelihood the moves would fail because of it. This is hardly surprising since there have been no large-scale human quarantines implemented in the U.S. in eight decades! (Barbera et al. 2001, 2712–13) Nevertheless, with time being so critical in the event of such an outbreak, there will be no time to "think things through on the fly" for government officials. Either the quarantine can be swiftly and effectively implemented, or it will fail—it is as simple as that.


## IMPROVING HOMELAND SECURITY

The task of upgrading domestic homeland security to reduce America's vulnerability to clandestine attacks (whether nuclear or biological) is a daunting one. Facing actors unlikely to attack using ICBMs that could possibly be intercepted (or traced back to their points of origin), the U.S. must come to grips with the likelihood that any attack on American cities would probably arrive by more inventive means.

For example, short- or medium-range missiles could be launched from platforms concealed on freighters or from launchers hidden among the 250 million ubiquitous shipping containers circling the globe daily (Easterbrook 2004, 1). Modified land-attack cruise missiles could be launched from surface ships or aircraft to strike deep into U.S. territory. Were these launched close to shore, even short-range systems could effectively target many of America's largest coastal cities with very little warning time or likelihood of detection. Weapons smuggled into neighboring countries sharing long land borders could also allow short-range delivery systems (hidden within cargo containers delivered inland) to be employed. On the other hand, nuclear weapons concealed inside cargo containers aboard ships or placed within the holds of large aircraft could be detonated in the harbors or above U.S. cities with no warning or chance of interception by customs officials. In fact, the CIA has concluded it is far more likely for a nuclear or biological weapon to arrive in the U.S. via shipping container than onboard missiles (Easterbrook 2004, 4). Materials for nuclear or biological weapons could be smuggled relatively easily into the U.S. for use by agents or terrorists against a wide variety of domestic soft targets. For planners seeking to reduce American vulnerability to "nonconventional" threats, the task is not only immense, but too little has been done in practice by the U.S. government to increase security through the allocation of funds nor by devoting prolonged attention to the problem.[7]

Indeed, the vast scale of the challenge is well illustrated by a brief review of a number of the logistical challenges awaiting planners attempting to close off some of the potential avenues of attack. For example, the problem of adequately monitoring America's borders, especially its seaports and coastline, is complicated by the fact the U.S. has 95,000 miles of coastline, more than a hundred seaports capable of handling the largest of container ships, and annually receives over 60,000 port calls by oceangoing ships unloading around 7 million cargo containers (Langewiesche 2003, 73–74; Shenon 2003). The U.S. Customs Service reports over 500 ships carrying 600,000 cargo containers enter one of the nation's 361 seaports daily, of which Customs inspects barely 2 percent (and often not until they reach their final destinations). And, while international trade has doubled since 1995, the number of Customs inspectors has remained constant, despite the fact seaports handle 95 percent of the cargo entering the U.S. from locations other than Canada and Mexico (Kilborn 2001). Along the 4,000-mile northern border with Canada, 6.5 million commercial trucks enter the U.S. annually, the vast majority of which go uninspected to any significant degree (Brinkley 2002).

Not only does the U.S. Coast Guard patrol 95,000 miles of shoreline, plus 3.36 million square miles of the U.S. "Exclusive Economic Zone" (that extends 200 miles offshore), they also do so with a fleet of antiquated ships and aircraft using a workforce the same size as the New York City Police Department (Flynn 2004, 39). And despite efforts, such as the $500 million spent since September 11th to improve security at seaports, Flynn (2004, 38) warns this is inadequate compared to the magnitude of the task:

> In 2002 alone, more than 400 million people, 122 million cars, 11 million trucks, 2.4 million rail freight cars, approximately 8 million maritime containers and 56,596 vessels entered the U.S. at more than 3,700 terminals and 301 ports of entry. In general, frontline agents have only a matter of seconds to make a go/no-go decision on whether to allow entry: 30 seconds for people and one minute for vehicles. And then there are the 7,000 miles of land borders and 95,000 miles of shoreline, which provide ample opportunities to walk, swim or sail into the nation. Official estimates place the number of illegal migrants living in America at 7 million.

At the moment, U.S. customs inspectors divide shipping containers into those coming from "trusted" sources (i.e., an importer or consolidator with no history of smuggling or other legal violations) and "untrusted" (i.e., shipments coming from unknown importers or regions deemed high risk) (Flynn 2004, 40). As Flynn (2004, 40) warns, "in the post-9/11 world, we should assume that bad guys will target a trusted box first." Moreover, the problems of controlling what is transported in shipping containers, or the ability to even ascertain the original points of origin of their contents, are extremely challenging. As research by Flynn (2004, 39–40) reveals:

> Port terminal operators have no way of confirming whether what is advertised as the contents of a box is what is actually there. The measure of a commercial

port's success, after all, is its ability to move cargo in and out of its turf as quickly as possible. . . . Anyone can lease one of the many millions of containers that circulate around the globe, then pack it with up to 65,000 lbs. of items, close the door and lock it with a seal that costs half a dollar. The box then enters the transportation system, with all the providers working diligently to get it where it needs to go as quickly as possible. Accompanying documents usually describe the contents in general terms. If the box moves through intermediate ports before it enters the U.S., the container manifest typically indicates only the details known to the final transportation carrier. . . . If a container is destined for a city inside the U.S., only in exceptional circumstances would it be inspected at the arrival port. On average, overseas containers will pass through 17 intermediate points before they arrive at their final U.S. destination, and often their contents come from several locations before they are even loaded into the box. Nearly 40% of all containers shipped to the U.S. are the maritime-transportation equivalent of the back of a UPS van. Intermediaries known as consolidators gather together goods or packages from a variety of customers or even other intermediaries and load them all into the container. They know only what their customers tell them about what they are shipping.

And, though the U.S. has put in place inspectors at major overseas ports, the simple reality is there are limits to how secure shipping can ever be made to be—regardless of the technology employed or the number of inspectors abroad (Easterbook 2004, 4). In fact, at present Flynn (2004, 40) estimates with current targeting and inspection practices, the odds are only about 10 percent that U.S. Customs would detect a nuclear device similar to a Russian nuclear warhead surrounded by shielding material. Boosting the probability of detection into the 90 percent range is possible, but costly:

> By using a mix of sensors and more vigorous monitoring, we could push the probability of detection into the 90% range. The cost of installing cargo-scanning equipment in all the world's marine container terminals would be $500 million to $600 million, or about the cost of four new F-22 fighters. A container outfitted with sensors and tracking equipment, and certified at its origin, would run approximately $50 per shipment or add 1.5% to the average overseas shipping cost.

In terms of the food supply, of the 3.7 million shipments of imported food arriving into the U.S. each year, only 1 percent are inspected by the U.S. Food and Drug Administration (FDA), a miniscule number of inspections similar to the percentage imposed on domestically produced or processed foods! (Begley "Food Supplies" 38–40) As noted by Caroline Smith DeWaal, head of food safety at the Center for Science in the Public Interest, "almost anyone can go into business, start producing food and ship it around the country with no federal oversight." While the processing undergone by many foodstuffs would render introduced pathogens harmless (such as sterilization of canned goods or the pasteurization of milk), were terrorists able to introduce agents into foodstuffs after the final processing step (where there are minimal inspections or safeguards), a potentially serious BW attack could be staged (Begley "Food Supplies" 39). Of course, adequately expanding inspectors for food imports, just as for border security, would be extremely costly.

Other areas of potential vulnerability would also be expensive to address. For example, the American airline industry boards 1.5 million passengers a day, a fraction of the 3.8 million passengers a day (boarding at 468 stations) who ride the New York subway system (Easterbrook 2004, 1). Noting at least $11 billion has been spent on improving airline security since September 11th, Easterbrook suggests adding comparable screening to the New York subway system might cost twice that amount. Of course, the potential economic costs of *failing* to prevent terrorist attacks using WMDs could also spiral into immense figures! For example, it has been estimated the economic costs associated with the September 11th attacks of just cleaning up lower Manhattan alone added up to $40 billion (plus the loss of economic activity for all the businesses involved) (Warrick 2004; Flynn 2004, 25). How much more expensive a mass-casualty nuclear or biological attack on a major U.S. city would be is difficult to assess—however, it seems safe to say such an event would quite easily dwarf the costs of the 9/11-related terrorism by many orders of magnitude.

Moreover, the threat is not limited to materials clandestinely smuggled into the U.S., since a number of domestic targets provide ample materials for would-be terrorists to exploit. Many chemical agents, for instance, are widely available due to their industrial uses (such as cyanide, chlorine, etc.) and could easily be employed by terrorists to produce mass-casualty attacks. Using a tanker filled with chlorine or cyanide gas in a downtown area avoids the problem terrorists face in seeking to weaponize more exotic BW agents, since toxic chemicals are already weaponized. As a 1999 federal study of dozens of facilities producing industrial chemicals notes, security ranged "from fair to very poor" at potentially dangerous facilities producing or handling flammable liquid pesticides, liquefied petroleum gases, chlorine, cyanide compounds, various acids, and butadiene (among other substances) (Begley "Chemical Plants" 2001, 33).

For example, each of the nearly 15,000 facilities producing toxic chemicals have long been required to file a report with the U.S. Environmental Protection Agency (EPA) specifying "worst-case scenarios" involving the release of the hazardous materials housed at their locations. The contents of these reports (removed from public view after the 9/11 attacks) illustrate the potential danger, with more than 2,000 facilities reporting a release of their agents could affect upwards of 100,000 people and hundreds of sites reporting the likelihood of a toxic cloud spreading up to fourteen miles from their plants (Begley "Chemical Plants" 2001, 33). In addition, there are more than 260,000 miles of natural gas pipelines and hundreds of pumping stations in the U.S., all of which are potential targets for terrorists (Johnston 2001). When one adds the number of pipelines that also carry hazardous liquids (in addition to natural gas), over 489,862 miles of pipelines snake across the U.S. (many running through populated areas). As Joe Caldwell, who originally set up the Office of Pipeline Safety (OPS) at the Department of Transportation in 1970 observes, a terrorist attack on a pipeline would be "a piece of cake," since the lines usually are only three or four feet beneath the surface (Begley "Chemical Plants" 2001, 33). And, as a recent Pentagon report noted, railroad tank cars and tanker trucks carrying toxic industrial chemicals "are moving targets of opportunity" (*Chemical and Biological Defense Primer*, 6).

Indeed, an analysis by the EPA warns at least 123 plants in the U.S. contain amounts of toxic chemical that would put 1 million people at risk if released in a catastrophic accident (Grimaldi and Gugliotta 2001; Pianin 2002). Another 700 plants could threaten 100,000 nearby residents, and more than 3,000 facilities pose a serious risk to at least 10,000 people in the surrounding area. Among the worst threats reported was a suburban California chemical plant which routinely loads ninety-ton railroad cars with chlorine, which if released would poison more than 4 million people in the surrounding Orange and Los Angeles counties. The 400,000 pounds of hydrogen fluoride at a Philadelphia refinery could asphyxiate up to 4 million nearby residents, and the release of a South Kearny, New Jersey, chemical company's 180,000 pounds of chlorine or sulfur dioxide could threaten nearly 12 million people. The Atofina Chemicals Inc. plant in Detroit would threaten up to 3 million people if one of its ninety-ton rail cars of chlorine were ruptured, and the Union Carbide Corp. factory near Charleston, West Virginia, could release a cloud of 200,000 pounds of methyl isocyanate (the same as was released in Bhopal, India) over around 60,000 local residents (Grimaldi and Gugliotta 2001). In fact, the deadly release of methyl isocyanate from the Union Carbide plant in Bhopal, India, in December 1984 was caused by a disgruntled employee (who merely added water to a storage tank) resulting in an explosion which killed nearly 4,000 and left around 11,000 with long-term disabilities (Stern 1999, 20).

More disturbing, of these 15,000 refineries, chemical plants, and other facilities storing hazardous materials that could place so many citizens at risk in the event of an accidental (or intentional) release of their contents—there exist only extremely limited federal security requirements. As Flynn (2004, 41) observes:

Basic measures such as posting warning signs and fencing, controlling access and maintaining 24-hour surveillance are required for only 21% of the 15,000 sites that store large quantities of hazardous materials. Chemical rail cars routinely sit parked for extended periods near residential areas or are shipped through the heart of urban centers. Each week shipments of such substances as deadly chloride are carried on slow-moving trains that pass within a few hundred yards of Capitol Hill in Washington. Chemical barges that move up and down America's inland waterways are unmonitored.

Obviously, while the focus of this book is upon nuclear and biological threats to U.S. security, the above discussion of the magnitude of the security challenges facing those seeking to reduce our current vulnerabilities to attack should illustrate we have a long way to go! At the same time, the logistical problems associated with our porous borders, and the difficulties we face in protecting "soft" transportation or industrial targets, all demonstrate areas of vulnerability "adaptive enemies" could exploit to use nuclear or biological weapons against us. And, it is another area where real political attention and resources should be applied.

## CONCLUSION

At the beginning of this book, it was suggested that nuclear and biological weapons proliferation had the potential to radically alter age-old security relationships between states, providing modern-day Melians with the means to deter the aggression of present day Athenians—of "lambs" being turned into "lions." Subsequent discussions introduced the current dynamics of this proliferation process, with technology and know-how spreading ever outward, like ripples on a pond, fundamentally transforming the surface of our existing security relationships. Across both state and nonstate actors, I have sought to illustrate the likely direction (or trajectory) of these changing capabilities and relationships, not only from the perspective of great powers, but from those of their potential small-power opponents as well. We explored the possible opportunities and constraints posed for these actors across varying security contexts and capability levels—illustrating across several chapters how the spread of advanced technologies and know-how, coupled with breakthroughs in biotechnology and genetic engineering, have led to unparalleled opportunities for small state and nonstate actors. And for the U.S., the reality which dawns at the beginning of the twenty-first century is that it will have to face redrawn security relationships with other states, ones which have the potential to seriously constrain American power and freedom of action abroad. Further, it will increasingly face unconventional threats from nonstate actors who

fall outside of the logic of deterrence theory, actors who better reflect the nuclear pessimist view of the impact of proliferation upon security and stability.

Unfortunately, whether we like it or not, this altered security environment is
largely unavoidable. It has become inevitable that state and nonstate actors
alike will eventually be able to obtain the technical capability to acquire
WMDs over time, regardless of counterproliferation efforts to prevent it. Indeed, the determining factor has become the actors' *motivation* to acquire
WMDs, rather than any limits which their industrial and technical development or the counterproliferation regime might pose. Especially in the realm of
bioweapons, which involve dual-use, widely available technology and know-
how, control efforts are doomed to failure. The new rule of thumb is simply
this: *A determined actor will be able to acquire WMDs if motivated to do so.*

Although this book has taken a decidedly theoretical and scholarly approach to the problem, it has also sought to maintain a *practical* edge, geared
toward providing realistic assessments of what is possible, while at the same
time integrating existing security theories into analytic frameworks to assist
practitioners and scholars alike in assessing these evolving nuclear and biological security relationships (see chapters 2 and 4). As a result, the practical
policy implications—to both the new proliferators and countries like the
U.S.—have been explored and discussed in-depth. Yet, at the same time, I
have sought to avoid taking a strongly normative or ethnocentric stance—at
least regarding the theoretical and substantive discussions of nuclear or biological weapons capabilities and their potential impact upon security—leaving it to the reader's own judgment as to whether these changes represent a
positive or negative development. To a great extent, this depends upon one's
viewpoint: Do you identify with the Melians or the Athenians?

In fact, the debates of proliferation pessimists and optimists aside, theory-
building efforts regarding the likely impact of these changing security relationships, and whether or not deterrence will work, must be considered to be
at an early stage in the security literature. How these new security relationships actually shape out, and whether or not they truly induce more stability
in cases where the central interests of states collide, will serve to better inform
our theories of deterrence and proliferation. There is obviously substantial
disagreement in the security field about the affects of proliferation upon deterrence and stability. Now we will observe in the "living laboratory" the truth
of the matter. We have not set up the experiment, we merely observe it. And
in the end, it may help us to rectify a common problem for security scholars
in this area—the problem of the "small-n" in our research.

Obviously, across the chapters in this book, and throughout the analytical
frameworks presented, it is clearly this author's assessment that (on the

whole) stability will be enhanced. At the same time, however, the analytical frameworks also point out areas where my model suggests pessimists are right as well, especially in the period of *nascent* WMD capabilities for states. Clearly, the theoretical frameworks presented in this book argue strongly for adoption of a *contingency* approach for studying these security relationships, one cognizant of the fact that both nuclear pessimist and optimist arguments may be correct, but only under certain contexts. It is hoped this work may serve as a bridge to begin the process of integrating the valuable research done by both camps of proliferation scholars.

At the same time, it should *not* be assumed by the reader that these changing security relationships represent the author's own personal views of what is desirable—especially from the standpoint of U.S. national security or foreign policy interests. Far from it. However, the best way to improve policy and reduce vulnerabilities to existing threats is to realistically appraise them—regardless of whether or not they conform to how we "wish" the world to be. Moreover, it is *absolutely critical* U.S. policy makers accurately comprehend the nature of these evolving, rapidly changing power relationships in the international system and how they will serve to constrain existing and future foreign policy. We must be realistic about what we can legitimately expect from counterproliferation efforts (whether centered around control regime efforts or preemptive military options). Otherwise, we may embark upon ill-advised policies that do not advance our national interests, due purely to miscalculations about what could realistically be accomplished by the policy. Policy makers need to be clear-eyed about the nature of the threat posed by nonstate actors employing nuclear or (more critically) biological weapons against U.S. interests or domestic targets. The only defense to this building threat is adequate preparation and attention to measures that reduce our vulnerability and limit the damage resulting from attacks.

In the final chapter, recommendations were made for addressing the vulnerabilities that exist for the U.S. in a world in which state and nonstate actors have at their disposal nuclear and biological weapons capabilities. That a perfect solution, or "silver bullet" is not produced may disappoint the reader, but it is a reflection of the true nature of the security problem we face. There are no perfect solutions, nor are there means for attaining perfect security from these threats. Our main defense against these threats is a realistic understanding of what they entail and what steps may be possible to avoid the worst outcomes. It is in this spirit that the policy recommendations in the last chapter are presented. It is by no means a comprehensive listing. However, it is hoped this book will contribute to a heightened awareness, across both the scholarly and practitioner communities, regarding the nature of current trends in nuclear and biological proliferation and how these may translate into dramatically altered security relationships. Ones which pose serious challenges to both theory and practical policy design alike. For great powers (like the U.S.), the inescapable reality of the new millennium will be one in which they face a drastically altered security environment. An environment which, over the decades to come, will increasingly provoke the realization that the "rules of the game" have been changed. That some of these small state and nonstate actors, Melians all, have undergone a transformation "from Lambs to Lions."

## NOTES

1. No doubt American policy makers' views of confrontational policies with the North would more resemble those of Seoul were the DMZ located thirty kilometers north of Washington D.C. in Maryland instead of on the Korean peninsula.

2. See also Altman October 2001 and Altman November 2001.

3. This move has been criticized by some as potentially expanding the number of people who could turn their knowledge to terror (given the possibility someone in the U.S. BW defensive program might have been behind the 2001 postal attacks) and increasing the chances dangerous pathogens might leak out (either accidentally or intentionally).

4. The first experimental vaccine that shows promise against Ebola was tested in 2005, yet another example of potentially valuable biodefense research.

5. Author interview with Ken Alibek.

6. See also Peng et al 2003, 405–19.

7. See, for example, Falkenrath, Newman, and Thayer 1998 and the series of reports U.S. Commission on National Security 1999, 2000, and 2001, also known as the Hart/Rudman Commission. In fact, the U.S. spends more every three days to finance the war in Iraq than it has over the preceding three years to improve security at U.S. seaports, and the fiscal year 2005 budget provides $7.6 billion to the Pentagon to improve security at military bases, but only $2.6 billion to the Department of Homeland Security to protect vital domestic systems. Flynn 2004, 22–23.

# References

Abelson, R. P. and A. Levi. "Decision-making and Decision Theory," Pp. 231–310 in *Handbook of Social Psychology*, edited by G. Lindzey and E. Aronson. New York: Random House, 1985.

Achen, Christopher H. and Duncan Snidal. "Rational Deterrence Theory and Comparative Case Studies." *World Politics* 41 (1989): 143–69.

Adams, Karen Ruth. "Attack and Conquer?: International Anarchy and the Offense-Defense-Deterrence Balance." *International Security* 28, no. 3 (Winter 2003/2004): 45–83.

Ahmed, Samina. "Pakistan's Nuclear Weapons Program: Turning Points and Nuclear Choices." *International Security* 23, no. 4 (Spring 1999): 178–204.

Albright, David. *South Africa's Secret Nuclear Weapons*. Washington, D.C.: Institute for Science and International Security, May 1994.

———. "The Shots Heard 'Round the World': India Conducted Three Nuclear Tests on May 11 and Two on May 13." *The Bulletin of the Atomic Scientists* 54, no.4 (July/August 1998): 20–25.

Albright, David and Mark Hibbs. "Iraq's Quest for the Nuclear Grail: What Can We Learn?" *Arms Control Today* (July/August 1992): 3–11.

Albright, David and Corey Hinderstein. "Iran: Furor over Fuel." *The Bulletin of the Atomic Scientists* 59, no. 3 (May/June 2003): 12–15.

———. "Iran, Player or Rogue?" *The Bulletin of the Atomic Scientists* 59, no. 5 (September/October 2003): 52–58.

———. "The Centrifuge Connection." *The Bulletin of the Atomic Scientists* 60, no.2 (March/April 2004): 61–66.

Albright, David, Frans Berkhout, and William Walker. *Plutonium and Highly Enriched Uranium 1996: World Inventories, Capabilities, and Policies*. Oxford: Oxford University Press for Stockholm International Peace Research Institute, 1997.

Alibek, Kenneth. "Russia's Deadly Expertise," *New York Times*, 27 March 1998, A19.

————. "Biological Weapons in the Former Soviet Union: An Interview with Dr. Kenneth Alibek." *The Nonproliferation Review* 6, no. 3 (Spring/Summer 1999): 1–10.

Alibek, Kenneth, with Stephen Handelman. *Biohazard*. New York: Random House, 1999.

Altman, Lawrence K., M.D. "C.D.C. Team Tackles Anthrax: Praise and Criticism for Agency's Response," *New York Times*, 16 October 2001, D1 and D7.

————. "When Everything Changed at the C.D.C.," *New York Times*, 13 November 2001, D1 and D4.

————. "New Tests Confirm Potency of Anthrax in Senate Office," *New York Times*, 11 December 2001, B6.

————. "C.D.C. Issues Challenge to Nation's Scientists to Find the Answers to Anthrax Mysteries," *New York Times*, 12 December 2001, B10.

Alvarez, Robert. "North Korea: No Bygones at Yongbyon." *The Bulletin of the Atomic Scientists* 59, no. 4 (July/August 2003): 38–45.

Archibold, Randal C. "Concerns Rise Over Safety of A-Plants," *New York Times*, 18 October 2001, B11.

Armon, Stephen S., Robert Schecter, Thomas V. Inglesby, Donald A. Henderson, John G. Bartlett, Michael S. Ascher, Edward Eitzen, Anne D. Fine, Jerome Hauer, Marcelle Layton, Scott Lillibridge, Michael T. Osterholm, Tara O'Toole, Gerald Parker, Trish M. Perl, Philip K. Russell, David L. Swerdlow, and Kevin Tonat. "Botulinum Toxin as a Biological Weapon: Medical and Public Health Management." *Journal of the American Medical Association* 285, no. 8 (February 28, 2001): 1059–70.

Arnett, Eric H. "Choosing Nuclear Arsenals: Prescriptions and Predictions for New Nuclear Powers." Special Issue on Opaque Nuclear Proliferation: Methodological and Policy Implications. *The Journal of Strategic Studies* 13, no. 3 (September 1990): 152–74.

Aron, Raymond. *The Great Debate*. New York: Doubleday, 1965.

Arthur, Max. *Forgotten Voices of the Great War*. London: Ebury Press, 2003.

Associated Press. "1999 Report Warned of Suicide Hijack," *New York Times*, 17 May 2002, A1.

Baer, Robert. "The Fall of the House of Saud." *The Atlantic Monthly*, May 2003.

Ball, H. L., D.S. King, F. E. Cohen, S. B. Prusiner, and M. A. Baldwin. "Engineering the Prion Protein Using Chemical Synthesis." *Journal of Peptide Research* 58 (2001): 357–374.

Balmer, Brian. *Britain and Biological Warfare: Expert Advice and Science Policy, 1930–65*. London: Palgrave, 2001.

Ban, Jonathan. *Agricultural Biological Warfare: An Overview*. Chemical and Biological Arms Control Institute. Number 9. June 2000.

Baram, Amatzia. "An Analysis of Iraqi WMD Strategy." *The Nonproliferation Review* 8, no. 2 (Summer 2001): 25–39.

Barbaro, Michael. "Bioshield Too Little for Drug Industry: Companies Want More Protection From Financial Loss," *Washington Post*, 26 July 2004, E01.

Barbera, Joseph, Anthony Macintyre, Larry Gostin, Tom Inglesby, Tara O'Toole, Craig DeAtley, Kevin Tonat, and Marci Layton. "Large-Scale Quarantine Following Biological Terrorism in the United States: Scientific Examination, Logistic and

Legal Limits, and Possible Consequences." *Journal of the American Medical Association* 286, no. 21 (December 5, 2001): 2711–17.

Barletta, Michael, Clay Bowen, Gaurav Kampani, and Tamara Robinson. "Nuclear- and Missile-Related Trade and Developments For Selected Countries, March–June 1998." *The Nonproliferation Review* 6, no. 1 (Fall 1998): 148–73.

———. "Nuclear- and Missile-Related Trade and Developments For Selected Countries, July–October 1998." *The Nonproliferation Review* 6, no. 2 (Winter 1999): 151–66.

Barletta, Michael, Amy Sands, and Jonathan B. Tucker. "Keeping Track of Anthrax: The Case for a Biosecurity Convention." *The Bulletin of the Atomic Scientists* 58, no. 3 (May/June 2002): 57–62.

Barnaby, Frank. *The Production of Primitive Nuclear Explosives From MOX Fuel.* London: The Oxford Research Group, May 2002.

Barringer, Felicity. "Inspectors in Iran Find Highly Enriched Uranium at an Electrical Plant," *New York Times*, 26 September 2003, A6.

Barry, John M. *The Great Influenza: The Epic Story of the Deadliest Plague in History.* New York, NY: Viking Penguin, 2004.

Barry, John and Mark Hosenball. "What Went Wrong." *Newsweek*, February 2004.

Bartholet, Jeffrey. "Al Qaeda Runs for the Hills." *Newsweek*, December 2001.

Basler, Christopher F., Ann H. Reid, Jody K. Dybing, Thomas A. Janczewski, Thomas G. Fanning, Hongyong Zheng, Mirella Salvatore, Michael L. Perdue, David E. Swayne, Adolfo Garcia-Sastre, Peter Palese, and Jeffery K. Taubenberger. "Sequence of the 1918 Pandemic Influenza Virus Nonstructural Gene (NS) Segment and Characterization of Recombinant Viruses Bearing the 1918 NS Gene." *Proceedings of the National Academy of Sciences* 98, no. 5 (February 27, 2001): 2746–51.

BBC News. "Mossad Warning Over Nuclear Iran." January 24, 2005, at http://news.bbc.co.uk/go/pr/fr/-/2/hi/middle-east/4203411.stm.

Beg, General Mirza Aslam. "Pakistan's Nuclear Programme: A National Security Perspective," Pp. 158–72 in *Nuclear Rivalry and International Order*, edited by J. Gjelstad and O. Njolstad. London: Sage Publications, 1996.

Begley, Sharon. "Tracking Anthrax." *Newsweek*, October 2001.

———. "Unmasking Bioterror." *Newsweek*, October 2001.

———. "Chemical Plants: Go Well Beyond 'Well Prepared'." *Newsweek*, November 2001.

———. "Food Supplies: Bar Handling by 'Almost Anyone'." *Newsweek*, November 2001.

———. "Mass Transit: Study the Lessons of Aum Shinrikyo." *Newsweek*, November 2001.

———. "Nuclear Power Plants: Keep Building on Three Mile Island." *Newsweek*, November 2001.

———. "Skyscrapers: Take the 'Immune Building' Challenge." *Newsweek*, November 2001.

Begley, Sharon and Michael Isikoff. "Anxious About Anthrax." *Newsweek*, October 2001.

Benn, Aluf. "Israel: Censoring the Past." *The Bulletin of the Atomic Scientists* 57, no. 4 (July/August 2001): 17–19.

Bermudez, Jr., Joseph S. "The Democratic People's Republic of Korea and Unconventional Weapons." Pp. 182–201 in *Planning the Unthinkable: How New Powers Will Use Nuclear, Biological, and Chemical Weapons*, edited by Lavoy, Sagan, and Wirtz. Ithaca, NY: Cornell University Press, 2000.

Betts, Richard K. "Paranoids, Pygmies, Pariahs and Nonproliferation Revisited." Pp. 100–24 in *The Proliferation Puzzle: Why Nuclear Weapons Spread and What Results*, edited by Z. Davis and B. Frankel. London: Frank Cass and Company Limited, 1993.

———. "Universal Deterrence or Conceptual Collapse?: Liberal Pessimism and Utopian Realism." Pp. 51–85 in *The Coming Crisis: Nuclear Proliferation, U.S. Interests, and World Order*, edited by Victor Utgoff. Cambridge, MA: MIT Press, 2000.

———. "Suicide From Fear of Death?" *Foreign Affairs* 82, no. 1 (January/February 2003): 34–43.

Blackwill, Robert D. and Ashton B. Carter. "The Role of Intelligence." Pp. 216–50 in *New Nuclear Nations: Consequences for U.S. Policy*, edited by R. Blackwill and A. Carnesale. New York: Council on Foreign Relations Press, 1993.

Blakeslee, Sandra. "Human Brains Examined for Clues About Mad Cow," *New York Times*, 27 January 2004, D6.

———. "Study Lends Support to Mad Cow Theory: Scientists Report Creating a Protein That Spread Disease in Mice," *New York Times*, 30 July 2004, A9.

Blechman, Barry M. and Stephen S. Kaplan. *Force without War: U.S. Armed Forces as a Political Instrument*. Washington, D.C.: Brookings Institution, 1976.

Blight, James G. *The Shattered Crystal Ball: Fear and Learning in the Cuban Missile Crisis*. Rowman & Littlefield Publishers, Inc., 1992.

Block, Steven M. "Living Nightmares: Biological Threats Enabled By Molecular Biology." Pp. 39–75 in *The New Terror: Facing the Threat of Biological and Chemical Weapons*, In S. Drell, A. Sofaer, and G. Wilson, eds., pp. 39–75. Stanford, CA: Hoover Institution Press, Stanford University, 1999.

Blumenthal, Ralph and Judith Miller. "Japanese Germ-War Atrocities: A Half-Century of Stonewalling the World." *The New York Times*, March 4, 1999, p. A10.

Bond, Horatio. "The Fire Attacks on German Cities." Pp. 76–97 in *Fire and the Air War*, edited by H. Bond. Boston: National Fire Protection Association, 1946.

Borio, Luciana, Thomas Inglesby, C. J. Peters, Alan L. Schmaljohn, James M. Hughes, Peter B. Jahrling, Thomas Ksiazek, Karl M. Johnson, Andrea Meyerhoff, Tara O'Toole, Michael S. Ascher, John Bartlett, Joel G. Breman, Edward M. Eitzen, Margaret Hamburg, Jerry Hauer, D. A. Henderson, Richard T. Johnson, Gigi Kwik, Marci Layton, Scott Lillibridge, Gary J. Nabel, Michael T. Osterholm, Trish M. Perl, Philip Russell, and Kevin Tonat. "Hemorrhagic Fever Viruses as Biological Weapons: Medical and Public Health Management." *Journal of the American Medical Association* 287, no.18 (May 8, 2002): 2391–2405.

Boureston, Jack and Charles D. Ferguson. "Schooling Iran's Atom Squad." *Bulletin of the Atomic Scientists* 60, no. 3 (May/June 2004): 31–35.

Bowen, Clayton P. and Daniel Wolven. "Command and Control Challenges in South Asia." *The Nonproliferation Review* 6, no. 3 (Spring-Summer 1999): 25–35.

Bozheyeva, Gulbarshyn, Yerlan Kunakbayev, and Dastan Yeleukenov. *Former Soviet Biological Weapons Facilities in Kazakstan: Past, Present, and Future.* Occasional Paper No. 1. Monterey, CA: Monterey Institute of International Studies, Center for Nonproliferation Studies. June 1999.

Bracken, Paul. "Nuclear Weapons and State Survival in North Korea." *Survival* 35, no. 3 (1993): 137–53.

———. *Fire in the East: The Rise of Asian Military Power and the Second Nuclear Age.* New York: HarperCollins Publishers, 1999.

Bray, Mike. "Defense Against Filoviruses Used As Biological Weapons." *Antiviral Research* 57 (2003): 53–60.

Brinkhoff, Thomas. City Population, http://www.citypopulation.de.

Brinkley, Joel. "Canada Wants Some Trucks Exempt from Border Inspection," *New York Times*, 1 February 2002, A12.

———. "U.S. and Allies Press U.N. Nuclear Agency to Criticize Iran," *New York Times*, 19 September 2005, A8.

Broad, William J. "Smallpox: The Once and Future Scourge?," *New York Times*, 15 June 1999, D1 and D4.

———. "Spy Photos of Korea Missile Site Bring Dispute," *New York Times*, 11 January 2000, A8.

———. "Australians Create a Deadly Mouse Virus," *New York Times*, 23 January 2001, A8.

———. "U.S. Acts to Make Vaccines and Drugs Against Smallpox," *New York Times*, 9 October 2001, D1 and D2.

———. "Obtaining Anthrax is Hard, but Not Impossible," *New York Times*, 10 October 2001, B12.

———. "Preparing America for the Reality of Germ Warfare," *New York Times*, 21 October 2001, 4.

———. "Terror Anthrax Linked to Type Made by U.S.," *New York Times*, 3 December 2001, A1 and B6.

———. "Interviews with Biowarriors: Bill Patrick," for the NOVA special *Bioterror*. December 2001.www.pbs.org/wgbh/nova/bioterror/biow_patrick.html.

———. "Key to Strains of Anthrax Is Discovered," *New York Times*, 27 March 2003, B14.

———. "Report Sees Risks in Push for Missile Defense," *New York Times*, 24 September 2003, A19.

———. "Plowshare or Sword?," *New York Times*, 25 May 2004, D1 and D4.

———. "In a Lonely Stand, a Scientist Takes On National Security Dogma," *New York Times*, 29 June 2004, D3.

Broad, William J., David Johnston, and Judith Miller. "Subject of Anthrax Inquiry Tied to Anti-Germ Training," *New York Times*, 2 July 2003, A11.

Broad, William J. and Judith Miller. "Bill Patrick: Once He Devised Germ Weapons; Now He Defends Against Them," *New York Times*, 3 November 1998, D1 and D5.

———. "Anthrax Itself May Point to Origin of Letter Sent to Daschle," *New York Times*, 18 October 2001, B5.

——. "Officials, Expanding Search, Warn Against Drawing Conclusions on Anthrax Source," *New York Times*, 26 October 2001, B7.

——. "U.S. Recently Produced Anthrax In a Highly Lethal Powder Form," *New York Times*, 13 December 2001, A1 and B7.

Broad, William J. and David E. Sanger. "U.N. Inspectors Report Evidence That Iran Itself Made Fuel That Could Be Used for A-Bombs," *New York Times*, 25 February 2004, A6.

——. "Iran Still Making Nuclear Materials, U.N. Agency Says," *New York Times*, 2 June 2004, A9.

——. "Iran Says It Will Not Give Up Uranium Enrichment Program," *The New York Times*, 1 August 2004, A8.

Broad, William J., David E. Sanger, and Raymond Bonner. "A Tale of Nuclear Proliferation: How Pakistani Built His Network," *New York Times*, 12 February 2004, A1 and A18.

Brodie, Bernard. *Strategy in the Missile Age.* Princeton, NJ: Princeton University Press, 1959a.

——. "The Anatomy of Deterrence." *World Politics* 11 (1959b): 173–91.

——. *Escalation and the Nuclear Option.* Princeton, N.J.: Princeton University Press, 1966.

——. *War and Politics.* New York: Macmillan, 1973.

Brooke, James. "DMZ Twist: U.S. Retreat Unsettles North Korea," *New York Times*, 16 June 2003, A8.

——. "North Korea Lashes Out at Neighbors and U.S.," *New York Times*, 19 August 2003, A7.

——. "Korean Claim Leaves U.S. Concerned, But Skeptical," *New York Times*, 3 October 2003, A6.

Brower, Jennifer and Peter Chalk. *The Global Threat of New and Reemerging Infectious Diseases: Reconciling U.S. National Security and Public Health Policy.* Santa Monica, CA: RAND, 2003.

Brown, David. "Agency With Most Need Didn't Get Anthrax Data: CDC Unaware of Canadian Study Before Attacks," *Washington Post*, 11 February 2002, A03.

——. "Smallpox Vaccine's Protection May Last Decades: People Inoculated More Than 30 Years Ago May Still Have Immunity to Fatal Virus, Study Finds," *Washington Post*, 18 August 2003, A02.

Brownlee, Shannon. "Clear and Present Danger," *Washington Post*, 28 October 2001, W08.

Bundy, McGeorge. "Existential Deterrence and Its Consequences." Pp. 3–13 in *The Security Gamble: Deterrence Dilemmas in the Nuclear Age*, edited by D. MacLean. Totowa, N.J.: Rowan and Allanheld, 1982.

——. *Danger and Survival: Choices About the Bomb in the First Fifty Years.* New York: Random House, 1988.

Burgess, Stephen and Helen Purkitt. *The Rollback of South Africa's Biological Warfare Program.* INSS Occasional Paper 37. Counterproliferation Series. USAF Institute for National Security Studies and USAF Academy, Colorado. February 2001.

Burke, John P. and Fred I. Greenstein. *How Presidents Test Reality: Decisions on Vietnam, 1954 and 1965*. New York: Russell Sage Foundation, 1991.

Burns, John F. "Iraq's Thwarted Ambitions Litter an Old Nuclear Plant," *New York Times*, 27 December 2002, A1 and A10

Burrows, William E. and Robert Windrem. *Critical Mass: The Dangerous Race for Superweapons in a Fragmenting World.* New York: Simon and Schuster, 1994.

Calabresi, Massimo and Melissa August. "Was Smallpox Overhyped?" *Time*, July 2004.

Calogero, Francesco. "Nuclear Terrorism." *The Bulletin of the Atomic Scientists* 58, no. 3 (May/June 2002): 5.

Cameron, Gavin, Jason Pate, Diana McCauley, and Lindsay DeFazio. "1999 WMD Terrorism Chronology: Incidents Involving Sub-National Actors and Chemical, Biological, Radiological, and Nuclear Materials." *The Nonproliferation Review* 7, no. 2 (Summer 2000): 157–74.

Cameron, Gavin, Jason Pate, and Kathleen Vogel. "Planting Fear: How Real is the Threat of Agricultural Terrorism?" *Bulletin of the Atomic Scientists* 57, no. 5 (September/October 2001): 38–44.

Carranza, Mario E. "An Impossible Game: Stable Nuclear Deterrence After the Indian and Pakistani Tests." *The Nonproliferation Review* 6, no. 3 (Spring–Summer 1999): 11–24.

Carus, W. Seth. *'The Poor Man's Atomic Bomb'?: Biological Weapons in the Middle East.* Policy Papers, Number 23. Washington, D.C.: The Washington Institute For Near East Policy, 1991.

———. *Bioterrorism and Biocrimes: The Illicit Use of Biological Agents Since 1900.* Washington, D.C.: Center for Counterproliferation Research, National Defense University, February 2001.

Casadevall, Arturo. "Passive Antibody Administration (Immediate Immunity) as a Specific Defense against Biological Weapons." *Emerging Infectious Diseases* 8, no. 8 (August 2002): 833–41.

Casagrande, Rocco. "Biological Terrorism Targeted at Agriculture: The Threat to U.S. National Security." *The Nonproliferation Review* 7, no. 3 (Fall/Winter 2000): 92–105.

"Casualties—US vs. NVA/VC." www.rjsmith.com/kia_tbl.html.

"Casualties in World War II." www.infoplease.com/ipa/A0004619.html; ragz-international.com/world_war_ii_casualties.htm.

"Casualty Figures, United Nations Forces." www.koreanwar-educator.org/topics/casualties/.

Cello, Jeronimo, Aniko V. Paul, and Eckard Wimmer. "Chemical Synthesis of Poliovirus cDNA: Generation of Infectious Virus in the Absence of Natural Template." *Science* 297 (August 9, 2002): 1016–18.

Center for Counterproliferation Research. *The Counterproliferation Imperative: Meeting Tomorrow's Challenges.* National Defense University. Washington, D.C., November 2001.

Chafetz, Glenn. "The End of the Cold War and the Future of Nuclear Proliferation: An Alternative to the Neorealist Perspective." Pp. 127–58 in *The Proliferation*

*Puzzle: Why Nuclear Weapons Spread and What Results*, edited by Z. Davis and B. Frankel. London: Frank Cass and Company Limited, 1993.

Chalk, Peter. *Hitting America's Soft Underbelly: The Potential Threat of Deliberate Biological Attacks Against the U.S. Agricultural and Food Industry.* National Defense Research Institute. Santa Monica, CA: RAND, 2004.

Chari, P. R. "India's Nuclear Doctrine: Confused Ambitions." *The Nonproliferation Review* 7, no. 3 (Fall/Winter 2000): 123–35.

Cheema, Zafar Iqbal. "Pakistan's Nuclear Use Doctrine and Command and Control." Pp. 158–81 in *Planning the Unthinkable: How New Powers Will Use Nuclear, Biological, and Chemical Weapons*, edited by Lavoy, Sagan, and Wirtz. Ithaca, NY: Cornell University Press, 2000.

Chellaney, Brahma. "South Asia's Passage to Nuclear Power." *International Security* 16, no. 1 (1991): 43–75.

Chevrier, Marie Isabelle. "The Aftermath of Aum Shinrikyo: A New Paradigm for Terror?" *Politics and the Life Sciences* 15, no. 2 (September 1996): 194–96.

Choe, Chong H., Selim S. Bouhaouala, Itzhak Brook, Thomas B. Elliott, and Gregory B. Knudson. "In Vitro Development of Resistance to Ofloxacin and Doxycycline in *Bacillus anthracis* Sterne." *Antimicrobial Agents and Chemotherapy* 44, no. 6 (June 2000): 1766.

Choffnes, Eileen. "Germs on the Loose: Bioweapons Tests Tainted Sites Around the Globe." *Bulletin of the Atomic Scientists* 57, no. 2 (March/April 2001): 57–61.

Chow, Brian G., Richard H. Speier, and Gregory S. Jones. *The Proposed Fissile-Material Production Cut-Off: Next Steps.* MR-586-OSD. Santa Monica, CA: RAND, 1995.

Christensen, Thomas J. "China, the U.S.–Japan Alliance, and the Security Dilemma in East Asia." *International Security* 23, no. 4 (Spring 1999): 49–80.

Chyba, Christopher F. "Biological Terrorism and Public Health." *Survival* 43, no. 1 (Spring 2001): 93–106.

Cimbala, Stephen J. *The Past and Future of Nuclear Deterrence.* Westport, Connecticut: Praeger, 1998.

Cirincione, Joseph. "Assessing the Assessment: The 1999 National Intelligence Estimate of the Ballistic Missile Threat." *The Nonproliferation Review* 7, no. 1 (Spring 2000): 125–137.

———. *Deadly Arsenals: Tracking Weapons of Mass Destruction.* Washington, D.C.: Carnegie Endowment for International Peace, 2002.

Clausewitz, Carl Von. *On War.* Harmondsworth, Middlesex, England: Penguin Books, Ltd., 1985.

Cochran, Thomas B. and Christopher E. Paine. *The Amount of Plutonium and Highly-Enriched Uranium Needed for Pure Fission Nuclear Weapons.* Washington, D.C.: National Resources Defense Council, Inc., 1995.

Cody, Edward. "N. Korea Vows to Quit Arms Program," *Washington Post*, 19 September 2005, A01.

Coffield, J.A., et. al. "Clostridial Neurotoxins in the Age of Molecular Medicine." *Trends in Microbiology* 2, no. 3 (March 1994): 67–69.

Cohen, Avner. *Israel and the Bomb.* New York: Columbia University Press, 1998.

——. "Nuclear Arms in Crisis under Secrecy: Israel and the Lessons of the 1967 and 1973 Wars." Pp. 104–24 in *Planning the Unthinkable: How New Powers Will Use Nuclear, Biological, and Chemical Weapons*, edited by Lavoy, Sagan, and Wirtz. Ithaca, NY: Cornell University Press, 2000.

——. "Israel and Chemical/Biological Weapons: History, Deterrence, and Arms Control." *The Nonproliferation Review* 8, no. 3 (Fall/Winter 2001): 27–53.

Cohen, Avner and Benjamin Frankel. "Opaque Nuclear Proliferation." Special Issue on Opaque Nuclear Proliferation: Methodological and Policy Implications. *The Journal of Strategic Studies* 13, no. 3 (September 1990): 14–44.

Cohen, Avner and Marvin Miller. "Nuclear Shadows in the Middle East: Prospects for Arms Control in the Wake of the Gulf Crisis." *Security Studies* 1, no. 1 (Autumn 1991): 54–77.

Cohen, Eliot A. "The Mystique of U.S. Air Power." *Foreign Affairs* 73, no. 1 (January/February 1994): 109–124.

Cohen, Jon. "Designer Bugs." *The Atlantic Monthly*, July/August 2002.

Cohen, William S. "Foreword." Pp. xi–xvi in *Biological Weapons: Limiting the Threat*, edited by Joshua Lederberg. Cambridge, Massachusetts: The MIT Press, 2001.

Coker, Pamala R., Kimothy L. Smith, Patricia F. Fellows, Galena Bybachuck, Konstantin G. Kousoulas, and Martin E. Hugh-Jones. "*Bacillus anthracis* Virulence in Guinea Pigs Vaccinated with Anthrax Vaccine Absorbed Is Linked to Plasmid Quantities and Clonality." *Journal of Clinical Microbiology* 41, no. 3 (March 2003): 1212–1218.

Cole, Leonard A. *Clouds of Secrecy: The Army's Germ Warfare Tests over Populated Areas*. Totowa, N.J.: Rowman & Littlefield, 1988.

——. *The Eleventh Plague: The Politics of Biological and Chemical Warfare*. New York: W. H. Freeman and Company, 1997.

Cook, Tim. *No Place To Run: The Canadian Corps and Gas Warfare in the First World War.* Vancouver: UBC Press, 1999.

Cookson, Clive. "Biowarfare Fear: Scientists Convert Virus Into Killer," *Financial Times*, 12 January 2001, 9.

Cordesman, Anthony H. *The Arab-Israeli Military Balance in 2002, Part Four: Trends in Chemical, Biological, Radiological, and Nuclear Weapons*. Washington, D.C.: Center for Strategic and International Studies, January 2002.

Cottam, Richard. *Foreign Policy Motivation: A General Theory and a Case Study*. Pittsburgh: University of Pittsburgh Press, 1977.

Cowell, Alan. "Nuclear Weapon Is Years Off For Iran, Research Panel Says," *New York Times*, 7 September 2005, A11.

Coyle, Philip E. "Why the Secrecy Shield?" *The Washington Post*, June 11, 2002, p. A25.

Crameri, A., et. al. "DNA Shuffling of a Family of Genes from Diverse Species Accelerates Directed Evolution." *Nature* 391 (15 January 1998): 288–91.

Croddy, Eric. "China's Role in the Chemical and Biological Disarmament Regimes." *The Nonproliferation Review* 9, no. 1 (Spring 2002): 16–47.

Cropsey, Seth. "The Only Credible Deterrent." *Foreign Affairs* 73, no. 2 (March/April 1994): 14–20.

Dando, Malcolm. *Biological Warfare in the 21ˢᵗ Century: Biotechnology and the Proliferation of Biological Weapons.* London: Brassey's (UK) Ltd., 1994.

———. "Benefits and Threats of Developments in Biotechnology and Genetic Engineering." Pp. 1–15 in *SIPRI Yearbook 1999: Armaments, Disarmament and International Security*, Appendix 13A. Oxford: Oxford University Press, 1999.

———. *The New Biological Weapons: Threat, Proliferation, and Control.* Boulder, CO: Lynne Rienner Publishers, 2001.

Danzig, Richard and Pamela B. Berkowsky. "Why Should We Be Concerned About Biological Warfare?" Pp. 9–14 in *Biological Weapons: Limiting the Threat*, edited by Joshua Lederberg. Cambridge, Massachusetts: The MIT Press, 2001.

*Dark Winter: Bioterrorism Exercise, Andrews Air Force Base, June 22–23, 2001.* John Hopkins Center for Civilian Biodefense, Center for Strategic and International Studies, ANSER, & Memorial Institute for the Prevention of Terrorism. www.upmc-biosecurity.org.

Dasey, Charles F. "Medical Benefits of the Biological Defense Research Program." *Politics and the Life Sciences* 9, no.1 (August 1990): 77–84.

Dashiell, Thomas R. "The Need for a Defensive Biological Research Program." *Politics and the Life Sciences* 9, no.1 (August 1990): 85–92.

Davies, Pete. *The Devil's Flu: The World's Deadliest Influenza Epidemic and the Scientific Hunt for the Virus That Caused It.* New York: Henry Holt and Company, 2000.

Davis, Christopher J. "Nuclear Blindness: An Overview of the Biological Weapons Programs of the Former Soviet Union and Iraq." *Emerging Infectious Diseases* 5, no. 4 (July–August 1999): 509–12.

Dawson, Jim. "Issues and Events." *Physics Today*, September 2003. www.physicstoday.org/vol-56/iss-9/p26.html.

De Mesquita, Bruce and William H. Riker. "An Assessment of the Merits of Selective Nuclear Proliferation." *Journal of Conflict Resolution* 26, no. 2 (1982): 283–306.

Demick, Barbara. "Seoul's Vulnerability Is Key to War Scenarios: A U.S. Strike on the North May Provoke a Catastrophic Retaliation Against South's Capital," *Los Angeles Times*, 27 May 2003, www.latimes.com/templates/misc/printstory.jsp?slug=la%2Dfg%2Dnorkor27may27,13188619.story?coll=la%2Dhome%2Dleftrail.

Dennis, Carina. "The Bugs of War." *Nature* 411 (17 May 2001): 232–35.

Dennis, David T., Thomas V. Inglesby, Donald A. Henderson, John G. Bartlett, Michael S. Ascher, Edward Eitzen, Anne D. Fine, Arthur M. Friedlander, Jerome Hauer, Marcelle Layton, Scott R. Lillibridge, Joseph E. McDade, Michael T. Osterholm, Tara O'Toole, Gerald Parker, Trish M. Perl, Philip K. Russell, and Kevin Tonat. "Tularemia as a Biological Weapon: Medical and Public Health Management." *Journal of the American Medical Association* 285, no. 21 (June 6, 2001): 2763–73.

DePalma, Anthony and Claudia Deutsch. "Postal Service Is Expected to Ask U.S. For Bailout," *New York Times*, 7 November 2001, B1 and B6.

De Rivera, Joseph. *The Psychological Dimension of Foreign Policy.* New York: Columbia University Press, 1968.

D'Esopo, Molly. "Hopkins Biodefense Center Outlines U.S. Strategy to Confront BW Threat." *Biodefense Quarterly* 2, no. 3 (December 2000/January 2001): 1–2.

Deutch, John, Harold Brown and John P. White. "National Missile Defense: Is There Another Way?." *Foreign Policy* (Summer 2000): 91–100.

Diamond, John. "N. Korea Keeps U.S. Intelligence Guessing," *USA Today*, 11 March 2003, 1.

Douglass, Nicola and Keith Dumbell. "Independent Evolution of Monkeypox and Variola Viruses." *Journal of Virology* 66, no.12 (December 1992): 7565–7567.

Duffy, Michael. "So Much For The WMD." *Time*, February 2004.

Dugger, Celia W. "As Mediators Seek Peace, India's Navy is Ready for War," *New York Times*, 17 January 2002, A3.

Dunlop, Lance R., Katherine A. Oehlberg, Jeremy J. Reid, Dilek Avci, and Ariella M. Rosengard. "Variola Virus Immune Evasion Proteins." *Microbes and Infection* 5 (2003): 1049–56.

Dunn, Lewis A. *Controlling the Bomb: Nuclear Proliferation in the 1980s.* New Haven: Yale University Press, 1982.

——. "New Nuclear Threats to U.S. Security." Pp. 20–50 in *New Nuclear Nations: Consequences for U.S. Policy*, edited by R. Blackwill and A. Carnesale. New York: Council on Foreign Relations Press, 1993.

——. "What Difference Will It Make?" Pp. 514–26 in *The Use of Force: Military Power and International Politics*, edited by Robert Art and Kenneth Waltz. Lanham, Maryland: Rowman & Littlefield Publishers, Inc., 1993.

Du Preez, Jean. "The Impact of the Nuclear Posture Review on the International Nuclear Nonproliferation Regime," *The Nonproliferation Review* 9, no. 3 (Fall/Winter 2002): 68–70.

Easterbrook, Gregg. "In an Age of Terror, Safety Is Relative." *The New York Times*, June 27, 2004, Section 4.

Eden, Lynn. *Whole World on Fire: Organizations, Knowledge, and Nuclear Weapons Devastation*. Ithaca: Cornell University Press, 2003.

——. "City on Fire." *The Bulletin of the Atomic Scientists* 60, no. 1 (January/February 2004): 33–43.

Elliott, Michael and John Barry. "Nothing Short of Doomsday." *Newsweek*, July 1994.

Engelberg, Stephen and Lawrence K. Altman. "Fighting a New Health Threat, on the Fly," *New York Times*, 24 October 2001, A1 and B8.

Engelberg, Stephen and Michael R. Gordon. "CIA Fears N. Korea Already Has Bomb," *San Jose Mercury News*, 26 December 1993, 1 and 20.

Engelberg, Stephen and Judith Miller. "Anthrax Mailed to Senate Found To Be Potent Strain; Case Tied to Illness at NBC: Sign of Escalating Threat: Experts Now Believe Someone Has Access to a Sophisticated Bioterrorism Weapon," *New York Times*, 17 October 2001, A1.

Erlanger, Steven. "Lax Nuclear Security in Russia Is Cited as Way for bin Laden to Get Arms," *New York Times*, 12 November 2001, B1 and B6.

Evron, Yair. "Opaque Proliferation: The Israeli Case." Special Issue on Opaque Nuclear Proliferation: Methodological and Policy Implications. *The Journal of Strategic Studies* 13, no. 3 (September 1990): 45–63.

Ewald, Paul W. "A Risky Policy On Smallpox Vaccinations," *New York Times*, 17 December 2001, A23.

Fainaru, Steve and Ceci Connolly. "Memo on Florida Case Roils Anthrax Probe: Experts Debate Theory Hijacker Was Exposed," *Washington Post*, 29 March 2002, A03.

Falkenrath, Richard A. "Chemical/Biological Terrorism: Coping with Uncertain Threats and Certain Vulnerabilities." *Politics and the Life Sciences* 15, no. 2 (September 1996): 201–02.

Falkenrath, Richard A., Robert D. Newman, and Bradley A. Thayer. *America's Achilles' Heel: Nuclear, Biological, and Chemical Terrorism and Covert Attack.* Cambridge, Massachusetts: The MIT Press, 1998.

Farr, Warner D. "The Third Temple's Holy of Holies: Israel's Nuclear Weapons." *Counterproliferation Papers*. Future Warfare Series, No. 2. Maxwell Air Force Base, AL: USAF Counterproliferation Center, 1999.

Fathi, Nazila. "Iran Confirms Test of Missile That Is Able to Hit Israel," *New York Times*, 8 July 2003, A9.

———. "Iran Parades New Missile on War Anniversary," *New York Times*, 23 September 2003, A6.

Feaver, Peter D. "Command and Control in Emerging Nuclear Nations." *International Security* 17, no. 3 (Winter 1992/1993): 160–87.

———. "Proliferation Optimism and Theories of Nuclear Operations." Pp. 159–91 in *The Proliferation Puzzle: Why Nuclear Weapons Spread and What Results*, edited by Z. Davis and B. Frankel. London: Frank Cass and Company Limited, 1993.

Feaver, Peter D. and Emerson M. S. Niou. "Managing Nuclear Proliferation: Condemn, Strike, or Assist?" *International Security* 40, no. 2 (1996): 209–34.

Feder, Barnaby J. and Andrew C. Revkin. "Post Office to Install Devices to Destroy Deadly Organisms at Mail-Processing Centers," *New York Times*, 25 October 2001, B5.

Feldman, Shai. *Israeli Nuclear Deterrence: A Strategy for the 1980s*. New York: Columbia University Press, 1982.

———. *Nuclear Weapons and Arms Control in the Middle East.* Cambridge, MA: The MIT Press, 1997.

Fennelly, Kevin P., Amy L. Davidow, Shelly L. Miller, Nancy Connell, and Jerrold J. Ellner. "Airborne Infection with *Bacillus anthracis* – from Mills to Mail." *Emerging Infectious Diseases* 10, no. 6 (June 2004): 996–1001.

Fetter, Steve. "Ballistic Missiles and Weapons of Mass Destruction: What is the Threat? What Should Be Done?" *International Security* 16, no. 1 (1991): 5–42.

Fetter, Steve and Devin T. Hagerty. "Correspondence: Nuclear Deterrence and the 1990 Indo-Pakistani Crisis." *International Security* 21, no. 1 (Summer 1996): 176–85.

*Financial Times*. 12 January 2001–8 July 2002.

Flournoy, Michele A. "Implications for U.S. Military Strategy." Pp. 135–61 in *New Nuclear Nations: Consequences for U.S. Policy*, edited by R. Blackwill and A. Carnesale. New York: Council on Foreign Relations Press, 1993.

Flynn, Stephen E. "Why America Is Still An Easy Target." *Time*, July 2004.

———. "The Neglected Home Front." *Foreign Affairs* 83, no. 5 (September/October 2004): 20–33.

Frankel, Benjamin. "The Brooding Shadow: Systemic Incentives and Nuclear Weapons Proliferation." Pp. 37–78 in *The Proliferation Puzzle: Why Nuclear Weapons Spread and What Results*, edited by Z. Davis and B. Frankel. London: Frank Cass and Company Limited, 1993.

Frantz, Douglas. "Nuclear Booty: More Smugglers Use Asia Route," *New York Times*, 11 September 2001, A1 and A8.

———. "Israel Now Has Capability to Launch Nukes From Subs," *Seattle Times*, 12 October 2003, A26.

Freedman, Lawrence. *The Evolution of Nuclear Strategy*. London: The Macmillan Press, Ltd., 1981.

Freedman, Lawrence and Efraim Karsh. "How Kuwait Was Won: Strategy in the Gulf War." *International Security* 16, no. 2 (1991): 5–41.

French, Howard W. "G.I.'s Gradually Are to Leave Korea DMZ to Cut War Risk," *New York Times*, 6 June 2003, A1 and A10.

Freudenheim, Milt. "Few Hospitals Are Ready for a Surge of Bioterror Victims," *New York Times*, 26 October 2001, B8.

Gaddis, John Lewis. "Nuclear Weapons and Cold War History." Pp. 40–54 in *Nuclear Rivalry and International Order*, edited by J. Gjelstad and O. Njolstad. London: Sage Publications, 1996.

Galimand, Marc, Annie Guiyoule, Guy Gerbaud, Bruno Rasoamanana, Suzanne Chanteau, Elisabeth Carniel, and Patrice Courvalin. "Multidrug Resistance in Yersinia Pestis Mediated By A Transferable Plasmid." *The New England Journal of Medicine* 337, no. 10 (September 4, 1997): 677–80.

Gallois, Pierre. *The Balance of Terror: Strategy for the Nuclear Age*. Boston: Houghton Mifflin Company, 1961.

Gamblin, S. J., L. F. Haire, R. J. Russell, D. J. Stevens, B. Xiao, Y. Ha, N. Vasisht, D. A. Steinhauer, R. S. Daniels, A. Elliot, D. C. Wiley, and J.J. Skehel. "The Structure and Receptor Binding Properties of the 1918 Influenza Hemagglutinin." *Science* 303 (March 19, 2004): 1838–42.

Ganguly, Sumit. "India's Pathway to Pokhran II: The Prospects and Sources of New Delhi's Nuclear Weapons Program." *International Security* 23, no. 4 (Spring 1999): 148–77.

Garwin, Richard L. "National Missile Defense: The Wrong Plan." *The Bulletin of the Atomic Scientists* 56, no. 2 (March/April 2000): 36–41.

Garwin, Richard L. and Vadim A. Simonenko. *Nuclear Weapon Development Without Nuclear Testing?* Paper prepared for the Pugwash Workshop on "Problems in Achieving a Nuclear-Weapon-Free World," London, England, October 25–27, 1996.

George, Alexander L. and Richard Smoke. *Deterrence in American Foreign Policy: Theory and Practice*. New York: Columbia University Press, 1974.

———. *Presidential Decision-making in Foreign Policy: The Effective Use of Information and Advice*. Boulder, CO: Westview, 1980.

———. "Incentives for U.S.–Soviet Security Cooperation and Mutual Adjustment," Pp. 644–50 in *U.S.–Soviet Security Cooperation: Achievements, Failures, and Lessons*, edited by A. L. George, P. J. Farley, and A. Dallin. New York: Oxford University Press, 1988.

———. "The Cuban Missile Crisis." Pp. 222–68 in *Avoiding War: Problems of Crisis Management*, edited by Alexander George. Boulder: Westview Press, 1991.

Gertz, Bill. "North Korea Tested A Cruise Missile," *Washington Times*, 27 February 2003, http://dynamic.washtimes.com/twt-print.cfm?ArticleID=20030227-615708.

———. "Nukes Option By U.S. in Korea," *Washington Times*, 18 November 2003, www.washingtontimes.com/functions/pring.php?StoryID=20031117-115816-2478r.

Gilbert, Martin. *The First World War: A Complete History*. New York: Henry Holt and Company, 1994.

Giles, Gregory F. "The Islamic Republic of Iran and Nuclear, Biological, and Chemical Weapons." Pp. 79–103 in *Planning the Unthinkable: How New Powers Will Use Nuclear, Biological, and Chemical Weapons*, edited by Lavoy, Sagan, and Wirtz. Ithaca, NY: Cornell University Press, 2000.

Gjelstad, Jorn, and Olav Njolstad, eds. *Nuclear Rivalry and International Order*. London: Sage Publications, 1996.

Glanz, James and David E. Rosenbaum. "Experts Say Spores Won't Spread in Ventilation System," *New York Times*, 18 October 2001, B6.

Glaser, Charles L. and Steve Fetter. "National Missile Defense and the Future of U.S. Nuclear Weapons Policy. *International Security* 26, no. 1 (Summer 2001): 40–92.

Goldstein, Avery. "Robust and Affordable Security: Some Lessons from the Second-Ranking Powers During the Cold War." *Journal of Strategic Studies* 15, no. 4 (December 1992): 475–527.

———. *Deterrence and Security in the 21st Century: China, Britain, France, and the Enduring Legacy of the Nuclear Revolution*. Stanford, CA: Stanford University Press, 2000.

Gormley, Dennis M. "Hedging Against the Cruise-Missile Threat." *Survival* 40, no. 1 (Spring 1998): 92–111.

———. "The Neglected Dimension: Controlling Cruise Missile Proliferation." *The Nonproliferation Review* 9, no. 2 (Summer 2002): 21–29.

Grace, Charles S. *Nuclear Weapons: Principles, Effects and Survivability*. London: Brassey's, 1994.

Graham, Bradley. "GAO Cites Risks in Missile Defense," *Washington Post*. 5 June 2003, A06.

Gray, Colin S. *The Second Nuclear Age*. Boulder, CO: Lynne Rienner Publishers, 1999.

Greenstein, Fred I. *Personality and Politics: Problems of Evidence, Inference, and Conceptualization*. Chicago: Markham Publishing Company, 1969.

Grimaldi, James V. and Guy Gugliotta. "Chemical Plants Feared as Targets," *Washington Post*, 16 December 2001, A01.

Guan, Y., L. L. M. Poon, C. Y. Cheung, T. M. Ellis, W. Lim, A. S. Lipatov, K. H. Chan, K. M. Sturm-Ramirez, C. L. Cheung, Y. H. C. Leung, R. G. Webster, and J. S. M. Peiris. "H5N1 Influenza: A Protean Pandemic Threat." *Proceedings of the National Academy of Sciences* 101, no. 21 (May 25, 2004): 8156–61.

*Guardian*. 18 June 2002–9 July 2003.

Gubser, Caroline and Geoffrey L. Smith. "The Sequence of Camelpox Virus Shows It Is Most Closely Related to Variola Virus, the Cause of Smallpox." *Journal of General Virology* 83 (2002): 855–72.

Guterl, Fred. "The Nagging Fear of Nukes." *Newsweek*, October 2001.

Haber, L. F. *The Poisonous Cloud: Chemical Warfare in the First World War.* Oxford: Clarendon Press, 2002.

Haberman, Clyde. "A Dark View of Anthrax, Errant Bombs, the Saudi Connection," *New York Times*, 25 October 2001, B1.

Hagerty, Devin T. "Nuclear Deterrence in South Asia: The 1990 Indo-Pakistani Crisis." *International Security* 20, no. 3 (Winter 1995/1996): 79–114.

———. *The Consequences of Nuclear Proliferation: Lessons from South Asia.* Cambridge, MA: The MIT Press, 1998.

Halpern, Orly. "New Estimates on Iranian Nukes," *The Jerusalem Post*, 1 August 2005, jpost.com/servlet/Satellite?pagename=Jpost/JPArticle/ShowFull&cid=1122776414371&p=1101615860782.

Hamilton, M. G. "Toxins: The Emerging Threat." *ASA Newsletter*, 98–3 (26 June 1998): 1, 20–28.

Hampton, Tracy. "Clues to the Deadly 1918 Flu Revealed." *Journal of the American Medical Association* 291, no. 13 (April 7, 2004): 1553.

Hanley, Charles J. "We Lied to Saddam About Nuke Development, Ex-Bombmakers Say," *USA Today*, 1 December 2003, www.usatoday.com/news/world/iraq/2003-12-01-iraq-arms_x.htm.

Hansen, Lynn M. "Biological and Toxin Weapons: Arms Control, Stability, and Western Security." *Politics and the Life Sciences* 9, no. 1 (August 1990): 47–58.

Harknett, Richard J. "The Logic of Conventional Deterrence and the End of the Cold War." *Security Studies* 4, no. 1 (Autumn 1994): 86–114.

———. "State Preferences, Systemic Constraints, and the Absolute Weapon." Pp. 47–72 in *The Absolute Weapon Revisited: Nuclear Arms and the Emerging International Order*, edited by T.V. Paul, R. Harknett, J. Wirtz. Ann Arbor, MI: University of Michigan Press, 1998.

Harris, Sheldon H. *Factories of Death: Japanese Biological Warfare, 1932–1945, and the American Cover-up.* New York: Routledge, 2002.

Hart, Paul 't. *Groupthink in Government: A Study of Small Groups and Policy Failure.* Baltimore: John Hopkins University Press, 1994.

Hart, Paul 't, Eric K. Stern, and Bengt Sundelius, eds. *Beyond Groupthink: Political Group Dynamics and Foreign Policymaking.* Ann Arbor, MI: University of Michigan Press, 1997.

Harvey, Frank P. *The Future's Back: Nuclear Rivalry, Deterrence Theory, and Crisis Stability after the Cold War.* Montreal: McGill-Queen's University Press, 1997a.

———. "Deterrence and Compellence in *Protracted* Crises: Methodology and Preliminary Findings." *International Studies Notes* 22, no. 1 (Winter 1997b): 12–23.

Harvey, John R. "Regional Ballistic Missiles and Advanced Strike Aircraft: Comparing Military Effectiveness." *International Security* 17, no. 2 (1992): 41–83.

Hass, Richard N. *Intervention: The Use of American Military Force in the Post-Cold War World.* Revised Edition. Washington, D.C.: Brookings Institution Press, 1999.

Heisbourg, Francois. "The Prospects for Nuclear Stability Between India and Pakistan." *Survival* 40, no. 4 (Winter 1998–1999): 77–92.

Henderson, Donald A., Thomas V. Inglesby, John G. Bartlett, Michael S. Ascher, Edward Eitzen, Peter B. Jahrling, Jerome Hauer, Marcelle Layton, Joseph McDade, Michael T. Osterholm, Tara O'Toole, Gerald Parker, Trish Perl, Philip K. Russell, and Kevin Tonat. "Smallpox as a Biological Weapon: Medical and Public Health Management." *Journal of the American Medical Association* 281, no. 22 (June 9, 1999): 2127–37.

Henry, Terrence. "Nuclear Iran." *The Atlantic Monthly*, December 2003.

Hermann, Margaret G. "Indicators of Stress in Policymaking During Foreign Policy Crises." *Political Psychology*, 1, (1979): 27–46.

——. "Explaining Foreign Policy Behavior Using Personal Characteristics of Political Leaders," 7–46; "Comments on Foreign Policy Makers Personality Attributes and Interviews: A Note on Reliability Procedures." *International Studies Quarterly*, 24 (1980): 67–73.

——. *Assessing Leadership Style: A Trait Analysis*. Columbus, OH: Social Science Automation, Inc., 1999.

Hermann, Margaret G. and Charles F. Hermann. "Hostage Taking, The Presidency, and Stress." Pp. 211–29 in *Origins of Terrorism: Psychologies, Ideologies, Theologies, States of Mind*, edited by W. Reich. Cambridge, MA: Cambridge University Press, 1990.

Hermann, Margaret G. and Charles W. Kegley, Jr. "Rethinking Democracy and International Peace: Perspectives from Political Psychology." *International Studies Quarterly* 39 (1995): 511–33.

Hermann, Margaret G. and Thomas Preston. "Presidents and Their Advisers: Leadership Style, Advisory Systems, and Foreign Policymaking," *Political Psychology* 15 (1994): 75–96.

Herring, Eric. *Danger and Opportunity: Explaining International Crisis Outcomes*. Manchester, NY: Manchester University Press, 1995.

Hersh, Seymour M. *The Samson Option: Israel's Nuclear Arsenal and American Foreign Policy*. New York: Random House, 1991.

——. "On the Nuclear Edge." *New Yorker*, March 1993.

——. "The Iran Game," *New Yorker,* 3 December 2001, 42–50.

Hoffman, Bruce. *Inside Terrorism*. New York: Columbia University Press, 1998.

——. "Terrorism, Trends, and Prospects." Pp. 7–38 in *Countering the New Terrorism*, edited by Brian M. Jenkins. Santa Monica, CA: RAND, 1999.

——. "One-Alarm Fire." *The Atlantic Monthly*, December 2001.

Holmes, Edward C. "1918 and All That." *Science* 303 (March 19, 2004): 1787–88.

Hopkins, John C. and Weixing Hu, eds. *Strategic Views From The Second Tier: The Nuclear Weapons Policies of France, Britain, and China*. New Brunswick, CT: Transaction Publishers, 1995.

Hosenball, Mark and Daniel Klaidman. "Clues on the Ground and in Custody." *Newsweek*, January 2002.

Houlder, Vanessa. "Farm Virus to Damage Economy by Up to $5.9 Billion," *Financial Times*, 30 August 2001, 9.

Huth, Paul. *Extended Deterrence and the Prevention of War.* New Haven, CT: Yale University Press, 1988.

Huth, Paul and Bruce Russett. "What Makes Deterrence Work?: Cases from 1900 to 1980." *World Politics* 36 (July 1984): 496–526.

Huth, Paul and Bruce Russett. "Testing Deterrence Theory: Rigor Makes a Difference." *World Politics* 42, no. 4 (1990): 466–501.

*Independent.* 10 June 2003.

"Indian Navy Compounds Military Stand-Off." January 16, 2002. www.cnn.com/2002/WORLD/asiapcf/south/01/16/pakistan.india.powell/index.html.

"Indian Prime Minister Defends Nuclear Test Decision." CNN. May 11, 1999. www.cnn.com/WORLD/asiapcf/9905/11/india.nuclear.01.

Inglesby, Thomas V., David T. Dennis, Donald A. Henderson, John G. Bartlett, Michael S. Ascher, Edward Eitzen, Anne D. Fine, Arther M. Friedlander, Jerome Hauer, John F. Koemer, Marcelle Layton, Joseph McDade, Michael T. Osterholm, Tara O'Toole, Gerald Parker, Trish M. Perl, Philip K. Russell, Monica Schoch-Spana, and Kevin Tonat. "Plague as a Biological Weapon: Medical and Public Health Management." *Journal of the American Medical Association* 283, no. 17 (May 3, 2000): 2281–90.

Inglesby, Thomas V., Rita Grossman, and Tara O'Toole. "A Plague on Your City: Observations from TOPOFF." *Clinical Infectious Diseases* 32 (2001): 436–45.

Inglesby, Thomas V., Tara O'Toole, Donald A. Henderson, John G. Bartlett, Michael S. Ascher, Edward Eitzen, Arthur M. Friedlander, Julie Gerberding, Jerome Hauer, James Hughes, Joseph McDade, Michael T. Osterholm, Gerald Parker, Trish M. Perl, Philip K. Russell, and Kevin Tonat. "Anthrax as a Biological Weapon, 2002: Updated Recommendations for Management." *Journal of the American Medical Association* 287, no. 17 (May 1, 2002): 2236–52.

*International Herald Tribune.* 7 August 2000–21 October 2003.

Jackson, Alan C., Mary J. Warrell, Charles E. Rupprecht, Hildegund C. J. Ertl, Bernard Dietzschold, Michael O'Reilly, Richard P. Leach, Zhen F. Fu, William H. Wunner, Thomas P. Bleck, and Henry Wilde. "Management of Rabies in Humans." *Clinical Infectious Diseases* 36 (January 1, 2003): 60–63.

Jackson, Paul J., Martin E. Hugh-Jones, Debra M. Adair, Gertrude Green, Karen K. Hill, Cheryl R. Kuske, Lev M. Grinberg, Faina A. Abramova, and Paul Keim. "PCR Analysis of Tissue Samples from the 1979 Sverdlovsk Anthrax Victims: The Presence of Multiple *Bacillus anthracis* Strains in Different Victims." *Proceedings of the National Academy of Sciences* 95 (February 1998): 1224–29.

Jackson, Ronald J., Alistair J. Ramsay, Carolina D. Christensen, Sandra Beaton, Diana F. Hall, and Ian A. Ramshaw. "Expression of Mouse Interleukin-4 by a Recombinant Ectromelia Virus Suppresses Cytolytic Lymphocyte Responses and Overcomes Genetic Resistance to Mousepox." *Journal of Virology* 75, no. 3 (February 2001): 1205–10.

Jahrling, Peter B., Gary M. Zaucha, and John W. Huggins. "Countermeasures to the Reemergence of Smallpox Virus as an Agent of Bioterrorism." Pp. 187–200 in *Emerging Infections 4*, edited by W. M. Scheld, W. A. Craig, and J. M. Hughes. Washington D.C.: ASM Press, 2000.

*Jane's Chem-Bio Handbook.* Second Edition, Alexandria, VA: Jane's Information Group, 2002.

Janis, Irving L. *Victims of Groupthink.* Boston: Houghton Mifflin, 1972.

Janis, Irving L. and L. Mann. *Decision Making: A Psychological Analysis of Conflict, Choice, and Commitment.* New York: Free Press, 1977.

Jehl, Douglas and Eric Schmitt. "Data Is Lacking On Iran's Arms, U.S. Panel Says," *New York Times*, 9 March 2005, A1.

Jenkins, Brian M. "Will Terrorists Go Nuclear?" *Orbis* 29, no. 1 (Autumn 1985): 507–515

*Jerusalem Post.* August 8, 2005.

Jervis, Robert. *Perception and Misperception in International Politics.* Princeton, N.J.: Princeton University Press, 1976.

———. *The Illogic of American Nuclear Strategy.* Ithaca, NY: Cornell University Press, 1986.

Ji, You. *The Armed Forces of China.* The Armed Forces of Asia Series. London: I.B. Tauris Publishers, 1999.

Joeck, Neil. "Tacit Bargaining and Stable Proliferation in South Asia." Special Issue on Opaque Nuclear Proliferation: Methodological and Policy Implications. *The Journal of Strategic Studies* 13, no. 3 (September 1990): 77–91.

Johnson, David E., Karl P. Mueller, and William H. Taft. *Conventional Coercion Across the Spectrum of Operations: The Utility of U.S. Military Forces in the Emerging Security Environment.* Santa Monica, CA: RAND, 2002.

Johnson, Larry C. "The Declining Terrorist Threat," *New York Times*, 10 July 2001, A23.

Johnston, Alastair Iain. "China's New 'Old Thinking': The Concept of Limited Deterrence." *International Security* 20, no.3 (Winter 1995/96): 5–42.

Johnston, David. "Careful Plan Devised for Anthrax Letter," *New York Times*, 27 November 2001, B8.

———. "Report Calls U.S. Agencies Understaffed For Bioterror," *New York Times*, 6 July 2003, A9.

Johnston, David and David Kocieniewski. "As Investigation Churns, More Attacks Are Expected," *New York Times*, 25 October 2001, B7.

Johnston, David and Alison Mitchell. "Particles Are Tiny: U.S. Suggest It Could Spread Easily in Air, Adding to Concern," *New York Times*, 17 October 2001, B5.

Jones, Rodney W. and Sumit Ganguly. "Correspondence: Debating New Delhi's Nuclear Decision." *International Security* 24, no. 4 (Spring 2000): 181–89.

Joseph, Robert G. and John F. Reichart. *Deterrence and Defense in a Nuclear, Biological, and Chemical Environment.* Center for Counterproliferation Research. Washington, D.C.: National Defense University Press, 1999.

Kahn, Joseph. "China Proposes a Deal to End North Korean Nuclear Standoff," *New York Times*, 17 September 2005, A4.

Kahneman, D., P. Slovic, and A. Tversky, eds. *Judgment Under Uncertainty: Heuristics and Biases.* Cambridge: Cambridge University Press, 1982.

Kahneman, D. and A. Tversky. "Prospect Theory: An Analysis of Decision Under Risk." *Econometrica* 47 (1979): 263–91.

Kaiser, Karl. "Non-proliferation and Nuclear Deterrence." *Survival* 31, no.2 (1989): 123–36.

Kampani, Gaurav. "From Existential to Minimum Deterrence: Explaining India's Decision to Test." *The Nonproliferation Review* 6, no. 1 (Fall 1998): 12–24.

Kaplan, Edward H., David L. Craft, and Lawrence M. Wein. "Emergency Response to a Smallpox Attack: The Case for Mass Vaccination." *Proceedings of the National Academy of Sciences* 99, no. 16 (August 6, 2002): 10935–40.

Kapur, Ashok. "Nuclear Development of India and Pakistan." Pp. 143–57 in *Nuclear Rivalry and International Order*, edited by J. Gjelstad and O. Njolstad. London: Sage Publications, 1996.

Karl, David J. "Proliferation Pessimism and Emerging Nuclear Powers." *International Security* 21, no. 3 (Winter 1996/97): 87–119.

Karp, Aaron. "Lessons of Iranian Missile Programs for U.S. Nonproliferation Policy." *The Nonproliferation Review* 5, no. 3 (Spring–Summer 1998): 17–26, cns.miis .edu/pubs/npr/karp53.htm.

———. "The Spread of Ballistic Missiles and the Transformation of Global Security." *The Nonproliferation Review* 7, no.3 (Fall/Winter 2000): 106–122.

Kaufmann, Arnold F., Martin I. Meltzer, and George P. Schmid. "The Economic Impact of a Bioterrorist Attack: Are Prevention and Post-Attack Intervention Programs Justifiable?" *Emerging Infectious Diseases* 3, no. 2 (April–June 1997): 83–94.

Kaysen, Carl, Robert McNamara, and George Rathjens. "Nuclear Weapons After the Cold War." *Foreign Affairs* 70, no. 4 (1991).

Keegan, John. *The First World War*. New York: Vintage Books, 1998.

Keller, Bill. "Nuclear Nightmares." *New York Times Magazine*, May 2002.

Kelley, Marylia and Jay Coghlan. "Mixing Bugs and Bombs." *Bulletin of the Atomic Scientists* 59, no.5 (September/October 2003): 25–31.

Kelly, Michael. "Slow Squeeze." *The Atlantic Monthly*, May 2002, pp. 20–21.

Kessler, Glenn. "N. Korea Still Denies Enriching Uranium: U.S. Delegation Told There Is No Secret Program," *Washington Post*, 13 January 2004, A12.

Khan, Feroz Hassan. "Challenges to Nuclear Stability in South Asia." *The Nonproliferation Review* 10, no. 1 (Spring 2003): 59–74.

Khong, Yuen F. *Analogies At War: Korea, Munich, Dien Bien Phu, and the Vietnam Decisions of 1965*. Princeton, N.J.: Princeton University Press, 1992.

Kilborn, Peter T. "The Seaports: On the Dock, Holes in the Security Net Are Gaping," *New York Times*, 7 November 2001, B5.

Kincade, William H. "Nuclear Weapons in Ukraine: Hollow Threat, Wasting Asset." *Arms Control Today* 6 (1993): 13–18.

Kiziah, Rex R., Lt. Col., USAF. *Assessment of the Emerging Biocruise Threat*. The Counterproliferation Papers. Future Warfare Series, No.6. USAF Counterproliferation Center, Air War College and the Air University, Maxwell Air Force Base, Alabama. August 2000.

———. "The Emerging Biocruise Threat." *Air & Space Power Journal* (Spring 2003). www.airpower.maxwell.af.mil/airchronicles/apj/apj03/spr03/kiziah.html.

Kleinfield, N. R. "Anthrax Investigators Are Hoping Bronx Case Leads Them to Source," *New York Times*, 6 November 2001, A1 and B6.

Kluger, Jeffrey. "The Nuke Pipeline," *Time*, December 2001.

Koblentz, Gregory. "Pathogens as Weapons: The International Security Implications of Biological Warfare." *International Security* 28, no. 3 (Winter 2003/2004): 84–122.

Koch, Andrew and Waheguru Pal Singh Sidhu. "Subcontinental Missiles." *The Bulletin of the Atomic Scientists* 54, no. 4 (July/August 1998): 44–49.

Kolata, Gina. *Flu: The Story of the Great Influenza Pandemic of 1918 and the Search for the Virus That Caused It.* New York: Farrar, Straus and Giroux, 1999.

——. "Gain in Hunt for How a Flu Turns Lethal: Team Finds Gene Changes that Let a Chicken Virus Kill 6 People," *New York Times*, 7 September 2001, A13.

Kramer, R. M. "Windows of Vulnerability or Cognitive Illusions?: Cognitive Processes and the Nuclear Arms Race." *Journal of Experimental Social Psychology* 25 (1988): 79–100.

Krepon, Michael. "Nuclear Risk Reduction: Is Cold War Experience Applicable to Southern Asia?" Pp. 1–14 in *The Stability-Instability Paradox: Nuclear Weapons and Brinkmanship in South Asia*, edited by M. Krepon and C. Gagne. Report No. 38. The Henry L. Stimson Center, June 2001.

Krepon, Michael and Chris Gagne, eds. *The Stability-Instability Paradox: Nuclear Weapons and Brinkmanship in South Asia*. Report No. 38. The Henry L. Stimson Center, June 2001.

Kristensen, Hans M. "Preemptive Posturing: What Happened to Deterrence?" *The Bulletin of the Atomic Scientists* 58, no.5 (September/October 2002): 54–59.

Kristof, Nicholas D. "A Nuclear 9/11," *New York Times*, 10 March 2004, A27.

——. "The Nuclear Shadow," *New York Times*, 14 August 2004, A27.

Kugler, Jacek. "Terror Without Deterrence." *Journal of Conflict Resolution* 28 (1984): 470–506.

Kwik, Gigi. "Weighing Scientific Advance Against Bioweapons Potential." *Biodefense Quarterly* (Autumn 2002): 4 and 10.

Kwik, Gigi, Joe Fitzgerald, Thomas V. Inglesby, and Tara O'Toole. "Biosecurity: Responsible Stewardship of Bioscience in an Age of Catastrophic Terrorism." *Biosecurity and Bioterrorism: Biodefense Strategy, Science, and Practice* 1, no. 1 (2003): 1–9.

Lamb, Gregory. "New Buffer for Bioterror's Tempest," Christian Science Monitor, July 1, 2004, p. 14.

Landler, Mark. "Nuclear Agency Expected to Back Weaker Rebuke to Iran," *New York Times*, 24 September 2005, A3.

Langewiesche, William. "Anarchy At Sea." *The Atlantic Monthly*, September 2003.

La Porte, Todd R. "Large Technical Systems, Instititional Surprise and Challenges to Political Legitimacy." *Technology in Society* 16, no. 3 (1994): 269–88.

La Porte, T. R. and P. Consolini. "Working In Practice But Not In Theory: Theoretical Challenges of High Reliability Organizations." *Journal of Public Administration Research and Theory* 1, no. 1 (Winter 1991): 19–47.

Lebow, Richard Ned. *Between Peace and War.* Baltimore: The Johns Hopkins University Press, 1981.

——. *Nuclear Crisis Management: A Dangerous Illusion*. Ithaca, NY: Cornell University Press, 1987.

Lebow, Richard Ned and Janice Gross Stein. "Rational Deterrence Theory: I Think, Therefore I Deter." *World Politics* 46, no. 2 (January 1989): 208–24.

——. "Deterrence: The Elusive Dependent Variable." *World Politics* 42 (April 1990): 336–69.

Lederberg, Joshua. "H1N1-Influenza As Lazarus: Genomic Resurrection from the Tomb of an Unknown." *Proceedings of the National Academy of Sciences* 98, no. 5 (February 27, 2001): 2115–16.

——. "Introduction." Pp. 1–8 in *Biological Weapons: Limiting the Threat*, edited by Joshua Lederberg. Cambridge, Massachusetts: The MIT Press, 2001.

——. "Epilogue." Pp. 321–29 in *Biological Weapons: Limiting the Threat*, edited by Joshua Lederberg. Cambridge, Massachusetts: The MIT Press, 2001.

Legault, Albert and George Lindsey. *The Dynamics of the Nuclear Balance.* Ithaca, NY: Cornell University Press, 1974.

Lewis, Dana. "Soviet Germ War Legacy Lives On," *MSNBC.com*, 20 October 1999.

Lewis, George, Lisbeth Gronlund and David Wright. "National Missile Defense: An Indefensible System." *Foreign Policy* (Winter 1999/2000): 120–37.

Lewis, John Wilson and Hua Di. "China's Ballistic Missile Programs: Technologies, Strategies, Goals." *International Security* 17, no. 2 (Fall 1992): 5–40.

Lewis, John Wilson and Litai Xue. *China Builds the Bomb*. Stanford, CA: Stanford University Press, 1988.

Li, K. S., Y. Guan, J. Wang, G. J. D. Smith, K. M. Xu, L. Duan, A. P. Rahardjo, P. Puthavathana, C. Buranathal, T. D. Nguyen, A. T. S. Estoepangestle, A. Chalsingh, P. Auewarakul, H. T. Long, N. T. H. Hanh, R. J. Webby, L. L. M. Poon, H. Chen, K. F. Shortridge, K. Y. Yuen, R. G. Webster, and J. S. M. Peiris. "Genesis of a Highly Pathogenic and Potentially Pandemic H5N1 Influenza Virus in Eastern Asia." *Nature* 430 (July 8, 2004): 209–13.

Lipton, Eric. "U.S. Say Thousands of Letters Might Be Tinged With Anthrax," *New York Times*, 4 December 2001, A1 and B6.

Loeb, Vernon. "U.S. Seeks Duplicate of Russian Anthrax: Microbe to Be Used to Check Vaccine," *Washington Post*, 5 September 2001, A16.

*Los Angeles Times.* 27 May 2003.

Lyall, Sarah. "Britain: Foot-and-Mouth Disease Gone," *New York Times*, 15 January 2002, A8.

Maass, Peter. "The Last Emperor: Kim Jong Il." *New York Times Magazine*, October 2003.

Mazaar, Michael J. "Going Just a Little Nuclear: Nonproliferation Lessons from North Korea." *International Security* 20, no. 2 (1995a): 92–122.

——. *North Korea and the Bomb: A Case Study in Nonproliferation*. London: Macmillan Press, Ltd., 1995b.

——. ed. *Nuclear Weapons in a Transformed World: The Challenge of Virtual Nuclear Arsenals*. New York: St. Martin's Press, 1997.

——. "The Notion of Virtual Arsenals." In M. Mazaar, ed., *Nuclear Weapons in a Transformed World: The Challenge of Virtual Nuclear Arsenals*, pp. 3–29. New York: St. Martin's Press, 1997a.

Mack, Andrew J. R. "Why Big Nations Lose Small Wars: The Politics of Asymmetric Conflict." *World Politics* 27, no. 2 (January 1975): 175–200.

Mackenzie, J. S., K. B. Chua, P. W. Daniels, B. T. Eaton, H. E. Field, R. A. Hall, K. Halpin, C. A. Johansen, P. D. Kirkland, S. K. Lam, P. McMinn, D.J. Nisbet, R. Paru, A. T. Pyke, S. A. Ritchie, P. Siba, D.W. Smith, G. A. Smith, A. F. van den Hurk, L. F. Wang, and D. T. Williams. "Emerging Viral Diseases of Southeast Asia and the Western Pacific." *Emerging Infectious Diseases* 7, no. 3 (June 2001): 497–504.

Mahnken, Thomas G. "The Arrow and the Shield: U.S. Responses to Ballistic Missile Proliferation." Pp. 321–35 in *U.S. Security in an Uncertain Era,* edited by B. Roberts. Cambridge, MA: MIT Press, 1993.

Mangold, Tom and Jeff Goldberg. *Plague Wars: A True Story of Biological Warfare.* New York: St. Martin's Press, 1999.

Manning, Anita. "Expect Germ Terrorism, Experts Warn," *USA Today,* 6 August 1997, 3D.

Mansoor, Ijaz and R. James Woolsey. "How Secure is Pakistan's Plutonium?," *New York Times,* 28 November 2001, A27

Maoz, Zeev. "The Mixed Blessing of Israel's Nuclear Policy." *International Security* 28, no. 2 (Fall 2003): 44–77.

Mark, J. Carson. *Reactor-Grade Plutonium's Explosive Properties.* Washington, D.C.: Nuclear Control Institute, August 1990.

Mark, J. Carson, Theodore Taylor, Eugene Eyster, William Maraman, and Jacob Wechsler. *Can Terrorists Build Nuclear Weapons?* Washington, D.C.: Nuclear Control Institute, 1986.

Martel, William C. "Deterrence and Alternative Images of Nuclear Possession." Pp. 213–34 in *The Absolute Weapon Revisited: Nuclear Arms and the Emerging International Order,* edited by T. V. Paul, R. Harknett, J. Wirtz. Ann Arbor, MI: University of Michigan Press, 1998.

Masood, Salman and David Rohde. "Pakistan Now Says Scientist Did Send Koreans Nuclear Gear," *New York Times,* 25 August 2005, A3.

Massung, R. F., L. I. Liu, J. Qi, J. C. Knight, T. E. Yuran, A.R. Kerlavage, J. M. Parsons, J. C. Venter, and J. J. Esposito. "Analysis of the Complete Genome of Smallpox Variola Major Virus Strain Bangladesh-1975." *Virology* 201 (1994): 215–40.

Mazaar, Michael J. "Going Just a Little Nuclear: Nonproliferation Lessons from North Korea." *International Security* 20, no. 2 (1995a): 92–122.

——. *North Korea and the Bomb: A Case Study in Nonproliferation.* London: Macmillan Press, Ltd., 1995b.

——. "The Notion of Virtual Arsenals." Pp. 3–29 in *Nuclear Weapons in a Transformed World: The Challenge of Virtual Nuclear Arsenals,* edited by Michael Mazaar. New York: St. Martin's Press, 1997.

McAvoy, Audrey. "Japan to Build Missile Defense System," *Washington Post,* 19 December 2003, A14.

McCarthy, Timothy V. and Jonathan B. Tucker. "Saddam's Toxic Arsenal: Chemical and Biological Weapons in the Gulf Wars." Pp. 47–78 in *Planning the Unthinkable: How New Powers Will Use Nuclear, Biological, and Chemical Weapons,* edited by Lavoy, Sagan, and Wirtz. Ithaca, NY: Cornell University Press, 2000.

McKinzie, Matthew G., Thomas B. Cochran, Robert S. Norris, and William M. Arkin. *The U.S. Nuclear War Plan: A Time For Change.* Washington, D.C.: Natural Resources Defense Council, June 2001.

McNamara, Robert S. "The Military Role of Nuclear Weapons: Perceptions and Misperceptions." *Foreign Affairs* (Fall 1983): 59–80.

McNaugher, Thomas L. "Ballistic Missiles and Chemical Weapons: The Legacy of the Iran-Iraq War." *International Security* 15, no. 1 (Fall 1990): 5–34.

Mearsheimer, John J. *Conventional Deterrence.* Ithaca, NY: Cornell University Press, 1983.

———. "Back to the Future: Instability in Europe After the Cold War." *International Security* 15, no. 1 (Summer 1990): 5–56.

———. "The Case For a Ukrainian Nuclear Deterrent." *Foreign Affairs* 72, no. 3 (1993): 50–66.

Meltzer, Martin I., Inger Damon, James W. LeDuc, and J. Donald Millar. "Modeling Potential Responses to Smallpox as a Bioterrorist Weapon." *Emerging Infectious Diseases* 7, no. 6 (November–December 2001): 959–969.

Miller, Judith. "Germ Warfare: Cold War Killer Emerges From Its Tomb," *Sydney Morning Herald*, 3 June 1999, 1.

———. "U.S. to Use Lab For More Study of Bioterrorism," *New York Times*, 22 September 1999, A1 and A25.

———. "In a Gamble, U.S. Supports Russian Germ Warfare Scientists," *New York Times*, 20 June 2000, D4.

———. "Next to Old Rec Hall, a 'Germ-Making Plant'," *New York Times*, 4 September 2001, A6.

———. "U.S. Set to Retain Smallpox Stocks," *New York Times*, 16 November 2001, A1 and B8.

———. "U.S. Has New Concerns About Anthrax Readiness: Drill Raises Questions About Antibiotics," *New York Times*, 28 December 2003, A16.

———. "Censored Study on Bioterror Doubts U.S. Preparedness," *New York Times*, 29 March 2004, A15.

———. "Wrangling Impedes Transfer of Civilian Anthrax Vaccine," *New York Times*, 20 August 2004, A18.

Miller, Judith and William J. Broad. "Iranians, Bioweapons in Mind, Lure Needy Ex-Soviet Scientists," *New York Times*, 8 December 1998, A1 and A12; Smithson, *Toxic Archipelago*, 15–17.

———. "Germ Weapons: In Soviet Past or In the New Russia's Future?," *New York Times*, 28 December 1998, 1.

Miller, Judith, Stephen Engelberg, and William Broad. *Germs: Biological Weapons and America's Secret War.* New York: Simon and Schuster, 2001.

Miller, Steven E. "The Case Against a Ukrainian Nuclear Deterrent." *Foreign Affairs* 72, no. 3 (1993): 67–80.

Millot, Marc Dean. "Facing the Emerging Reality of Regional Nuclear Adversaries." *The Washington Quarterly* 17, no. 3 (Summer 1994): 41–71.

Ministry of National Defense, Republic of Korea. *Defense White Paper 1998.* Seoul: Korean Institute for Defense Analysis, 1999.

Mistry, Dinshaw. "Beyond the MTCR: Building a Comprehensive Regime to Contain Ballistic Missile Proliferation." *International Security* 27, no. 4 (Spring 2003): 119–49.

Moodie, Michael. "The Soviet Union, Russia, and the Biological and Toxin Weapons Convention." *The Nonproliferation Review* 8, no.1 (Spring 2001): 59–69.

Moore, Mike. "Unintended Consequences." *Bulletin of the Atomic Scientists* 56, no. 1 (January/February 2000): 58–64.

Moore, Richard. "Britain's Bacteria." *Bulletin of the Atomic Scientists* 58, no.4 (July/August 2002): 66–67.

Monath, Thomas P. "Ecology of Marburg and Ebola Viruses: Speculations and Directions for Future Research." *The Journal of Infectious Diseases* 179 (Suppl 1) (1999): S127–S138.

Morgenthau, Hans J. *Politics Among Nations: The Struggle for Power and Peace.* New York: Alfred A. Knopf, 1948.

Morris, Jefferson. "Commercial Satellite Systems At Risk From Nuclear After-Effects." *Aerospace Daily*, May 11, 2001. http://home.datawest.net/dawog/Space/s20010511nuc_effects_on_comm_sats.htm

Mueller, John. "Nine Propositions about the Historical Impact of Nuclear Weapons." Pp. 55–74 in *Nuclear Rivalry and International Order*, edited by J. Gjelstad and O. Njolstad. London: Sage Publications, 1996.

——. "The Escalating Irrelevance of Nuclear Weapons." Pp.73–98 in *The Absolute Weapon Revisited: Nuclear Arms and the Emerging International Order*, edited by T.V. Paul, R. Harknett, J. Wirtz. Ann Arbor, MI: University of Michigan Press, 1998.

Mueller, John and Karl Mueller. "Sanctions of Mass Destruction." *Foreign Affairs* 78, no. 3 (May/June 1999): 43–53.

Mufson, Steven. "U.S. Says Iraq, Others Pursue Germ Warfare," *Washington Post*, 20 November 2001, A8.

Muhlberger, Elke, Michael Weik, Viktor E. Volchkov, Hans-Dieter Klenk, and Stephan Becker. "Comparison of the Transcription and Replication Strategies of Marburg Virus and Ebola Virus by Using Artificial Replication Systems." *Journal of Virology* 73, no. 3 (March 1999): 2333–42.

Mullbacher, Arno and Mario Lobigs. "Creation of Killer Poxvirus Could Have Been Predicted." *Journal of Virology* 75, no. 18 (September 2001): 8353–55.

Mullen, Robert K. "Mass Destruction and Terrorism." *Journal of International Affairs* 32, no. 1 (Spring/Summer 1978): 63–89.

Mulvenon, James C. and Andrew N. D. Yang. *A Poverty of Riches: New Challenges and Opportunities in PLA Research.* RAND National Security Research Division. Santa Monica, CA: RAND Corporation, 2003.

Nair, Vijai K. *Nuclear India.* New Delhi: Lancer International, 1992.

Natural Resources Defense Council. "The U.S. Nuclear War Plan: A Time for Change." Washington, D.C.: 2001.

Nelson, Robert W. "Low-Yield Earth-Penetrating Nuclear Weapons." *Science and Global Security* 10, no. 1 (January–April 2002): 1–20.

Nesirky, Martin. "North Korea Says It Is Making Nuclear Bombs: Analysts See Pre-Negotiation Gambit," *Washington Post*, 2 October 2003, A32.

*New York Times.* 26 October 1994 – 24 September 2005.

Nicoll, Alexander. "Nuclear Theft Causes Global Alert," *Financial Times*, 8 July 2002, http://news.ft.com/s01/servlet/ContentServer?pagename=FT.com/StoryFT/FullStory&c=StoryFT&cid=1025793406726&p=1021991059913.

"North Korea Makes New Bomb Boasts." CBSNEWS.com, June 2, 2003. www.cbsnews.com/stories/2003/05/23/world/printable555243.shtml.

"North Korea 'Reprocessing Nuclear Fuel.'" *Guardian*, 9 July 2003, www.guardian.co.uk/Print/0,3858,4709005,00.html.

NRDC Nuclear Notebook. "French Nuclear Forces, 2001." *The Bulletin of the Atomic Scientists* 57, no. 4 (July/August 2001): 70–71.

———. "Pakistan's Nuclear Forces, 2001." *The Bulletin of the Atomic Scientists* 58, no.1 (January/February 2002): 70–71.

———. "India's Nuclear Forces, 2002." *The Bulletin of the Atomic Scientists* 58, no.2 (March/April 2002): 70–72.

———. "Israeli Nuclear Forces, 2002." *The Bulletin of the Atomic Scientists* 58, no. 5 (September/October 2002): 73–75.

———. "North Korea's Nuclear Program, 2003." *The Bulletin of the Atomic Scientists* 59, no. 2 (March/April 2003): 74–77.

———. "China's Nuclear Forces, 2003." *The Bulletin of the Atomic Scientists* 59, no. 6 (November/December 2003): 77–80.

"Nuclear Appraisal." *Online Newshour.* January 21, 2004. www.pbs.org/newshour/bb/asia/jan-june04/northkorea_01-21.html.

Nunn-Lugar Cooperative Threat Reduction Program. "Nunn-Lugar in an Election Year." Speech delivered by Senator Richard G. Lugar, Chairman of the Senate Committee on Foreign Relations at the National Press Club, Washington, D.C., August 11, 2004. www.lugar.senate.gov/nunnlugar.html.

Ochmanek, David. *Military Operations Against Terrorist Groups Abroad: Implications for the United States Air Force.* RAND Project Air Force. Santa Monica, CA: RAND, 2003.

Oh, Kongdan and Ralph C. Hassig. *North Korea Through the Looking Glass.* Washington, D.C.: Brookings Institution Press, 2000.

O'Hanlon, Michael. "Stopping a North Korean Invasion: Why Defending South Korea is Easier than the Pentagon Thinks." *International Security* 22, no. 4 (1998): 135–70.

Osvold-Doppelhauer, E., C. Lakmann, K. Thomas, H. Birk, S. Menezes, M. O'Brien, L. Dayton, D. Schnurr, S. Honarmand, C. Kohlmeier, L. Orciari, and M. Niezgoda. "Human Death Associated with Bat Rabies – California, 2003." *Journal of the American Medical Association* 291, no. 7 (Feburary 18, 2004): 816–17.

O'Toole, Tara. "Smallpox: An Attack Scenario." *Emerging Infectious Diseases* 5, no. 4 (July–August 1999): 540–46.

Overbye, Dennis and James Glanz. "Arrested Pakistani Atom Expert Is a Taliban Advocate," *New York Times*, 2 November 2001, B4.

"Pakistan: Musharraf Says Nuclear Weapons Are an Option." April 8, 2002. www.nti.org/d_newswire/issues/2002/4/8/6p.html.

Parker, Henry. *Agricultural Bioterrorism: A Federal Strategy to Meet the Threat.* McNair Paper 65, Washington, D.C.: Institute for National Strategic Studies, National Defense University, March 2002.

Parker, Laura, Steve Sternberg, and Kevin Johnson. "Science Reveals Much About Spores, Except Attacker," *USA Today*, 26 October 2001, 3.

Parkhill, J., B. W. Wren, N. R. Thomson, R. W. Titball, M. T. G. Holden, M. B. Prentice, M. Sebaihia, K. D. James, C. Churcher, K. L. Mungall, S. Baker, D. Basham, S. D. Bentley, K. Brooks, A. M. Cerdeno-Tarraga, T. Chillingworth, A. Cronin, R. M. Davis, P. Davis, G. Dougan, T. Feltwell, N. Hamlin, S. Holroyd, K. Jaels, A. V. Karlyshev, S. Leather, S. Moule, P. C. F. Oyston, M. Quail, K. Rutherford, M. Simmonds, J. Skelton, K. Stevens, S. Whitehead, and B. G. Barrell. "Genome Sequence of *Yersinia pestis*, The Causative Agent of Plague." *Nature* 413 (October 4, 2001): 523–27.

Pasternak, Douglas. "A Nuclear Nightmare: They Look Tough, But Some Plants Are Easy Marks for Terrorists." *U.S. News & World Report*, September 2001.

Pate, Jason and Gavin Cameron. *Covert Biological Weapons Attacks against Agricultural Targets: Assessing the Impact against U.S. Agriculture.* BCSIA Discussion Paper 2001-9, ESDP Discussion Paper ESDP-2001-05, John F. Kennedy School of Government, Harvard University, August 2001.

Patrick, William C. "Biological Terrorism and Aerosol Dissemination." *Politics and the Life Sciences* 15, no. 2 (September 1996): 208–10.

Paul, T.V. "Power, Influence, and Nuclear Weapons: A Reassessment." Pp. 19–45 in *The Absolute Weapon Revisited: Nuclear Arms and the Emerging International Order*, edited by T.V. Paul, R. Harknett, J. Wirtz. Ann Arbor, MI: University of Michigan Press, 1998.

———. "The Systemic Bases of India's Challenge to the Global Nuclear Order." *The Nonproliferation Review* 6, no. 1 (Fall 1998): 1–11.

Pavlov, V. M., A. N. Mokrievich, and K. Volkovoy. "Cryptic Plasmid pFNL10 from *Francisella novicida*-like F6168: The Base of Plasmid Vectors For *Francisella tularensis*." FEMS Immunology and Medical Microbiology 13, no. 3 (March 1996): 253–56.

Pearson, Graham S. "Chemical/Biological Terrorism: How Serious a Risk?" *Politics and the Life Sciences* 15, no. 2 (September 1996): 210–12.

Peng, X., J. Peccia, P. Fabian, J. W. Martyny, K. P. Fennelly, M. Hernandez. "Efficacy of Ultraviolet Germicidal Irradiation of Upper-Room Air in Inactivating Airborne Bacterial Spores and Mycobacteria in Full-Scale Studies." *Atmospheric Environment* 37, no. 3 (January 2003): 405–19.

Peres, Shimon. *The New Middle East.* New York: Henry Holt, 1993.

Perkovich, George. *India's Nuclear Bomb: The Impact on Global Proliferation.* Berkeley, CA: University of California Press, 1999.

———. "Bhabha's Quest for the Bomb." *The Bulletin of the Atomic Scientists* 56, no. 3 (May/June 2000): 54–63.

Perrow, Charles. *Normal Accidents: Living with High-Risk Technologies.* New York, Basic Books, 1984.

Peters, C. J. "Are Hemorrhagic Fever Viruses Practical Agents for Biological Terorrism?" Pp. 201–09 in *Emerging Infections 4*, edited by W. M. Scheld, W. A. Craig, and J. M. Hughes. Washington, D.C.: ASM Press, 2000.

Peters, C.J. and D.M. Hartley. "Anthrax Inhalation and Lethal Human Infection." *Lancet* 359 (2002): 710–11.

Peters, C. J. and J. W. LeDuc. "An Introduction to Ebola: The Virus and the Disease." *The Journal of Infectious Diseases* 179 (Suppl 1) (1999): ix–xvi.

Pianin, Eric. "U.S. Faulted on Chemical Plants' Security: Government Inaction Leaves Industry Vulnerable Target to Terrorists, Critics Say," *Washington Post*, 13 June 2002, A10.

Pilat, Joseph F. "Chemical and Biological Terrorism after Tokyo: Assessing Threats and Response." *Politics and the Life Sciences* 15, no. 2 (September 1996): 213–15.

Pincus, Walter. "U.S. Explores Developing Low-Yield Nuclear Weapons," *Washington Post*, 20 February 2003, A09.

———. "Future of U.S. Nuclear Arsenal Debated: Arms Control Experts Worry Pentagon's Restructuring Plan Means More Weapons," *Washington Post*, 4 May 2003, A06.

"Plague Strain Found Immune to Antibiotics." *New York Times*, 4 September 1997, A12.

Pollack, Andrew. "Scientists Ponder Limits On Access to Germ Research," *New York Times*, 27 November 2001, D6.

———. "With Biotechnology, a Potential to Harm," *New York Times*, 27 November 2001, D6.

———. "Scientists Create a Live Polio Virus," *New York Times*, 12 July 2002, D1.

Pomerantsev, A. P., N. A. Staritsin, Y. V. Mockov, and L. I. Marinin. "Expression of Cereolysine AB Genes in Bacillus Anthracis Vaccine Strain Ensures Protection Against Experimental Hemolytic Anthrax Infection." *Vaccine* 15, nos. 17–18 (December 1997): 1846–50.

Posen, Barry R. "What If Iraq Had Had Nuclear Weapons? Pp. 353–69 in *The Use of Force: Military Power and International Politics*, edited by Robert Art and Kenneth Waltz. Lanham, Maryland: Rowman and Littlefield Publishers, Inc., 2004.

"Post Office Needs $5 Billion in Aid, Chief Tells Congress." *New York Times*, 9 November 2001, B9.

Postol, Theodore A. "Possible Fatalities from Superfires Following Nuclear Attacks In or Near Urban Areas." Pp. 15–72 in *The Medical Implications of Nuclear War*, edited by F. Solomon and R. Marston. Washington, D.C.: National Academy Press, 1986.

———. "Lessons of the Gulf War Patriot Experience." *International Security* 16, no. 3 (1991/1992): 119–171.

———. "Patriot Experience in the Gulf War." *International Security* 17, no. 1 (1992): 225–240.

———. "Why Missile Defense Won't Work." Special Report on Missile Defense. *Technology Review* (April 2002): 42–51.

Poulose, T. T. "India's Deterrence Doctrine: A Nehruvian Critique." *The Nonproliferation Review* 6, no. 1 (Fall 1998): 77–84.

Powell, Michael and Ceci Connolly. "Experts Warn Bioterrorism Could Expand," *Washington Post*, 1 November 2001, A01.

Powell, Robert. *Nuclear Deterrence Theory: The Search for Credibility.* Cambridge: Cambridge University Press, 1990.

———. "Nuclear Deterrence Theory, Nuclear Proliferation, and National Missile Defense." *International Security* 27, no. 4 (Spring 2003): 86–118.

Preez, Jean Du. "The Impact of the Nuclear Posture Review on the International Nuclear Nonproliferation Regime." *The Nonproliferation Review* 9, no.3 (Fall/Winter 2002): 67–81.

Preston, Bob, Dana J. Johnson, Sean J. A. Edwards, Michael Miller, and Calvin Ship-baugh. *Space Weapons Earth Wars*. Project Air Force. Santa Monica, CA: Rand Corporation, 2002.

Preston, Richard. *The Cobra Event*. New York: Ballantine Books, 1997.

——. "Biology Gone Bad," *New York Times*, 7 November 1997, 17.

——. "The Bioweaponeers." *The New Yorker*, March 1998.

——. *The Demon in the Freezer: A True Story*. New York: Random House, 2002.

Preston, Thomas. " 'From Lambs to Lions': Nuclear Proliferation's Grand Reshuffling of Interstate Security Relationships." *Cooperation and Conflict* 32, no. 1 (March 1997): 79–117.

Preston, Thomas. *The President and His Inner Circle: Leadership Style and the Advisory Process in Foreign Policy Making*. New York: Columbia University Press, 2001.

Preston, Thomas and Margaret G. Hermann. "Presidential Leadership Style and the Foreign Policy Advisory Process." Pp. 363–80 in *The Domestic Sources of American Foreign Policy: Insights and Evidence*, edited by Eugene R. Wittkopf and James M. McCormick. Lanham, Maryland: Roman & Littlefield, 2004.

Preston, Thomas and Paul 't Hart. Understanding and Evaluating Bureaucratic Politics: The Nexus Between Political Leaders and Advisory Systems. *Political Psychology* 20, no. 1 (March 1999): 49–98.

Quester, George H. "Nuclear Proliferation and Stability." Pp.101–116 in *Strategies for Managing Nuclear Proliferation*, edited by M. D. Intriligator and A. E. Wicks. Lexington, MA: D.C. Heath, 1983.

——. *The Future of Nuclear Deterrence*. Lexington, Massachusetts: Lexington Books, 1986.

——. "Some Thoughts on Deterrence Failures." Pp. 62–65 in *Perspectives on Deterrence*, edited by P. Stern, R. Axelrod, and R. Radner. New York: Oxford University Press, 1989.

——. "The Continuing Debate on Minimal Deterrence." Pp.176–78 in *The Absolute Weapon Revisited: Nuclear Arms and the Emerging International Order*, edited by T. V. Paul, R. Harknett, J. Wirtz. Ann Arbor, MI: University of Michigan Press, 1998.

Quinlan, Michael. "How Robust is India–Pakistan Deterrence?" *Survival* 42, no. 4 (Winter 2000-01): 141–54.

"Rabin Warns Arabs against Use of Chemical Weapons." *Jerusalem Domestic Service in Hebrew*, 20 July 1988, in FBIS-NES-88-140 (21 July 1988), 29.

Raghavan, V. R. "Limited War and Nuclear Escalation in South Asia." *The Nonproliferation Review* 8, no. 3 (Fall–Winter 2001): 82–98.

Ramana, M.V. and A. H. Nayyar. "India, Pakistan, and the Bomb." *Scientific American* (December 2001): 72–83.

Ray, J. L. "Wars Between Democracies: Rare or Nonexistent?" *International Interactions* 18 (1993): 251–76.

——. *Democracy and International Conflict: An Evaluation of the Democratic Peace Proposition*. Columbia: University of South Carolina Press, 1995.

Reeves, Phil. "North Korea Wants Nuclear Arms 'To Cut Size of Army'," *Independent*, 10 June 2003, http://news.independent.co.uk/low_res/story.jsp?story=414101&host=3&dir=71.

Regis, Ed. *The Biology of Doom: The History of America's Secret Germ Warfare Project.* New York: Henry Holt and Company, 1999.

Rehbein, Robert E. "Managing Proliferation in South Asia: A Case for Assistance to Unsafe Nuclear Arsenals." *The Nonproliferation Review* 9, no. 1 (Spring 2002): 92–111.

Reichart, John F. "Adversary Use of NBC Weapons: A Neglected Challenge." *Strategic Forum.* Institute for National Strategic Studies, National Defense University, no. 187, (December 2001): 1–4.

Renlemann, C. and C. Spinelli. "An Economic Assessment of the Costs and Benefits of African Swine Fever Prevention." *Animal Health Insight* (Spring/Summer) 1994.

"Responding to Anthrax Attacks." *New York Times*, 16 October 2001, A30.

Rettig, Richard A. and Jennifer Brower. *The Acquisition of Drugs and Biologics for Chemical and Biological Warfare Defense: Department of Defense Interactions with the Food and Drug Administration.* National Defense Research Institute. Santa Monica, CA: RAND, 2003.

Revkin, Andrew C. and Lawrence K. Altman. "Clues, Overlooked, to a Coming Threat," *New York Times*, 3 December 2001, B6.

Reynolds, Gretchen. "Why Were Doctors Afraid to Treat Rebecca McLester?: When a 10-Year-Old Contracted Monkeypox, Medical Professionals Had To Confront Their Own Fears." *New York Times Magazine*, April 2004.

Rhodes, Edward. *Power and MADness: The Logic of Nuclear Coercion.* New York: Columbia University Press, 1989.

Riemenschneider, Jenny, Aura Garrison, Joan Geisbert, Peter Jahrling, Michael Hevey, Diane Negley, Alan Schmaljohn, John Lee, Mary Kate Hart, Lorna Vanderzanden, David Custer, Mike Bray, Albert Ruff, Bruce Ivins, Anthony Bassett, Cynthia Rossi, and Connie Schmaljohn. "Comparison of Individual and Combination DNA Vaccines for *B. anthracis*, Ebola virus, Marburg virus and Venezuelan equine encephalitis Virus." *Vaccine* 21 (2003): 4071–80.

Rimmington, Anthony. "Fragmentation and Proliferation?: The Fate of the Soviet Union's Offensive Biological Weapons Programme," *Contemporary Security Policy* 20, no. 1 (April 1999): 100.

Risen, James. "Doubts Yield Discord on North Korea Arms: U.S. Officials and Analysts Differ on Threat," *International Herald Tribune*, 7 August 2000, 4.

———. "C.I.A. Lacked Iraq Arms Data, Ex-Inspector Says: Recent Search Indicates Weapons Programs Were in Disarray," *New York Times*, 26 January 2004, A1 and A10.

Risen, James and Judith Miller. "No Illicit Arms Found in Iraq, U.S. Inspector Tells Congress," *New York Times*, 3 October 2003, A1 and A12.

Roberts, Brad. "Terrorism and Weapons of Mass Destruction: Has the Taboo Been Broken?" *Politics and the Life Sciences* 15, no. 2 (September 1996): 216–17.

———. "Proliferation and Nonproliferation in the 1990s: Looking for the Right Lessons." *The Nonproliferation Review* 6, no. 4 (Fall 1999): 70–82.

Rochlin, Gene I. "Defining 'High Reliability' Organizations in Practice: A Taxonomic Prologue." Pp. 11–32 in *New Challenges to Organization Research: High Reliability Organizations*, edited by K. H. Roberts. New York: Macmillan, 1993.

Rochlin, G. I., T. R. La Porte, and K. H. Roberts. "The Self-Designing High-Reliability Organization: Aircraft Carrier Flight Operations at Sea." *Naval War College Review* 40, no. 4 (1987): 76–90.

Rodriguez, L. L., A. De Roo, Y. Guimard, S.G. Trappier, A. Sanches, D. Bressler, A. J. Williams, A. K. Rowe, J. Bertolli, A. S. Khan, T. G. Ksiazek, C.J. Peters, and S. T. Nichol. "Persistence and Genetic Stability of Ebola Virus During the Outbreak in Kikwit, Democratic Republic of the Congo, 1995." *The Journal of Infectious Disease* 179 (Suppl 1) (1999): S170–76.

Rosen, Steven J. "A Stable System of Mutual Nuclear Deterrence in the Arab-Israeli Conflict." *American Political Science Review* 7, no. 4 (1977): 1367–83.

Rosenbaum, David E. "Anthrax Danger Delays Inspection of Millions of Letters," *New York Times*, 6 November 2001, B6.

Rosengard, Ariella M., Yu Liu, Zhiping Nie, and Robert Jimenez. "Variola Virus Immune Evasion Design: Expression of a Highly Efficient Inhibitor of Human Complement." *Proceedings of the National Academy of Sciences* 99, no. 13 (June 25, 2002): 8808–13.

Rosovitz, M. J. and Stephen H. Leppla. "Virus Deals Anthrax a Killer Blow." *Nature* 418 (August 22, 2002): 825–26.

Roth, George S. and Leonard T. Roth. "No Time for NMD." *The Bulletin of the Atomic Scientists* 57, no. 3 (May/June 2001): 76–77.

Rubin, Rita. "Decades-old smallpox vaccinations may still protect," *USA Today*, 8 November 2001.

Russett, Bruce. "Controlling the Soviet–US Enduring Rivalry: What was the Role of Nuclear Weapons?" Pp. 75–84 in *Nuclear Rivalry and International Order*, edited by J. Gjelstad and O. Njolstad. London: Sage Publications, 1996.

Russett, Bruce and J. R. O'Neal. *Triangulating Peace: Democracy, Independence, and International Organizations.* New York: Norton, 2001.

"Russia Says It Foiled Illegal Sale of Weapons-Grade Uranium." *New York Times*, 7 December 2001, A8.

Ryzhko, I.V., A. I. Shcerbaniuk, and E. D. Samokhodkina. "Virulence of Rifampicin and Quinolone Resistant Mutants of Strains of Plague Microbe with Fra+ and Fra- Phenotypes." *Antibiot Khimioter* 39 (1994): 32–36.

Sadek, Ramses F., Ali S. Khan, Gary Stevens, C. J. Peters, and Thomas G. Ksiazek. "Ebola Hemorrhagic Fever, Democratic Republic of the Congo, 1995: Determinants of Survival." *The Journal of Infectious Diseases* 179 (Suppl 1) (1999): S24–27.

Sagan, Scott D. *The Limits of Safety: Organizations, Accidents, and Nuclear Weapons.* Princeton: Princeton University Press, 1993.

———. "The Perils of Proliferation: Organization Theory, Deterrence Theory, and the Spread of Nuclear Weapons." *International Security* 18, no. 4 (1994): 66–107.

———. "Why Do States Build Nuclear Weapons?: Three Models in Search of a Bomb." *International Security* 21, no. 3 (Winter 1996/1997): 54–86.

———. "The Commitment Trap: Why the United States Should Not Use Nuclear Threats to Deter Biological and Chemical Weapons Attacks." *International Security* 24, no. 4 (Spring 2000): 85–115.

———. "Nuclear Instability in South Asia." Pp. 370–81 in *The Use of Force: Military Power and International Politics*, edited by Robert Art and Kenneth Waltz. Lanham, Maryland: Rowman & Littlefield Publishers, Inc., 2004.

Sagan, Scott D. and Jeremi Suri. "The Madman Nuclear Alert: Secrecy, Signaling, and Safety in October 1969." *International Security* 27, no. 4 (Spring 2003): 150–183.

Sagan, Scott D. and Kenneth N. Waltz. *The Spread of Nuclear Weapons: A Debate Renewed*. New York: Norton, 2003.

Sandoval, R. Robert. "Consider the Porcupine: Another View of Nuclear Proliferation." *Bulletin of the Atomic Scientists* 32, no.5 (1976): 17–19.

Salik, Naeem Ahmad. "Missile Issues in South Asia." *The Nonproliferation Review* 9, no. 2 (Summer 2002): 47–55.

Sandoval, R. Robert. "Consider the Porcupine: Another View of Nuclear Proliferation." *Bulletin of the Atomic Scientists* 32, no. 5 (1976): 17–19.

*San Jose Mercury News*. 26 December 1993.

Sanger, Christian, Elke Mulhberger, Elena Ryabchikova, Larissa Kolesnikova, Hans-Dieter Klenk, and Stephan Becker. "Sorting of Marburg Virus Surface Protein and Virus Release Take Place at Opposite Surfaces of Infected Polarized Epithelial Cells. *Journal of Virology* 75, no. 3 (February 2001): 1274–83.

Sanger, David E. "Nuclear Experts in Pakistan May Have Links to Al Qaeda," *New York Times*, 9 December 2001, A1 and B5

———. "Bush Shifts Focus To Nuclear Sales By North Korea," *New York Times*, 5 May 2003, A16.

———. "North Korea Says It Seeks To Develop Nuclear Arms," *New York Times*, 10 June 2003, A9.

———. "CIA Said To Detect North Korean Gains In Atom Technology," *New York Times*, 1 July 2003, A1.

———. "Intelligence Puzzle: North Korean Bombs," *New York Times*, 14 October 2003, A7.

———. "North Korea's Bomb: Untested but Ready, CIA Concludes," *New York Times*, 9 November 2003, A4.

———. "In Face of Report, Iran Acknowledges Buying Nuclear Components," *New York Times*, 23 February 2004, A6.

———. "Bush Envoy Briefs Panel After Talks On A-Bombs," *New York Times*, 3 March 2004, A8.

———. "Pakistani Tells of North Korean Nuclear Devices," *New York Times*, 13 April 2004, A1 and A14.

———. "Pakistan Found to Aid Iran Nuclear Efforts: U.N. Agency Also Learns Tehran Has Tested Centrifuge Parts," *New York Times*, 2 September 2004, A7.

———. "Yes, Parallel Tracks to North, But Parallel Tracks Don't Meet," *New York Times*, 20 September 2005, A6.

Sanger, David E. and William J. Broad. "Iran Admits That It Has Plans for a Newer Centrifuge," *New York Times*, 13 February 2004, A11.

Sanger, David E. and Howard W. French. "North Korea Prompts U.S. To Investigate Nuclear Boast," *New York Times*, 1 May 2003, A18.

Saunders, Phillip C. "Confronting Ambiguity: How to Handle North Korea's Nuclear Program." *Arms Control Today*, March 2003. www.armscontrol.org/act/2003_03/saunders_mar03.asp.

Sayed, Abdulhay. "The Future of the Israeli Nuclear Force and the Middle East Peace Process." *Security Dialogue* 28 (March 1997): 31–48.

Scales, Jr., Robert H. "Adaptive Enemies: Dealing With The Strategic Threat After 2010." *Strategic Review* 27, no. 1 (Winter 1999): 5–14.

Schelling, Thomas C. *The Strategy of Conflict*. Cambridge, MA: Harvard University Press, 1960.

———. *Arms and Influence*. New Haven, CT: Yales University Press, 1966.

———. "The Diplomacy of Violence." Pp. 1–26 in *The Use of Force: Military Power and International Politics*, edited by Robert Art and Kenneth Waltz. Lanham, Maryland: Rowman & Littlefield Publishers, Inc., 1988.

Schemo, Diana Jean. "Laboratory Security: Bill Would Require Laboratories to Adopt Strict Security," *New York Times*, 25 January 2002, A11.

Schlesinger, James R. "The Impact of Nuclear Weapons on History." Pp. 15–21 in *Nuclear Rivalry and International Order*, edited by J. Gjelstad and O. Njolstad. London: Sage Publications, 1996.

Schmitt, Eric and James Dao. "Use of Pinpoint Air Power Comes of Age in New War." *The New York Times*, December 24, 2001, pp. A1 and B3.

Schneider, Barry R. "Nuclear Proliferation and Counter-Proliferation: Policy Issues and Debates." *Mershon International Studies Review* 38, no. 2 (1994): 209–34.

Schock-Spana, Monica. "Implications of Pandemic Influenza for Bioterrorism Response." *Clinical Infectious Diseases* 31 (December 2000): 1409–13.

Schuch, Raymond, Daniel Nelson, and Vincent A. Fischetti. "A Bacteriolytic Agent That Detects and Kills *Bacillus anthracis*." *Nature* 418 (August 22, 2002): 884–87.

Schwarz, Benjamin. "The Real War." *The Atlantic Monthly*, June 2001.

———. "A Job for Rewrite: Stalin's War." *The New York Times*, February 21, 2004, pp. A17 and A19

Sciolino, Elaine. "Nuclear Ambitions Aren't New for Iran," *New York Times*, 22 June 2003, WK 4.

Scoblic, Peter. "Nuclear Weapons We Don't Need," *Washington Post*, 14 May 2003, A29.

———. "Iran Will Allow U.N. Inspections of Nuclear Sites," *New York Times*, 22 October 2003, A1.

*Seattle Times*. 12 October 2003.

Selden, Zachary. "Assessing the Biological Weapons Threat." Special Report. Washington, D.C.: Business Executives for National Security, February 1997.

Shanker, Thom. "Lessons From Iraq Include How to Scare Korean Leader," *New York Times*, 12 May 2003, A17.

———. "F.D.A. Rules Shots Effective For Anthrax That Is Inhaled," *New York Times*, 31 December 2003, A13.

———. "Regime Thought War Unlikely, Iraqis Tell U.S.," *New York Times*, 12 February 2004, A1 and A12.

———. "Korean Missile Said to Advance: U.S. Is Unworried," *New York Times*, 5 August 2004, A3.

Shanker, Thom and David E. Sanger. "North Korea Hides New Nuclear Site, Evidence Suggests A 2nd Reprocessing Unit," *New York Times*, 20 July 2003, A1 and A6.

Shchelkunov, S. N., R. F. Massung, and J. J. Esposito. "Comparison of the Genome DNA Sequences of Bangladesh-1975 and India-1967 Variola Viruses." *Virus Research* 36 (1995): 107–118.

Shchelkunov, Sergei N., Alexei V. Totmenin, Igor V. Babkin, Pavel F. Safronov, Olga I. Ryazankina, Nikolai A. Petrov, Valery V. Gutorov, Elena A. Uvarova, Maxim V. Mikheev, Jerry R. Sisler, Joseph J. Esposito, Peter B. Jahrling, Bernard Moss, and Lev S. Sandakhchiev. "Human Monkeypox and Smallpox Viruses: Genomic Comparison." *FEBS Letters* 509 (2001): 66–70.

Shchelkunov, S. N., A. V. Totmenin, P. F. Safronov, M. V. Mikheev, V. V. Gutorov, O. I. Ryazankina, N. A. Petrov, I. V. Babkin, E. A. Uvarova, L. S. Sandakhchiev, J. R. Sisler, J. J. Esposito, I. K. Damon, P. B. Jahrling, and B. Moss. "Analysis of the Monkeypox Virus Genome." *Virology* 297 (2002): 172–94.

Shenon, Philip. "Suspected North Korean Atom Site Is Empty, U.S. Finds," *New York Times*, 28 May 1999, A3.

———. "U.S. Plans to Toughen Rules for Cargo Shipping Industry," *New York Times*, 19 November 2003, A18.

Shoham, Dany. "Chemical/Biological Terrorism: An Old, But Growing Threat in the Middle East and Elsewhere." *Politics and the Life Sciences* 15, no. 2 (September 1996): 218–19.

Shulsky, Abram N. *Deterrence Theory and Chinese Behavior.* Report MR-1161-AF, 2000. RAND's Project Air Force, 2000.

Sidhu, Waheguru Pal Singh. "India's Nuclear Use Doctrine." Pp. 125–57 in *Planning the Unthinkable: How New Powers Will Use Nuclear, Biological, and Chemical Weapons*, edited by Lavoy, Sagan, and Wirtz. Ithaca, NY: Cornell University Press, 2000.

Sigal, Leon V. *Disarming Strangers: Nuclear Diplomacy With North Korea*. Princeton University Press, 1998.

Simons, Lewis M. "Weapons of Mass Destruction: An Ominous New Chapter Opens on the Twentieth Century's Ugliest Legacy." *National Geographic* (November 2002): 2–35.

Singer, John D. "Threat Perception and the Armament-Tension Dilemma." *Journal of Conflict Resolution* 2 (1958): pp. 90–105.

Smee, Donald F., Robert W. Sidwell, Debbie Kefauver, Mike Bray, and John W. Huggins. "Characterization of Wild-Type and Cidofovir-Resistant Strains of Camelpox, Cowpox, Monkeypox, and Vaccinia Viruses." *Antimicrobial Agents and Chemotherapy* 46, no. 5 (May 2002): 1329–35.

Smith, Bradley T., Thomas V. Inglesby, and Tara O'Toole. "Biodefense R&D: Anticipating Future Threats, Establishing a Strategic Environment." *Biosecurity and Bioterrorism: Biodefense Strategy, Practice, and Science* 1, no. 3 (2003): 193–202.

Smith, Dan. "The Uselessness and the Role of Nuclear Weapons: An Exercise in Pseudo-problems and Disconnection." Pp. 85–101 in *Nuclear Rivalry and International Order*, edited by J. Gjelstad and O. Njolstad. London: Sage Publications, 1996.

Smith, Hamilton O., Clyde A. Hutchison III, Cynthia Pfannkoch, and J. Craig Venter. "Generating a Synthetic Genome By Whole Genome Assembly: OX174 Bacteriophage from Synthetic Oligonucleotides." *Proceedings of the National Academy of Sciences* 100, no. 26 (December 23, 2003): 15440–45.

Smithson, Amy E. *Toxic Archipelago: Preventing Proliferation from the Former Soviet Chemical and Biological Weapons Complexes*. Report No. 32, Washington, D.C.: The Henry L. Stimson Center, December 1999.

Smithson, Amy E. and Leslie-Anne Levy. *Ataxia: The Chemical and Biological Terrorism Threat and the U.S. Response*. Report No. 35, Washington, D.C.: The Henry L. Stimson Center, October 2000.

Snyder, Glenn H. *Deterrence and Defense*. Princeton, NJ: Princeton University Press, 1961.

Snyder, Scott. *Negotiating on the Edge: North Korean Negotiating Behavior*. Washington, D.C.: United States Institute of Peace Press, 1999.

Sontag, Deborah. "Israeli Lawmakers Hold Quick Debate on Nuclear Arms," *New York Times*, 3 February 2000, A3.

"South Africa's Apartheid-Era Germ Warfare Program Investigated." The Henry L. Stimson Center. *The CBW Chronicle* 2, No. 5 (January 1999): 1–3.

Spector, Leonard S. "Foreign-Supplied Combat Aircraft: Will They Drop the Third World Bomb?" *Journal of International Affairs* 40, no. 1 (Summer 1986): 143–58.

———. *The Undeclared Bomb*. Cambridge, MA: Ballinger, 1988.

Spiers, Edward M. *Weapons of Mass Destruction: Prospects for Proliferation*. London: Macmillan Press Ltd., 2000.

Stein, Janice Gross. "Extended Deterrence in the Middle East: American Strategy Reconsidered." *World Politics* 39 (April 1987): 326-52.

Stein, Robert M. "Patriot Experience in the Gulf War." *International Security* 17, no. 1 (1992): 199–225.

Steinberg, Gerald M. "Parameters of Stable Deterrence in a Proliferated Middle East: Lessons from the 1991 Gulf War." *The Nonproliferation Review* 7, no. 3 (Fall/Winter 2000): 43–60.

Stepanov, A. V., L. I. Marinin, A. P. Pomerantsev, and N. A. Staritsin. "Development of Novel Vaccines Against Anthrax in Man." *Journal of Biotechnology* 44 (1996): 155–60.

Stern, Jessica. "Weapons of Mass Impact: A Growing and Worrisome Danger." *Politics and the Life Sciences* 15, no. 2 (September 1996): 222–25.

———. *The Ultimate Terrorists*. Cambridge, Massachusetts: Harvard University Press, 1999.

———. "Dreaded Risks and the Control of Biological Weapons." *International Security* 27, no. 3 (Winter 2002/2003): 89–123.

Stevens, James, Adam L. Corper, Christopher F. Basler, Jeffery K. Taubenberger, Peter Palese, and Ian A. Wilson. "Structure of the Uncleaved Human H1 Hemagglutinin from the Extinct 1918 Influenza Virus. *Science* 303 (March 19, 2004): 1866–70.

Stober, Dan. "No Experience Necessary." *The Bulletin of the Atomic Scientists* 59, no. 2 (March/April 2003): 57–63.

Stolberg, Sheryl Gay. "U.S. Seeks to Build a Stock of Vaccine Against Smallpox," *New York Times*, 18 October 2001, A1 and B8.

———. "Health Officials Put Cost of Germ-Warfare Defense at Almost Twice Bush Plan," *New York Times*, 30 November 2001, B8.

———. "Civilians Are Reluctant to Join U.S. Test of Anthrax Vaccine," *New York Times*, 8 January 2002, A14.

———. "States' Preparedness: U.S. Will Give States $1 Billion to Improve Bioterrorism Defense," *New York Times*, 25 January 2002, A11.

Struck, Doug. "North Korea Says It Will Renew Work at Reactors," *Washington Post*, 13 December 2002, A01.

———. "North Korea 'Successfully Reprocessing' Fuel Rods," *Washington Post*, 18 April 2003, A50.

Subrahmanyam, K. "Nuclear Policy, Arms Control and Military Cooperation," paper presented at the Carnegie Endowment for International Peace – India International Centre conference on India and the United States after the Cold War, New Delhi, March 7–9, 1993.

———. "Talbott is Stuck in Pre-'85 Nuclear Groove," *Times of India*, 17 November 1998, 1.

Sullivan, Kevin and Mary Jordan. "N. Korea Building New Missile Site, South Says," *Washington Post*, 8 July 1999, A17.

Sullivan, Nancy, Zhi-Yong Yang, and Gary J. Nabel. "Ebola Virus Pathogenesis: Implications for Vaccines and Therapies." *Journal of Virology* 77, no. 18 (September 2003): 9733–37.

Sundarji, General K. "India's Nuclear Weapons Policy." Pp. 173–95 in *Nuclear Rivalry and International Order*, edited by J. Gjelstad and O. Njolstad. London: Sage Publications, 1996.

Swamy, M.R. Narayan. "Indian Lashes West for 'Hypocrisy' of Anti-Nuclear Stance," *Washington Times*, 21 May 1998, A17.

*Sydney Morning Herald*. 3 June 1999.

Tagliabue, John. "A Warning From an Official About an Increased Possibility of Nuclear Terror," *New York Times*, 2 November 2001, B4.

Taubes, Gary. "Postol vs. the Pentagon." *Technology Review*. Special Report/Missile Defense. (April 2003): 52–61.

Technical Annex. March 1997 report, www.defenselink.mil/pubs/prolif97/annex.html.

Tellis, Ashley J. *Stability in South Asia*. Santa Monica, CA: RAND, 1997.

———. *India's Emerging Nuclear Posture: Between Recessed Deterrent and Ready Arsenal*. Santa Monica, CA: RAND, 2001.

Tellis, Ashley J., C. Christine Fair, and Jamison Jo Medby. *Limited Conflicts Under the Nuclear Umbrella: Indian and Pakistani Lessons from the Kargil Crisis*. National Security Research Division. Santa Monica, CA: RAND, 2001.

Tetlock, Philip E. "Accountability: The Neglected Social Context of Judgment and Choice." Pp. 297–332 in *Research in Organizational Behavior*, edited by K. L. Cummings and B. M. Staw. Greenwich, CT: JAI Press, 1985.

Tetlock, Philip E., Charles B. McGuire, and Gregory Mitchell. "Psychological Perspectives on Nuclear Deterrence." *Annual Review of Pschology* 42 (1991): 239–76.

"The First Defence Against Biological Attack." *Financial Times*, 12 October 2001, 11.

*Theater Missile Defenses in the Asia-Pacific Region*. Working Group Report, No. 34. Washington, D.C.: The Henry L. Stimson Center, June 2000.

Thomas, Jo. "U.S. Groups Have Some Ties to Germ Warfare," *New York Times*, 2 November 2001, B8.

Thucydides. *The Peloponnesian War*. Harmondsworth, U.K.: Penguin Books, Ltd., 1985.

*Times of India*. 11 January 2002.

*Times of London*. 17 October 2001.

Traub, James. "The Netherworld of Nonproliferation." *New York Times Magazine*, June 2004.

Tucker, Jonathan B. "Lessons of Iraq's Biological Warfare Programme." *Arms Control* 14, no. 3 (December 1993): 229–71.

———. "Chemical/Biological Terrorism: Coping With a New Threat." *Politics and the Life Sciences* 15, no. 2 (September 1996): 167–83.

———. "Historical Trends Related to Bioterrorism: An Empirical Analysis." *Emerging Infectious Diseases* 5, no. 4 (July/August 1999): 498–504.

———. *Scourge: The Once and Future Threat of Smallpox*. New York: Grove Press, 2001.

———. "How to Regulate the Trade in Toxins." *New York Times*, 26 October 2001, A23.

Tucker, Jonathan B. and Amy Sands. "An Unlikely Threat." *The Bulletin of the Atomic Scientists* 55, no. 4 (July/August 1999): 46–52.

———. "A Farewell to Germs: The U.S. Renunciation of Biological and Toxin Warfare, 1969–70." *International Security* 27, no.1 (Summer 2002): 107–48.

Tucker, Jonathan B. and Kathleen M. Vogel. "Preventing the Proliferation of Chemical and Biological Weapon Materials and Know-How." *The Nonproliferation Review* 7, no. 1 (Spring 2000): 88–96.

Tumpey, Terrence M., Adolfo Garcia-Sastre, Andrea Mikulasova, Jeffery K. Taubenberger, David E. Swayne, Peter Palese, and Christopher F. Basler. "Existing Antivirals Are Effective Against Influenza Viruses With Genes from the 1918 Pandemic Virus." *Proceedings of the National Academy of Sciences* 99, no. 21 (October 15, 2002): 13849–54.

Tversky, A. and D. Kahneman. "Rational Choice and the Framing of Decisions." *Journal of Business* 59 (1986): 251–78.

Tyler, Patrick E. "A Case Shows Russia's Quandary in Preventing Leaks of Arms Lore," *New York Times*, 10 May 2000, www.nytimes.com/library/world/europe/051000russia-missile.htm.

Tzu, Sun. *The Art of War*. London: Oxford University Press, 1963.

Underwood, Anne. "Scary Lessons of 1918." *Newsweek*, February 2004.

*USA Today*. 6 August 1997 – 1 December 2003.

Van Aken, Jan and Edward Hammond. "Genetic Engineering and Biological Weapons: New Technologies, Desires and Threats From Biological Research." *European Molecular Biology Organization Reports* 4 (2003): 57–60.

Van Benthem van den Bergh, Godfried. "The Nuclear Revolution into its Second Phase." Pp. 22–39 in *Nuclear Rivalry and International Order*, edited by J. Gjelstad and O. Njolstad. London: Sage Publications, 1996.

Van Cleave, William R. and S. T. Cohen. *Tactical Nuclear Weapons: An Examination of the Issues.* New York: Crane, Russak and Company, Inc., 1978.

Vergano, Dan. "Bioterrorism Defense Under Fire: Doctors Say Military Plans Are Wrong Approach," *USA Today*, 21 June 2000, 10D.

Vertzberger, Yaacov. *The World In Their Minds: Information Processing, Cognition, and Perception in Foreign Policy Decisionmaking.* Stanford, CA: Stanford University Press, 1990.

Vick, Karl. "Iran Says It Will Abandon Development of Longer-Range Missile," *Washington Post*, 7 November 2003, A26.

Volchkov, V. E., V. A. Volchkova, A. A. Chepurnov, V. M. Blinov, O. Dolnik, S. V. Netesov, and H. Feldmann. "Characterization of the L gene and 5' trailer region of Ebola Virus." *Journal of General Virology* 80 (1999): 355–62.

Volchkov, Viktor E., Valentina A. Volchkova, Elke Muhlberger, Larissa V. Kolesnikova, Michael Weik, Olga Dolnik, and Hans-Dieter Klenk. "Recovery of Infectious Ebola Virus from Complementary DNA: RNA Editing of the GP Gene and Viral Cytotoxicity." *Science* 291 (March 9, 2001): 1965–69.

Vorobeychikov, E. V., G. M. Kurtzer, A. Z. Vasilenko, and O. P. Misnikov. "Probabilistic Evaluation of Aspirating Doses of a Q Fever Pathogen." *Annals of the New York Academy of Sciences* 990 (2003): 743–50.

Wade, Nicholas. "Anthrax Findings Fuel Worry on Vaccine," *New York Times*, 3 February 1998, A6.

———. "Tests With Anthrax Raise Fears That American Vaccine Can Be Defeated," *New York Times*, 26 March 1998, A22.

———. "DNA Map for Bacterium of Plague is Decoded," *New York Times*, 4 October 2001, A9.

———. "Clusters of Illness Suggest that Most Infections Came from Two Mailings," *New York Times*, 2 November 2001, B9.

Waitt, Brigadier-General Alden H. *Gas Warfare: The Chemical Weapon, Its Use, and Protection Against It.* New York: Duell, Sloan and Pearce, 1943.

Wald, Matthew L. "Nuclear Sites Ill-Prepared For Attacks, Group Says," *New York Times*, 17 December 2001, B6.

———. "Suicidal Nuclear Threat Is Seen at Weapons Plants," *New York Times*, 23 January 2002, A9.

Walker, David H. "Principles of the Malicious Use of Infectious Agents to Create Terror: Reasons for Concern for Organisms of the Genus *Rickettsia*." *Annals of the New York Academy of Sciences* 990 (2003): 739–42.

Waltz, Kenneth N. "The Spread of Nuclear Weapons: More May Be Better." *Adelphi Paper*, no. 171. London: International Institute of Strategic Studies, Autumn, 1981.

———. "Toward Nuclear Peace." Pp. 684–712 in *The Use of Force: Military Power and International Politics*, edited by Robert Art and Kenneth Waltz. Lanham, Maryland: Rowman & Littlefield Publishers, Inc., 1988.

——. "Nuclear Myths and Political Realities." *American Political Science Review* 84, no. 3 (September 1990): 731–44.

——. "Missile Defenses and the Multiplication of Nuclear Weapons." Pp. 347–52 in *The Use of Force: Military Power and International Politics*, edited by Robert Art and Kenneth Waltz. Lanham, Maryland: Rowman & Littlefield Publishers, Inc., 2004.

——. "Nuclear Stability in South Asia." Pp.382–93 in *The Use of Force: Military Power and International Politics*, edited by Robert Art and Kenneth Waltz. Lanham, Maryland: Rowman & Littlefield Publishers, Inc., 2004.

Warrick, Joby. "Russia's Poorly Guarded Past: Security Lacking at Facilities Used for Soviet Bioweapons Research," *Washington Post*, 17 June 2002, A01.

——. "Iran Said to Be Producing Bioweapons: Opposition Group Names Anthrax as First of Six Pathogens in Intensive Effort," *Washington Post*, 15 May 2003, A22.

——. "Study Raises Projection For 'Dirty Bomb' Toll," *Washington Post*, 13 January 2004, A2.

Warrick, Joby and John Mintz. "Lethal Legacy: Bioweapons for Sale," *Washington Post*, 20 April 2003, A01.

*Washington Post*. 8 July 1999 – 19 September 2005.

*Washington Times*. 27 February 2003 – 18 November 2003.

Watts, Jonathan. "North Korean Nuclear Missile 'Could Reach US'," *Guardian*, 4 August 2004, 23.

Weart, S. R. "Peace Among Democratic and Oligarchic Republics." *Journal of Peace Research* 31 (1994): 299–316.

——. *Never at War.* New Haven, CT: Yale University Press, 1998.

Weaver, G. and J. David Glaes. *Inviting Disaster: How Weapons of Mass Destruction Undermine U.S. Strategy for Projecting Military Power.* McLean, Va: AMCODA Press, 1997.

Weaver, Scott C., Cristina Ferro, Roberto Barrera, Jorge Boshell, and Juan-Carlos Navarro. "Venezuelan Equine Encephalitis." *Annual Review of Entomology* 49 (2004): 141–74.

Webb, G. F. "A Silent Bomb: The Risk of Anthrax as a Weapon of Mass Destruction." *Proceedings of the National Academy of Sciences* 100, no. 8 (April 15, 2003): 4355–56.

Wein, Lawrence M., David L. Craft, and Edward H. Kaplan. "Emergency Response to an Anthrax Attack." *Proceedings of the National Academy of Sciences* 100, no.7 (April 1, 2003): 4346–51.

Weisman, Steven R. "South Korea, Once a Solid Ally, Now Poses Problems for the U.S.: Seoul Challenges American Policy on the North," *New York Times*, 2 January 2003, A1 and A9.

Weisman, Steven R. and Douglas Jehl. "Estimate Revised on When Iran Could Make Nuclear Bomb," *New York Times*, 3 August 2005, A8.

Weiss, Rick. "Germ Tests Point Away From Iraq: Hill, N.Y. Post Spores Lack Telltale Compound," *Washington Post*, 30 October 2001, A09.

——. "Anthrax Response Plans Inadequate, Study Warns: Modeling of Bio-Attack on Large City Predicts Mass Casualties Without Prior Distribution of Antibiotics," *Washington Post*, 18 March 2003, A23.

Weiss, Rick and Dan Eggen. "Additive Made Spores Deadlier: 3 Nations Known to be Able to Make Sophisticated Coating," *Washington Post*, 25 October 2001, A1.

Weiss, Rick and Joby Warrick. "Army Working on Weapons-Grade Anthrax: Utah Facility Quietly Developed Formulation; Spores Sent Back and Forth to Md," *Washington Post*, 13 December 2001, A16.

Weltman, John J. "Nuclear Devolution and World Order." *World Politics* 32, no. 2 (January 1980): 169–93.

———. "Managing Nuclear Multipolarity." *International Security* 6, no. 3 (Winter 1981/82): 182–94.

Wheelis, Mark. "Biotechnology and Biochemical Weapons." *The Nonproliferation Review* 9, no. 1 (Spring 2002): 48–53.

Wheelis, Mark and Malcolm Dando. "Back to Bioweapons?" *The Bulletin of the Atomic Scientists* 59, no. 1 (January/February 2003): 41–46.

Whitby, Simon. *Biological Warfare Against Crops.* London: Palgrave Macmillan, 2002.

Whitworth, Damian. "America Paralysed by 2,300 Anthrax Scares," *Times of London*, 17 October 2001, 1.

Wirtz, James J. "Beyond Bipolarity: Prospects for Nuclear Stability after the Cold War." Pp. 137–65 in *The Absolute Weapon Revisited: Nuclear Arms and the Emerging International Order*, edited by T.V. Paul, R. Harknett, J. Wirtz. Ann Arbor, MI: University of Michigan Press, 1998.

Wiseman, Paul. "Steep Price Tag Expected For Victory in N. Korea: War Would Be 'Military's Nightmare,' Expert Says," *USA Today*, 28 February 2003, 13A.

Wohlstetter, Albert. "The Delicate Balance of Terror." *Foreign Affairs* 37 (January 1959): 211–35.

Wohlstetter, Roberta. "Terror on a Grand Scale." *Survival* 18, no. 3 (1978): 98–104

Wolfinger, Kirk. "Interviews with Biowarriors: Bill Patrick and Ken Alibek," for the NOVA special *Bioterror*. December 21, 2001. www.pbs.org/wgbh/nova/bioterror/biow_alibek.html.

———. "Interviews with Biowarriors: Sergei Popov," for the NOVA special *Bioterror*. December 21, 2001. www.pbs.org/wgbh/nova/bioterror/biow_popov.html.

Wolfsthal, Jon B. "Estimates of North Korea's Unchecked Nuclear Weapons Production Potential." Non-Proliferation Project. Carnegie Endowment for International Peace. July 28, 2003. www.ceip.org/files/nonprolif/default.asp.

World Health Organization. *Health Aspects of Chemical and Biological Weapons: Report of a WHO Group of Consultants.* Geneva: World Health Organization, 1970.

Yashina, Lyudmila, Irina Petrova, Sergei Seregin, Oleg Vyshemirskii, Dmitri Lvov, Valeriya Aristova, Jens Kuh, Sergey Morzunov, Valery Gutorov, Irina Kuzina, Georgii Tyunnikov, Sergei Netesov, and Vladimir Petrov. "Genetic Variability of Crimean-Congo Haemorrhagic Fever Virus in Russia and Central Asia." *Journal of General Virology* 84 (2003): 1199–1206.

Yuan, Jing-Dong. "Chinese Reponses to U.S. Missile Defenses: Implications for Arms Control and Regional Security." *The Nonproliferation Review* 10, no.1 (Spring 2003): 75–96.

Zagare, Frank C. and D. Marc Kilgour. "Asymmetric Deterrence." *International Studies Quarterly* 37 (1993): 1–27.

Zelicoff, Alan P. "An Epidemiological Analysis of the 1971 Smallpox Outbreak in Aralsk, Kazakstan." Pp. 12–21 in *The 1971 Smallpox Epidemic in Aralsk, Kazakstan, and the Soviet Biological Warfare Program*, edited by Jonathan B. Tucker and Raymond A. Zilinskas. Occasional Paper No. 9. Monterey, CA: Monterey Institute of International Studies Center for Nonproliferation Studies, July 2002.

Zelikow, Philip. "Offensive Military Options." Pp. 162–95 in *New Nuclear Nations: Consequences for U.S. Policy*, edited by R. Blackwill and A. Carnesale. New York: Council on Foreign Relations Press, 1993.

Zhang, Ming. "What Threat?" *The Bulletin of the Atomic Scientists* 55, no. 5 (September/October 1999): 52–57.

Zielbauer, Paul and William J. Broad. "In Utah, a Government Hater Sells a Germ-Warfare Book," *New York Times*, 21 November 2001, B1 and B6.

Zilinskas, Raymond A. "Aum Shinrikyo's Chemical/Biological Terrorism as a Paradigm?" *Politics and the Life Sciences* 15, no. 2 (September 1996): 237–39.

Zimmerman, Peter D. "Technical Barriers to Nuclear Proliferation." Pp. 345–56 in *The Proliferation Puzzle: Why Nuclear Weapons Spread and What Results*, edited by Z. Davis and B. Frankel. London: Frank Cass and Company Limited, 1993.

Zimmerman, Peter D. and Charles D. Ferguson. "Sweeping the Skies." *The Bulletin of the Atomic Scientists* 59, no. 6 (November/December 2003): 57–61.

Zue, Litai. "Evolution of China's Nuclear Strategy." Pp. 167–89 in *Strategic Views From The Second Tier: The Nuclear Weapons Policies of France, Britain, and China*, edited by J.C. Hopkins and W. Hu. New Brunswick, CT: Transaction Publishers, 1995.

Zuger, Abigail. "A Baffling Viral Outbreak?: He's on the Trail," *New York Times*, 14 August 2001, D1 and D2.

## GOVERNMENT DOCUMENTS
## UNITED STATES GOVERNMENT

Abt Associates. "The Economic Impact of Nuclear Terrorist Attacks on Freight Transport Systems in an Age of Seaport Vulnerability," executive summary, April 30, 2003.www.abtassociates.com/reports/ES-Economic_Impact_of_Nuclear_Terrorist_Attacks.pdf.

Central Intelligence Agency. *The Chemical and Biological Weapons Threat*. Washington, D.C.: Nonproliferation Center, March 1996.

———. National Intelligence Council. "Foreign Missile Developments and the Ballistic Missile Threat to the United States Through 2015." Key Points. September 1999. www.cia.gov/cia/publications/nie/nie99msl.html#rtoc2.

———. "Unclassified Report to Congress on the Acquisition of Technology Relating to Weapons of Mass Destruction and Advanced Conventional Munitions, 1 July Through 31 December 2001. cia.gov/cia/reports/721_reports/july_dec2001.htm.

———. National Intelligence Council. "Foreign Missile developments and the Ballistic Missile Threat Through 2015." (Unclassified Summary of a National Intelligence Estimate). December 2001. www.fas.org/irp/nie/bmthreat-2015.htm.

———. "Unclassified Report to Congress on the Acquisition of Technology Relating to Weapons of Mass Destruction and Advanced Conventional Munitions, 1 January Through 30 June 2002. cia.gov/cia/reports/721_reports/jan_june2002.htm.

———. National Intelligence Council. "Annual Report to Congress on the Safety and Security of Russian Nuclear Facilities and Military Forces." February 2002. www.odci.gov/nic/pubs/other_products/icarussiansecurity.htm.

———. Directorate of Intelligence. *The Darker Bioweapons Future.* (Unclassified Report Prepared by Office of Transnational Issues). November 3, 2003.

*Chemical and Biological Defense Primer.* Prepared by The Deputy Assistant to the Secretary of Defense for Chemical and Biological Defense. Washington, D.C., October 2001.

Defense Intelligence Agency. *North Korea: The Foundations for Military Strength Update 1995.* December 1995.

———. *Military Threats and Security Challenges Through 2015.* Statement for the Record, Senate Select Committee on Intelligence, by Vice Admiral Thomas R. Wilson, Director, Defense Intelligence Agency, February 2, 2000.

Department of the Army. *U.S. Army Activity in the U.S. Biological Warfare Programs: 1942–1977.* Vol. 2. Washington, D.C.: U.S. Government Printing Office, 24 February 1977.

Department of Defense. United States Atomic Energy Commission. *The Effects of Nuclear Weapons.* Revised Edition. Washington, D.C.: United States Government Printing Office, February 1964.

———. Defense Civil Preparedness Agency. *Radiological Defense Textbook.* SM-11.22-2. Washington, D.C.: United States Government Printing Office, June 1974.

———. Nuclear/Biological/Chemical (NBC) Defense Annual Report to Congress, March 1997. www.defenselink.mil/pubs/prolif97/.

———. Office of the Secretary of Defense. *Proliferation: Threat and Response.* Washington, D.C.: United States Government Printing Office, January 2001.

———. The Deputy Assistant to the Secretary of Defense for Chemical and Biological Defense. *Chemical and Biological Defense Primer.* Washington, D.C.: United States Government Printing Office, October 2001.

———. Office of the Secretary of Defense. *Nuclear Posture Review [Excerpts].* December 31, 2001. www.globalsecurity.org/wmd/library/policy/dod/npr.htm.

Feickert, Andrew and K. Alan Kronstadt. *Missile Proliferation and the Strategic Balance in South Asia.* Congressional Research Service (CRS) Report for Congress, Received through the CRS Web, October 17, 2003.

*First Annual Report to the President and the Congress of the Advisory Panel to Assess Domestic Response Capabilities for Terrorism Involving Weapons of Mass Destruction: I. Assessing the Threat.* Washington, D.C.: 15 December 1999. [also known as the Gilmore Report]

Grim, B. S. and W. H. Rose. *Biological Vulnerability Assessment: The U.S. East Coast.* DPG-S-84-503. U.S. Army: Dugway Proving Ground, Utah, 1983.

*Gulf War Air Power Survey: Operations and Effects and Effectiveness.* Directed by Eliot A. Cohen. Vol. II. Washington, D.C.: U.S. Government Printing Office, 1993.

Heyman, David. *Anthrax Attacks: Implications for U.S. Bioterrorism Preparedness.* Report Prepared for the Defense Threat Reduction Agency and the Center for Strategic and International Studies. DTRA01-02-C-0013. Washington, D.C.: Center for Strategic and International Studies, April 2002.

House National Security Committee. Hearings on Ballistic Missile Defense, Statement for the Record by Richard N. Cooper, Chairman, National Intelligence Council for Hearings of 28 February 1996, "Emerging Missile Threats to North America During the Next 15 Years." www.ceip.org/programs/npp/ciacooper.htm.

Jones, Rodney W. *Minimum Nuclear Deterrence Postures in South Asia: An Overview.* Report Prepared for the Defense Threat Reduction Agency Advanced Systems and Concepts Office, U.S. Department of Defense. October 1, 2001.

Medalia, Jonathan. *Terrorist Nuclear Attacks on Seaports: Threats and Response.* Congressional Research Service. CRS Report for Congress, Received through the CRS Web, August 2003.

*Military Threats and Security Challenges Through 2015.* Statement for the Record by Vice Admiral Thomas R. Wilson, Director, Defense Intelligence Agency. Senate Select Committee on Intelligence, February 2, 2000, 5–10.

Morrison, John H. *DTC Test 68-50. Test Report.* Volume I. Department of the Army. Fort Douglas, Utah: Deseret Test Center, March 1969. (Redacted edition of secret document; 44 pages; U.S. Army Dugway Proving Ground Archives. Ft. Belvoir, Virginia: Defense Technical Information Center: AD 500676.)

———. *DTC Test 68-50. Test Report.* Volume II. Department of the Army. Fort Douglas, Utah: Deseret Test Center, April 1969. (Redacted edition of secret document; 200 pages; U.S. Army Dugway Proving Ground Archives. Ft. Belvoir, Virginia: Defense Technical Information Center: AD 501487.)

Nuclear Regulatory Commission. "Issue 20: Effects of Electromagnetic Pulse on Nuclear Power Plants." 23 June 2003. www.nrc.gov/reading-rm/doccollections/nuregs/staff/sr0933/sec3/020r1.html.

Office of Counterproliferation and Chemical and Biological Defense. *Biotechnology and Genetic Engineering: Implications for the Development of New Warfare Agents*, 1996. www.acq.osd.mil/cp/biotech96.html.

U.S. Army Medical Research Institute of Infectious Diseases. *USAMRIID's Medical Management of Biological Casualties Handbook.* Fourth Edition. Fort Detrick, Maryland: USAMRIID. February 2001.

U.S. Commission on National Security/21st Century. *New World Coming: American Security in the 21st Century – Major Themes and Implications.* Phase I Report. September 15, 1999.

———. *Seeking A National Strategy: A Concert For Preserving Security and Promoting Freedom.* Phase II Report. April 15, 2000.

———. *Road Map for National Security: Imperative for Change.* Phase III Report. February 15, 2001.

U.S. Congress. Office of Technology Assessment. *The Effects of Nuclear War.* Washington, D.C.: U.S. Government Printing Office, May 1979.

———. Office of Technology Assessment. *Technology Against Terrorism: The Federal Effort.* Washington, D.C.: U.S. Government Printing Office, 1991.

———. Office of Technology Assessment. *Proliferation of Weapons of Mass Destruction: Assessing the Risks, OTA-ISC-559.* Washington, D.C.: U.S. Government Printing Office, August 1993.

———. Office of Technology Assessment. *Technologies Underlying Weapons of Mass Destruction, OTA-BP-ISC-115.* Washington, D.C.: U.S. Government Printing Office, December 1993.

———. House of Representatives. *Electromagnetic Pulse Threats to U.S. Military and Civilian Infrastructure.* Hearing Before the Military Research and Development Subcommittee of the Committee on Armed Services. One Hundred Sixth Congress, First Session. October 7, 1999.

———. House of Representatives. *Prepared Testimony of Mr. Gordon K. Soper, Group Vice President, Defense Group, Inc.* Hearing Before the Committee on Small Business. One Hundred Sixth Congress, First Session. 1999.

———. U.S. Senate. *Testimony of Donald A. Henderson, MD, MPH, Director, Center for Civilian Biodefense Studies, The John Hopkins University, Schools of Public Health and Medicine.* Hearing on the Threat of Bioterrorism and the Spread of Infectious Diseases Before the Senate Foreign Relations Committee, September 5, 2001.

———. House of Representatives. *Nuclear Power Reactors Are Inadequately Protected Against Terrorist Attack.* Statement of Paul Leventhal on Behalf of Nuclear Control Institute and Committee to Bridge the Gap. Hearing Before the House Committee on Energy and Commerce Subcommittee on Oversight and Investigations on "A Review of Security Issues at Nuclear Power Plants." December 5, 2001.

———. Senate. Testimony to the Senate Committee on Foreign Relations on "Visit to the Yongbyon Nuclear Scientific Research Center in North Korea" by Siegfried S. Hecker, Senior Fellow, Los Alamos National Laboratory, University of California. January 21, 2004.

U.S. Department of State. Office of the Coordinator for Counterterrorism. *Patterns of Global Terrorism 1999.* Washington, D.C.: U.S. Department of State, 2000.

U.S. General Accounting Office. *Missile Defense: Additional Knowledge Needed in Developing System for Intercepting Long-Range Missiles.* Report to the Ranking Minority Member, Subcommittee on Financial Management, the Budget, and International Security, Committee on Governmental Affairs, U.S. Senate. GAO-03-600. August 2003.

U.S. Strategic Bombing Survey. Physical Damage Division. *Effects of Incendiary Bomb Attacks on Japan: A Report on Eight Cities.* April 1947.

NON U.S. GOVERNMENT

International Atomic Energy Agency. *Implementation of the NPT Safeguards Agreement in the Islamic Republic of Iran.* Report by the Director General. November 10, 2003.

United Nations. UNSCOM Report on Iraq Disarmament. 29 January 1999. www.un.org/Depts/unscom/s99-94.htm.

Washington Headquarters Services, Directorate for Information Operations and Report. "Korean War—Casualty Summary: As of June 15, 2004"

Washington Headquarters Services, Directorate for Information Operations and Report. "Vietnam Conflict—Casualty Summary: As of June 15, 2004"

INTERVIEWS WITH AUTHOR
Interview with Dr. Ken Alibek, Manasis, VA, April 4, 2002.
Interview with Dr. Sergei Popov, Manasis, VA, April 4, 2002.
Interview with James Woolsey, Washington, D.C., April 4, 2002.

# Index

# About the Author

Thomas Preston is associate professor of international relations in the Department of Political Science at Washington State University, Pullman. He is also a faculty research associate at the Moynihan Institute of Global Affairs at the Maxwell School, Syracuse University, New York. He received his MA at the University of Essex (United Kingdom) and his PhD from The Ohio State University (Columbus, OH). A specialist in security policy, foreign affairs, and political psychology, Preston is the author of *The President and His Inner Circle: Leadership Style and the Advisory Process in Foreign Affairs* (Columbia University Press, 2001) and the coauthor of *Introduction to Political Psychology* (Erlbaum, 2004). He has written numerous refereed journal articles and book chapters on leadership, advisory relations, international security, and foreign policy analysis. He frequently serves as a consultant for various U.S. governmental departments and agencies.